Folk-Lore in the Old Testament

Studies in Comparative Religion, Legend and Law

By

Sir George Frazer

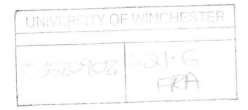
Published by Forgotten Books 2012
Originally Published 1918

PIBN 1000075448

FOLK-LORE IN THE OLD TESTAMENT

MACMILLAN AND CO., Limited
LONDON · BOMBAY · CALCUTTA · MADRAS
MELBOURNE

THE MACMILLAN COMPANY
NEW YORK · BOSTON · CHICAGO
DALLAS · SAN FRANCISCO

THE MACMILLAN CO. OF CANADA, Ltd.
TORONTO

FOLK-LORE IN
THE OLD TESTAMENT

STUDIES IN COMPARATIVE RELIGION
LEGEND AND LAW

BY

Sir JAMES GEORGE FRAZER

HON. D.C.L., OXFORD ; HON. LL.D., GLASGOW ; HON. LITT.D., DURHAM
FELLOW OF TRINITY COLLEGE, CAMBRIDGE

IN THREE VOLUMES
VOL. I

MACMILLAN AND CO., LIMITED
ST. MARTIN'S STREET, LONDON
1918

SANCTAE TRINITATIS APUD CANTABRIGIENSES

COLLEGIO VENERABILI

MAGNIS MAGNORUM INGENIORUM INCUNABULIS

SPLENDIDO LITTERARUM DOCTRINARUMQUE LUMINI

TUTO VIRORUM DOCTORUM ADVERSUS FORTUNAE TEMPESTATES

PORTUI AC PERFUGIO

PARVULUM PRO TANTIS IN ME COLLATIS BENEFICIIS MUNUSCULUM

PIO GRATOQUE ANIMO

MORTALIS IMMORTALI OFFERO

PREFACE

MODERN researches into the early history of man, conducted on different lines, have converged with almost irresistible force on the conclusion, that all civilized races have at some period or other emerged from a state of savagery resembling more or less closely the state in which many backward races have continued to the present time ; and that, long after the majority of men in a community have ceased to think and act like savages, not a few traces of the old ruder modes of life and thought survive in the habits and institutions of the people.   Such survivals are included under the head of folk-lore, which, in the broadest sense of the word, may be said to embrace the whole body of a people's traditionary beliefs and customs, so far as these appear to be due to the collective action of the multitude and cannot be traced to the individual influence of great men.   Despite the high moral and religious development of the ancient Hebrews, there is no reason to suppose that they formed an exception to this general law.   They, too, had probably passed through a stage of barbarism and even of savagery ; and this probability, based on the analogy of other races, is confirmed by an examination of their literature, which contains many references to beliefs and practices that can hardly be explained except on the supposition that they are rudimentary survivals from a far lower level of culture.   It is to the illustration and explanation of a few such relics of ruder times, as they are preserved like fossils in the Old Testament, that I have addressed myself in the present work.

Elsewhere I have had occasion to notice other similar survivals of savagery in the Old Testament, such as the sacrifice of the firstborn, the law of the uncleanness of women, and the custom of the scapegoat; but as I am unwilling to repeat what I have said on these topics, I content myself with referring readers, who may be interested in them, to my other writings.

The instrument for the detection of savagery under civilization is the comparative method, which, applied to the human mind, enables us to trace man's intellectual and moral evolution, just as, applied to the human body, it enables us to trace his physical evolution from lower forms of animal life. There is, in short, a Comparative Anatomy of the mind as well as of the body, and it promises to be no less fruitful of far-reaching consequences, not merely speculative but practical, for the future of humanity. The application of the comparative method to the study of Hebrew antiquities is not novel. In the seventeenth century the method was successfully employed for this purpose in France by the learned French pastor Samuel Bochart, and in England by the learned divine John Spencer, Master of Corpus Christi College, Cambridge, whose book on the ritual laws of the ancient Hebrews is said to have laid the foundations of the science of Comparative Religion. In our own age, after a lapse of two centuries, the work initiated by these eminent scholars and divines was resumed in Cambridge by my revered master and friend William Robertson Smith, and the progress which the study made during his lifetime and since his too early death is due in large measure to the powerful impulse it received from his extraordinary genius and learning. It has been my ambition to tread in the footsteps of these my illustrious predecessors in this department of learning, and to carry on what I may be allowed to call the Cambridge tradition of Comparative Religion.

It is a familiar truth that the full solution of any one problem involves the solution of many more ; nay, that nothing short of omniscience could suffice to answer all the questions implicitly raised by the seemingly simplest inquiry. Hence the investigation of a point of folk-lore, especially in the present inchoate condition of the study, naturally opens up lines of inquiry which branch out in many directions ; and in following them we are insensibly drawn on into wider and wider fields of inquiry, until the point from which we started has almost disappeared in the distance, or, to speak more correctly, is seen in its proper perspective as only one in a multitude of similar phenomena. So it befell me when, many years ago, I undertook to investigate a point in the folk-lore of ancient Italy ; so it has befallen me now, when I have set myself to discuss certain points in the folk-lore of the ancient Hebrews. The examination of a particular legend, custom, or law has in some cases gradually broadened out into a disquisition and almost into a treatise. But I hope that, apart from their immediate bearing on the traditions and usages of Israel, these disquisitions may be accepted as contributions to the study of folk-lore in general. That study is still in its infancy, and our theories on the subjects with which it deals must probably for a long time to come be tentative and provisional, mere pigeon-holes in which temporarily to sort the multitude of facts, not iron moulds in which to cast them for ever. Under these circumstances a candid inquirer in the realm of folk-lore at the present time will state his inferences with a degree of diffidence and reserve corresponding to the difficulty and uncertainty of the matter in hand. This I have always endeavoured to do. If anywhere I have forgotten the caution which I recommend to others, and have expressed myself with an appearance of dogmatism which the evidence does not warrant, I would request the reader to correct all such particular statements by this general and sincere profession of scepticism.

Throughout the present inquiry I have sought to take account of the conclusions reached by the best modern critics with regard to the composition and dates of the various books of the Old Testament ; for I believe that only in the light of these conclusions do many apparent discrepancies in the sacred volume admit of a logical and historical explanation. Quotations are generally made in the words of the Revised English Version, and as I have occasionally ventured to dissent from it and to prefer a different rendering or even, in a very few places, a different reading, I wish to say that, having read the whole of the Old Testament in Hebrew attentively, with the English Version constantly beside me, I am deeply impressed by the wonderful felicity with which Translators and Revisers alike have done their work, combining in an extraordinary degree fidelity to the letter with justice to the spirit of the original. In its union of scrupulous accuracy with dignity and beauty of language the English Revised Version of the Old Testament is, as a translation, doubtless unsurpassed and probably unequalled in literature.

The scope of my work has obliged me to dwell chiefly on the lower side of ancient Hebrew life revealed in the Old Testament, on the traces of savagery and superstition which are to be found in its pages. But to do so is not to ignore, far less to disparage, that higher side of the Hebrew genius which has manifested itself in a spiritual religion and a pure morality, and of which the Old Testament is the imperishable monument. On the contrary the revelation of the baser elements which underlay the civilization of ancient Israel, as they underlie the civilization of modern Europe, serves rather as a foil to enhance by contrast the glory of a people which, from such dark depths of ignorance and cruelty, could rise to such bright heights of wisdom and virtue, as sunbeams appear to shine with a greater effulgence of beauty when they break through the murky clouds of a winter evening than when they flood the earth from the serene splendour of a summer noon. The annals of savagery and superstition unhappily compose a large part of human literature ; but in what other volume shall we find, side by side with that melancholy record, psalmists who poured forth their. sweet and solemn strains of meditative piety in the solitude of the hills or in green pastures and beside still waters ; prophets who lit up their beatific visions of a blissful future with the glow of an impassioned imagination ; historians who bequeathed to distant ages the scenes of a remote past embalmed for ever in the amber of a pellucid style ? These are the true glories of the Old Testament and of Israel ; these, we trust and believe, will live to delight and inspire mankind, when the crudities recorded alike in sacred and profane literature shall have been purged away in a nobler humanity of the future.

J. G. FRAZER.

1 BRICK COURT, TEMPLE, LONDON,
    26th May 1918.

CONTENTS

PART I

THE EARLY AGES OF THE WORLD

CHAPTER I

THE CREATION OF MAN

PAGE

Two different accounts of the creation of man in Genesis . . 3
The Priestly and the Jehovistic narratives . . . 4
The Jehovistic the more primitive 5
Babylonian and Egyptian parallels 5
Greek legend of the creation of man out of clay . . . 6
Australian and Maori stories of the creation of man out of clay . . 8
Tahitian tradition : creation of woman out of man's rib . . 9
Similar stories of the creation of woman in Polynesia . . . 10
Similar Karen and Tartar stories 10
Other stories of the creation of man in the Pacific . . 11
Melanesian legends of the creation of men out of clay . . . 12
Stories of the creation of man in Celebes . . . 12
Stories told by the Dyaks of Borneo 14
Legend told by the natives of Nias 15
Stories told by the natives of the Philippines . . . 16
Indian legends of the creation of man . . . 17
Cheremiss story of the creation of man . . . 22
African stories of the creation of man 22
American stories of the creation of man 24
Our first parents moulded out of red clay . . . 29
Belief of savages in the evolution of man out of lower animals . . 29
American Indian stories of the evolution of men out of animals . . 29
African and Malagasy stories of the evolution of men . . . 32
Evolution of men out of fish in Africa and Borneo . . . 33
Descent of men from trees and animals in the Indian Archipelago 34
Descent of men from animals in New Guinea . . 36
Descent of men from fish and grubs in the Pacific . . . 40

xiii

PAGE

Evolution of men out of animals in Australia 41

Evolutionary hypothesis of Empedocles . . 44

Creation or evolution? . . 44

CHAPTER II

THE FALL OF MAN

§ 1. *The Narrative in Genesis*

The temptation and the fall, the woman and the serpent . . 45

The two trees 46

The Tree of Life and the Tree of Death . . 47

The Creator's good intention frustrated by the serpent . . 48

The serpent's selfish motive for deceiving the woman . 49

Widespread belief in the immortality of serpents . 49

Story of the Fall, a story of the origin of death . 51

§ 2. *The Story of the Perverted Message*

Hottentot story of the Moon and the hare . . . 52

Bushman story of the Moon and the hare . . 53

Nandi story of the Moon and the dog . . . 54

Hottentot story of the Moon, the insect, and the hare : 55

Bushman story of the Moon, the tortoise, and the hare . 56

Louyi story of the Sun and Moon, the chameleon and the hare . 57

Ekoi story of God, the frog, and the duck . . . 58

Gold Coast story of God, the sheep, and the goat . . 58

Ashantee story of God, the sheep, and the goat . 59

Akamba story of God, the chameleon, and the thrush 61

Togoland story of God, the dog, and the frog . 62

Calabar story of God, the dog, and the sheep . 63

Bantu story of God, the chameleon, and the lizard . 63

The miscarriage of the message of immortality . 65

§ 3. *The Story of the Cast Skin*

Supposed immortality of animals that cast their skins . . 66

How men missed immortality and serpents, etc., obtained it 66

Belief that men formerly cast their skins and lived for ever 68

Belief that men used to rise from the dead after three days . 71

How men missed immortality and the Moon obtained it . 73

Bahnar story how men used to rise from the dead . 73

Rivalry between men and serpents, etc., for immortality . 74

§ 4. *The Composite Story of the Perverted Message and the Cast Skin*

Galla story of God, the blue bird, and the serpent . . 74

Stories of the Good Spirit, men, and serpents . 75

§ 5. *Conclusion*

Original form of the story of the Fall of Man . . 76

CHAPTER III

THE MARK OF CAIN

	PAGE
The theory that the mark was a tribal badge	78
Homicides shunned as infected	79
Attic law concerning homicides	80
Seclusion of murderers in Dobu	80
Belief in the infectiousness of homicides in Africa	81
Earth supposed to spurn the homicide	82
Wanderings of the matricide Alcmaeon	83
Earth offended by bloodshed and appeased by sacrifice	84
The homicide's mark perhaps a danger-signal to others	85
The mark perhaps a protection against the victim's ghost	86
Ceremonies to appease the ghosts of the slain	86
Seclusion of murderer through fear of his victim's ghost	88
Fear of ghosts of the murdered, a motive for executing murderers	89
Protection of executioners against the ghosts of their victims	89
Bodily marks to protect people against ghosts of the slain	91
Need of guarding warriors against the ghosts of the slain	92
Various modes of guarding warriors against the ghosts of the slain	93
Faces or bodies of manslayers painted in diverse colours	95
The mark of Cain perhaps a disguise against the ghost of Abel	98
Advantage of thus interpreting the mark	100
The blood rather than the ghost of Abel prominent in the narrative	101
Fear of leaving blood of man or beast uncovered	101
Superstition a crutch of morality	103

CHAPTER IV

THE GREAT FLOOD

§ 1. *Introduction*

Huxley on the Great Flood	104
The present essay a study in folk-lore	105
Bearing of flood stories on problems of origin and diffusion	106

§ 2. *The Babylonian Story of a Great Flood*

Babylonian tradition recorded by Berosus	107
Nicolaus of Damascus on the flood	110
Modern discovery of the original Babylonian story	110
The Gilgamesh epic	111
Journey of Gilgamesh to Ut-napishtim	112
Ut-napishtim's story of the Great Flood	113
The building of the ship—the embarkation—the storm	114

The sending forth of the dove and the raven—the landing   .   .   116
Other fragmentary versions of the Babylonian story   .   118
Sumerian version of the flood story   .   .   .   120
The flood story borrowed by the Semites from the Sumerians   .   124
The scene of the story laid at Shurippak on the Euphrates   .   124

§ 3. *The Hebrew Story of a Great Flood*

The story in Genesis   .   .   125
The story compounded of two different narratives   .   .   130
The Priestly Document and the Jehovistic Document   .   .   131
Late date and ecclesiastical character of the Priestly Document .   131
Its contrast with the Jehovistic Document   .   .   .   134
Verbal differences between the Priestly and the Jehovistic Documents .   136
Material differences between the documents in the flood story   .   137
The Jehovistic document the older of the two   .   .   .   139
Dependence of the Hebrew on the Babylonian story of the flood . .   140
Fanciful additions made to the flood story in later times .   .   143

§ 4. *Ancient Greek Stories of a Great Flood*

Deucalion and Pyrrha   146
The grounding of the ark on Parnassus   .   .   148
Aristotle and Plato on Deucalion's flood   .   .   148
Ovid's rhetorical account of the flood   .   .   149
Athenian legend of Deucalion's flood   .   .   151
The grave of Deucalion and the Water-bearing Festival at Athens   152
Story of Deucalion's flood at Hierapolis on the Euphrates   .   153
Water festival and prayers at Hierapolis .   .   .   154
Deucalion, the ark, and the dove   .   .   154
Phrygian story of a flood associated with King Nannacus .   155
Noah's flood on coins of Apamea Cibotos in Phrygia   .   156
Greek traditions of three great floods.   The flood of Ogyges   157
Dates assigned by ancient authorities to the flood of Ogyges   158
The flood of Ogyges and the vicissitudes of the Copaic Lake   .   160
The ruins of Gla on a stranded island of the lake   .   161
The flood of Dardanus.   Home of Dardanus at Pheneus .   163
Alternations of the valley of Pheneus between wet and dry   .   164
The water-mark on the mountains of Pheneus   .   .   . 165
Samothracian story of great flood consequent on opening of Dardanelles .   167
The Samothracian story partially confirmed by geology   .   .   168
The Samothracian story probably a speculation of an early philosopher   170
Story of Deucalion's flood perhaps an inference from the configuration of
    Thessaly   171
The Vale of Tempe   .   172
The Greek flood stories probably myths of observation·   .   174

§ 5. *Other European Stories of a Great Flood*

Icelandic story of a deluge of blood   174
Welsh story of a flood   175

PAGE
Lithuanian story of a great flood . . . 176
Flood story told by the gipsies of Transylvania . . . 177
Vogul story of a great flood 178
Relics of the flood in Savoy 179

§ 6. *Supposed Persian Stories of a Great Flood*

Supposed traces of a flood story in ancient Persian literature . . 179
The sage Yima and his blissful enclosure 180

§ 7. *Ancient Indian Stories of a Great Flood*

The story in the *Satapatha Brahmana.* Manu and the fish 183
The story in the *Mahabharata* 185
The story in the Sanscrit *Purānas* 187

§ 8. *Modern Indian Stories of a Great Flood*

Stories told by the Bhils and Kamars of Central India . . . 193
Stories told by the Hos and Mundas of Bengal . . . 195
Stories told by the Santals of Bengal 196
Stories told by the Lepchas of Sikhim and tribes of Assam . . 198
Shan story of a great flood 199
Tradition concerning the Vale of Cashmeer . . . 204
Geological confirmation of the tradition 205
The tradition probably a myth of observation 206

§ 9. *Stories of a Great Flood in Eastern Asia*

Stories told by the Karens and Singphos of Burma . . 208
Story told by the Bahnars or Bannavs of Cochin China . . . 209
Stories told by the aborigines of the Malay Peninsula . 211
Story told by the Lolos of Southern China . . . 212
Chinese tradition of a great flood 214
A Chinese emperor on Noah's flood 215
Kamchadale story of a great flood . . . 216
Mongolian story of a great flood 217

§ 10. *Stories of a Great Flood in the Indian Archipelago*

Stories told by the Battas of Sumatra . . . 217
Stories told by the natives of Nias and Engano . . . 219
Stories told by the Dyaks of Borneo . . . 220
Stories told by the natives of Celebes . . . 222
Stories told by the natives of Ceram and Rotti . . . 223
Story told by the natives of Flores 224
Stories told by the Philippine Islanders 225
Stories told by the wild tribes of Formosa . . 225
Story told by the Andaman Islanders . . . 233

§ 11. *Stories of a Great Flood in Australia*

PAGE

Story told by the Kurnai of Victoria . . . 234
Stories told by other tribes of Victoria . . . 235
Stories told by the aborigines of South Australia and Queensland . 236

§ 12. *Stories of a Great Flood in New Guinea and Melanesia*

Stories told by the natives of New Guinea 237
R. Neuhauss on stories of a flood in New Guinea . 238
Fijian story of a great flood 239
Melanesian story of a great flood 240

§ 13. *Stories of a Great Flood in Polynesia and Micronesia*

Wide diffusion of such stories in the Pacific . . . 241
Tahitian legends of a great flood . . . 242
Hawaiian legends of a great flood 245
Mangaian story of a great flood . . . 246
Samoan traditions of a great flood . . . 249
Maori stories of a great flood 250
Story of a great flood told by the Pelew Islanders . . 253

§ 14. *Stories of a Great Flood in South America*

Stories told by the Indians near Rio de Janeiro 254
Story told by the Caingangs of Southern Brazil . . . 256
Story told by the Carayas of Brazil . . . 257
Story told by the Ipurina of the Purus River . . 259
Story told by other Indians of the Purus River . . 260
Story told by the Jibaros of the Upper Amazon . 260
Story told by the Muratos of Ecuador . . 261
Story told by the Araucanians of Chili . . 262
Story told by the Ackawois of British Guiana . . 263
Story told by the Arawaks of British Guiana . . . 265
Story told by the Macusis of British Guiana . . 265
Stories told by the Indians of the Orinoco . 266
Stories told by the Muyscas or Chibchas of Bogota . 267
Geological evidence as to the valley of Bogota . 268
Story told by the Canaris of Ecuador . . . 268
Stories told by the Peruvian Indians . 269
Story told by the Chiriguanos of Bolivia . . 272
Story told by the Fuegians . . . 273

§ 15. *Stories of a Great Flood in Central America and Mexico*

Stories told by the Indians of Panama and Nicaragua . . 273
Mexican tradition of a great flood 274
Michoacan legend of a great flood . . . 275
Story of a great flood in the *Popol Vuh* . . . 276
Story told by the Huichol Indians of Mexico . . 277

                                               PAGE
Stories told by the Cora Indians of Mexico   .   .   .   279
Story told by the Tarahumares of Mexico   .   .   280
Story told by the Caribs of the Antilles   281

§ 16. *Stories of a Great Flood in North America.*

Story told by the Papagos of Arizona   281
Stories told by the Pimas   282
Story told by the Zuñi Indians of New Mexico   287
Stories told by the Californian Indians   .   .   .   288
Story told by the Natchez of the Lower Mississippi   .   .   .   291
Story told by the Mandan Indians   292
Annual Mandan ceremonies commemorative of the flood .   .   .   293
Story told by the Cherokee Indians   294
Story of a Great Flood widely spread among the Algonquins   .   .   295
Story told by the Montagnais Indians of Canada .   .   295
Story told by the Crees   297
The Algonquin story told in full by the Chippeways   .   .   297
An Ojibway version of the same story   301
Another Ojibway version of the same story   305
Another Ojibway version of the same story   307
Another version of the same story told by the Blackfoot Indians   .   308
Another version of the same story told by the Ottawas .   .   .   308
Another version of the same story told by the Crees   .   .   .   309
Another version of the same story told by the Dogrib and Slave Indians .   310
Another version of the same story told by the Hareskin Indians .   310
Stories of a Great Flood told by the Tinneh Indians   .   .   .   312
Stories told by the Tlingit Indians of Alaska   316
Story told by the Haida Indians of Queen Charlotte Islands   .   319
Story told by the Tsimshian Indians of British Columbia .   319
Story told by the Bella Coola Indians of British Columbia   .   320
Story told by the Kwakiutl Indians of British Columbia .   .   .   320
Story told by the Lillooet Indians of British Columbia .   .   .   321
Story told by the Thompson Indians of British Columbia   .   .   322
Story told by the Kootenay Indians of British Columbia .   .   .   323
Stories told by the Indians of Washington State .   .   323
Story told by the Indians of the Lower Columbia River .   325
Stories told by the Eskimo and Greenlanders   326

§ 17. *Stories of a Great Flood in Africa*

General absence of flood stories in Africa   329
Reported traces of such stories   329
Stories of a Great Flood reported in East Africa   330

§ 18. *The Geographical Diffusion of Flood Stories*

Absence of flood stories in a great part of Asia 332
Rarity of flood stories in Europe   333
Absence of flood stories in Africa   333

PAGE

Presence of flood stories in the Indian Archipelago, New Guinea, Australia
    Melanesia, Polynesia, and America   333
The Hebrew flood story derived from the Babylonian   .   .   .   334
Most other flood stories apparently independent of the Babylonian   .   334
Greek flood stories not borrowed from the Babylonian   .   .   .   335
Ancient Indian story probably independent of the Babylonian   .   .   335
Wide diffusion of the Algonquin story in North America .   .   337
Evidence of diffusion in South America and Polynesia   .   .   338

§ 19. *The Origin of Stories of a Great Flood*

Old theory of a universal deluge supported by evidence of fossils .   .   338
Survivals of the theory of a universal deluge in the nineteenth century   .   340
Stories of a Great Flood interpreted as solar, lunar, or stellar myths   .   341
Evidence of geology against a universal deluge   .   .   .   342
Philosophical theories of a universal primeval ocean   .   .   .   343
Many flood stories probably reminiscences of real events .   .   .   343
Memorable floods in Holland   344
Floods caused by earthquake waves in the Pacific   .   .   347
Some flood stories in the Pacific probably reminiscences of earthquake
    waves   351
Inundations caused by heavy rains   .   .   .   352
Babylonian story explained by annual inundation of the Euphrates valley   353,
Suess's theory of a flood caused by an earthquake and a typhoon .   .   356
Objections to the theory   356
Diluvial traditions partly legendary, partly mythical   .   .   359
Myths of observation based on geological configuration and fossils   360
All flood stories probably comparatively recent   .   .   .   360

CHAPTER V

THE TOWER OF BABEL

The Tower of Babel and the confusion of tongues   .   .   .   362
Later Jewish legends as to the Tower of Babel   .   .   .   364
The Tower of Babel probably a reminiscence of a temple-tower .   .   365
Two such ruined temple-towers at Babylon   .   .   .   365
The mound of Babil, formerly a temple of Marduk   .   .   366
Inscriptions of Nabopolassar and Nebuchadnezzar at Babil   .   367
The mound of Birs-Nimrud, formerly a temple of Nebo .   .   .   369
Inscription of Nebuchadnezzar at Birs-Nimrud   .   .   .   370
Ruined temple-tower at Ur of the Chaldees   .   .   .   371
Inscription of Nabonidus at Ur   372
The temple-tower at Ur perhaps seen by Abraham   .   .   373
Theories as to the primitive language of mankind   .   .   374
Experimental attempts to determine the primitive language   .   .   375
African stories like that of the Tower of Babel   .   .   .   377

PAGE

Story told by the Anals of Assam . . . 378
Story told of the pyramid of Cholula in Mexico . . 379
Story told by the Toltecs of Mexico . . 382
Karen and Mikir versions of the Tower of Babel . 383
Admiralty Islands' version of the Tower of Babel . . 383
Stories as to the origin of the diversity of tongues in Greece, Africa,
    Assam, Australia, and America 384

PART II

THE PATRIARCHAL AGE

CHAPTER I

THE COVENANT OF ABRAHAM

The Patriarchal Age described in Genesis 391
God's covenant with Abraham 392
Hebrew covenant by cutting a sacrificial victim in two . . . 392
Similar Greek modes of ratifying oaths 393
Similar modes of swearing among the Scythians . . . 394
Similar ceremonies at peacemaking in East Africa . . . 394
Ceremonies at peacemaking in South Africa . . 397
Similar ceremonies among tribes of Assam 398
Two theories of the ceremonies, the retributive and the sacramental or
    purificatory 399
The retributive theory implied in some cases 399
Ceremony at peacemaking among the Awome of Calabar . . 400
Retributive theory confirmed by Greek and Roman practice . 401
Retributive theory illustrated by an Assyrian inscription . . . 401
Similar sacrifices and imprecations in the ritual of barbarous tribes . 402
The slaughter of the victim symbolizes the fate of the perjurer . . 407
The sacramental or purificatory theory . . . 408
Bisection of victims in purificatory ceremonies . . . 408
The purificatory theory confirmed by a modern Arab rite . 409
Similar rites observed by Chins, Koryaks, and gipsies . . 410
Significance of the passage between the pieces of the victim . 411
Robertson Smith's sacramental interpretation of the Hebrew rite . 412
The interpretation confirmed by savage rituals . . . 413
Half-skeleton of bisected human body found at Gezer . 416
The half-skeleton probably a relic of human sacrifice . 417
Alternative explanations, the purificatory and the covenantal, of the bisec
    tion of human victims 418
The purificatory or protective explanation of the rite . . 418
Discovery of another half-skeleton of a human victim at Gezer . . 421

PAGE

The half-skeleton not explicable as a foundation sacrifice   .   421
Covenantal explanation of half-skeletons confirmed by Wachaga practice .   422
Retributive theory of Hebrew rite confirmed by Wachaga parallel   .   424
Retributive and sacramental theories complementary   .   425
Theory of vicarious sacrifice in modern Syria   .   .   .   425
Vicarious aspect of bisected victims in ritual   .   .   .   428

CHAPTER II

THE HEIRSHIP OF JACOB OR ULTIMOGENITURE

§ 1. *Traces of Ultimogeniture in Israel*

The character of Jacob   429
His alleged frauds on his brother and father   .   430
Theory that Jacob, as the younger son, was the heir   .   431
Traces of junior right or ultimogeniture in patriarchal history   431
Traces of ultimogeniture in the history of David .   .   433

§ 2. *Ultimogeniture in Europe*

Borough English in England   433
Ultimogeniture in France   .   .   436
Ultimogeniture in Friesland and Germany   .   437
Ultimogeniture in Russia   .   .   .   438
Ultimogeniture in Hungary   439

§ 3. *The Question of the Origin of Ultimogeniture*

Blackstone on the origin of Borough English   .   .   .   439
Ultimogeniture among the Turks and Mongols   .   .   441

§ 4. *Ultimogeniture in Southern Asia*

The Lushais of Assam, their migratory cultivation   .   .   442
Youngest son a chief's heir among the Lushais   .   .   444
Ultimogeniture in private families among the Lushais   .   .   445
Ultimogeniture among the Angamis of Assam   .   .   .   445
Ultimogeniture among the Naga tribes of Manipur   .   .   .   446
Ultimogeniture among the Meitheis of Assam   .   .   .   448
Ultimogeniture among the Kachins or Singphos of Burma   449
Systems of ownership dependent on systems of agriculture . .   450
Economic advance from migratory agriculture and communal ownership to
    permanent agriculture and individual ownership   .   .   451
The Kachins practise both migratory and permanent agriculture . .   452
Ultimogeniture among the Kachins of China   .   .   .   454
Ultimogeniture among the Shans of China   .   .   .   455
Ultimogeniture among the Chins   456
Compromise between ultimogeniture and primogeniture among the Hkamies   457

PAGE

Ultimogeniture among the Lolos of China . 458
Heirship of youngest daughter among the Khasis and Garos of Assam . 458
Mother-kin among the Khasis . . 459
Youngest daughter the heir among the Khasis 460
Why daughters rather than sons are heirs among the Khasis . 461
The Garos . 462
Mother-kin among the Garos . . . 463
Heirship of the youngest daughter among the Garos . 464
Original home of Mongolian tribes practising ultimogeniture . 465
Ultimogeniture among the Mrus . . . 466
The Hos or Larka Coles of Bengal . 467
Ultimogeniture and primogeniture among the Hos 469
The Bhils of Central India . 470
Ultimogeniture among the Bhils 471
Ultimogeniture among the Badagas of Southern India . . 472
Traces of ultimogeniture in the Malay region and Georgia . . 472

§ 5. *Ultimogeniture in North-Eastern Asia*

Ultimogeniture among the Yukaghirs . . 473
Ultimogeniture among the Chukchee 475
Ultimogeniture among the Koryaks . 476

§ 6. *Ultimogeniture in Africa*

Rarity of ultimogeniture in Africa 476
Rights of youngest sons among the Bogos, Suks, and Turkanas . 477
Ultimogeniture among the Ibos of Southern Nigeria . . 477
Ultimogeniture among the Ba-Ngoni of Mozambique 479
Why some chiefs are reluctant to see their grandsons . . 480

§ 7. *The Origin of Ultimogeniture*

Why youngest sons are preferred as heirs . 481
Why youngest daughters are preferred as heirs . 482
Preference for youngest sons natural among pastoral tribes 482
Ultimogeniture tends to pass into primogeniture . . . 484

§ 8. *Ultimogeniture and Jus Primae Noctis*

Theory of the illegitimacy of the eldest child . . . 485
Robert Plot on Borough English . . . 485
Plot's erroneous interpretation of *Marcheta mulierum* . . 486
Plot's theory rejected by modern historians of English law . 487
King Evenus and the so-called *jus primae noctis* in Scotland . 488
The legislation of Evenus a fable . . . 490
The fable born of a misinterpretation of the *merchet* . . 491
Modern legal authorities on the *merchet* 492
No evidence of the so-called *jus primae noctis* in Britain . . 495
Survival of the *merchet* in the highlands of Scotland . 495

African parallel to the *merchet* 495
The so-called *jus primae noctis* equally fabulous on the Continent . 496
Misapprehension of the real *jus primae noctis* . . 497
The " Tobias Nights " enjoined by the Catholic Church . . . 497
The story of Tobias and his wife Sarah 498
The remission of the " Tobias Nights " the real *jus primae noctis* . 501
Lawsuit between Abbeville and the Bishop of Amiens . . . 501
Survival of " Tobias Nights " in modern Europe 503
The practice of continence after marriage older than Christianity . 505
Continence for several nights after marriage in Vedic India . 505
Continence after marriage in non-Aryan tribes of India . . . 507
Continence after marriage in hill tribes of Assam and Burma . 508
Continence after marriage in the Indian Archipelago and New Guinea . 509
Continence after marriage among the aborigines of Australia . . 512
Continence after marriage in African tribes 513
Continence after marriage among American Indians . . . 514
The function of bridesmen and bridesmaids 516
" Tobias Nights " probably borrowed from paganism . . . 516
The " Tobias Nights " an interpolation in *The Book of Tobit* . . 517
Continence after marriage probably based on fear of demons . 519
Precautions against demons at marriage in many lands . 520
Precautions at the marriage of widowers and widows . . . 523
Mock marriages of widowers and widows in India . . . 525
No real evidence of alleged seignorial right in Europe . . . 530
Ultimogeniture not derived from alleged seignorial right . . . 530
Slight ground for such a derivation among the Lolos . 531
Marco Polo on the defloration of virgins in Tibet . . 532
Liberty accorded to Lolo brides after marriage . . . 533
Defloration of brides could not explain ultimogeniture . . 534

§ 9. *Ultimogeniture and Polygamy*

Ultimogeniture traced to preference for youngest wife in a polygamous
    family 534
The theory not supported by the evidence 535
The first wife the chief wife of a polygamous family in West Africa . 536
The first wife the chief wife in Central and East Africa . . . 540
The first wife the chief wife in South Africa . . 544
In some Kafir tribes a chief's principal wife not the first wife . . 547
Superiority of a later wife explained by chief's reluctance to see his grand-
    child 548
Suggested explanation of this reluctance 548
" Great wife," " Right-hand wife," " Left-hand wife " in Kafir tribes 551
In Kafir law succession regulated by primogeniture . . 553
In India the first wife of a polygamous family generally the chief wife . 554
In other parts of Asia the first wife generally the chief wife . . 556
In the Indian Archipelago the first wife generally the chief wife . 557
Among the American Indians the first wife generally the chief wife . 559

CONTENTS

PAGE

Among the Eskimo and Greenlanders the first wife generally the chief wife   561

In polygamous families generally the first wife the chief wife   .   .   561

Tendency of polygamy to favour primogeniture   .   562

§ 10. *Ultimogeniture and Infanticide*

Ultimogeniture and the killing of the firstborn   .   . 562

The two customs probably unconnected 563

§ 11. *Superstitions about youngest children*

Superstitions about youngest children in many lands   . 564

Youngest sons in ritual among the Akikuyu   .   . 565

Youngest sons in ritual among the Taiyals of Formosa   . 565

ADDENDA   567

PART I

THE EARLY AGES OF THE WORLD

CHAPTER I

THE CREATION OF MAN

ATTENTIVE readers of the Bible can hardly fail to remark a striking discrepancy between the two accounts of the creation of man recorded in the first and second chapters of Genesis. In the first chapter, we read how, on the fifth day of creation, God created the fishes and the birds, all the creatures that live in the water or in the air ; and how on the sixth ¹day he created all terrestrial animals, and last of all man, whom he fashioned in his own image, both male and female. From this narrative we infer that man was the last to be created of all living beings on earth, and incidentally we gather that the distinction of the sexes, which is characteristic of humanity, is shared also by the divinity ; though how the distinction can be reconciled with the unity of the Godhead is a point on which the writer vouchsafes us no information. Passing by this theological problem, as perhaps too deep for human comprehension, we turn to the simpler question of chronology and take note of the statements that God created the lower animals first and human beings afterwards, and that the human beings consisted of a man and a woman, produced to all appearance simultaneously, and each of them reflecting in equal measure the glory of their divine original. So far we read in the first chapter. But when we proceed to peruse the second chapter, it is somewhat disconcerting to come bolt on a totally different and, indeed, contradictory account of the same momentous transaction. For here we learn with surprise that God created man first, the lower animals next, and woman last of all, fashioning her as a mere afterthought out of a rib which he abstracted from

3

man in his sleep. The order of merit in the two narratives is clearly reversed. In the first narrative the deity begins with fishes and works steadily up through birds and beasts to man and woman. In the second narrative he begins with man and works downwards through the lower animals to woman, who apparently marks the nadir of the divine workmanship. And in this second version nothing at all is said about man and woman being made in the image of God. We are simply told that "the Lord God formed man of the dust of the ground, and breathed into his nostrils the breath of life ; and man became a living soul."[1] Afterwards, to relieve the loneliness of man, who wandered without a living companion in the beautiful garden which had been created for him, God fashioned all the birds and beasts and brought them to man, apparently to amuse him and keep him company. Man looked at them and gave to them all their names ; but still he was not content with these playmates, so at last, as if in despair, God created woman out of an insignificant portion of the masculine frame, and introduced her to man to be his wife.[2]

The flagrant contradiction between the two accounts is explained very simply by the circumstance that they are derived from two different and originally independent documents, which were afterwards combined into a single book by an editor, who pieced the two narratives together without always taking pains to soften or harmonize their discrepancies. The account of the creation in the first chapter is derived from what is called the Priestly Document, which was composed by priestly writers during or after the Babylonian captivity. The account of the creation of man and the animals in the second chapter is derived from what is called the Jehovistic Document, which was written several hundred years before the other, probably in the ninth or eighth century before our era.[3] The difference between the religious standpoints of the two writers is manifest. The later or priestly writer conceives God in an abstract form as withdrawn from human sight, and creating all things by a simple fiat. The earlier or Jehovistic writer conceives God in a very concrete form as acting and speak-

---

[1] Genesis ii. 7.   [2] Genesis ii. 18-24.   [3] See below, pp. 131 *sqq.*

ing like a man, modelling a human being out of clay, planting a garden, walking in it at the cool of the day, calling to
the man and woman to come out from among the trees
behind which they had hidden themselves, and making coats
of skin to replace the too scanty garments of fig-leaves with
which our abashed first parents sought to conceal their
nakedness.[1] The charming naïvety, almost the gaiety, of
the earlier narrative contrasts with the high seriousness of
the later ; though we cannot but be struck by a vein of
sadness and pessimism running under the brightly coloured
picture of life in the age of innocence, which the great
Jehovistic artist has painted for us. Above all, he hardly
attempts to hide his deep contempt for woman. The late-
ness of her creation, and the irregular and undignified
manner of it—made out of a piece of her lord and master,
after all the lower animals had been created in a regular
and decent manner—sufficiently mark the low opinion he
held of her nature ; and in the sequel his misogynism, as we
may fairly call it, takes a still darker tinge, when he ascribes
all the misfortunes and sorrows of the human race to the
credulous folly and unbridled appetite of its first mother.[2]

Of the two narratives, the earlier or Jehovistic is not
only the more picturesque but also the richer in folk-lore,
retaining. many features redolent of primitive simplicity
which have been- carefully effaced by the later writer.
Accordingly, it offers more points of comparison with the
childlike stories by which men in many ages and countries
have sought to explain the great mystery of the beginning
of life on earth. Some of these simple tales I will adduce
in the following pages.

The Jehovistic writer seems to have imagined that God
moulded the first man out of clay, just as a potter might do,
or as a child moulds a doll out of mud ; and that having
kneaded and patted the clay into the proper shape, the deity
animated it by breathing into the mouth and nostrils of the
figure, exactly as the prophet Elisha is said to have restored
to life the dead child of the Shunammite by lying on him,
and putting his eyes to the child's eyes and his mouth to
the child's mouth, no doubt to impart his breath to the

[1] Genesis ii. 7-9 ; iii. 8-10, 21.   [2] Genesis iii.

corpse ; after which the child sneezed seven times and opened its eyes.[1]   To the Hebrews this derivation of our species from the dust of the ground suggested itself all the more naturally because, in their language, the word for " ground " (*adamah*) is in form the feminine of the word for " man " (*adam*).[2]   From various allusions in Babylonian literature it would seem that the Babylonians also conceived man to have been moulded out of clay.[3]   According to Berosus, the Babylonian priest, whose account of creation has been preserved in a Greek version, the god Bel cut off his own head, and the other gods caught the flowing blood, mixed it with earth, and fashioned men out of the bloody paste ; and that, they said, is why men are so wise, because their mortal clay is tempered with blood divine.[4]   In Egyptian mythology Khnoumou, the Father of the Gods, is said to have moulded men out of clay on his potter's wheel.[5]

So in Greek legend the sage Prometheus is said to have moulded the first men out of clay at Panopeus in Phocis. When he had done his work, some of the clay was left over, and might be seen on the spot long afterwards in the shape of two large boulders lying at the edge of a ravine.   A Greek traveller, who visited the place in the second century of our era, thought that the boulders had the colour of clay, and that they smelt strongly of human flesh.[6]   I, too, visited the spot some seventeen hundred and fifty years later.   It is

[1] 2 Kings iv. 34 *sq.*   Among the Nilotic Kavirondo, of British East Africa, it sometimes happens that a person supposed to be dead sneezes and .revives.   In such a case the sneeze is taken as a sign that the spirit, which had gone away on a journey, has re turned to its body.   See John Roscoe *The Northern Bantu* (Cambridge 1915), p. 288.

[2] S. R. Driver and W. H. Bennett in their commentaries on Genesis ii. 7

[3] H. Zimmern, in E. Schrader's *Die Keilinschriften und das Alte Testament*[3] (Berlin, 1902), p. 506 ; Paul Dhorme, *La Religion Assyro-Babyloni enne* (Paris, 1910), p. 75.

[4] Eusebius, *Chronicon*, ed. A Schoene, vol. i. (Berlin, 1875) col. 16

[5] (Sir) Gaston Maspero, *Histoire Ancienne des Peuples de l'Orient Clas-*

sique, Les Origines (Paris, 1895), p. 128, compare 157.

[6] Pausanias x. 4. 4.   Compare Apollodorus, *Bibliotheca*, i. 7. 1 ; Ovid, *Metamorph.* i. 82 *sq.* ; Juvenal, *Sat.* xiv. 35.   According to another version of the tale the creation took place not at Panopeus, but at Iconium in Ly-caonia.   See below, p. 155.   It is said that Prometheus fashioned the animals as well as men, giving to each kind of beast its proper nature.   See Philemon, quoted by Stobaeus, *Florilegium*, ii. 27 The creation of man by Prometheus is figured on ancient works of art.   See J. Toutain, *Études de Mythologie et d'Histoire des Religions Antiques* (Paris, 1909), p. 190.   The late Greek rheto-rician Libanius confessed that, though he knew that all human bodies were moulded out of the same clay, he did

a forlorn little glen, or rather hollow, on the southern side
of the hill of Panopeus, below the long line of ruined but
still stately walls and towers which crowns the grey rocks of
the summit.   It was a hot day in late autumn—the first
of November—and after the long rainless summer of Greece
the little glen was quite dry ; no water trickled down its
bushy sides, but in the bottom I found a reddish crumbling
earth, perhaps a relic of the clay out of which Prometheus
modelled our first parents.   The place was solitary and
deserted : not a human being, not a sign of human
habitation was to be seen ; only the line of mouldering
towers and battlements on the hill above spoke of the busy
life that had long passed away.   The whole scene, like so
many else in Greece, was fitted to impress the mind with a
sense of the transitoriness of man's little bustling existence
on earth compared with the permanence and, at least, the
outward peace and tranquillity of nature.   The impression
was deepened when I rested, in the heat of the day, on the
summit of the hill under the shade of some fine holly-oaks,
and surveyed the distant prospect, rich in memories of the
past, while the sweet perfume of the wild thyme scented all
the air.   To the south the finely cut peak of Helicon peered
over the low intervening ridges.   In the west loomed the
mighty mass of Parnassus, its middle slopes darkened by
pine-woods like shadows of clouds brooding on the mountain
side ; while at its skirts nestled the ivy-mantled walls of
Daulis overhanging the deep glen, whose romantic beauty
accords so well with the loves and sorrows of Procne and
Philomela, which Greek legend associated with the spot.
Northwards, across the broad plain to which the steep bare
hill of Panopeus descends, the eye rested on the gap in the
hills through which the Cephissus winds his tortuous way to
flow under grey willows, at the foot of barren stony hills,
till his turbid waters lose themselves, no longer in the vast
reedy swamps of the now vanished Copaic Lake, but in a
dark cavern of the limestone rock.   Eastward, clinging to

not know who had moulded them ;
however, he was content to accept the
traditional ascription of our creation to
Prometheus (Libanius, *Orat.* xxv. 31,
vol. ii. p. 552, ed. R. Foerster, Leipsic, 1904). According to Hesiod
(*Works and Days*, 60 *sqq.*), it was the
smith-god Hephaestus who, at the bidding of Zeus, moulded the first woman
out of moist earth.

the slopes of the bleak range of which the hill of Panopeus
forms part, were the ruins of Chaeronea, the birthplace of
Plutarch ; and out there in the plain was fought the fatal
battle which laid Greece at the feet of Macedonia. There,
too, in a later age, East and West met in deadly conflict,
when the Roman armies under Sulla defeated the Asiatic
hosts of Mithridates. Such was the landscape spread out
before me on one of those farewell autumn days of almost
pathetic splendour, when the departing summer seems to
linger fondly, as if loth to resign to winter the enchanted
mountains of Greece. Next day the scene had changed :
summer was gone. A grey November mist hung low on
the hills which only yesterday had shone resplendent in the
sun, and under its melancholy curtain the dead flat of the
Chaeronean plain, a wide, treeless expanse shut in by
desolate slopes, wore an aspect of chilly sadness befitting the
battlefield where a nation's freedom was lost.

Australian
. . . ri
stories of
the creation
en ou
of clay.

We cannot doubt that such rude conceptions of the
origin of mankind, common to Greeks, Hebrews, Babylonians,
and Egyptians, were handed down to the civilized peoples of
antiquity by their savage or barbarous forefathers. Certainly
stories of the same sort have been recorded among the
savages and barbarians of to-day or yesterday. Thus the
Australian blacks in the neighbourhood of Melbourne said
that Pund-jel, the Creator, cut three large sheets of bark with
his big knife. On one of these he placed some clay and
worked it up with his knife into a proper consistence. He
then laid a portion of the clay on one of the other pieces of
bark and shaped it into a human form ; first he made the
feet, then the legs, then the trunk, the arms, and the head.
Thus he made a clay man on each of the two pieces of bark ;
and being well pleased with his handiwork, he danced round
them for joy. Next he took stringy bark from the eucalyptus
tree, made hair of it, and stuck it on the heads of his clay
men. Then he looked at them again, was pleased with his
work, and again danced round them for joy. He then lay
down on them, blew his breath hard into their mouths, their
noses, and their navels ; and presently they stirred, spoke,
and rose up as full-grown men.[1] The Maoris of New Zealand

---

[1] R. Brough Smyth, *The Aborigines of Victoria* (Melbourne, 1878), i. 424.

say that a certain god, variously named Tu, Tiki, and Tane, took red riverside clay, kneaded it with his own blood into a likeness or image of himself, with eyes, legs, arms, and all complete, in fact, an exact copy of the deity ; and having perfected the model, he animated it by breathing into its mouth and nostrils, whereupon the clay effigy at once came to life and sneezed. "Of all these things," said a Maori, in relating the story of man's creation, "the most important is the fact that the clay sneezed, forasmuch as that sign of the power of the gods remains with us even to this day in order that we may be reminded of the great work Tu accomplished on the altar of the Kauhanga-nui, and hence it is that when men sneeze the words of Tu are repeated by those who are present" ; for they say, "Sneeze, O spirit of life."[1] So like himself was the man whom the Maori Creator Tiki fashioned that he called him *Tiki-ahua*, that is, Tiki's likeness.[2]

A very generally received tradition in Tahiti was that the first human pair was made by Taaroa, the chief god. They say that after he had formed the world he created man out of red earth, which was also the food of mankind until bread-fruit was produced. Further, some say that one day Taaroa called for the man by name, and when he came he made him fall asleep. As he slept, the Creator took out one of his bones (*ivi*) and made of it a woman, whom he gave to the man to be his wife, and the pair became the progenitors of mankind. This narrative was taken down from the lips of the natives in the early years of the mission to Tahiti. The missionary who records it observes: "This always appeared to me a mere recital of the Mosaic account of creation, which they had heard from some European, and I never placed any reliance on it, although they have repeatedly told me it was a tradition among them before any foreigner arrived. Some have also stated that the woman's

Tahitian tr o the creation of man out of woman out of man's rib.

---

[1] Lieut.-Colonel W. E. Gudgeon "Maori Religion" *Journal of the Polynesian Society*, vol. xiv. (1905), pp. 125 *sq.* ; R. Taylor, *Te Ika a Maui. or New Zealand and its Inhabitants.* Second Edition (London, 1870), p. 117. Compare E. Shortland, *Maori Religion and Mythology* (London,

1882), pp. 21 *sq.* The name of the Creator varies in the three versions : in the first it is Tu, in the second Tiki, in the third Tane. The red colour of the clay, and the kneading of it with the god's blood, are mentioned only by Taylor, a good authority.

[2] R. Taylor, *l.c.*

name was Ivi, which would be by them pronounced as if written *Eve*. Ivi is an aboriginal word, and not only signifies a bone, but also a widow, and a victim slain in war. Notwithstanding the assertion of the natives, I am disposed to think that *Ivi*, or Eve, is the only aboriginal part of the story, as far as it respects the mother of the human race." [1] However,

Similar stories as to of woman in other parts of Polynesia. the same tradition has been recorded in other parts of Polynesia besides Tahiti. Thus the natives of Fakaofo or Bowditch Island say that the first man was produced out of a stone. After a time he bethought him of making a woman. So he gathered earth and moulded the figure of a woman out of it, and having done so he took a rib out of his left side and thrust it into the earthen figure, which thereupon started up a live woman. He called her Ivi (Eevee) or "rib" and took her to wife, and the whole human race sprang from this pair.[2] The Maoris also are reported to believe that the first woman was made out of the first man's ribs.[3] This wide diffusion of the story in Polynesia raises a doubt whether it is merely, as Ellis thought, a repetition of the Biblical narrative learned from Europeans.

Similar story of the creation of woman told by the Karens of Burma. However, the story of the creation of the first woman out of a rib of the first man meets us elsewhere in forms so closely resembling the Biblical account that they can hardly be independent of it. Thus the Karens of Burma say that God "created man, and of what did he form him? He created man at first from the earth, and finished the work of creation. He created woman, and of what did he form her? He took a rib from the man and created the woman." Again they say, "He created spirit or life. How did he create spirit? Father God said : 'I love these my son and daughter. I will bestow my life upon them.' He took a particle of his life, and breathed it into their nostrils, and they came to life and were men. Thus God created man. God made food and drink, rice, fire and water, cattle, elephants and

[1] William Ellis, *Polynesian Researches*, Second Edition (London, 1832-1836), i. 110 *sq*. *Ivi* or *iwi* is the regular word for "bone" in the various Polynesian languages. See E. Tregear, *The Maori - Polynesian Comparative Dictionary* (Wellington, New Zealand, 1891), p. 109.

[2] George Turner, *Samoa a Hundred Years ago and long before* (London, 1884), pp. 267 *sq*.

[3] J. L. Nicholas, *Narrative of a Voyage to New Zealand* (London, 1817), i. 59, who writes, "and to add still more to this strange coincidence the general term for bone is *Hevee*."

birds."[1] The suspicion that we have here to do with missionary
or at all events European influence, is confirmed, if not raised
to a certainty, by other traditions current among the Ghaikos,
a branch of the Karens. For the Ghaikos trace their genealogy to Adam, and count thirty generations from him to the
building of a great tower and the confusion of tongues.
According to them "in the days of Pan-dan-man, the people
determined to build a pagoda that should reach up to heaven.
The place they suppose to be somewhere in the country of
the Red Karens, with whom they represent themselves as
associated until this event. When the pagoda was half way
up to heaven, God came down and confounded the language
of the people, so that they could not understand each other.
Then the people scattered, and Than-mau-rai, the father of
the Ghaiko tribe, came west, with eight chiefs, and settled in
the valley of the Sitang."[2] Again, the Bedel Tartars of
Siberia have a tradition that God at first made a man, who
lived quite alone on the earth. But once, while this solitary
slept, the devil touched his breast ; then a bone grew out
from his ribs, and falling to the ground it grew long and
became the first woman.[3] Thus these Tartars have deepened
the cynicism of the writer in Genesis by giving the devil
a hand in the creation of our common mother.[4] But to return
to the Pacific.

Tartar
tra-
dition of the
creation of
woman out
of
man's rib

In Nui, or Netherland Island, one of the Ellice Islands,
they say that the god Aulialia made models of a man and
a woman out of earth, and when he raised them up they
came to life. He called the man Tepapa and the woman
Tetata.[5] The Pelew Islanders relate that a brother and
sister made men out of clay kneaded with the blood of
various animals, and that the characters of these first men

Other
stori-
es of
th creation
of man in
the Pacific.

[1] Rev. E. B. Cross, "On the
Karens," *Journal of the American
Oriental Society*, vol. iv. No. 2 (New
York, 1854), pp. 300 *sq.* The trans-
lations from the Karen are by the
Rev. F. Mason, D.D.

[2] Rev. F. Mason, D.D., "On
Dwellings, Works of Art, etc., of the
Karens,' *Journal of the Asiatic Society
of Bengal*, N.S. xxxvii. (1868) pp.
163 *sq.*

[3] W. Radloff, *Aus Sibirien* (Leipsic,
1884), i. 360.

[4] In Namoluk, one of the Caroline
Islands, there is a story of a man who
in the early age of the world was
created out of the rib of a man and
married the daughter of the Creator.
See Max Girschner, "Die Karolinen-
insel Namoluk und ihre Bewohner,"
Baessler-Archiv. ii. (Leipsic and Berlin,
1912) p. 187.

[5] G. Turner, *Samoa* (London, 1884),
pp. 300 *sq.*

and of their descendants were determined by the characters of the animals whose blood had been mingled with the primordial clay ; for instance, men who have rat's blood in them are thieves, men who have serpent's blood in them are sneaks, and men who have cock's blood in them are brave.[1]

Melanesian legends of the creation of men out of red clay. According to a Melanesian legend, told in Mota, one of the Banks' Islands, the hero Qat moulded men of clay, the red clay from the marshy riverside at Vanua Lava. At first he made men and pigs just alike, but his brothers remonstrated with him, so he beat down the pigs to go on all fours and made man walk upright. Qat fashioned the first woman out of supple twigs, and when she smiled he knew she was a living woman.[2] A somewhat different version of the Melanesian story is told at Lakona, in Santa Maria. There they say that Qat and another spirit (vui) called Marawa both made men. Qat constructed them out of the wood of dracaena-trees. Six days he worked at them, carving their limbs and fitting them together. Then he allowed them six days to come to life. Three days he hid them away, and three days more he worked to make them live. He set them up and danced to them and beat his drum, and little by little they stirred, till at last they could stand all by themselves. Then Qat divided them into pairs and called each pair husband and wife. Marawa also constructed men out of the wood of a tree, but it was a different tree, the tavisoviso. He likewise worked at them six days, beat his drum, and made them live, just as Qat did. But when he saw them move, he dug a pit and buried them in it for six days, and then, when he scraped away the earth to see what they were doing, he found them all rotten and stinking. That was the origin of death.[3] The natives of Malekula, one of the New Hebrides, give the name of Bokor to the great being who kneaded the first man and woman out of clay.[4]

Stories of the creation of man in the Indian Archipelago. The Toradja version in Celebes. The inhabitants of Noo-hoo-roa, in the Kei Islands, say that their ancestors were fashioned out of clay by the supreme

[1] J. Kubary, "Die Religion der Pelauer," in A. Bastian's *Allerlei aus Volks- und Menschenkunde* (Berlin, 1888), i. 3, 56.

[2] R. H. Codrington, *The Melanesians* (Oxford, 1891), p. 158.

[3] R. H. Codrington, *The Melan-*

esians, pp. 157 sq.

[4] Rev. T. Watt Leggatt, "Malekula, New Hebrides," *Report of the Fourth Meeting of the Australasian Association for the Advancement of Science, held at Hobart, Tasmania, in January 1892* (Hobart, 1893), pp. 707 sq.

god, Dooadlera, who breathed life into the clay figures.[1]
According to the Bare'e-speaking Toradjas of Central Celebes
there were at first no human beings on the earth.   Then
i Lai, the god of the upper world, and i Ndara, the goddess
of the under world, resolved to make men.   They committed
the task to i Kombengi, who made two models, one of a man
and the other of a woman, out of stone or, according to others,
out of wood.   When he had done his work, he set up his
models by the side of the road which leads from the upper
to the under world, so that all spirits passing by might see
and criticize his workmanship.   In the evening the gods
talked it over, and agreed that the calves of the legs of the
two figures were not round enough.   So Kombengi went to
work again, and constructed another pair of models which he
again submitted to the divine criticism.   This time the gods
observed that the figures were too pot-bellied, so Kombengi
produced a third pair of models, which the gods approved
of, after the maker had made a slight change in the anatomy
of the figures, transferring a portion of the male to the female
figure.   It now only remained to make the figures live.   So
the god Lai returned to his celestial mansion to fetch eternal
breath for the man and woman ; but in the meantime the
Creator himself, whether from thoughtlessness or haste, had
allowed the common wind to blow on the figures, and they
drew their breath and life from it.   That is why the breath
returns to the wind when a man dies.[2]

The aborigines of Minahassa, in the north of Celebes,
say that two beings called Wailan Wangko and Wangi
were alone on an island, where grew a coco-nut tree.
Said Wailan Wangko to Wangi, "Remain on earth while
I climb up the tree."   Said Wangi to Wailan Wangko,
"Good."   But then a thought occurred to Wangi, and he
climbed up the tree to ask Wailan Wangko why he, Wangi,
should remain down there all alone.   Said Wailan Wangko
to Wangi, "Return and take earth and make two images, a
man and a woman."   Wangi did so, and both images were

The
Mi aba san
version n
Celebes.

[1] C. M. Pleyte, "Ethnographische
Beschrijving der Kei-Eilanden," *Tijdschrift van het Nederlandsch Aardrijkskundig Genootschap*, Tweede Serie,
x. (1893) p. 564.

[2] N. Adriani en Alb. C. Kruijt,
*De Bare'e - sprekende Toradja's van
Midden-Celebes* (Batavia, 1912-1914),
i. 3, 245 *sq.*

men who could move but not speak. So Wangi swarmed up the tree again to ask Wailan Wangko, " How now? The two images are made, but they cannot speak." Said Wailan Wangko to Wangi, " Take this ginger and go and blow it on the skulls and the ears of these two images, that they may be able to speak ; call the man Adam and the woman Ewa."[1] In this narrative the names of the man and woman betray Christian or Mohammedan influence, but the rest of the story may be aboriginal.

The Dyaks of Sakarran in British Borneo say that the first man was made by two large birds. At first they tried to make men out of trees, but in vain. Then they hewed them out of rocks, but the figures could not speak. Then they moulded a man out of damp earth and infused into his veins the red gum of the kumpang-tree. After that they called to him and he answered ; they cut him and blood flowed from his wounds, so they gave him the name of Tannah Kumpok or " moulded earth."[2] Some of the Sea Dyaks, however, are of a different opinion. They think that a certain god named Salampandai is the maker of men. He hammers them into shape out of clay, thus forming the bodies of children who are to be born into the world. There is an insect which makes a curious clinking noise at night, and when the Dyaks hear it, they say that it is the clink of Salampandai's hammer at his work. The story goes that he was commanded by the gods to make a man, and he made one of stone ; but the figure could not speak and was therefore rejected. So he set to work again, and made a man of iron ; but neither could he speak, so the gods would have none of him. The third time Salampandai made a man of clay, and he had the power of speech. Therefore the gods were pleased and said, " The man you have made will do well. Let him be the ancestor of the human race, and you must make others like him." So Salampandai set about fashioning human beings, and he is still fashioning them at his anvil, working away with his

---

[1] N. Graafland, *De Minahassa* (Rotterdam, 1869), i. 96 *sq.*
[2] Horsburgh, quoted by H. Ling Roth, *The Natives of Sarawak and of British North Borneo* (London, 1896), i. 299 *sq.* Compare the Lord Bishop of Labuan, "On the Wild Tribes of the North-West Coast of Borneo," *Transactions of the Ethnological Society of London*, New Series, ii. (1863) p. 27.

tools in unseen regions. There he hammers out the clay babies, and when one of them is finished he brings it to the gods, who ask the infant, " What would you like to handle and use? " If the child answers, " A sword," the gods pronounce it a male; but if the child replies, " Cotton and a spinning-wheel," they pronounce it a female. Thus they are born boys or girls, according to their own wishes.[1]

The natives of Nias, an island to the south-west of Sumatra, have a long poem descriptive of the creation, which they recite at the dances performed at the funeral of a chief. In this poem, which is arranged in couplets after the style of Hebrew poetry, the second verse repeating the idea of the first in somewhat different language, we read how the supreme god, Luo Zaho, bathed at a celestial spring which reflected his figure in its clear water as in a mirror, and how, on seeing his image in the water, he took a handful of earth as large as an egg, and fashioned out of it a figure like one of those figures of ancestors which the people of Nias construct. Having made it, he put it in the scales and weighed it; he weighed also the wind, and having weighed it, he put it on the lips of the figure which he had made; so the figure spoke like a man or like a child, and God gave him the name of Sihai. But though Sihai was like God in form, he had no offspring; and the world was dark, for as yet there was neither sun nor moon. So God meditated, and sent Sihai down to earth to live there in a house made of tree-fern. But while as yet he had neither wife nor child, he one day died at noon. However, out of his mouth grew two trees, and the trees budded and blossomed, and the wind shook the blossoms from the trees, and blossoms fell to the ground and from them arose diseases. And from Sihai's throat grew a tree, from which gold is derived; and from his heart grew another tree, from which men are descended. Moreover, out of his right eye came the sun, and out of his left eye came the moon.[2] In this legend the idea of creating man in his own image appears to have been

---

[1] Edwin H. Gomes, *Seventeen Years among the Sea Dyaks of Borneo* (London, 1911), p. 197, compare p. 174.

[2] H. Sunderman, *Die Insel Nias und die Mission daselbst* (Barmen, 1905), pp. 65 *sqq.*, 200 *sqq.*

suggested to the Creator by the accident of seeing his own
likeness reflected in a crystal spring.

Story of
the creation
of man told
by the
Bila-an
in the
Philippine
Islands.

The Bila-an, a wild tribe of Mindanao, one of the Philippine Islands, relate the creation of man as follows. They
say that in the beginning there was a certain being named
Melu, of a size so huge that no known thing can give any
idea of it ; he was white in colour, and had golden teeth,
and he sat upon the clouds, occupying all the space above.
Being of a very cleanly habit, he was constantly rubbing
himself in order to preserve the whiteness of his skin un-
sullied.   The scurf which he thus removed from his person
he laid on one side, till it gathered in such a heap as to
fidget him.   To be rid of it he constructed the earth out of
it, and being pleased with his work he resolved to make
two beings like himself, only much smaller in size.   He
fashioned them accordingly in his own likeness out of the
leavings of the scurf whereof he had moulded the earth, and
these two were the first human beings.   But while the
Creator was still at work on them, and had finished one of
them all but the nose, and the other all but the nose and one
other part, Tau Dalom Tana came up to him and demanded
to be allowed to make the noses.   After a heated argument
with the Creator, he got his way and made the noses, but in
applying them to the faces of our first parents he unfortunately placed them upside down.   So warm had been the
discussion between the Creator and his assistant in regard
to the noses, that the Creator quite forgot to finish the other
part of the second figure, and went away to his place above
the clouds, leaving the first man or the first woman (for we
are not told which) imperfect ; and Tau Dalom Tana also
went away to his place below the earth.   After that a heavy
rain fell, and the two first of human kind nearly perished,
for the rain ran off the tops of their heads into their up-
turned nostrils.   Happily the Creator perceived their plight
and coming down from the clouds to the rescue he took off
their noses and replaced them right end up.[1]

A variant of the foregoing legend told by the Bila-an
runs thus.   In the beginning four beings, two male and two

[1] Fay-Cooper Cole, *The Wild Tribes*
of Davao District, Mindanao (Chicago,
1913), pp. 135 *sq.*   (*Field Museum
of Natural History, Publication 170.*)

female, lived on a small island no bigger than a hat. Neither trees nor grass grew on the island, but one bird lived on it. So the four beings sent the bird to fetch some earth, the fruit of the rattan, and the fruit of trees. When it brought the articles, Melu, who was one of the two male beings, took the earth and moulded it into land, just as a woman moulds pots ; and having fashioned it he planted the seeds in it, and they grew. But after a time he said, " Of what use is land without people ? " The others said, " Let us make wax into people." They did so, but when the waxen figures were set near the fire, they melted. So the Creators perceived that they could not make man out of wax. Not to be baffled, they resolved to make him out of dirt, and the two male beings accordingly addressed themselves to the task. All went well till it came to fashioning the noses. The Creator who was charged with this operation put the noses on upside down, and though his colleague Melu pointed out his mistake, and warned him that the people would be drowned if they went about with their noses in that position, he refused to repair his blunder and turned his back in a huff. His colleague seized the opportunity and the noses at the same instant, and hastily adjusted these portions of the human frame in the position which they still occupy. But on the · bridge of the nose you can see to this day the print left by the Creator's fingers in his hurry.[1]

The Bagobos, a pagan tribe of South-Eastern Mindanao, say that in the beginning a certain Diwata made the sea and the land, and planted trees of many sorts. Then he took two lumps of earth, shaped them like human figures, and spat on them ; so they became man and woman. The old man was called Tuglay, and the old woman, Tuglibung. They married and lived together, and the old man made a great house and planted seeds of different kinds, which the old woman gave him.[2] *Bagobo ry t creation of man.*

The Kumis, who inhabit portions of Arakan and the Chittagong hill tracts in eastern India, told Captain Lewin the following story of the creation of man. God made the world and the trees and the creeping things first, and after *Indian l of the creation of man.*

[1] Fay-Cooper Cole, *op. cit.* pp. 136 *sq.*
[2] Laura Watson Benedict, " Bagobo

Myths," *Journal of American Folk-lore,* xxvi. (1913) p. 15.

Kumi story how God created man with the assistance of a dog.

that he made one man and one woman, forming their bodies of clay ; but every night, when he had done his work, there came a great snake, which, while God was sleeping, devoured the two images. This happened twice or thrice, and God was at his wits' end, for he had to work all day, and could not finish the pair in less than twelve hours ; besides, if he did not sleep, " he would be no good," as the native narrator observed with some show of probability. So, as I have said, God was at his wits' end. But at last he got up early one morning and first made a dog and put life into it ; and that night, when he had finished the images, he set the dog to watch them, and when the snake came, the dog barked and frightened it away. That is why to this day, when a man is dying, the dogs begin to howl ; but the Kumis think that God sleeps heavily nowadays, or that the snake is bolder, for men die in spite of the howling of the dogs. If God did not sleep, there would be neither sickness nor death ; it is during the hours of his slumber that the snake comes and carries us off.[1] A similar tale is told by the

Khasi version of the tale.

Khasis of Assam. In the beginning, they say, God created man and placed him on earth, but on returning to look at the work of his hands he found that the man had been destroyed by the evil spirit. This happened a second time, whereupon the deity created first a dog and then a man ; and the dog kept watch and prevented the devil from destroying the man. Thus the work of the deity was preserved.[2]

Korku version of the tale.

The same story also crops up, with a slight varnish of Hindoo mythology, among the Korkus, an aboriginal tribe of the Central Provinces of India. According to them, Rawan, the demon king of Ceylon, observed that the Vindhyan and Satpura ranges were uninhabited, and he besought the great god Mahadeo to people them. So Mahadeo, by whom they mean Siva, sent a crow to find for him an ant-hill of red earth, and the bird discovered such an ant-hill among the mountains of Betul. Thereupon the god repaired to the spot, and taking a handful of the red

[1] Captain T. H. Lewin, *Wild Races of South - Eastern India* (London, 1870), pp. 224-226.

[2] Lieut.-Colonel P. R. T. Gurdon, *The Khasis*, Second Edition (London, 1914), p. 106. Compare A. Bastian, *Volkerstämme am Brahmaputra und verwandtschaftliche Nachbarn* (Berlin, 1883), p. 8.

earth he fashioned out of it two images, in the likeness of a man and a woman. But no sooner had he done so than two fiery horses, sent by Indra, rose from the earth and trampled the images to dust. For two days the Creator persisted in his attempts, but as often as the images were made they were dashed in pieces by the horses. At last the god made an image of a dog, and breathed into it the breath of life, and the animal kept off the fiery steeds of Indra. Thus the god was able to make the two images of man and woman undisturbed, and bestowing life upon them, he called them Mula and Mulai. These two became the ancestors of the Korku tribe.[1]

A like tale is told, with a curious variation, by the Mundas, a primitive aboriginal tribe of Chota Nagpur. They say that the Sun-god, by name Singbonga, first fashioned two clay figures, one meant to represent a man and the other a woman. But before he could endow the figures with life, the horse, apprehensive of what in future he might endure at their hands, trampled them under its hoofs. In those days the horse had wings and could move about much faster than now. When the Sun-god found that the horse had destroyed his earthen figures of men, he first created a spider and then fashioned two more clay figures like those which the horse had demolished. Next he ordered the spider to guard the effigies against the horse. Accordingly the spider wove its web round the figures in such a way that the horse could not break them again. After that, the Sun-god imparted life to the two figures, which thus became the first human beings.[2]

A story of the same sort, in fuller form and with material variations, is told by the Santals of Bengal. They say that in the beginning there was a certain Thakur Jiu. There was no land visible, all was covered with water. Then Thakur Jiu's servants said to him, "How shall we create human beings?" He replied, "If it be so desired,

Munda
\rs of
the tale

Santal
rj t
creation of
man.

[1] R. V. Russell, *The Tribes and Castes of the Central Provinces of India* (London, 1916), iii. 551 *sq.*

[2] Sarat Chandra Roy, "The Divine Myths of the Mundas," *Journal of the Bihar and Orissa Research Society*, ii.

(Bankipore, 1916) pp. 201 *sq.* The writer adds in a note, " The Bir-hors and the Asurs of Chota Nagpur substitute the dog for the spider. The dog would bark at the horse and frighten him away whenever he attempted to approach the clay figures."

we can create them." They then said, "If you give us a blessing (or the gift), we shall be able to do so." Thakur Jiu then said, "Go, call Malin Budhi. She is to be found in a rock cave under the water." When she came, she received the order to form two human beings. Some say she made them of a kind of froth which proceeded from a supernatural being who dwelt at the bottom of the sea, but others say she made them of a stiff clay. Thakur Jiu was a spectator of what was being done. At length Malin Budhi made the bodies of two human beings, and laid them out to dry. In the meantime Day-horse (Singh Sadom) passed that way, and trampling them under foot destroyed them. After an interval Thakur Jiu demanded of Malin Budhi whether she had prepared the figures. She replied, "I made them, but I have many enemies." Thakur Jiu inquired who they were, and she answered, "Who but Day-horse?" Thakur Jiu then said, "Kick the pieces into the Sora Nai and the Samud Nai." At this point the reciter of the story chants the following staves :—

How the clay images were trampled to pieces by Day-horse

> " *Oh! the Day-horse. Oh! the Day-horse,*
> *The Day-horse has gone to the river Gang,*
> *The Day-horse has floated to the Sora Sea,*
> *Oh! the Day-horse.*"

The creation of two birds.

Thakur Jiu then said to Malin Budhi, "I again give you a blessing ; go, make two human beings." Having prepared them, she went to Thakur Jiu, who said, "Well, have you got them ready?" She replied, "They are ready ; give them the gift of life." He said, "Above the door-frame is the life (or spirit) of birds ; do not bring that. Upon the cross-beam is the life of human beings ; bring it." So she went, but being low of stature she could not reach the cross-beam ; hence she brought the birds' life from above the door. No sooner had she given the birds' life to the figures than they flew up into the heavens, where they continued to course about, whether for twelve years or for twelve months is doubtful. The names of the birds were Has and Hasin. At length the desire to breed came upon them, and they went to Thakur Jiu and said, "You gave us being, but we cannot find a place on which to rest." He answered, "I will prepare a place for you."

Living in the water were Sole-fish, Crab, Prince Earth-worm, and Lendom Kuar. Thakur Jiu called them and ordered them to raise the earth above the water. Sole-fish said, " I will raise the earth above the water," but though he tried and tried again, he could not do it. Then Crab came and said, " I will do it," but he also failed. Prince Earth-worm then came and undertook to accomplish it. So he ducked his head under water and swallowed earth, and the earth passed through him and came out at the other end ; but when it fell on the surface of the water, it immediately sank to the bottom again. Then Prince Earth-worm said, " Within the water resides Prince Tortoise ; if we fasten him at the four corners with chains, and then raise the earth on his back, it will remain and not fall into the water again." So Prince Earth-worm secured Prince Tortoise with chains and raised the earth on his back, and in a short time there was an island in the midst of the waters. Thakur Jiu then caused a *karam* tree [1] to spring up, and at the foot of the *karam* tree he caused *sirom* grass [2] to grow. He then caused *dhobi* grass [3] to spring up, after which he covered the earth with all kinds of trees and herbs. In this manner the earth became firm and stable.

Then the birds Has and Hasin came and alighted on the *karam* tree, and afterwards made their nest among the *sirom* grass at its foot. There the female laid two eggs, and Raghop Buar came and ate them. Again she laid other two eggs, and again Raghop Buar came and devoured them. Then Has and Hasin went to Thakur Jiu and informed him that Raghop Buar had twice eaten their eggs. On hearing this Thakur Jiu said, " I shall send some one to guard your eggs." So, calling Jaher-era, he committed the eggs of the two birds to her care. So well did she perform her task that the female was allowed to hatch her eggs, and from the eggs emerged two human beings, a male and a female ; their names were Pilchu Haram and Pilchu Budhi. These were the parents of mankind. Here the reciter of the story bursts out into song as follows :—

The raising of the earth out of the water.

Human being hatched out of birds eggs.

---

[1] *Adina cordifolia*, Hook. f. Benth.   [2] *Andropogon muricatus*, Retz.
[3] *Cynodon dactylon*, Pers.

> " *Hae, hae, two human beings,*
> *Hae, hae, are born in the water,*
> *Hae, hae, how can I bring them up ?*
> *Hae, hae, where can I place them ?*
> *My mother gave me birth among the* sirom *grass,*
> *My father had his dwelling at the* karma *tree foot."* [1]

Creation and evolution combined in the Santal story.

This Santal story of the origin of man combines the principles of creation and evolution, for according to it mankind is ultimately derived from two images, which were modelled in human form out of froth or damp clay, but were afterwards accidentally transformed into birds, from whose eggs the first man and woman of flesh and blood were hatched.

Cheremiss story of the creation of man.

The Cheremiss of Russia, a Finnish people, tell a story of the creation of man which recalls episodes in the Toradjan and Indian legends of the same event. They say that God moulded man's body of clay and then went up to heaven to fetch the soul, with which to animate it. In his absence he set the dog to guard the body. But while he was away the Devil drew near, and blowing a cold wind on the dog he seduced the animal by the bribe of a fur-coat to relax his guard. Thereupon the fiend spat on the clay body and beslavered it so foully, that when God came back he despaired of ever cleaning up the mess and saw himself reduced to the painful necessity of turning the body outside in. That is why a man's inside is now so dirty. And God cursed the dog the same day for his culpable neglect of duty.[2]

African stories of the creation of man. The Shilluk version of the tale.

Turning now to Africa, we find the legend of the creation of mankind out of clay among the Shilluks of the White Nile, who ingeniously explain the different complexions of the various races by the differently coloured clays out of which they were fashioned. They say that the creator Juok moulded all men out of earth, and that while he was engaged in the work of creation he wandered about the world. In the land of the whites he found a pure white earth or sand, and out of it he shaped white men. Then he came to the land of Egypt and out of the mud of the Nile he made red

[1] Rev. A. Campbell, D.D., "The Traditions of the Santals," *The Journal of the Bihar and Orissa Research Society,* ii. (Bankipore, 1916) pp. 15-17.

[2] Jean N. Smirnov, *Les Populations Finnoises des Bassins de la Volga et de la Kama,* Première Partie (Paris 1898) p. 200.

or brown men.   Lastly, he came to the land of the Shilluks,
and finding there black earth he created black men out of it.
The way in which he modelled men was this.   He took a
lump of earth and said to himself, " I will make man, but he
must be able to walk and run and go out into the fields, so
I will give him two long legs, like the flamingo."   Having
done so, he thought again, " The man must be able to cultivate his millet, so I will give him two arms, one to hold the
hoe, and the other to tear up the weeds."   So he gave him
two arms.   Then he thought again, " The man must be able
to see his millet, so I will give him two eyes."   He did so
accordingly.   Next he thought to himself, " The man must
be able to eat his millet, so I will give him a mouth."   And
a mouth he gave him accordingly.   After that he thought
within himself, " The man must be able to dance and speak
and sing and shout, and for these purposes he must have a
tongue."   And a tongue he gave him accordingly.   Lastly,
the deity said to himself, " The man must be able to hear the
noise of the dance and the speech of great men, and for that
he needs two ears."   So two ears he gave him, and sent
him out into the world a perfect man.[1]   The Fans of West
Africa say that God created man out of clay, at first in the
shape of a lizard, which he put in a pool of water and left
there for seven days.   At the end of the seven days God
cried, " Come forth," and a man came out of the pool instead
of a lizard.[2]   The Ewe-speaking tribes of Togo-land, in West
Africa, think that God still makes men out of clay.   When
a little of the water with which he moistens the clay remains
over, he pours it on the ground, and out of that he makes
the bad and disobedient people.   When he wishes to make
a good man he makes him out of good clay ; but when he
wishes to make a bad man, he employs only bad clay for
the purpose.   In the beginning God fashioned a man and
set him on the earth ; after that he fashioned a woman.
The two looked at each other and began to laugh, whereupon God sent them into the world.[3]

*The Fan
v s   f
the story*

*The Ewe
v rs
the story*

[1] W. Hofmayr, "Die Religion der
Schilluk," *Anthropos*, vi. (1911) pp.
128 *sq.*

[2] Günter Tessmann, *Die Pangwe*

(Berlin, 1913), ii. 18.
[3] Jakob Spieth, *Die Ewe-Stämme,
Material zur Kunde des Ewe-Volkes
in Deutsch-Togo* (Berlin, 1906), pp.
828, 840.

American
o   of
the crea ion
of man.
sk m
versions of
the story.

The story of the creation of mankind out of clay occurs also in America, both among the Eskimo and the Indians, from Alaska to Paraguay. Thus the Eskimo of Point Barrow, in Alaska, tell of a time when there was no man in the land, till a certain spirit named *à se lu*, who resided at Point Barrow, made a clay man, set him up on the shore to dry, breathed into him, and gave him life.[1] Other Eskimo of Alaska relate how the Raven made the first woman out of clay, to be a companion to the first man ; he fastened water-grass to the back of the head to be hair, flapped his wings over the clay figure, and it arose, a beautiful young woman.[2]

Californian
nd a
stories of
the creation
of man.

The Acagchemem Indians of California said that a powerful being called Chinigchinich created man out of clay which he found on the banks of a lake ; male and female created he them, and the Indians of the present day are the descendants of the clay man and woman.[3]

Maidu
version
of the
story.

According to the Maidu Indians of California the first man and woman were created by a mysterious personage named Earth-Initiate, who descended from the sky by a rope made of feathers. His body shone like the sun, but his face was hidden and never seen. One afternoon he took dark red earth, mixed it with water, and fashioned two figures, one of them a man and the other a woman. He laid the man on his right side and the woman on his left side, in his house. He lay thus and sweated all that afternoon and all that night. Early in the morning the woman began to tickle him in the side. He kept very still and did not laugh. By and by he arose, thrust a piece of pitch-wood into the ground, and fire burst out. The two people were very white. No one to-day is so white as they were. Their eyes were pink, their hair was black, their teeth shone brightly, and they were very handsome. It is said that Earth-Initiate did not finish the hands of the people, because he did not know how best to do it. The coyote, or prairie-wolf, who plays a great part in the myths of the Western Indians, saw the

---

[1] *Report of the International Expedition to Point Barrow* (Washington, 1885), p. 47.

[2] E. W. Nelson, "The Eskimo about Bering Strait," *Eighteenth Annual Report of the Bureau of American Ethno-* *logy*, Part i. (Washington, 1899) p. 454.

[3] Father Geronimo Boscana, "Chinigchinich," appended to [A. Robinson's] *Life in California* (New York, 1846), p. 247.

people and suggested that they ought to have hands like his. But Earth-Initiate said, " No, their hands shall be like mine." Then he finished them. When the coyote asked why their hands were to be like that, Earth-Initiate answered, " So that, if they are chased by bears, they can climb trees." The first man was called Kuksu, and the first woman was called Morning-Star Woman.[1]

The Diegueno Indians or, as they call themselves, the Kawakipais, who occupy the extreme south-western corner of the State of California, have a myth to explain how the world in its present form and the human race were created. They say that in the beginning there was no earth or solid land, nothing but salt water, one vast primeval ocean. But under the sea lived two brothers, of whom the elder was named Tcaipakomat. Both of them kept their eyes shut, for if they had not done so, the salt water would have blinded them. After a while the elder brother came up to the surface and looked about him, but he could see nothing but water. The younger brother also came up, but on the way to the surface he incautiously opened his eyes, and the salt water blinded him ; so when he emerged he could see nothing at all, and therefore he sank back into the depths. Left alone on the face of the deep, the elder brother now undertook the task of creating a habitable earth out of the waste of waters. First of all he made little red ants, which produced land by filling up the water solid with their tiny bodies. But still the world was dark, for as yet neither sun nor moon had been created. Tcaipakomat now caused certain black birds with flat bills to come into being ; but in the darkness the birds lost their way and could not find where to roost. Next Tcaipakomat took three kinds of clay, red, yellow, and black, and thereof he made a round flat thing, which he took in his hand and threw up against the sky. It stuck there, and beginning to shed a dim light became the moon. Dissatisfied with the faint illumination of this pallid orb, Tcaipakomat took more clay, moulded it into another round flat disc, and tossed it up against the other side of the sky. It stuck there and became the sun,

The
¹
of man
according
Diegueno
Indians of
California.

---

[1] Roland B. Dixon, "Maidu Myths," *Bulletin of the American Museum of* *Natural History*, xvii. Part ii. (New York, 1902), pp. 39, 41 *sq.*

lighting up everything with his beams.   After that Tcaipakomat took a lump of light-coloured clay, split it partly up,
and made a man of it.   Then he took a rib from the man
and made a woman of it.   The woman thus created out of
the man's rib was called Sinyaxau or First Woman (from
siny, " woman," and *axau,* " first ").   From this first man
and woman, modelled by the Creator out of clay, mankind
is descended.   At first people lived at a great mountain
called Wikami.   If you go there and put your ear to the
ground, you will hear the sound of dancing ; it is. made by
the spirits of all the dead people footing it away.   For when
people die, they go back to the place where all things were at
first created, and there they dance, just as live folks do here.[1]

The Hopi
story of the
creation of
man.   The Hopi or Moqui Indians of Arizona similarly believe
that in the beginning there was nothing but water everywhere, and that two deities, apparently goddesses, both
named Huruing Wuhti, lived in houses in the ocean, one of
them in the east, and the other in the west ; and these two
by their efforts caused dry land to appear in the midst of
the water.   Nevertheless the sun, on his daily passage across
the newly created earth, noticed that there was no living
being of any kind on the face of the ground, and he brought
this radical defect to the notice of the two deities.   Accordingly the divinities met in consultation, the eastern goddess
passing over the sea on the rainbow as a bridge to·visit her
western colleague.   Having laid their heads together they
resolved to make a little bird ; so the goddess of the east
made a wren of clay, and together they chanted an incantation over it, so that the clay bird soon came to life.   Then
they sent out the wren to fly over the world and see whether
he could discover any living being on the face of the earth ;
but on his return he reported that no such being existed
anywhere.   Afterwards the two deities created many sorts
of birds and beasts in like manner, and sent them forth to
inhabit the world.   Last of all the two goddesses made up
their mind to create man.   Thereupon the eastern goddess
took clay and moulded out of it first a woman and after-

[1] T. T. Waterman, *The Religious
Practices of the Diegueño Indians* (Berkeley, 1910), pp. 338 *sq.* (*University of California Publications in
American Archaeology and Ethnology,*
vol. viii. No. 6.)

wards a man ; and the clay man and woman were brought
to life just as the birds and beasts had been so before them.[1]

The Pima Indians, another tribe of Arizona, allege
that the Creator took clay into his hands, and mixing
it with the sweat of his own body, kneaded the whole
into a lump. Then he blew upon the lump till it began
to live and move and became a man and a woman.[2] A
priest of the Natchez Indians in Louisiana told Du Pratz
"that God had kneaded some clay, such as that which
potters use, and had made it into a little man ; and that
after examining it, and finding it well formed, he blew
upon his work, and forthwith that little man had life, grew,
acted, walked, and found himself a man perfectly well
shaped." As to the mode in which the first woman was
created, the priest frankly confessed that he had no information, the ancient traditions of his tribe being silent as to any
difference in the creation of the sexes ; he thought it likely,
however, that man and woman were made in the same way.
So Du Pratz corrected his erroneous ideas by telling him the
tale of Eve and the rib, and the grateful Indian promised to
bruit it about among the old men of his tribe.[3]

The Michoacans of Mexico said that the great god
Tucapacha first made man and woman out of clay, but that
when the couple went to bathe in a river they absorbed so
much water that the clay of which they were composed all
fell to pieces. To remedy this inconvenience the Creator
applied himself again to his task and moulded them afresh out
of ashes, but the result was again disappointing. At last,
not to be baffled, he made them of metal. His perseverance
was rewarded. The man and woman were now perfectly
watertight ; they bathed in the river without falling in pieces,
and by their union they became the progenitors of mankind.[4]

[1] H. R. Voth, *The Traditions of
the Hopi* (Chicago, 1905), pp. 1 *sq.*
(*Field Columbian Museum, Publication, 96*).

[2] H. H. Bancroft, *The Native Races
of the Pacific States* (London, 1875–
1876), iii. 78.

[3] Le Page du Pratz, *The History of
Louisiana* (London, 1774), p. 330.

[4] A. de Herrera, *General History*

of the vast Continent and Islands of
America, translated into English by
Capt. J. Stevens (London, 1725–1726),
iii. 254 ; Brasseur de Bourbourg, *Histoire des Nations civilisées du Mexique
et de l'Amérique-Centrale* (Paris, 1857–
1859), iii. 80 *sq.* ; compare *id.*, i. 54
sq. A similar story of the successive
creation of the human race out of
materials is told in the *Popol Vuh*.
See below, p. 276.

According to a legend of the Peruvian Indians, which was told to a Spanish priest in Cuzco about half a century after the conquest, it was in Tiahuanaco that the human race was restored after the great flood which had destroyed them all, except one man and woman. There in Tiahuanaco, which is about seventy leagues from Cuzco, "the Creator began to raise up the people and nations, that are in that region, making one of each nation of clay, and painting the dresses that each one was to wear. Those that were to wear their hair, with hair; and those that were to be shorn, with hair cut; and to each nation was given the language that was to be spoken, and the songs to be sung, and the seeds and food that they were to sow. When the Creator had finished paint-ing and making the said nations and figures of clay, he gave life and soul to each one, as well men as women, and ordered that they should pass under the earth. Thence each nation came up in the places to which he ordered them to go."[1] The Lengua Indians of Paraguay believe that the Creator, in the shape of a beetle, inhabited a hole in the earth, and that he formed man and woman out of the clay which he threw up from his subterranean abode. At first the two were joined together, "like the Siamese twins," and in this very inconvenient posture they were sent out into the world, where they contended, at great disadvantage, with a race of powerful beings whom the beetle had previously created. So the man and woman besought the beetle to separate them. He complied with their request and gave them the power to propagate their species. So they became the parents of mankind. But the beetle, having created the world, ceased to take any active part or interest in it.[2] We are reminded of the fanciful account which Aristophanes, in the *Symposium* of Plato, gives of the original condition of mankind; how man and woman at first were knit together in one composite being, with two heads, four arms, and four legs, till Zeus cleft them down the middle and so separated the sexes.[3]

[1] Christoval de Molina, "The Fables and Rites of the Yncas," in *Narratives of the Rites and Laws of the Yncas*, translated and edited by (Sir) Clements R. Markham (London, 1873), p. 4.

[2] W. Barbrooke Grub, *An Unknown People in an Unknown Land* (London, 1911), pp. 114 sq.

[3] Plato, *Symposium*, pp. 189 D–191 D.

It is to be observed that in a number of these stories the
clay out of which our first parents were moulded is said to
have been red.   The colour was probably intended to explain
the redness of blood.   Though the Jehovistic writer in Genesis
omits to mention the colour of the clay which God used in
the construction of Adam, we may perhaps, without being
very rash, conjecture that it was red.   For the Hebrew word
for man in general is *adam*, the word for ground is *adamah*,
and the word for red is *adom* ; so that by a natural and
almost necessary concatenation of causes we arrive at the
conclusion that our first parent was modelled out of red
earth.   If any lingering doubt could remain in our mind on
the subject, it would be dissipated by the observation that
down to this day the soil of Palestine is of a dark reddish
brown, " suggesting," as the writer who notices it justly
remarks, " the connection between Adam and the ground
from which he was taken ; especially is this colour noticeable
when the soil is newly turned, either by the plough or in
digging." [1]   So remarkably does nature itself bear witness to
the literal accuracy of Holy Writ.

However, it is noteworthy that in regard to the origin of
the human species many savages reject the hypothesis of
creation in favour of the theory of evolution.   They believe,
in fact, that men in general, or their own tribespeople in
particular, have been developed out of lower forms of animal
life.   The theory of evolution is particularly popular among
totemic tribes who imagine that their ancestors sprang from
their totemic animals or plants, but it is by no means confined to them.   For example, some of the Californian Indians,
in whose mythology the coyote or prairie-wolf is a leading
personage, think that they are descended from coyotes.   At
first they walked on all fours ; then they began to have some
members of the human body, one finger, one toe, one eye,
one ear, and so on ; then they got two fingers, two toes, two
eyes, two ears, and so forth ; till at last, progressing from
period to period, they became perfect human beings.   The
loss of their tails, which they still deplore, was produced by
the habit of sitting upright. [2]   Similarly Darwin thought that

---

[1] Rev. T. C. Wilson, *Peasant Life in the Holy Land* (London, 1906), p. 189.

[2] H. R. Schoolcraft, *Indian Tribes of the United States*, iv. (Philadelphia,

"the tail has disappeared in man and the anthropomorphous apes, owing to the terminal portion having been injured by friction during a long lapse of time ; the basal and embedded portion having been reduced and modified, so as to become suitable to the erect or semi-erect position."[1] The Turtle clan of the Iroquois think that they are descended from real mud turtles which used to live in a pool. One hot summer the pool dried up, and the mud turtles set out to find another. A very fat turtle, waddling after the rest in the heat, was much incommoded by the weight of his shell, till by a great effort he heaved it off altogether. After that he gradually developed into a human being and became the progenitor of the Turtle clan.[2] The Crawfish clan of the Choctaws are in like manner descended from real crawfish, which used to live underground, only coming up occasionally through the mud to the surface. Once a party of Choctaws smoked them out, taught them to speak the Choctaw language and to walk on two legs, and made them cut off their toe nails and pluck the hair from their bodies, after which they adopted them into the tribe. But the rest of their kindred, the crawfish, are crawfish under the ground to this day.[3] The Osage Indians universally believed that they were descended from a male snail and a female beaver. A flood swept the snail down to the Missouri and left him high and dry on the bank, where the sun ripened him into a man. He met and married a beaver maid, and from the pair the tribe of the Osages is descended. For a long time these Indians retained a pious reverence for their animal ancestors and refrained from hunting beavers, because in killing a beaver they killed a brother of the Osages. But when white men came among them and offered high prices for beaver skins, the Osages yielded to the temptation and took the lives of their furry brethren.[4] The

Iroquois story.
Choctaw story.
Osage story.

1856) pp. 224 *sq.* ; compare *id.*, v. 217.   The descent of some, not all, Indians from coyotes is mentioned also by Friar Boscana in [A Robinson'] *Life in California* (New York, 1846), p. 2

[1] Charles Darwin, *The Descent of Man*, Second Edition (London, 1879), p. 60.

[2] E. A. Smith, "Myths of the Iroquois," *Second Annual Report of*

the Bureau of Ethnology (Washington, 1883), p. 77.

[3] Geo. Catlin, *Letters and Notes on the Manners Customs and Conditions of the North American Indians*, Fourth Edition (London, 1844), ii. 128.

[4] M. Lewis and W. Clark, *Travels to the Source of the Missouri River* (London, 1815), i. 12 (vol. i. pp. 44 *sq.* of the London reprint, 1905).

Carp clan of the Ootawak (Ottawa) Indians are descended Ottawa story.
from the eggs of a carp which had been deposited by the fish
on the banks of a stream and warmed by the sun.[1]   The Crane
clan of the Ojibways are sprung originally from a pair of Ojibway story.
cranes, which after long wanderings settled on the rapids at
the outlet of Lake Superior, where they were changed by
the Great Spirit into a man and woman.[2]   The members of
two Omaha clans were at first buffaloes and lived under Omaha story.
water, which they splashed about, making it muddy.   And
at death all the members of these clans went back to their
ancestors the buffaloes.   So when one of them lay a-dying,
his friends used to wrap him up in a buffalo skin with the
hair outside and say to him, " You came hither from the
animals and you are going back thither.   Do not face this
way again.   When you go, continue walking." [3]   The Haida Haida story.
Indians of the Queen Charlotte Islands believe that long ago
the raven, who is the chief figure in the mythology of North-
Western America, took a cockle from the beach and married it ;
the cockle gave birth to a female child, whom the raven took
to wife, and from their union the Indians were produced.[4]
Speaking of these Indians, a writer who lived among them
tells us that " their descent from the crows is quite gravely
affirmed and steadfastly maintained.   Hence they never will
kill one, and are always annoyed, not to say angry, should
we whites, driven to desperation by the crow-nests on every
side of us, attempt to destroy them.   This idea likewise
accounts for the coats of black paint with which young and
old in all those tribes constantly besmear themselves.   The
crow-like colour affectionately reminds the Indians of their re-
puted forefathers, and thus preserves the national tradition." [5]
The Delaware Indians called the rattlesnake their grand- Delaware s ory.
father and would on no account destroy one of these reptiles,
believing that were they to do so the whole race of rattle-
snakes would rise up and bite them.   Under the influence

---

[1] *Lettres Édifiantes et Curieuses,*
Nouvelle Édition, vi. (Paris, 1781)
p. 171.
[2] L. H. Morgan, *Ancient Society*
(London, 1877), p. 180.
[3] J. Owen Dorsey, "Omaha Sociology," *Third Annual Report of the
Bureau of Ethnology* (Washington,

1884), pp. 229, 233.
[4] G. M. Dawson, *Report on the
Queen Charlotte Islands* (Montreal,
1880), pp. 149B *sq.* (*Geological Survey
of Canada*).
[5] Francis Poole, *Queen Charlotte
Islands*, edited by John W. Lyndon
(London, 1872), p. 136.

of the white man, however, their respect for their grandfather the rattlesnake gradually died away, till at last they killed him without compunction or ceremony whenever they met him.   The writer who records the old custom observes that he had often reflected on the curious connexion which appears to subsist in the mind of an Indian between man and the brute creation ; " all animated nature," says he, " in whatever degree, is in their eyes a great whole, from which they have not yet ventured to separate themselves." [1]   However, the title of grandfather, which these Indians bestowed on the rattlesnake, hardly suffices to prove that they believed themselves to be actually descended from the creature ; it may have only been a polite form of address intended to soothe and gratify the formidable reptile.   Some of the

Peruvian story.

Indians of Peru boasted of being descended from the puma or American lion ; hence they adored the lion as a god, and appeared at festivals, like Hercules, dressed in the skins of lions with the heads of the beasts fixed over their own. Others claimed to be descended from condors and attired themselves in great black and white wings, like that huge bird.[2]

African and asy stories of the u of men out of animals.

The Wanika of East Africa look upon the hyena as one of their ancestors or as associated in some way with their origin and destiny.   The death of a hyena is mourned by the whole people, and the greatest funeral ceremonies which they perform are performed for this brute.   The wake held over a chief is as nothing compared to the wake held over a hyena ; one tribe alone mourns the death of its chief, but all the tribes unite to celebrate the obsequies of a hyena.[3] Some Malagasy families claim to be descended from the babacoote (*Lichanotus brevicaudatus*), a large lemur of grave appearance and staid demeanour which lives in the depth of the forest.   When they find one of these creatures dead,

[1] Rev. John Heckewelder, "An Account of the History, Manners, and Customs of the Indian Nations, who once inhabited Pennsylvania and the Neighbouring States," *Transactions of the Historical and Literary Committee of the American Philosophical Society* (Philadelphia, 1819), pp. 245, 247, 248.

[2] Garcilasso de la Vega, *First Part of the Royal Commentaries of the Yncas*, translated and edited by (Sir) Clements R. Markham (London, 1869-1871), i. 323, ii. 156.

[3] Charles New, *Life, Wanderings, and Labours in Eastern Africa* (London, 1873), p. 122.

his human descendants bury it solemnly, digging a grave for it, wrapping it in a shroud, and weeping and lamenting over its carcase. A doctor who had shot a babacoote was accused by the inhabitants of a Betsimisaraka village of having killed " one of their grandfathers in the forest," and to appease their indignation he had to promise not to skin the animal in the village but in a solitary place where nobody could see him.[1] Many of the Betsimisaraka believe that the curious nocturnal animal called the aye-aye (*Cheiromys madagascariensis*) " is the embodiment of their forefathers, and hence will not touch it, much less do it an injury. It is said that when one is discovered dead in the forest, these people make a tomb for it and bury it with all the forms of a funeral. They think that if they attempt to entrap it, they will surely die in consequence."[2] Some Malagasy tribes believe themselves descended from crocodiles and accordingly they deem the ferocious reptiles their brothers. If one of these scaly brothers so far forgets the ties of kinship as to devour a man, the chief of the tribe, or in his absence an old man familiar with the tribal customs, repairs at the head of the people to the edge of the water, and summons the family of the culprit to deliver him up to the arm of justice. A hook is then baited and cast into the river or lake. Next day the guilty brother, or one of his family, is dragged ashore, formally tried, sentenced to death, and executed. The claims of justice being thus satisfied, the erring brother is lamented and buried like a kinsman ; a mound is raised over his grave, and a stone marks the place of his head.[3]

Amongst the Tshi-speaking tribes of the Gold Coast in West Africa the Horse-mackerel family traces its descent from a real horse-mackerel whom an ancestor of theirs once

Stories ie evolution of men out of fish told in West Africa and Borneo.

---

[1] Father Abinal, "Croyances fabu- leuses des Malgaches," *Les Missions Catholiques*, xii. (1880) p. 526 ; G. H. Smith, "Some Betsimisaraka Super- stitions," *The Antananarivo Annual and Madagascar Magazine*, No. 10 (Antananarivo, 1886), p. 239 ; H. W. Little, *Madagascar, its History and People* (London, 1884), pp. 321 *sq.* ; A. van Gennep, *Tabou et Totémisme a Madagascar* (Paris, 1904), pp. 214 *sqq.*

[2] G. A. Shaw, "The Aye-aye," *The Antananarivo Annual and Madagascar Magazine*, vol. ii. (Antananarivo, 1896), pp. 201, 203 (Reprint of the Second Four Numbers). Compare A. van Gennep, *Tabou et Totémisme à Mada- gascar*, pp. 281 *sq.*

[3] Father Abinal, "Croyances fabu- leuses des Malgaches," *Les Missions Catholiques*, xii. (1880) p. 527 ; A. van Gennep, *Tabou et Totémisme a Mada- gascar*, pp. 281 *sq.*

took to wife. She lived with him happily in human shape on shore, till one day a second wife, whom the man had married, cruelly taunted her with being nothing but a fish. That hurt her so much that, bidding her husband farewell, she returned to her old home in the sea, with her youngest child in her arms, and never came back again. But ever since the Horse-mackerel people have refrained from eating horse-mackerels because the lost wife and mother was a fish of that sort.[1] Some of the Land Dyaks of Borneo tell a similar tale to explain a similar custom. " There is a fish which is taken in their rivers called a *puttin*, which they would on no account touch, under the idea that if they did they would be eating their relations. The tradition respecting it is, that a solitary old man went out fishing and caught a *puttin*, which he dragged out of the water and laid down in his boat. On turning round, he found it had changed into a very pretty little girl. Conceiving the idea she would make, what he had long wished for, a charming wife for his son, he took her home and educated her until she was fit to be married. She consented to be the son's wife, cautioning her husband to use her well. Some time after their marriage, however, being out of temper, he struck her, when she screamed, and rushed away into the water ; but not without leaving behind her a beautiful daughter, who became afterwards the mother of the race."[2] The Kayans of Borneo think that the first man and woman were born from a tree, which had been fertilized by a creeper swaying backwards and forwards in the wind. The man was named Kaluban Gai and the woman Kalubi Angai. However, they were incomplete, for they had no legs, and even the lower half of their trunks was wanting, so that their entrails protruded. Nevertheless they married and became the progenitors of mankind.[3] Thus the Kayans suppose the human race to

Kayan story of the evolution of men out of a tree.

[1] (Sir) A. B. Ellis, *The Tshi-speaking Peoples of the Gold Coast of West Africa* (London, 1887), pp. 208-211. A similar tale is told by another fish family who abstain from eating the species of fish (*appei*) from which they take their name (A. B. Ellis, *op. cit.* pp. 211 *sq.*).

[2] The Lord Bishop of Labuan, " On the Wild Tribes of the North-West Coast of Borneo," *Transactions of the Ethnological Society of London*, New Series, ii. (London, 1863) pp. 26 *sq.* Such stories conform to a well-known type which may be called the Swan-maiden type of story, or Beauty and the Beast, or Cupid and Psyche.

[3] Ch Hose and W. McDougall, *The Pagan Tribes of Borneo* (London 1912), ii. 138.

have been directly evolved from plants without passing through the intermediate stage of animals.

Members of a clan in Mandailing, on the west coast of Sumatra, allege that they are descended from a tiger, and at the present day, when a tiger is shot, the women of the clan are bound to offer betel to the dead beast. When members of this clan come upon the tracks of a tiger, they must, as a mark of homage, enclose them with three little sticks. Further, it is believed that the tiger will not attack or lacerate his kinsmen, the members of the clan.[1] The Battas or Bataks of Central Sumatra are divided into a number of clans which have for their totems white buffaloes, goats, wild turtle-doves, dogs, cats, apes, tigers, and so forth ; and one of the explanations which they give of their totems is that these creatures were their ancestors, and that their own souls after death can transmigrate into the animals.[2]

Stories of ~~~ e cent of men from ~~~ ~~ Sumatra.

Some of the natives of Minahassa, a district at the northeastern extremity of Celebes, believe that they are descended from apes, and that the parent stock of these animals still inhabits the woods of Menado toowah, or Old Menado, an island which rises out of the sea in the shape of a conical mountain. The old inhabitants of Menado, a town on the mainland of Celebes, stoutly affirmed that the apes on that island were their forefathers. In former times they used to send offerings of rice, bananas, and so forth, every year to their simian ancestors in the woods, but afterwards they found it more convenient to place their offerings on a raft of bamboo stems and then, in the darkness of night, illuminated by the glare of torches, to let the frail bark drift down the river amid a hubbub of noises and the clamour of multitudinous voices wishing it good speed. A similar belief in their descent from these apes is cherished by the inhabitants of Tanawangko, another town of Minahassa distant somewhat farther from the ancestral island. These people sometimes repair to the island

Stories of cent of men from Apes in Celebes.

[1] H. Ris, "De Onderafdeeling Klein Mandailing Oeloe en Pahantan en hare Bevolking met uitzondering van de Oeloes," *Bijdragen tot de Taal- Land- en Volkenkunde van Nederlandsch-Indie*, xlvi. (1896) p. 473.

[2] J. B. Neumann, " Het Pane en Bila - stroomgebied op het eiland Sumatra," *Tijdschrift van het Nederlandsch Aardrijkskundig Genootschap*, Tweede Serie, iii. Afdeeling, Meer uitgebreide Artikelen, No. 2 (Amsterdam, 1886), pp. 311 *sq.* ; *id., op. cit.*, Tweede Serie, iv. Afdeeling Meer uitgebreide Artikelen, No. 1 (Amsterdam, 1887), pp. 8 *sq.*

for the purpose of felling timber, and it is said that, rather than chase away or injure the apes which infest the forest, they suffer the thievish animals to steal their rice, bananas, and clothes, believing that sickness or death would be the inevitable consequence of any attempt to defend their property against the monkeys.[1]

In Amboyna and the neighbouring islands the inhabitants of some villages aver that they are descended from trees, such as the *Capellenia moluccana*, which had been fertilized by the *Pandion Haliaetus*. Others claim to be sprung from pigs, octopuses, crocodiles, sharks, and eels. People will not burn the wood of the trees from which they trace their descent, nor eat the flesh of the animals which they regard as their ancestors. Sicknesses of all sorts are believed to result from disregarding these taboos.[2] Similarly in Ceram persons who think they are descended from crocodiles, serpents, iguanas, and sharks will not eat the flesh of these animals.[3] Many other peoples of the Molucca Islands entertain similar beliefs and observe similar taboos.[4]

The Bukaua of North-Eastern New Guinea appear to trace their descent from their totemic animals. Thus the inhabitants of one village will not eat a certain sea-fish (*ingo*), because they allege that they are all descended from it. Were one of them to eat the fish, they believe that the doom of all the villagers would be sealed. Another clan revere white parrots as their totems, and never eat the bird, though they are glad to deck themselves with its feathers. If they see other people eating a white parrot, they are grieved, sprinkle themselves with ashes in token of sorrow for the death of the bird, and expect compensation from the murderers. If one of themselves ate a white parrot, he would suffer from sore eyes. The members of a particular family refuse to eat pig, because they owe their existence to a sow, which farrowed babies and little pigs at the same birth.[5] Similarly some of the natives of Astrolabe

[1] N. Graafland, *De Minahassa* (Rotterdam, 1869), i. 8 *sq.*

[2] J. G. F. Riedel, *De sluik- en kroesharige rassen tusschen Selebes en Papua* (The Hague, 1886), pp. 32, 61 ; G. W. W. C. Baron van Hoevell, *Ambon en meer bepaaldelijk de Oeliasers* (Dordrecht, 1875), p. 152.

[3] J. G. F. Riedel, *op. cit.* p. 122.

[4] J. G. F. Riedel, *op. cit.* pp. 253, 334, 341, 348, 412, 414, 432.

[5] Stefan Lehner, " Bukaua," in R. Neuhauss, *Deutsch Neu-Guinea* (Berlin, 1911), iii. 428.

Bay in Northern New Guinea believe that they are descended from a crocodile, which a human ancestress of theirs
brought forth along with a twin girl.   Hence they refuse
to eat the flesh of crocodiles, and they tell a long story
about the vicious behaviour of their crocodile forefather.[1]

A somewhat different account of the origin of man is Story of
given by the Marindineeze, a tribe who occupy the dreary, of man
monotonous treeless flats on the southern coast of Dutch told by the
New Guinea, not far from the border of the British territory. dineeze of
They say that one day a crane or stork (*dik*) was busy Dutch New
picking fish out of the sea.   He threw them on the beach,
where the clay covered and killed them.   So the fish were
no longer anything but shapeless lumps of clay.   They were
cold and warmed themselves at a fire of bamboos.   Every
time that a little bamboo burst with a pop in the heat, the
lumps of clay assumed more and more the shape of human
beings.   Thus the apertures of their ears, eyes, mouth, and
nostrils were opened, but as yet they could not speak, they
could only utter a murmuring sound.   Their fingers were
still joined by membranes like those in the wings of bats.
However, with a bamboo knife they severed the membranes
and threw them into the sea, where they turned into leeches.
When the nature spirit (*dema*) saw the human beings, he
was wroth, and enviously asked the crane, why he had
bestowed life on these creatures.   So the crane ceased to
peck at the fish and pecked at a log of wood instead ; and
that is why his beak has been bent ever since.   At last,
while the first men were sitting round the fire, a big bamboo
burst with a louder crack than usual, which frightened the
people so that they gave a loud shriek, and that was the
beginning of human speech.   You may still hear shrieks of
the same sort at the present day, when in time of sickness
the descendants of these first parents are sitting by the fire
and throwing bamboos into it, in order that the crackling
and popping of the bamboos in the flames may put the
spirit of disease to flight.   Every time a bamboo bursts
with a pop, all the people shout and load the demon with
curses.   And this Papuan narrative of the descent of man

[1] Otto Dempwolff, " Sagen und Marchen aus Bilbili," *Baessler-Archiv*
i. (1911) pp. 63-66.

usually winds up with the words, "So the stork or crane (*dik*) bestowed life on us."[1]

A somewhat different version of the story is told by other members of the tribe. They say that before the first human pair appeared on earth, there were spirits (*demas*) residing at Wegi, near Kondo-miraaf which is near the extreme south-eastern corner of the tribal territory. Now the spirits owned a dog and a bird (*diegge*), which may be presumed to be the same crane or stork (*dik, diek*) which figures in the former version. One day the dog, snuffing about, was attracted by the scent to a certain spot, and there with his paws he scraped a hole in the ground, from which the first human pair, a man and a woman, came forth. They possessed all animal instincts, but their minds were very imperfectly developed. They lived like beasts, without experience and without feeling the need of communicating with each other by speech. As for the necessaries of life, they received them from the spirits. Roaming about one day they came to a river, and in their ignorance of the nature of water they walked straight into it and might have been drowned, if the bird had not flown to their rescue and drawn them out of the stream. That is how they came to be acquainted with water ; but still they were ignorant of fire. Their knowledge of that element they acquired from watching a fire which the spirits had kindled to warm themselves at in cold weather ; and it was the astonishment our first parents felt at the sight of the devouring flames, and the alarm they experienced at the loud crackling of the bamboos in the heat, which elicited from them the first cry of fear and wonder and so unloosed their tongues. Henceforth they could speak. The hole from which these ancestors of mankind emerged on that memorable day has

[1] Jos. Viegen (Pastoor te Merauke), "Oorsprongs- en afstammingslegenden van den Marindinees (Zuid Niew-Guinea)," *Tijdschrift van het Koninklijk Nederlandsch Aardrijkskundig Genootschap*, Tweede Serie, xxix. (1912) pp. 137, 145 *sq.*; A. J. Gooszen, "De Majo-mysterien ter Nieuw-Guinea's Zuidkust," *Bijdragen tot de Taal- Land- en Volkenkunde van* *Nederlandsch-Indie*, lxix. (1914) p. 375. There seems to be some doubt as to the identification of the bird which plays so important a part in the legend. The natives call it *dik* (*diek*). According to Pastor Viegen, it is a crane ; Mr. Gooszen describes it as a stork or crane ; Mr. O. G. Heldring (see the reference in the next note) calls it a stork (*ooievaar*, p. 466).

continued to be a hole ever since ; but water has gathered in it, and it is now the sacred pool of Wegi. Even in seasons of the greatest drought the water in that pool never fails ; and all the animals and plants about it, every thing that runs or flies or grows there, is holy.[1]

The legend which in one or other of these versions the Marindineeze tell to account for the origin of the human species is said to be represented dramatically by them at the mysteries or rites of initiation which they celebrate every year, and on the celebration of which they apparently believe the fertility of the land, of man, and of beast to be dependent.   Thus the story that the bird picked the first human beings from the water in the likeness of fish and threw them on the beach, is acted by an initiated man who comes hopping along on two sticks, picks up the novices one by one and throws them into the sacred enclosure.   There they must lie motionless ; they are stripped of all their orna-ments, and coated from head to foot with a thick layer of clay ; more than that, lumps of clay are thrust into their mouths by initiated men, and these they have after-wards to spit out into holes dug in the ground.   This scene of the mysteries seems to recall either the clay which is said to have covered our fishy ancestors when they were first cast on the beach, or the earth from which they emerged when the dog had scraped away the soil from above them. The subsequent stages of the mysteries consist for the most part in a series of lessons designed to initiate the novices successively into the various occupations of ordinary life, of which, like newborn babes or their ancestors when they first emerged from the water or the earth, they are presumed to be entirely ignorant.[2]

The origin
la
represented
at the
dineeze
mysteries.

[1] O. G. Heldring, " Bijdrage tot de ethnografische kennis der Mariende-Anim," *Tijdschrift voor Indische Taal-Land- en Volkenkunde*, lv. (1913) p. 429 *sq.*; A. J. Gooszen, " De Majo-mysterien ter Nieuw-Guinea's Zuid-kust," *Bijdragen tot de Taal- Land- en Volkenkunde van Nederlandsch-Indie*, lxix. (1914) pp. 375 *sq.*

[2] Jos. Viegen, " Oorsprongs- en afstammingslegenden van den Marin-dinees (Zuid Nieuw-Guinea)," *Tijd-*

schrift van het Koninklijk Nederlandsch Aardrijkskundig Genootschap, Tweede Serie, xxix. (1912) pp. 147 *sqq.*; O. G. Heldring, " Bijdrage tot de ethno-grafische kennis der Mariende-Anim," *Tijdschrift voor Indische Taal- Lana-en Volkenkunde*, lv. (1913) pp. 440 *sqq.*; A. J. Gooszen, " De Majo-mysterien ter Nieuw-Guinea's Zuid-kust," *Bijdragen tot de Taal- Land- en Volkenkunde van Nederlandsch-Indie*, lxix. (1914) pp. 366 *sqq.*   The name

Stories
of the
descent of
men from
an
grubs in
the Pacific.
Again, in Ponape, one of the Caroline Islands, "the different families suppose themselves to stand in a certain relation
to animals, and especially to fishes, and believe in their descent
from them.   They actually name these animals ' mothers ' ;
the creatures are sacred to the family and may not be injured.
Great dances, accompanied with the offering of prayers, are
performed in their honour.   Any person who killed such an
animal would expose himself to contempt and punishment,
certainly also to the vengeance of the insulted deity." Blind-
ness is commonly supposed to be the consequence of such a
sacrilege.[1]   The Samoans have a tradition that the first two
men were developed out of two grubs, which were produced
through the rotting of a convolvulus torn up by its roots.
But the transformation of the grubs into men was carried
out by two divine beings under the direction of Tuli (a species
of plover), who was himself the son of the great god Tangaloa
of the Skies.   When the two men had received all their
human limbs and features complete at the hands of the
deities, they dwelt in the land where they had been formed,
but being both males they could not continue the species.
However, it chanced that one day, while he was fishing, one
of the two men received a mortal hurt from a little fish and
died ; whereupon the great god Tangaloa caused the dead
man to be changed into a woman and to be brought to life
again.   So the man and the woman married and became
the parents of mankind.[2]   This Samoan story of the origin
of man combines the processes of evolution and creation ;

---

of the initiatory rites or mysteries is
Mayo (*Majo*).   They are described
most fully by Mr. Heldring, whose
description is based partly on personal
observation, but mainly on information
furnished by a native Government interpreter, who attended all the ceremonies in the villages to the east of
the Marau River (pp. 443 *sq.*).   Mr.
Heldring lays stress on the importance
which the natives attach to the performance of the rites as a means to
ensure the fertility of man and beast as
well as of the land (p. 460).   "All
accounts," he tells us, "agree that the
holding of the *Mayo* rites is always
followed by good harvests.   It is,

therefore, the foremost duty of the
Mariende tribes to celebrate the rites
every year, though not in the same
group of villages two years running."
At the same time he points out the
great part which the dramatic representation of the creation myth plays
in the mysteries.   The parallelism
between the myth and the ritual is
drawn out most fully by Pastor Viegen.

[1] Dr. Hahl, "Mittheilungen über
Sitten und rechtliche Verhältnisse auf
Ponape," *Ethnologisches Notizblatt*,
vol. ii. Heft 2 (Berlin, 1901), p. 10.

[2] Rev. John B. Stair, *Old Samoa*
(London, 1897), pp. 213 *sq.*

for while it represents the first men as developed out of grubs, it attributes their final perfection to the formative action of divine beings.

Some of the aborigines of Western Australia believe that their ancestors were swans, ducks, or various other species of water-fowl before they were transformed into men.[1] The Dieri tribe of Central Australia, who are divided into totemic clans, explain their origin by the following legend. They say that in the beginning the earth opened in the midst of Perigundi Lake, and the totems (*murdus* or *madas*) came trooping out one after the other. Out came the crow, and the shell parakeet, and the emu, and all the rest. Being as yet imperfectly formed and without members or organs of sense, they laid themselves down on the sandhills which surrounded the lake then, just as they do now. It was a bright day, and the totems lay basking in the sunshine, till at last, refreshed and invigorated by it, they stood up as human beings and dispersed in all directions. That is why people of the same totem are now scattered all over the country. You may still see the island in the lake out of which the totems came trooping long ago.[2] Another Dieri legend relates how Paralina, one of the *Mura-Muras* or mythical predecessors of the Dieri, perfected mankind. He was out hunting kangaroos, when he saw four incomplete beings cowering together. So he went up to them, smoothed their bodies, stretched out their limbs, slit up their fingers and toes, formed their mouths, noses, and eyes, stuck ears on them, and blew into their ears in order that they might hear. Having perfected their organs and so produced mankind out of these rudimentary beings, he went about making men everywhere.[3] Yet another Dieri tradition sets forth how the *Mura-Mura* produced the race of man out of a species of small black lizards, which may still be met with under dry bark. To do this he divided the feet of the lizards into fingers and toes, and, applying his forefinger to the middle of their faces, created a nose ; likewise he gave

Stories
evolution
of men out
among the
aborigines
Australia.

[1] Captain G. Grey, *A Vocabulary of the Dialects of South Western Australia*, Second Edition (London, 1840), pp. 29, 37, 61, 63, 66, 71.

[2] A. W. Howitt, *Native Tribes of South-East Australia* (London, 1904), pp. 476, 779 *sq.*

[3] A. W. Howitt, *op. cit.* pp. 476, 780 *sq.*

them human eyes, mouths, and ears.   He next set one of them upright, but it fell down again because of its tail ; so he cut off its tail, and the lizard then walked on its hind legs. That is the origin of mankind.[1]

Arunta
rs n
of the
evolution of
their out of
rudi-
mentary
creatures.

The Arunta tribe of Central Australia similarly tell how in the beginning mankind was developed out of various rudi-mentary forms of animal life.   They say that in those days two beings called *Ungambikula*, that is, "out of nothing," or "self-existing," dwelt in the western sky.   From their lofty abode they could see, far away to the east, a number of *inapertwa* creatures, that is, rudimentary human beings or incomplete men, whom it was their mission to make into real men and women.   For at that time there were no real men and women ; the rudimentary creatures (*inapertwa*) were of various shapes and dwelt in groups along the shore of the salt water which covered the country.   These embryos, as we may call them, had no distinct limbs or organs of sight, hearing, and smell ; they did not eat food, and they presented the appearance of human beings all doubled up into a rounded mass, in which only the outline of the different parts could be vaguely perceived.   Coming down from their home in the western sky, armed with great stone knives, the *Ungambikula* took hold of the embryos, one after the other.   First of all they released the arms from the bodies, then making four clefts at the end of each arm they fashioned hands and fingers ; afterwards legs, feet, and toes were added in the same way.   The figure could now stand ; a nose was then moulded and the nostrils bored with the fingers.   A cut with the knife made the mouth, which was pulled open several times to render it flexible.   A slit on each side of the face separated the upper and lower eyelids, disclosing the eyes, which already existed behind them ; and a few strokes more completed the body.   Thus out of the rudimentary creatures were formed men and women.   These rudimentary creatures or embryos, we are told, "were in

[1] S. Gason, "The Manners and Customs of the Dieyerie tribe of Australian Aborigines," in J. D. Woods's *Native Tribes of South Australia* (Adelaide, 1879), p. 260.   This writer made the mistake of regarding the *Mura-Mura* (*Mooramoora*) as a Good Spirit instead of as one of the mythical but more or less human predecessors of the Dieri in the country.   See A. W. Howitt, *Native Tribes of South-East Australia*, pp. 475 *sqq.*

reality stages in the transformation of various animals and plants into human beings, and thus they were naturally, when made into human beings, intimately associated with the particular animal or plant, as the case may be, of which they were the transformations—in other words, each individual of necessity belonged to a totem the name of which was of course that of the animal or plant of which he or she was a transformation." However, it is not said that all the totemic clans of the Arunta were thus developed ; no such tradition, for example, is told to explain the origin of the important Witchetty Grub clan. The clans which are known, or said, to have originated out of embryos in the way described are the Plum Tree, the Grass Seed, the Large Lizard, the Small Lizard, the Alexandra Parakeet, and the Small Rat clans. When the *Ungambikula* had thus fashioned people out of these totems, they circumcised them all, except the Plum Tree men, by means of a fire-stick. After that, having done the work of creation or evolution, the *Ungambikula* turned themselves into little lizards which bear a name meaning "snappers-up of flies."[1]

This Arunta tradition of the origin of man, as Messrs. Spencer and Gillen, who have recorded it, justly observe, "is of considerable interest ; it is in the first place evidently a crude attempt to describe the origin of human beings out of non-human creatures who were of various forms ; some of them were representatives of animals, others of plants, but in all cases they are to be regarded as intermediate stages in the transition of an animal or plant ancestor into a human individual who bore its name as that of his or her totem."[2] In a sense these speculations of the Arunta on their own origin may be said, like a similar myth of the Samoans,[3] to combine the theory of creation with the theory of evolution ; for while they represent men as developed out of much simpler forms of life, they at the same time assume that this development was effected by the agency of two powerful beings, whom so far we may call creators. It is well known

The tradition of the origin of man compared with that of the Greek philosopher Empedocles.

[1] (Sir) Baldwin Spencer and F. J. Gillen, *Native Tribes of Central Australia* (London, 1899), pp. 388 *sq.* ; compare *iid., Northern Tribes of Central Australia* (London, 1904), p. 150.

[2] (Sir) Baldwin Spencer and F. J. Gillen, *Native Tribes of Central Australia*, pp. 391 *sq.*

[3] Above, p. 40.

that at a far higher stage of culture a crude form of the evolutionary hypothesis was propounded by the Greek philosopher Empedocles. He imagined that shapeless lumps of earth and water, thrown up by the subterranean fires, developed into monstrous animals, bulls with the heads of men, men with the heads of bulls, and so forth ; till at last, these hybrid forms being gradually eliminated, the various existing species of animals and men were evolved.[1] The theory of the civilized Greek of Sicily may be set beside the similar theory of the savage Arunta of Central Australia. Both represent gropings of the human mind in the dark abysses of the past ; both were in a measure grotesque anticipations of the modern theory of evolution.

The opinions of mankind divided between the theory of creation and the theory of evolution.

The foregoing examples may serve to illustrate two very different views which primitive man has taken of his own origin. They may be distinguished as the theory of creation and the theory of evolution. According to the one, the human race was fashioned in its present form by a great artificer, whether a god or a hero ; according to the other, it was evolved by a natural process out of lower forms of animal or even vegetable life. Roughly speaking, these two theories still divide the civilized world between them. The partisans of each can appeal in support of their view to a large consensus of opinion ; and if truth were to be decided by weighing the one consensus against the other, with *Genesis* in the one scale and *The Origin of Species* in the other, it might perhaps be found, when the scales were finally trimmed, that the balance hung very even between creation and evolution.

[1] E. Zeller, *Die Philosophie der Griechen*, i.[4] (Leipsic, 1876), pp. 718 *sq.*; H. Ritter und L. Preller, *Historia Philosophiae Graecae et Latinae ex fontium locis contexta*[6] (Gothae, 1875), pp. 102 *sq.* ; H. Diels, *Die Fragmente der Vorsokratiker*,[2] i. (Berlin, 1906), pp. 190 *sqq.* Compare Lucretius, *De rerum natura*, v. 837 *sqq.* Another ancient Greek philosopher, Anaximander of Miletus, thought that men were developed out of fishes. See Plutarch, *Symposium*, viii. 8. 4 ; Censorinus, *De die natali*, iv. 7 ; H. Diels, *op. cit.* i. 17.

CHAPTER II

THE FALL OF MAN

§ 1. *The Narrative in Genesis*

WITH a few light but masterly strokes the Jehovistic writer depicts for us the blissful life of our first parents in the happy garden which God had created for their abode. There every tree that was pleasant to the sight and good for food grew abundantly ; there the animals lived at peace with man and with each other ; there man and woman knew no shame, because they knew no ill : it was the age of innocence.[1] But this glad time was short, the sunshine was soon clouded. From his description of the creation of Eve and her intro-duction to Adam, the writer passes at once to tell the sad story of their fall, their loss of innocence, their expulsion from Eden, and the doom of labour, of sorrow, and of death pronounced on them and their posterity. In the midst of the garden grew the tree of the knowledge of good and evil, and God had forbidden man to eat of its fruit, saying, ",In the day that thou eatest thereof thou shalt surely die." But the serpent was cunning, and the woman weak and credulous : he persuaded her to eat of the fatal fruit, and she gave of it to her husband, and he ate also. No sooner had they tasted it than the eyes of both of them were opened, they knew that they were naked, and filled with shame and confusion they hid their nakedness under aprons of fig-leaves : the age of innocence was gone for ever. That woeful day, when the heat of noon was over and the shadows were growing long in the garden, God walked there, as was his wont, in the

[1] Genesis ii. 8-25.

45

cool of the evening. The man and woman heard his foot-steps,[1] perhaps the rustling of the fallen leaves (if leaves could fall in Eden) under his tread, and they hid behind the trees, ashamed to be seen by him naked. But he called them forth from the thicket, and learning from the abashed couple how they had disobeyed his command by eating of the tree of knowledge, he flew into a towering passion. He cursed the serpent, condemning him to go on his belly, to eat dust, and to be the enemy of mankind all the days of his life : he cursed the ground, condemning it to bring forth thorns and thistles : he cursed the woman, condemning her to bear children in sorrow and to be in subjection to her husband : he cursed the man, condemning him to wring his daily bread from the ground in the sweat of his brow, and finally to return to the dust out of which he had been taken. Having relieved his feelings by these copious maledictions, the irascible but really kind-hearted deity relented so far as to make coats of skins for the culprits to replace their scanty aprons of fig-leaves, and clad in these new garments the shamefaced pair retreated among the trees ; while in the west the sunset died away, and the shadows deepened on Paradise Lost.[2]

The tree
t e
kn wl d
of good
/i
and the tree
of life.

In this account everything hinges on the tree of the knowledge of good and evil : it occupies, so to say, the centre of the stage in the great tragedy, with the man and woman and the talking serpent grouped round it. But when we look closer we perceive a second tree standing side by side with the other in the midst of the garden. It is a very remarkable tree, for it is no less than the tree of life, whose fruit confers immortality on all who eat of it. Yet in the actual story of the fall this wonderful tree plays no part. Its fruit hangs there on the boughs ready to be plucked ; unlike the tree of knowledge, it is hedged about by no divine prohibition, yet no one thinks it worth while to taste of the luscious fruit and live for ever. The eyes of the actors are all turned on the tree of knowledge ; they appear

---

[1] Genesis iii. 8, " they heard the sound of the Lord God walking in the garden." The " sound " is clearly that of his footsteps, not of his voice, as the English version translates it. The Hebrew word for sound (קוֹל) is ambiguous ; it may signify either "sound" or "voice."

[2] Genesis iii.

not to see the tree of life.   Only, when all is over, does God
bethink himself of the wondrous tree standing there neglected,
with all its infinite possibilities, in the midst of the garden ;
and fearing lest man, who has become like him in knowledge
by eating of the one tree, should become like him in immortality by eating of the other, he drives him from the
garden and sets an angelic squadron, with flaming swords,
to guard the approach to the tree of life, that none henceforth may eat of its magic fruit and live for ever.   Thus,
while throughout the moving tragedy in Eden our attention
is fixed exclusively on the tree of knowledge, in the great
transformation scene at the end, where the splendours of Eden
fade for ever into the light of common day, the last glimpse
we catch of the happy garden shows the tree of life alone lit
up by the lurid gleam of brandished angelic falchions.[1]

It appears to be generally recognized that some confusion
has crept into the account of the two trees, and that in the
original story the tree of life did not play the purely passive
and spectacular part assigned to it in the existing narrative.
Accordingly, some have thought that there were originally
two different stories of the fall, in one of which the tree of
knowledge figured alone, and in the other the tree of life
alone, and that the two stories have been unskilfully fused
into a single narrative by an editor, who has preserved the
one nearly intact, while he has clipped and pared the other
almost past recognition.[2]   It may be so, but perhaps the
solution of the problem is to be sought in another direction.
The gist of the whole story of the fall appears to be an
attempt to explain man's mortality, to set forth how death
came into the world.   It is true that man is not said to
have been created immortal and to have lost his immortality
through disobedience ; but neither is he said to have been
created mortal.   Rather we are given to understand that
the possibility alike of immortality and of mortality was
open to him, and that it rested with him which he would
choose ; for the tree of life stood within his reach, its fruit
was not forbidden to him, he had only to stretch out his
hand, take of the fruit, and eating of it live for ever.

We may
suppose
that in the
original
o   e
narrative
there were
w
a Tree of
Life and a
Death, and
that man
allowed to
eat of the
Life but
forbidden
the Tree
of Death.

[1] Genesis iii. 22-24.
[2] J. Skinner, *Critical and Exegetical*

Commentary on Genesis (Edinburgh,
1910), pp. 52 *sq.*. 94.

Indeed, far from being prohibited to eat of the tree of life, man was implicitly permitted, if not encouraged, to partake of it by his Creator, who had told him expressly, that he might eat freely of every tree in the garden, with the single exception of the tree of the knowledge of good and evil.[1] Thus by planting the tree of life in the garden and not prohibiting its use, God apparently intended to give man the option, or at least the chance, of immortality, but man missed his chance by electing to eat of the other tree, which God had warned him not to touch under pain of immediate death. This suggests that the forbidden tree was really a tree of death, not of knowledge, and that the mere taste of its deadly fruit, quite apart from any question of obedience or disobedience to a divine command, sufficed to entail death on the eater. The inference is entirely in keeping with God's warning to man, "Thou shalt not eat of it : for in the day that thou eatest thereof thou shalt surely die."[2] Accordingly we may suppose that in the original story there were two trees, a tree of life and a tree of death ; that it was open to man to eat of the one and live for ever, or to eat of the other and die ; that God, out of good will to his creature, advised man to eat of the tree of life and warned him not to eat of the tree of death ; and that man, misled by the serpent, ate of the wrong tree and so forfeited the immortality which his benevolent Creator had designed for him.

This hypothesis sets the character of the Creator in a more amiable light by making it probable that he intended to confer the boon of immortality on his

At least this hypothesis has the advantage of restoring the balance between the two trees and of rendering the whole narrative clear, simple, and consistent. It dispenses with the necessity of assuming two original and distinct stories which have been clumsily stitched together by a botching editor. But the hypothesis is further recommended by another and deeper consideration. It sets the character of the Creator in a far more amiable light : it clears him entirely of that suspicion of envy and jealousy, not to say malignity and cowardice, which, on the strength of the narrative in Genesis, has so long rested like a dark blot

[1] Genesis ii. 16 *sq.*, "And the Lord God commanded the man, saying, Of every tree of the garden thou mayest freely eat : but of the tree of the knowledge of good and evil, thou shalt not eat of it : for in the day that thou eatest thereof thou shalt surely die."
[2] Genesis ii. 17.

on his reputation.   For according to that narrative, God grudged man the possession both of knowledge and of immortality ; he desired to keep these good things to himself, and feared that if man got one or both of them, he would be the equal of his maker, a thing not to be suffered at any price.   Accordingly he forbade man to eat of the tree of knowledge, and when man disregarded the command, the deity hustled him out of the garden and closed the premises, to prevent him from eating of the other tree and so becoming immortal.   The motive was mean, and the conduct despicable.   More than that, both the one and the other are utterly inconsistent with the previous behaviour of the deity, who, far from grudging man anything, had done all in his power to make him happy and comfortable, by creating a beautiful garden for his delectation, beasts and birds to play with, and a woman to be his wife.   Surely it is far more in harmony both with the tenor of the narrative and with the goodness of the Creator to suppose, that he intended to crown his kindness to man by conferring on him the boon of immortality, and that his benevolent intention was only frustrated by the wiles of the serpent.

But we have still to ask, why should the serpent practise this deceit on man ? what motive had he for depriving the human race of the great privilege which the Creator had planned for them ?   Was his interference purely officious ? or had he some deep design behind it ?   To these questions the narrative in Genesis furnishes no answer.   The serpent gains nothing by his fraud ; on the contrary he loses, for he is cursed by God and condemned thenceforth to crawl on his belly and lick the dust.   But perhaps his conduct was not so wholly malignant and purposeless as appears on the surface.   We are told that he was more subtle than any beast of the field ; did he really show his sagacity by blasting man's prospects without improving his own ?   We may suspect that in the original story he justified his reputation by appropriating to himself the blessing of which he deprived our species ; in fact, that while he persuaded our first parents to eat of the tree of death, he himself ate of the tree of life and so lived for ever.   The supposition is not so extravagant as it may seem.   In not a few savage

Marginal notes: creature m n, d was only frustrated amiable intention cunning of the serpent. In the original narrative the se e t's motive for beguiling woman was probably men of the boon of ity and to confer it on which are commonly to be immo al, be se they cast k n and thereby renew their yout .

stories of the origin of death, which I will relate immediately, we read that serpents contrived to outwit or intimidate man and so to secure for themselves the immortality which was meant for him ; for many savages believe that by annually casting their skins serpents and other animals renew their youth and live for ever. The belief appears to have been shared by the Semites ; for, according to the ancient Phoenician writer Sanchuniathon, the serpent was the longest-lived of all animals, because it cast its skin and so renewed its youth.[1] But if the Phoenicians held this view of the serpent's longevity and the cause of it, their neighbours and kinsfolk the Hebrews may well have done the same. Certainly the Hebrews seem to have thought that eagles renew their youth by moulting their feathers ;[2] and if so, why not serpents by casting their skins? Indeed, the notion that the serpent cheated man of immortality by getting possession of a life-giving plant which the higher powers had destined for our species, occurs in the famous Gilgamesh epic, one of the oldest literary monuments of the Semitic race and far more ancient than Genesis. In it we read how the deified Ut-napishtim revealed to the hero Gilgamesh the existence of a plant which had the miraculous power of renewing youth and bore the name "the old man becomes young" ; how Gilgamesh procured the plant and boasted that he would eat of it and so renew his lost youth ;

[1] Sanchuniathon, quoted by Eusebius, *Praeparatio Evangelii*, i. 10, καὶ πολυχρονιώτατον δέ ἐστιν οὐ μόνον τῷ ἐκδυόμενον τὸ γῆρας νεάζειν. Here γῆρας is used in the sense of "old or cast skin," as in Aristotle, *Histor. Animal.* vii. 18 (vol. i. pp. 600 a-601 b, of Im. Bekker's Berlin edition), who discusses the subject at length. The use of γῆρας ("old age") in the sense of "cast skin" is a clear indication that the Greeks shared the widespread belief in the renewal of an animal's youth by the casting of its skin.

[2] Psalm ciii. 5, "Thy youth is renewed like the eagle." The commentators rightly explain the belief in the renewal of the eagle's youth by the moulting of its feathers. Compare J. Morgenstern, "On Gilgames-Epic, xi. 274-320," *Zeitschrift für Assyriologie*, xxix. (1915) p. 294, " Baethgen quotes a tradition from Bar Hebraeus, that when the eagle grows old he casts off his feathers and clothes himself with new ones. Rashi, commenting on this same verse, is even more specific. He says that from year to year the eagle casts off his old wings and feathers and puts on new, and thereby renews his youth constantly." Strictly speaking, the bird referred to in this passage of the Psalms (נשר) is not the eagle but the great griffon-vulture, which abounds in Palestine. See H. B. Tristram, *The Natural History of the Bible*, Ninth Edition (London, 1898), pp. 172 *sqq.*

how, before he could do so, a serpent stole the magic plant
from him, while he was bathing in the cool water of a well
or brook ; and how, bereft of the hope of immortality,
Gilgamesh sat down and wept.[1]   It is true that nothing is
here said about the serpent eating the plant and so obtaining immortality for himself; but the omission may be due
merely to the state of the text, which is obscure and
defective, and even if the poet were silent on this point, the
parallel versions of the story, which I shall cite, enable us to
supply the lacuna with a fair degree of probability.   These
parallels further suggest, though they cannot prove, that in
the original of the story, which the Jehovistic writer has
mangled and distorted, the serpent was the messenger sent
by God to bear the glad tidings of immortality to man,
but that the cunning creature perverted the message to
the advantage of his species and to the ruin of ours.   The
gift of speech, which he used to such ill purpose, was lent
him in his capacity of ambassador from God to man.

To sum up, if we may judge from a comparison of the
versions dispersed among many peoples, the true original
story of the Fall of Man ran somewhat as follows.   The
benevolent Creator, after modelling the first man and
woman out of mud and animating them by the simple
process of blowing into their mouths and noses, placed the
happy pair in an earthly paradise, where, free from care and
toil, they could live on the sweet fruits of a delightful
garden, and where birds and beasts frisked about them in
fearless security.   As a crowning mercy he planned for our
first parents the great gift of immortality, but resolved to
make them the arbiters of their own fate by leaving them
free to accept or reject the proffered boon.   For that purpose
he planted in the midst of the garden two wondrous trees
that bore fruits of very different sorts, the fruit of the one

*The story
of the Fall
of Man in
its original
an explana-
tion of the
death.*

---

[1] P. Jensen, *Assyrisch-Babylonische
Mythen und Epen* (Berlin, 1900), pp.
251 *sqq.* ; R. F. Harper, *Assyrian and
Babylonian Literature* (New York,
1901), pp. 361 *sq.* ; P. Dhorme, *Choix
de Textes Religieux Assyro-Babyloniens*
(Paris, 1907), pp. 311 *sqq.* ; A. Ungnad
und H. Gressmann, *Das Gilgamesch-
Epos* (Göttingen, 1911), pp. 62 *sq.* ;
L. W. King, *Babylonian Religion and
Magic* (London, 1899), pp. 173 *sq.*
The first, so far as I know, to point
out the parallelism between this passage
and the narrative in Genesis was Rabbi
Julian Morgenstern. See his instructive
article, " On Gilgameš-Epic, xi. 274-
320 " *Zeitschrift fur Assyriologie*, xxix.
(1915) pp. 284 *sqq.*

being fraught with death to the eater, and the other with life eternal. Having done so, he sent the serpent to the man and woman and charged him to deliver this message: " Eat not of the Tree of Death, for in the day ye eat thereof ye shall surely die ; but eat of the Tree of Life and live for ever." Now the serpent was more subtle than any beast of the field, and on his way he bethought him of changing the message ; so when he came to the happy garden and found the woman alone in it, he said to her, "Thus saith God : Eat not of the Tree of Life, for in the day ye eat thereof ye shall surely die ; but eat of the Tree of Death, and live for ever." The foolish woman believed him, and ate of the fatal fruit, and gave of it to her husband, and he ate also. But the sly serpent himself ate of the Tree of Life. That is why men have been mortal and serpents immortal ever since, for serpents cast their skins every year and so renew their youth. If only the serpent had not perverted God's good message and deceived our first mother, we should have been immortal instead of the serpents ; for like the serpents we should have cast our skins every year and so renewed our youth perpetually.

That this, or something like this, was the original form of the story is made probable by a comparison of the following tales, which may conveniently be arranged under two heads, " The Story of the Perverted Message " and " The Story of the Cast Skin."

§ 2. *The Story of the Perverted Message*

Hottentot story of the origin of death : the hare and

Like many other savages, the Namaquas or Hottentots associate the phases of the moon with the idea of immortality, the apparent waning and waxing of the luminary being understood by them as a real process of alternate disintegration and reintegration, of decay and growth repeated perpetually. Even the rising and setting of the moon is interpreted by them as its birth and death.[1] They say that once on a time the Moon wished to send to mankind a message of immortality, and the hare undertook to act as

[1] C. J. Andersson, *Lake Ngami*, Second Edition (London, 1856), p. 328 note [1], " When speaking of the moon, the Namaquas do not say, like ourselves, that it rises and sets, but that ' it dies and is born again.' "

messenger. So the Moon charged him to go to men and say, "As I die and rise to life again, so shall you die and rise to life again." Accordingly the hare went to men, but either out of forgetfulness or malice he reversed the message and said, "As I die and do not rise to life again, so you shall also die and not rise to life again." Then he went back to the Moon, and she asked him what he had said. He told her, and when she heard how he had given the wrong message, she was so angry that she threw a stick at him which split his lip. That is why the hare's lip is still cloven. So the hare ran away and is still running to this day. Some people, however, say that before he fled he clawed the Moon's face, which still bears the marks of the scratching, as anybody may see for himself on a clear moonlight night. But the Namaquas are still angry with the hare for robbing them of immortality. The old men of the tribe used to say, "We are still enraged with the hare, because he brought such a bad message, and we will not eat him." Hence from the day when a youth comes of age and takes his place among the men, he is forbidden to eat hare's flesh, or even to come into contact with a fire on which a hare has been cooked. If a man breaks the rule, he is not infrequently banished the village. However, on the payment of a fine he may be readmitted to the community.[1]

A similar tale, with some minor differences, is told by the Bushmen. According to them, the Moon formerly said to men, "As I die and come to life again, so shall ye do; when ye die, ye shall not die altogether but shall rise again." But one man would not believe the glad tidings of immortality, and he would not consent to hold his tongue. For his mother had died, he loudly lamented her, and nothing could persuade him that she would come to life again. A heated altercation ensued between him and the Moon on this painful subject. "Your mother's asleep," says the Moon. "She's dead," says the man, and at it they went

Bushman story of the origin of death : the Moon and the hare

---

[1] Sir J. E. Alexander, *Expedition of Discovery into the Interior of Africa* (London, 1838), i. 169; C. J. Andersson, *Lake Ngami*, Second Edition (London, 1856), pp. 328 *sq.*; W. H. I. Bleek, *Reynard the Fox in South Africa* (London, 1864), pp. 71-73; Th. Hahn, *Tsuni- ‖ Goam, the Supreme Being of the Khoi-Khoi* (London, 1881), p. 52.

again, hammer and tongs, till at last the Moon lost patience and struck the man on the face with her fist, cleaving his mouth with the blow. And as she did so, she cursed him saying, "His mouth shall be always like this, even when he is a hare. For a hare he shall be. He shall spring away, he shall come doubling back. The dogs shall chase him, and when they have caught him they shall tear him in pieces. He shall altogether die. And all men, when they die, shall die outright. For he would not agree with me, when I bid him not to weep for his mother, for she would live again. ' No,' says he to me, ' my mother will not live again.' Therefore he shall altogether become a hare. And the people, they shall altogether die, because he contradicted me flat when I told him that the people would do as I do, returning to life after they were dead." So a righteous retribution overtook the sceptic for his scepticism, for he was turned into a hare, and a hare he has been ever since. But still he has human flesh in his thigh, and that is why, when the Bushmen kill a hare, they will not eat that portion of the thigh, but cut it out, because it is human flesh. And still the Bushmen say, " It was on account of the hare that the Moon cursed us, so that we die altogether. If it had not been for him, we should have come to life again when we died. But he would not believe what the Moon told him, he contradicted her flat." [1] In this Bushman version of the story the hare is not the animal messenger of God to men, but a human sceptic who, for doubting the gospel of eternal life, is turned into a hare and involves the whole human race in the doom of mortality. This may be an older form of the story than the Hottentot version, in which the hare is a hare and nothing more.

Nandi yo‾ ‾e origin of death : the Moon and the dog.

The Nandi of British East Africa tell a story in which the origin of death is referred to the ill-humour of a dog, who brought the tidings of immortality to men, but, not being received with the deference due to so august an embassy, he changed his tune in a huff and doomed mankind to the sad fate to which they have ever since been subject.

---

[1] W. H. I. Bleek and L. C. Lloyd, *Specimens of Bushman Folklore* (London, 1911), pp. 57-65. The part of the hare's thigh which the Bushmen cut out is believed to be the *musculus biceps femoris*.

The story runs thus. When the first men lived upon the
earth, a dog came to them one day and said, " All people
will die like the Moon, but unlike the Moon you will not
return to life again unless you give me some milk to drink
out of your gourd and beer to drink through your straw.
If you do this, I will arrange for you to go to the river when
you die and to come to life again on the third day." But
the people laughed at the dog, and gave him some milk and
beer to drink off a stool. The dog was angry at not being
served in the same vessels as a human being, and though
he put his pride in his pocket and drank the milk and beer
from the stool, he went away in high dudgeon, saying, " All
people will die, and the Moon alone will return to life."
That is why, when people die, they stay away, whereas when
the Moon goes away she comes back again after three days'
absence. If only people had given that dog a gourd to
drink milk out of, and a straw to suck beer through, we
should all have risen from the dead, like the moon, after
three days.[1] In this story nothing is said as to the personage who sent the dog with the message of immortality to
men ; but from the messenger's reference to the Moon, and
from a comparison with the parallel Hottentot story, we
may reasonably infer that it was the Moon who employed
the dog to run the errand, and that the unscrupulous
animal misused his opportunity to extort privileges for
himself to which he was not strictly entitled.

In these stories a single messenger is engaged to carry
the momentous message, and the fatal issue of the mission
is set down to the carelessness or malice of the missionary.
However, in some narratives of the origin of death, two
messengers are despatched, and the cause of death is said to
have been the dilatoriness or misconduct of the messenger
who bore the glad tidings of immortality. There is a
Hottentot story of the origin of death which is cast in this
form. They say that once the Moon sent an insect to men
with this message, " Go thou to men and tell them, ' As I
die, and dying live, so ye shall also die, and dying live.' "
The insect set off with this message, but as he crawled
along, the hare came leaping after him, and stopping beside

*In some
stories of
the origin
of death
messengers
appear.*

*Hottentot
origin of
death : the
Moon, the
insect, and
the hare.*

[1] A. C. Hollis, *The Nandi* (Oxford, 1909), p. 98.

him asked, " On what errand art thou bound ? " The insect
answered, " I am sent by the Moon to men, to tell them that
as she dies, and dying lives, they also shall die, and dying·
live." The hare said, " As thou art an awkward runner,
let me go." And away he tore with the message, while the
insect came creeping slowly behind. When he came to men,
the hare perverted the message which he had officiously
taken upon himself to deliver, for he said, " I am sent by
the Moon to tell you, ' As I die, and dying perish, in the
same manner ye shall also die and come wholly to an end.' "
Then the hare returned to the Moon, and told her what he
had said to men. The Moon was very angry and reproached
the hare, saying, " Darest thou tell the people a thing which
I have not said ? " With that she took a stick and hit him
over the nose. That is why the hare's nose is slit down to
this day.[1]

Tati
story of the
origin of
death :
the Moon,
the tortoise,
and the
hare.

The same tale is told, with some slight variations, by the
Tati Bushmen or Masarwas, who inhabit the Bechuanaland
Protectorate, the Kalahari desert, and portions of Southern
Rhodesia. The men of old time, they say, told this story.
The Moon wished to send a message to the men of the early
race, to tell them that as she died and came to life again, so
they would die, and dying come to life again. So the Moon
called the tortoise and said to him, " Go over to those men
there, and give them this message from me. Tell them that
as I dying live, so they dying will live again." Now the
tortoise was very slow, and he kept repeating the message
to himself, so as not to forget it. The Moon was very vexed
with his slowness and with his forgetfulness ; so she called
the hare and said to her, " You are a swift runner. Take
this message to the men over yonder : ' As I dying live again,
so you will dying live again.' " So off the hare started, but
in her great haste she forgot the message, and as she did not
wish to show the Moon that she had forgotten, she delivered
the message to men in this way, " As I dying live again, so
you dying will die for ever." Such was the message delivered
by the hare. In the meantime the tortoise had remembered
the message, and he started off a second time. " This time,"

[1] W. H. I. Bleek, *Reynard the Fox in South Africa* (London, 1864),
pp. 69 *sq.*

said he to himself, " I won't forget." He came to the place where the men were, and he delivered his message. When the men heard it they were very angry with the hare, who was sitting at some distance. She was nibbling the grass after her race. One of the men ran and lifted a stone and threw it at the hare. It struck her right in the mouth and cleft her upper lip ; hence the lip has been cleft ever since. That is why every hare has a cleft upper lip to this day, and that is the end of the story.[1]

In a story told by the A-Louyi tribe of the Upper Zambesi, the messengers of death and of life respectively are the chameleon and the hare. They say that Nyambe, whom they identify with the sun, used to dwell on earth with his wife Nasilele, whom they identify with the moon. But Nyambe retired to heaven from fear of men. Whenever he carved wood, men carved it also ; when he made a wooden plate, so did they. After he had withdrawn to the sky, it happened that Nyambe's dog died. He loved the animal, and said, " Let the dog live." But his wife said, " No, I won't have it. He's a thief." Nyambe still persisted. " For my part," said he, " I love my dog." But his wife said, " Throw him out." So they threw him out. By and by Nyambe's mother-in-law died, and his wife said to him, " Let her live," just as Nyambe himself had said to her about his dog. But Nyambe answered, " No, let her die and be done with it. I said to you that my dog should live, and you refused. It is my wish that your mother should die for good and all." So die she did for good and all. After that the husband and wife sent two messengers, a chameleon and a hare, to men on the earth. To the chameleon they said, " When thou art come to men, say to them, 'Ye shall live'; but as for thee, O hare, when thou art come to men, say to them, 'Ye shall die once, for all.'" The chameleon and the hare set off with their messages. Now the chameleon, as he went, kept constantly turning about, but the hare ran. So the hare arrived first, and said that men should die once for all. Having delivered his message, the hare returned. That is why, when men die, they die once for

Louyi story of the origin of death : and moon, the chameleon and the hare.

---

[1] Rev. S. S. Dornan, "The Tati Bushmen (Masarwas) and their Lan- guage," *Journal of the Royal Anthropological Institute*, xlvii. (1917) p. 80.

all.[1]   From this Louyi legend it would appear that human
mortality resulted from a domestic jar in heaven, the deity
falling out with his wife over his dead dog and mother-in-
law.   From such seemingly trivial causes may flow such
momentous consequences.

Ekoi story
origin of
death :
...
frog, and
the duck.

   The Ekoi of Southern Nigeria, on the border of the
Cameroons, attribute human mortality to the gross misconduct of a duck.   It happened in this way.   The
sky-god Obassi Osaw one day thought to himself, " Men
fear to die.   They do not know that perhaps they may
come to life again.   I will tell them that sometimes such
a thing may happen, then they will have less dread of
death."   So he stood up in his house in the sky, and
called a frog and a duck before him.   To the frog he said,
" Go to earth and say to the people, ' When a man dies, it
is the end of all things ; he shall never live again.' "   To the
duck he said, " Go tell the earth folk that if a man dies he
may come to life again."   He then led them a little way
and showed them the road, saying, " Take my message.
Duck, you may go to the left hand.   Frog, keep to the
right."   So the frog kept on to the right, and when he came
to the earth he delivered his message of death to the first
men he met, telling them that when they died it would be
an end of them.   In due time the duck also reached the
earth, but happening to arrive at a place where the people
were making palm oil, she fell to gobbling it up and forgot
all about the message of immortality which the good god
had charged her to deliver to mankind.   That is why we
are all mortal down to this day.   We are bound to go by
the message of the frog ; we cannot go by the message of
the duck, which never reached us.[2]

Gold Coast
y o he
origin of
death :
...
the sheep,
and the
goat.

   The story of the two messengers is related also by the
negroes of the Gold Coast, and in their version the two messengers are a sheep and a goat.   The following is the form in
which the tale was told by a native to a Swiss missionary at
Akropong.   In the beginning, when sky and earth existed,

[1] E. Jacottet, *Études sur les langues
du Haut-Zambèze*, Troisieme Partie,
Textes Louyi (Paris, 1901), pp. 116
sq.   As to the identification of Nyambe and Nasilele with the sun and

moon respectively, see E. Jacottet, *op.
cit.* p. 118, note [3].

[2] P. Amaury Talbot, *In the Shadow
of the Bush* (London, 1912), p. 229.

but there were as yet no men on earth, there fell a great rain, and soon after it had ceased a great chain was let down from heaven to earth with seven men hanging on it. These men had been created by God, and they reached the earth by means of the chain. They brought fire with them and cooked their food at it. Not long afterwards God sent a goat from heaven to deliver the following message to the seven men, " There is something that is called Death ; it will one day kill some of you ; but though you die, you will not perish utterly, but you will come to me here in heaven." The goat went his way, but when he came near the town he lit on a bush which seemed to him good to eat ; so he lingered there and began to browse. When God saw that the goat lingered by the way, he sent a sheep to deliver the same message. The sheep went, but did not say what God had commanded her to say ; for she perverted the message and said, " When you once die, you perish, and have no place to go to." Afterwards the goat came and said, " God says, you will die, it is true, but that will not be the end of you, for you will come to me." But the men answered, " No, goat, God did not say that to you. What the sheep first reported, by that we shall abide." [1] In another version of the story, also told at Akropong, the parts of the goat and the sheep are inverted ; it is the sheep that bears the good tidings and loiters by the way to browse, and it is the goat that bears the evil tidings, and is the first to deliver them. The story ends with the melancholy reflection that " if only the sheep had made good speed with her message, man would have died but returned after death ; but the goat made better speed with the contrary message, so man returns no more." [2]

In an Ashantee version of the story the two messengers are also a sheep and a goat, and the perversion of the message of immortality is ascribed sometimes to the one animal and sometimes to the other. The Ashantees say that long ago men were happy, for God dwelt among them and talked with them face to face. However, these blissful days did not last for ever. One unlucky day it chanced that some

Ashantee origin of death: the sheep, and the goat.

[1] J. G. Christaller, " Negersagen von der Goldküste," *Zeitschrift fur Afrikan-ische Sprachen*, i. (Berlin, 1887–88) p. 55.
[2] J. G. Christaller, *op. cit.* p. 58.

women were pounding a mash with pestles in a mortar, while God stood by looking on. For some reason they were annoyed by the presence of the deity and told him to be off; and as he did not take himself off fast enough to please them, they beat him with their pestles. In a great huff God retired altogether from the world and left it to the direction of the fetishes; and still to this day people say, "Ah, if it had not been for that old woman, how happy we should be!" However, God was very good-natured, and even after he had gone up aloft, he sent a kind message by a goat to men on earth, saying, "There is something which they call Death. He will kill some of you. But even if you die, you will not perish completely. You will come to me in heaven." So off the goat set with this cheering intelligence. But before he came to the town, he saw a tempting bush by the wayside, and stopped to browse on it. When God looked down from heaven and saw the goat loitering by the way, he sent off a sheep with the same message to carry the joyful news to men without delay. But the sheep did not give the message aright. Far from it: she said, "God sends you word that you will die, and that will be an end of you." When the goat had finished his meal, he also trotted into the town and delivered his message, saying, "God sends you word that you will die, certainly, but that will not be the end of you, for you will go to him." But men said to the goat, "No, goat, that is not what God said. We believe that the message which the sheep brought us is the one which God sent to us." That unfortunate misunderstanding was the beginning of death among men.[1] However, in another Ashantee version of the tale the parts played by the sheep and goat are reversed. It is the sheep who brings the tidings of immortality from God to men, but the goat overruns him, and offers them death instead. In their innocence men accepted death with enthusiasm, not knowing what it was, and naturally they have died ever since.[2]

In a version of the story which is told by the Akamba

[1] E. Perregaux, *Chez les Achanti* (Neuchatel, 1906), pp. 198 *sq.*
[2] E. Perregaux, *op. cit.* p. 199.

of British East Africa the two gospel messengers are a Akamba
chameleon and a thrush, whom God sent out together to o he
origin of
find people who died one day and came to life the next, and death :
to bear the glad tidings of immortality to men.   So off they chameleon,
set, the chameleon leading the way, for in those days he was and the
thrush.
a very high and mighty person indeed.   As they went along,
what should they see but some people lying like dead by
the wayside.   The chameleon went up to them and said
softly, " *Niwe, niwe, niwe."*   But the thrush asked him testily
what he was making that noise for.   The chameleon mildly
answered, " I am only calling the people who go forward and
then come back," and he explained to the thrush that these
seemingly dead folk would rise from the dead, just as he
himself in walking lurches backward and forward before he
takes a step.   This argument from analogy, which might
have satisfied a Butler, had no effect on the sceptical thrush.
He derided the idea of the resurrection.   Undeterred by
this blatant infidelity the chameleon persisted in calling to
the dead people, and sure enough they opened their eyes
and listened to him.   But the thrush rudely interrupted
him and told the dead people that dead they were and
dead they would remain, nothing could bring them to life.
With that he flew away, and though the chameleon stayed
behind and preached to the corpses, telling them that he
had come from God on purpose to bring them to life again,
and that they were not to believe the lies of that shallow
sceptic the thrush, they turned a deaf ear to his message ;
not one of those dead corpses would so much as budge.   So
the chameleon returned crestfallen to God and reported the
failure of his mission, telling him how, when he preached
the glad tidings of resurrection to the corpses, the thrush
had roared him down, so that the corpses could not hear a
word he said.   Thereupon God cross-questioned the thrush,
who stated that the chameleon had so bungled the message
that he, the thrush, felt it to be his imperative duty to
interrupt him.   The simple-minded deity believed the lying
thrush, and being very angry with the honest chameleon he
degraded him from his high position and made him walk
very slow, lurching this way and that, as he does down to
this very day.   But the thrush he promoted to the office of

wakening men from their slumber every morning, which he still does punctually at 2 A.M. before the note of any other bird is heard in the tropical forest.[1]

Togoland story of the origin of death : ~~C~~ dog and the frog.

In all these versions of the story the message is sent from God to men but in another version, reported from Togoland in West Africa, the message is despatched from men to God. They say that once upon a time men sent a dog to God to say that when they died they would like to come to life again. So off the dog trotted to deliver the message. But on the way he felt hungry and turned into a house, where a man was boiling magic herbs. So the dog sat down and thought to himself, " He is cooking food." Meantime the frog had set off to tell God that when men died they would prefer not to come to life again. Nobody had asked him to give that message ; it was a piece of pure officiousness and impertinence on his part. However, away he tore. The dog, who still sat hopefully watching the hellbroth brewing, saw him hurrying past the door, but he thought to himself, " When I have had something to eat, I will soon catch froggy up." However, froggy came in first, and said to the deity, " When men die, they would prefer not to come to life again." After that, up comes the dog, and says he, " When men die, they would like to come to life again." God was naturally puzzled, and said to the dog, " I really do not understand these two messages. As I heard the frog's request first, I will comply with it. I will not do what you said." That is the reason why men die and do not come to life again. If the frog had only minded his own business instead of meddling with other people's, the dead would all have come to life again to this day. But frogs come to life again when it thunders at the beginning of the rainy season, after they have been dead all the dry season while the Harmattan wind was blowing. Then, while the rain falls and the thunder peals, you may hear them quacking in the marshes.[2] Thus we see that the frog had his own private ends to serve

[1] C. W. Hobley, *Ethnology of A-Kamba and other East African Tribes* (Cambridge, 1910), pp. 107-109. The bird's native name is *itoroko* or *siotoroka*. It is a small bird of the thrush tribe (*Cossypha imolaens*), with a black head, bluish-black back, and a buff-coloured breast. Its Luganda name is *nyonza* and its Swahili name *kurumbizi*.

[2] Fr. Müller, "Die Religionen Togos in Einzeldarstellungen," *Anthropos*, ii. (1907) p. 203.

in distorting the message.   He gained for himself the
immortality of which he robbed mankind.

In Calabar a somewhat different version of the same
widespread story is told.   The messengers are a dog and a
sheep, and they go backwards and forwards between God
and men.   They say that for a long time after the creation
of the world there was no death in it.   At last, however, a
man sickened and died.   So the people sent a dog to God
to ask him what they should do with the dead man.   The
dog stayed so long away that the people grew tired of waiting
and sent off a sheep to God with the same question.   The
sheep soon returned, and reported that God said, " Let the
dead man be buried."   So they buried him.   Afterwards the
dog returned also and reported that God said, " Put warm
ashes on the dead man's belly, and he will rise again."
However, the people told the dog that he came too
late ; the dead man was already buried according to the
instructions of the sheep.   That is why men are buried
when they die.   But as for the dog, he is driven from
men and humiliated, because it is through his fault that we
all die.[1]

In these stories the origin of death is ascribed to the
blunder or wilful deceit of one of the two messengers.   However, according to another version of the story, which is widely
current among the Bantu tribes of Africa, death was caused,
not by the fault of the messenger, but by the vacillation of
God himself, who, after deciding to make men immortal,
changed his mind and resolved to make or leave them
mortal ; and unluckily for mankind the second messenger,
who bore the message of death, overran the first messenger,
who bore the message of immortality.   In this form of the tale
the chameleon figures as the messenger of life, and the lizard
as the messenger of death.   Thus the Zulus say that in the
beginning Unkulunkulu, that is, the Old Old One, sent the
chameleon to men with a message, saying, " Go, chameleon,
go and say, Let not men die."   The chameleon set out, but
it crawled very slowly and loitered by the way to eat the
purple berries of the *ubukwebezane* shrub or of a mulberry

Marginal notes: Calabar story of the death : dog and the sheep. Bantu story of the origin of death : God, chameleon, and the lizard.

[1] "Calabar Stories," *Journal of the African Society*, No. 18 (January 1906),
p. 194.

tree ; however, some people say that it climbed up a tree
to bask in the sun, filled its belly with flies, and fell fast
asleep.   Meantime the Old Old One had thought better of
it and sent a lizard post-haste after the chameleon with a
very different message to men, for he said to the animal,
" Lizard, when you have arrived, say, Let men die." So the
lizard ran, passed the dawdling chameleon, and arriving first
among men delivered his message of death, saying, " Let
men die." Then he turned and went back to the Old Old
One who had sent him.   But after he was gone, the chameleon at last arrived among men with his joyful news of
immortality, and he shouted, saying, " It is said, Let not
men die ! " But men answered, " Oh ! we have heard the
word of the lizard ; it has told us the word, ' It is said, Let
men die.' We cannot hear your word.   Through the word
of the lizard, men will die." And died they have ever since
from that day to this.   So the Zulus hate the lizard and
kill it whenever they can, for they say, " This is the very
piece of deformity which ran in the beginning to say that
men should die." But others hate and hustle or kill the
chameleon, saying, " That is the little thing which delayed
to tell the people that they should not die.   If he had only
told us in time, we too should not have died ; our ancestors
also would have been still living ; there would have been no
diseases here on earth.   It all comes from the delay of the
chameleon." [1]

The same story is told in nearly the same form by other

[1] H. Callaway, The Religious System
of the Amazulu, Part i. (Springvale,
Natal, etc., 1868) pp. 1, 3 sq.,
Part ii. (Springvale, Natal, etc.,
1869) p. 138 ; Rev. L. Grout, Zulu-
land, or Life among the Zulu-Kafirs
(Philadelphia, N.D.), pp. 148 sq. ;
Dudley Kidd, The Essential Kafir
(London, 1904), pp. 76 sq.   Compare
A. F. Gardiner, Narrative of a Journey
to the Zoolu Country (London, 1836),
pp. 178 sq. ; T. Arbousset et F.
Daumas, Relation d'un voyage d'exploration au Nord-Est de la Colonie du
Cap de Bonne-Espérance (Paris, 1842),
p. 472 ; Rev. F. Shooter, The Kafirs
of Natal and the Zulu Country (London, 1857), p. 159 ; W. H. I. Bleek,

Reynard the Fox in South Africa
(London, 1864), p. 74 ; D. Leslie,
Among the Zulus and Amatongas,
Second Edition (Edinburgh, 1875), p.
209 ; F. Merensky, Beiträge zur Kenntniss Süd-Afrikas (Berlin, 1875), p.
124 ; F. Speckmann, Die Hermanns-
burger Mission in Afrika (Hermanns-
burg, 1876), p. 164.   According to
Callaway, the lizard is hated much
more than the chameleon and is invariably killed.   On the other hand,
according to Arbousset and Daumas,
it was the grey lizard that brought the
message of life, and the chameleon
that brought the message of death ;
hence the chameleon is hated, but the
harmless grey lizard beloved.

Bantu tribes such as the Bechuanas,[1] the Basutos,[2] the
Baronga,[3] the Ngoni,[4] and apparently by the Wa-Sania of
British East Africa.[5] It is found, in a slightly altered form,
even among the Hausas, who are not a Bantu people.[6] To
this day the Baronga and the Ngoni owe the chameleon a
grudge for having brought death into the world by its dilatoriness. Hence, when they find a chameleon slowly climbing
on a tree, they tease it till it opens its mouth, whereupon
they throw a pinch of tobacco on its tongue, and watch with
delight the creature writhing and changing colour from
orange to green, from green to black in the agony of death ;
for so they avenge the great wrong which the chameleon did
to mankind.[7]

Thus the belief is widespread in Africa, that God at one
time purposed to make mankind immortal, but that the
benevolent scheme miscarried through the fault of the
messenger to whom he had entrusted the gospel message.

[1] J. Chapman, *Travels in the Interior
of South Africa* (London, 1868), i. 47.

[2] E. Casalis, *The Basutos* (London,
1861), p. 242 ; E. Jacottet, *The
Treasury of Ba-suto Lore*, i. (Morija,
Basutoland, 1908) pp. 46 *sqq*. According to the Basutos it was the grey
lizard that was sent first with the
message of immortality, and the chameleon that was sent after him with
the message of mortality. Compare
above, p. 64, note.

[3] Henri A. Junod, *Les Chants et les
Contes des Ba-ronga* (Lausanne, N.D.),
p. 137 ; *id.*, *Les Ba-Ronga* (Neuchatel, 1898), pp. 401 *sq.* ; *id.*, *The
Life of a South African Tribe* (Neuchatel, 1912-1913), ii. 328 *sq*.

[4] W. A. Elmslie, *Among the Wild
Ngoni* (Edinburgh and London, 1899),
p. 70.

[5] See Captain W. E. R. Barrett,
"Notes on the Customs and Beliefs of
the Wa-giriama, etc., of British East
Africa," *Journal of the Royal Anthropological Institute*, xli. (1911) p. 37,
"The Wa-Sania believe that formerly
human beings did not die until one day
a lizard (Dibleh) appeared and said to

them, 'All of you know that the moon
dies and rises again, but human beings
will die and rise no more.' They say
that from that day human beings commenced to die." This is probably
only an abridged form of the story of
the two messages sent to man by the
Moon through the lizard and the
chameleon.

[6] J. G. Christaller, "Negersagen
von der Goldküste," *Zeitschrift für
Afrikanische Sprachen*, i. (Berlin,
1887-1888) p. 61. In this Hausa version the message sent by God to men
through the chameleon is as follows,
"When a man dies, you must touch
him with bread, and he will rise again."
This message the chameleon faithfully
delivered, but men refused to accept
it, because the lizard, outrunning the
chameleon, had brought them this
word, "When a man dies, you must
bury him."

[7] H. A. Junod and W. A. Elmslie,
ll.cc.; see above, notes [3] and [4]. The
particular species of lizard which according to the Thonga (Baronga) outran the
chameleon and brought the message of
death, is a large animal with a blue
head.

§ 3. *The Story of the Cast Skin*

Savage
belief that
which cast
their skins
renew their
youth and
never die.

Many savages believe that, in virtue of the power of periodically casting their skins, certain animals and in particular serpents renew their youth and never die. Holding this belief, they tell stories to explain how it came about that these creatures obtained, and men missed, the boon of immortality.

Various
stories of
how men
missed the
gift of im-
mortality
and
rpe
and lizards
obtained it.

Thus, for example, the Wafipa and Wabende of East Africa say that one day God, whom they name Leza, came down to earth, and addressing all living creatures said, ' Who wishes not to die?" Unfortunately man and the other animals were asleep ; only the serpent was awake and he promptly answered, " I do." That is why men and all other animals die. The serpent alone does not die of himself. He only dies if he is killed. Every year he changes his skin, and so renews his youth and his strength.[1] In like manner the Dusuns of British North Borneo say that when the Creator had finished making all things, he asked, " Who is able to cast off his skin ? If any one can do so, he shall not die." The snake alone heard and answered, " I can." For that reason down to the present day the snake does not die unless he is killed by man. The Dusuns did not hear the Creator's question, or they also would have thrown off their skins, and there would have been no death.[2] Similarly the Todjo-Toradjas of Central Celebes relate that once upon a time God summoned men and animals for the purpose of determining their lot. Among the various lots proposed by the deity was this, " We shall put off our old skin." Unfortunately mankind on this momentous occasion was represented by an old woman in her dotage, who did not hear the tempting proposal. But the animals which slough their skins, ' such as serpents and shrimps, heard it and closed with the offer.[3] Again, the natives of Vuatom, an island in the Bismarck Archipelago, say that a certain To Konokonomiange bade two lads fetch fire, promising that if they did so they should

[1] Mgr. Lechaptois, *Aux Rives-du Tanganika* (Algiers, 1913), p. 195.

[2] Ivor H. N. Evans, " Folk Stories of the Tempassuk and Tuaran Districts, British North Borneo," *Journal of the Royal Anthropological Institute*, xliii. (1913) p. 478.

[3] N. Adriani en Alb. C. Kruijt, *De Bare'e-sprekende Toradja's van Midden-Celebes* (Batavia, 1912-1914), ii. 83.

never die, but that, if they refused, their bodies would perish, though their shades or souls would survive. They would not hearken to him, so he cursed them, saying, "What! you would all have lived! Now you shall die, though your soul shall live. But the iguana (*Goniocephalus*) and the lizard (*Varanus indicus*) and the snake (*Enygrus*), they shall live, they shall cast their skin and they shall live for evermore." When the lads heard that, they wept, for bitterly they rued their folly in not going to fetch the fire for To Konokono-miange.[1]

The Arawaks of British Guiana relate that once upon a time the Creator came down to earth to see how his creature man was getting on. But men were so wicked that they tried to kill him ; so he deprived them of eternal life and bestowed it on the animals which renew their skin, such as serpents, lizards, and beetles.[2] A somewhat different version of the story is told by the Tamanachiers, an Indian tribe of the Orinoco. They say that after residing among them for some time the Creator took boat to cross to the other side of the great salt water from which he had come. Just as he was shoving off from the shore, he called out to them in a changed voice, "You will ,change your .skins," by which he meant to say, "You will renew your youth like the serpents and the beetles." But unfortunately an old woman, hearing these words, cried out "Oh!" in a tone of scepticism, if not of sarcasm, which so annoyed the Creator that he changed his tune at once and said testily, "Ye shall die." That is why we are all mortal.[3]

The people of Nias, an island to the west of Sumatra, say that, when the earth was created, a certain being was sent down from above to put the finishing touches to the work. He ought to have fasted, but, unable to withstand the pangs of hunger, he ate some bananas. The choice of food was very unfortunate, for had he only eaten river crabs, men would have cast their skins like crabs, and so, renewing their youth perpetually, would never have died. As it is, death has come upon us all through the eating of those

---

[1] Otto Meyer, "Mythen und Erzahlungen von der Insel Vuatom (Bismarck-Archipel, Südsee)," *Anthropos*, v. (1910) p. 724.

[2] R. Schomburgk, *Reisen in Britisch-Guiana* (Leipsic, 1847–1848), ii. 319.

[3] R. Schomburgk, *op. cit.* ii. 320.

bananas.[1]   Another version of the Niasian story adds that
"the serpents on the contrary ate the crabs, which in the
opinion of the people of Nias cast their skins but do not
die ; therefore serpents also do not die but merely cast their
skin."[2]

Samoan
story of
how men
missed the
gift of im-

In this last version the immortality of serpents is ascribed
to their having partaken of crabs, which by casting their
skins renew their youth and live for ever.   The same belief
in the immortality of shell-fish occurs in a Samoan story of
the origin of death.   They say that the gods met in council
to determine what should be the end of man.   One proposal
was that men should cast their skins like shellfish, and so
renew their youth.   The god Palsy moved, on the contrary,
that shellfish should cast their skins, but that men should
die.   While the motion was still before the meeting a shower
of rain unfortunately interrupted the discussion, and as the
gods ran to take shelter, the motion of Palsy was carried
unanimously.   That is why shellfish still cast their skins
and men do not.[3]

Some
peoples
believe
that
formerly
men cast
their skins
and lived
for ever.

Thus not a few peoples appear to believe that the happy
privilege of immortality, obtainable by the simple process of
periodically shedding the skin, was once within reach of our
species, but that through an unhappy chance it was transferred to certain of the lower creatures, such as serpents,
crabs, lizards, and beetles.   According to others, however,
men were at one time actually in possession of this priceless
boon, but forfeited it through the foolishness of an old woman.

Melanesian
story of
how men
ceased to
renew their
youth by
casting
their skins.

Thus the Melanesians of the Banks' Islands and the New
Hebrides say that at first men never died, but that when
they advanced in life they cast their skins like snakes and
crabs, and came out with youth renewed.   After a time a
woman, growing old, went to a stream to change her skin ;
according to some, she was the mother of the mythical or
legendary hero Qat, according to others, she was Ul-ta-
marama, Change-skin of the world.   She threw off her old

[1] H. Sundermann, *Die Insel Nias
und die Mission daselbst* (Barmen,
1905), p. 68 ; E. Modigliani, *Un
viaggio a Nias* (Milan, 1890), p. 295.
   [2] A. Fehr, *Der Niasser im Leben
und Sterben* (Barmen, 1901), p. 8.

[3] George Brown, D.D., *Melanesians
and Polynesians* (London, 1910), p.
365 ; George Turner, *Samoa a Hundred Years ago and long before* (London, 1884), pp. 8 sq.

skin in the water, and observed that as it floated down it caught against a stick. Then she went home, where she had left her child. But the child refused to recognize her, crying that its mother was an old woman, not like this young stranger. So to pacify the child she went after her cast integument and put it on. From that time mankind ceased to cast their skins and died.[1] A similar story of the origin of death is told in the Shortlands Islands[2] and by the Kai, a Papuan tribe of north-eastern New Guinea. The Kai say that at first men did not die but renewed their youth. When their old brown skin grew wrinkled and ugly, they stepped into water, and stripping it off got a new, youthful white skin instead. In those days there lived an old grandmother with her grandchild. One day the old woman, weary of her advanced years, bathed in the river, cast off her withered old hide, and returned to the village, spick and span, in a fine new skin. Thus transformed, she climbed up the ladder and entered her house. But when her grandchild saw her, he wept and squalled, and refused to believe that she was his granny. All her efforts to reassure and pacify him proving vain, she at last went back in a rage to the river, fished her wizened old skin out of the water, put it on, and returned to the house a hideous old hag again. The child was glad to see his granny come back, but she said to him, "The locusts cast their skins, but ye men shall die from this day forward." And sure enough, they have done so ever since.[3] The same story, with some trivial variations, is told by natives of the Admiralty Islands. They say that once on a time there was an old woman, and she was frail. She had two sons, and they went a-fishing, while she herself went to bathe. She stripped off her wrinkled old skin and came forth as young as she had been long ago. When her sons came from the fishing they were astonished to see her. The one said, "It is our mother"; but the other said, "She may be your mother, but she shall be my wife." Their mother overheard

A similar
story of the
origin of
death told
ᴄᴀɪ
of New
Guinea.

Similar
old
by the
natives of
Admiralty
Islands.

[1] R. H. Codrington, *The Melanesians* (Oxford, 1891), p. 265; W. Gray, "Some Notes on the Tannese," *Internationales Archiv für Ethnographie*, vii. (1894) p. 232.

[2] C. Ribbe, *Zwei Jahre unter den Kannibalen der Salomo-Inseln* (Dresden-Blasowitz, 1903), p. 148.

[3] Ch. Keysser, "Aus dem Leben der Kaileute," in R. Neuhauss's *Deutsch Neu-Guinea* (Berlin, 1911), iii. 161 *sq.*

them and said, "What were you two saying?" The two said, "Nothing! We only said that you are our mother." "You are liars," she retorted, "I heard you both. If I had had my way, we should have grown to be old men and women, and then we should have cast our skin and been young men and young women. But you have had your way. We shall grow old men and old women, and then we shall die." With that she fetched her old skin, and put it on, and became an old woman again. As for us, her descendants, we grow up and we grow old. But if it had not been for those two young scapegraces, there would have been no end of our days, we should have lived for ever and ever.[1]

A similar story of the ig death told by a tribe in Celebes.

Still farther away from the Banks Islands the very same story is repeated by the To Koolawi, a mountain tribe of Central Celebes. As reported by the Dutch missionaries who discovered it, the Celebes version of this widely diffused tale runs thus. In the olden time men had, like serpents and shrimps, the power of casting their skin, whereby they became young again. Now there was an old woman who had a grandchild. Once upon a time she went to the water to bathe, and thereupon laid aside her old skin and hung it up on a tree. With her youth quite restored she returned to the house. But her grandchild did not know her again, and would have nothing to do with his grandmother; he kept on saying, "You are not my grandmother; my grandmother was old, and you are young." Then the woman went back to the water and drew on her old skin again. But ever since that day men have lost the power of renewing their youth and must die.[2]

A variant of the Melanesian story.

A variant form of the Melanesian story is told in Aneityum, one of the New Hebrides. There they say that once an old man took off his skin before he began to work in his garden. He then looked young. But one day his two grandchildren, finding his skin folded away, pierced it through, making many holes therein. When the old man put it on again he shivered with cold, and seeing the holes in his skin he said to his grandchildren, "I thought we should live for

[1] Josef Meier, "Mythen und Sagen der Admiralitätsinsulaner," *Anthropos*, iii. (1908) p. 193.
[2] N. Adriani en Alb. C. Kruijt, *De Bare'e-sprekende Toradja's van Midden-Celebes* (Batavia, 1912–1914), ii. 83.

ever and cast our skins and become young again ; but as you have done this we shall all die." Thus death came into the world.[1]

Another Melanesian tradition ascribes the introduction of death to purely economic causes. In the days when men changed their skins and lived for ever, the permanence of property in the same hands was found to be a great inconvenience ; it bore very hard on the heirs, who were perpetually tantalized by the prospect of an inheritance to which it was legally and physically impossible that they should ever succeed. All this time Death had resided either in a shadowy underground region called Panoi or by the side of a volcanic vent in Santa Maria, it is not quite certain which ; but now in answer to the popular demand he was induced to come abroad and show himself. He was treated to a handsome funeral of the usual sort ; that is to say, he was laid out on a board and covered with a pall, a pig was killed, and the mourners enjoyed a funeral feast and divided the property of the deceased. Afterwards, on the fifth day, the conch shell was blown to drive away the ghost. In short, nothing was left undone to soothe and gratify the feelings of the departed. So Death returned down the road to the underground region from which he had emerged ; and all mankind have since followed him thither.[2]

While some peoples have supposed that in the early ages of the world men were immortal in virtue of periodically casting their skins, others have ascribed the same high privilege to a certain lunar sympathy, in consequence of which mankind passed through alternate states of growth and decay, of life and death, corresponding to the phases of the moon, without ever coming to an end. On this view, though death in a sense actually occurred, it was speedily repaired by resurrection, generally, it would seem, by resurrection after three days, since three days is the period between the disappearance of the old moon and the reappearance of the new. Thus the Mentras or Mantras, a shy tribe of savages in the jungles of the Malay Peninsula, allege that in the early ages of the world men did not die, but only grew

A different es story of the origin of death.

Some es believe that men on to rise from the dead days, as the moon appears to do in the sky.

[1] William Gunn, *The Gospel in Futuna* (London, 1914), pp. 217 *sq.*

[2] R. H. Codrington, *The Melanesians* (Oxford, 1891), pp. 265 *sq.*

thin at the waning of the moon and then waxed fat again
as she waxed to the full.   Thus there was no check whatever
on the population, which increased to an alarming extent.
So a son of the first man brought this state of things to his
father's notice, and asked him what was to be done.   The
first man, a good easy soul, said, "Leave things as they are";
but his younger brother, who took a more Malthusian view
of the matter, said, "No, let men die like the banana, leaving
their offspring behind."   The question was submitted to the
Lord of the Underworld, and he decided in favour of death.
Ever since then men have ceased to renew their youth like
the moon and have died like the banana.[1]   In the Caroline
Islands it is said that in the olden time death was unknown, or
rather it was only a short sleep.   Men died on the last day of
the waning moon and came to life again on the appearance of
the new moon, just as if they had wakened from a refreshing
slumber.   But an evil spirit somehow contrived that when
men slept the sleep of death they should wake no more.[2]
The Wotjobaluk, a tribe of south-eastern Australia, related
that when all animals were men and women, some of them
died and the moon used to say, "You up again," whereupon
they came to life again.   But once on a time an old man
said, "Let them remain dead"; and since then nobody has
ever come to life again, except the moon, which still continues to do so down to this very day.[3]   The Unmatjera and
Kaitish, two tribes of central Australia, say that their dead
used to be buried either in trees or underground, and that
after three days they regularly rose from the dead.   The
Kaitish tell how this happy state of things came to an end.
It was all the fault of a man of the Curlew totem, who found
some men of the Little Wallaby totem in the act of burying
a man of that ilk.   For some reason the Curlew man flew
into a passion and kicked the corpse into the sea.   Of
course after that the dead man could not come to life again,
and that is why nowadays nobody rises from the dead after

[1] D. F. A. Hervey, "The Mentra
Traditions," *Journal of the Straits
Branch of the Royal Asiatic Society*,
No. 10 (December, 1882), p. 190;
W. W. Skeat and C. O. Blagden,
Pagan Races of the Malay Peninsula
(London, 1906), ii. 337 *sq.*

[2] *Lettres Édifiantes et Curieuses*,
Nouvelle Édition, xv. (Paris, 1781)
pp. 305 *sq.*

[3] A. W. Howitt, *Native Tribes of
South-East Australia* (London, 1904),
pp. 428 *sq.*

three days, as everybody used to do long ago.[1]   Though
nothing is said about the moon in this narrative of the
origin of death, the analogy of the preceding stories makes
it probable that the three days, during which the dead used
to lie in the grave, were the three days during which the
moon lay " hid in her vacant interlunar cave."   The Fijians
also associated the possibility, though not the actual enjoyment, of human immortality with the phases of the moon.
They say that of old two gods, the Moon and the Rat, discussed the proper end of man.   The Moon said, " Let him
be like me, who disappear awhile and then live again."   But
the Rat said, " Let man die as a rat dies."   And he prevailed.[2]

The Upotos of the Congo tell how men missed and
the Moon obtained the boon of immortality.   One day God,
whom they call Libanza, sent for the people of the moon and
the people of the earth.   The people of the moon hastened
to the deity, and were rewarded by him for their alacrity.
" Because," said he, addressing the moon, " thou camest to me
at once when I called thee, thou shalt never die.   Thou
shalt be dead for but two days each month, and that only
to rest thee ; and thou shalt return with greater splendour."
But when the people of the earth at last appeared before
Libanza, he was angry and said to them, " Because you
came not at once to me when I called you, therefore you
will die one day and not revive, except to come to me."[3]

The Bahnars of eastern Cochin China explain the immortality of primitive man neither by the phases of the
moon nor by the custom of casting the skin, but apparently
by the recuperative virtue of a certain tree.   They say that
in the beginning, when people died, they used to be buried
at the foot of a tree called Long Blo, and that after a time
they always rose from the dead, not as infants, but as full-
grown men and women.   So the earth was peopled very
fast, and all the inhabitants formed but one great town
under the presidency of our first parents.   In time men
multiplied to such an extent that a certain lizard could not
take his walks abroad without somebody treading on his tail.

Upoto, how men missed the mortality and the obtained it.

Bahnar y, how men used to ir the dead by being the foot of a certain ...

[1] (Sir) Baldwin Spencer and F. J.
Gillen, *Northern Tribes of Central
Australia* (London, 1904), pp. 513 *sq.*
[2] Thomas Williams, *Fiji and the*
Fijians, Second Edition (London,
1860), i. 205.
[3] M. Lindeman, *Les Upotos* (Brussels,
1906), pp. 23 *sq.*

This vexed him, and the wily creature gave an insidious hint
to the gravediggers. "Why bury the dead at the foot of the
Long Blo tree?" said he; "bury them at the foot of Long
Khung, and they will not come to life again. Let them die
outright and be done with it." The hint was taken, and
from that day men have not come to life again.[1]

Rivalry for
immortal-
ity between
men and
creatures
that cast
their skins,
such as
serpents
and lizards.

In this last story, as in many African tales, the instrument of bringing death among men is a lizard. We may
conjecture that the reason for assigning the invidious office
to a lizard was that this animal, like the serpent, casts its
skin periodically, from which primitive man might infer, as
he infers with regard to serpents, that the creature renews its
youth and lives for ever. Thus all the myths which relate
how a lizard or a serpent became the maleficent agent of
human mortality may perhaps be referred to an old idea of
a certain jealousy and rivalry between men and creatures
which cast their skins, notably serpents and lizards; we may
suppose that in all such cases a story was told of a contest
between man and his animal rivals for the possession of immortality, a contest in which, whether by mistake or guile,
the victory always remained with the animals, who thus
became immortal, while mankind was doomed to mortality.

§ 4. *The Composite Story of the Perverted Message and the Cast Skin*

Stories
which
combine
the
incidents
of the
perverted
message
and the
cast skin.
Galla story
of God and
the blue
bird.

In some stories of the origin of death the incidents of
the perverted message and the cast skin are combined.
Thus the Gallas of East Africa attribute the mortality of
man and the immortality of serpents to the mistake or malice
of a certain bird which falsified the message of eternal life
entrusted to him by God. The creature which did this
great wrong to our species is a black or dark blue bird, with
a white patch on each wing and a crest on its head. It
perches on the tops of trees and utters a wailing note like
the bleating of a sheep; hence the Gallas call it *holawaka*
or "the sheep of God," and explain its apparent anguish by
the following tale. Once upon a time God sent that bird to

---

[1] Guerlach, "Mœurs et Superstitions des sauvages Ba-hnars," *Les Missions
Catholiques*, xix. (1887) p. 479.

tell men that they should not die, but that when they grew old and weak they should slip off their skins and so renew their youth. In order to authenticate the message God gave the bird a crest to serve as the badge of his high office. Well, off the bird set to deliver the glad tidings of immortality to man, but he had not gone far before he fell in with a snake devouring carrion in the path. The bird looked longingly at the carrion and said to the snake, "Give me some of the meat and blood, and I will tell you God's message." " I don't want to hear it," said the snake tartly, and continued his meal. But the bird pressed him so to hear the message that the snake rather reluctantly consented. " The message," then said the bird, " is this. When men grow old they will die, but when you grow old you will cast your skin and renew your youth." That is why people grow old and die, but snakes crawl out of their old skins and renew their youth. But for this gross perversion of the message God punished the heedless or wicked bird with a painful internal malady, from which he suffers to this day ; that is why he sits wailing on the tops of trees.[1] Again, the Melanesians, who inhabit the coast of the Gazelle Peninsula in New Britain, say that To Kambinana, the Good Spirit, loved men and wished to make them immortal. So he called his brother To Korvuvu and said to him, "Go to men and take them the secret of immortality. Tell them to cast their skin every year. So will they be protected from death, for their life will be constantly renewed. But tell the serpents that they must thenceforth die." However, To Korvuvu acquitted himself badly of his task ; for he commanded men to die, and betrayed to the serpents the secret of immortality. Since then all men have been mortal, but the serpents cast their skins every year and never die.[2] A similar story of the origin of death is told in Annam. They say that Ngoc hoang sent a messenger from heaven to men to say that when they reached old age they should change their skins and live for ever, but that when serpents grew old they must die. The messenger came down to earth and said, rightly enough, "When man is old he shall cast his skin ;

Melanesian story of To Kambinana and To Korvuvu.

Annamite story of Ngoc hoang and his message to men.

[1] Miss A. Werner, "Two Galla Legends," *Man*, xiii. (1913) pp. 90 sq.

[2] P. A. Kleintitschen, *Die Küstenbewohner der Gazellehalbinsel* (Hiltrup bei Munster, N.D.), p. 334.

but when serpents are old they shall die and be laid in coffins." So far so good. But unluckily there happened to be a brood of serpents within hearing, and when they learned the doom pronounced on their kind, they fell into a fury and said to the messenger, "You must say it over again and just the contrary, or we will bite you." That frightened the messenger, and he repeated his message, changing the words thus, "When the serpent is old he shall cast his skin ; but when man is old he shall die and be laid in the coffin." That is why all creatures are now subject to death, except the serpent, who, when he is old, casts his skin and lives for ever.[1]

§ 5. *Conclusion*

In its gin form the Hebrew ... o' ... Fall o Man probably the serpent, by eating of the Tree of Life, obtained the boon of immor- a ity or his eci-

Thus, arguing from the analogy of the moon or of animals which cast their skins, the primitive philosopher has inferred that in the beginning a perpetual renewal of youth was either appointed by a benevolent being for the human species or was actually enjoyed by them, and that but for a crime, an accident, or a blunder it would have been enjoyed by them for ever. People who pin their faith in immortality to the cast skins of serpents, lizards, beetles, and the like, naturally look on these animals as the hated rivals who have robbed us of the heritage which God or nature intended that we should possess ; consequently they tell stories to explain how it came about that such low creatures contrived to oust us from the priceless possession. Tales of this sort are widely diffused throughout the world, and it would be no matter for surprise to find them among the Semites. The story of the Fall of Man in the third chapter of Genesis appears to be an abridged version of this savage myth. Little is wanted to complete its resemblance to the similar myths still told by savages in many parts of the world. The principal, almost the only, omission is the silence of the narrator as to the eating of the fruit of the tree of life by the serpent, and the consequent attainment of immortality by the reptile. Nor is it difficult to account for the lacuna. The vein of rationalism, which runs through the Hebrew account of creation and has stripped

[1] A. Landes, "Contes et Legendes Annamites," *Cochinchine française*,   *Excursions et Reconnaissances*, No. 25 (Saigon, 1886) pp. 108 *sq.*

it of many grotesque features that adorn or disfigure the corresponding Babylonian tradition, could hardly fail to find a stumbling-block in the alleged immortality of serpents ; and the redactor of the story in its final form has removed this stone of offence from the path of the faithful by the simple process of blotting out the incident entirely from the legend. Yet the yawning gap left by his sponge has not escaped the commentators, who look in vain for the part which should have been played in the narrative by the tree of life. If my interpretation of the story is right, it has been left for the comparative method, after thousands of years, to supply the blank in the ancient canvas, and to restore, in all their primitive crudity, the gay barbaric colours which the skilful hand of the Hebrew artist had softened or effaced.

THE MARK OF CAIN

Mark set
by God on
Cain.
WE read in Genesis that when Cain had murdered his brother Abel he was driven out from society to be a fugitive and a vagabond on earth. Fearing to be slain by any one who might meet him, he remonstrated with God on the hardness of his lot, and God had so far compassion on him that he "set a mark upon Cain, lest any finding him should kill him."[1] What was the mark that God put on the first murderer? or the sign that he appointed for him?

The theory that the mark was a tribal badge seems inadequate.
That we have here a reminiscence of some old custom observed by manslayers is highly probable; and, though we cannot hope to ascertain what the actual mark or sign was, a comparison of the customs observed by manslayers in other parts of the world may help us to understand at least its general significance. Robertson Smith thought that the mark in question was the tribal mark, a badge which every member of the tribe wore on his person, and which served to protect him by indicating that he belonged to a community that would avenge his murder.[2] Certainly such marks are

[1] Genesis iv. 8-15 (Authorized Version). The Revised Version renders: "and the Lord appointed a sign for Cain." The former rendering, which I have adopted, appears to be demanded by the context, as Principal J. Skinner observes in his commentary on Genesis (p. 110). The most literal translation would be "set a sign to (or for) Cain." Modern commentators on Genesis (Dillmann, Driver, Bennett, Skinner, Gunkel, Ryle) are rightly agreed that the mark was intended for the protection of Cain, and that it was

either imprinted on his body or at all events closely attached to his person.

[2] W. Robertson Smith, *Kinship and Marriage in Early Arabia*, New Edition (London, 1903), p. 251. B. Stade has argued that the mark was the tribal mark of the Kenites, of whom he believes Cain to have been the eponymous ancestor; further, he holds that it had a religious as well as a tribal significance, stamping the Kenites as worshippers of Jehovah. From a variety of indications he concludes that the mark was probably tattooed on the

common among peoples who have preserved the tribal system. For example, among the Bedouins of to-day one of the chief tribal badges is a particular mode of wearing the hair.[1]   In many parts of the world, notably in Africa, the tribal mark consists of a pattern tattooed or incised on some part of the person.[2]   That such marks might serve as a protection to the tribesman in the way supposed by Robertson Smith seems probable ; though on the other hand it is to be remembered that in a hostile country they might, on the contrary, increase his danger by advertising him as an enemy.   But even if we concede the protective value of a tribal mark, still the explanation thus offered of the mark of Cain seems hardly to fit the case.   It is too general.   Every member of a tribe was equally protected by such a mark, whether he was a manslayer or not.   The whole drift of the narrative tends to show that the mark in question was not worn by every member of the community, but was peculiar to a murderer.   Accordingly we seem driven to seek for an explanation in another direction.

From the narrative itself we gather that Cain was thought to be obnoxious to other dangers than that of being slain as an outlaw by any one who met him.   God is represented saying to him, " What hast thou done ? the voice of thy brother's blood crieth unto me from the ground. And now cursed art thou from the ground, which hath opened her mouth to receive thy brother's blood from thy hand ; when thou tillest the ground, it shall not henceforth yield unto thee her strength ; a fugitive and a wanderer shalt thou be in the earth." [3]   Here it is obvious that the blood of his murdered brother is regarded as constituting a physical danger to the murderer ; it taints the ground and prevents it from yielding its increase.   Thus the murderer is thought to have poisoned the sources of life and thereby jeopardized the supply of food for himself, and perhaps for

Homicides ed because they are o g be infected by a ..:.. of death.

---

forehead of the tribesmen. See B. Stade, " Das Kainszeichen," *Zeitschrift fur die alttestamentliche Wissenschaft,* xiv. (1894) pp. 250-318 ; *id., Biblische Theologie des Alten Testaments,* i. (Tübingen, 1905) pp. 42, 146.   But the view is open to serious objections. See Principal J. Skinner, *Critical and*

Exegetical Commentary on Genesis (Edinburgh, 1910), pp. 111 *sqq.*
[1] W. Robertson Smith, *l.c.*
[2] J. G. Frazer, *Totemism and Exogamy* (London, 1910), i. 28 *sq.*, iv. 197 *sqq.*
[3] Genesis iv. 10-12 (Revised Version).

others. On this view it is intelligible that a homicide should be shunned and banished the country, to which his presence is a continual menace. He is plague-stricken, surrounded by a poisonous atmosphere, infected by a contagion of death ; his very touch may blight the earth.

Attic law concerning banished homicides. Hence we can understand a certain rule of Attic law. A homicide who had been banished, and against whom in his absence a second charge had been brought, was allowed to return to Attica to plead in his defence ; but he might not set foot on the land, he had to speak from a ship, and even the ship might not cast anchor or put out a gangway. The judges avoided all contact with the culprit, for they judged the case sitting or standing on the shore.[1] Clearly the intention of this rule of law was to put the manslayer in quarantine, lest by touching Attic earth even indirectly through the anchor or the gangway he should blast it. For the same reason, if such a man, sailing the sea, had the misfortune to be cast away on the country where his crime had been perpetrated, he was allowed indeed to camp on the shore till a ship came to take him off, but he was expected to keep his feet in sea-water all the time,[2] evidently in order to counteract, or at least dilute, the poison which he was supposed to instil into the soil.

Seclusion of murderers in Dobu. The quarantine which Attic law thus imposed on the manslayer has its counterpart in the seclusion still enforced on murderers by the savages of Dobu, an island off the south-eastern extremity of New Guinea. On this subject a missionary, who resided for seventeen years in the island, writes as follows : " War may be waged against the relatives of the wife, but the slain must not be eaten. The person who kills a relation by marriage must never after partake '

[1] Demosthenes, *Orat.* xxiii. 77 *sq.*, pp. 645 *sq.* ; Aristotle, *Constitution of Athens*, 57 ; Pausanias, i. 28. 11 ; Julius Pollux, *Onomasticon*, viii. 120 ; Helladius, quoted by Photius, *Bibliotheca*, p. 535*a*, lines 28 *sqq.*, ed. Im. Bekker (Berlin, 1824). The rule which forbade the ship to cast anchor or to put out a gangway is mentioned only by Pollux. But Pollux had access to excellent authorities, and the rule bears the stamp of genuine antiquity. We may therefore safely dismiss as unauthorized the statement of Helladius that the ship cast anchor.

[2] Plato, *Laws*, ix. 8, p. 866 C D. In ancient Greece, for a different reason, when a man died of dropsy, his children were made to sit with their feet in water until the body was burnt (Plutarch, *De sera numinis vindicta*, 14). Compare *The Magic Art and the Evolution of Kings*, i. 78 (*The Golden Bough*, Third Edition, Part i.).

of the general food or fruit from his wife's village. His
wife alone must cook his food. If his wife's fire goes out
she is not allowed to take a fire-stick from a house in her
village. The penalty for breaking this tabu is that the
husband dies of blood-poisoning! The slaying of a blood
relation places an even stricter tabu on the slayer. When
the chief Gaganumore slew his brother (mother's sister's
son) he was not allowed to return to his own village,
but had to build a village of his own. He had to have a
separate lime-gourd and spatula; a water-bottle and cup of
his own; a special set of cooking pots; he had to get his
drinking cocoanuts and fruit elsewhere; his fire had to be
kept burning as long as possible, and if it went out it could
not be relit from another fire, but by friction. If the chief
were to break this tabu, his brother's blood would poison
his blood so that his body would swell, and he would die a
terrible death." [1]

In these Dobuan cases the blood of the slain man is
supposed to act as a physical poison on the slayer, should
he venture to set foot in, or even to hold indirect communication with, the village of his victim. His seclusion is therefore a precaution adopted in his own interest rather than in
that of the community which he avoids; and it is possible
that the rules of Attic law in the matter of homicide ought
to be similarly interpreted. However, it is more probable
that the danger was believed to be mutual; in other words,
that both the homicide and the persons with whom he came
into contact were thought liable to suffer from blood-poisoning caused by contagion. Certainly the notion that a manslayer can infect other people with a malignant virus is held
by the Akikuyu of British East Africa. They think that if
a man who has killed another comes and sleeps at a village
and eats with a family in their hut, the persons with whom
he has eaten contract a dangerous pollution (*thahu*), which
might prove fatal to them, were it not removed in time by
a medicine-man. The very skin on which the homicide
slept has absorbed the taint and might infect any one else

*Belief in the
nf tious
state of
homicides
tu
b" Kikuyu
notions.*

[1] Rev. W. E. Bromilow, "Some
manners and customs of the Dobuans
of S.E. Papua," *Report of the Twelfth
Meeting of the Australasian Association*
*for the Advancement of Science held at
Brisbane, 1909* (Brisbane, 1910), p.
478.

who slept on it.   So a medicine-man is called in to purify the hut and its inmates.[1]

Similarly among the Moors of Morocco a manslayer " is considered in some degree unclean for the rest of his life. Poison oozes out from underneath his nails ; hence anybody who drinks the water in which he has washed his hands will fall dangerously ill.   The meat of an animal which he has killed is bad to eat, and so is any food which is partaken of in his company.   If he comes to a place where people are digging a well, the water will at once run away.   In the Hiáina, I was told, he is not allowed to go into a vegetable garden or an orchard, nor to tread on a threshing-floor or enter a granary, nor to go among the sheep.   It is a common, although not universal, rule that he must not perform the sacrifice at the Great Feast with his own hands ; and in some tribes, mostly Berber-speaking ones, there is a similar prohibition with reference to a person who has killed a dog, which is an unclean animal.   All blood which has left the veins is unclean and haunted by *jnun* " [2] (jinn).

But in the Biblical narrative of the murder of Abel the blood of the murdered man is not the only inanimate object that is personified.   If the blood is represented as crying aloud, the earth is represented as opening her mouth to receive the blood of the victim.[3]   To this personification of the earth Aeschylus offers a parallel, for he speaks of the ground drinking the blood of the murdered Agamemnon.[4]   But in Genesis the attribution of personal qualities to the earth seems to be carried a step further, for we are told that the murderer was " cursed from the ground " ; and that when he tilled it, the land would not yield him her strength, but that a fugitive and a wanderer should he be in the world.

The implication apparently is that the earth, polluted by blood and offended by his crime, would refuse to allow the seed sown by the murderer to germinate and bear fruit ; nay,

[1] C. W. Hobley, " Kikuyu Customs and Beliefs," *Journal of the Royal Anthropological Institute*, xl. (1910) p. 431.   I have already cited this and more evidence to the same effect in *Psyche's Task*, Second Edition (London, 1913), pp. 115 *sqq.*

[2] Edward Westermarck, *The Moorish Conception of Holiness* (Helsingfors, 1916), pp. 130 *sq.*

[3] Genesis iv. 11.

[4] Aeschylus, *Choephor.* 63 (58), δι' αἱμά τ' ἐκποθὲν ὑπὸ χθονὸς τροφου.

that it would expel him from the cultivated soil on which he had hitherto prospered, and drive him out into the barren wilderness, there to roam a houseless and hungry vagabond. The conception of earth as a personal being, who revolts against the sin of the dwellers upon it and spurns them from her bosom, is not foreign to the Old Testament. In Leviticus we read that, defiled by human iniquity, " the land vomiteth out her inhabitants ";[1] and the Israelites are solemnly warned to keep God's statutes and judgments, "that the land vomit not you out also, when ye defile it, as it vomited out the nation that was before you." [2]

The ancient Greeks apparently entertained similar notions as to the effect of polluting earth by the shedding of human blood, or, at all events, the blood of kinsfolk ; for tradition told how the matricide Alcmaeon, haunted by the ghost of his murdered mother Eriphyle, long wandered restlessly over the world, till at last he repaired to the oracle at Delphi, and the priestess told him, that " the only land whither the avenging spirit of Eriphyle would not dog him was the newest land, which the sea had uncovered since the pollution of his mother's blood had been incurred ;"[3] or, as Thucydides puts it, " that he would never be rid of his terrors till he had found and settled in a country which, when he slew his mother, the sun had not yet shone on, and which at that time was not yet dry land ; for all the rest of the earth had been polluted by him." [4] Following the directions of the oracle, he discovered at the mouth of the Achelous the small and barren Echinadian Islands which, by washing down the soil from its banks, the river was supposed to have created since the perpetration of his crime; and there he took up his abode.[5] According to one version of the legend, the murderer had found rest for a time in the bleak upland valley of Psophis, among the solemn Arcadian mountains, but even

Ancient legend of the ...ngs of the matricide Alcmaeon.

[1] Leviticus xviii. 25.
[2] Leviticus xviii. 28, compare xx. 22.
[3] Pausanias viii. 24. 8.
[4] Thucydides ii. 102.
[5] Thucydides ii. 102 ; Pausanias viii. 24. 7-9. Miss J. E. Harrison has ingeniously conjectured that the Aleïan plain in Cilicia (Herodotus vi. 95), over which Bellerophon wandered (Homer, *Iliad*, vi. 201), after he had accidentally slain his brother (Apollodorus, *Bibliotheca*, ii. 3. 1), may have consisted, like the Echinadian Islands, of new land formed by alluvial soil and but lately recovered from the sea. See her *Prolegomena to the Study of Greek Religion*, Second Edition (Cambridge, 1908), pp. 220 *sq.*

there the ground refused to yield its increase to the matricide, and he was forced, like Cain, to resume his weary wanderings.[1]

Belief entertained by some tribes of Upper Senegal that the offended by bloodshed may be appeased by sacrifice.

customs of the Bobos.

The belief that the earth is a powerful divinity, who is defiled and offended by the shedding of human blood and must be appeased by sacrifice, prevails, or prevailed till lately, among some tribes of Upper Senegal, who exact expiation even for wounds which have merely caused blood to flow without loss of life. Thus at Laro, in the country of the Bobos, "the murderer paid two goats, a dog, and a cock to the chief of the village, who offered them in sacrifice to the Earth on a piece of wood stuck in the ground. Nothing was given to the family of the victim. All the villagers, including the chief, afterwards partook of the flesh of the sacrificial victims, the families of the murderer and his victim alone being excluded from the banquet. If it was an affair of assault and wounds, but blood had not been shed, no account was taken of it. But when blood had been spilt, the Earth was displeased at the sight, and therefore it was necessary to appease her by a sacrifice. The culprit gave a goat and a thousand cowries to the chief of the village, who sacrificed the goat to the Earth and divided the cowries among the elders of the village. The goat, after being offered to the Earth, was also divided among the village elders. But the injured party throughout the affair was totally forgotten and received nothing at all, and that, too, logically enough. For the intention was not to compensate the injured party for his wrong at the cost of the wrongdoer, but to appease the Earth, a great and redoubtable divinity, who was displeased at the sight of bloodshed. In these circumstances there was nothing for the injured party to get. It sufficed that the Earth was pacified by eating the soul of the goat that had been sacrificed to her;"[2] for "among the Bobos, as among the other blacks, the Earth is esteemed a great goddess of justice."[3]

Similar beliefs and customs of the Nou-noumas concerning bloodshed.

Among the Nounoumas, another tribe of Upper Senegal, the customs and beliefs in regard to bloodshed were similar.

[1] Apollodorus, *Bibliotheca*, iii. 7. 5, γενομένης δὲ ὕστερον τῆς γῆς δι' αὐτὸν ἀφθόου κτλ.

[2] L. Tauxier, *Le Noir du Soudan* (Paris, 1912), p. 64.

[3] L. Tauxier, *op. cit.* p. 73.

A murderer was banished for three years and had to pay a heavy fine in cowries and cattle, not as a blood-wit to the family of his victim, but to appease the Earth and the other local divinities, who had been offended by the sight of spilt blood. The ox or oxen were sacrificed to the angry Earth by a priest who bore the title of the Chief of the Earth, and the flesh, together with the cowries, was divided among the elders of the village, the family of the murdered man receiving nothing, or at most only a proportionate share of the meat and money. In the case of brawls where no life had been taken, but blood had flowed, the aggressor had to pay an ox, a sheep, a goat, and four fowls, all of which were sacrificed to pacify the anger of the local deities at the sight of bloodshed. The ox was sacrificed to the Earth by the Chief of the Earth in presence of all the elders of the village ; the sheep was sacrificed to the River ; and the fowls to the Rocks and the Forest. As for the goat, it was sacrificed by the chief of the village to his private fetish. If these expiatory sacrifices were not offered, it was believed that the gods in their wrath would slay the culprit and all his family. The Chief of the Earth received as his due the intestines, hide, head, horns, and one shoulder of the sacrificial ox ; the rest of the ox and the remaining victims were divided between the chief of the village, the headmen of the various wards, and the elders. Every one carried off his portion of flesh to his own house and ate it there. In some places the assailant had also to pay a fine in cowries proportioned to the seriousness of the wound which he had inflicted.[1]

The foregoing facts suggest that a mark put on a homicide might be intended primarily, not for his protection, but for the protection of the persons who met him, lest by contact with his pollution they should defile themselves and incur the wrath of the god whom he had offended, or of the ghost by whom he was haunted ; in short, the mark might be a danger-signal to warn people off, like the special garb prescribed in Israel for lepers.[2]

However, there are other facts which tend to show that the

Thus the mark a homicide might be a danger signal to warn others away.

[1] L. Tauxier, *Le Noir du Soudan*, pp. 176-178. For more evidence of expiatory sacrifices offered to appease the anger of Earth at bloodshed, see *id.*, pp. 100 *sq.*, 227, 228, 239 *sq.*, 263, 264, 290, 313-315, 352.

[2] Leviticus xiii. 45.

murderer's mark was designed, as the story of Cain implies, for the benefit of the murderer alone, and further that the real danger against which it protected him was not the anger of his victim's kinsfolk, but the wrath of his victim's ghost. Here again, as in the Athenian customs already mentioned, we seem to touch the bed-rock of superstition in Attica. Plato tells us that according to a very ancient Greek belief the ghost of a man who had just been killed as angry with his slayer and troubled him, being enraged at the sight of the homicide stalking freely about in his, the ghost's, old familiar haunts ; hence it was needful for the homicide to depart from his country for a year until the wrath of the ghost had cooled down, nor might he return before sacrifices had been offered and ceremonies of purification performed. If the victim chanced to be a foreigner, the slayer had to shun the native land of the dead man as well as his own, and in going into banishment he had to follow a prescribed road ;[1] for clearly it would never do to let him rove about the country with the angry ghost at his heels.

Again, we have seen that among the Akikuyu a murderer is believed to be tainted by a dangerous pollution (*thahu*) which he can communicate to other people by contact. That this pollution is connected with his victim's ghost appears from one of the ceremonies which are performed to expiate the deed. The elders of the village sacrifice a pig beside one of those sacred fig-trees which play a great part in the religious rites of the tribe. There they feast on the more succulent parts of the animal, but leave the fat, intestines, and some of the bones for the ghost, who is supposed to come that very night and devour them in the, likeness of a wild cat ; his hunger being thus stayed, he considerately refrains from returning to the village to trouble the inhabitants. It deserves to be noticed that a Kikuyu homicide incurs ceremonial pollution (*thahu*) only through the slaughter of a man of his own clan ; there is no ceremonial pollution incurred by the slaughter of a man of another clan or of another tribe.[2]

[1] Plato, *Laws*, ix. 8, pp. 865 D-866 A ; Demosthenes, *Orat.* xxiii. pp. 643 *sq.* ; Hesychius, *s.v.* ἀπενιαυτισμός.

[2] C. W. Hobley, "Kikuyu Customs and Beliefs," *Journal of the Royal Anthropological Institute*, xl. (1910)

Among the Bagesu of Mount Elgon, in British East Africa, when a man has been guilty of manslaughter and his victim was a member of the same clan and village, he must leave the village and find a new home elsewhere, even though he may settle the matter amicably with the relations of the deceased. Further, he must kill a goat, smear the contents of its stomach on his chest, and throw the remainder upon the roof of the house of the murdered man "to appease the ghost."[1] In this tribe very similar ceremonies of expiation are performed by a warrior who has slain a man in battle; and we may safely assume that the intention of the ceremonies is to appease the ghost of his victim. The warrior returns to his village, but he may not spend the first night in his own house, he must lodge in the house of a friend. In the evening he kills a goat or sheep, deposits the contents of the stomach in a pot, and smears them on his head, chest, and arms. If he has any children, they must be smeared in like manner. Having thus fortified himself and his progeny, the warrior proceeds boldly to his own house, daubs each door-post with the stuff, and throws the rest on the roof, probably for the benefit of the ghost who may be supposed to perch, if not to roost, there. For a whole day the slayer may not touch food with the hands which shed blood; he conveys the morsels to his mouth with two sticks cut for the purpose. On the second day he is free to return home and resume his ordinary life. These restrictions are not binding on his wife; she may even go and mourn over the slain man and take part in his obsequies.[2] Such a pretence of sorrow may well mollify the feelings of the ghost and induce him to spare her husband.

Again, among the Nilotic Kavirondo, another tribe of British East Africa, a murderer is separated from the members of his village and lives in a hut with an old woman, who attends to his wants, cooks for him, and also feeds him, because he may not touch his food with his hands. This separation lasts for three days, and on the fourth day a man,

Bagesu m... y to appease the ghost ...a... man.

Similar expiation observed gesu warriors who have enemies in battle.

Nilotic 'o ceremony to rid a of his victim's ghost.

---

pp. 438 *sq.* As to the sanctity of the fig-tree (*mugumu*) among the Akikuyu, see M. W. H. Beech, "The sacred fig-tree of the A-kikuyu of East Africa," *Man*, xiii. (1913) pp. 4-6.

[1] J. Roscoe, *The Northern Bantu* (Cambridge, 1915), p. 171.

[2] J. Roscoe, *The Northern Bantu*, p. 190.

who is himself a murderer, or who has at some time killed a man in battle, takes the murderer to a stream, where he washes him all over. He then kills a goat, cooks the meat, and puts a piece of it on each of four sticks ; after which he gives the four pieces to the murderer to eat in turn. Next he puts four balls of porridge on the sticks, and these also the murderer must swallow. Finally, the goat-skin is cut into strips, and one strip is put on the neck, and one strip round each of the wrists of the homicide. This ceremony is per- formed by the two men alone at the river. After the per- formance the murderer is free to return home. It is said that, until this ceremony is performed, the ghost cannot take its departure for the place of the dead, but hovers about the murderer.[1]

Customs observed by a Boloki murderer to mollify his victim s ghost.

Among the Boloki of the Upper Congo a homicide is not afraid of the ghost of the man whom he has killed, when his victim belongs to any of the neighbouring towns, because the area within which Boloki ghosts can travel is extremely limited ; but murder, which in that case he might commit with an easy mind, assumes a much more serious complexion when it is perpetrated on a man of the same town, for then he knows himself to be within striking distance of the ghost. The fear of ghostly vengeance now sits heavy on him. There are unfortunately no rites by the observance of which he could allay these terrors, but in default of them he mourns for his victim as though he were a brother, neglecting his toilet, shaving his head, fasting, and lamenting with torrents of crocodile tears.[2] Thus the symptoms of sorrow, which the ingenuous European might take for signs of genuine repentance and remorse of conscience, are nothing but shams intended to deceive the ghost.

Among the Omaha has the seclusion of a murderer seems to spring from a fear of h victim's host.

Once more among the Omaha Indians of North America a murderer, whose life was spared by the kinsmen of his victim, had to observe certain stringent regulations for a period which varied from two to four years. He must walk barefoot, and he might eat no warm food, nor raise his voice, nor look around. He had to pull his robe about him and to keep it tied at the neck, even in warm weather ; he might

---

[1] J. Roscoe, *The Northern Bantu*, pp. 279 *sq.*

[2] John H Weeks, *Among Congo Cannibals* (London, 1913), p. 268.

not let it hang loose or fly open. He might not move his hands about, but had to keep them close to his body. He might not comb his hair, nor allow it to be blown about by the wind. No one would eat with him, and only one of his kindred was allowed to remain with him in his tent. When the tribe went hunting, he was obliged to pitch his tent about a quarter of a mile from the rest of the people, "lest the ghost of his victim should raise a high wind which might cause damage." [1] The reason here alleged for banishing the murderer from the camp probably gives the key to all the similar restrictions laid on murderers and manslayers among primitive peoples ; the seclusion of such persons from society is dictated by no moral aversion to their crime : it springs purely from prudential motives, which resolve themselves into a simple dread of the dangerous ghost by which the homicide is supposed to be pursued and haunted.

This fear of the wrathful ghost of the slain is probably at the root of many ancient customs observed in connexion with homicide ; it may well have been one of the principal motives for inflicting capital punishment on murderers. For if such persons are dogged by a powerful and angry spirit, which makes them a danger to their fellows, society can obviously protect itself very simply by sacrificing the murderer to the ghost ; in other words, by putting him to death. But then it becomes necessary to guard the executioners in their turn against the ghosts of their victims, and various precautions are adopted for this purpose. For example, among the Bakongo, of the Lower Congo, when a man has been executed for murder, his body is burnt to ashes. "By reducing the body to ashes they believe that they thereby destroy his spirit, and thus prevent the spirit from seeking revenge by bewitching his executioners." [2] At Porto Novo, on the coast of Guinea, the public executioner used to decorate the walls of his house with the jawbones of his victims in order to prevent their ghosts from troubling him at night. [3] At Issini, on the Gold Coast, executioners used to remain

The fear of he g osts of the murdered m e been one motive for murderers.

Necessity fo o e - i g ex cu- tioners g e ghosts of their m Precau- tions taken xecu tioners in Africa and Burma.

[1] Rev. J. Owen Dorsey, "Omaha Sociology," *Third Annual Report of the Bureau of Ethnology* (Washington, 1884), p. 369.

[2] John H. Weeks, *Among the Primi- tive Bakongo* (London, 1914), pp. 62 *sq.*

[3] Father Baudin, "Feticheurs ou ministres religieux des Negres de la Guinée " *Les Missions Catholiques*, xvi. (1884) p. 332.

in seclusion for three days after doing their office ; during that time they lived in a hut built for the purpose at a distance from the village. When the three days were up, they proceeded to the place of execution, and there called thrice by name on the criminal whom they had put to death.[1] The invocation was probably supposed to protect the executioners against the ghost of their victim. Another mode of effecting the same purpose is to taste of his blood ; this has been customary with executioners on the Lower Niger in West Africa, and among the Shans of Burma. The alleged intention of the custom is to prevent the executioner from being affected by a kind of homicidal madness or otherwise contracting a fatal illness ;[2] but these effects are in all probability believed to be wrought by the ghost of the slain man, who has entered into and taken possession of the body of his slayer, and the motive for tasting of his blood is to bring about a reconcilement between the slayer and the slain by establishing a blood covenant between them.[3] Among the Tupi Indians of Brazil a man who had publicly executed a prisoner had to fast and lie in his hammock for three days, without setting foot on the ground ; further, he had to make incisions in his breast, arms, and other parts of his body, and a black powder was rubbed into the wounds, which left indelible scars so artistically arranged that they presented the appearance of a tight-fitting garment. It was believed that he would die if he did not observe these rules and draw blood from his own body after slaughtering the captive.[4]

The Tupi Indians invited a condemned man to avenge himself before his death, and the executioner had to cut marks on his own body, perhaps for the satisfaction of the ghost.

[1] G. Loyer, "Voyage to Issini on the Gold Coast," in T. Astley's *New General Collection of Voyages and Travels*, ii. (London, 1745) p. 444.

[2] Major A. G. Leonard, *The Lower Niger and its Tribes* (London, 1906), pp. 180, 181 *sq.* ; Mrs. Leslie Milne, *Shans at Home* (London, 1910), p. 192.

[3] See further *Psyche's Task*, Second Edition (London, 1913), pp. 117 *sqq.*

[4] F. A. Thevet, *Les Singularitez de la France Antarctique, autrement nommée Amerique* (Antwerp, 1558), pp. 74-76 ; *id.*, *Cosmographie Universelle* (Paris, 1575), pp. 944 [978] *sq.* ; Pero de Magalhanes de Gandavo, *Histoire de la province de Sancta-Cruz*

(Paris, 1837), pp. 134-141 (H. Ternaux-Compans, *Voyages, relations, et mémoires originaux pour servir à l'histoire de la découverte de l'Amérique ;* the original of Gandavo's work was published in Portuguese at Lisbon in 1576) ; J. Lery, *Historia navigationis in Brasiliam, quae et America dicitur* (1586), pp. 183-194 ; *The Captivity of Hans Stade of Hesse, in A.D. 1547-1555, among the Wild Tribes of Eastern Brazil*, translated by A. Tootal (London, 1874), pp. 155-159 ; J. F. Lafitau, *Mœurs des Sauvages Ameriquains* (Paris, 1724), ii. 292 *sqq.* ; R. Southey, *History of Brazil*, i.[2] (London, 1822) p. 232. Compare G. Friederici, "Über eine als Couvade gedeutete

The fear of his victim's ghost is not indeed mentioned by our authorities as the motive for practising these customs ; but that it was the real motive is not only suggested by the analogy of the West African customs, but is practically proved by a custom which these same Brazilian Indians observed before the execution.   They formally invited the doomed man to avenge his death, and for this purpose they supplied him with stones or potsherds, which he hurled at his guards, while they protected themselves against the missiles with shields made of hide.[1]   The form of the invitation, which ran thus, " Avenge your death before your decease," clearly implies a hope that if a man had thus satisfied his thirst for vengeance in his lifetime, his ghost would not trouble them after death.   But to make assurance doubly sure the executioner secluded himself, and observed the curious precautions which I have described.   The drawing of blood from his own body, which was regarded as essential to the preservation of his life,[2] may have been intended to satisfy the ghost's demand of blood for blood, or possibly to form a blood covenant with him, while the permanent marks left on the slayer's body would be a standing evidence that he had given satisfaction to his victim and made his peace with him.   Could any reasonable ghost ask for more ?

This interpretation of the marks on the executioner's body is confirmed by the following custom.   Among the Yabim, on the north-eastern coast of New Guinea, when the kinsmen of a murdered man have accepted a blood-wit instead of avenging his death, they take care to be marked with chalk on the forehead by the relatives of the murderer, " lest the ghost should trouble them for failing to avenge his death, and should carry off their pigs or loosen their teeth." [3]

The Yabim pu   wh mark on the foreheads ers who have accepted a vit for the murder of the mark is supposed to prevent the ghost from troubling them.

Widergeburtszeremonie bei den Tupi," *Globus,* lxxxix. (1906) pp. 59 - 63, who interprets the incised marks on the executioner's body as intended to disguise him from his victim's ghost. As to marks made with this intention see below, pp. 92 *sqq.*

[1] J. Lery *op. cit.* p. 18ç.

[2] P. de Magalhanes de Gandavo, *op. cit.* p. 139.

[3] K. Vetter, in *Nachrichten über*

Kaiser Wilhelms-Land und den Bismarck-Archipel (Berlin, 1897), p. 99 ; B. Hagen, *Unter den Papuas* (Wiesbaden, 1899), p. 254.   In the same tribe, at the conclusion of hostilities, the bravest of the victors puts a chalk mark on the brows of the vanquished " in order that they may not be exposed to the caprice of the ghosts." See H. Zahn, " Die Jabim," in R. Neuhauss's *Deutsch Neu-Guinea* (Berlin, 1911), iii. 318.

In this custom it is not the murderer but the kinsmen of his victim who are marked, but the principle is the same.   The ghost of the murdered man naturally turns in fury on his heartless relatives who have not exacted blood for his blood. But just as he is about to swoop down on them to loosen their teeth, or steal their pigs, or make himself unpleasant in other ways, he is brought up short by the sight of the white mark on their black or coffee-coloured brows.   It is the receipt for the payment in full of the blood-wit ; it is the proof that his kinsfolk have exacted a pecuniary, though not a sanguinary, compensation for his murder ; with this crumb of consolation he is bound to be satisfied, and to spare his family any molestation in future.   The same mark might obviously be put for the same purpose on the murderer's brows to prove that he had paid in cash, or whatever may be the local equivalent for cash, for the deed he had done, and that the ghost therefore had no further claim upon him.   Was the mark of Cain a mark of this sort ?   Was it a proof that he had paid the blood-wit ?   Was it a receipt for cash down ?

Not only murderers but warriors who have slain enemies have to guard themselves against the ghosts of their victims.

It may have been so, but there is still another possibility to be considered.   On the theory which I have just indicated it is obvious that the mark of Cain could only be put on a homicide when his victim was a man of the same tribe or community as himself, since it is only to men of the same tribe or community that compensation for homicide is paid. But the ghosts of slain enemies are certainly not less dreaded than the ghosts of slain friends ; and if you cannot pacify them with a sum of money paid to their kinsfolk, what are you to do with them ?   Many plans have been adopted for the protection of warriors against the spirits of the men whom they have sent out of the world before their due time. Apparently one of these precautions is to disguise the slayer so that the ghost may not recognize him ; another is to render his person in some way so formidable or so offensive that the spirit will not meddle with him.   One or other of these motives may explain the following customs, which I select from a large number of similar cases.[1]

Among the Ba-Yaka, a Bantu people of the Congo Free

---

[1] For more examples see *Taboo and the Perils of the Soul*, pp. 157 *sqq.* ;   *Psyche's Task*, Second Edition (London, 1913), pp. 120 *sqq.*

State, "a man who has been killed in battle is supposed to
send his soul to avenge his death on the person of the man
who killed him ; the latter, however, can escape the vengeance of the dead by wearing the red tail-feathers of the
parrot in his hair, and painting his forehead red." [1]   The
Thonga of south-eastern Africa believe that a man who has
killed an enemy in battle is exposed to great danger from
his victim's ghost, who haunts him and may drive him mad.
To protect himself from the wrath of the ghost, the slayer
must remain in a state of taboo at the capital for several
days, during which he may not go home to his wife, and
must wear old clothes and eat with special spoons off special
plates.   In former times it was customary to tattoo such a
man between the eyebrows, and to rub in medicines into the
incisions, so as to raise pimples and to give him the appearance of a buffalo when it frowns.[2]   Among the Basutos
"warriors who have killed an enemy are purified.   The
chief has to wash them, sacrificing an ox in the presence of
the whole army.   They are also anointed with the gall of
the animal, which prevents the ghost of the enemy from
pursuing them any farther." [3]

Among the Wawanga, of the Elgon district in British
East Africa, a man on returning from a raid, on which he
has killed one of the enemy, may not enter his hut until he
has taken cow's dung and rubbed it on the cheeks of the
women and children of the village, and has purified himself
by the sacrifice of a goat, from whose forehead he cuts a strip
of skin and wears it round his right wrist for the next four
days.[4]   Among the Bantu tribes of Kavirondo, in British
East Africa, when a man has killed a foe in battle he
shaves his head on his return home, and his friends rub a
medicine, which generally consists of cow's dung, over his
body to prevent the spirit of the slain man from troubling

Precau-
on taken
b he
Ba-Yaka,
and   nga,
Basutos
n   e
ghosts of
men slain
in battle.

Precau-
tions taken
b he
Wawanga
g nst t e
ghos s of
slain
enemies.

Precau-
ns aken
by the
Bantu
Kavirondo
against the
ghosts of
slain
enemies.

[1] E. Torday and T. A. Joyce,
"Notes on the Ethnography of the
Ba-Yaka," Journal of the Anthropological Institute, xxxvi. (1906) pp.
50 sq.
[2] Henri A. Junod, The Life of a
South African Tribe (Neuchâtel, 1912–
1913), i. 453 sq.
[3] Father Porte, "Les réminiscences

d'un missionnaire du Basutoland," Les
Missions Catholiques, xxviii. (1896) p.
371.

[4] Hon. Kenneth R. Dundas, "The
Wawanga and other tribes of the Elgon
District, British East Africa," Journal
of the Royal Anthropological Institute,
xliii. (1913) p. 47.

Precautions
taken by
the Nilotic
tribes of
aviron
against the
ghosts of
slain
enemies. him.[1] In these cases the cow's dung may serve either to
wipe off the ghost or to disgust and repel him.   Among the
Ja-Luo, a Nilotic tribe of Kavirondo, the warrior who has
slain a foe in battle shaves his head three days after his
return from the fight; and before he enters his village he
must hang a live fowl, head uppermost, round his neck ;
then the bird is decapitated and its head left hanging round
his neck.   Soon after his return a feast is made for the slain
man, in order that his ghost may not haunt his slayer.[2]
According to another account the ceremonies observed on
such occasions by the Nilotic tribes of Kavirondo are as
follows. "When a warrior kills another in battle, he is
isolated from his village, lives in a separate hut some four
days, and an old woman cooks his food and feeds him like a
child because he is forbidden to touch any food.   On the
fifth day he is escorted to the river by another man, who
washes him ; a white goat is killed and cooked by the
attendant, who feeds the man with the meat ; the goat-skin
is cut into strips and put upon the man's wrists and round
his head, and he returns to his temporary home for the night.
The next day he is again taken to the river and washed,
and a white fowl is presented to him.   He kills it and it is
cooked for him, and he is again fed with the meat.   He is
then pronounced to be clean and may return to his home.
It sometimes happens that a warrior spears another man in
battle, and the latter dies from the wound some time after.
When death takes place, the relatives go to the warrior and
tell him of the death, and he is separated at once from the community until the ceremonies above described have been performed.   The people say that the ceremonies are necessary in
order to release the ghost of the dead man, which is bound to
the warrior who slew him, and is only released on the fulfilment of the ceremonies.   Should a warrior refuse to fulfil the
ceremonies, the ghost will ask, ' Why don't you fulfil the ceremonies and let me go ? '   Should a man still refuse to comply,
the ghost will take him by the throat and strangle him."[3]

[1] Sir H. Johnston, *The Uganda
Protectorate* (Lodon, 1902), ii. 743
sq.; C. W. Hobley, *Eastern Uganda*
(London, 1902), p. 20.
[2] Sir H. Johnston, *The Uganda*

Protectorate, ii. 794 ; C. W. Hobley,
Eastern Uganda, p. 20.

[3] J. Roscoe, *The Northern Bantu*
(Cambridge, 1915), p. 289.

We have seen that among the Nilotic tribes of Kavirondo
a very similar ceremony is observed by a murderer for the
avowed purpose of freeing himself from the ghost of his
victim, which otherwise haunts him.[1]   The close resemblance
of the ritual in both cases, together with the motives expressly
assigned for it, set in the clearest light the essential purpose
of the purificatory ceremonies observed by a homicide, whether
he is a warrior or a murderer : that purpose is simply to
rid the man of his victim's ghost, which will otherwise be his
undoing.   The intention of putting strips of goat-skin round
his head and wrists may be to disguise him from the ghost.
A similar custom is observed by other tribes of East Africa
on a variety of occasions, which will be noticed later on.[2]
Even when no mention is made of the ghosts of the slain
by our authorities, we may still safely assume that the purificatory rites performed by or for warriors after bloodshed are
intended to appease or repel or deceive these angry spirits.
Thus among the Ngoni of British Central Africa, when a
victorious army approaches the royal village, it halts by the
bank of a stream, and all the warriors who have killed
enemies smear their bodies and arms with white clay, but
those who were not the first to dip their spears in the blood
of the victims, but merely helped to despatch them, whiten
their right arms only.   That night the manslayers sleep in
the open pen with the cattle, and do not venture near their
own homes.   In the early morning they wash off the white
clay from their bodies in the river.   The witch-doctor attends
to give them a magic potion, and to smear their persons with
a fresh coating of clay.   This process is repeated on six
successive days, till their purification is complete.   Their
heads are then shaved, and being pronounced clean they are
free to return to their own homes.[3]   Among the Borana
Gallas, when a war-party has returned to the village, the
victors who have slain a foe are washed by the women
with a mixture of fat and butter, and their faces are painted
red and white.[4]   Masai warriors, who have killed barbarians in a fight, paint the right half of their bodies red and

The
nt n
purificatory
ceremonies
serve d
by
homicides,

murderers
or warriors,
is to free
the slayers
from the
ghosts of
the slain.

Some
Af an
tribes aint
the faces or
od
manslayers
in various
co ours.

[1] See above, pp. 87 *sq.*
[2] See below, vol. ii. pp. 7 *sqq.*
[3] Donald Fraser, *Winning a Primitive People* (London, 1914), pp. 39 *sq.*

[4] Ph.   Paulitschke, *Ethnographie
Nord-ost-Afrikas : die materielle Cul-
tur der Danâkil, Galla und Somâl*
(Berlin, 1893), p. 258.

the left half white.[1]   Similarly a Nandi, who has slain a
man of another tribe, paints one side of his body red, and
the other side white ; for four days after the slaughter
he is deemed unclean and may not go home.   He must
build a small shelter by the river and live there ; he may not
associate with his wife or sweetheart, and he may only eat
porridge, beef, and goat's flesh.   At the end of the fourth
day he must purify himself by drinking a strong purge made
from the *segetet* tree, and by drinking goat's milk mixed
with bullock's blood.[2]   Among the Wagogo, of German East
Africa, a man who has killed an enemy in battle paints a
red circle round his right eye and a black circle round his
left eye.[3]

In some
Indian
tribes of
North
America
it is
customary
for a
manslayer
to blacken
his face,
paint it red,
or plaster
his head
with mud.

Among the Thompson Indians of British Columbia it
used to be customary for men who had slain enemies to
blacken their faces.   If this precaution were neglected, it
was believed that the spirits of their victims would blind
them.[4]   A Pima Indian who slew one of his hereditary foes,
the Apaches, had regularly to undergo a rigid seclusion and
purification, which lasted sixteen days.   During the whole
of that time he might not touch meat or salt, nor look at a
blazing fire, nor speak to a human being.   He lived alone
in the woods attended by an old woman, who brought him
his scanty dole of food.   He kept his head covered almost
the whole time with a plaster of mud, and he might not
touch it with his fingers.[5]   A band of Tinneh Indians, who
had massacred a helpless party of Eskimo at the Copper
River, considered themselves to be thereby rendered unclean,
and they observed accordingly a number of curious restrictions
for a considerable time afterwards.   Those who had actually
shed blood were strictly prohibited from cooking either for
themselves or for others ; they might not drink out of any

[1] A. C. Hollis, *The Masai* (Oxford,
1905), p. 353.
[2] A. C. Hollis, *The Nandi* (Oxford,
1909), p. 74.
[3] Rev. H. Cole, "Notes on the
Wagogo of German East Africa,"
*Journal of the Anthropological Insti-
tute*, xxxii. (1902) p. 314.
[4] J. Teit, "The Thompson Indians
of British Columbia," *Memoirs of the
American Museum of Natural History*,

vol. ii., *Anthropology*, i. [Part] iv.
([New York], April 1900) p. 357.
[5] H. H. Bancroft, *Native Races of
the Pacific States* (London, 1875–1876),
i. 553 ; Capt. Grossman, cited in *Ninth
Annual Report of the Bureau of Ethnology* (Washington, 1892), pp. 475 *sq.* ;
F. Russell, "The Pima Indians,"
*Twenty-Sixth Annual Report of the
Bureau of American Ethnology* (Washington, 1908), pp. 204 *sq.*

dish nor smoke out of any pipe but their own ; they might eat no boiled flesh, but only flesh that was raw or had been broiled at a fire or dried in the sun ; and at every meal, before they would taste a morsel, they had to paint their faces with red ochre from the nose to the chin and across the cheeks almost to the ears.[1]

Among the Chinook Indians of Oregon and Washington a man who had killed another had his face painted black with grease and charcoal, and wore rings of cedar bark round his head, his ankles, knees, and wrists. After five days the black paint was washed off his face and replaced by red. During these five days he might not sleep nor even lie down ; he might not look at a child nor see people eating. At the end of his purification he hung his head-ring of cedar bark on a tree, and the tree was then supposed to dry up.[2] Among the Eskimo of Langton Bay the killing of an Indian and the killing of a whale were considered to be equally glorious achievements. The man who had killed an Indian was tattooed from the nose to the ears ; the man who had killed a whale was tattooed from the mouth to the ears. Both heroes had to refrain from all work for five days, and from certain foods for a whole year ; in particular, they might not eat the heads nor the intestines of animals.[3] Among the Southern Massim of British New Guinea a warrior who has slain a man remains secluded in his house for six days. During the first three days he may eat only roasted food and must cook it for himself. Then he bathes and blackens his face for the remaining three days.[4] When a party of Arunta, in Central Australia, are returning from a mission of vengeance, on which they have taken the life of an enemy, they stand in fear of the ghost of their victim, who is believed to pursue them in the likeness of a small bird, uttering a plaintive cry. For some days after their return they will not speak of their deed, and continue to paint themselves all over with powdered charcoal, and to

In other customary for ~~ic~~ to blacken or tattoo ~~laces~~ or to blacken the whole of their bodies.

[1] S. Hearne, *Journey from Prince of Wales's Fort in Hudson's Bay to the Northern Ocean* (London, 1795), pp. 204-206.

[2] Franz Boas, *Chinook Texts* (Washington, 1894), p. 258.

[3] V. Stefansson, *My Life with the Eskimo* (London, 1913), p. 367.

[4] C. G. Seligmann, *The Melanesians of British New Guinea* (Cambridge, 1910), pp. 563 *sq.*

decorate their foreheads and noses with green twigs. Finally,
they paint their bodies and faces with bright colours, and
become free to talk of the affair; but still of nights
they must lie awake listening for the plaintive cry of
the bird in which they fancy they hear the voice of their
victim.[1]

In Fiji
mans ayers
painted red
all over.

In Fiji any one who had clubbed a human being to
death in war was consecrated or tabooed. He was smeared
red by the king with turmeric from the roots of his hair to
his heels. A hut was built, and in it he had to pass the
next three nights, during which he might not lie down, but
must sleep as he sat. Till the three nights had elapsed he
might not change his garment, nor remove the turmeric, nor
enter a house in which there was a woman.[2] That these
rules were intended to protect the Fijian warrior from his
victim's ghost is strongly suggested, if not proved, by another
Fijian custom. When these savages had buried a man alive,
as they often did, they used at nightfall to make a great
uproar by means of bamboos, trumpet-shells, and so forth,
for the purpose of frightening away his ghost, lest he should
attempt to return to his old home. And to render his house
unattractive to him they dismantled it and clothed it with
everything that to their thinking seemed most repulsive.[3]

Some
peoples
forcibly
expel the
g o s f
the slain

So the North American Indians used to run through the
village with hideous yells, beating on the furniture, walls,
and roofs of the huts to drive away the angry ghost of an
enemy whom they had just tortured to death.[4] A similar
custom is still observed in various parts of New Guinea and
the Bismarck Archipelago.[5]

Thus the mark of Cain may have been a mode of dis-

[1] (Sir) Baldwin Spencer and F. J. Gillen, *Native Tribes of Central Australia* (London, 1899), pp. 493-495; *iid., Northern Tribes of Central Australia* (London, 1904), pp. 563-568. The writers suggest that the practice of painting the slayers black is meant to render them invisible to the ghost.

[2] T. Williams, *Fiji and the Fijians*, Second Edition (London, 1860), i. 55 *sq.*

[3] John Jackson, quoted by Captain J. E. Erskine, *Journal of a Cruise among the Islands of the Western Pacific* (London, 1853), p. 477.

[4] Charlevoix, *Histoire de la Nouvelle France* (Paris, 1744), vi. 77, 122 *sq.*; J. F. Lafitau, *Mœurs des Sauvages Ameriquains* (Paris, 1724), ii. 279. Compare W. H. Keating, *Narrative of an Expedition to the Source of St. Peter's River* (London, 1825), i. 109.

[5] R. E. Guise, "On the tribes inhabiting the mouth of the Wanigela River, New Guinea," *Journal of the Anthropological Institute*, xxviii. (1899) pp. 213 *sq.*; J. L. D. van der Roest, "Uit het leven der bevolking van Windessi," *Tijdschrift voor Indische*

guising a homicide, or of rendering him so repulsive or formidable in appearance that his victim's ghost would either not know him or at least give him a wide berth. Elsewhere I have conjectured that mourning costume in general was originally a disguise adopted to protect the surviving relatives from the dreaded ghost of the recently departed.[1] Whether that be so or not, it is certain that the living do sometimes disguise themselves to escape the notice of the dead. Thus in the western districts of Timor, a large island of the Indian Archipelago, before the body of a man is coffined, his wives stand weeping over him, and their village gossips must also be present, "all with loosened hair in order to make themselves unrecognizable by the *nitu* (spirit) of the dead."[2] Again, among the Herero of South-West Africa, when a man is dying he will sometimes say to a person whom he does not like, "Whence do you come? I do not wish to see you here," and so saying he presses the fingers of his left hand together in such a way that the tip of the thumb protrudes between the fingers. "The person spoken to, now knows that the other has decided upon taking him away (*okutuaerera*) after his death, which means that he must die. In many cases, however, he can avoid this threatening danger of death. For this purpose he hastily leaves the place of the dying man, and looks for an *onganga* (*i.e.* 'doctor,' 'magician'), in order to have himself undressed, washed, and greased again, and dressed with other clothes. He is now quite at ease about the threatening of death caused by the deceased ; for, says he, 'Now, our father does not know me' (*Nambano tate ke ndyi i*). He has no longer any reason to fear the dead."[3]

Taal- Land- en Volkenkunde, xl. (1898) pp. 157 *sq.*; H. von Rosenberg, *Der Malayische Archipel* (Leipsic, 1878), p. 461 ; K. Vetter, "Uber papuanische Rechtsverhaltnisse," in *Nachrichten uber Kaiser Wilhelms-Land und den Bismarck-Archipel* (Berlin, 1897), p. 94 ; B. Hagen, *Unter den Papuas* (Wiesbaden, 1899), p. 266 ; Stefan Lehner, "Bukaua," in R. Neuhauss's *Deutsch Neu-Guinea* (Berlin, 1911), iii. 44 ; George Brown, D.D., *Melanesians and Polynesians* (London, 1910), pp.

142, 145.

[1] J. G. Frazer, "On certain Burial Customs as illustrative of the Primitive Theory of the Soul," *Journal of the Anthropological Institute*, xv. (1886) p. 73.

[2] J. G. F. Riedel, "Die Landschaft Dawan oder West-Timor," *Deutsche Geographische Blatter*, x. 286.

[3] Rev. G Viehe, "Some Customs of the Ovaherero," (*South African*) *Folk-lore Journal*, i. (Capetown, 1879) pp. 51 *sq.*

In like manner we may suppose that, when Cain had been marked by God, he was quite easy in his mind, believing that the ghost of his murdered brother would no longer recognize and trouble him. What the mark exactly was which the divinity affixed to the first murderer for his protection, we have no means of knowing ; at most we can hazard a conjecture on the subject. If it is allowable to judge from the similar practices of savages at the present day, the deity may have decorated Cain with red, black, or white paint, or perhaps with a tasteful combination of these colours. For example, he may have painted him red all over, like a Fijian ; or white all over, like a Ngoni ; or black all over, like an Arunta ; or one half of his body red and the other half white, like the Masai and the Nandi. Or if he confined his artistic efforts to Cain's countenance, he may have painted a red circle round his right eye and a black circle round his left eye, in the Wagogo style ; or he may have embellished his face from the nose to the chin, and from the mouth to the ears, with a delicate shade of vermilion, after the manner of the Tinneh Indians. Or he may have plastered his head with mud, like the Pimas, or his whole body with cow's dung, like the Kavirondo. Or again, he may have tattooed him from the nose to the ears, like the Eskimo, or between the eyebrows, like the Thonga, so as to raise pimples and give him the appearance of a frowning buffalo. Thus adorned the first Mr. Smith—for Cain means Smith [1]—may have paraded the waste places of the earth without the least fear of being recognized and molested by his victim's ghost.

This explanation of the mark of Cain has the advantage of relieving the Biblical narrative from a manifest absurdity. For on the usual interpretation God affixed the mark to Cain in order to save him from human assailants, apparently forgetting that there was nobody to assail him, since the earth was as yet inhabited only by the murderer himself and his parents. Hence by assuming that the foe of whom the

---

[1] T. K. Cheyne, in *Encyclopaedia Biblica* (Edinburgh, 1899–1903), i. col. 620, *s.v.* "Cain" ; F. Brown, S. R. Driver, and Ch. A. Briggs, *Hebrew and English Lexicon* (Oxford, 1906), p. 883, *s.v.* קין.

first murderer went in fear was a ghost instead of a living man, we avoid the irreverence of imputing to the deity a grave lapse of memory little in keeping with the divine omniscience.   Here again, therefore, the comparative method approves itself a powerful *advocatus Dei*.

To this explanation of the mark of Cain it may be objected, with some show of reason, that the ghost of the murdered Abel is nowhere alluded to in the Biblical narrative, according to which it was not the ghost, but the blood, of his victim which endangered the murderer by calling aloud from the ground for vengeance.   It is true that the conception of blood thus endowed with a voice and with a thirst for vengeance differs from the conception of a ghost, being a simpler and possibly a more primitive idea ; yet in practice it perhaps made little material difference to the manslayer whether he believed himself to be pursued by the bloody phantom or only by the dolorous voice of his victim's blood shrieking after him.   Still it cannot be denied that in the Old Testament it is the actual blood, and not the ghost, of the murdered person which figures prominently in the references to manslaughter and to the retribution which should overtake the slayer.   Thus in the Priestly Document we read, with regard to homicide, that " blood, it polluteth the land : and no expiation can be made for the land for the blood that is shed therein, but by the blood of him that shed it." [1]   The notion seems to have been, that so long as the blood lay exposed to the air and had not run away or soaked into the ground, it continued to call aloud for vengeance on the murderer, but that its mouth could be stopped and its voice stifled by a handful of earth.   Hence Job, looking for death and passionately appealing against the injustice of his fate, cries out in his agony, " O earth, cover not my blood, and let my cry have no *resting* place." [2] And in denouncing the wrath of God on Jerusalem for all the innocent blood shed in the city, the prophet Ezekiel exclaims, " Woe to the bloody city, to the caldron whose rust is therein, and whose rust is not gone out of it ! bring it out piece by piece ; no lot is fallen upon it.   For her blood is in

In the narrative it is rather the blood than the ghost of the Abel which cries for vengeance.

Fear of leaving bl uncovered on the ground.

---

[1] Numbers xxxv. 33.   [2] Job xvi. 18.

the midst of her ; she set it upon the bare rock ; she poured
it not on the ground to cover it with dust ; that it might
cause fury to come up to take vengeance, I have set her
blood upon the bare rock, that it should not be covered." [1]
Here it is mentioned as a great aggravation alike of the
guilt and of the danger of Jerusalem, that the blood shed in
her midst still weltered in clotted pools, like rust, on her
rocky surface instead of being mercifully covered with dust
or allowed to soak into the ground ; for so long as it lay
there festering in the sun, the multitudinous voices of the
slain would ascend up to heaven, clamouring in a doleful
chorus for vengeance on their slayers. [2]   The belief that
unavenged human blood cries aloud from the ground is still
held by the Arabs of Moab.   A Bedouin of that country told
a preaching friar that "the blood cries from the earth, and it
continues to cry until the blood of an enemy has been shed." [3]

The dread
of un-
covered
blood,
whether of
man or of
beast.

So scrupulous indeed were the ancient Hebrews about
leaving blood of any sort exposed to the air, that the
Levitical law commands the hunter or fowler to cover
up with dust the blood of the beast or fowl which he
has poured out on the ground. [4]   The precept may well
embody a traditional usage based on an ancient belief that
animals, like men, acknowledged the obligation of avenging
the death of their kind on their murderer or his kinsfolk,
and that consequently if their blood was left uncovered, it
would cry aloud to all beasts or birds of the same sort to
exact retribution from the guilty hunter or fowler who had
spilt it on the ground.   At all events similar notions as to
the practice of blood revenge by animals and birds are
common among savages in modern times, [5] and they may
well have prevailed among the Semites in antiquity, though
we need not suppose that they were consciously present to
the mind of the author or editor of Leviticus.   It would
appear that in the opinion of some savages not only may

Even the
blood of
beasts
may be
supposed
to cry
aloud for
vengeance.

---

[1] Ezekiel xxiv. 6-8.

[2] So Aeschylus tells us that "vengeful gore sets hard and will not run away." See *Choephor.* 65 (59), τίτας φόνος πέπηγεν οὐ διαρρύδαν, with the commentaries of Paley and Verrall in their editions. The words οὐ διαρρύδαν imply that the blood will not disappear by *running through* the soil.

[3] A. Jaussen, *Coutumes des Arabes au pays de Moab* (Paris, 1908), p. 227.

[4] Leviticus xvii. 13.

[5] For examples I may refer the reader to *Spirits of the Corn and of the Wild*, ii. 204 *sqq.* (*The Golden Bough*, Third Edition, Part v.).

the blood of animals cry to heaven for vengeance, but if its cry is not answered, the slayer of the beast may be compelled, like Cain, to roam an outlaw from land to land for the rest of his life.   Thus in a legend of the Waboungou, a tribe of German East Africa, we hear of a skilful hunter who one day killed an elephant with his arrows.   Thereupon a mysterious personage called the Great Sultan appeared to him and said, " The smell of spilt blood has reached even to me. That blood calls for vengeance.   If you do not bring me the bones of the elephant, there can be no peace between us. I will tell all the Sultans to drive you from their countries, so that you will henceforth find no place where to build a hut." But the obstinate hunter refused to bring the bones of the elephant to the Great Sultan.   Therefore the Sultan drove him from his kingdom, and the wretch went roving from land to land till the day of his death.[1]

We may smile if we please at these quaint fancies of vengeful ghosts, shrieking gore, and Earth opening her mouth to drink blood or to vomit out her guilty inhabitants ; nevertheless it is probable that these and many other notions equally unfounded have served a useful purpose in fortifying the respect for human life by the adventitious aid of superstitious terror.   The venerable framework of society rests on many pillars, of which the most solid are nature, reason, and justice ; yet at certain stages of its slow and laborious construction it could ill have dispensed with the frail prop of superstition.[2]   If the day should ever come when the great edifice has been carried to completion and reposes in simple majesty on adamantine foundations, it will be possible, without risk to its stability, to cut away and destroy the rotten timbers that shored it up in the process of building.

These al fancies ma have served a useful purpose in the morality by reinforcing of human life.

Mgr. Lechaptois, *Aux Rives du Tanganika* (Algiers, 1913), pp. 194 *sq.*

[2] In *Psyche's Task* (Second Edition, 1913) I have attempted to illustrate the support which in the course of their evolution the fundamental institutions of society (government, private property, marriage, and the security of human life) have received from superstition, that is, from the purely imaginary and baseless fears of mankind.

CHAPTER IV

THE GREAT FLOOD [1]

§ 1. *Introduction*

The Huxley lecture.

WHEN the Council of the Royal Anthropological Institute invited me to deliver the annual Huxley lecture, I gratefully accepted the invitation, esteeming it a high honour to be thus associated with one for whom, both as a thinker and as a man, I entertain a deep respect, and with whose attitude towards the great problems of life I am in cordial sympathy. His own works will long keep his memory green; but it is fitting that our science should lay, year by year, a wreath on the grave of one of the most honoured of its exponents.

Huxley's essay on the Great Flood.

Casting about for a suitable subject, I remembered that in his later life Huxley devoted some of his well-earned leisure to examining those traditions as to the early ages of the world which are recorded in the Book of Genesis; and accordingly I thought that I might appropriately take one of them for the theme of my discourse. The one which I have chosen is the familiar story of the Great Flood. Huxley himself discussed it in an instructive essay written with all the charm of his lucid and incisive style.[2] His aim was to show that, treated as a record of a deluge which overwhelmed the whole world, drowning almost all men and animals, the story conflicts with the plain teaching of geology and must be rejected as a fable. I shall not attempt either to reinforce or to criticize his arguments and his conclusions, for the simple reason that

[1] The part of this chapter which deals with the ancient flood stories of Babylonia, Palestine, and Greece, was delivered as the annual Huxley lecture before the Royal Anthropological In- stitute of Great Britain and Ireland, November, 1916.

[2] "Hasisadra's Adventure," *Collected Essays*, vol. iv. (London, 1911), pp. 239-286.

I am no geologist, and that for me to express an opinion
on such a matter would be a mere impertinence. I have
approached the subject from a different side, namely, from
that of tradition. It has long been known that legends of
a great flood, in which almost all men perished, are widely
diffused over the world ; and accordingly what I have tried
to do is to collect and compare these legends, and to inquire
what conclusions are to be deduced from the comparison.
In short, my discussion of the stories is a study in comparative folk-lore. My purpose is to discover how the
narratives arose, and how they came to be so widespread
over the earth ; with the question of their truth or falsehood
I am not primarily concerned, though of course it cannot be
ignored in considering the problem of their origin. The
inquiry thus defined is not a novel one. It has often been
attempted, especially in recent years, and in pursuing it I
have made ample use of the labours of my predecessors,
some of whom have discussed the subject with great learning
and ability. In particular, I would acknowledge my debt
to the eminent German geographer and anthropologist, the
late Dr. Richard Andree, whose monograph on diluvial
traditions, like all his writings, is a model of sound learning
and good sense, set forth with the utmost clearness and
conciseness.[1]

The present
discussion na-
tion o
diluvial
is a study in
compara-
folk-lore.

[1] R. Andree, *Die Flutsagen* (Bruns-
wick, 1891). Other notable discussions
of the same theme in recent years are
the following : H. Usener, *Die Sintflutsagen* (Bonn, 1899) ; *id.*, "Zu den
Sintfluthsagen," *Kleine Schriften*, iv.
(Berlin, 1913) pp. 382-396 ; M.
Winternitz, *Die Flutsagen des Alterthums und der Naturvolker* (Vienna,
1901) (reprinted from *Mittheilungen
der anthropologischen Gesellschaft in
Wien*, vol. xxxi.) ; E. Boklen, "Die
Sintflutsage, Versuch einer neuen Er-
klarung," *Archiv für Religionswissenschaft*, vi. (1903) pp. 1-61, 97-150 ;
G. Gerland, *Der Mythus von der Sintflut* (Bonn, 1912). Of these works,
that of Winternitz contains a useful
list of flood legends, with references to
the authorities and a full analysis of
the principal incidents in the legends.
Like the treatise of R. Andree, it is
characterized by the union of accurate
learning and good sense. On the
other hand, the works of Usener,
Boklen, and Gerland are vitiated
by their fanciful and improbable
theories as to the origin of the
legends in solar or lunar myths. But
in spite of this defect Gerland's treatise
is valuable for the number of parallel
legends which the author's ethnological
learning has collected from many races.
Among earlier discussions of the same
theme may be mentioned Philipp Buttmann, "Ueber den Mythos der Sünd-
flut," *Mythologus* (Berlin, 1828–1829),
i. 180-214 ; François Lenormant, *Les
Origines de l'Histoire d'après la Bible,
de la Création de l'Homme au Déluge*
(Paris, 1880), pp. 382-491 ; (Sir)
Henry H. Howorth, *The Mammoth
and the Flood* (London, 1887).

Apart from the intrinsic interest of such legends as professed records of a catastrophe which destroyed at a blow
almost the whole human race, they deserve to be studied
for the sake of their bearing on a general question which is
at present warmly debated among anthropologists. That
question is, How are we to explain the numerous and striking
similarities which obtain between the beliefs and customs
of races inhabiting distant parts of the world ? Are such
resemblances due to the transmission of the customs and
beliefs from one race to another, either by immediate
contact or through the medium of intervening peoples ? Or
have they arisen independently in many different races
through the similar working of the human mind under
similar circumstances ? Now, if I may presume to offer an
opinion on this much-debated problem, I would say at once
that, put in the form of an antithesis between mutually
exclusive views, the question seems to me absurd. So far
as I can judge, all experience and all probability are in
favour of the conclusion, that both causes have operated
extensively and powerfully to produce the observed similarities of custom and belief among the various races of
mankind : in other words, many of these resemblances are
to be explained by simple transmission, with more or less of
modification, from people to people, and many are to be
explained as having originated independently through the
similar action of the human mind in response to similar
environment. If that is so—and I confess to thinking that
this is the only reasonable and probable view--it will follow
that in attempting to account for any particular case of
resemblance which may be traced between the customs and
beliefs of different races, it would be futile to appeal to the
general principle either of transmission or of independent
origin ; each case must be judged on its own merits after an
impartial scrutiny of the facts and referred to the one or
the other principle, or possibly to a combination of the two,
according as the balance of evidence inclines to the one
side or to the other, or hangs evenly between them.

This general conclusion, which accepts the two principles of transmission and independent origin as both of
them true and valid within certain limits, is confirmed by

the particular investigation of diluvial traditions. For it is certain that legends of a great flood are found dispersed among many diverse peoples in distant regions of the earth, and so far as demonstration in such matters is possible, it can be demonstrated that the similarities which undoubtedly exist between many of these legends are due partly to direct transmission from one people to another, and partly to similar, but quite independent, experiences either of great floods or of phenomena which suggested the occurrence of great floods, in many different parts of the world. Thus the study of these traditions, quite apart from any conclusions to which it may lead us concerning their historical credibility, may serve a useful purpose if it mitigates the heat with which the controversy has sometimes been carried on, by convincing the extreme partisans of both principles that in this as in so many other disputes the truth lies wholly neither on the one side nor on the other, but somewhere between the two.

This co sion is confirmed by s of diluvial traditions.

§ 2. *The Babylonian Story of a Great Flood*

Of all the legends of a Great Flood recorded in literature, by far the oldest is the Babylonian or rather the Sumerian ; for we now know that, ancient as was the Babylonian version of the story, it was derived by the Babylonians from their still more ancient predecessors, the Sumerians, from whom the Semitic inhabitants of Babylonia appear to have derived the principal elements of their civilization.

The oldest legend of a C eat Flood is the iabylo an or rather Sumerian.

The Babylonian tradition of the Great Flood has been known to Western scholars from the time of antiquity, since it was recorded by the native Babylonian historian Berosus, who composed a history of his country in the first half of the third century before our era. Berosus wrote in Greek and his work has not come down to us, but fragments of it have been preserved by later Greek historians, and among these fragments is fortunately his account of the deluge. It runs as follows :—[1]

The Babylonian tradition of the flood as d by Berosus

The great flood took place in the reign of Xisuthrus,

[1] Eusebius, *Chronicorum Liber Prior*, ed. A. Schoene (Berlin, 1875), coll. 19 *sqq.* ; *Fragmenta Historicorum Graecorum*, ed. C. Müller, ii. (Paris, 1878) pp. 501 *sq.* Eusebius had not the original work of Berosus before

the tenth king of Babylon. Now the god Cronus appeared to him in a dream and warned him that all men would be destroyed by a flood on the fifteenth day of the month Daesius, which was the eighth month of the Macedonian. calendar.[1] Therefore the god enjoined him to write a history of the world from the beginning and to bury it for safety in Sippar, the city of the Sun.[2] Moreover, he was to build a ship and embark in it with his kinsfolk and friends, and to lay up in it a store of meat and drink, and to bring living things, both fowls and four-footed beasts, into the ship, and when he had made all things ready he was to set sail. And when he asked, " And whither shall I sail ? " the

---

him. He copied from Julius Africanus, who copied from Alexander Polyhistor (a contemporary of Sulla in the first century B.C.), who copied from Apollodorus, who may have copied from Berosus himself. See C. Muller, *Fragmenta Historicorum Graecorum*, ii. 496. Even the original Greek text of Eusebius is lost and is known only through an Armenian translation, of which a Latin version is printed by A. Schoene and C. Müller, *l.cc.* A Greek version of the Babylonian legend is preserved in the chronicle of the Christian writer Georgius Syncellus, who lived at the end of the eighth and the beginning of the ninth century. The Greek version of Syncellus is printed side by side with the Latin translation of Eusebius's version in A. Schoene's edition of Eusebius's *Chronicle* and in C. Müller's *Fragmenta Historicorum Graecorum, l.cc.*

[1] L. Ideler, *Handbuch der mathematischen und technischen Chronologie* (Berlin, 1825), i. 393, 402 *sq.* ; W. Smith, *Dictionary of Greek and Roman Antiquities*, Third Edition (London, 1890-1891), i. 338 *sq.*, *s.v.* " Calendar." The date is probably derived from Berosus himself, who, writing in Greek under the Macedonian empire, would naturally use the Macedonian calendar. However, we cannot say at what time of the year the month Daesius fell at Babylon in the time of Berosus, and consequently we do not know at what time of the year he supposed the deluge

to have occurred. For though the order of the months in the Macedonian calendar was the same everywhere, their *dates* fell differently in different' places. See *The Dying God*, p. 116, *n.*[1]. In one passage (*Aratus*, 53) Plutarch tells us that the Macedonian month Daesius was equivalent to the Attic month Anthesterion, which roughly corresponded to our February. But elsewhere he says that the battle of Granicus was fought in the Macedonian month Daesius (*Alexander*, 16) and the Attic month Thargelion (*Camillus*, 19), which was approximately equivalent to our May.

[2] Κελεῦσαι οὖν διὰ γραμμάτων πάντων ἀρχὰς καὶ μέσα καὶ τελευτὰς ὀρύξαντα θεῖναι ἐν πόλει ἡλίου Σιππάροις. The Greek is peculiar and ambiguous. ὀρύξαντα, "having dug," might mean either that he was to bury the record in the ground or to dig it up. The corresponding word in the Armenian version of Eusebius is said to be equally ambiguous. I have preferred the former sense as more appropriate and as confirmed by the sequel (see below, p. 109). Σιππάροις is a correction of Scaliger for the manuscript reading Σισπάροις. In modern times many thousands of clay tablets, containing records of legal transactions, have been found in the ancient Babylonian city of Sippar. See Morris Jastrow, *The Religion of Babylonia and Assyria* (Boston, 1898), p. 10.

god answered him, "To the gods; but first thou shalt pray for all good things to men." So he obeyed and built the ship, and the length of it was five furlongs,[1] and the breadth of it was two furlongs; and when he had gathered all things together he stored them in the ship and embarked his children and friends. And when the flood had come and immediately abated, Xisuthrus let fly some of the birds. But as they could find no food nor yet a place to rest, they came back to the ship. And again after some days Xisuthrus let fly the birds; and they returned again to the ship with their feet daubed with clay. A third time he let them fly, and they returned no more to the vessel. Then Xisuthrus perceived that the land had appeared above the water; so he parted some of the seams of the ship, and looking out he saw the shore, and drove the ship aground on a mountain, and stepped ashore with his wife, and his daughter, and the helmsman. And he worshipped the ground, and built an altar, and when he had sacrificed to the gods, he disappeared with those who had disembarked from the ship. And when those who had remained in the ship saw that he and his company returned not, they disembarked likewise and sought him, calling him by name. But Xisuthrus himself was nowhere to be seen. Yet a voice from the air bade them fear the gods, for that he himself for his piety was gone to dwell with the gods, and that his wife, and his daughter, and the helmsman partook of the same honour. And he commanded them that they should go to Babylon, and take up the scriptures which they had buried, and distribute them among men. Moreover, he told them that the land in which they stood was Armenia. And when they heard these things, they sacrificed to the gods and journeyed on foot to Babylon. But of the ship that grounded on the mountains of Armenia a part remains to this day,[2]

[1] The Armenian text of Eusebius stretches the length of the ship to *fifteen* furlongs, or nearly two miles, which seems exorbitant when we consider the state of the shipbuilding industry in the days before the flood. No modern dock could hold such a vessel.

[2] When Lord Bryce ascended Mount Ararat in 1876, he found, on a bare rocky slope, at a height of over 13,000 feet, an isolated log, which he humorously proposed to identify as one of the timbers of Noah's ark. See (Lord) James Bryce, *Transcaucasia and Ararat*, Fourth Edition (London, 1896), p. 280. In this work (pp. 211 *sqq.*) Lord Bryce has discussed at length the traditional association of Mount Ararat with Noah's flood.

and some people scrape the bitumen off it and use it in charms. So when they were come to Babylon they dug up the scriptures in Sippar, and built many cities, and restored the sanctuaries, and repeopled Babylon.

Nicolaus of Damascus on the flood.

According to the Greek historian Nicolaus of Damascus, a contemporary and friend of Augustus and of Herod the Great, "there is above Minyas in Armenia a great mountain called Baris, to which, as the story goes, many people fled for refuge in the flood and were saved; they say too that a certain man, floating in an ark, grounded on the summit, and that remains of the timbers were preserved for a long time. The man may have been he who was recorded by Moses, the legislator of the Jews."[1] Whether Nicolaus of Damascus drew this information from Babylonian or Hebrew tradition, may be doubted; the reference to Moses seems to show that he was acquainted with the narrative in Genesis, which he may easily have learned through his patron Herod.

Modern discovery of the original Babylonian version of the flood story in the ruins of Nineveh.

For many centuries the Babylonian tradition of a great flood was known to Western scholars only through its preservation in the Greek fragments of Berosus; it was reserved for modern times to recover the original Babylonian version from the long-lost archives of Assyria. In the course of those excavations at Nineveh, which were one of the glories of the nineteenth century and which made an epoch in the study of ancient history, the English explorers were fortunate enough to discover extensive remains of the library of the great king Ashurbanipal, who reigned from 668 to 626 B.C. in the splendid sunset of the Assyrian empire, carrying the terror of his arms to the banks of the Nile, embellishing his capital with magnificent structures, and gathering within its walls from far and near a vast literature, historical, scientific, grammatical and religious, for the enlightenment of his people.[2] The literature, of which

---

[1] Nicolaus Damascenus, quoted by Josephus, *Antiquit. Jud.* i. 3, 6; *Fragmenta Historicorum Graecorum*, ed. C. Muller, ii. 415, Frag. 76. For Minyas some scholars would substitute Milyas in the text, comparing Pliny, *Nat. Hist.* v. 147, "*Attingit Galatia et Pamphyliae Cabaliam et Milyas*

qui circa Barim sunt." The reading Minyas is retained by C. Müller and defended by A. Reinach, *Noé Sangariou* (Paris, 1913), pp. 47 *sqq.*

[2] Morris Jastrow, *The Religion of Babylonia and Assyria* (Boston, U.S.A., 1898), p. 43.

a great part was borrowed from Babylonian originals, was inscribed in cuneiform characters on tablets of soft clay, which were afterwards baked hard and deposited in the library. Apparently the library was arranged in an upper story of the palace, which, in the last sack of the city, collapsed in the flames, shattering the tablets to pieces in its fall. Many of them are still cracked and scorched by the heat of the burning ruins. In later ages the ruins were ransacked by antiquaries of the class of Dousterswivel, who sought among them for the buried treasures not of learning, but of gold, and by their labours contributed still further to the disruption and disintegration of the precious records. To complete their destruction the rain, soaking through the ground every spring, saturates them with water containing chemicals, which form in every crack and fissure crystals that by their growth split the already broken tablets into minuter fragments. Yet by laboriously piecing together a multitude of these fragments George Smith, of the British Museum, was able to recompose the now famous epic of Gilgamesh in twelve cantos, or rather tablets, the eleventh of which contains the Babylonian story of the deluge. The great discovery was announced by Mr. Smith at a meeting of the Society of Biblical Archaeology on December the 3rd, 1872.[1]

It was ingeniously conjectured by Sir Henry Rawlinson that the twelve cantos of the Gilgamesh epic corresponded to the twelve signs of the zodiac, so that the course of the poem followed, as it were, the course of the sun through the twelve months of the year. The theory is to some extent confirmed by the place assigned to the flood legend in the eleventh canto ; for the eleventh Babylonian month fell at the height of the rainy season, it was dedicated to the storm-god Ramman, and its name is said to signify "month of the curse of rain."[2] Be that as it may, the story as it stands is

The Gilgamesh

---

[1] George Smith, *The Chaldean Account of Genesis*, a new edition revised and corrected by A. H. Sayce (London, 1880), pp. 1 *sqq.*

[2] E. Schrader, *The Cuneiform Inscriptions and the Old Testament*, translated by O. C. Whitehouse (London and Edinburgh, 1885), i. 47 ; M. Jastrow, *Religion of Babylonia and Assyria* (Boston, 1898), pp. 463, 484, 510 ; *id., Hebrew and Babylonian Myths* (London, 1914), p. 325 note [1]. According to Schrader, " the Akkadian name of the month, *iti asa ségi* = As-

an episode or digression destitute of all organic connexion with the rest of the poem.   It is introduced as follows :—[1]

The journey of to consult his deified ancestor Ut-napishtim.

The hero of the poem, Gilgamesh, has lost his dear friend Engidu [2] by death, and he himself has fallen grievously sick. Saddened by the past and anxious for the future, he resolves to seek out his remote ancestor Ut-napishtim,[3] son of Ubara-Tutu, and to inquire of him how mortal man can attain to eternal life.   For surely, he thought, Ut-napishtim must know the secret, since he has been made like to the gods and now dwells somewhere far away in blissful immortality.   A weary and a perilous journey must Gilgamesh accomplish to come at him.   He passes the mountain, guarded by a scorpion man and woman, where the sun goes down : he traverses a dark and dreadful road never trodden before by mortal man : he is ferried across a wide sea : he crosses the Water of Death by a narrow bridge, and at last he enters the presence

syrian *arah arratzunni*, signifies 'month of the curse of rain,' *i.e.* 'month of the judgment of the Flood.'" Further correspondences between the cantos and the months are noted by Professor Jastrow, *ll.cc.*

[1] For translations or summaries of the deluge legend, see Eberhard Schrader, *The Cuneiform Inscriptions and the Old Testament*, translated by Rev. Owen C. Whitehouse (London and Edinburgh, 1885-1888), i. 46 *sqq.* ; M. Jastrow, *The Religion of Babylonia and Assyria* (Boston, 1898), pp. 495 *sqq.* ; *id.*, *Hebrew and Babylonian Traditions* (London, 1914), pp. 325 *sqq.* ; L. W. King, *Babylonian Religion and Mythology* (London, 1899), pp. 127 *sqq.* ; P. Jensen, *Assyrisch-Babylonische Mythen und Epen* (Berlin, 1900), pp. 229 *sqq.* ; W. Muss-Arnolt, in R. F. Harper's *Assyrian and Babylonian Literature* (New York, 1901), pp. 350 *sqq.* ; H. Zimmern, in E. Schrader's *Die Keilinschriften und das Alte Testament*, Dritte Auflage (Berlin, 1902), pp. 544 *sqq.* ; Alfred Jeremias, *Das Alte Testament im Lichte des Alten Orients*, Zweite Auflage (Berlin, 1906), pp. 228 *sqq.* ; P. Dhorme, *Choix de Textes Religieux Assyro-Babyloniens* (Paris, 1907), pp. 100 *sqq.* ; Arthur Ungnad,

in H. Gressmann's *Altorientalische Texte und Bilder zum Alten Testamente* (Tubingen, 1909), i. 50 *sqq.* ; A. Ungnad und H. Gressmann, *Das Gilgamesch-Epos* (Gottingen, 1911), pp. 52 *sqq.* ; R. W. Rogers, *Cuneiform Parallels to the Old Testament* (Oxford [1912]), pp. 90 *sqq.* Of these works the translations of Jensen, Dhorme, and Rogers are accompanied by the original Babylonian text printed in Roman characters.   The version in the text is based on a comparison of these various renderings.

[2] The name is said to be Sumerian, meaning "Enki (Semitic Ea) is Creator." See A. Ungnad und H. Gressmann, *Das Gilgamesch-Epos*, pp. 75 *sq.* The name was formerly read as Eabani.

[3] The name is said to mean "He saw (*uta, ût*) life," in the sense of "He found life." See H. Zimmern, in E. Schrader's *Die Keilinschriften und das Alte Testament*[3], p. 545 note 2.   Compare P. Jensen, *Assyrisch-Babylonische Mythen und Epen*, p. 466 ; A. Ungnad und H. Gressmann, *Das Gilgamesch-Epos*, p. 80.   The name was formerly read as Par-napishtim, Per-napishtim, or Tsit-napishtim.

of Ut-napishtim.[1]   But when he puts to his great ancestor the question, how man may attain to eternal life, he receives a discouraging reply : the sage tells him that immortality is not for man.   Surprised at this answer from one who had been a man and was now himself immortal, Gilgamesh naturally asks his venerable relative to explain how he had contrived to evade the common doom.   It is in answer to this pointed question that Ut-napishtim tells the story of the great flood, which runs as follows :—

Ut-napishtim spoke to him, to Gilgamesh : "I will reveal to thee, O Gilgamesh, a hidden word, and the purpose [2] of the gods will I declare to thee.   Shurippak, a city which thou knowest, which lies on the bank of the Euphrates, that city was old ;[3] and the gods within it, their heart prompted the great gods to send a flood.[4]   There was their father Anu, their counsellor the warrior Enlil,[5] their messenger Ninib, their prince Ennugi.   The Lord of Wisdom, Ea, sat also with them, he repeated their word to the hut [6] of reeds, saying, 'O reed hut, reed hut, O wall, wall, O reed hut hearken, O wall attend.   O man of Shurippak, son of

(margin) Ut-napishtim tells Gilgamesh the story of the great flood.

Gilgamesh is warned by the god Ea to build a ship and save himself in it.

[1] As to the journey, narrated in the ninth and tenth cantos of the poem, see M. Jastrów, *The Religion of Babylonia and Assyria*, pp. 487-492 ; L. W. King, *Babylonian Religion and Mythology*, pp. 165-171 ; A. Ungnad und H. Gressmann, *Das Gilgamesch-Epos*, pp. 134-139.

[2] Or "decision" (M. Jastrow, R. W. Rogers), "secret" (P. Jensen, A. Jeremias, P. Dhorme, A. Ungnad), "mystery" (W. Muss-Arnolt).   The same Assyrian word (*pirishtu*) occurs again twice towards the end of the canto.   See below, pp. 117, 118. It may be connected with the Hebrew verb *parash* (פרש), "make distinct, declare," with which the lexicographers compare the Assyrian *parâsu*. See W. Gesenius, *Hebräisches und Aramäisches Hand-wörterbuch*,[14] bearbeitet von F. Buhl (Leipsic, 1905), p. 604.   The "purpose" or "decision" in question is the resolve of the gods to bring a flood upon the world.

[3] H. Zimmern proposed, by a slight change of reading, to translate "that city was not pious" (E. Schrader, *Die*

Keilinschriften und das Alte Testament,[3] p. 546, note [6]).   This would assign the wickedness of the city as the cause of its destruction by the flood. But the suggested reading and rendering have not been accepted by later editors and translators.

[4] Or "the gods thereof induced the great gods to bring a cyclone over it" (M. Jastrow, *Hebrew and Babylonian Traditions*, p. 326).

[5] Or Illil, less correctly Ellil. The name was formerly read Bel (so Jensen and Dhorme, and formerly Jastrow). Enlil is the Sumerian name of the god, Bel is his Semitic name.   Together with Anu, the Father of the Gods, and Enki (the Semitic Ea), he made up the highest trinity of the ancient Sumerians. See L. W. King, *Babylonian Religion and Mythology*, p. 14 ; A. Ungnad und H. Gressmann, *Das Gilgamesch-Epos*, p. 76.

[6] Or perhaps rather "fence." So Dhorme translates it "*haie de roseaux.*" As to the hut or wall of reeds, see below, p. 122.

Ubara-Tutu, pull down thy house, build a ship, forsake thy possessions, take heed for thy life! Thy gods abandon, save thy life, bring living seed of every kind into the ship. As for the ship which thou shalt build, well planned must be its dimensions, its breadth and its length shall bear proportions each to each, and thou shalt launch it in the ocean.'[1] I took heed and spake unto Ea, my lord, saying, 'The command, O my lord, which thou hast given, I will honour and will fulfil. But how shall I make answer unto the city, the people and the elders thereof?' Ea opened his mouth and spake, and he said unto me his servant, 'Thus shalt thou answer and say unto them: Because Enlil hates me, no longer may I abide in your city nor lay my head on Enlil's earth. Down into the deep sea must I go with Ea,

The building of the ship.

my lord, to dwell.'" So Ut-napishtim obeyed the god Ea and gathered together the wood and all things needful for the building of the ship, and on the fifth day he laid down the hull. In the shape of a barge he built it, and on it he set a house a hundred and twenty cubits high, and he divided the house into six stories, and in each story he made nine rooms. Water-plugs he fastened within it; the outside he daubed with bitumen, and the inside he caulked with pitch. He caused oil to be brought, and he slaughtered oxen and lambs. He filled jars with sesame-wine and oil and grape-wine; he gave the people to drink like a river and he made a feast like to the feast of the New Year.

The lading of the ship and the embarkation.

And when the ship was ready he filled it with all that he had of silver, and all that he had of gold, and all that he had, of living seed. Also he brought up into the ship all his family and his household, the cattle of the field likewise and the beasts of the field, and the handicraftsmen: all of them he brought in. A fixed time the sun-god Shamash had appointed, saying, "'At eventide the lord of darkness will send a heavy rain. Then enter thou into the ship and shut thy door.' The time appointed drew near, and at eventide the lord of darkness sent a heavy rain. Of the storm, I

The beginning of the storm.

saw the beginning, to look upon the storm I was afraid. I entered into the ship and shut the door. To the pilot of

[1] Or "On a level with the deep, provide it with a covering" (M. Jastrow, *Hebrew and Babylonian Traditions*, p. 326). ". . . the ocean, cover it with a roof" (R. W. Rogers). Similarly A. Ungnad (*Das Gilgamesch-Epos*, p. 53).

the ship, even to Puzur-Amurri, the sailor, I committed the (floating) palace [1] and all that therein was.   When the early dawn appeared there came up from the horizon a black cloud.   Ramman [2] thundered in the midst thereof, the gods Mujati [3] and Lugal [4] went before.   Like messengers they passed over mountain and land; Irragal [5] tore away the ship's post.   There went Ninib and he made the storm to burst.   The Anunnaki lifted up flaming torches, with the brightness thereof they lit up the earth.   The whirlwind of Ramman [2] mounted up into the heavens, and all light was turned into darkness."   A whole day the tempest raged, and the waters rose on the mountains.   " No man beheld his fellow, no more could men know each other.   In heaven the gods were afraid of the deluge, they drew back, they climbed up into the heaven of Anu.   The gods crouched like dogs, they cowered by the walls.   Ishtar cried out like a woman in travail, loudly lamented the queen of the gods with her beautiful voice : ' Let that day be turned to clay, when [6] I commanded evil in the assembly of the gods ! Alas, that I commanded evil in the assembly of the gods, that for the destruction of my people I commanded battle ! That which I brought forth, where is it ?   Like the spawn of fish it filleth the sea.'   The gods of the Anunnaki [7] wept with her, the gods were bowed down, they sat down weeping.

The fear and lamentation of the gods.

---

[1] The ship is so called because of its many stories and apartments.   The Assyrian word here employed (*ekallu*) is the same with the ordinary Hebrew word for a palace or temple (היכל *hekal*). See E. Schrader, *The Cuneiform Inscriptions and the Old Testament*, i. 56 ; P. Dhorme, *Choix de Textes Religieux Assyro-Babyloniens*, p. 109, note ⁹⁶ ; Fr. Brown, S. R. Driver, and Ch. A. Briggs, *Hebrew and English Lexicon* (Oxford, 1906), p. 228.

[2] So L. W. King and A. Ungnad (*Das Gilgamesch-Epos*, p. 56). Others read " Adad " (so Jensen, Jeremias, and formerly Ungnad).   Ramman or Adad was the god of thunder and storms.   His name is written AN.IM. See A. Ungnad und H. Gressmann, *Das Gilgamesch-Epos*, p. 79.

[3] A minor deity, afterwards identified with Nabu (Nebo).   See A. Ungnad

und H. Gressmann, *Das Gilgamesch-Epos*, p. 78.

[4] A minor deity, the herald of the gods.   His name means " King," a title bestowed on Marduk.   Hence some translators render it by "Marduk" in the present passage. See A. Ungnad und H. Gressmann, *Das Gilgamesch-Epos*, p. 78.

[5] Irragal or Irrakal is " the Great Irra," the god of pestilence, more commonly known as Nergal.   See A. Ungnad und H. Gressmann, *Das Gilgamesch-Epos*, pp. 77, 78.

[6] So Jensen, Dhorme, and Jastrow (*Hebrew and Babylonian Traditions*, p. 331).   Others translate, " The former time (that is, the old race of man) has been turned into clay, because," etc.

[7] Or " because of the Anunnaki " (P. Dhorme), " over the Anunnaki " (W. Muss-Arnolt).

Their lips were pressed together. For six days and six nights the wind blew, and the deluge and the tempest over-whelmed the land. When the seventh day drew nigh, then ceased the tempest and the deluge and the storm, which had fought like a host. Then the sea grew quiet, it went down ; the hurricane and the deluge ceased. I looked upon the sea, there was silence come,[1] and all mankind was turned back into clay. Instead of the fields a swamp lay before me.[2] I opened the window and the light fell upon my cheek ; I bowed myself down, I sat down, I wept, over my cheek flowed my tears. I looked upon the world, and behold all was sea. After twelve (days ?)[3] an island arose, to the land Nisir the ship made its way. The mount of Nisir[4] held the ship fast and let it not slip. The first day, the second day, the mountain Nisir held the ship fast : the third day, the fourth day, the mountain Nisir held the ship fast : the fifth day, the sixth day, the mountain Nisir held the ship fast. When the seventh day drew nigh, I sent out a dove, and let her go forth. The dove flew hither and thither, but there was no resting-place for her, and she returned. Then I sent out a swallow and let her go forth. The swallow flew hither and thither, but there was no resting-place for her, and she returned. Then I sent out a raven and let her go forth. The raven flew away, she beheld the abatement of the waters, she ate,[5] she waded, she croaked, but she did not return. Then I brought all out unto the four winds, I offered an offering, I made a libation on the peak of the mountain. By sevens I set out the vessels,

The end of the storm and the sinking of the sea.

The ship grounds on Mount Nisir.

The dove sent forth from the ship.

The raven sent forth from the ship.

The disembarkation and the sacrifice.

---

[1] Or "and cried aloud" (so L. W. King, W. Muss-Arnolt, and doubtfully A. Jeremias).

[2] "The swamp reached to the roofs" (so P. Dhorme), "Like a roof the plain lay level" (R. W. Rogers).

[3] "Double hours" (so P. Jensen and H. Zimmern). Dhorme thinks that the number refers to distance : the island appeared twelve miles or leagues (?) away. This interpretation is now accepted by M. Jastrow (*Hebrew and Babylonian Traditions*, p. 332).

[4] If Haupt and Delitsch are right, the name Nisir is derived from the same root as the Hebrew *nasar* (נצר)

meaning, "to guard, keep, preserve"; so that Mount Nisir would be "the Mount of Salvation or Deliverance." See E. Schrader, *The Cuneiform Inscriptions and the Old Testament*, translated by O. C. Whitehouse (London and Edinburgh, 1885), i. 54. Similarly in Greek legend, Deucalion is said to have dedicated an altar to Zeus the Deliverer on the mountain where he landed after the great flood. See below, p. 148.

[5] So P. Jensen, H. Zimmern, P. Dhorme, and A. Ungnad. "She drew near" (R. W. Rogers). "She came near" (L. W. King).

under them I heaped up reed, and cedar-wood, and myrtle.[1]
The gods smelt the savour, the gods smelt the sweet savour.
The gods gathered like flies about him that offered up the
sacrifice. Then the Lady of the gods drew nigh, she lifted
up the great jewels which Anu had made according to her
wish. She said, 'Oh ye gods here, as truly as I will not
forget the jewels of *lapis lazuli* which are on my neck, so
truly will I remember these days, never shall I forget them!
Let the gods come to the offering, but Enlil[2] shall not come
to the offering, for he took not counsel and sent the deluge,
and my people he gave to destruction.' Now when Enlil[2] Anger of
drew nigh, he saw the ship; then was Enlil[2] wroth. He Enlil at the
was filled with anger against the gods, the Igigi (saying), escape
'Who then hath escaped with his life? No man shall live napishtim.
after the destruction.' Then Ninib opened his mouth and
spake, he said to the warrior Enlil,[2] 'Who but Ea could have
done this thing? For Ea knoweth every matter.' Then Ea
opened his mouth and spake, he said to the warrior Enlil,[2]
'Thou art the governor of the gods,[3] O warrior, but thou
wouldst not take counsel and thou hast sent the deluge!
On the sinner visit his sin, and on the transgressor visit his
transgression. But hold thy hand, that all be not destroyed!
and forbear, that all be not confounded! Instead of sending
a deluge, let a lion come and minish mankind! Instead of
sending a deluge, let a leopard[4] come and minish mankind!
Instead of sending a deluge, let a famine come and waste
the land! Instead of sending a deluge, let the Plague-god
come and slay mankind! I did not reveal the purpose[5] of
the great gods. I caused Atrakhasis[6] to see a dream, and

[1] Or "incense" (so L. W. King).

[2] Or "Bel." So M. Jastrow, L. W.
King, P. Jensen, and P. Dhorme.
See above, p. 113, note [5].

[3] Or "Thou wise one among the
gods" (so W. Muss-Arnolt, H. Zimmern, A. Jeremias, P. Dhorme, A. Ungnad, R. W. Rogers). This rendering certainly gives more point, as P. Dhorme
observes, to what follows : "You so
wise, yet to be so rash and unjust
as to send the deluge!" The doubtful
Assyrian word is *abkallu*, which, according to Delitsch, means "commander,"
"ruler," but according to others has the

sense of "wise." See P. Jensen, *Assyrisch-Babylonische Mythen und Epen*,
p. 320; P. Dhorme, *Choix de Textes
religieux Assyro-Babyloniens*, p. 117.

[4] The meaning of the Assyrian word
(*barbaru*) here translated "leopard" is
uncertain. Ungnad and Rogers render
"wolf"; Jeremias prefers a panther,
Jastrow a jackal, and Muss-Arnolt a
tiger. The rendering "leopard" is
strongly defended by P. Dhorme.

[5] Or "secret." See above, p. 113.

[6] "The very prudent one," a name
or title applied to Ut-napishtim. See
below, pp. 118 *sq.*

thus he heard the purpose [1] of the gods.' Thereupon Enlil [2] arrived at a decision, and he went up into the ship. He took my hand and brought me forth, he brought my wife forth, he made her to kneel at my side, he turned towards us,[3] he stood between us, he blessed us (saying), ' Hitherto hath Ut-napishtim been a man, but now let Ut-napishtim and his wife be like unto the gods, even us, and let Ut-napishtim dwell afar off at the mouth of the rivers ! ' Then they took me, and afar off, at the mouth of the rivers, they made me to dwell."

Such is the long story of the deluge interwoven into the Gilgamesh epic, with which, to all appearance, it had originally no connexion. A fragment of another version of the tale is preserved on a broken tablet, which, like the tablets of the Gilgamesh epic, was found among the ruins of Ashurbanipal's library at Nineveh. It contains a part of the conversation which is supposed to have taken place before the flood between the god Ea and the Babylonian Noah, who is here called Atrakhasis, a name which, as we saw, is incidentally applied to him in the Gilgamesh epic, though elsewhere in that version he is named not Atrakhasis but Ut-napishtim. The name Atrakhasis is said to be the

[1] Or " secret." See above, p. 113.
[2] Or " Bel." So M. Jastrow, L. W. King, P. Jensen, W. Muss-Arnolt, H. Zimmern, A. Jeremias, and P. Dhorme. Ungnad and Rogers read " Ea " instead of Enlil (Bel). But the sense given by the former reading is incomparably finer. Enlil (Bel) is at first enraged at the escape of Ut-napishtim and his family, but, moved by Ea's eloquent pleading on their behalf, he experiences a revulsion of feeling, and entering the ship he magnanimously takes Ut-napishtim by the hand and leads him forth. The dramatic situation thus created is worthy of a great literary artist, and reminds us of the famous meeting of Achilles and Priam in Homer, " His hand he placed in the old man's hand, and pushed him gently away " (*Iliad*, xxiv. 508). The phrase rendered "arrived at a decision" (so L. W. King, W. Muss-Arnolt, and apparently H. Zimmern) is variously translated

"came to his senses" (so A. Jeremias and formerly M. Jastrow), " then they took his counsel " (P. Jensen and P. Dhorme), and " Now take counsel for him " (so A. Ungnad, R. W. Rogers, and now M. Jastrow, in *Hebrew and Babylonian Traditions*, p. 334). This last rendering (" Now take counsel for him ") puts the words in the mouth of the preceding speaker Ea : so understood, they are at once feeble and otiose, whereas understood to refer to the sudden revulsion of feeling in Enlil (Bel), they are eminently in place and add a powerful stroke to the picture.

[3] Or " turned us face to face " (W. Muss-Arnolt), "turned us toward each other " (R. W. Rogers), " touched our face " (P. Dhorme), " touched our fore-heads " (A. Ungnad, M. Jastrow, in *Hebrew and Babylonian Traditions*, p. 334), " touched our *shoulder* " (P. Jensen).

Babylonian original which in Berosus's Greek version of the deluge legend is represented by Xisuthrus.[1] In this fragment the god Ea commands Atrakhasis, saying, " Go in and shut the door of the ship. Bring within thy corn, thy goods and thy possessions, thy (wife ?), thy family, thy kinsfolk, and thy craftsmen, the cattle of the field, the beasts of the field, as many as eat grass." [2] In his reply the hero says that he has never built a ship before, and he begs that a plan of the ship be drawn for him on the ground, which he may follow in laying down the vessel.[3]

Thus far the Babylonian versions of the flood legend date only from the time of Ashurbanipal in the seventh century before our era, and might therefore conceivably be of later origin than the Hebrew version and copied from it. However, conclusive evidence of the vastly greater antiquity of the Babylonian legend is furnished by a broken tablet, which was discovered at Abu-Habbah, the site of the ancient city of Sippar, in the course of excavations undertaken by the Turkish Government. The tablet contains a very mutilated version of the flood story, and it is exactly dated ; for at the end there is a colophon or note recording that the tablet was written on the twenty-eighth day of the month Shabatu (the eleventh Babylonian month) in the eleventh year of King Ammizaduga, or about 1966 B.C. Unfortunately the text is so fragmentary that little information can be

Fragment of another version of the flood to an flood to y, in which t is called Atrakhasis.

---

[1] Atrakhasis, "the very Prudent One," in the inverted form Khasis-atra is identified with Xisuthrus by E. Schrader, H. Zimmern, P. Dhorme, and A. Ungnad. See E. Schrader, *The Cuneiform Inscriptions and the Old Testament*, i. 56 ; H. Zimmern, in E. Schrader's *Die Keilinschriften und das Alte Testament*, Dritte Auflage, pp. 532, 551 ; P. Dhorme, *Choix de Textes religieux Assyro-Babyloniens*, pp. 119 note [196], 132 note [63] ; A. Ungnad, in H. Gressmann's *Altorientalische Texte und Bilder zum Alten Testamente*, i. 39 note [15], 46 note [4] ; A. Ungnad und H. Gressmann, *Das Gilgamesch-Epos*, pp. 59, 74 *sq.* As to the name Atrakhasis, see further P. Jensen, *Assyrisch-Babylonische Mythen und Epen*, pp. 276 *sq.* ; H. Usener, *Die Sintflutsagen*, p. 15.

[2] "As many as eat grass." So P. Jensen, A. Jeremias, A. Ungnad, and R. W. Rogers. Others render simply, "all kinds of herbs," understanding the words as a direction to Atrakhasis to take on board a supply of vegetables. So P. Dhorme and M. Jastrow.

[3] P. Jensen, *Assyrisch-Babylonische Mythen und Epen*, pp. 255, 257 ; A. Jeremias, *Das Alte Testament im Lichte des alten Orients*,[2] p. 233 ; P. Dhorme, *Choix de Textes religieux Assyro-Babyloniens*, pp. 126 *sq.* ; A. Ungnad, in H. Gressmann's *Altorientalische Texte und Bilder zum Alten Testamente*, i. 57 ; A. Ungnad und H. Gressmann, *Das Gilgamesch-Epos*, p. 69 ; R. W. Rogers, *Cuneiform Parallels to the Old Testament*, pp. 103 *sq.* ; M. Jastrow, *Hebrew and Babylonian Traditions*, pp. 343-345.

extracted from it ; but the name of Atrakhasis occurs in it, together with references to the great rain and apparently to the ship and the entrance into it of the people who were to be saved.[1]

Fragment
of another
very ancient
version
of the
Babylonian
flood story
found at
Nippur.

Yet another very ancient version of the deluge legend came to light at Nippur in the excavations conducted by the University of Pennsylvania. It is written on a small fragment of unbaked clay, and on the ground of the style of writing and of the place where the tablet was found it is dated by its discoverer, Professor H. V. Hilprecht, not later than 2100 B.C. In this fragment a god appears to announce that he will cause a deluge which will sweep away all mankind at once ; and he warns the person whom he addresses to build a great ship, with a strong roof, in which he is to save his life, and also to bring into it the beasts of the field and the birds of heaven.[2]

Fragment
of another
very ancient
version
of the
Babylonian
flood story
written
in the
Sumerian
language
about
2100 B.C.

All these versions of the flood story are written in the Semitic language of Babylonia and Assyria ; but another fragmentary version, found by the American excavators at Nippur and recently deciphered, is written in Sumerian, that is, in the non-Semitic language of the ancient people who appear to have preceded the Semites in Babylonia and to

[1] L. W. King, *Babylonian Religion and Mythology*, pp. 124-126 ; P. Jensen, *Assyrisch-Babylonische Mythen und Epen*, pp. 289, 291 ; H. Zimmern, in E. Schrader's *Die Keilinschriften und das Alte Testament*,[3] p. 552 ; P. Dhorme, *Choix de Textes religieux Assyro-Babyloniens*, pp. 120-125 ; A. Ungnad, in H. Gressmann's *Altorientalische Texte und Bilder zum Alten Testamente*, i. 57 *sq.* ; A. Ungnad und H. Gressmann, *Das Gilgamesch-Epos*, pp. 5 *sq.*, 69 *sq.* ; R. W. Rogers, *Cuneiform Parallels to the Old Testament*, pp. 104-107 ; M. Jastrow, *Hebrew and Babylonian Traditions*, pp. 340 *sq.* The date of King Ammizaduga, the tenth monarch of the first Babylonian dynasty, is variously given as 2100 B.C. (so H. Zimmern) or somewhat later than 2000 B.C. (so A. Ungnad, *Das Gilgamesch-Epos*, p. 5). Professor Ed. Meyer assigns the king's reign to the years 1812-1792 B.C. (*Geschichte des Altertums*,[2] i. 2. p.

574) ; and accordingly R. W. Rogers and M. Jastrow date the king roughly at 1800 B.C. According to the latest calculation, based on elaborate astronomical data, the year of Ammizaduga's accession is now assigned by Mr. L. W. King to the year 1977 B.C., and in this dating ordinary students may provisionally acquiesce. See L. W. King, *A History of Babylon* (London, 1915), pp. 107 *sqq.*

[2] A. Ungnad und H. Gressmann, *Das Gilgamesch-Epos*, pp. 6, 73 ; R. W. Rogers, *Cuneiform Parallels to the Old Testament*, pp. 108 *sq.* ; M. Jastrow, *Hebrew and Babylonian Traditions*, pp. 342 *sq.* These scholars incline to date the tablet later than 2100 B.C. "The tablet may well be as old as Professor Hilprecht argues, but the suggestion of a date so late as the early Kassite period (1700 B.C.) can hardly be excluded" (R. W. Rogers, *op. cit.* p. 108).

have founded in the lower valley of the Euphrates that remarkable system of civilization which we commonly call Babylonian.[1]   The city of Nippur, where the Sumerian version of the deluge legend has been discovered, was the holiest and perhaps the oldest religious centre in the country, and the city-god Enlil was the head of the Babylonian pantheon.   The tablet which records the legend would seem, from the character of the script, to have been written about the time of the famous Hammurabi, king of Babylon, that is, about 2100 B.C.   But the story itself must be very much older ; for by the close of the third millennium before our era, when the tablet was inscribed, the Sumerians as a separate race had almost ceased to exist, having been absorbed in the Semitic population, and their old tongue was already a dead language, though the ancient literature and sacred texts embalmed in it were still studied and copied by the Semitic priests and scribes.[2]   Hence the discovery of a Sumerian version of the deluge legend raises a presumption that the legend itself dates from a time anterior to the occupation of the Euphrates valley by the Semites, who after their immigration into the country appear to have borrowed the story from their predecessors the Sumerians. It is of interest to observe that the Sumerian version of the flood story formed a sequel to an account, unfortunately very fragmentary, of the creation of man, according to which men were created by the gods before the animals.   Thus the Sumerian story agrees with the Hebrew account in

[1] The tablet containing the Sumerian version of the story was first read by Dr. Arno Poebel, of the Johns Hopkins University, in 1912. See A. Poebel, "The Babylonian Story of the Creation and the Earliest History of the World," *The Museum Journal*, Philadelphia, June 1913, pp. 41 *sqq.* ; *id.*, in *University of Pennsylvania, Publications of the Babylonian Section of the University Museum*, vol. iv. No. 1 (Philadelphia, 1914), pp. 7-70 ; M. Jastrow, *Hebrew and Babylonian Traditions*, pp. 335 *sqq.* ; L. W. King, "Recent Babylonian Research and its Relation to Hebrew Studies," *Church Quarterly Review*, No. 162, January 1916, pp. 271 *sqq.*

[2] L. W. King, "Recent Babylonian Research and its Relation to Hebrew Studies," *Church Quarterly Review*, No. 162, January 1916, pp. 274, 275. As to the date of Hammurabi (about 2100 B.C.) see Principal J. Skinner, *Commentary on Genesis* (Edinburgh, 1910), p. xiv note †; S. R. Driver, *The Book of Genesis*,[10] (London, 1916), p. 156 ; R. Kittel, *Geschichte des Volkes Israel*,[2] i. (Gotha, 1912), p. 77 ; L. W. King, *A History of Babylon* (London, 1915), pp. 111, 320, who assigns the king's reign to 2123-2081 B.C. A later date (1958-1916 B.C.) is assigned to Hammurabi's reign by Professor Ed. Meyer (*Geschichte des Altertums*,[2] i. 2, p. 557).

Genesis, in so far as both of them treat the creation of man and the great flood as events closely connected with each other in the early history of the world ; and further the Sumerian narrative agrees with the Jehovistic against the Priestly Document in representing the creation of man as antecedent to the creation of the animals.[1]

In this Sumerian version the hero Ziudsuddu is warned by Ea of the coming deluge and escapes in a ship, after which he worships the gods and is rewarded with immortality.

Only the lower half of the tablet on which this Sumerian Genesis was inscribed has as yet come to light, but enough remains to furnish us with the main outlines of the flood story. From it we learn that Ziugiddu, or rather Ziudsuddu,[2] was at once a king and a priest of the god Enki, the Sumerian deity who was the equivalent of the Semitic Ea ;[3] daily he occupied himself in the god's service, prostrating himself in humility and constant in his observance at the shrine. To reward him for his piety Enki informs him that at the request of Enlil it has been resolved in the council of the gods to destroy the seed of mankind by a rain-storm. Before the holy man receives this timely warning, his divine friend bids him take his stand beside a wall, saying, " Stand by the wall on my left side, and at the wall I will speak a word with thee." These words are evidently connected with the curious passage in the Semitic version, where Ea begins his warning to Ut-napishtim, " O reed hut, reed hut, O wall, wall, O reed hut hearken, O wall attend."[4] Together the parallel passages suggest that the friendly god, who might not directly betray the resolution of the gods to a mortal man, adopted the subterfuge of whispering it to a wall of reeds, on the other side of which he had first stationed Ziudsuddu. Thus by eavesdropping the good man learned the fatal secret, while his divine patron was able afterwards to protest that he had not revealed the counsel of the gods. The subterfuge reminds us of the well-known story, how the

[1] See above, pp. 1 *sq.*

[2] So Mr. L. W. King would read the name (*Church Quarterly Review*, No. 162, January 1916, p. 277).

[3] L. W. King, *Babylonian Religion and Mythology*, p. 14. See above, p. 113, note [6].

[4] Above, p. 113. With reference to the collocation of reeds and wall, it is well to remember that in ancient Babylonian buildings mats made of reed were regularly interposed between the layers of brick, at intervals of four or five feet, in order to protect the earthen mass from disintegration. So well known is this to the modern Arabs, that they give the name of *Buwariyya* or "reed mats" to ancient mounds in which this mode of construction is discernible. See W. K. Loftus, *Travels and Researches in Chaldaea and Susiana* (London, 1857), p. 168.

servant of King Midas detected the ass's ears of his master, and, unable to contain himself, whispered the secret into a hole in the ground and filled up the hole with earth ; but a bed of reeds grew up on the spot, and rustling in the wind, proclaimed to all the world the king's deformity.[1]   The part of the tablet which probably described the building of the ship and Ziudsuddu's embarkation is lost, and in the remaining portion we are plunged into the midst of the deluge.   The storms of wind and rain are described as raging together.   Then the text continues : " When for seven days, for seven nights, the rain-storm had raged in the land, when the great boat had been carried away by the wind-storms on the mighty waters, the Sun-god came forth, shedding light over heaven and earth."   When the light shines into the boat, Ziudsuddu prostrates himself before the Sun-god and sacrifices an ox and a sheep.   Then follows a gap in the text, after which we read of Ziudsuddu, the King, prostrating himself before the gods Anu and Enlil.   The anger of Enlil against men appears now to be abated, for, speaking of Ziudsuddu, he says, " Life like that of a god I give to him," and " an eternal soul like that of a god I create for him," which means that the hero of the deluge legend, the Sumerian Noah, receives the boon of immortality, if not of divinity.   Further, he is given the title of " Preserver of the Seed of Mankind," and the gods cause him to dwell on a mountain, perhaps the

---

[1] Ovid, *Metamorphoses*, xi. 174 *sqq.* Parallels to the story are found, with trifling variations of detail, in Ireland, Brittany, Serbia, Bulgaria, Greece, India, and among the Mongols.   See Grimm's *Household Tales*, translated by Margaret Hunt (London, 1884), ii. 498 ; Patrick Kennedy, *Legendary Fictions of the Irish Celts* (London, 1866), pp. 248 *sqq.*; Alfred de Nore, *Coutumes, Mythes et Traditions des Provinces de France* (Paris and Lyons, 1846), pp. 219 *sq.*; W. S. Karadschitsch, *Volksmärchen der Serben* (Berlin, 1854), pp. 225 *sqq.*; Adolf Strausz, *Die Bulgaren* (Leipsic, 1898), pp. 250 *sqq.*; Bernhard Schmidt, *Griechische Märchen, Sagen und Volkslieder* (Leipsic, 1877), pp. 70 *sv.*, 224 *sq.*; *North Indian Notes and Queries*, iii. No. 6 (September, 1893), p. 104, § 218 (story told at Kon, in Mirzapur); Ghulam Muhammad, *Festivals and Folklore of Gilgit* (Calcutta, 1905), pp. 113 *sq.* (*Memoirs of the Asiatic Society of Bengal*, vol. i. No. 7) ; Bernard Jülg, *Mongolische Märchen-Sammlung* (Innsbruck, 1868), No. 22, pp. 182 *sqq.*; *Sagas from the Far East* (London, 1873), No. 21, pp. 206 *sqq.*   In some versions of the story the king's ears are those of a horse or a goat instead of an ass.   In the Gilgit version the king's feet, not his ears, are shaped like those of an ass.   Benfey thought that the story was borrowed by the East from the West.   See Theodor Benfey, *Pantschatantra* (Leipsic, 1859), i. p. xxii, note [1].

mountain of Dilmun, though the reading of the name is uncertain. The end of the legend is wanting.

Resemblance of the Sumerian version of the flood story to the version in the Gilgamesh epic.

Thus in its principal features the Sumerian version of the deluge legend agrees with the much longer and more circumstantial version preserved in the Gilgamesh epic. In both a great god (Enlil or Bel) resolves to destroy mankind by flooding the earth with rain ; in both another god (Enki or Ea) warns a man of the coming catastrophe, and the man, accepting the admonition, is saved in a ship ; in both the flood lasts at its height for seven days ; in both, when the deluge has abated, the man offers a sacrifice and is finally raised to the rank of the gods. The only essential difference is in the name of the hero, who in the Sumerian version is called Ziudsuddu, and in the Semitic version Ut-napishtim or Atrakhasis. The Sumerian name Ziudsuddu resembles the name Xisuthrus, which Berosus gives as that of the hero who was saved from the flood ; if the two names are really connected, we have fresh ground for admiring the fidelity with which the Babylonian historian followed the most ancient documentary sources.

The Semites probably borrowed their story of the deluge from the Sumerians.

The discovery of this very interesting tablet, with its combined accounts of the creation and the deluge, renders it highly probable that the narratives of the early history of the world which we find in Genesis did not originate with the Semites, but were borrowed by them from the older civilized people whom, some thousands of years before our era, the wild Semitic hordes, swarming out of the Arabian desert, found in possession of the fat lands of the lower Euphrates valley, and from whom the descendants of these primitive Bedouins gradually learned the arts and habits of civilization, just as the northern barbarians acquired a varnish of culture through their settlement in the Roman empire.

The scene of the story in the Gilgamesh epic laid at on the Euphrates.

The various fragmentary versions, Babylonian and Sumerian, of the deluge story confirm the conclusion that the legend circulated independently of the Gilgamesh epic, into which the poet loosely inserted it as an episode. In the epic the original scene of the disaster is laid, as we saw, at the city of Shurippak on the Euphrates. Recent excavations of the German Oriental Society have revealed the site of the ancient city. The place is at the hill of Fara, to the north of Uruk ; and the remains which have come to light there seem to show that Shurippak was among the very oldest Sumerian settlements yet discovered ; for the inscribed clay tablets which have been excavated on the spot are of a very archaic character, and are believed to have been written not much later than 3400 B.C.[1] The site is now a long way from the sea and at some distance from the Euphrates ; but we know that in the course of ages the river has repeatedly changed its bed, and that the sea has retreated, or rather that the land has advanced, in consequence of the vast quantities of soil annually washed down by the Euphrates and the Tigris.[2] Apparently the ancient city perished, not by water, but by fire ; for the ruins are buried under a thick layer of ashes. After the conflagration the greater part of the hill seems to have remained desolate, though a small town existed on the spot during the Sumerian and Accadian periods. From about the time of Hammurabi, that is, from about 2100 B.C. onward, the very name of Shurippak vanishes from Baby-lonian history.[3] Thus the story of the great flood which destroyed the city cannot have originated later than the end of the third millennium before Christ, and it may well have been very much older. In the Sumerian version of the deluge legend Shurippak is named, along with Eridu, Larak, and Sippar, as cities before the flood ; but in the frag-mentary state of the text it is impossible to say whether or not it was the city of Ziudsuddu, the Sumerian Noah.[4]

§ 3. *The Hebrew Story of a Great Flood*

The ancient Hebrew legend of a great flood, as it is recorded in the book of Genesis,[5] runs thus :—

" And the Lord saw that the wickedness of man was great

[1] A. Ungnad und H. Gressmann, *Das Gilgamesch-Epos*, pp. 190 sq.

[2] T. H. Huxley, "Hasisadra's Adventure," *Collected Essays*, vol. iv. (London, 1911) pp. 250 sq. ; Eduard Suess, *The Face of the Earth*, i. (Oxford, 1904) pp. 24 sq. ; G. Maspero, *Histoire Ancienne des peuples de l'Orient Classique, Les Origines* (Paris, 1895), pp. 552 sq. ; Ed. Meyer, *Geschichte des Altertums*,[2] i. 2. (Stutt-gart und Berlin, 1909) pp. 398 sq.

[3] A. Ungnad und H. Gressmann, *Das Gilgamesch-Epos*, p. 191.

[4] A. Poebel, in *The University of Pennsylvania, Publications of the Babylonian Section of the University Museum*, vol. iv. No. 1 (Philadelphia, 1914), pp. 18, 44.

[5] Genesis vi. 5-ix. 17, Revised Version.

in the earth, and that every imagination of the thoughts of his heart was only evil continually. And it repented the Lord that he had made man on the earth, and it grieved him at his heart. And the Lord said, I will destroy man whom I have created from the face of the ground ; both man, and beast, and creeping thing, and fowl of the air ; for it repenteth me that I have made them. But Noah found grace in the eyes of the Lord.

Noab, warned by God of tbe coming deluge, builds an ark.

" These are the generations of Noah. Noah was a righteous man and perfect in his generations : Noah walked with God. And Noah begat three sons, Shem, Ham, and Japheth. And the earth was corrupt before God, and the earth was filled with violence. And God saw the earth, and, behold, it was corrupt ; for all flesh had corrupted his way upon the earth. And God said unto Noah, The end of all flesh is come before me ; for the earth is filled with violence through them ; and, behold, I will destroy them with the earth.

The con-

of the ark.

Make thee an ark of gopher wood ; rooms shalt thou make in the ark, and shalt pitch it within and without with pitch. And this is how thou shalt make it : the length of the ark three hundred cubits, the breadth of it fifty cubits, and the height of it thirty cubits. A light shalt thou make to the ark, and to a cubit shalt thou finish it upward ; and the door of the ark shalt thou set in the side thereof ; with lower, second, and third stories shalt thou make it. And I, behold, I do bring the flood of waters upon the earth, to destroy all flesh, wherein is the breath of life, from under heaven ; every thing that is in the earth shall die. But I will establish my covenant with thee ; and thou shalt come into the ark, thou, and thy sons, and thy wife, and thy sons' wives

The animals to be taken into the ark.

with thee. And of every living thing of all flesh, two of every sort shalt thou bring into the ark, to keep them alive with thee ; they shall be male and female. Of the fowl after their kind, and of the cattle after their kind, of every creeping thing of the ground after its kind, two of every sort shall come unto thee, to keep them alive. And take thou unto thee of all food that is eaten, and gather it to thee ; and it shall be for food for thee, and for them. Thus did Noah ; according to all that God commanded him, so did he.

" *And the Lord said unto Noah, Come thou and all thy house into the ark ; for thee have I seen righteous before me in this generation. Of every clean beast thou shalt take to thee seven and seven, the male and his female; and of the beasts that are not clean two, the male and his female; of the fowl also of the air, seven and seven,* male and female *: to keep seed alive upon the face of all the earth. For yet seven days, and I will cause it to rain upon the earth forty days and forty nights; and every living thing that I have made will I destroy from off the face of the ground. And Noah did according unto all that the Lord commanded him.* And Noah was six hundred years old when the flood of waters was upon the earth. *And Noah went in, and his sons, and his wife, and his sons' wives with him, into the ark, because of the waters of the flood. Of clean beasts, and of beasts that are not clean, and of fowls, and of every thing that creepeth upon the ground, there went in* two and two *unto Noah into the ark,* male and female, *as* God *commanded Noah. And it came to pass after the seven days, that the waters of the flood were upon the earth.* In the six hundredth year of Noah's life, in the second month, on the seventeenth day of the month, on the same day, were all the fountains of the great deep broken up, and the windows of heaven were opened. *And the rain was upon the earth forty days and forty nights.* In the selfsame day entered Noah, and Shem, and Ham, and Japheth, the sons of Noah, and Noah's wife, and the three wives of his sons with them, into the ark; they, and every beast after its kind, and all the cattle after their kind, and every creeping thing that creepeth upon the earth after its kind, and every fowl after its kind, every bird of every sort. And they went in unto Noah into the ark, two and two of all flesh, wherein is the breath of life. And they that went in, went in male and female of all flesh, as God commanded him : *and the Lord shut him in.* And the flood was forty days upon the earth ; *and the waters increased, and bare up the ark, and it was lift up above the earth.* And the waters prevailed, and increased greatly upon the earth ; and the ark went upon the face of the waters. And the waters prevailed exceedingly upon the earth ; and all the high mountains that were under the whole heaven were covered. Fifteen cubits upward did the waters prevail ; and the mountains were covered. And all flesh died that moved upon the earth, both fowl, and cattle, and beast, and

Noah, his m a the beasts enter into the ark.

Duration and depth of the flood.

Destruction of all life n earth

every creeping thing that creepeth upon the earth, and every man : *all in whose nostrils was the breath of the spirit of life, of all that was in the dry land, died.   And every living thing was destroyed which was upon the face of the ground, both man, and cattle, and creeping thing, and fowl of the heaven ; and they were destroyed from the earth : and Noah only was left, and they that were with him in the ark.*   And the waters prevailed upon the earth an hundred and fifty days.

Cessation of the rain and assuage- ment of tne waters.
" And God remembered Noah, and every living thing, and all the cattle that were with him in the ark : and God made a wind to pass over the earth, and the waters assuaged ; the fountains also of the deep and the windows of heaven were stopped, *and the rain from heaven was restrained ; and the waters returned from off the earth continually :* and after the end of an hundred and fifty days the waters decreased.

The ark gr(s on Ararat
And the ark rested in the seventh month, on the seventeenth day of the month, upon the mountains of Ararat.   And the waters decreased continually until the tenth month : in the tenth month, on the first day of the month, were the tops of the mountains seen.   *And it came to pass at the end of forty days, that Noah opened the window of the ark which he had*

Noah sends out a raven and a dove.
made : and he sent forth a raven, and it went forth to and fro, until the waters were dried up from off the earth.   And he sent forth a dove from him, to see if the waters were abated from off the face of the ground ; but the dove found no rest for the sole of her foot, and she returned unto him to the ark, for the waters were on the face of the whole earth : and he put forth his hand, and took her, and brought her in unto him into the ark.   And he stayed yet other seven days ; and again he sent forth the dove out of the ark ; and the dove came in to him at eventide ; and, lo, in her mouth an olive leaf pluckt off : so Noah knew that the waters were abated from off the earth.   And he stayed yet other seven days ; and sent forth the dove ; and she returned not again unto him any more.   And it came to pass in the six hundred and first year, in the first month, the first day of the month, the waters were dried up from off the earth : *and Noah removed the covering of the ark, and looked, and, behold, the face of the ground was dried.*   And in the second month, on the seven and twentieth day of the month, was the earth dry.

"And God spake unto Noah, saying, Go forth of the ark, thou, and thy wife, and thy sons, and thy sons' wives with thee. Bring forth with thee every living thing that is with thee of all flesh, both fowl, and cattle, and every creeping thing that creepeth upon the earth ; that they may breed abundantly in the earth, and be fruitful, and multiply upon the earth. And Noah went forth, and his sons, and his wife, and his sons' wives with him : every beast, every creeping thing, and every fowl, whatsoever moveth upon the earth, after their families, went forth out of the ark. *And Noah builded an altar unto the Lord ; and took of every clean beast, and of every clean fowl, and offered burnt offerings on the altar. And the Lord smelled the sweet savour ; and the Lord said in his heart, I will not again curse the ground any more for man's sake, for that the imagination of man's heart is evil from his youth ; neither will I again smite any more every thing living, as I have done. While the earth remaineth, seedtime and harvest, and cold and heat, and summer and winter, and day and night shall not cease.* And God blessed Noah and his sons, and said unto them, Be fruitful, and multiply, and replenish the earth. And the fear of you and the dread of you shall be upon every beast of the earth, and upon every fowl of the air ; with all wherewith the ground teemeth, and all the fishes of the sea, into your hand are they delivered. Every moving thing that liveth shall be food for you ; as the green herb have I given you all. But flesh with the life thereof, which is the blood thereof, shall ye not eat. And surely your blood, the blood of your lives, will I require ; at the hand of every beast will I require it : and at the hand of man, even at the hand of every man's brother, will I require the life of man. Whoso sheddeth man's blood, by man shall his blood be shed : for in the image of God made he man. And you, be ye fruitful, and multiply ; bring forth abundantly in the earth, and multiply therein.

"And God spake unto Noah, and to his sons with him, saying, And I, behold, I establish my covenant with you, and with your seed after you ; and with every living creature that is with you, the fowl, the cattle, and every beast of the earth with you ; of all that go out of the ark, even every beast of the earth. And I will establish my covenant with

you ; neither shall all flesh be cut off any more by the waters
of the flood ; neither shall there any more be a flood to destroy
the earth. And God said, This is the token of the covenant
which I make between me and you and every living creature
that is with you, for perpetual generations : I do set my bow
'n the cloud, and it shall be for a token of a covenant between me and the earth. And it shall come to pass, when
I bring a cloud over the earth, that the bow shall be seen in
the cloud, and I will remember my covenant, which is
between me and you and every living creature of all flesh ;
and the waters shall no more become a flood to destroy all
flesh. And the bow shall be in the cloud ; and I will look
upon it, that I may remember the everlasting covenant
between God and every living creature of all flesh that is
upon the earth. And God said unto Noah, This is the token
of the covenant which I have established between me and all
flesh that is upon the earth."

The bow in the cloud.

In this account of the deluge Biblical critics are now
agreed in detecting the presence of two originally distinct
and partially inconsistent narratives, which have been
combined so as to present the superficial appearance of a
single homogeneous story. Yet the editorial task of uniting
them has been performed so clumsily that the repetitions
and inconsistencies left standing in them can hardly fail to
attract the attention even of a careless reader. In repro-
ducing the text of the legend from the English Revised
Version I have distinguished the two strands of the composite narrative by printing them in different types ; the
analysis thus exhibited is the one now generally accepted by
critics.[1]

The story of i Genesi is com- out of two distinct and a y inconsistent narratives.

[1] W. Robertson Smith, *The Old Testament in the Jewish Church*[2] (London and Edinburgh, 1892), pp. 329 *sq.* ; E. Kautsch und A. Socin, *Die Genesis, mit äusserer Unterschei-dung der Quellenschriften*[2] (Freiburg i. B., 1891), pp. 11 *sqq.* ; E. Kautsch, *Die heilige Schrift des Alten Testa-ments übersetzt und herausgegeben* (Freiburg i. B. und Leipzig, 1894), pp. 6 *sqq.* ; J. Estlin Carpenter and G. Harford-Battersby, *The Hexateuch* (London, 1900), ii. 9 *sqq.* ; W. H. Bennett, *Genesis*, pp. 135 *sqq.* (*The* *Century Bible*) ; W. H. Bennett and W. F. Adeney, *A Biblical Introduc-tion*[5] (London, 1908), pp. 27 *sqq.* ; S. R. Driver, *The Book of Genesis*[10] (London, 1916), pp. 85 *sqq.* ; *id.*, *Introduction to the Literature of the Old Testament*[9] (Edinburgh, 1913), p. 14 ; K. Budde, *Geschichte der alt-hebraischen Litteratur* (Leipzig, 1906), pp. 47 *sqq.* ; H. Gunkel, *Genesis über-setzt und erklärt*[3] (Gottingen, 1910), pp. 59 *sqq.*; J. Skinner, *Critical and Exegetical Commentary on Genesis* (Edinburgh, 1910), pp. 147 *sqq.* ;

Of the two versions of the legend thus artificially combined, the one, printed in ordinary Roman type, is derived
from what the critics call the Priestly Document or
Code (usually designated by the letter P); the other,
printed in italic type, is derived from what the critics
call the Jehovistic or Jahwistic Document (usually designated by the letter J), which · is characterized by the
use of the divine name Jehovah (Jahweh, or rather
Yahweh). ' The two documents differ conspicuously in
character and style, and they belong to different ages ; for
while the Jehovistic narrative is probably the oldest, the
Priestly Code is now generally admitted to be the latest, of
the four principal documents which have been united to
form the Hexateuch.   The Jehovistic document is believed
to have been written in Judea in the early times of the
Hebrew monarchy, probably in the ninth or eighth century
before our era ; the Priestly Code dates from the period
after the year 586 B.C., when Jerusalem was taken by
Nebuchadnezzar, king of Babylon, and the Jews were carried
away by him into captivity.   Both documents are in their
form historical, but while the Jehovistic writer displays a
genuine interest in the characters and adventures of the men
and women whom he describes, the Priestly writer appears
to concern himself with them only so far as he deemed them
instruments in the great scheme of Providence for conveying
to Israel a knowledge of God and of the religious and social
institutions by which it was his gracious will that the Chosen
People should regulate their lives.   The history which he
writes is sacred and ecclesiastical rather than secular and
civil ; his preoccupation is with Israel as a church rather
than as a nation.   Hence, while he dwells at comparative
length on the lives of the patriarchs and prophets to whom
the deity deigned to reveal himself, he hurries over whole
generations of common mortals, whom he barely mentions
by name, as if they were mere links to connect one religious
epoch with another, mere packthread on which to string at
rare intervals the splendid jewels of revelation.   His attitude

One of the
native
is derived
from the
Code[t] and
the other
Jehovistic
(Jahwistic)
document.

Difference
between
the two
documents
probable
dates.

The ecclesi-
astical[1]
character of
the history
recorded
in the
Priestly
explained
by the cir-
cumstances[s]
of the age
in which
it was
composed.

A. T. Chapman, *An Introduction to the Pentateuch* (Cambridge, 1911), pp. 74-81 ; H. E. Ryle, *The Book of Genesis* (Cambridge, 1914), pp. 96 *sqq.*; M. Jastrow, *Hebrew and Babylonian Traditions* (London, 1914), pp. 348 *sqq.*

to the past is sufficiently explained by the circumstances of
the times in which he lived. The great age of Israel was
over ; its independence was gone, and with it the hopes of
worldly prosperity and glory. The rosy dreams of empire,
which the splendid reigns of David and Solomon had con-
jured up in the hearts of the people, and which may have
lingered for a while, like morning clouds, even after the
disruption of the monarchy, had long ago faded in the
clouded evening of the nation's day, under the grim reality
of foreign domination. Barred from all the roads of purely
mundane ambition, the irrepressible idealism of the national
temperament now found a vent for itself in another direction.
Its dreams took a different cast. If earth was shut upon
it, heaven was still open ; and like Jacob at Bethel, with
enemies behind him and before, the dreamer beheld a ladder
stretching up beyond the clouds, by which angelic hosts
might descend to guard and comfort the forlorn pilgrim.
In short, the leaders of Israel sought to console and compensate their nation for the humiliations she had to endure
in the secular sphere by raising her to a position of supremacy in the spiritual. For this purpose they constructed or
perfected an elaborate system of religious ritual designed to
forestall and engross the divine favour, and so to make Zion
the holy city, the joy and centre of God's kingdom on earth.
With these aims and ambitions the tone of public life became
more and more clerical, its interests ecclesiastical, its predominant influence priestly. The king was replaced by
the high priest, who succeeded even to the purple robes and
golden crown of his predecessor.[1] The revolution which
thus substituted a line of pontiffs for a line of temporal
rulers at Jerusalem, was like that which converted the Rome
of the Cæsars into the Rome of the mediæval Popes.

The r~~n~~ tly C de deals rather with he f rmal side of religion ha w th its deeper problems.

It is this movement of thought, this current of religious
aspirations setting strongly in the direction of ecclesiasticism,
which is reflected, we may almost say arrested and crystal-
lized, in the Priestly Code. The intellectual and moral
limitations of the movement are mirrored in the corresponding limitations of the writer. It is the formal side of
religion in which alone he is really interested ; it is in the

[1] W. Robertson Smith, *The Old Testament in the Jewish Church*,[2] p. 445.

details of rites and ceremonies, of ecclesiastical furniture and garments, that he revels with genuine gusto. The deeper side of religion is practically a sealed book for him : its moral and spiritual aspects he barely glances at : into the profound problems of immortality and the origin of evil, which have agitated inquiring spirits in all the ages, he never enters. With his absorption in the minutiæ of ritual, his indifference to purely secular affairs, his predilection for chronology and genealogy, for dates and figures, in a word, for the dry bones rather than the flesh and blood of history, the priestly historian is like one of those monkish chroniclers of the Middle Ages who looked out on the great world through the narrow loophole of a cloistered cell or the many-tinted glass of a cathedral window. His intellectual horizon was narrowed, the atmosphere in which he beheld events was coloured, by the medium through which he saw them. Thus the splendours of the Tabernacle in the wilderness, invisible to all eyes but his, are as if they had loomed on his heated imagination through the purple lights of a rose-window or the gorgeous panes of some flamboyant oriel. Even in the slow processes or sudden catastrophes which have fashioned or transformed the material universe he discerned little more than the signs and wonders vouchsafed by the deity to herald new epochs of religious dispensation. For him the work of creation was a grand prelude to the institution of the sabbath.[1] The vault of heaven itself, spangled with glorious luminaries, was a magnificent dial-plate on which the finger of God pointed eternally to the correct seasons of the feasts in the ecclesiastical calendar.[2] The deluge, which swept away almost the whole of mankind, was the occasion which the repentant deity took to establish a covenant with the miserable survivors ; and the rainbow, glowing in iridescent radiance against the murky storm-cloud, was nothing but the divine seal appended to the covenant as a guarantee of its genuine and irrevocable character.[3]

---

[1] Genesis ii. 1 *sq.*

[2] Genesis i. 14. The Hebrew word here translated " seasons " (מוֹעֲדִים) "appears never (certainly not in P) to be used of the natural seasons of the year, but always of a time conventionally agreed upon, or fixed by some circumstance. The commonest application is to the *sacred seasons* of the ecclesiastical year, which are fixed by the moon " (Principal Skinner, in his *Critical and Exegetical Commentary on Genesis*, p. 26).

[3] Genesis ix. 8-17.

Legal bent
of the
writer ; his
insistence
on
covenants. For the priestly historian was a lawyer as well as an ecclesiastic, and as such he took great pains to prove that the friendly relations of God to his people rested on a strictly legal basis, being authenticated by a series of contracts into which both parties entered with all due formality. He is never so much in his element as when he is expounding these covenants ; he never wearies of recalling the long series of Israel's title-deeds. Nowhere does this dryasdust antiquary, this rigid ritualist, so sensibly relax his normal severity, nowhere does he so nearly unbend and thaw, as when he is expatiating on the congenial subject of contracts and conveyances. His masterpiece of historical narrative is acknowledged to be his account of the negotiations into which the widowed Abraham entered with the sons of Heth in order to obtain a family vault in which to bury his wife.[1] The lugubrious nature of the transaction does not damp the professional zest of the narrator ; and the picture he has drawn of it combines the touches of no mean artist with the minute exactitude of a practised conveyancer. At this distance of time the whole scene still passes before us, as similar scenes may have passed before the eyes of the writer, and as they may still be witnessed in the East, when two well-bred Arab sheikhs fence dexterously over a point of business, while they observe punctiliously the stately forms and courtesies of Oriental diplomacy. But such pictures are rare indeed in this artist's gallery. Landscapes he hardly attempted, and his portraits are daubs, lacking all individuality, life, and colour. In that of Moses, which he laboured most, the great leader is little more than a lay-figure rigged out to distribute ecclesiastical upholstery and millinery.[2]

High
literary
quality
of the
~~Jehovistic~~
document.   Very different are the pictures of the patriarchal age bequeathed to us by the author of the Jehovistic document. In purity of outline, lightness and delicacy of touch, and warmth of colouring, they are unsurpassed, perhaps unequalled, in literature. The finest effects are produced by the fewest strokes, because every stroke is that of a master who knows instinctively just what to put in and what to leave out. Thus, while his whole attention seems to be

---

[1] Genesis xxiii.
[2] W. Robertson Smith, *The Old Testament in the Jewish Church*,[2] p. 409.

given to the human figures in the foreground, who stand out from the canvas with lifelike truth and solidity, he contrives simultaneously, with a few deft, almost imperceptible touches, to indicate the landscape behind them, and so to complete a harmonious picture which stamps itself indelibly on the memory.   The scene, for example, of Jacob and Rachel at the well, with the flocks of sheep lying round it in the noontide heat, is as vivid in the writer's words as it is in the colours of Raphael.

And to this exquisite picturesqueness in the delineation of human life he adds a charming naïvety, an antique simplicity, in his descriptions of the divine.   He carries us back to the days of old, when no such awful gulf was supposed to yawn between man and the deity.   In his pages we read how God moulded the first man out of clay, as a child shapes its mud baby ;[1] how he walked in the garden in the cool of the evening and called to the shamefaced couple who had been skulking behind trees ;[2] how he made coats of skin to replace the too scanty fig-leaves of our first parents ;[3] how he shut the door behind Noah, when the patriarch had entered into the ark ;[4] how he sniffed the sweet savour of the burning sacrifice ;[5] how he came down to look at the tower of Babel,[6] apparently because, viewed from the sky, it was beyond his reach of vision ; how he conversed with Abraham at the door of his tent, in the heat of the day, under the shadow of the whispering oaks.[7]   In short, the whole work of this delightful writer is instinct with a breath of poetry, with something of the freshness and fragrance of the olden time, which invests it with an ineffable and immortal charm.[8]

Naive anthropomorphism of the [Jehov]istic [w]riter.

---

[1] Genesis ii. 7.
[2] Genesis iii. 8 *sq.*
[3] Genesis iii. 21.
[4] Genesis vii. 16.
[5] Genesis viii. 21.
[6] Genesis xi. 5 and 7.
[7] Genesis xviii. 1 *sqq.*   In the English Authorized Version the trees have disappeared from the picture and been replaced by plains.   They are rightly restored in the Revised Version, though the correct rendering of the Hebrew word is perhaps rather " tere-binths " than " oaks."   See below,

Part iv. chap. xv., " Sacred Oaks and Terebinths."

[8] As to the two documents, the Jehovistic (J) and the Priestly (P), see W. Robertson Smith, *The Old Testament in the Jewish Church,*[2] pp. 319 *sqq.*, 381 *sqq.*, 442 *sqq.* ; J. Estlin Carpenter and G. Harford-Battersby, *The Hexateuch,* i. 33 *sqq.*, 97 *sqq.*, 121 *sqq.* ; E. Kautsch, *Die heilige Schrift des Alten Testaments* (Freiburg i. B. und Leipzig, 1894), ii. 150 *sqq.*, 188 *sqq.* ; W. H. Bennett, *Genesis,* pp. 9 *sqq.*, 22 *sqq.*, 34 *sqq.* ; W. H.

Verbal
ff en
between the
Jehovistic
and the
Priestly
documents.

In the composite narrative of the Great Flood which we possess in Genesis, the separate ingredients contributed by the Jehovistic and the Priestly documents respectively are distinguishable from each other both by verbal and by material differences. To take the verbal differences first, the most striking is that in the Hebrew original the deity is uniformly designated, in the Jehovistic document by the name of *Jehovah* (*Jahweh*), and in the Priestly document by the name of *Elohim*, which in the English version are rendered respectively by the words " Lord " and " God." In representing the Hebrew *Jehovah* (*Jahweh*) by " Lord," the English translators follow the practice of the Jews, who, in reading the Scriptures aloud, uniformly substitute the title *Adonai* or " Lord " for the sacred name of Jehovah, wherever they find the latter written in the text. Hence the English reader may assume as a general rule that in the passages of the English version, where the title " Lord " is applied to the

---

Bennett and W. F. Adeney, *A Biblical Introduction*,[5] pp. 20 *sqq.*; S. R. Driver, *Introduction to the Literature of the Old Testament*,[9] pp. 10 *sqq.*, 116 *sqq.*; *id., The Book of Genesis*,[10] Introduction, pp. iv. *sqq.*; K. Budde, *Geschichte der althebräischen Litteratur*, pp. 45-65, 183-205; J. Skinner, *Critical and Exegetical Commentary on Genesis*, pp. xxxii-lxvii; H. Gunkel, *Genesis übersetzt und erklärt*[3] (Gottingen, 1910), pp. lxxx *sqq.*, xcii *sqq.*; A. T. Chapman, *Introduction to the Pentateuch* (Cambridge, 1911), pp. 50 *sqq.*, 207 *sqq.*; R. Kittel, *Geschichte des Volkes Israel*[2] (Gotha, 1909-1912), i. 273-333, ii. 398 *sqq.*; H. E. Ryle, *The Book of Genesis* (Cambridge, 1914), pp. xviii *sqq.* Critics seem generally to agree that the Priestly Code is the framework into which the three other main constituents of the Hexateuch have been fitted, and that it was substantially " the book of the law of Moses " which was publicly promulgated by Ezra at Jerusalem in 444 B.C. and accepted by the people as the basis of a new reformation (Nehemiah viii.). But the work of combining the Priestly Code with the other documents, so as to form our present Hexateuch, appears to have been carried out at a later date, perhaps about 400 B.C. See J. Estlin Carpenter and G. Harford-Battersby, *The Hexateuch*, i. 176 *sqq.*; W. H. Bennett and F. W. Adeney, *op. cit.*, pp. 56 *sqq.* Besides the Priestly Code (P) and the Jehovistic document (J), the two main constituents of the Hexateuch are Deuteronomy (the D of the critics) and the Elohistic document (the E of the critics). Of these, the Elohistic is the older; it is generally believed to have been composed in Northern Israel not very long after the Jehovistic document, perhaps early in the eighth century B.C. In style and character it is akin to the Jehovistic document, but the writer is not so great a literary artist, though his religious and moral standpoint is somewhat more advanced. Unlike the Jehovistic writer, he uses the divine name *Elohim* for God instead of Jehovah. It is generally believed that the main part of Deuteronomy is " the book of the law " which was found in the temple at Jerusalem in 621 B.C. and formed the basis of Josiah's reformation (2 Kings xxii. 8 *sqq.*). On these matters the reader will find the evidence stated and discussed in the works mentioned at the beginning of this note.

deity, the name Jehovah stands for it in the written or printed Hebrew text.[1]   But in the narrative of the flood and throughout Genesis the Priestly writer avoids the use of the name Jehovah and substitutes for it the term *Elohim*, which is the ordinary Hebrew word for God ; and his reason for doing so is that according to him the divine name Jehovah was first revealed by God to Moses,[2] and therefore could not have been applied to him in the earlier ages of the world.   On the other hand, the Jehovistic writer has no such theory as to the revelation of the name Jehovah ; hence he bestows it on the deity without scruple from the creation onwards.

Apart from this capital distinction between the documents, there are verbal differences which do not appear in the English translation.   Thus, one set of words is used for "male and female" in the Jehovistic document, and quite a different set in the Priestly.[3]   Again, the words translated "destroy" in the English version are different in the two documents,[4] and similarly with the words which the English translators represent by "die"[5] and "dried."[6]

But the material differences between the Jehovistic and the Priestly narratives are still more remarkable, and as they amount in some cases to positive contradictions, the proof that they emanate from separate documents may be regarded as complete.   Thus in the Jehovistic narrative the clean animals are distinguished from the unclean, and while seven of every sort of clean animals are admitted to the ark, only a pair of each sort of unclean animals is suffered to enter.[7]   On the other hand, the Priestly writer makes no

Material differences between the Jehovistic Priestly narratives Their discrepancies as to the animals.

[1] See E. Kautsch, in *Encyclopædia Biblica*, ii. 3320 *sqq., s.v.* "Names"; A. T. Chapman, *Introduction to the Pentateuch*, pp. 51 *sq.*

Exodus vi. 2 *sq.*

יִכָּר וּנְקֵבָה in J (vii. 2), אִישׁ וְאִשְׁתּוֹ in P (vi. 19, vii. 9. 16).

מָחָה in J (vi. 7, vii. 4, 23), שׁחת in P (vi. 13, 17, ix. 11, 15).   The former word means properly "blot out," as it is rendered in the margin of the English Revised Version ; the latter is the ordinary Hebrew word for "destroy."

[5] מוּת in J (vii. 22), גּוע in P (vi. 17, vii. 21).   The former is the ordinary Hebrew word for "die" ; the latter is

sometimes translated "give up the ghost."

[6] חרב in J (viii. 13), יָבֵשׁ in P (viii. 14).   All the foregoing and other verbal differences between the two documents are noted by Principal J. Skinner in his *Critical and Exegetical Commentary on Genesis*, p. 148.   Compare H. Gunkel, *Genesis übersetzt und erklärt*[3] (Gottingen, 1910), p. 138.

[7] Genesis vii. 2, compare viii. 20.   The Hebrew phrase (שׁבְעָה שׁבְעָה) in vii. 2 is commonly understood to mean seven *pairs*; but in accordance with Hebrew idiom it can only mean seven *individuals* of each sort, as my teacher

such invidious distinction between the animals, but admits them to the ark on a footing of perfect equality, though at the same time he impartially limits them all alike to a single couple of each sort.[1] The explanation of this discrepancy is that in the view of the Priestly writer the distinction between clean and unclean animals was first revealed by God to Moses,[2] and could not therefore have been known to his predecessor Noah ; whereas the Jehovistic writer, untroubled by any such theory, naively assumes the distinction between clean and unclean animals to have been familiar to mankind from the earliest times, as if it rested on a natural difference too obvious to be overlooked by anybody.

Discrep-ancy between the Jehovistic and the Priestly writers as to the duration of the flood.

Another serious discrepancy between the two writers relates to the duration of the flood. In the Jehovistic narrative the rain lasted forty days and forty nights,[3] and afterwards Noah passed three weeks in the ark before the water had subsided enough to let him land.[4] On this reckoning the flood lasted sixty-one days. On the other hand, in the Priestly narrative it was a hundred and fifty days before the water began to sink,[5] and the flood lasted altogether for twelve months and ten days.[6] As the Hebrew months were lunar, twelve of them would amount to three hundred and fifty-four days, and ten days added to them would give a solar year of three hundred and sixty-four days.[7] Since the Priestly writer thus assigns to the duration of the flood the approximate length of a solar year, we may safely assume that he lived at a time when the Jews were able to correct the serious error of the lunar calendar by observation of the sun.

Again, the two writers differ from each other in the

and friend, the Rev. Professor R. H. Kennett, has kindly pointed out to me in a letter. See Gesenius' *Hebrew Grammar as edited and enlarged by E. Kautsch*, Second English Edition, revised by A. E. Cowley (Oxford, 1910), p. 436, § 134 *q*. The phrase, as was to be expected, is rightly understood by W. Robertson Smith (*The Old Testament in the Jewish Church*,[2] p. 329), and Principal J. Skinner (*Commentary on Genesis*, p. 152).

[1] Genesis vi. 19 *sq.*, vii. 15 *sq.*
[2] Leviticus xi. ; Deuteronomy xiv.

4-20.
[3] Genesis vii. 12, 17.
[4] Genesis viii. 6-13.
[5] Genesis viii. 3.
[6] Genesis vii. 11 compared with viii. 14.
[7] S. R. Driver, *The Book of Genesis*,[10] p. 85 ; J. Skinner, *Critical and Exegetical Commentary on Genesis*, pp. 167 *sqq.* ; H. Gunkel, *Genesis übersetzt und erklärt*,[3] pp. 146 *sq.* ; A. T. Chapman, *Introduction to the Pentateuch*, p. 79 ; H. E. Ryle, *The Book of Genesis*, p. 113.

causes which they allege for the flood ; for whereas the
Jehovistic writer puts it down to rain only,[1] the Priestly
writer speaks of subterranean waters bursting forth as well
as of sheets of water descending from heaven.[2]

Discrep-
a y as t
the cause of
the flood.

Lastly, the Jehovistic writer represents Noah as building
an altar and sacrificing to God in gratitude for his escape
from the flood.[3] The Priestly writer, on the other hand,
makes no mention either of the altar or of the sacrifice ; no
doubt because from the standpoint of the Levitical law, which
he occupied, there could be no legitimate altar anywhere but
in the temple at Jerusalem, and because for a mere layman
like Noah to offer a sacrifice would have been an unheard-of
impropriety, a gross encroachment on the rights of the clergy
which he could not for a moment dream of imputing to the
respectable patriarch.

Discrep-
a
the building
of an altar
offering of
sacrifice.

Thus a comparison of the Jehovistic and the Priestly
narratives strongly confirms the conclusion of the critics that
the two were originally independent, and that the Jehovistic
is considerably the older. For the Jehovistic writer is clearly
ignorant of the law of the one sanctuary, which forbade the
offering of sacrifice anywhere but at Jerusalem ; and as that
law was first clearly enunciated and enforced by King Josiah
in 021 B.C., it follows that the Jehovistic document must
have been composed some time, probably a long time, before
that date. For a like reason the Priestly document must
have been composed some time, probably a considerable time,
after that date, since the writer implicitly recognizes the law
of the one sanctuary by refusing to impute a breach of it to
Noah. Thus, whereas the Jehovistic writer betrays a certain
archaic simplicity in artlessly attributing to the earliest ages
of the world the religious institutions and phraseology of his
own time, the Priestly writer reveals the reflection of a later
age, which has worked out a definite theory of religious
evolution and applies it rigidly to history.

A compari-
the two
narratives
d
confirms
the
....clusion
that the
Jehovistic
and Priestly
documents
were
'in all
indepen-
d   nd
that the
Jehovistic
'   r
of the two.

A very cursory comparison of the Hebrew with the
Babylonian account of the Deluge may suffice to convince us
that the two narratives are not independent, but that one of
them must be derived from the other, or both from a common

---

[1] Genesis vii. 12.   [2] Genesis vii. 11, compare viii. 2.
[3] Genesis viii. 20 *sq.*

original.   The points of resemblance between the two are far
too numerous and detailed to be accidental.   In both narratives the divine powers resolve to destroy mankind by a
great flood ; in both the secret is revealed beforehand to a
man by a god, who directs him to build a great vessel, in
which to save himself and seed of every kind.   It is probably
no mere accidental coincidence that in the Babylonian story,
as reported by Berosus, the hero saved from the flood was
the *tenth* King of Babylon, and that in the Hebrew story
Noah was the *tenth* man in descent from Adam.   In both
narratives the favoured man, thus warned of God, builds a
huge vessel in several stories, makes it water-tight with pitch
or bitumen, and takes into it his family and animals of all
sorts : in both, the deluge is brought about in large measure
by heavy rain, and lasts for a greater or less number of days:
in both, all mankind are drowned except the hero and his
family : in both, the man sends forth birds, a raven and a
dove, to see whether the water of the flood has abated : in
both, the dove after a time returns to the ship because it
could find no place in which to rest : in both, the raven does
not return : in both, the vessel at last grounds on a mountain:
in both, the hero, in gratitude for his rescue, offers sacrifice
on the mountain : in both, the gods smell the sweet savour,
and their anger is appeased.

So much for the general resemblance between the Babylonian story as a whole and the Hebrew story as a
whole.   But if we take into account the separate elements
of the Hebrew story, we shall see that the Jehovistic
narrative is in closer agreement than the Priestly with the
Babylonian.   Alike in the Jehovistic and in the Babylonian
narrative special prominence is given to the number seven.
In the Jehovistic version, Noah has a seven days' warning
of the coming deluge : he takes seven of every sort of
clean animals with him into the ark : he allows intervals of
seven days to elapse between the successive despatches of
the dove from the ark.   In the Babylonian version the flood
lasts at its greatest height for seven days ; and the hero sets
out the sacrificial vessels by sevens on the mountain.   Again,
alike in the Jehovistic and the Babylonian version, special
mention is made of shutting the door of the ship or ark

when the man, his family, and the animals have entered into it : in both alike we have the picturesque episode of sending forth the raven and the dove from the vessel, and in both alike the offering of the sacrifice, the smelling of it by the gods, and their consequent appeasement. On the other hand, in certain particulars the Priestly narrative in Genesis approaches more closely than the Jehovistic to the Babylonian. Thus, in both the Priestly and the Babylonian version exact directions are given for the construction of the vessel : in both alike it is built in several stories, each of which is divided into numerous cabins : in both alike it is made water-tight by being caulked with pitch or bitumen : in both alike it grounds on a mountain ; and in both alike on issuing from the vessel the hero receives the divine blessing.

But if the Hebrew and Babylonian narratives are closely related to each other, how is the relation to be explained ? The Babylonian cannot be derived from the Hebrew, since it is older than the Hebrew by at least eleven or twelve centuries. Moreover, " as Zimmern has remarked, the very essence of the Biblical narrative presupposes a country liable, like Babylonia, to inundations : so that it cannot be doubted that the story was ' indigenous in Babylonia, and transplanted to Palestine.' " [1] But if the Hebrews derived the story of the great flood from Babylonia, when and how did they do so? We have no information on the subject, and the question can only be answered conjecturally. Some scholars of repute have supposed that the Jews first learned the legend in Babylon during the captivity, and that the Biblical narrative is consequently not older than the sixth century before our era.[2] This view might be tenable if we only possessed the Hebrew version of the Deluge legend in the Priestly recension ; for the Priestly Code, as we saw, was probably composed during or after the captivity, and it is perfectly possible that the writers of it acquired a knowledge of the Babylonian tradition either orally or from Babylonian literature during their exile or perhaps after their return to Palestine ; for it

[marginal note: The Hebrew story of the flood may have been ultimately derived from Babylonia; but the Hebrews were acquainted with it long before the Babylonian captivity.]

[1] S. R. Driver, *The Book of Genesis*,[10] p. 107.
[2] This is, or was, the opinion of P. Haupt and Fr. Delitsch, as reported by E. Schrader, *The Cuneiform Inscriptions and the Old Testament*, i. 55. The view is rightly rejected by Schrader.

is reasonable to suppose that the intimate relations which the conquest established between the two countries may have led to a certain diffusion of Babylonian literature in Palestine, and of Jewish literature in Babylonia. On this view some of the points in which the Priestly narrative departs from the Jehovistic and approximates to the Babylonian may conceivably have been borrowed directly by the Priestly writers from Babylonian sources. Such points are the details as to the construction of the ark, and in particular the smearing of it with pitch or bitumen, which is a characteristic product of Babylonia.[1] But that the Hebrews were acquainted with the story of the great flood, and that too in a form closely akin to the Babylonian, long before they were carried away into captivity, is abundantly proved by the Jehovistic narrative in Genesis, which may well date from the ninth century before our era and can hardly be later than the eighth.

How and when the Hebrews learned the flood we do not know.

Assuming, then, that the Hebrews in Palestine were familiar from an early time with the Babylonian legend of the deluge, we have still to ask, how and when did they learn it? Two answers to the question have been given. On the one hand, it has been held that the Hebrews may have brought the legend with them, when they migrated from Babylonia to Palestine about two thousand years before Christ.[2] On the other hand, it has been suggested that, after their settlement in Palestine, the Hebrews may have borrowed the story from the native Canaanites, who in their turn may have learned it through the medium of Babylonian literature sometime in the second millennium before our era.[3] Which, if either, of these views is the true one, we have at present no means of deciding.

[1] Herodotus i. 179, with the note in George Rawlinson's translation (Fourth Edition, vol. i., London, 1880, p. 300).

[2] This is the view of Professor M. Jastrow (*Hebrew and Babylonian Traditions*, pp. 13 *sqq.*), who identifies Abraham's contemporary, Amraphel, King of Shinar (Genesis xiv. 1), with Hammurabi, King of Babylon, thus dating Abraham and his migration from Babylonia to Palestine about 2100 B.C. As to Hammurabi's date, see

above, p. 121, note 2.

[3] H. Gressmann, in *Das Gilgamesch-Epos ubersetzt und erklart* von A. Ungnad und H. Gressmann, p. 220. On this theory see Principal J. Skinner, *Critical and Exegetical Commentary on Genesis*, p. x, who objects to it that "there are no recognisable traces of a specifically Canaanite medium having been interposed between the Babylonian originals and the Hebrew accounts of the Creation and the Flood, such as we may surmise in the case of the Paradise myth."

In later times Jewish fancy tricked out the story of the flood with many new and often extravagant details designed apparently to satisfy the curiosity or tickle the taste of a degenerate age, which could not rest satisfied with the noble simplicity of the narrative in Genesis. Among these tawdry or grotesque additions to the ancient legend we read how men lived at ease in the days before the flood, for by a single sowing they reaped a harvest sufficient for the needs of forty years, and by their magic arts they could compel the sun and moon to do them service. Instead of nine months children were in their mothers' wombs only a few days, and immediately on their birth could walk and talk and set even the demons at defiance. It was this easy luxurious life that led men astray and lured them into the commission of those sins, especially the sins of wantonness and rapacity, which excited the wrath of God and determined him to destroy the sinners by a great flood. Yet in his mercy he gave them due warning ; for Noah, instructed by the deity, preached to them to mend their ways, threatening them with the flood as the punishment of their iniquity ; and this he did for no less than one hundred and twenty years. Even at the end of that period God gave mankind another week's grace, during which, strange to say, the sun rose in the west every morning and set in the east every night. But nothing could move these wicked men to repentance ; they only mocked and jeered at the pious Noah when they saw him building the ark. He learned how to make it from a holy book, which had been given to Adam by the angel Raziel and which contained within it all knowledge, human and divine. It was made of sapphires, and Noah enclosed it in a golden casket when he took it with him into the ark, where it served him as a time-piece to distinguish night from day ; for so long as the flood prevailed neither the sun nor the moon shed any light on the earth. Now the deluge was caused by the male waters from the sky meeting the female waters which issued forth from the ground. The holes in the sky by which the upper waters escaped were made by God when he removed two stars out of the constellation of the Pleiades ; and in order to stop this torrent of rain God had afterwards to bung up the two holes with a couple of stars borrowed

from the constellation of the Bear. That is why the Bear
runs after the Pleiades to this day : she wants her children
back, but she will never get them till after the Last Day.

The
animals
taken into
the ark.

When the ark was ready, Noah proceeded to gather
the animals into it. They came trooping in such numbers
that the patriarch could not take them all in, but
had to sit at the door of the ark and make a choice ; the
animals which lay down at the door he . took in, and the
animals which stood up he shut out. Even after this principle of natural selection had been rigidly enforced, the
number of species of reptiles which were taken on board
was no less than three hundred and sixty-five, and the
number of species of birds thirty-two. No note was taken,
at least none appears to have been recorded, of the number
of mammals, but many of them were among the passengers,
as we shall see presently. Before the flood the unclean animals
far outnumbered the clean, but after the flood the proportions
were reversed, because seven pairs[1] of each of the clean sorts
were preserved in the ark, but only two pairs of the unclean.
One creature, the *reem*, was so huge that there was no room for
it in the ark,so Noah tethered it to the outside of the vessel,and

Og, King
of Bashan,
on the top
of the ark ;
Falsehood
and
Misfortune
in the ark.

the animal trotted behind. The giant Og, king of Bashan, was
also much too big to go into the ark, so he sat on the top of
it, and in that way escaped with his life. With Noah himself
in the ark were his wife Naamah, daughter of Enosh, and
his three sons and their wives. An odd pair who also found
refuge in the ark were Falsehood and Misfortune. At first
Falsehood presented himself alone at the door of the ark,
but was refused a passage on the ground that there was no
admission except for married couples. So he went away,
and meeting with Misfortune induced her to join him, and
the pair were received into the ark. When all were aboard,
and the flood began, the sinners gathered some seven hundred
thousand strong round about the ark and begged and prayed
to be taken in. When Noah sternly refused to admit them,
they made a rush at the door as if to break it in, but the
wild beasts that were on guard round about the ark fell upon
them and devoured some of them, and all that escaped the
beasts were drowned in the rising flood. A whole year the

[1] But see above, p. 137, note 7.

ark floated on the face of the waters ; it pitched and tossed
on·the heaving billows, and all inside of it were shaken up
like lentils in a pot.   The lions roared, the oxen lowed, the
wolves howled, and the rest bellowed after their several
sorts.   But the great difficulty with which Noah had to
struggle in the ark was the question of victuals.   Long afterwards his son Shem confided to Eliezer, the servant of
Abraham, the trouble his father had had in feeding the
whole menagerie.   The poor man was up and down, up and
down, by day and by night.   For the daylight animals had
to be fed by day and the nocturnal animals by night ; and
the giant Og had his rations served out to him through a
hole in the roof.   Though the lion suffered the whole time
from a fever, which kept him comparatively quiet, yet he
was very surly and ready to fly out on the least pro-
vocation.   Once when Noah did not bring him his dinner
fast enough, the noble animal gave him such a blow with his
paw that the patriarch was lame for the rest of his natural
life and therefore incapable of serving as a priest.   It was on
the tenth day of the month Tammuz that Noah sent forth
the raven to see and report on the state of the flood.   But
the raven found a corpse floating on the water and set to
work to devour it, so that he quite forgot to return and hand
in his report.   A week later Noah sent out the dove, which
at last, on its third flight, brought back in its bill an olive
leaf plucked on the Mount of Olives at Jerusalem ; for the
Holy Land had not been ravaged by the deluge.   When he
stepped out of the ark Noah wept to see the widespread
devastation wrought by the flood.   A thank-offering for his
delivery was offered by his son Shem, for the patriarch himself was still suffering from the effects of his encounter with
the lion and could not officiate in person.[1]

From another late account we learn some interesting
particulars as to the internal arrangements of the ark and
the distribution of the passengers.   The beasts and cattle
were battened down in the hold, the middle deck was occupied
by the birds, and the promenade deck was reserved for Noah
and his family.   But the men and the women were kept
strictly apart.   The patriarch and his sons lodged in the east

*The diffi-
culty of
feeding the
animals in
the ark.*

*Another
a e ew 1
version of
the flood
story.*

L. Ginzberg, *The Legends of the Jews*, i. (Philadelphia, 1909) pp. 151-167.

end of the ark, and his wife and his sons' wives lodged in
the west end ; and between them as a barrier was interposed
the dead body of Adam, which was thus rescued from a
watery grave.   This account, which further favours us with
the exact dimensions of the ark in cubits and the exact
day of the week and of the month when the passengers
got aboard, is derived from an Arabic manuscript found in
the library of the Convent of St. Catherine on Mount Sinai.
The author would seem to have been an Arab Christian,
who flourished about the time of the Mohammedan conquest, though the manuscript is of later date.[1]

§ 4. *Ancient Greek Stories of a Great Flood*

Greek
legend of
a flood as
told by
Apollo-
dorus.
How
Deucalion
and Pyrrha,
warned by
Zeus of the
coming
flood, saved
themselves
in an ark,
and
afterwards
re-peopled
the world
by throwing
~~stones~~
over their
shoulders.

Legends of a destructive deluge, in which the greater
part of mankind perished, meet us in the literature of ancient
Greece.   As told by the mythographer Apollodorus, the
story runs thus : "Deucalion was the son of Prometheus.
He reigned as king in the country about Phthia and married
Pyrrha, the daughter of Epimetheus and Pandora, the first
woman fashioned by the gods.   But when Zeus wished to
destroy the men of the Bronze Age, Deucalion by the advice
of Prometheus constructed a chest or ark, and having stored
in it what was needful he entered into it with his wife.   But
Zeus poured a great rain from the sky upon the earth and
washed down the greater part of Greece, so that all men
perished except a few, who flocked to the high mountains
near.   Then the mountains in Thessaly were parted, and all
the world beyond the Isthmus and Peloponnese was overwhelmed.   But Deucalion in the ark, floating over the sea
for nine days and as many nights, grounded on Parnassus,
and there, when the rains ceased, he disembarked and·
sacrificed to Zeus, the God of Escape.   And Zeus sent

---

[1] *Studia Sinaitica*, No. viii., *Apo-
crypha Arabica*, edited and translated
into English by Margaret Dunlop
Gibson (London and Cambridge,
1901), pp. 23-30, with the Editor's
Introduction, pp. vii *sqq.* According
to this account the ark was 300 cubits
long by 50 cubits broad and 30 cubits
high.   It was Friday the 17th of
March or, according to others, of May,
when the body of Adam was brought
into the ark ; and all the passengers,
both animal and human, got on board
the next day.   The flood fell, and
Noah and his company quitted the ark,
on a day in Nisan (April).

Hermes to him and allowed him to choose what he would, and he chose men. And at the bidding of Zeus he picked up stones and threw them over his head; and the stones which Deucalion threw became men, and the stones which Pyrrha threw became women. That is why in Greek people are called *laoi* from *laas*, 'a stone.' "[1]

In this form the Greek legend is not older than about the middle of the second century before our era, the time when Apollodorus wrote, but in substance it is much more ancient, for the story was told by Hellanicus, a Greek historian of the fifth century B.C., who said that Deucalion's ark drifted not to Parnassus but to Mount Othrys in Thessaly.[2] The other version has the authority of Pindar, who wrote earlier than Hellanicus in the fifth century B.C.; for the poet speaks of Deucalion and Pyrrha descending from Parnassus and creating the human race afresh out of stones.[3] According to some, the first city which they founded after the great flood was Opus, situated in the fertile Locrian plain between the mountains and the Euboic Gulf. But Deucalion is reported to have dwelt at Cynus, the port of Opus, distant a few miles across the plain; and there his wife's tomb was shown to travellers down to the beginning of our era. Her husband's dust is said to have rested at Athens.[4] The coast of Locris, thus associated with traditions of the great flood, is rich in natural beauties. The road runs at the foot of the mountains, which are of soft and lovely outlines, for the most part covered with forest; while the low hills and glades by the sea are wooded with pines, plane-trees, myrtles, lentisks, and other trees and shrubs, their luxuriant verdure fed by abundant springs. Across the blue waters of the gulf the eye roams to the island of Euboea, with its winding shores and long line of finely cut mountains standing out against the sky. The home of Deucalion was on a promontory jutting into the gulf. On it, and on the isthmus which joins it to the land, may still be seen the mouldering ruins of Cynus: a line of fortification walls, built of sandstone, runs round the edge of the height, and the

(marginal notes) Hellanicus on Deucalion's flood.

Deucalion at Cynus on the Euboic Gulf.

[1] Apollodorus, *Bibliotheca*, i. 7. 2.
[2] Scholiast on Pindar, *Olymp.* ix. 64; *Fragmenta Historicorum Graecorum*, ed. C. Muller, i. 48.
[3] Pindar, *Olymp.* ix. 64 *sqq.*
[4] Strabo, ix. 4. 2, p. 425, ed. Casaubon.

summit is crowned by the remains of a mediæval tower. The ground is littered with ancient potsherds.[1]

Deucalion's ark variously said to have grounded on Parnassus and on a mountain in Argolis.

It is said that an ancient city on Parnassus was overwhelmed by the rains which caused the deluge, but the inhabitants, guided by the howling of wolves, found their way to the peaks of the mountain, and when the flood had subsided they descended and built a new city, which they called Lycorea or Wolf-town in gratitude for the guidance of the wolves.[2] Lucian speaks of Deucalion's ark, with the solitary survivors of the human race, grounding on what was afterwards the site of Wolf-town, while as yet all the rest of the world was submerged.[3] But according to another account, the mountain to which Deucalion escaped was a peak in Argolis, which was afterwards called Nemea from the cattle which cropped the greensward on its grassy slopes. There the hero built an altar in honour of Zeus the Deliverer, who had delivered him from the great flood.[4] The mountain on which he is said to have alighted is probably the table-mountain, now called Phouka, whose broad flat top towers high above the neighbouring hills and forms a conspicuous landmark viewed from the plain of Argos.[5]

Megarian story of the flood.

Aristotle on the flood.

The Megarians told how in Deucalion's flood Megarus, son of Zeus, escaped by swimming to the top of Mount Gerania, being guided by the cries of some cranes, which flew over the rising waters and from which the mountain afterwards received its new name.[6] According to Aristotle, writing in the fourth century B.C., the ravages of the deluge in Deucalion's time were felt most sensibly " in ancient Hellas, which is the country about Dodona and the river Achelous, for that river has changed its bed in many places. In those days the land was inhabited by the Selli·and the people who were then called Greeks (*Graikoi*) but are now named Hellenes." [7] Some people thought that the sanctuary

<hr/>

[1] Ludwig Ross, *Wanderungen in Griechenland* (Halle, 1851), i. 94 *sq.*

[2] Pausanias, x. 6. 2.

[3] Lucian, *Timon*, 3. Elsewhere he refers to the ark and to the creation of men out of stones (*De Saltatione*, 39).

[4] *Etymologicum Magnum*, p. 176, *s.v.* Ἀφέσιος, referring to the Second Book of Arrian's *Bithyniaca*.

[5] The modern Phouka seems to be the Apesas of the ancients (Pausanias, ii. 5. 3, with the note in my commentary), which again appears to be connected with Zeus *Aphesios* (Deliverer), to whom Deucalion built an altar on the mountain.

[6] Pausanias, i. 40. 1 (Gerania from *geranoi*, " cranes ").

[7] Aristotle, *Meteorolog.* i. 14, p. 352, ed. Im. Bekker (Berlin, 1831).

of Zeus at Dodona was founded by Deucalion and Pyrrha, who
dwelt among the Molossians of that country.[1]   In the fourth
century B.C.   Plato also mentions, without describing, the   Plato on
flood which took place in the time of Deucalion and Pyrrha,   the flood.
and he represents the Egyptian priests as ridiculing the
Greeks for believing that there had been only one deluge,
whereas there had been many.[2]   The Parian chronicler, who
drew up his chronological table in the year 265 B.C.,[3] dated
Deucalion's flood one thousand two hundred and sixty-five   Deucalion's
years before his own time;[4] according to this calculation   flood dated
the cataclysm occurred in the year 1539 B.C.   in 1539 B.C.

At a later age the Roman poet Ovid decked out the   Ovid's
tradition of the great flood in the pinchbeck rhetoric which   rhetorical
betrayed the decline of literary taste.   He tells us that   Deucalion's
Jupiter, weary of the wickedness and impiety of the men of   Jupiter
the Iron Age, resolved to destroy the whole of mankind at   resolves to
one fell swoop.   His first idea was to overwhelm them under   destroy the
the flaming thunderbolts which he brandished in his red   men of the
right hand; but on reflection he laid these dangerous   by a flood.
weapons aside, lest the upper air and heaven itself should
catch fire from the great conflagration which they would
kindle on earth; and in this prudent resolution he was confirmed by an imperfect recollection of an old prophecy that
the whole world, sky and earth alike, was destined to perish
in a grand and final combustion.   Accordingly he decided
on the safer course of turning on the celestial taps and
drowning the whole wicked race under the tremendous
shower bath.   So he shut up the North Wind in the cave
of Aeolus, to prevent him from sweeping the murky clouds   Description
from the blue sky, and he let loose the South Wind, who   of the
flew abroad, rigged out in all the stage properties calculated   deluge.
to strike terror into the beholder.   He flapped his dripping
wings: his dreadful face was veiled in pitchy blackness:
mists sat on his forehead, his beard was soaking wet, and
water ran down from his hoary hair.   In his train the sky
lowered, thunder crashed, and the rainbow shone in spangled
glory against the dark rain-clouds.   To help the sky-god in

[1] Plutarch, *Pyrrhus*, 1.
[2] Plato, *Timaeus*, pp. 22A, 23B.
[3] L. Ideler, *Handbuch der mathe-matischen und technischen Chronologie*
(Berlin, 1825–1826), i. 380 *sqq.*
[4] *Marmor Parium*, 6 *sqq.*, in *Frag-menta Historicorum Graecorum*, ed. C. Müller, i. 542.

his onslaught on mankind his sea-blue brother Neptune
summoned an assembly of the rivers and bade them roll in
flood over the land, while he himself fetched the earth a
swashing blow with his trident, causing it to quake like
a jelly. The fountains of the great deep were now opened.
The deluge poured over the fields and meadows, whirling
away trees, cattle, men and houses. Far and wide nothing
was to be seen but a shoreless sea of tossing, turbid water.
The farmer now rowed in a shallop over the field where he
had lately guided the oxen at the plough-tail, and peering
down he could discern his crops and the roof of his farm-
house submerged under the waves. He dropped his anchor
on a green meadow, his keel grated on his own vineyard, and
he fished for trout in the tops of the tall elms. Seals now
lolled and sprawled where goats had lately nibbled the
herbage, and dolphins gambolled and plunged in the woods.
When at last nothing remained above the waste of waters
but the two peaks of Parnassus, toppling over the heaving
billows and reaching up above the clouds, Deucalion and his
wife drifted in a little boat to the mountain, and landing
adored the nymphs of the Corycian cave and the prophetic
goddess Themis, who managed the business of the oracle
before it was taken over by Apollo. A righteous and god-
fearing man was Deucalion, and his wife was just such
another. Touched with compassion at the. sight of the
honest pair, the sole survivors of so many thousands, Jupiter
now dispersed the clouds and the deluge, revealing the blue
sky and the green earth to each other once more. So
Neptune also laid aside his trident, and summoning the
bugler Triton, his back blue with the growth of the purple-
shell, he ordered him to sound the " Retire." The bugler
obeyed, and putting the shell to his lips he blew from his
puffed cheeks such a blast that at the sound of it all the
waves and rivers fell back and left the land high and dry.
This was all very well, but what were Deucalion and Pyrrha
to do now, left solitary in a desolate world, where not a
sound broke the dreadful silence save the melancholy lapping
of the waves on the lonely shore ? They shed some natural
tears, and then wiping them away they resolved to consult
the oracle. So, pacing sadly by the yellow turbid waters of

Deucalion
lands on
Parnassus.

On the
advice of
the Delphic
oracle

the Cephisus, they repaired to the temple of the goddess.
The sacred edifice presented a melancholy spectacle, its walls
still overgrown with moss and sea-weed, its courts still deep
in slime ; and naturally no fire flamed or smouldered on the
defiled altars.   However, the goddess was fortunately at
home, and in reply to the anxious inquiries of the two suppliants she instructed them, as soon as they had quitted the
temple, to veil their heads, unloose their robes, and throw
behind their backs the bones of their great parent.   This
strange answer bewildered them, and for a long time they
remained silent.   Pyrrha was the first to find her voice, and
when at last she broke silence it was to declare respectfully
but firmly that nothing would induce her to insult her
mother's ghost by flinging her bones about.   Her husband,
more discerning, said that perhaps by their great parent the
goddess meant them to understand the earth, and that by
her bones she signified the rocks and stones embedded in the
ground.   They were not very hopeful of success, but nothing
else occurring to them to do, they decided to make the attempt.
So they carried out the instructions of the oracle to the letter,
and sure enough the stones which Deucalion threw turned
into men, and the stones which Pyrrha threw turned into
women.   Thus was the earth repeopled after the great flood.[1]

Any one who compares the laboured ingenuity of this
account of the deluge with the majestic simplicity of the
corresponding narrative in Genesis is in a position to
measure the gulf which divides great literature from its
tinsel imitation.

In his account of the catastrophe Ovid so far followed
ancient Greek tradition as to represent Deucalion and Pyrrha
landing on the peak of Parnassus.   Later Roman writers
carried the pair much further afield ; one of them landed
the voyagers on Mount Athos,[2] and another conveyed them
as far as Mount Etna.[3]

Various places in Greece, as we have seen, claimed the
honour of having been associated in a particular manner
with Deucalion and the great flood.   Among the claimants,

[1] Ovid, *Metamorphoses*, i. 125-415.   i. 9 *sq.*).
The fish sticking in the tops of the   [2] Servius, on Virgil, *Eclog.* vi. 41.
elms are borrowed from Horace (*Odes*,   [3] Hyginus, *Fabulae*, 153.

as might have been expected, were the Athenians, who, pluming themselves on the vast antiquity from which they had inhabited the land of Attica, had no mind to be left out in the cold when it came to a question of Deucalion and the deluge. They annexed him accordingly by the simple expedient of alleging that when the clouds gathered dark on Parnassus and the rain came down in torrents on Lycorea, where Deucalion reigned as king, he fled for safety to Athens, and on his arrival founded a sanctuary of Rainy Zeus, and offered thank-offerings for his escape.[1] In this brief form of the legend there is no mention of a ship, and we seem to be left to infer that the hero escaped on foot. Be that as it may, he is said to have founded the old sanctuary of Olympian Zeus and to have been buried in the city. Down to the second century of our era the local Athenian guides pointed with patriotic pride to the grave of the Greek Noah near the later and far statelier temple of Olympian Zeus, whose ruined columns, towering in solitary grandeur above the modern city, still attract the eye from far, and bear silent but eloquent witness to the glories of ancient Greece.[2]

The grave of Deucalion at Athens.

Festival of the Water-bearing at Athens in honour of the victims of the flood. Nor was this all that the guides had to show in memory of the tremendous cataclysm. Within the great precinct overshadowed by the vast temple of Olympian Zeus they led the curious traveller to a smaller precinct of Olympian Earth, where they pointed to a cleft in the ground a cubit wide. Down that cleft, they assured him, the waters of the deluge ran away, and down it every year they threw cakes of wheaten meal kneaded with honey.[3] These cakes would seem to have been soul-cakes destined for the consumption of the poor souls who perished in the great flood; for we know that a commemoration service or requiem mass was celebrated every year at Athens in their honour. It was called the Festival of the Water-bearing,[4] which suggests that charitable people

[1] *Marmor Parium*, 6 *sq.*, in *Historicorum Graecorum Fragmenta*, ed. C. Müller, i. 542.

[2] Pausanias, i. 18. 8. The tomb of Deucalion at Athens is mentioned also by Strabo, ix. 4. 2, p. 425, ed. Casaubon.

[3] Pausanias, i. 18. 7.

[4] Plutarch, *Sulla*, 14 ; *Etymologicum Magnum*, p. 774, *s.v.* ὑδροφορία ; Hesychius, *s.v.* ὑδροφόρια. The festival fell at the new moon in the month of Anthesterion (Plutarch, *l.c.*). Compare the Scholiasts on Aristophanes, *Acharnians*, 1076, and on *Frogs*, 218 ; August Mommsen, *Feste der Stadt Athen im Altertum* (Leipsic, 1898), pp. 424 *sq.*

not only threw cakes but poured water down the cleft in the
ground to slake the thirst as well as to stay the hunger of
the ghosts in the nether world.

Another place where the great flood was commemorated
by a similar ceremony was Hierapolis on the Euphrates.
There down to the second century of our era the ancient
Semitic deities were worshipped in the old way under a
transparent disguise imposed on them, like modern drapery
on ancient statues, by the nominally Greek civilization
which the conquests of Alexander had spread over the East.
Chief among these aboriginal divinities was the great Syrian
goddess Astarte, who to her Greek worshippers masqueraded
under the name of Hera. Lucian has bequeathed to us a
very valuable description of the sanctuary and the strange
rites performed in it.[1] He tells us that according to the
general opinion the sanctuary was founded by Deucalion, in
whose time the great flood took place. This gives Lucian
occasion to relate the Greek story of the deluge, which
according to him ran as follows. The present race of men,
he says, are not the first of human kind ; there was another
race which perished wholly. We are of the second breed,
which multiplied after the time of Deucalion. As for the
folk before the flood, it is said that they were exceedingly
wicked and lawless ; for they neither kept their oaths, nor
gave hospitality to strangers, nor respected suppliants, wherefore the great calamity befell them. So the fountains of the
deep were opened, and the rain descended in torrents, the
rivers swelled, and the sea spread far over the land, till there
was nothing but water, water everywhere, and all men perished. But Deucalion was the only man who, by reason of
his prudence and piety, survived and formed the link between
the first and the second race of men ; and the way in which
he was saved was this. He had a great ark, and into it he
entered with his wives and children ; and as he was entering
there came to him pigs, and horses, and lions, and serpents,
and all other land animals, all of them in pairs. He received
them all, and they did him no harm ; nay, by God's help
there was a great friendship between them, and they all sailed

[1] *De dea Syria.* The modern
scepticism as to Lucian's authorship
of this treatise rests, in my judgment,
on no firm foundation.

in one ark so long as the flood prevailed on the earth. Such, says Lucian, is the Greek story of Deucalion's deluge ; but the people of Hierapolis, he goes on, tell a marvellous thing.

The chasm that received the water of the flood.

They say that a great chasm opened in their country, and all the water of the flood ran away down it. And when that happened, Deucalion built altars and founded a holy temple of Hera beside the chasm. " I have seen the chasm," he proceeds, " and a very small one it is under the temple. Whether it was large of old and .has been reduced to its present size in course of time, I know not, but what I saw is undoubtedly small. In memory of this legend they perform

Water festival at

in memory of the flood.

the following ceremony ; twice a year water is brought from the sea to the temple. It is brought not by the priests only, but by all Syria and Arabia, ay and from beyond the Euphrates many men go to the sea, and all of them bring water. The water is poured into the chasm, and though the chasm is small yet it receives a mighty deal of water. In doing this they say that they comply with the custom which Deucalion instituted in the sanctuary for a memorial at once

Prayers offered from the tops of two obelisks at

of calamity and of mercy."[1] Moreover, at the north gate of the great temple there stood two tall columns, or rather obelisks, each about three hundred and sixty feet high ; and twice a year a man used to ascend one of them and remain for seven days in that airy situation on the top of the obelisk. Opinions differed as to why he went there, and what he did up aloft. Most people thought that at that great height he was within hail of the gods in heaven, who were near enough to hear distinctly the prayers which he offered on behalf of the whole land of Syria. Others, however, opined that he clambered up the obelisk to signify how men had ascended to the tops of mountains and of tall trees in order to escape from the waters of Deucalion's flood.[2]

Deucalion, the ark, and the dove.

In this late Greek version of the deluge legend the resemblances to the Babylonian version are sufficiently close ;

---

[1] Lucian, *De dea Syria*, 12 *sq.* In the opening words of this passage (οἱ μὲν ὦν πολλοὶ Δευκαλίωνα τὸν Σισύθεα τὸ ἱρὸν εἴσασθαι λέγουσι) the name Σισύθεα is an emendation of Buttmann's for the MS. reading Σκύθεα. See Ph. Buttmann, *Mythologus* (Berlin, 1828–1829), i. 191 *sq.* If the emenda-

tion is correct the name Sisythes may be, as scholars suppose, a variant of Xisuthrus, the name of the hero in Berosus's Greek version of the flood legend. See, above, pp. 107 *sqq.*; and H. Usener, *Die Sintflutsagen*, pp. 47 *sq.*

[2] Lucian, *De dea Syria*, 28.

and a still nearer trait is supplied by Plutarch, who says that Deucalion let loose a dove from the ark in order to judge by its return or its flight whether the storm still continued or had abated.[1] In this form the Greek legend of the great flood was unquestionably coloured, if not moulded, by Semitic influence, whether the colours and the forms were imported from Israel or from Babylon.

But Hierapolis on the Euphrates was not the only place in Western Asia which Greek tradition associated with the deluge of Deucalion. There was, we are told, a certain Nannacus, king of Phrygia, who lived before the·time of Deucalion, and, foreseeing the coming catastrophe, gathered his people into the sanctuaries, there to weep and pray. Hence "the age of Nannacus" became a proverbial expression for great antiquity or loud lamentations.[2] According to another account Nannacus or Annacus, the Phrygian, lived over three hundred years, and when his neighbours, apparently tired of the old man, inquired of the oracle how much longer he might be expected to live, they received the discouraging reply that when the patriarch died, all men would perish with him. So the Phrygians lamented bitterly, which gave rise to the old proverb about "weeping for Nannacus."[3] The Greek satyric poet Herodas puts the proverb in the mouth of a mother, who brings her brat to the schoolmaster to receive a richly deserved thrashing ; and in so doing she refers sorrowfully to the cruel necessity she was under of paying the school fees, even though she were to "weep like Nannacus."[4] When the deluge had swept away the whole race of mankind, and the earth had dried up again, Zeus commanded Prometheus and Athena to fashion images of mud, and then summoning the winds he bade them breathe into the mud images and make them live. So the place was called Iconium after the images (*eikones*) which were made there.[5] Some have thought that the patriarchal Nannacus or Annacus was no other than the Biblical Enoch or Hanoch,[6] who lived before the flood for three hundred

Phrygian legend of a flood associated w K Nannacus.

After the mankind are said to cu created afresh out Iconium.

---

[1] Plutarch, *De sollertia animalium,* 13.

[2] Suidas, *s.v.* Ναννακος ; Zenobius, *Cent.* vi. 10 ; Macarius, *Cent.* ii. 23, viii. 4 ; Apostolius, *Cent.* xv. 100.

[3] Stephanus Byzantius, *s.v.* Ἰκόνιον.

[4] Herodas, *Mimes.* iii. 10.

[5] Stephanus Byzantius, *s.v.* Ἰκόνιον.

[6] חנוך.

and sixty-five years and was then removed from the world in a mysterious fashion.[1] But against this identification it is to be said that the name Nannacus would seem to be genuine Greek, since it occurs in Greek inscriptions of the island of Cos.[2]

The story of Noah's flood represented on the Apamea Cibotos in Phrygia.
Another city of Asia Minor which appears to have boasted of its connexion with the great flood was Apamea Cibotos in Phrygia. The surname of Cibotos, which the city assumed, is the Greek word for chest or ark[3]; and on coins of the city, minted in the reigns of Severus, Macrinus, and Philip the Elder, we see the ark floating on water with two passengers in it, whose figures appear from the waist upwards; beside the ark two other human figures, one male and the other female, are represented standing; and lastly, on the top of the chest are perched two birds, one of them said to be a raven and the other a dove carrying an olive-branch. As if to remove all doubt as to the identification of the legend, the name Noe, the Greek equivalent of Noah, is inscribed on the ark. No doubt, the two human figures represent Noah and his wife twice over, first in the ark, and afterwards outside of it.[4] These coin types prove unquestionably that in the third century of our era the people of Apamea were acquainted with the Hebrew tradition of the Noachian deluge in the form in which the story is narrated in the Book of Genesis. They may easily have learned it from their Jewish fellow-citizens, who in the first century before our era were so numerous or so wealthy that on one occasion they contributed no less than a hundred pounds weight of

[1] Genesis v. 23 *sq.* The identification, first suggested by Ph. Buttman (*Mythologus*, Berlin, 1828-1829, i. 175 *sqq.*, 187 *sq.*), is accepted by E. Babelon. See E. Babelon, "La tradition Phrygienne du Déluge," *Revue de l'Histoire des Religions*, xxiii. (1891) p. 180. Buttmann even identified Aeacus, the righteous hero of Aegina, with Nannacus and Enoch.

[2] H. Collitz und F. Bechtel, *Sammlung der griechischen Dialekt-Inschriften*, iii. 1. (Gottingen, 1899), p. 342, Inscr. No. 3623 c. 51; G. Dittenberger, *Sylloge Inscriptionum Graecarum*,[2] (Leipsic, 1898-1901), ii. p.

732, No. 885.

[3] Strabo, xi. 6. 3, and 8. 13, pp. 569, 576, ed. Casaubon; Pliny, *Nat. Hist.* v. 106. Adolphe Reinach preferred to suppose that the name is a native Asiatic word assimilated by popular etymology to a Greek one. He compared Kibyra, Kibyza, Kybistra, and Kybela. See his *Noé Sangariou* (Paris, 1913), pp. 38 *sq.*

[4] Barclay V. Head, *Historia Numorum* (Oxford, 1887), p. 558; E. Babelon, "La tradition Phrygienne du Deluge," *Revue de l'Histoire des Religions*, xxiii. (1891) pp. 180 *sq.*

gold to be sent as an offering to Jerusalem.[1] Whether
at Apamea the tradition of the deluge was purely Jewish in
origin, or whether it was grafted upon an old native legend of
a great flood, is a question on which scholars are not agreed.[2]

Though the deluge associated with the name of Deucalion
was the most familiar and famous, it was not the only one
recorded by Greek tradition. Learned men, indeed, distinguished between three such great catastrophes, which had
befallen the world at different epochs. The first, we are told,
took place in the time of Ogyges, the second in the time of
Deucalion, and the third in the time of Dardanus.[3] Ogyges
or Ogygus, as the name is also spelled, is said to have founded
and reigned over Thebes in Boeotia,[4] which, according to the
learned Varro, was the oldest city in Greece, having been
built in antediluvian times before the earliest of all the
floods.[5] The connexion of Ogyges with Boeotia in general
and with Thebes in particular is further vouched for by the
name Ogygian which was bestowed on the land,[6] on the city,[7]
and on one of its gates.[8] Yet the Athenians, jealous of the
superior antiquity which this tradition assigned to their
hated rival, claimed the ancient Boeotian hero as an aboriginal

Greek
recorded
three great
the days of
Ogyges,
Deucalion,
and
Dardanus
respec-
tively. Of
the three,
the flood
associated
with t e
name of
Ogyges,
Thebes
was
p o
to be the
earliest.

---

[1] Cicero, *Pro Flacco*, 28. We know
from Josephus (*Antiquit. Jud.* xii.
3. 4) that Antiochus the Great issued
orders for transplanting two thousand
Jewish families from Mesopotamia and
Babylonia to Lydia and Phrygia, and
for settling them there as colonists on
very liberal terms. This may well have
been the origin of the Jewish settlement
at Apamea, as E. Babelon has pointed
out ("La tradition Phrygienne du
Déluge," *Revue de l'Histoire de la
Religion*, xxiii. (1891) pp. 177 *sq.*).

[2] The view that the flood legend of
Apamea was purely Jewish, without
any basis of local tradition, is maintained by E. Babelon ("La tradition
Phrygienne du Deluge," *Revue de
l'Histoire des Religions*, xxiii. (1891)
pp. 174-183). On the other hand the
composite character of the Apamean
legend is maintained by H. Usener
(*Die Sintflutsagen*, pp. 48-50) and
advocated, with a great array of learning, by Adolphe Reinach in his treatise
Noé Sangariou (Paris, 1913). I confess that the arguments adduced in

favour of an aboriginal flood legend
at Apamea appear to me to carry little
weight, resting rather on a series of
doubtful combinations than on any
solid evidence.

[3] Nonnus, *Dionys.* iii. 202-219 ;
Scholiast on Plato, *Timaeus*, p. 22 A.
That the deluge of Ogyges was prior
to the deluge of Deucalion is affirmed
also by Augustine (*De civitate Dei*,
xviii. 8) and Servius (on Virgil, *Eclog.*
vi. 41), neither of whom, however,
mentions the deluge of Dardanus.

[4] Pausanias, ix. 5. 1 ; Servius, on
Virgil, *Eclog.* vi. 41, " *sub Ogyge,
rege Thebanorum.*"

[5] Varro, *Rerum Rusticarum*, iii. 1.

[6] Strabo, ix. 2. 18, p. 407, ed.
Casaubon ; Stephanus Byzantius, *s.v.*
Βοιωτία.

[7] Pausanias, ix. 5. 1 ; Apollonius
Rhodius, *Argonaut.* iii. 1178 ; Fes-
tus, *De verborum significatione*, *s.v.*
"Ogygia," p. 179, ed. C. O. Müller.

[8] Euripides, *Phoenissae*, 1113 ; Pausanias, ix. 8. 5 ; Scholiast on Apollonius Rhodius, *Argonaut.* iii. 1178.

of their country ;[1] one tradition describes Ogyges as a king of Attica,[2] and another represents him as the founder and king of Eleusis.[3]   So great was the devastation wrought in Attica by the flood that the country remained without kings from the time of Ogyges down to the reign of Cecrops.[4]   If we may trust the description of a rhetorical poet, the whole earth was submerged by the deluge, even the lofty peaks of Thessaly were covered, and the snowy top of Parnassus itself

was lashed by the snowy billows.[5]   With regard to the date of the catastrophe, some writers of antiquity profess to give us more or less exact information.   The learned Roman scholar Varro tells us that the Boeotian Thebes was built about two thousand one hundred years before the time when he was writing, which was in or about the year 36 B.C. ; and as the deluge, according to him, took place in the lifetime of Ogyges but after he had founded Thebes, we infer that in Varro's opinion the great flood occurred in or soon after the year 2136 B.C.[6]   Still more precise is the statement of Julius

Africanus, a Christian author who drew up a chronicle of the world from the Creation down to the year 221 A.D.   He affirms that the deluge of Ogyges happened just one thousand and twenty years before the first Olympiad, from which the Greeks dated their exact reckoning ; and as the first Olympiad fell in the year 776 B.C., we arrive at the year 1796 B.C. as the date to which the Christian chronicler referred the great Ogygian flood.   It happened, he tells

---

[1] Africanus, quoted by Eusebius, *Praeparatio Evangelica*, x. 10. 4.

[2] Scholiast on Plato, *Timaeus*, p. 22 A.

[3] Africanus, quoted by Eusebius, *Praeparatio Evangelica*, x. 10. 7 ; Eusebius, *Chronic.*, ed. A. Schoene, vol. ii. p. 17 ; Isidorus Hispalensis, *Origines*, xiii. 22. 3.   Some said that the hero Eleusis, from whom the city took its name, was a son of Ogygus (Pausanias, i. 38. 7).

[4] Africanus, quoted by Eusebius, *Praeparatio Evangelica*, x. 10. 9. Among the authorities cited by Africanus (in Eusebius, *op. cit.* x. 10. 5) are the Attic historians Hellanicus and Philochorus.

[5] Nonnus, *Dionys.* iii. 206-208.

[6] Varro, *Rerum Rusticarum*, iii. 1. 3.   In his preface to this treatise on agriculture (bk. i. ch. i.) Varro indicates that it was written in his eightieth year ; and as he was born in 116 B.C., he must have been composing the work in question in or about 36 B.C. From Arnobius (*Adversus Gentes*, v. 8) we learn that Varro reckoned less than two thousand years from Deucalion's flood to the consulship of Hirtius and Pansa in 43 B.C., which seems to show that he dated Deucalion's flood fully a hundred years later than that of Ogyges. Compare the commentary of Meursius on Varro, printed in J. G. Schneider's edition of the *Scriptores Rei Rusticae Veteres Latini* (Leipsic, 1794-1796), vol. i. part 2, p. 491.

us, in the reign of Phoroneus, king of Argos. He adds
for our further information that Ogyges, who survived the
deluge to which he gave his name, was a contemporary
of Moses and flourished about the time when that great
prophet led the children of Israel out of Egypt ; and he
clinches his chain of evidence by observing that at a time
when God was visiting the land of Egypt with hailstorms
and other plagues, it was perfectly natural that distant parts
of the earth should simultaneously feel the effects of the
divine anger, and in particular it was just and right that
Attica should smart beneath the rod, since according to some
people, including the historian Theopompus, the Athenians
were in fact colonists from Egypt and therefore shared the
guilt of the mother-country.[1] According to the Church Eusebius
historian Eusebius, the great flood in the time of Ogyges dates of
occurred about two thousand two hundred years after the the floods
Noachian deluge and two hundred and fifty years before the and
similar catastrophe in the days of Deucalion.[2] It would seem Deucalion.
indeed to have been a point of honour with the early
Christians to claim for the flood recorded in their sacred
books an antiquity far more venerable than that of any
flood described in mere profane writings. We have seen
that Julius Africanus depresses Ogyges from the age of
Noah to that of Moses ; and Isidore, the learned bishop of
Seville at the beginning of ,the seventh century, heads his
list of floods with the Noachian deluge, while the second
and third places in order of time are assigned to the floods
of Ogyges and Deucalion respectively ; according to him,
Ogyges was a contemporary of the patriarch Jacob, while
Deucalion lived in the days of Moses. The bishop was,
so far as I am aware, the first of many writers who have
appealed to fossil shells imbedded in remote mountains as
witnesses to the truth of the Noachian tradition.[2]

---

[1] Julius Africanus, quoted by Eusebius, *Praeparatio Evangelica*, x. 10.
That the deluge of Ogyges happened
in the reign of Phoroneus, king of
Argos, is mentioned also by the Christian writers Tatian (*Oratio ad Graecos*,
p. 150, ed. J. C. T. Otto) and Clement
of Alexandria (*Strom.* i. 21 § 102, p.
379, ed. Potter). Compare H. Fynes

Clynton, *Fasti Hellenici*, i. (Oxford,
1834) pp. 5-8.
[2] Eusebius, *Chronic.*, ed. A. Schoene,
vol. i. col. 71.
[3] Isidorus Hispalensis, *Origines*,
xiii. 22, "*cujus indicium hactenus
videmus in lapidibus, quos in remotis
montibus conchis et ostreis concretos, saepe
etiam cavatos aquis visere solemus*"

The story
of Ogyges
perhaps
if a e
in the
annual
vicissitudes
of the
Copaic
Lake.

Yearly

the Copaic
Lake in
n ern
times.

If Ogyges was originally, as seems probable, a Boeotian rather than an Attic hero, the story of the deluge in his time may well have been suggested by the vicissitudes of the Copaic Lake which formerly occupied a large part of Central Boeotia.[1] For, having no outlet above ground, the lake depended for its drainage entirely on subterranean passages or chasms which the water had hollowed out for itself in the course of ages through the limestone rock, and according as these passages were clogged or cleared the level of the lake rose or fell. In no lake, perhaps, have the annual changes been more regular and marked than in the Copaic ; for while in winter it was a reedy mere, the haunt of thousands of wild fowl, in summer it was a more or less marshy plain, where cattle browsed and crops were sown and reaped. So well recognized were the vicissitudes of the seasons that places on the bank of the lake such as Orchomenus, Lebadea, and Copae, had summer roads and winter roads by which they communicated with each other, the winter roads following the sides of the hills, while the summer roads struck across the plain. With the setting in of the heavy autumnal rains in November the lake began to rise and reached its greatest depth in February or March, by which time the mouths of the emissories were completely submerged and betrayed their existence only by swirls on the surface of the mere. Yet even then the lake presented to the eye anything but an unbroken sheet of water. Viewed from a height, such as the acropolis of Orchomenus, it appeared as an immense fen, of a vivid green colour, stretching away for miles and miles, overgrown with sedge, reeds, and canes, through which the river Cephisus or Melas might be seen sluggishly oozing, while here and there a gleam of sunlit water, especially towards the north-east corner of the mere, directed the eye to what looked like ponds in the vast green swamp. Bare grey mountains on the north and east, and the beautiful wooded slopes of Helicon on the south, bounded the fen. In spring the water began to sink. Isolated brown patches, where no reeds grew, were the first to show as islands in the mere ; and as the season advanced they expanded more and more till they met. By the middle of summer great

[1] Ed. Meyer, *Geschichte des Alterthums*, ii. (Stuttgart, 1896) p. 194.

stretches, especially in the middle and at the edges, were bare. In the higher parts the fat alluvial soil left by the retiring waters was sown by the peasants and produced crops of corn, rice, and cotton ; while the lower parts, overgrown by rank grass and weeds, were grazed by herds of cattle and swine. In the deepest places of all, the water often stagnated the whole summer, though there were years when it retreated even from these, leaving behind it only a bog or perhaps a stretch of white clayey soil, perfectly dry, which the summer heat seamed with a network of minute cracks and fissures. By the end of August the greater part of the basin was generally dry, though the water did not reach its lowest point till October. At that time what had lately been a fen was only a great brown expanse, broken here and there by a patch of green marsh, where reeds and other water-plants grew. In November the lake began to fill again fast.

Such was the ordinary annual cycle of changes in the Copaic Lake in modern times, and we have no reason to suppose that it was essentially different in antiquity. But at all times the water of the lake has been liable to be raised above or depressed below its customary level by unusually heavy or scanty rainfall in winter or by the accidental clogging or opening of the chasms. As we read in ancient authors of drowned cities on the margin of the lake,[1] so a modern traveller tells of villagers forced to flee before the rising flood, and of vineyards and corn-fields seen under water.[2] One such inundation, more extensive and destructive than any of its predecessors, may have been associated ever after with the name of Ogyges.

Among the dead cities whose ruins are scattered in and around the wide plain that was once the Copaic Lake, none is more remarkable or excites our curiosity more keenly than one which bears the modern name of Goulas or

An extensive inundation of Copaic Lake may have given rise the of the flood of Ogyges.

The ruins o nd palace of Gla in a and now stranded the Copaic Lake.

[1] Strabo, ix. 2. 18, p. 407, ed. Casaubon ; Pausanias, ix. 24. 2.

[2] On the Copaic Lake in antiquity see the excellent account in Strabo, ix. 2. 16-18, pp. 406 *sq.* Compare Pausanias, ix. 24. 1 *sq.* For modern accounts of it see C. Neumann und J. Partsch, *Physikalische Geographie von Griechenland* (Breslau, 1885), pp. 244-

247 ; and especially A. Philippson, "Der Kopais-See in Griechenland und seine Umgebung," *Zeitschrift der Gesellschaft für Erdkunde zu Berlin,* xxix. (1894) pp. 1-90. I have allowed myself to quote from the description of the lake in my commentary on Pausanias (vol. v. pp. 110 *sqq*), where I have cited the modern literature on the subject.

Gla.   Its ancient name and history are alike unknown : even legend is silent on the subject.   The extensive remains occupy the broad summit of a low rocky hill or tableland which rises abruptly on all sides from the dead flat of the surrounding country.   When the lake was full, the place must have been an island, divided by about a mile of shallow and weedy water from the nearest point in the line of cliffs which formed the eastern shore of the lake.   A fortification wall, solidly built of roughly squared blocks of stone, encircles the whole edge of the tableland, and is intersected by four gates flanked by towers of massive masonry.   Within the fortress are the ruins of other structures, including the remains of a great palace constructed in the style, though not on the plan, of the prehistoric palaces of Mycenae and Tiryns.   The fortress and palace of Gla would seem to have been erected in the Mycenaean age by a people akin in civilization, if not in race, to the builders of Tiryns and Mycenae, though less skilled in the science of military engineering ; for the walls do not exhibit the enormous stones of Tiryns, and the gates are arranged on a plan far less formidable to an assailant than the gates of the two Argive citadels.   The scanty remains of pottery and other domestic furniture on the plateau appear to indicate that it was occupied only for a short time, and the traces of fire on the palace point to the conclusion that its end was sudden and violent.   Everything within the place bears the imprint of a single plan and a single period : there is no trace of an earlier or a later settle-ment.   Created at a blow, it would seem to have perished at a blow and never to have been inhabited again.   In its solitude and silence, remote from all human habitations, looking out from its grey old walls over the vast Copaic plain to the distant mountains which bound the horizon on all sides, this mysterious fortress is certainly one of the most impressive sights in Greece.[1]

Was Gla the city of Ogyges before he founded Thebes?   Can it be that this ancient and forgotten town, once lapped on all sides by the waters of the Copaic Lake, was the home of the legendary Ogyges, and that he forsook it,

[1] For a fuller account of the place, which I have described from personal observation, I may refer the reader to   my commentary on Pausanias (vol. v. pp. 120 *sqq.*).

perhaps in consequence of an inundation, to migrate to the higher and drier site which was afterwards known as Thebes? The hypothesis would go some way to explain the legends which gathered round his memory; but it is no more than a simple guess, and as such I venture to hazard it.

The theory which would explain the great flood of Ogyges by an extraordinary inundation of the Copaic Lake, is to some extent supported by an Arcadian parallel. We have seen that in Greek legend the third great deluge was associated with the name of Dardanus. Now according to one account, Dardanus at first reigned as a king in Arcadia, but was driven out of the country by a great flood, which submerged the lowlands and rendered them for a long time unfit for cultivation. The inhabitants retreated to the mountains, and for a while made shift to live as best they might on such food as they could procure; but at last, concluding that the land left by the water was not sufficient to support them all, they resolved to part; some of them remained in the country with Dimas, son of Dardanus, for their king; while the rest emigrated under the leadership of Dardanus himself to the island of Samothrace.[1] According to a Greek tradition, which the Roman Varro accepted, the birthplace of Dardanus was Pheneus in north Arcadia.[2] The place is highly significant, for, if we except the Copaic area, no valley in Greece is known to have been from antiquity subject to inundations on so vast a scale and for such long periods as the valley of Pheneus.[3] The natural conditions in the two regions are substantially alike. Both are basins in a limestone country without any outflow above ground: both receive the rain water which pours into them from the surrounding mountains: both are drained by subterranean channels which the water has worn or which earthquakes have opened through the rock; and whenever these outlets are silted up or otherwise closed, what at other times is a plain becomes converted for the time being into a lake. But with these substantial resemblances are combined some striking differences between the two landscapes. For while

The third great deluge was associated with the name of Dardanus, who is said to have been driven by it from and to have fled to Samothrace.

Dardanus is said to have been born at Pheneus, which, lying in a basin encircled by mountains, has always been subject to inundations.

---

[1] Dionysius Halicarnasensis, *Antiquitates Romanae*, i. 61.

[2] Servius, on Virgil, *Aen.* iii. 167.

[3] C. Neumann und J. Partsch, *Physikalische Geographie von Griechenland* (Breslau, 1885), p. 252.

the Copaic basin is a vast stretch of level ground little above sea-level and bounded only by low cliffs or gentle slopes, the basin of Pheneus is a narrow upland valley closely shut in on every side by steep frowning mountains, their upper slopes clothed with dark pine woods and their lofty summits capped with snow for many months of the year. The river which drains the basin through an underground channel is the Ladon, the most romantically beautiful of all the rivers of Greece. Milton's fancy dwelt on "sanded Ladon's lilied banks"; even the prosaic Pausanias exclaimed that there was no fairer river either in Greece or in foreign lands;[1] and among the memories which I brought back from Greece I recall none with more delight than those of the days I spent in tracing the river from its birthplace in the lovely lake, first to its springs on the far side of the mountain, and then down the deep wooded gorge through which it hurries, brawling and tumbling over rocks in sheets of greenish-white foam, to join the sacred Alpheus. Now the passage by which the Ladon makes its way underground from the valley of Pheneus has been from time to time blocked by an earthquake, with the result that the river has ceased to flow. When I was at the springs of the Ladon in 1895, I learned from a peasant on the spot that three years before, after a violent shock of earthquake, the water ceased to run for three hours, the chasm at the bottom of the pool was exposed, and fish were seen lying on the dry ground. After three hours the spring began to flow a little, and three days later there was a loud explosion, and the water burst forth in immense volume. Similar stoppages of the river have been reported both in ancient and modern times; and whenever the obstruction has been permanent, the valley of Pheneus has been occupied by a lake varying in extent and depth with the more or less complete stoppage of the subterranean outlet. According to Pliny there had been down to his day five changes in the condition of the valley from wet to dry and from dry to wet, all of them caused by earthquakes.[2] In Plutarch's time the flood rose so high that the whole valley was under water, which pious folk attributed to the somewhat belated wrath of Apollo at

Alternations of the valley of Pheneus between wet and dry in ancient modern times.

---

[1] Pausanias, viii. 25. 13.   [2] Pliny, *Nat. Hist.* xxxi. 54.

Hercules, who had stolen the god's prophetic tripod from Delphi and carried it off to Pheneus about a thousand years before.[1]   However, later in the same century the waters had again subsided, for the Greek traveller Pausanias found the bottom of the valley to be dry land, and knew of the former existence of the lake only by tradition.[2]   At the beginning of the nineteenth century the basin was a swampy plain, for the most part covered with fields of wheat or barley.   But shortly after the expulsion of the Turks, through neglect of the precautions which the Turkish governor had taken to keep the mouth of the subterranean outlet open, the channel became blocked, the water, no longer able to escape, rose in its bed, and by 1830 it formed a deep lake about five miles long by five miles wide.   And a broad lake of greenish-blue water it still was when I saw it in the autumn of 1895, with the pine-clad mountains descending steeply in rocky declivities or sheer precipices to the water's edge, except for a stretch of level ground on the north, where the luxuriant green of vine-yards and maize-fields contrasted pleasingly with the blue of the lake and the sombre green of the pines.   The whole scene presented rather the aspect of a Swiss than of a Greek landscape.   A few years later and the scene was changed. Looking down into the valley from a pass on a July after-noon, a more recent traveller beheld, instead of an expanse of sea-blue water, a blaze of golden corn with here and there a white point of light showing where a fustanella'd reaper was at his peaceful toil.   The lake had disappeared, perhaps for ever ; for we are told that measures have now been taken to keep the subterranean outlets permanently open, and so to preserve for the corn the ground which has been won from the water.[3]

A permanent mark of the height to which the lake of Pheneus attained in former days and at which, to all appear-ance, it must have stood for many ages, is engraved on the sides of the mountains which enclose the basin.   It is a

[1] Plutarch, *De sera numinis vin-dicta*, 12.

[2] Pausanias, viii. 14. 1-3.

[3] C. Neumann und J. Partsch, *Physikalische Geographie von Griechen-land*, pp. 252 sq. ; A. Philippson, *Der Peloponnes* (Berlin, 1892), pp. 144 - 146 ; J. ff. Baker - Penoyre, " Pheneus and the Pheneatiké," *Journal of Hellenic Studies*, xxii. (1902) pp. 228 - 240.   For further details I may refer the reader to my commentary on Pausanias (vol. iv. pp. 230 sqq., 262 sq., 287 sqq.).

sharply drawn line running round the contour of the mountains
at a uniform level of not less than a hundred and fifty feet
above the bottom of the valley. The trees and shrubs
extend down the steep slopes to this line and there stop
abruptly. Below the line the rock is of a light-yellow colour
and almost bare of vegetation ; above the line the rock is of
a much darker colour. The attention of travellers has been
drawn to this conspicuous mark from antiquity to the present day. The ancient traveller Pausanias noticed it in the
second century of our era, and he took it to indicate the line
to which the lake rose at the time of its highest flood, when
the city of Pheneus was submerged.[1] This interpretation has
been questioned by some modern writers, but there seems
to be little real doubt that the author of the oldest extant
guide-book to Greece was substantially right ; except that
the extremely sharp definition of the line and its permanence
for probably much more than two thousand years appear to
point to a long-continued persistence of the lake at this high
level rather than to a mere sudden and temporary rise in a
time of inundation. " It is evident," says the judicious
traveller Dodwell, " that a temporary inundation could not
effect so striking a difference in the superficies of the rock,
the colour of which must have been changed from that of
the upper parts by the concreting deposit of many ages."[2]

These inun-
dations of
the valley
of Pheneus
lend
probability
to the story
of the
flood of
Dardanus.

In a valley which has thus suffered so many alternations
between wet and dry, between a broad lake of sea-blue water

[1] Pausanias, viii. 14. 1.

[2] E. Dodwell, *Classical and Topographical Tour through Greece* (London,
1819), ii. 436. This is the view also
of the latest writer on the subject, Mr.
Baker - Penoyre. See his article,
"Pheneus and the Pheneatiké," *Journal of Hellenic Studies*, xxii. (1902)
pp. 231 *sqq.* The German geologist,
Mr. A. Philippson, took the line to
mark the level to which the lake rose
in 1830 (*Der Peloponnes*, p. 146).
But as the lake suddenly fell again in
1834, it seems hardly possible that a
flood lasting for only a few years should
have scored its record so deep on the
sides of the mountains. As to the
water-line see further Sir William Gell,
Narrative of a Journey in the Morea
(London, 1823), p. 374 ; W. M.

Leake, *Travels in the Morea* (London,
1830), iii. 147 *sqq.* ; E. Pouillon
Boblaye, *Recherches Géographiques sur
les ruines de la Morée* (Paris, 1835),
p. 153 note [2]; E. Curtius, *Peloponnesos*
(Gotha, 1851), ii. 188 *sq.* ; W. G.
Clark, *Peloponnesus* (London, 1858),
pp. 317 *sq.* The height of the water-
line has been variously estimated.
Dodwell and Curtius put it at several
hundreds of feet ; W. G. Clark guessed
that it might be about fifty feet above
the level of the lake when he saw it.
I roughly estimated the line by the eye
at 200 or 300 feet above the lake, the
level of which was probably lower than
at the time of W. G. Clark's visit.
Mr. Baker-Penoyre's estimate of the
height is 150 feet above the bottom of
the valley.

and broad acres of yellow corn, the traditions of great floods cannot be lightly dismissed ; on the contrary everything combines to confirm their probability.   The story, therefore, that Dardanus, a native of Pheneus, was compelled to emigrate by a great inundation which swamped the lowlands, drowned the fields, and drove the inhabitants to the upper slopes of the mountains, may well rest on a solid foundation of fact.   And the same may be true of the flood recorded by Pausanias, which rose and submerged the ancient city of Pheneus at the northern end of the lake.[1]

From his home in the highlands of Arcadia, the emigrant Dardanus is said to have made his way to the island of Samothrace.[2]   According to one account, he floated thither on a raft ;[3] but according to another version of the legend, the great flood overtook him, not in Arcadia, but in Samothrace, and he escaped on an inflated skin, drifting on the face of the waters till he landed on Mount Ida, where he founded Dardania or Troy.[4]   Certainly, the natives of Samothrace, who were great sticklers for their antiquity, claimed to have had a deluge of their own before any other nation on earth.   They said that the sea rose and covered a great part of the flat land in their island, and that the survivors retreated to the lofty mountains which still render Samothrace one of the most conspicuous features in the northern Aegean and are plainly visible in clear weather from Troy.[5]   As the sea still pursued them in their retreat, they prayed to the gods to deliver them, and on being saved they set up landmarks of their salvation all round the island and built altars on which they continued to sacrifice down to later ages. And many centuries after the great flood fishermen still occasionally drew up in their nets the stone capitals of columns, which told of cities drowned in the depths of the

According to one account the great flood Dardanus in Samothrace whence he escaped to Ida.

Samothracian tradition of a great flood caused by the bursting of barriers which till then divided the Black Sea from the Mediterranean.

[1] Pausanias, viii. 14. 1.

[2] Dionysius Halicarnasensis, *Antiquitates Romanae*, i. 61. 3.

[3] Scholiast on Plato, *Timaeus*, p. 22 A.

[4] Lycophron, *Cassandra*, 72 *sqq.*, with the scholia of Tzetzes ; Scholia on Homer, *Iliad*, xx. 215 (p. 558, ed. Im Bekker, Berlin, 1825).

[5] W. Smith, *Dictionary of Greek*

and Roman Geography, ii. 901, *s.v.* "Samothrace."   Seen from the neighbouring island of Imbros, the mighty mass of Samothrace rises from the sea like the side of a Norwegian mountain, which indeed it closely resembles when the clouds and mists hang low on it in winter.   See Alan G. Ogilvie, "Notes on the Geography of Imbros," *The Geographical Journal*, xlviii. (1916) p. 144.

sea. The causes which the Samothracians alleged for the inundation were very remarkable. The catastrophe happened, according to them, not through a heavy fall of rain, but through a sudden and extraordinary rising of the sea occasioned by the bursting of the barriers which till then had divided the Black Sea from the Mediterranean. At that time the enormous volume of water dammed up behind these barriers broke bounds, and cleaving for itself a passage through the opposing land created the straits which are now known as the Bosphorus and the Dardanelles, through which the waters of the Black Sea have ever since flowed into the Mediterranean. When the tremendous torrent first rushed through the new opening in the dam, it washed over a great part of the coast of Asia, as well as the flat lands of Samothrace.[1]

The Samothracian tradition partially confirmed by geology, which proves that the Black Sea was once really separated from the Mediterranean by a barrier of land.

Now this Samothracian tradition is to some extent confirmed by modern geology. "At no very distant period," we are told, "the land of Asia Minor was continuous with that of Europe, across the present site of the Bosphorus, forming a barrier several hundred feet high, which dammed up the waters of the Black Sea. A vast extent of eastern Europe and of western central Asia thus became a huge reservoir, the lowest part of the lip of which was probably situated somewhat more than 200 feet above the sea-level, along the present southern watershed of the Obi, which flows into the Arctic Ocean. Into this basin, the largest rivers of Europe, such as the Danube and the Volga, and what were then great rivers of Asia, the Oxus and Jaxartes, with all the intermediate affluents, poured their waters. In addition, it received the overflow of Lake Balkash, then much larger; and, probably, that of the inland sea of Mongolia. At that time, the level of the Sea of Aral stood at least 60 feet higher than it does at present. Instead of the separate Black, Caspian, and Aral seas, there was one vast Ponto-Aralian Mediterranean, which must have been prolonged into arms and fiords along the lower valleys of the Danube, and the Volga (in the course of which Caspian shells are now

---

[1] Diodorus Siculus, v. 47. Among the proofs of the great antiquity of the Samothracians, according to this his- torian, was their archaic dialect, of which many examples survived in their religious ritual down to his time.

found as far as the Kuma), the Ural, and the other affluent rivers—while it seems to have sent its overflow, northward, through the present basin of the Obi." [1]   This enormous reservoir or vast inland sea, bounded and held up by a high natural dam joining Asia Minor to the Balkan Peninsula, appears to have existed down to the Pleistocene period ; and the erosion of the Dardanelles, by which the pent-up waters at last found their way into the Mediterranean, is believed to have taken place towards the end of the Pleistocene period or later. [2]   But man is now known for certain to have inhabited Europe in the Pleistocene period ; some hold that he inhabited it in the Pliocene or even the Miocene period. [3]   Hence it seems possible that the inhabitants of Eastern Europe should have preserved a traditional memory of the vast inland Ponto-Aralian sea and of its partial desiccation through the piercing of the dam which divided it from the Mediterranean, in other words, through the opening of the Bosphorus and the Dardanelles.   If that were so, the Samothracian tradition

[1] T. H. Huxley, "The Aryan Question," *Collected Essays*, vol. vii. (London, 1906) pp. 300 *sq.*

[2] T. H. Huxley, "Hasisadra's Adventure," *Collected Essays*, vol. iv. (London, 1911) pp. 275, 276.

[3] Sir Charles Lyell, *The Student's Elements of Geology*, Third Edition (London, 1878), pp. 128 *sqq.* ; A. de Quatrefages, *The Human Species* (London, 1879), pp. 142-153 ; Sir John Lubbock (Lord Avebury), *Prehistoric Times*, Fifth Edition (London and Edinburgh, 1890), pp. 422 *sqq.* ; W. J. Sollas, *Ancient Hunters* (London, 1915), pp. 59-86 ; Arthur Keith, *The Antiquity of Man* (London, 1915), pp. 509-511, H. F. Osborn, *Men of the Old Stone Age* (London, 1916), p. 60. Of these writers, Professors Keith and Osborn definitely pronounce in favour of man's existence in the Pliocene period ; indeed Professor Keith admits the possibility of a still greater antiquity of the human species on earth. He says (p. 511), "The human origin of eoliths is still being called in question, but the more these shaped flints of Pliocene date are investigated and discussed, the greater becomes the number of those who regard them as the work of the hands and brain of Pliocene man. It is also maintained that flints, similar in shape and chipping, have been discovered in deposits of Miocene and even of Oligocene age. If it be proved that such are of human origin, then we must extend still further the period covered by the antiquity of man. There is not a single fact known to me which makes the existence of a human form in the Miocene period an impossibility." Professor Sollas sums up his conclusion (p. 85) as follows : "We have seen that the order of succession in time of fossil remains of the Mammalia and especially of apes and men suggests that man, in the strictest sense, *Homo Sapiens*, is a creature of Pleistocene time ; as we look backwards into the past we lose sight of him before the close of that age and encounter in his place forms specifically and even generically distinct ; that other species of the human family might have already come into existence in the Pliocene epoch seems possible, but scarcely in the Miocene, and still less in the Oligocene epoch."

might be allowed to contain a large element of historical truth in regard to the causes assigned for the catastrophe.

On the other hand geology seems to lend no support to the tradition of the catastrophe itself. For the evidence tends to prove that the strait of the Dardanelles was not opened suddenly, like the bursting of a dam, either by the pressure of the water or the shock of an earthquake, but that on the contrary it was created gradually by a slow process of erosion which must have lasted for many centuries or even thousands of years; for the strait "is bounded by undisturbed Pleistocene strata forty feet thick, through which, to all appearance, the present passage has been quietly cut."[1] Thus the lowering of the level of the Ponto-Aralian sea to that of the Mediterranean can hardly have been sudden and catastrophic, accompanied by a vast inundation of the Asiatic and European coasts; more probably it was effected so slowly and gradually that the total amount accomplished even in a generation would be imperceptible to ordinary observers or even to close observers unprovided with instruments of pre-

cision. Hence, instead of assuming that Samothracian tradition preserved a real memory of a widespread inundation consequent on the opening of the Dardanelles, it seems safer to suppose that this story of a great flood is nothing but the guess of some early philosopher, who rightly divined the origin of the straits without being able to picture to himself the extreme slowness of the process by which nature had excavated them. As a matter of fact, the eminent physical philosopher Strato, who succeeded Theophrastus as head of the Peripatetic school in 287 B.C., actually maintained this view on purely theoretical grounds, not alleging it as a tradition which had been handed down from antiquity, but arguing in its favour from his observations of the natural features of the Black Sea. He pointed to the vast quantities of mud annually washed down by great rivers into the Euxine, and he inferred that but for the outlet of the Bosphorus the basin of that sea would in time be silted up. Further, he conjectured that in former times the same rivers had forced for themselves a passage through the Bosphorus, allowing

---

[1] T. H. Huxley, "Hasisadra's Adventure," *Collected Essays*, vol. iv. (London, 1911) p. 281.

their collected waters to escape first to the Propontis, and then from it through the Dardanelles to the Mediterranean. Similarly he thought that the Mediterranean had been of old an inland sea, and that its junction with the Atlantic was effected by the dammed up water cutting for itself an opening through the Straits of Gibraltar.[1] Accordingly we may conclude that the cause which the Samothracians alleged for the great flood was derived from an ingenious speculation rather than from an ancient tradition.

There are some grounds for thinking that the flood story which the Greeks associated with the names of Deucalion and Pyrrha may in like manner have been, not so much a reminiscence of a real event, as an inference founded on the observation of certain physical facts. We have seen that in one account the mountains of Thessaly are said to have been parted by the deluge in Deucalion's time, and that in another account the ark, with Deucalion in it, is reported to have drifted to Mount Othrys in Thessaly. These references seem to indicate Thessaly as the original seat of the legend; and the indication is greatly strengthened by the view which the ancients took of the causes that had moulded the natural features of the country. Thus Herodotus relates a tradition that in ancient times Thessaly was a great lake or inland sea, shut in on all sides by the lofty mountains of Ossa and Pelion, Olympus, Pindus, and Othrys, through which there was as yet no opening to allow the pent-up waters of the rivers to escape. Afterwards, according to the Thessalians, the sea-god Poseidon, who causes earthquakes, made an outlet for the lake through the mountains, by cleaving the narrow gorge of Tempe, through which the river Peneus has ever since drained the Thessalian plain. The pious historian intimates his belief in the truth of this local tradition. "Whoever believes," says he, "that Poseidon shakes the earth, and that chasms caused by earthquakes are his handiwork, would say, on seeing the gorge of the Peneus, that Poseidon had made it. For the separation of the mountains, it seems to me, is certainly the effect of an earth-

---

[1] Strabo, i. 3. 4, pp. 49-50, ed. Casaubon. Compare Sir Charles Lyell, *Principles of Geology*[12] (London, 1875), i. 24; E. H. Bunbury, *History of Ancient Geography*[2] (London, 1883), i. 658 *sq.*

quake."[1] The view of the father of history was substantially accepted by later writers of antiquity,[2] though one of them would attribute the creation of the gorge and the drainage of the lake to the hero Hercules, among whose beneficent labours for the good of mankind the construction of water-works on a gigantic scale was commonly reckoned.[3] More cautious or more philosophical authors contented themselves with referring the origin of the defile to a simple earthquake, without expressing any opinion as to the god or hero who may have set the tremendous disturbance in motion.[4]

The g n the cenery of Tempe naturally suggest the idea that the gorge had originated in some great ca a t oh ; whereas g shows that like the Dar- e e was created by the slow erosion of water.

Yet we need not wonder that popular opinion in this matter should incline to the theory of divine or heroic agency, for in truth the natural features of the pass of Tempe are well fitted to impress the mind with a religious awe, with a sense of vast primordial forces which, by the gigantic scale of their operations, present an overwhelming contrast to the puny labours of man. The traveller who descends at morning into the deep gorge from the west, may see, far above him, the snows of Olympus flushed with a golden glow under the beams of the rising sun, but as he pursues the path downwards the summits of the mountains disappear from view, and he is confronted on either hand only by a stupendous wall of mighty precipices shooting up in prodigious grandeur and approaching each other in some places so near that they almost seem to meet, barely leaving room for the road and river at their foot, and for a strip of blue sky overhead. The cliffs on the side of Olympus, which the traveller has constantly before his eyes, since the road runs on the south or right bank of the river, are indeed the most magnificent and striking in Greece, and in rainy weather they are rendered still more impressive by the waterfalls that pour down their sides to swell the smooth and steady current of the stream. The grandeur of the scenery culminates about the middle of the pass, where an enormous crag rears its colossal form high in air, its soaring summit crowned with the ruins of a Roman castle. Yet the sublimity of the landscape is tempered and softened by the richness and verdure of the vegetation. In

[1] Herodotus, vii. 129.
[2] Philostratus, *Imag.* ii. 14.
[3] Diodorus Siculus, iv. 18. 6.

[4] Strabo, ix. 5. 2, p. 430, ed. Casaubon ; Seneca, *Natur. Quaest.* vi. 25. 2.

some parts of the defile the cliffs recede sufficiently to leave
little grassy flats at their foot, where thickets of evergreens
—the laurel, the myrtle, the wild olive, the arbutus, the agnus
castus—are festooned with wild vines and ivy, and variegated
with the crimson bloom of the oleander and the yellow gold
of the jasmine and laburnum, while the air is perfumed by
the luscious odours of masses of aromatic plants and flowers.
Even in the narrowest places the river bank is overshadowed
by spreading plane-trees, which stretch their roots and dip
their pendent boughs into the stream, their dense foliage
forming so thick a screen as almost to shut out the sun.
The scarred and fissured fronts of the huge cliffs themselves
are tufted with dwarf oaks and shrubs, wherever these can
find a footing, their verdure contrasting vividly with the bare
white face of the limestone rock ; while breaks here and there
in the mountain wall open up vistas of forests of great oaks
and dark firs mantling the steep declivities.   The overarching
shade and soft luxuriance of the vegetation strike the traveller
all the more by contrast if he comes to the glen in hot
summer weather after toiling through the dusty, sultry plains
of Thessaly, without a tree to protect him from the fierce
rays of the southern sun, without a breeze to cool his brow,
and with little variety of hill and dale to relieve the dull
monotony of the landscape.[1]   No wonder that speculation
should have early busied itself with the origin of this grand
and beautiful ravine, and that primitive religion and science
alike should have ascribed it to some great primeval cataclysm, some sudden and tremendous outburst of volcanic
energy, rather than to its true cause, the gradual and age-
long erosion of water.[2]

[1] E. Dodwell, *Classical and topographical Tour through Greece* (London,
1819), ii. 109 *sqq.* ; Sir William Gell,
The Itinerary of Greece (London, 1819),
pp. 275 *sqq.* ; W. M. Leake, *Travels
in Northern Greece* (London, 1835), iii.
390 *sqq.* ; C. Bursian, *Geographie von
Griechenland* (Leipsic, 1862–1872), i.
58 *sqq.* ; Christopher Wordsworth,
*Greece, Pictorial, Descriptive, and
Historical*, New Edition, revised by
H. F. Tozer (London, 1882). pp. 295
sqq. For ancient descriptions of Tempe
see Aelian, *Var. Hist.* iii. 1 ; Livy,
xliv. 6 ; Pliny, *Nat. Hist.* iv. 31 ;
Catullus, lxiv. 285 *sqq.* ; Ovid, *Metamorph.* i. 568 *sqq.* Of these descriptions that of Aelian is the most copious
and most warmly coloured. He dwells
with particular delight on the luxuriance of the vegetation.

[2] "That Olympus and Ossa were
torn asunder and the waters of the
Thessalian basin poured forth, is a very
ancient notion, and an often cited ' confirmation ' of Deucalion's flood.   It
has not yet ceased to be in vogue,
apparently because those who entertain

Hence the
f
Deucalion's
flood may
a
genuine
tradition,
u   r y
a myth of
observa-
tion.

Hence we may with some confidence conclude that the cleft in the Thessalian mountains, which is said to have been rent by Deucalion's flood, was no other than the gorge of Tempe. Indeed, without being very rash, we may perhaps go farther and conjecture that the story of the flood itself was suggested by the desire to explain the origin of the deep and narrow defile. For once men had pictured to themselves a great lake dammed in by the circle of the Thessalian mountains, the thought would naturally occur to them, what a vast inundation must have followed the bursting of the dam, when the released water, rushing in a torrent through the newly opened sluice, swept over the subjacent lowlands carrying havoc and devastation in its train! If there is any truth in this conjecture, the Thessalian story of Deucalion's flood and the Samothracian story of the flood of Dardanus stood exactly on the same footing : both were mere inferences drawn from the facts of physical geography : neither of them contained any reminiscences of actual events. In short, both were what Sir Edward Tylor has called myths of observation rather than historical traditions.[1]

§ 5. *Other European Stories of a Great Flood*

Few diluvial
legends in
Europe.

Icelandic
ory f
d :li e f
blood in
which the
giants were
drowned.

Apart from the ancient Greek stories of a great flood, it is remarkable that very few popular traditions of a universal or widespread deluge have been recorded in Europe. An Icelandic version of the tradition occurs in the Younger Edda, the great collection of ancient Norse myths and legends which was put together by Snorri Sturluson about 1222 A.D.[2] We there read how the god Bor had three divine sons, Odin, Wili, and We, and how these sons slew the giant Ymir. From the wounds of the dying giant there gushed such a stream of blood that it drowned all the other giants except one, named Bergelmir, who escaped with his wife in a boat,

---

it are not aware that modern geological investigation has conclusively proved that the gorge of the Peneus is as typical an example of a valley of erosion as any to be seen in Auvergne or in Colorado " (T. H. Huxley, " Hasisadra's Adventure," *Collected Essays,*

vol. iv. pp. 281 *sq.*).

[1] (Sir) Edward B. Tylor, *Researches into the Early History of Mankind* (London, 1878), pp. 306 *sqq.*

[2] *Encyclopædia Britannica,* Ninth Edition, vol. vii. (Edinburgh, 1877) p. 649, *s.v.* " Edda."

and from whom the later race of giants is descended. After- But this sto s ra her cosmogonic diluvial, and resembles the Babylonian cosmogony recorded by Berosus.
wards the sons of Bor took the carcase of the giant Ymir
and fashioned the world out of it, for down to that time the
world, as we see it now, did not exist. Out of his flowing
blood they made the ocean, the seas, and all waters ; out of
his flesh the earth ; out of his bones the mountains ; out of
his teeth and broken bones the rocks and stones : and out
of his skull the vault of the sky, which they set up on four
horns, with a dwarf under each horn to prop it up.[1]   However, this Norse tale differs from the Babylonian, the Hebrew,
and the Greek in dating the great flood before the creation
of the world and of mankind ; it hardly therefore belongs to
the same class of legends.[2]   In it the formation of the world
out of the body and blood of a giant has been compared to
the Babylonian cosmogony recorded by Berosus, according
to which the god Bel made the world by splitting a giantess
in two and converting one half of her into the earth and the
other half of her into the sky, after which he cut off his own
head, and from the flowing blood mingled with earth the
other gods moulded the human race.[3]   The resemblance
between the two cosmogonies is fairly close, but whether, as
some think, this proves a direct Babylonian influence on the
Norse legend may be doubted.[4]

A Welsh legend of a deluge runs thus. Once upon a Welsh legend of a deluge.
time the lake of Llion burst and flooded all lands, so that
the whole human race was drowned, all except Dwyfan and
Dwyfach, who escaped in a naked or mastless ship and repeopled the island of Prydain (Britain). The ship also
contained a male and a female of every sort of living
creature, so that after the deluge the animals were able to
propagate their various kinds and restock the world.[5]

[1] *Die Edda, übersetzt und mit Erläuterungen begleitet von* Karl Sim-rock, Achte Auflage (Stuttgart, 1882), p. 253 ; J. Grimm, *Deutsche Mytho-logie,*[4] i. (Berlin, 1875) pp. 463 *sqq.* In this Norse legend the word trans-lated "boat" (*lúdr*) is obscure ; it might also mean "cradle." See K. Simrock, *Handbuch der deutschen Mythologie,* Fünfte Auflage (Bonn, 1878), pp. 20 *sq.*

[2] Compare K. Simrock, *Handbuch der deutschen Mythologie,*[5] p. 20.

[3] Eusebius, *Chronicon,* ed. A. Schoene, vol. i. col. 16.

[4] Eugen Mogk, "Mythologie," in H. Paul's *Grundriss der Germanischen Philologie,*[2] iii. (Strasburg, 1900) p. 377.

[5] Edward Davies, *The Mythology and Rites of the British Druids* (Lon-don, 1809), p. 95 ; (Sir) John Rhys, *Celtic Folklore, Welsh and Manx* (Oxford, 1901), ii. 429 (referring to the

A Lithuanian story of a great flood is also reported.
One day it chanced that the supreme god Pramzimas was
looking out of a window of his heavenly house, and surveying the world from this coign of vantage he could see nothing
but war and injustice among mankind.   The sight so vexed
his righteous soul that he sent two giants, Wandu and Wejas,
down to the sinful earth to destroy it.   Now the two giants
were no other than Water and Wind, and they laid about
them with such hearty good will, that after twenty nights
and twenty days there was very little of the world left standing.   The deity now looked out of the window again to see
how things were progressing, and, as good luck would have
it, he was eating nuts at the time.   As he did so, he threw
down the shells, and one of them happened to fall on the
top of the highest mountain, where animals and a few pairs
of human beings had sought refuge from the flood.   The
nutshell came, in the truest sense of the word, as a godsend;
everybody clambered into it, and floated about on the surface
of the far-spreading inundation.   At this critical juncture
the deity looked out of the window for the third time, and,
his wrath being now abated, he gave orders for the wind to
fall and the water to subside.   So the remnant of mankind
were saved, and they dispersed over the earth.   Only a single
couple remained on the spot, and from them the Lithuanians
are descended.   But they were old and naturally a good
deal put out by their recent experience ; so to comfort them
God sent the rainbow, which advised them to jump over the
bones of the earth nine times.   The aged couple did as they
were bid ; nine times they jumped, and nine other couples
sprang up in consequence, the ancestors of the nine Lithuanian tribes.[1]

---

late Triads, iii. 13 and iii. 97).   Sir
John Rhys adds (pp. 440 *sq.*) : "From
the names Dwyfan and Dwyfach I infer
that the writer of Triad iii. 13 has developed his universal deluge on the
basis of the scriptural account of it, for
those names belonged in all probability
to wells and rivers : in other terms,
they were the names of water divinities.
At any rate there seems to be some
evidence that two springs, whose waters
flow into Bala Lake, were at one time

called Dwyfan and Dwyfach, these
names being borne both by the springs
themselves and the rivers flowing from
them."

[1] J. Grimm, *Deutsche Mythologie,*[4]
i. 480 *sq.*, referring to *Dzieje starozytne
narodu litewskiego*, przez Th. Narbutta
(Wilno, 1835), i. 2.   According to H.
Usener (*Die Sintflutsagen*, p. 3) the
genuineness of this Lithuanian legend
is not above suspicion.

The gipsies of Transylvania are reported to tell the fol- lowing legend of a deluge. There was a time, they say, when men lived for ever, and knew neither trouble nor cold, neither sickness nor sorrow. The earth brought forth the finest fruits : flesh grew on many trees, and milk and wine flowed in many rivers. Men and animals lived happily with each other, and they had no fear of death. But one day it happened that an old man came into the country and begged a cottager to give him a night's lodging. He slept in the cottage and was well entertained by the cottager's wife. Next day, on taking his leave, the old man gave his host a small fish in a little vessel, and said, " Keep this fish and do not eat it. In nine days I will return, and if you give me the fish back, I will reward you." Then away he went. The housewife looked at the little fish and said to her husband, "Goodman, how would it be if we roasted the fish?" Her husband answered, " I promised the old man to give him back the fish. You must swear to me to spare the fish and to keep it till the old man returns." The wife swore, saying, " I will not kill the fish, I will keep it, so help me God ! " After two days the woman thought, " The little fish must taste uncommonly well, since the old man sets such store on it, and will not let it be roasted, but carries it with him about the world." She thought about it a long time, till at last she took the little fish out of the vessel, and threw it on the hot coals. Hardly had she done so than the first flash of lightning came down from heaven and struck the woman dead. Then it began to rain. The rivers overflowed their beds and swamped the country. On the ninth day the old man appeared to his host and said, " Thou hast kept thine oath and not killed the fish. Take thee a wife, gather thy kins-folk together, and build thee a boat in which ye can save yourselves. All men and all living things must be drowned, but ye shall be saved. Take with thee also animals and seeds of trees and herbs, that ye may afterwards people the earth again." Then the old man disappeared, and the man did as he was bidden. It rained for a whole year, and nothing was to be seen but water and sky. After a year the water sank, and the man, with his wife and kinsfolk, and the animals, disembarked. They had now to work, tilling and

sowing the earth, to gain a living.   Their life was now labour
and sorrow, and worse than all came sickness and death.
So they multiplied but slowly, and many, many thousands
of years passed before mankind was as numerous as they had
been before the flood, and as they are now.[1]   The incident
of the fish in this story reminds us of the fish which figures
prominently in the ancient Indian legend of a great flood;[2]
and accordingly it seems possible that, as Dr. H. von
Wlislocki believes,[3] the ancestors of the gipsies brought the
legend with them to Transylvania from their old home in
India.

A story of a great flood has also been recorded among
the Voguls, a people of the Finnish or Ugrian stock, who
inhabit the country both on the east and the west of the
Ural Mountains, and who therefore belong both to Asia and
Europe.[4]   The story runs thus.   After seven years of drought
the Great Woman said to the Great Man, "It has rained
elsewhere.   How shall we save ourselves?   The other giants
are gathered in a village to take counsel.   What shall we
do?"   The Great Man answered, "Let us cut a poplar in
two, hollow it out, and make two boats.   Then we shall
weave a rope of willow roots five hundred fathoms long.
We shall bury one end of it in the earth and fasten the other
to the bow of our boats.   Let every man with children embark in the boat with his family, and let them be covered in
with a tarpaulin of cowhide, let victuals be made ready for
seven days and seven nights and put under the tarpaulin.
And let us place pots of melted butter in each boat."   Having
thus provided for their own safety, the two giants ran about
the villages, urging the inhabitants to build boats and weave
ropes.   Some did not know how to set about it, and the
giants showed them how it should be done.   Others preferred
to seek a place of refuge, but they sought in vain, and the
Great Man, to whom they betook themselves because he was
their elder, told them that he knew no place of refuge large
enough to hold them.   "See," said he, "the holy water will

The ... e t of the fi h the story analog in the ancient story of the flood.

Vogul story great flood.

[1] H. v. Wlislocki, *Vom wandernden Zigeunervolke* (Hamburg, 1890), pp. 267-269.

[2] See below, pp. 183 *sqq.*

[3] *Op. cit.* p. 269.

[4] *Encyclopædia Britannica*, Ninth Edition, xxii. 8, *s.v.*, "Siberia;" J. Deniker, *The Races of Man* (London, 1900), p. 351.

soon be on us ; for two days we have heard the rumble of
its waves. Let us embark without delay." The earth was
soon submerged, and the people who had not built boats
perished in the hot water. The same fate befell the owners
of boats whose ropes were too short, and likewise those who
had not provided themselves with liquid butter wherewith to
grease the rope as it ran out over the gunwale. On the
seventh day the water began to sink, and soon the survivors
set foot on dry ground. But there were neither trees nor
plants on·the face of the earth ; the animals had perished ;
even the fish had disappeared. The survivors were on the
point of dying of hunger, when they prayed to the great
god Numi-târom to create anew fish, animals, trees, and
plants, and their prayer was heard.[1]

Some curious relics of the great flood are still pointed
out in Savoy. Here and there a huge iron or bronze ring
may be seen fixed into a steep rock in some apparently inac-
cessible position. Tradition runs that when the water of the
deluge had covered all the low-lying parts of Savoy, such
persons as were lucky enough to own boats fastened them to
these rings, which afforded them a temporary security. There
are three of these rings in the Mont de Saleve, which over-
looks Julien in the Haute-Savoie, and there is another in the
mountains of Voirons. Again, in the Passo del Cavollo there
is a well-known stone bearing great hoof-marks. These,
the peasants say, were made by a horse, for which Noah
could find no room in the ark. When the flood rose, the
animal leaped on to this rock, which was the highest he
could see ; and as fast as the drowning people tried to
clamber up it, the horse beat them off, till the water overwhelmed him also.[2]

Relics of great flood pointed out in Savoy.

§ 6. *Supposed Persian Stories of a Great Flood*

Some scholars have held that in ancient Persian literature they can detect the elements of diluvial traditions.

[1] François Lenormant, *Les Origines de l'Histoire d'après la Bible : de la Création de l'Homme au Déluge* (Paris, 1880), pp. 455 *sq.*, quoting Lucien Adam in *Revue de Philologie et d'Ethnographie*, vol. i. pp. 12 *sq.*

[2] Estella Canziani, *Costumes, Traditions and Songs of Savoy* (London, 1911), p. 98.

Ancient
a
tradition
of a flood

overspread
the world,

before the
appearance
of man on
earth.

Another
e
Persian
story relates
how t e
gods
resolved
most living
creatures
winter and
deep snow,
and how,
warned by
them the
sage Yima
took refuge
)
threatened
calamity in
a blissful
enclosure,
into which
he gathered
the seeds
of men, of
animals,
and of fire.

Thus in the *Bundahis*, a Pahlavi work on cosmogony, mythology, and legendary history, we read of a conflict which the angel Tistar, an embodiment of the bright star Sirius, waged with the Evil Spirit apparently in the early ages of the world.   When the sun was in the sign of Cancer, the angel converted himself successively into the forms of a man, a horse, and a bull, and in each form he produced rain for ten days and nights, every drop of the rain being as big as a bowl ; so that at the end of the thirty days the water stood at the height of a man all over the world, and all noxious creatures, the breed of the Evil Spirit, were drowned in the caves and dens of the earth.   It is the venom of these noxious creatures, diffused in the water, which has made the sea salt to this day.[1]   But this story has all the appearance of being a cosmogonic myth devised to explain why the sea is salt ; it is certainly not a diluvial tradition of the ordinary type, since nothing is said in it about mankind ; indeed we are not even given to understand that the human race had come into existence at the time when the angelic battle with the principle of evil took place.[2]

Another ancient Persian story recorded in the *Zend-Avesta*, has sometimes been adduced as a diluvial tradition. We read that Yima was the first mortal with whom the Creator Ahura Mazda deigned to converse, and to whom the august deity revealed his law.   For nine hundred winters the sage Yima, under the divine superintendence, reigned over the world, and during all that time there was neither cold wind nor hot wind, neither disease nor death ; the earth was replenished with flocks and herds, with men and dogs and birds, and with red blazing fires.   But as there was neither disease nor death mankind and animals increased at

[1] *Pahlavi Texts*, translated by E. W. West (Oxford, 1880), pp. 25-28 (*Sacred Books of the East*, vol. v.) ; Fr. Spiegel, *Erânische Alterthumskunde* (Leipsic, 1871–1878), i. 479-481. As to Tistar or Tistrya, the angel of Sirius, see *The Zend-Avesta*, Part ii., translated by J. Darmesteter (Oxford, 1883), pp. 92 *sqq.* (*Sacred Books of the East*, vol. xxiii.).

[2] This is also the view of the eminent Iranian scholar, Fr. Spiegel (*Erânische Alterthumskunde*, i. 48) and of R. Andree, *Die Flutsagen*, p. 15, who says, "This seems to me so clear and simple, that I cannot understand how any one can here assume Semitic influence." François Lenormant also treats the story as a cosmogonic myth, which has no reference to humanity and no connexion with the Biblical narrative (*Les Origines de l'Histoire d'après la Bible*, pp. 430 *sqq.*).

such an alarming rate that on two occasions, at intervals of three hundred years, it became absolutely necessary to enlarge the earth in order to find room for the surplus population. The necessary enlargement was successfully carried out by Yima with the help of two instruments, a golden ring and a gold-inlaid dagger, which he had received as insignia of royalty at the hands of the Creator. However, after the third enlargement it would seem that either the available space of the universe or the patience of the Creator was exhausted; for he called a council of the celestial gods, and as a result of their mature deliberations he informed Yima that "upon the material world the fatal winters are going to fall, that shall bring the fierce, foul frost; upon the material world the fatal winters are going to fall, that shall make snow-flakes fall thick, even an *aredvi* deep on the highest tops of mountains. And all the three sorts of beasts shall perish, those that live in the wilderness, and those that live on the tops of the mountains, and those that live in the bosom of the dale, under the shelter of stables." Accord-
-ingly the Creator warned Yima to provide for himself a place of refuge in which he could find safety from the threatened calamity. He was told to make a square enclosure (*Vara*), as long as a riding-ground on every side, and to convey into it the seeds of sheep and oxen, of men, of dogs, of birds, and of red blazing fires. "There thou shalt establish dwelling places, consisting of a house with a balcony, a courtyard, and a gallery. Thither thou shalt bring the seeds of men and women, of the greatest, best, and finest kinds on this earth; thither thou shalt bring the seeds of every kind of cattle, of the greatest, best, and finest kinds on this earth. Thither thou shalt bring the seeds of every kind of tree, of the greatest, best, and finest kinds on this earth; thither thou shalt bring the seeds of every kind of fruit, the fullest of food and sweetest of odour. All those seeds shalt thou bring, two of every kind, to be kept inexhaustible there, so long as those men shall stay in the enclosure (*Vara*). There shall be no humpbacked, none bulged forward there; no impotent, no lunatic; no poverty, no lying; no meanness, no jealousy; no decayed tooth, no leprous to be confined, nor any of the brands

wherewith Angra Mainyu stamps the bodies of mortals."
Yima obeyed the divine command, and made the enclosure,
and gathered into it the seeds of men and animals, of trees
and fruits, the choicest and the best. On that blissful abode
the sun, moon, and stars rose only once a year, but on the
other hand a whole year seemed only as one day. Every
fortieth year to every human couple were born two children,
a male and a female, and so it was also with every sort of
cattle. And the men in Yima's enclosure lived the happiest
life.[1]

But this
not
strictly a
tradition
of a flood.

In all this it is hard to see any vestige of a flood story.
The destruction with which the animals are threatened is to
be the effect of severe winters and deep snow, not of a
deluge ; and nothing is said about repeopling the world
after the catastrophe by means of the men and animals who
had been preserved in the enclosure. It is true that the
warning given by the Creator to Yima, and the directions
to bestow himself and a certain number of animals in a
place of safety, resemble the warning given by God to
Noah and the directions about the building and use of the
ark. But in the absence of any reference to a deluge we
are not justified in classing this old Persian story with
diluvial traditions.[2]

---

[1] *The Zend-Avesta*, Part i., translated by J. Darmesteter (Oxford, 1880),
pp. 11-20 (*Sacred Books of the East*,
vol. iv.) ; Fr. Spiegel, *Eranische
Alterthumskunde*, i. 478 *sq.*

[2] In this opinion I am supported by
the authority of Fr. Spiegel (*Eranische
Alterthumskunde*, i. 479). On the other
hand the story is treated as a variation
of the Babylonian flood legend by Fr.
Lenormant (*Les Origines de l'Histoire
d'après la Bible : de la Création de
l'Homme au Déluge*, Paris, 1880, p.
430), and by M. Winternitz (*Die Flutsagen*, pp. 328 *sq.*). According to James
Darmesteter (*The Zend-Avesta*, Part i.,
Oxford, 1880, pp. 10 *sq.*) "the tale in
the first part refers to Yima as the first
man, the first king, and the founder of
civilisation ; the tale in the second part
is a combination of the myths of Yima,

as the first dead and the king of the
dead over whom he rules in a region
of bliss, and of old myths about the
end of the world. The world, lasting
a long year of twelve millenniums, was
to end by a dire winter, like the Eddic
Fimbul winter, to be followed by an
everlasting spring, when men, sent back
to earth from the heavens, should enjoy,
in an eternal earthly life, the same happiness that they had enjoyed after their
death in the realm of Yima. But as in
the definitive form which was taken by
Mazdean cosmology the world was made
to end by fire, its destruction by winter
was no longer the last incident of its
life, and therefore, the *Var* of Yima,
instead of remaining, as it was originally, the paradise that gives back to
earth its inhabitants, came to be nothing
more than a sort of Noah's ark."

§ 7. *Ancient Indian Stories of a Great Flood*

No legend of a great flood is to be found in the Vedic hymns, the most ancient literary monuments of India, which appear to have been composed at various dates between 1500 and 1000 B.C., while the Aryans were still settled in the Punjab and had not yet spread eastward into the valley of the Ganges. But in the later Sanscrit literature a well-marked story of a deluge repeatedly occurs in forms which combine a general resemblance with some variations of detail. The first record of it meets us in the *Satapatha Brahmana*, an important prose treatise on sacred ritual, which is believed to have been written not long before the rise of Buddhism, and therefore not later than the sixth century before Christ. The Aryans then occupied the upper valley of the Ganges as well as the valley of the Indus ; but they were probably as yet little affected by the ancient civilizations of Western Asia and Greece. Certainly the great influx of Greek ideas and Greek art came centuries later with Alexander's invasion in 326 B.C.[1] As related in the *Satapatha Brahmana* the story of the great flood runs as follows :—

"In the morning they brought to Manu water for washing, just as now also they are wont to bring water for washing the hands. When he was washing himself, a fish came into his hands. It spake to him the word, 'Rear me, I will save thee!' 'Wherefrom wilt thou save me?' 'A flood will carry away all these creatures: from that I will save thee!' 'How am I to rear thee? It said, 'As long as we are small, there is great destruction for us : fish devours fish. Thou wilt first keep me in a jar. When I outgrow that, thou wilt dig a pit and keep me in it. When I outgrow that, thou wilt take

The story
ea
flood occurs
in the later
literature
of India ;
recorded
in the
S t brtha
Brahmana,
probably
not later
ian the
sixth
century
B.C.

The story
e re
flood in the
Satapatha
Brahmana.
Manu
warned by
a fish, saves
himself
from the
flood in a
shi

[1] *The Imperial Gazetteer of India, The Indian Empire* (Oxford, 1909), i. 402 *sqq.*, 417 *sq.* (W. Crooke), ii. 206 *sqq.*, 229 *sq.* (A. A. Macdonell). The *Satapatha Brahmana* belong to a series of priestly treatises on ritual and theology, which form the most ancient body of Sanscrit prose literature ; they are, however, a good deal later than the Vedic hymns, and are believed to have been composed between 800 and 500 B.C. See, in addition to the foregoing authorities, A. Weber, *Akademische Vorlesungen über Indische Literaturgeschichte* (Berlin, 1876), pp. 12 *sqq.*; J. Eggeling, *The Satapatha Brahmana*, Part i. (Oxford, 1882) Introduction, pp. i. *sqq.* (*The Sacred Books of the East*, vol. xii.).

me down to the sea, for then I shall be beyond destruction.'
It soon became a *ghasha* (a large fish) ; for that grows largest
of all fish.   Thereupon it said, ' In such and such a year that
flood will come.   Thou shalt then attend to me by preparing
a ship ;[1] and when the flood has risen thou shalt enter into
the ship, and I will save thee from it.'   After he had reared
it in this way, he took it down to the sea.   And in the same
year which the fish had indicated to him, he attended to the
advice of the fish by preparing a ship ;[2] and when the flood
had risen, he entered into the ship.   The fish then swam up
to him, and to its horn he tied the rope of the ship, and
by that means he passed swiftly up to yonder northern
mountain.   It then said, ' I have saved thee.   Fasten the
ship to a tree ; but let not the water cut thee off, whilst
thou art on the mountain.   As the water subsides, thou
mayest gradually descend !'   Accordingly he gradually descended, and hence that slope of the northern mountain is
called ' Manu's descent.'   The flood then swept away all
these creatures, and Manu alone remained here.

How after
the flood
~~Manu~~
obtained a
daughter
through
sacrifice.

" Being desirous of offspring, he engaged in worshipping
and austerities.   During this time he also performed a *pâka*-
sacrifice : he offered up in the waters clarified butter, sour
milk, whey, and curds.   Thence a woman was produced in
a year : becoming quite solid she rose ; clarified butter
gathered in her footprint.   Mitra and Varuna met her.
They said to her, ' Who art thou ? '   ' Manu's daughter,' she
replied.   ' Say thou art ours,' they said.   ' No,' she said, ' I am
the daughter of him who begat me.'   They desired to have a
share in her.   She either agreed or did not agree, but passed
by them.   She came to Manu.   Manu said to her, ' Who
art thou ? '   ' Thy daughter,' she replied.   ' How, illustrious
one, art thou my daughter ? ' he asked.   She replied, ' Those
offerings of clarified butter, sour milk, whey, and curds, which
thou madest in the waters, with them thou hast begotten
me.   I am the blessing ; make use of me at the sacrifice !
If thou wilt make use of me at the sacrifice, thou wilt become
rich in offspring and cattle.   Whatever blessing thou shalt

---

[1] " Build a ship then and worship
me " (Max Müller) ; " Thou shalt,
therefore, construct a ship and resort
to me " (J. Muir).

[2] " Manu had built a ship, and worshipped the fish " (Max Muller) ; " he
constructed a ship and resorted to him "
(J. Muir).

invoke through me, all that shall be granted to thee!' He accordingly made use of her as the benediction in the middle of the sacrifice; for what is intermediate between the fore-offerings and the after-offerings, is the middle of the sacrifice. With her he went on worshipping and performing austerities, wishing for offspring. Through her he generated this race, which is this race of Manu; and whatever blessing he invoked through her, all that was granted to him."[1]

The next record of the flood legend in Sanscrit literature meets us in the *Mahabharata*, the vast Indian epic, which, in the form in which we now possess it, is about eight times as long as the *Iliad* and *Odyssey* put together. The nucleus of this huge compilation may date from the fifth century before Christ; through successive expansions it attained its present enormous bulk in the early centuries of our era. The evidence of inscriptions proves that by the year 500 A.D. the poem was complete.[2] As told in the epic, the legend runs thus :—

"There was a great sage [*rishi*] Manu, son of Vivasvat, majestic, in lustre equal to Prajapati. In energy, fiery vigour, prosperity, and austere fervour he surpassed both his father and his grandfather. Standing with uplifted arm, on one foot, on the spacious Badari, he practised intense austere fervour. This direful exercise he performed, with his head downwards, and with unwinking eyes, for ten thousand years. Once, when, clad in dripping rags, with matted hair, he was so engaged, a fish came to him on the banks of the Chīrinī, and spake : ' Lord, I am a small fish; I dread the stronger ones, and from them you must save me. For the stronger fish devour the weaker; this has been immemorially ordained as our means of subsistence. Deliver me from this flood of apprehension in which I am sinking, and I will requite the deed.' Hearing this, Manu,

(marginal notes:) The story ˌe ˈre flood in the *Maha-onarata.*

How the as ˌic sage Manu rescued a was warned by it of the g deluge,

[1] *The Satapatha Brāhmana*, translated by Julius Eggeling, Part i. (Oxford, 1882) pp. 216-219 (*The Sacred Books of the East*, vol. xii.). For other translations of the legend see F. Max Muller, *History of Sanscrit Literature* (London and Edinburgh, 1859), pp. 425-427 ; *id. India, what can it teach us?* (London, 1892) pp. 134 *sqq.* ; J. Muir, *Original Sanskrit*

Texts, vol. i. Third Edition (London, 1890), pp. 182-184 ; H. Usener, *Die Sintflutsagen*, pp. 26 *sq.* (Ad. Weber's German translation).

[2] A. A. Macdonell, "Sanskrit Literature," in *The Imperial Gazetteer of India, The Indian Empire* (Oxford, 1909), ii. 234 *sqq.* ; H. Oldenberg, *Die Literatur des alten Indien* (Stuttgart and Berlin, 1903), pp. 146 *sqq.*

filled with compassion, took the fish in his hand, and bringing him to the water threw him into a jar bright as a moon-
beam.   In it the fish, being excellently tended, grew ; for
Manu treated him like a son.   After a long time he became
very large, and could not be contained in the jar.   Then,
seeing Manu, he said again : ' In order that I may thrive,
remove me elsewhere.'   Manu then took him out of the jar,
brought him to a large pond, and threw him in.   There he
continued to grow for very many years.   Although the pond
was two *yojanas* long, and one *yojana* broad, the lotus-eyed
fish found in it no room to move ; and again said to Manu :
' Take me to Ganga, the dear queen of the ocean-monarch ;
in her I shall dwell ; or do as thou thinkest best, for I must
contentedly submit to thy authority, as through thee I have
exceedingly increased.'   Manu accordingly took the fish and
threw him into the river Ganga.   There he waxed for some
time, when he again said to Manu : ' From my great bulk I
cannot move in the Ganga ; be gracious and remove me
quickly to the ocean.'   Manu took him out of the Ganga ;
and cast him into the sea.   Although so huge, the fish was
easily borne, and pleasant to touch and smell, as Manu
carried him.   When he had been thrown into the ocean he
said to Manu : ' Great lord, thou hast in every way preserved
me : now hear from me what thou must do when the time
arrives.   Soon shall all these terrestrial objects, both fixed
and moving, be dissolved.   The time for the purification of
the worlds has now arrived.   I therefore inform thee what
is for thy greatest good.   The period dreadful for the universe,
moving and fixed, has come.   Make for thyself a strong ship,
with a cable attached ; embark in it with the seven sages
[*rishis*], and stow in it, carefully preserved and assorted, all
the seeds which have been described of old by Brahmans.
When embarked in the ship, look out for me : I shall come
recognizable by my horn.   So shalt thou do ; I greet thee and
depart.   These great waters cannot be crossed over without
me.   Distrust not my word.'   Manu replied, ' I shall do as
thou hast said.'   After taking mutual leave they departed
each on his own way.   Manu then, as enjoined, taking with
him the seeds, floated on the billowy ocean in the beautiful
ship.   He then thought on the fish, which, knowing his

How, on
d
of the fish
Manu
m
in a hi
with
se' sag s
and many
kinds of
seeds.

desire arrived with all speed, distinguished by a horn. How Manu
When Manu saw the horned leviathan, lofty as a mountain, d th ship's cable
he fastened the ship's cable to the horn. Being thus attached, to the horn
the fish dragged the ship with great rapidity, transporting it and how the
across the briny ocean which seemed to dance with its waves fish towed
and thunder with its waters. Tossed by the tempests, the the peak of
ship whirled like a reeling and intoxicated woman. Neither Himavat.
the earth, nor the quarters of the world appeared; there was
nothing but water, air, and sky. In the world thus confounded, the seven sages [*rishis*], Manu, and the fish were
beheld. So, for very many years, the fish, unwearied, drew
the ship over the waters; and brought it at length to the
highest peak of Himavat. He then, smiling gently, said to
the sages, 'Bind the ship without delay to this peak.' They
did so accordingly. And that highest peak of Himavat is
still known by the name of Naubandhana ('the Binding of
the Ship'). The friendly fish (or god, *animisha*) then said How the
to the sages, 'I am the Prajapati Brahma, than whom nothing revealed
higher can be reached. In the form of a fish I have delivered itself as
you from this great danger. Manu shall create all living Brahma,
beings, gods, demigods [*asuras*], men, with all worlds, and all and
things moving and fixed. By my favour and through severe Manu to
austere fervour, he shall attain perfect insight into his creative create all
work, and shall not become bewildered.' Having thus spoken, beings, both
the fish in an instant disappeared. Manu, desirous to call gods and men.
creatures into existence and bewildered in his work, performed
a great act of austere fervour; and then began visibly to
create all living beings. This which I have narrated is
known as the Matsyaka Purana (or 'Legend of the Fish')." [1]

In this latter version Manu is not a common man but a
great seer, who by his religious austerities and the favour of
the Supreme Being is promoted to the dignity of Creator of
the world and of all living things, including gods and men.

The same legend is repeated, with minor variations, in The story of
the later class of Sanscrit books known as the *Purānas.* the Sanscrit
These are epic works, didactic in character and sectarian in *Purānas.*
purpose, generally designed to recommend the worship of

[1] J. Muir, *Original Sanskrit Texts*, vol. i. Third Edition (London, 1890), pp. 199-201. Compare H. Jacobi's   German translation of the passage in H. Usener's *Die Sintflutsagen* (Bonn, 1899), pp. 29-31.

Vishnu, though some of them inculcate the religion of Siva.
So far as they deal with the legends of ancient days, they
derive their materials mainly from the *Mahabharata.* The
Vāyu Purana, which may be the oldest of them, is believed
to date from about 320 A.D.[1] In the *Matsyu* (" Fish ")
Purāna the legend of the deluge runs thus :—

The story of
flo d
the *Matsvu*
Purâna.   " Formerly a heroic king called Manu, the patient son of
the Sun, endowed with all good qualities, indifferent to pain
and pleasure, after investing his son with royal authority,
practised intense austere fervour, in a certain region of
Malaya (Malabar), and attained to transcendent union with
the Deity (*yoga*). When a million years had elapsed,
Brahma became pleased and disposed to bestow a boon,
which he desired Manu to choose. Bowing before the father
of the world the monarch said, ' I desire of thee this one
incomparable boon, that when the dissolution of the universe
arrives I may have the power to preserve all existing things,
whether moving or stationary.' ' So be it,' said the Soul of
all things, and vanished on the spot ; when a great shower
of flowers, thrown down by the gods, fell from the sky.
Manu saves
a
is warned
by it of the
ng
flood. Once as, in his hermitage, Manu offered the oblation to the
Manes, there fell upon his hands, along with some water, a
S'apharı fish (a carp), which the kind-hearted king perceiving,
strove to preserve in his water-jar. In one day and night
the fish grew to the size of sixteen fingers, and cried, ' Preserve me, preserve me.' Manu then took and threw him
into a large pitcher, where in one night he increased three
cubits, and again cried, with the voice of one distressed, to
the son of Vivasvat, ' Preserve me, preserve me, I have sought
refuge with thee.' Manu next put him into a well, and
when he could not be contained even in that, he was thrown
into a lake, where he attained to the size of a *yojana* ; but
still cried in humble tones, ' Preserve me, preserve me.'
When, after being flung into the Ganga, he increased there
also, the king threw him into the ocean. When he filled the
entire ocean, Manu said, in terror, ' Thou art some god, or
thou art Vasudeva ; how can any one else be like this?
Whose body could equal two hundred thousand *yojanas*?

[1] A. A. Macdonell, "Sanskrit
Literature," in *The Imperial Gazetteer* *of India, The Indian Empire* (Oxford,
1909), ii. 236 *sq.*

Thou art recognised under this form of a fish, and thou tormentest me, Keśava ; reverence be to thee, Hrishikesa, lord of the world, abode of the universe ! ' Thus addressed, the divine Janardana, in the form of a fish, replied : ' Thou hast well spoken, and hast rightly known me.   In a short time the earth with its mountains, groves, and forests, shall be submerged in the waters.   This ship has been constructed by the company of all the gods for the preservation of the vast host of living creatures.   Embarking in it all living creatures, both those engendered from moisture and from eggs as well as the viviparous, and plants, preserve them from calamity.   When driven by the blasts at the end of the *vura*,[1] the ship is swept along, thou shalt bind it to this horn of mine.   Then at the close of the dissolution thou shalt be the Prajapati (lord of creatures) of this world, fixed and moving.   When this shall have been done, thou, the omniscient, patient sage [*rishi*], and lord of the *Manvantara*[2] shalt be an object of worship to the gods.'   2nd. Adhyaya : Suta said : Being thus addressed, Manu asked the slayer of the Asura, ' In how many years shall the (existing) *Manvantara*[2] come to an end ?   And how shall I preserve the living creatures? or how shall I meet again with thee ? '   The fish answered : ' From this day forward a drought shall visit the earth for a hundred years and more, with a tormenting famine.   Then the seven direful rays of the sun, of little power, destructive, shall rain burning charcoal.   At the close of the *yuga* the submarine fire shall burst forth, while the poisonous flame issuing from the mouth of Sankarshana (shall blaze) from Patala, and the fire from Mahadeva's third eye shall issue from his forehead.   Thus kindled the world shall become confounded.   When, consumed in this manner, the earth shall become like ashes, the aether too shall be scorched with heat.   Then the world, together with the gods and planets, shall be destroyed.   The seven clouds of the period of dissolution, called Samvartta, Bhimanada, Drona, Chanda, Balahaka, Vidyutpataka, and Sonambu, produced from the steam of the fire, shall inundate

He is told to embark in a ship with all iv creatures and plants, in order to save them from the flood.

---

[1] A great mundane period. See J. Muir, *Original Sanscrit Texts*, vol. i. Third Edition (London, 1890), pp. 43 *sqq.*

[2] A great mundane period, vastly longer than a *yuga.* See J. Muir, *l.c.*

the earth. The seas agitated, and joined together, shall reduce these entire three worlds to one ocean. Taking this celestial ship, embarking on it all the seeds, and through contemplation fixed on me fastening it by a rope to my horn, thou alone shalt remain, protected by my power, when even the gods are burnt up. The sun and moon, I Brahma with the four worlds, the holy river Narmada [Nerbudda], the great sage Markandeya, Mahadeva, the Vedas, the Purana, with the sciences,—these shall remain with thee at the close of the *Manvantara*. The world having thus become one ocean at the end of the *Chākshusha manvantara*, I shall give currency to the Vedas at the commencement of thy creation.' Suta continued : Having thus spoken, the divine Being vanished on the spot ; while Manu fell into a state of

The deluge come, Manu draws all s into the ship.

contemplation (*yoga*) induced by the favour of Vasudeva. When the time announced by Vasudeva had arrived, the predicted deluge took place in that very manner. Then Janardana appeared in the form of a horned fish ; (the serpent) Ananta came to Manu in the shape of a rope. Then he who was skilled in duty (*i.e.* Manu) drew towards himself all creatures by contemplation (*yoga*) and stowed them in the ship, which he then attached to the fish's horn by the serpent-rope, as he stood upon the ship, and after he had made obeisance to Janardana. I shall now declare the *Purana* which, in answer to an enquiry from Manu, was uttered by the deity in the form of the fish, as he lay in a sleep of contemplation till the end of the universal inundation : Listen." The *Matsya Purana* says nothing more about the progress and results of the deluge.[1]

Another ancient Indian work of the same class, the *Bhāgavata Purana*, gives the same story with variations as follows :—

The story of the flood in the *Bhāgavata Purāna*.

"At the close of the past *Kalpa*[2] there occurred an occasional dissolution of the universe arising from Brahma's nocturnal repose ; in which the Bhurloka and other worlds

---

[1] J Muir, *Ancient Sanscrit Texts*, vol. i. Third Edition (London, 1890), pp. 205-207.

[2] A *Kalpa* was counted a day of the great god Brahma. It was equivalent to a period of 4,320,000,000 human years. At the end of each such period the universe was supposed to collapse and to remain in a state of dissolution for a night of the same length, till the Creator awoke from his sleep and created the world anew. See J. Muir, *op. cit.* i. 43 *sqq.*

were submerged in the ocean. When the creator, desirous
of rest, had under the influence of time been overcome by
sleep, the strong Hayagrīva coming near, carried off the
Vedas which had issued from his mouth. Discovering this
deed of the prince of the Danavas, the divine Hari, the Lord,
took the form of a S'aphari fish. At that time a certain
great royal sage [*rishi*], called Satyavrata, who was devoted
to Narayana, practised austere fervour, subsisting on water.
He was the same who in the present great *Kalpa* is the son
of Visvasvat, called S'raddhadeva,[1] and was appointed by
Hari to the office of Manu. Once, as in the river Kritamala How the
he was offering the oblation of water to the Pitris [ancestral sage Satya-
vrata saved
spirits], a S'aphari fish came into the water in the hollow of a fish and
his hands. The lord of Dravida, Satyavrata, cast the fish in by it to
his hands with the water into the river. The fish very rescue
piteously cried to the merciful king, 'Why dost thou abandon from the
me poor and terrified to the monsters who destroy their coming
deluge by
kindred in this river?' [Satyavrata then took the fish from embarking
the river, placed it in his waterpot, and as it grew larger and in a ship
with plants
larger, threw it successively into a larger vessel, a pond, and seeds.
various lakes, and at length into the sea. The fish objects
to be left there on the plea that it would be devoured ; but
Manu replies that it can be no real fish, but Vishnu himself ;
and with various expressions of devotion enquires why he
had assumed this disguise.] The god replies : ' On the
seventh day after this the three worlds Bhurloka, etc., shall
sink beneath the ocean of the dissolution. When the universe
is dissolved in that ocean, a large ship, sent by me, shall
come to thee. Taking with thee the plants and various seeds,
surrounded by the seven sages [*rishis*], and attended by all
existences, thou shalt embark on the great ship, and shalt
without alarm move over the one dark ocean, by the sole
light of the sages [*rishis*]. When the ship shall be vehemently
shaken by the tempestuous wind, fasten it by the great serpent
to my horn—for I shall come near. So long as the night of
Brahma lasts, I shall draw thee with the sages [*rishis*] and
the ship over the ocean.' [The god then disappears after
promising that Satyavrata shall practically know his great-
ness and experience his kindness, and Satyavrata awaits the

---

[1] "Manu is called S'raddhadeva in the *Mahabharata* also."

predicted events.]   Then the sea, augmenting as the great
clouds poured down their waters, was seen overflowing its
shores and everywhere inundating the earth.   Meditating on
the injunctions of the deity, Satyavrata beheld the arrival of
the ship, on which he embarked with the Brahmans, taking
along with him the various kinds of plants.   Delighted, the
Munis said to him, ' Meditate on Keśava ; he will deliver us
from this danger, and grant us prosperity.'   Accordingly
when the king had meditated on him, there appeared on the
ocean a golden fish, with one horn, a million *yojanas* long.
Binding the ship to his horn with the serpent for a rope, as
he had been before commanded by Hari, Satyavrata landed
Madhusudana.   [The hymn follows.]   When the king had
thus spoken, the divine primeval Male, in the form of a fish,
moving on the vast ocean declared to him the truth ; the
celestial collection of Puranas, with the Sankhya, Yoga, the
ceremonial, and the mystery of the soul.   Seated on the ship
with the sages [*rishis*], Satyavrata heard the true doctrine of
the soul, of the eternal Brahma, declared by the god.   When
Brahma arose at the end of the past dissolution, Hari restored
to him the Vedas, after slaying Hayagrīva.   And King
Satyavrata, master of all knowledge, sacred and profane,
became, by the favour of Vishnu, the son of Vivasvat, the
Manu in this *Kalpa*" [1]

Story of the flood in the *Agni Purāna*. How Manu saved a fish and was arn it to escape from the m ng deluge in a ship.

Yet another ancient Indian version of the deluge legend
meets us in the *Agni Purāna* : it runs thus :—

"Vasishtha said : ' Declare to me Vishnu, the cause of
the creation, in the form of a Fish and his other incarnations;
and the Puranic revelation of Agni, as it was originally heard
from Vishnu.'   Agni replied : ' Hear O Vasishtha, I shall
relate to thee the Fish-incarnation of Vishnu, and his acts
when so incarnate for the destruction of the wicked, and protection of the good.   At the close of the past *Kalpa* there
occurred an occasional dissolution of the universe caused by
Brahma's sleep, when the Bhurloka and other worlds were
inundated by the ocean.   Manu, the son of Vivasvat, practised austere fervour for the sake of worldly enjoyment as
well as final liberation.   Once, when he was offering the

[1] J. Muir, *Ancient Sanskrit Texts*, vol. i. Third Edition (London, 1890),
pp. 209 *sq*.

libation of water to the Pitris [ancestral spirits] in the river
Kritamala, a small fish came into the water in the hollow of
his hands, and said to him when he sought to cast it into
the stream, ' Do not throw me in, for I am afraid of alligators
and other monsters which are here.'   On hearing this Manu
threw it into a jar.   Again, when grown, the Fish said to
him, ' Provide me a large place.'   Manu then cast it into a
larger vessel (?).   When it increased there, it said to the
king, ' Give me a wide space.'   When, after being thrown
into a pond, it became as large as its receptacle, and cried
out for greater room, he flung it into the sea.   In a moment
it became a hundred thousand *yojanas* in bulk.   Beholding
the wonderful Fish, Manu said in astonishment : ' Who art
thou ?   Art thou Vishnu ?   Adoration be paid to thee, O
Narayana.   Why, O Janardana, dost thou bewilder me by thy
illusion ? '   The Fish, which had become incarnate for the
welfare of this world and the destruction of the wicked, when
so addressed, replied to Manu, who had been intent upon its
preservation : ' Seven days after this the ocean shall inundate
the world.   A ship shall come to thee, in which thou shalt
place the seeds, and accompanied by the sages [*rishis*] shalt
sail during the night of Brahma.   Bind it with the great
serpent to my horn, when I arrive.'   Having thus spoken the
Fish vanished.   Manu awaited the promised period, and
embarked on the ship when the sea overflowed its shores.
(There appeared) a golden Fish, a million *yojanas* long, with
one horn, to which Manu attached the ship, and heard from
the Fish the *Matsya Purāna*, which takes away sin, together
with the Veda.   Keśava then slew the Danava Hayagrīva
who had snatched away the Vedas, and preserved its mantras
and other portions." [1]

§ 8. *Modern Indian Stories of a Great Flood*

The Bhils, a wild jungle tribe of Central India, relate
that once upon a time a pious man (*dhobi*), who used to
wash his clothes in a river, was warned by a fish of the
approach of a great deluge.   The fish informed him that,
out of gratitude for his humanity in always feeding the

[1] J. Muir, *Ancient Sanskrit Texts*, vol. i. Third Edition (London, 1890),
pp. 211 *sq.*

fish, he had come to give him this warning, and to urge him to prepare a large box in which he might escape. The pious man accordingly made ready the box and embarked in it with his sister and a cock. After the deluge Rama sent out his messenger to inquire into the state of affairs. The messenger heard the crowing of the cock and so discovered the box. Thereupon Rama had the box brought before him, and asked the man who he was and how he had escaped. The man told his tale. Then Rama made him face in turn north, east, and west, and swear that the woman with him was his sister. The man stuck to it that she was indeed his sister. Rama next turned him to the south, whereupon the man contradicted his former statement and said that the woman was his wife. After that, Rama inquired of him who it was that told him to escape, and on learning that it was the fish, he at once caused the fish's tongue to be cut out for his pains ; so that sort of fish has been tongueless ever since. Having executed this judgment on the fish for blabbing, Rama ordered the man to repeople the devastated world. Accordingly the man married his sister and had by her seven sons and seven daughters. The firstborn received from Rama the present of a horse, but, being unable to ride, he left the animal in the plain and went into the forest to cut wood. So he became a woodman, and woodmen his descendants the Bhils have been from that day to this.[1] In this Bhil story the warning of the coming flood given by the fish to its human benefactor resembles the corresponding incident in the Sanscrit story of the flood too closely to be independent. It may be questioned whether the Bhils borrowed the story from the Aryan invaders, or whether on the contrary the Aryans may not have learned it from the aborigines whom they encountered in their progress through the country. In favour of the latter view it may be pointed out that the story of the flood does not occur in the most ancient Sanscrit literature, but only appears in books written long after the settlement of the Aryans in India.

[1] *The Ethnographical Survey of the Central India Agency,* Monograph II., *The Jungle Tribes of Malwa,* compiled by Captain C. E. Luard (Lucknow, 1909), p. 17.

The Kamars, a small Dravidian tribe of the Raipur District and adjoining States, in the Central Provinces of India, tell the following story of a great flood. They say that in the beginning God created a man and woman, to whom in their old age two children were born, a boy and a girl. But God sent a·deluge over the world in order to drown a jackal which had angered him. The old couple heard of the coming deluge, so they shut up their children in a hollow piece of wood with provision of food to last them till the flood should subside. Then they closed up the trunk, and the deluge came and lasted for twelve years. The old couple and all other living things on earth were drowned, but the trunk floated on the face of the waters. After twelve years God created two birds and sent them to see whether his enemy the jackal had been drowned. The birds flew over all the corners of the world, and they saw nothing but a log of wood floating on the surface of the water. They perched on it, and soon heard low and feeble voices coming from inside the log. It was the children saying to each other that they had only provisions for three days left. So the birds flew away and told God, who then caused the flood to subside, and taking out the children from the log of wood he heard their story. Thereupon he brought them up, and in due time they were married, and God gave the name of a different caste to every child who was born to them, and from them all the inhabitants of the world are descended.[1] In this story the incident of the two birds suggests a reminiscence of the raven and the dove in the Biblical legend, which may have reached the Kamars through missionary influence.

The Hos or Larka Kols, an aboriginal race who inhabit Singbhum, in south-western Bengal, say that after the world was first peopled mankind grew incestuous and paid no heed either to God or to their betters. So Sirma Thakoor, or Sing Bonga, the Creator, resolved to destroy them all, and he carried out his intention, some say by water, others say by fire. However, he spared sixteen people, and from them presumably the present race of mortals is descended.[2] A

Story of a great flood told by the Kamars of a[?] *Provinces, India.*

Story of a great flood told by the Hos and Mundas of Bengal.

---

[1] R. V. Russell, *Tribes and Castes of the Central Provinces of India* (London, 1916), iii. 326 *sq.*

[2] Lieut. Tickell, "Memoir on the Hodesum (improperly called Kolehan)," *Journal of the Asiatic Society of Bengal,* ix. (Calcutta, 1840) Part ii. p. 798.

fuller version of this legend is reported to be current among
the Mundaris or Mundas, a tribe of Kols akin to the Hos,
who inhabit the tableland of Chọta Nagpur to the north of
Singbhum. According to the Mundas, God created mankind
out of the dust of the ground. But soon mankind grew
wicked ; they would not wash themselves, or work, or do anything but dance and sing perpetually. So it repented Sing
Bonga that he had made them, and he resolved to destroy
them by a great flood. For that purpose he sent down a
stream of fire-water (*Sengle-Daa*) from heaven, and all men
died. Only two, a brother and a sister, were saved by hiding
under a *tiril* tree ; hence the wood of a *tiril* tree is black
and charred with fire to this day. But God thought better
of it, and to stop the fiery rain he created the snake Lurbing,
which puffed its soul up into the shape of a rainbow, thereby
holding up the showers. So when the Mundaris see a rainbow they say, " It will rain no more. Lurbing has destroyed
the rain." [1]

Story of a
grea fi
flc d te ld
by the
te s of
Bençal
The Santals, another aboriginal race of Bengal, have also
a legend that in the early ages of the world almost the whole
human race was destroyed by fire from heaven. There are
various traditions concerning this great calamity. Some say
that it occurred soon after the creation of the first man and
woman. Others assign it to a later period, and mention
different places as the scene of the catastrophe. Different
reasons, too, are alleged for the visitation. Some say it was
sent by God as a punishment for the sins of the people ;
others affirm that two discontented members of the Marndi
tribe invoked the vengeance of the Creator Thakur upon
those who had offended them. The account which dates the
event immediately after the creation makes no reference to
the causes which operated to bring it about. It runs as

[1] R. Andree, *Die Flutsagen*, pp. 25
sq., citing Nottrott, *Die Gossnerische
Mission unter den Kohls* (Halle, 1874),
p. 59. However, compare Colonel E.
T. Dalton, *Descriptive Ethnology of
Bengal* (Calcutta, 1872), pp. 188 sq. :
" It has been said that the Hos and
Mundas, like the Karens, have a tradition of the destruction of the human
race, all but two persons, by deluge,
but of this I have not been able to discover a trace, and it appears incom-
patible with their tradition of the origin
of different races. *Lúrbeng* is in their
language a serpent, properly a water-
snake, and the name is poetically given
by them to the rainbow, and by a
simple reasoning on cause and effect,
they say ' the serpent stops the rain,'
but it requires stronger imaginative
powers than I possess to eliminate from
this a tradition of the deluge."

follows.   When Pilchu Haram and Pilchu Budhi, the first
man and woman, had reached adolescence, it rained fire-rain
for seven days and seven nights.   They sought refuge from
the burning liquid in a cave in a rock, from which, when the
flood was over, they came forth unscathed.   Jaher-era then
came and inquired of them where they had been.   They
answered, " We were underneath a rock."   The following
verse, we are told, completes the description :—

> " *Seven days and seven nights it rained fire-rain,*
> *Where were you, ye two human beings :*
> *Where did you pass the time ?* "

The other Santal story, which explains the fire-flood by
the discontent of the Marndi tribe, is as follows.   When the
different social distinctions and duties were assigned to the
various tribes, the Marndis were overlooked.   Two members
of the tribe, by name Ambir Singh and Bir Singh, who
dwelt on Mount Here, were incensed at the slight thus put
upon their fellows, and they prayed that fire from heaven
might descend and destroy the other tribes.   Their prayer
was answered : one half of the country was destroyed, and
one half of the population perished.   The house in which
Ambir Singh and Bir Singh lived was of stone, with a door
of the same material.   It therefore resisted the fire which
was devastating the country far and wide, and the two inmates
escaped unhurt.   At this point the reciter of the tale sings
the following verses :—

Another
Santal story
of a great
fire-flood.

> " *Thou art shut in with a stone door,*
> *Ambir Singh, thou art shut in with a stone door,*
> *Ambir Singh, the country is burning,*
> *Ambir Singh, the country is burnt up.*"

When Kisku Raj heard of what had happened, he inquired
who had done it.   They told him it was the work of Ambir
Singh and Bir Singh.   He at once ordered them into his
presence and asked why they had brought .such a disaster
upon the people.   They answered, " In the distribution of
distinctions and offices all were considered but ourselves."
To that Kisku Raj replied, " Yes, yes, do not act thus, and
you also shall receive an office."   Then they caused the fire
to be extinguished.   So Kisku Raj, addressing them, said,

" I appoint you treasurers and stewards over all the property
and possessions of all kings, princes, and nobles. All the
rice and the unhusked rice will be under your charge. From
your hands will all the servants and dependents receive their
daily portion." Thus was the fire-flood stayed, and thus did
the Marndi tribe attain to its present rank.

A third
Santal
version of
the fire-
flood story.
    Yet a third Santal version of the fire-flood story has it
that, while the people were at Khojkaman, their iniquity rose
to such a pitch that Thakur Jiu, the Creator, punished them
by sending fire-rain upon earth. Out of the whole race two
individuals alone escaped destruction by hiding in a cave on
Mount Haradata.[1]

Lepcha and
Tibetan
stories of a
flood.
    The Lepchas of Sikhim have a tradition of a great flood
during which a couple escaped to the top of a mountain
called Tendong, near Darjeeling.[2] Captain Samuel Turner,
who went on an embassy from India to the court of the
Teshoo Lama at the close of the eighteenth century, reports
that according to a native legend Tibet was long ago almost
totally inundated, until a deity of the name of Gya, whose
chief temple is at Durgeedin, took compassion on the survivors, drew off the waters through Bengal, and sent teachers
to civilize the wretched inhabitants, who were destined to
repeople the land, and who up to that time had been very
little better than monkeys.[3]

Stories of
a flood
told by the
Singphos
and Lushais
of Assam.
    The Singphos of Assam relate
that once on a time mankind was destroyed by a flood
because they omitted to offer the proper sacrifices at the
slaughter of buffaloes and pigs. Only two men, Khun litang
and Chu liyang, with their wives, were saved, and being
appointed by the gods to dwell on Singrabhum hill, they
became the progenitors of the present human race.[4] The
Lushais of Assam have a legend that the king of the water
demons fell in love with a woman named Ngai-ti (Loved One),
but she rejected his addresses and ran away ; so he pursued

[1] Rev. A. Campbell, D.D., "The
Traditions of the Santals," *The Journal
of the Bihar and Orissa Research
Society*, ii. (Bankipore, 1916) pp. 23-25.
    [2] Sir Joseph Hooker, *Himalayan
Journals* (London, 1891), chapter v.
p. 86 (Minerva Library edition).
    [3] Captain Samuel Turner, *An Ac-
count of an Embassy to the Court of*
*the Teshoo Lama in Tibet, containing
a Narrative of a Journey through
Bootan and part of Tibet* (London,
1800), p. 224. Durgeedin is perhaps
Darjeeling. If that is so, the legends
briefly recorded by Hooker and Turner
may coincide.
    [4] A. Bastian, *Die Voelker des Oest-
lichen Asien*, i. (Leipsic, 1866) p. 87.

her, and surrounded the whole human race with water on the top of a hill called Phun-lu-buk, which is said to be far away to the north-east.   As the water continued to rise, the people took Ngai-ti and threw her into the flood, which thereupon receded.   In flowing away, the water hollowed out the deep valleys and left standing the high mountains which we see to this day ; for down to the time of the great flood the earth had been level.[1]   Again, the Anals of Assam say that once upon a time the whole world was flooded.   All the people were drowned except one man and one woman, who ran to the highest peak of the Leng hill, where they climbed up a high tree and hid themselves among the branches. The tree grew near a large pond, which was as clear as the eye of a crow.   They spent the night perched on the tree, and in the morning, what was their astonishment to find that they had been changed into a tiger and a tigress ! Seeing the sad plight of the world, the Creator, whose name is Pathian, sent a man and a woman from a cave on a hill to repeople the drowned world.   But on emerging from the cave, the couple were terrified at the sight of the huge tiger and tigress, and they said to the Creator, " O Father, you have sent us to repeople the world, but we do not think that we shall be able to carry out your intention, as the whole world is under water, and the only spot on which we could make a place of rest is occupied by two ferocious beasts, which are waiting to devour us ; give us strength to slay these animals."   After that, they killed the tigers, and lived happily, and begat many sons and daughters, and from them the drowned world was repeopled.[2]

Story of a o old by the Anals of m.

A long story of a great flood is told by the Ahoms of Assam, a branch of the great Shan race of Indo-China, from which their ancestors crossed over the Patkoi mountains about 1228 A.D. to settle in their present abode.[3]   The Ahom, or rather Shan, legend runs as follows :—

Shan story of a gr flood told by the s of Assam.

Long, long ago there were many worlds beneath the sky,

[1] Lieut.-Colonel J. Shakespear, *The Lushei Kuki Clans* (London, 1912), p. 95.

[2] Lieut.-Colonel J. Shakespear, *The Lushei Kuki Clans*, pp. 176 *sq.*

[3] *Census of India, 1891, Assam*, by E. A. Gait (Shillong, 1892), p. 280. Compare Colonel P. R. Gurdon, " The Origin of the Ahoms," *Journal of the Royal Asiatic Society for 1913* (London, 1913), pp. 283-287.

How by
ne   ng
o offer
sacrifices,
      a
excited the
wrath of
the storm-
god.
but in the world of men, the middle world, there was as yet
no race of kings (the Shans). The earth was like a wild
mountainous jungle. On a time, bamboos cracked and
opened, and from them came forth animals. They lived in
deep forests, far from the haunts of men. Thereafter, a king
and queen from heaven, Hpi-pok and Hpi-mot, came down
to earth and found their way to Mong-hi on the Cambodia
River's banks. They were the ancestors of the kingly race
of Shans. But a time came when they made no sacrificial
offerings to their gods. Therefore the storm-god, Ling-
lawn, was angry at their impiety, and he sent down great
cranes to eat them up. The cranes came, but could not eat
all the people up, because there were so many of them.
Then the storm-god sent down great tawny lions, but they
too found more Shans than they could devour. Next he
sent down great serpents to swallow the whole impious
race ; but all the people, from palace to hamlet, from the
oldest to the youngest, attacked the serpents with their
swords, and killed them. The storm-god was enraged, he
snorted threateningly, and the battle was not over.

How there
was a very
great
drought
and the
eo le
died.
        The old year passed, and from the first to the third
month of the new year, which was the nineteenth of the
cycle, there was a great drought. In the fourth month
(March, well on in the dry season) the parched earth cracked
open in wide seams, and many people died of thirst and
famine. But in whatever country they were, there they
must stay. There was no water, and they could not pass
from one country to another. The water dried up in the
deepest ponds and in the broadest rivers ; where elephants
had bathed, the people now dug wells for drinking water.
What had been their watering-places, where many people
had gathered together like swarms of bees in their search
for water, now stank with the bodies of the dead.

How the
storm-god
sent down
the
water-god
to warn the
sage Lip-
g
the coming
flood.
        Then Ling-lawn, the storm-god, called his counsellors—
Kaw-hna and Hseng-kio, old Lao-hki, Tai-long and Bak-
long, and Ya-hseng-hpa, the smooth talker, and many others.
At his court they gathered together. Entering his palace,
they bowed down to worship. Over the head of the god
was an umbrella, widely spread and beautiful as a flower.
They talked together in the language of men (Shan), and

they took counsel to destroy the human race. " Let us send for Hkang-hkak," said they. He was the god of streams and of ponds, of crocodiles and of all water animals. Majestically came he in, and the storm-god gave him instructions, saying, " Descend with the clouds. Tarry not. Straightway report to Lip-long the distinguished lord."

Soon thereafter the water-god Hkang-hkak appeared before the sage Lip-long, who had been consulting his chicken bones. The omens were evil. When the sage came down from his house, the sky was dry as an oven. He knew that some great calamity was impending. On meeting the water-god, therefore, the sage was not surprised to hear him say that Ling-lawn, the storm-god, was about to send a flood to overwhelm the earth. The divine messenger declared that the people of every land would be destroyed, that trees would be uprooted and houses submerged or float bottom up on the water. Even great cities would be overwhelmed. None could escape. Every living thing would be drowned. But against the coming of the flood the sage was commanded to make a strong raft, binding it firmly together with ropes. A cow, too, he was to take with him on the raft, and though all things else should be destroyed, yet would he and the cow escape. He might not even warn his loving wife and dear children of the coming destruction.

Musing on the water-god's sad instructions, the sage went homeward with bowed head in deep dejection. He caught up his little son in his arms and wept aloud. He longed to tell his eldest son, but he feared the cruel vengeance of the gods. Too sore at heart to eat, he went down in the morning hungry and bent to the river's bank. There he toiled day by day, gathering the parts of his raft and firmly binding them side by side. Even his own wife and children jeered at his finished but futile task. From house to house the scoffers mocked and railed. " Quit it, thou fool, thou ass," they cried ; " if this come to the ear of the governors, they will put thee out of the way ; if it come to the ear of the king, he will command thy death." Over the great kingdoms then reigned Hkun Chao and Hkun Chu.

A few days more and the flood came, sweeping on and

How the came and destroyed e ng thing but the sage and the cow.

increasing in violence like the onward rush of a forest fire. Fowls died in their coops. The crying of children was hushed in death. The bellowing of bulls and the trumpeting of elephants ceased as they sank in the water. There was confusion and destruction on every side. All animals were swept away, and the race of men perished. There was no one left in the valleys or on the mountains. The strong raft, bearing the sage Lip-long and the cow, alone floated safe upon the water. Drifting on, he saw the dead bodies of his wife and children. He caught and embraced them, and let them fall back again into the water. As he cast them from him into the deep he wept bitterly ; bitterly did he lament that the storm-god had not given him leave to warn them of the impending doom. Thus perished the kingly race (the Shans). Paying their ferry-hire, their spirits passed over to the mansions of heaven. There they heard the reverberations of the celestial drums. They came by tens of thousands, and eating cold crab they were refreshed. When they reached the spirit-world they looked round and said, " Spirit-land is as festive and charming as a city of wine and women."

How the storm-god sent down the fire-god d ip the flood.

But now the stench of dead bodies, glistering in the su⁻, filled the earth. The storm-god Ling-lawn sent down serpents innumerable to devour them, but they could not, so many were the corpses. The angry god would have put the serpents to death, but they escaped by fleeing into a cave. Then he sent down nine hundred and ninety-nine thousand tigers, but even they could make little headway in the consumption of the corpses and retired discomfited. More angry than ever, the god hurled showers of thunderbolts at the retreating tigers, but they too fled into caves, growling so fiercely that the very sky might have fallen. Then the storm-god sent down Hsen-htam and Hpa-hpai, the god of fire. As they descended, riding their horses, they viewed all the country round. Alighting on a mountain they could see but three elevations of land. They sent forth a great conflagration, scattering their fire everywhere. The fire swept over all the earth, and the smoke ascended in clouds to heaven.

When he saw the fire coming, the sage Lip-long snatched

up a stick and knocked down the cow at one blow. With How the
his sword he ripped up her belly and crawled in. There he g escaped
saw seed of the gourd plant, white as leavened bread. The from the
fire swept over the dead cow, roaring as it went. When it r planted the
was gone, Lip-long came forth, the only living man beneath seeds of a wondrous
the sun. He asked the great water-god Hkang-hkak what gourd vine.
he should do, and the god bade him plant the seed of the
gourd on a level plot of ground. He did so, and one gourd-
vine climbed up a mountain and was scorched by the fierce
rays of the sun. Another vine ran downward, and, soaked
in the water of the flood, it rotted and died. A third vine,
springing upwards with clinging tendrils, twined about the
bushes and trees. News of its rapid growth reached the
ears of Ling-lawn, the storm-god, and he sent down his
gardener to care for the vine. The gardener made haste
and arrived in the early morning at cock-crow. He dug
about and manured the vine. He trailed up its branches
with his own hand. When the rainy season came, the vine
grew by leaps and bounds. It spread far and wide, coiling
itself like a serpent about the shrubs and trees. It blossomed
and bore fruit, great gourds such as no man may see again.

Then Ling-lawn, the rain-god, sent down Sao-pang, the How from
god of the clear sky, to prepare the earth for human habita- the gourds of that he
tion. From him went forth waves of heat to dry up what mankind,
remained of the flood. When the earth was dry once more be sts birds, and
and fit for habitation, the storm-god threw thunderbolts to plants were
break the gourds in pieces. A bolt struck and broke open restore to life.
a gourd. The people within the gourd cried out, " What is
this ? a bolt from a clear sky ; let us go forth to till the
land." Stooping low, they came forth. Again, another
bolt struck another gourd, breaking it open, and the Shans
therein said, " What shall we do, lord ? " He replied, " You
shall come forth to rule many lands." Thus the thunderbolts struck gourd after gourd, and from them came rivers
of water, animals, both tame and wild, domestic fowls and
birds of the air, and every useful plant. So was the earth
filled again with life in all its varied forms.[1]

According to another version of the Shan legend, the Another
persons who survived the deluge were seven men and seven v rs f the Shan legend.

[1] W. W. Cochrane, *The Shans*, i. (Rangoon, 1915) pp. 121-125.

women, who were more righteous than their neighbours and
escaped death by crawling into the dry shell of a gigantic
gourd, which floated on the face of the waters. On emerging
from this ark of safety, they were fruitful and replenished the
drowned earth.[1]

Tradition
that the
valley of
Cashmeer
was once
occupied
by a great
lake, and
that the
water was
raised
away by the
interposi-
tion of
Vishnu.

The secluded Alpine valley of Cashmeer, which by its
delightful climate and beautiful scenery, at once luxuriant
and sublime, has earned for itself the title of the Earthly
Paradise of India, is almost completely surrounded by the
lofty mountain-ranges of the Himalayas, their sides belted
with magnificent forests, above which extend rich Alpine
pastures close up to the limit of eternal snow. A native
tradition, recorded by the early chroniclers of Cashmeer,
relates that the whole of the valley was once occupied by a
great lake. One of the oldest of these annals, called the
Nilamata Purāna, claims to give the sacred legends regarding
the origin of the country, together with the special ordin-
ances which Nila, the lord of the Cashmeerian Nagas, laid
down for the regulation of its religious worship and ceremonies. In this chronicle, which may date from the sixth
or seventh century of our era, we read how at the beginning of the present *Kalpa*, or great era of the world, the
valley was filled by a lake called Satisaras, that is, the Lake
of Sati. Now in the period of the seventh Manu, a certain
demon named Jalodbhava or "water-born," resided in the
lake and caused great distress to all neighbouring countries,
by the devastations which he spread far and wide. But it
so happened that the wise Kasyapa, the father of all Nagas,
went on pilgrimage to the holy places of northern India, and
there he learned of the ravages of the demon from his son
Nila, the king of the Cashmeerian Nagas. The sage promised to punish the evil-doer, and accordingly repaired to
the seat of the great god Brahman to implore his help. His
prayer was granted. At Brahman's command, the whole
host of gods set off for the lake and took up their posts on
the lofty peaks of the Naubandhana Mountain, overlooking
the lake ; that is, on the very same mountain on which,
according to the *Mahabharata*, Manu anchored his ship after
the great flood. But it was vain to challenge the demon to

[1] W. W. Cochrane, *The Shans.* i. 120.

single combat; for in his own element he was invincible, and he was too cunning to quit it and come forth.   In this dilemma the god Vishnu called upon his brother Balabhadra to drain the lake.   His brother did so by piercing the mountains with his weapon, the ploughshare ; the water drained away, and in the dry bed of the lake the demon, now exposed to the assaults of his enemies, was attacked by Vishnu, and after a fierce combat was slain by the deity with his war-disc.   After that King Kasyapa settled the land of Cashmeer, which had thus been born of the waters.   The gods also took up their abode in it, and the various goddesses adorned the country in the shape of rivers.[1]   And a land of rivers and lakes it has been from that day to this.   The same legend is told in a briefer form by the Cashmeerian chronicler Kalhana, who wrote in the middle of the twelfth century of our era, and whose work displays an extremely accurate knowledge both of the topography of the valley and of the popular legends still current among the natives.[2]   And the same story is told, in nearly the same form, by the Mohammedan writers Beddia and Dien :[3] it is alluded to, in a Buddhistic setting, by the famous Chinese pilgrim of the sixth century, Hiuen Tsiang, who lived as an honoured guest for two full years in the happy valley ;[4] and it survives to this day in popular tradition.[5]

Now there are physical facts which seem at first sight to support the belief that in comparatively late geological times the valley of Cashmeer was wholly or in great part occupied by a vast lake ; for undoubted lacustrine deposits are to be seen on some of the tablelands of the valley.[6]   Moreover, "the aspect of the province confirms the truth of the legend, the subsidence of the waters being distinctly defined by horizontal lines on the face of the mountains : it is also not

There is geological evidence that the Cashmeer was once occupied by a lake.

---

[1] (Sir) M. A. Stein, *Kalhana's Rajatarangini, a Chronicle of the Kings of Kaśmir, translated with an Introduction, Commentary and Appendices* (Westminster, 1900), ii. 388 *sq.* Compare M. Winternitz, *Die Flutsagen des Alterthums und der Naturvölker,* p. 307 *n.*[3].   As to the *Nilamata Purana,* see M. A. Stein, *op. cit.* ii. 376 *sqq.*

[2] As to the legend see M. A.

Stein, *op. cit.* vol. i. p. 5 (Book i. §§ 25-27 of the *Rajatarangini*) ; as to Kalhana and his chronicle, see *id.* vol. i. Introduction, pp. 6 *sqq.,* vol. ii. pp. 366 *sqq.*

[3] C. Freiherr von Hügel, *Kaschmir und das Reich der Siek,* ii. (Stuttgart, 1840) pp. 16 *sq.*

[4] M. A. Stein, *op. cit.* ii. 355, 389.

[5] M. A. Stein, *op. cit.* ii. 389.

[6] M. A Stein, *ob. cit.* ii. 389 *sq.*

at all unlikely to have been the scene of some great convulsion of nature, as indications of volcanic action are not
unfrequent : hot springs are numerous : at particular seasons
,the ground in various places is sensibly hotter than the
atmosphere, and earthquakes are of common occurrence."[1]
Are we then to suppose that a tradition of the occupation of
the Vale of Cashmeer by a great lake has survived among
the inhabitants from late geological times to the present
day ? It is true that in Cashmeer the popular local traditions appear to be peculiarly tenacious of life and to outlive
the written traditions of the learned. From the experience
gained on his antiquarian tours, Sir Marc Aurel Stein is
convinced that, when collected with caution and critically
sifted, these local legends may safely be accepted as supple-
ments to the topographical information of our written
records ; and their persistence he attributes in large measure
to the secluded position of the valley and to the naturally
conservative habits of life and thought, which mountain
barriers and consequent isolation tend everywhere to foster
in Alpine countries. Certainly for ages Cashmeer remained,
like Tibet, a hermit land, little known to the outer world
and jealously exclusive of strangers. The army of Alexander, on its victorious march through India, passed almost
within sight of the gates of Cashmeer ; yet the great captain,
thirsting for new worlds to conquer, seems to have heard no
whisper of the earthly paradise that lay beyond these snow-
capped mountains.[2]

Yet the
story of the
existence of
the lake
is more
probably an
inference
from the
natural
features
of the
country
than a
genuine
tradition.

Yet we may reasonably doubt whether any memory of
an event so remote as the comparative desiccation of the
valley of Cashmeer should survive in human tradition even

[1] W. Moorcroft and G. Trebeck,
*Travels in the Himalayan Provinces of
Hindustan and the Panjab ; in Ladakh
and Kashmir ; in Peshawar, Kabul,
Kunduz, and Bokhara* (London, 1841),
ii. 109.

[2] M. A. Stein, *op. cit.* ii. 351, 385.
As to the exclusiveness of the Cashmeerians in the Middle Ages, the great
Arab geographer Albiruni, in his work
on India, writes as follows : " They are
particularly anxious about the natural
strength of their country, and therefore
take always much care to keep a strong
hold upon the entrances and roads
leading into it. In consequence it is
very difficult to have any commerce
with them. In former times they used
to allow one or two foreigners to enter
their country, particularly Jews, but at
present they do not allow any Hindu
whom they do not know personally to
enter, much less other people." See
Albiruni's *India*, English Edition, by
Dr. Edward C. Sachau (London, 1888),
i. 206.

under circumstances so favourable to its preservation. It is far more likely that the legend owes its origin to a natural inference, based partly on observation of the general features of the country, partly on a knowledge of the drainage operations which within the memory of man have extended the area of arable land and reduced the area covered by lakes and marshes. " To any one, however ignorant of geology, but acquainted with the latter fact," says Sir Marc Aurel Stein, " the picture of a vast lake originally covering the whole valley might naturally suggest itself. It would be enough for him to stand on a hillside' somewhere near the Volur, to look down on the great lake and the adjoining marshes, and to glance then beyond towards that narrow gorge of Baramula where the mountains scarcely seem to leave an opening. It is necessary to bear in mind the singular flights of Hindu imagination as displayed in the *Purānas, Māhātmyas* and similar texts. Those acquainted with them will, I think, be ready to allow that the fact of that remarkable gorge being the single exit for the drainage of the country might alone even have sufficed as a starting-point for the legend." [1]

Thus we may fairly conclude that, like the Samothracian legend of a great flood caused by the bursting of the Black Sea and its consequent union with the Mediterranean, the Cashmeer legend furnishes no evidence of human tradition stretching back into the mists of geological time, but is simply the shrewd guess of intelligent observers, who used their wits to supplement the evidence of their eyes. However, it is to be observed that the Cashmeer story hardly falls under the head of flood legends, since it recounts the desiccation rather than the inundation of a mountain basin. No doubt if the event really happened as it is said to have done, it must have caused a tremendous flood in the lowlands beyond the valley ; but as the disastrous consequences can only have concerned other people, the Cashmeerians naturally say nothing about it.

Such stories furnish no evidence of human tradition dating from remote geological eras

[1] M. A. Stein, *op. cit.* ii. 390.

§ 9. *Stories of a Great Flood in Eastern Asia*

According to the Karens of Burma the earth was of old deluged with water, and two brothers saved themselves from the flood on a raft. The waters rose till they reached to heaven, when the younger brother saw a mango-tree hanging down from the celestial vault. With great presence of mind he clambered up it and ate of the fruit, but the flood, suddenly subsiding, left him suspended in the tree. Here the narrative breaks off abruptly, and we are left to conjecture how he extricated himself from his perilous position.[1] The Chingpaws or Singphos of Upper Burma, like their brethren in Assam, have a tradition of a great flood. They say that when the deluge came, a man Pawpaw Nan-chaung and his sister Chang-hko saved themselves in a large boat. They had with them nine cocks and nine needles. After some days of rain and storm they threw overboard one cock and one needle to see whether the waters were falling. But the cock did not crow and the needle was not heard to strike bottom. They did the same thing day after day, but with no better result, till at last on the ninth day the last cock crew and the last needle was heard to strike on a rock. Soon after the brother and sister were able to leave their boat, and they wandered about till they came to a cave inhabited by two elves or fairies (*nats*), a male and a female. The elves bade them stay and make themselves useful in clearing the jungle,

tilling the ground, hewing wood, and drawing water. The brother and sister did so, and soon after the sister gave birth to a child. While the parents were away at work, the old elfin woman, who was a witch, used to mind the baby ; and whenever the infant squalled, the horrid wretch would threaten, if it did not stop bawling, to make mince meat of it at a place where nine roads met. The poor child did not understand the dreadful threat and persisted in giving tongue, till one day the old witch in a fury snatched it up, hurried it to the meeting-place of nine roads, and there hewed it in pieces, and sprinkled the blood and strewed the bits all over the

[1] Rev. E. B. Cross, "On the Karens," *Journal of the American Oriental Society*, vol. iv. no. 2 (1854), p. 304, quoting Mr. Mason (the Rev. F. Mason, D.D.).

roads and the country round about. But some of the titbits she carried back to her cave and made into a savoury curry. Moreover, she put a block of wood into the baby's empty cradle. And when the mother came back from her work in the evening and asked for her child, the witch said, " It is asleep. Eat your rice." So the mother ate the rice and curry, and then went to the cradle, but in it she found nothing but a block of wood. When she asked the witch .where the child was, the witch replied tartly, " You have eaten it." The poor mother fled from the house, and at the cross-roads she wailed aloud and cried to the Great Spirit to give her back her child or avenge its death. The Great Spirit appeared to her and said, " I cannot piece your baby together again, but instead I will make you the mother of all nations of men." And then from one road there sprang up the Shans, from another the Chinese, from others the Burmese, and the Bengalees, and all the races of mankind ; and the bereaved mother claimed them all as her children, because they all sprang from the scattered fragments of her murdered babe.[1]

The Bahnars, a primitive tribe of Cochin China, tell how once on a time the kite quarrelled with the crab, and pecked the crab's skull so hard that he made a hole in it, which may be seen down to this very day. To avenge this injury to his skull, the crab caused the sea and the rivers to swell till the waters reached the sky, and all living beings perished except two, a brother and a sister, who were saved in a huge chest. They took with them into the chest a, pair of every sort of animal, shut the lid tight, and floated on the waters for seven days and seven nights. Then the brother heard a cock crowing outside, for the bird had been sent by the spirits to let our ancestors know that the flood had abated, and that they could come forth from the chest. So the brother let all the birds fly away, then he let loose the animals, and

Story of a
gre   o
told by the
Bahnars of
China.

---

[1] (Sir) J. George Scott and J. P. Hardiman, *Gazetteer of Upper Burma and the Shan States* (Rangoon, 1900–1901), Part i. vol. i. pp. 417 *sq.* For a somewhat fuller version of the legend see Ch. Gilhodes, " Mythologie et Religion des Katchins (Birmanie)," *Anthropos*, iii. (1908) pp. 683-686. The story has also been briefly recorded by Major C. R. Macgregor, who travelled through the country of the Singphos. See his article, " Journey of the Expedition under Colonel Woodthorpe, R. E., from Upper Assam to the Irawadi and return over the Patkoi Range," *Proceedings of the Royal Geographical Society*, New Series, ix. (1887) p. 23.

last of all he and his sister walked out on the dry land. They did not know how they were to live, for they had eaten up all the rice that was stored in the chest. However, a black ant brought them two grains of rice : the brother planted them, and next morning the plain was covered with a rich crop. So the brother and sister were saved.[1]

Story of a
g   o
told by he
Bannavs of
e   me
regioni

A legend of a deluge has been recorded by a French missionary among the Bannavs, one of the savage tribes which inhabit the mountains and tablelands between Cochin China, Laos, and Cambodia. " If you ask them respecting the origin of mankind, all they tell you is, that the father of the human race was saved from an immense inundation by means of a large chest in which he shut himself up ; but of the origin or creator of this father they know nothing. Their traditions do not reach beyond the Deluge ; but they will tell you that in the beginning one grain of rice sufficed to fill a saucepan and furnish a repast for a whole family. This is a souvenir of the first age of the world, that fugitive period of innocence and happiness which poets have called the golden age." [2] The tradition is probably only an abridged form of the deluge legend which, as we have just seen, is recorded by another French missionary among the Bahnars, who may be supposed to be the same with the Bannavs. As to the racial affinity of the tribe, the missionary writes : " To what race do the Bannavs belong ? That is the first question I asked myself on arriving here, and I must confess that I cannot yet answer it ; all I can say is, that in all points they differ from the Annamites and Chinese ; neither do they resemble the Laotians or Cambodians, but appear to have a common origin with the Cédans, Halangs, Reungao, and Giaraïe, their neighbours. Their countenances, costumes, and belief are nearly the same ; and the language, although it differs in each tribe, has yet many words common to all ; the construction, moreover, is perfectly

[1] Guerlach, " Mœurs et superstitions des sauvages Ba-hnars," *Les Missions Catholiques*, xix. (Lyons, 1887) p. 479. Compare Combes in *Annales de la Propagation de la Foi*, xxvii. (1855) pp. 432 *sq.* ; A. Bastian, " Beiträge zur Kenntniss der Gebirgsstamme in Kambodia," *Zeitschrift der Gesellschaft für Erdkunde zu Berlin*, i. (1866) p. 42.

[2] Henri Mouhot, *Travels in the Central Parts of Indo-China (Siam), Cambodia, and Laos* (London, 1864), ii. 28 *sq.*, quoting the letter of a French missionary, M. Comte, who lived among these savages for several years.

identical. I have not visited the various tribes of the south, but from all I have heard I conclude that these observations apply to them also, and that all the savages inhabiting the vast country lying between Cochin China, Laos, and Cambodia, belong to the same great branch of the human family." [1]

The Benua-Jakun, a primitive aboriginal tribe of the Malay Peninsula, in the State of Johor, say that the ground on which we stand is not solid, but is merely a skin covering an abyss of water. In ancient times Pirman, that is the deity, broke up this skin, so that the world was drowned and destroyed by a great flood. However, Pirman had created a man and a woman and put them in a ship of *pulai* wood, which was completely covered over and had no opening. In this ship the pair floated and tossed about for a time, till at last the vessel came to rest, and the man and woman, nibbling their way through its side, emerged on dry ground and beheld this our world stretching away on all sides to the horizon. At first all was very dark, for there was neither morning nor evening, because the sun had not yet been created. When it grew light, they saw seven small shrubs of rhododendron and seven clumps of the grass called *sambau*. They said one to another, "Alas, in what a sad plight are we, without either children or grandchildren!" But some time afterwards the woman conceived in the calves of her legs, and from her right calf came forth a male, and from her left calf came forth a female. That is why the offspring of the same womb may not marry. All mankind are the descendants of the two children of the first pair. [2]

In Kelantan, a district of the Malay Peninsula, they say that one day a feast was made for a circumcision, and all manner of beasts were pitted to fight against one another. There were fights between elephants, and fights between buffaloes, and fights between bullocks, and fights between goats; and at last there were fights between dogs and cats. And when the fights took place between dogs and cats,

Story of a great flood told by the Benua-Jakun of Johor, in the Malay Peninsula.

Another story of a great flood told in the Malay Peninsula

M. Comte (missionary), quoted by H. Mouhot, *Travels in the Central Parts of Indo-China (Siam), Cambodia, and Laos*, ii. 25.

[note] J. R. Logan, "The Orang Binua of Johore "*Journal of the Indian Archipelago*, i. (1847) p. 278; W. W. Skeat and C. O. Blagden, *Pagan Races of the Malay Peninsula* (London, 1906), ii. 355-357.

a great flood came down from the mountains, and overwhelmed the people that dwelt in the plains. And they
were all drowned in that flood, save only some two or three
menials who had been sent up into the hills to gather firewood. Then the sun, moon, and stars were extinguished,
and there was a great darkness. And when light returned,
there was no land but a great sea, and all the abodes of men
had been overwhelmed.[1]

The
Lolos, an
aboriginal
race of
Southern
China.

The legend of a great flood plays an important part in
the traditionary lore of the Lolos, an aboriginal race who
occupy the almost impregnable mountain fastnesses of
Yunnan and other provinces of South-Western China, where
they have succeeded in maintaining their independence
against the encroachments of the Chinese. A robust and
warlike people, they not only make raids into Chinese territory for the purpose of levying blackmail and carrying off
prisoners, whom they hold to ransom, but they actually
maintain a large population of slaves entirely composed of
Chinese captives. Yet in spite of their hostility to the
Chinese, with whom they never intermarry, they appear to
belong to the same race ; at least they speak a monosyllabic
language of extreme simplicity, which belongs to the Tibeto-
Burman branch of the Tibeto-Chinese family. They are
so far from being savages that they have even invented
a mode of writing, pictographic in origin, in which they
have recorded their legends, songs, genealogies, and religious
ritual. Their manuscripts, copied and recopied, have been
handed down from generation to generation.[2] They bear
family surnames, which are said always to signify a plant or
an animal ; the members of each family believe that they
are descended from the species of animal or plant whose
name they bear, and they will neither eat nor even touch it.
These facts suggest the existence of totemism among the

[1] Walter Skeat, *Fables and Folk-
tales from an Eastern Forest* (Cambridge, 1901), pp. 62 *sq.*

[2] E. C. Baber, "China, in some of
its Physical and Social Aspects," *Proceedings of the Royal Geographical
Society*, N.S., v. (1883) p. 445 ; A.
Henry, "The Lolos and other Tribes
of Western China," *Journal of the*
Anthropological Institute, xxxiii. (1903)
pp. 96, 98 *sqq.* Their script is
arranged in vertical columns, which
are read from left to right, instead of,
as in Chinese, from right to left. As
to the affinity of the Lolo language
with Chinese, see E. A. Gait in *Census
of India, 1911*, vol. i. Part i. (Calcutta, 1913) pp. 329 *sq.*

Lolos. At the same time the Lolos believe in patriarchs
who now live in the sky, but who formerly dwelt on earth,
where they attained to the great ages of six hundred and
sixty and even nine hundred and ninety years, thereby
surpassing Methusaleh himself in longevity. Each family,
embracing the persons united by a common surname, pays
its devotions to a particular patriarch. The most famous of
these legendary personages is a certain Tse-gu-dzih, who
enjoys many of the attributes of divinity. He it was who
brought death into the world by opening the fatal box which
contained the seeds of mortality ; and he too it was who
caused the deluge. The catastrophe happened thus. Men
were wicked, and Tse-gu-dzih sent down a messenger to
them on earth, asking for some flesh and blood from a mortal.
No one would give them except only one man, Du-mu by
name. So Tse - gu - dzih in wrath locked the rain - gates,
and the waters mounted to the sky. But Du-mu, who
complied with the divine injunction, was saved, together with
his four sons, in a log hollowed out of a *Pieris* tree ; and
with them in the log were likewise saved otters, wild ducks
and lampreys. From his four sons are descended the
civilized peoples who can write, such as the Chinese and the
Lolos. But the ignorant races of the world are the descendants of the wooden figures whom Du-mu constructed after
the deluge in order to repeople the drowned earth. To this
day the ancestral tablets which the Lolos worship on set days
of the year and on all the important occasions of life, are
made out of the same sort of tree as that in which their great
forefather found safety from the waters of the deluge ; and
nearly all the Lolo legends begin with some reference to him
or to the great flood. In considering the origin of this flood
legend it should be mentioned that the Lolos generally keep a
Sabbath of rest every sixth day, when ploughing is forbidden,
and in some places women are not allowed to sew or wash
clothes. Taken together with this custom, the Lolo traditions of the patriarchs and of the flood appear to betray
Christian influence ; and Mr. A. Henry may well be right in
referring them all to the teaching of Nestorian missionaries ;
for Nestorian churches existed in Yunnan in the thirteenth
century when Marco Polo travelled in the country, and the

Nestorian Alopen is said to have arrived in China as early as 635 A.D.[1]

Chinese tradition of a great flood.

The Chinese have a tradition of a great flood which happened in the reign of the emperor Yao, who reigned in the twenty-fourth century before our era. In his distress the emperor addressed his prime minister, saying, "Ho! President of the Four Mountains, destructive in their overflow are the waters of the inundation. In their vast extent they embrace the hills and overtop the great heights, threatening the heavens with their floods, so that the lower people groan and murmur! Is there a capable man to whom I can assign the correction of this calamity?" All the court replied to the emperor, saying, "Is there not Khwan?" But the emperor answered, "Alas! how perverse is he! He is disobedient to orders, and tries to injure his peers." The prime minister rejoined, "Well, but try whether he can accomplish the work." So the emperor employed Khwan, and said to him, "Go, and be reverent!" Thus put on his mettle Khwan worked assiduously for nine years, but he laboured in vain, for at the end of the nine years the work was still unaccomplished, the floods were still out. Yet did his son Yu afterwards cope successfully with the inundation, accomplishing all that he had undertaken and showing his superiority to other men.[2] This Chinese tradition has been by some people forcibly identified with the Biblical account of the Noachian deluge, but in truth it hardly belongs to the class of diluvial legends at all, since it obviously records merely a local, though widespread, inundation, not a

The tradition seems to contain the reminiscence of a local inundation caused by the Yellow River.

---

[1] A. Henry, "The Lolos and other Tribes of Western China," *Journal of the Anthropological Institute*, xxxiii. (1903) pp. 103, 105 *sq.* As to the spread of Nestorian Christianity among the Tartars on the borders of China, see J. L. Mosheim, *Ecclesiastical History* (London, 1819), ii. 372 *sqq.* According to that historian (pp. 373 *sq.*) it is certain that the monarchs of the Karit nation, "which makes a large part of the empire of the Mogul, and is by some denominated a province of the Turks, and by others a tribe of Tartars," embraced Christianity in the tenth century, and that a considerable part of Tartary lived under the spiritual jurisdiction of bishops who were sent thither by the Nestorian pontiff. See further Gibbon, *Decline and Fall of the Roman Empire*, ch. xlvii. (vol. vi. pp. 68 *sqq.*, London, 1838), who says (p. 70) that "under the reign of the caliphs, the Nestorian church was diffused from China to Jerusalem and Cyprus; and their numbers, with those of the Jacobites, were computed to surpass the Greek and Latin communions."

[2] *The Sacred Books of China*, translated by James Legge, Part i. (Oxford, 1879) pp. 34 *sq.*, 49 (*The Sacred Books of the East*, vol. iii.).

universal cataclysm in which the greater part· of mankind perished. The event it describes may well have been a real flood caused by the Yellow River, a great and very rapid stream, partially enclosed by artificial and ill-constructed banks and dykes, which in modern times have often burst and allowed the water to spread devastation over the surrounding country. Hence the river is a source of perpetual anxiety and expense to the Chinese Government; and it is the opinion of a modern observer that a repetition of the great flood of Yao's time might still occur and lay the most fertile and populous plains of China under water.[1]

That the Chinese were, totally unacquainted with traditions of a universal deluge may be affirmed on the high authority of a Chinese emperor. In the ninth century of our era an Arab traveller, named Ibn-Wahab, of Koraishite origin, of the family of Habbar Ben el-Aswad, made his way by sea from Bassorah to India and thence to China. Arrived there, he sought an interview with the Chinese emperor, alleging as part of his credentials that he was of the family of the Prophet Mohammed. The emperor caused inquiries to be instituted on this point, and being satisfied as to the truth of the allegation, he admitted the traveller to his presence and held a long conversation with him through an interpreter. The Arab has recorded at some length what passed between him and his august interlocutor. Amongst other things the emperor asked him, through the interpreter, whether he could recognize his Lord, that is to say, the Prophet Mohammed, if he should see him. " How can I see him ? " said the Arab, " he is with God." " I do not mean it literally," replied the emperor, " but in a representation." The Arab answered that he could. The emperor then ordered a box to be brought ; and when it was before him, he took a casket out of it, and said to the interpreter, " Show him his Lord." The Arab looked. " And I saw," he tells us, " in the casket, the images of the prophets. My lips muttered benedictions upon them. The king did not know that I knew them ; hence, he said to

(marginal note:) That the e have no traditions ni· versal deluge was affirmed by a Chinese Emperor in a discussion with an Arab traveller.

[1] John Francis Davis, *The Chinese* (London, 1845–1851), i. 137, 140 *sq.*; Sir Charles Lyell, *Principles of Geo- logy*, Twelfth Edition (London, 1875) i. 10 *sq.*; R. Andree, *Die Flutsagen* pp. 35-38.

the interpreter, 'Ask him why he moves his lips.' He interrogated me, and I answered him that I was pronouncing benedictions upon the prophets. He asked me further how I recognized them, and I told him that I knew them by the attributes with which they were represented. 'This,' I exclaimed, 'is Nuh in the ark; he has been saved with those who were with him whilst God submerged the whole earth, and all that was on it.' He smiled and said, 'It is Nuh, as thou sayest, but it is not true that the whole earth was inundated. The flood occupied only a part of the globe, and did not reach our country. Your traditions are correct, as far as that part of the earth is concerned which you inhabit; but we, the inhabitants of China, of India, of es-Sind, and other nations, do not agree with your account; nor have our forefathers left us a tradition agreeing with yours on this head. As to thy belief that the whole earth was covered with water, I must remark that this would be so remarkable an event that the terror would keep up its recollection, and all the nations would have handed it down to their posterity.' I endeavoured to answer him, and to bring forth arguments against his assertion in defence of my statement."[1] The Arab has not reported the arguments with which he maintained the truth of the Noachian tradition, but we may surmise that they did not succeed in shaking the incredulity of the sceptical emperor.

Kamchad-
es
of a great
flood.

The Kamchadales have a tradition of a great flood which covered the whole land in the early days of the world. A remnant of the people saved themselves on large rafts made of tree-trunks bound together; on these they loaded their property and provisions, and on these they drifted

---

[1] El-Mas'udí's *Historical Encyclopædia, entitled "Meadows of Gold and Mines of Gems"* translated from the Arabic by Alois Sprenger, i. (London, 1841) pp. 335 *sq.* Compare *Ancient Accounts of India and China by Two Mohammedan Travellers, who went to those parts in the ninth century*, translated from the Arabic by Eusebius Renaudot (London, 1733), pp. 54 *sq.*; John Pinkerton, *General Collection of Voyages and Travels* (London, 1808–1814), vii. 204 *sq.* Mohammed acknowledged Noah to be a great prophet, but the references in the Koran to the deluge and the ark, though frequent enough, are all comparatively slight and cursory. See *The Koran*, chapters vii., x., xi., xxiii., xxvi., xxix., liv., lxxi.; *The Qur'ân*, translated by E. H. Palmer (Oxford, 1880), Part i. pp. 144 *sq.*, 200 *sq.*, 207-210, Part ii. pp. 66, 94, 119, 255 *sq.*, 302-304 (*The Sacred Books of the East*, vols. vi. and ix.).

about, dropping stones tied to straps instead of anchors in order to prevent the flood from sweeping them away out to sea. When at last the water of the deluge sank, it left the people and their rafts stranded high and dry on the tops of the mountains.[1]

In a Chinese Encyclopaedia there occurs the following passage : "*Eastern Tartary.*—In travelling from the shore of the Eastern Sea toward Che-lu, neither brooks nor ponds are met with in the country, although it is intersected by mountains and valleys. Nevertheless there are found in the sand very far away from the sea, oyster-shells and the shields of crabs. The tradition of the Mongols who inhabit the country is, that it has been said from time immemorial that in remote antiquity the waters of the deluge flooded the district, and when they retired, the places where they had been made their appearance covered with sand." [2]

Mongolian
ry
great flood

§ 10. *Stories of a Great Flood in the Indian Archipelago*

The Battas or Bataks of Sumatra say that in the beginning of time the earth rested on the head, or rather on the three horns, of Naga Padoha, a monster who is described as a serpent with the horns of a cow, but who appears to have been also provided with hands and feet. When Naga Padoha grew weary of supporting the earth on his horns, he shook his head, and the earth sank into the water. Thereupon the high god Batara Guru set about recovering it from the watery abyss. For that purpose he sent down his daughter Puti-orla-bulan ; indeed she requested to be despatched on this beneficent mission. So down she came, riding on a white owl and accompanied by a dog. But she found all the nether world so covered with water that there was no ground for the soles of her feet to rest upon. In this emergency her divine father Batara Guru came to the rescue of his child, and let Mount Bakarra fall from heaven to be an abode for her. It may be seen in the land of the

Story of a
gre   o
told by the
Battas or
s
Sumatra.

---

[1] G. W. Steller, *Beschreibung von dem Lande Kamtschatka* (Frankfort and Leipsic, 1774), p. 273.

" (Sir) E. B. Tylor, *Researches into the Early History of Mankind*, Third Edition (London, 1878), pp. 328 *sq.*, referring to *Mémoires concernant. les Chinois*, vol. iv. p. 481, and to G. Klemm, *Allgemeine Cultur-Geschichte*, vi. 467.

Battas to this day, and from it gradually sprang all the rest
of the habitable earth.   Batara Guru's daughter had afterwards three sons and three daughters, from whom the whole
of mankind are descended, but who the father of them all
may have been is not revealed by the legend.   The restored
earth was again supported on the horns of Naga Padoha;
and from that time forward there has been a constant
struggle between him and Batara Guru, the monster always
trying to rid himself of his burden, and the deity always
endeavouring to prevent him from so doing.   Hence come
the frequent earthquakes, which shake the world in general
and the island of Sumatra in particular.   At last, when the
monster proved obstreperous, Batara Guru sent his son
Layang-layang mandi (which means the diving swallow [1])
to tie Naga Padoha's hands and feet.   But even when he
was thus fettered, the monster continued to shake his head,
so that earthquakes have not ceased to happen.   And he
will go on shaking himself till he snaps his fetters.   Then
the earth will again sink into the sea, and the sun will
approach to within an ell of this our world.   The men of
that time will, according to their merit, either be transported
to heaven or cast into the flaming cauldron in which Batara
Guru torments the wicked until they have expiated their
sins.   At the destruction of the world, the fire of the
cauldron will join with the fire of the sun to consume the
material universe.[2]

Another
version of
the Batta
story.

A less grandiose version of the Batta belief, which in the
preceding form unites the reminiscence of a universal flood
with the prophecy of a future destruction of the earth by
water and fire, is recorded by a modern traveller, who visited
the Battas in their mountain home.   According to him, the
people say that, when the earth grew old and dirty, the
Creator, whom they call Debata, sent a great flood to destroy
every living thing.   The last human pair had taken refuge
on the top of the highest mountain, and the waters of the
deluge had already reached to their knees, when the Lord of
All repented of his resolution to make an end of mankind.
So he took a clod of earth, kneaded it into shape, tied it to

---

[1] In German, *die Taucherschwalbe.*   *Kawi - Sprache auf der Insel Java*
[2] W. von Humboldt, *Uber die*   (Berlin, 1836–1839), i. 239-241.

a thread, and laid it on the rising flood, and the last pair stepped on it and were saved. As the descendants of the couple multiplied, the clod increased in size till it became the earth which we all inhabit at this day.[1]

The natives of Nias, an island to the west of Sumatra, say that in days of old there was a strife between the mountains of their country as to which of them was the highest. The strife vexed their great ancestor Balugu Luomewona, and in his vexation he went to the window and said, " Ye mountains, I will cover you all ! " So he took a golden comb and threw it into the sea, and it became a huge crab, which stopped up the sluices whereby the waters of the sea usually run away. The consequences of the stoppage were disastrous. The ocean rose higher and higher till only the tops of two or three mountains in Nias still stood above the heaving billows. All the people who with their cattle had escaped to these mountains were saved, and all the rest were drowned. That is how the great ancestor of the islanders settled the strife between the mountains ; and the strife is proverbial among his descendants to the present day.[2]

The natives of Engano, another island to the west of Sumatra, have also their story of a great flood. Once on a time, they say, the tide rose so high that it overflowed the island and every living being was drowned, except one woman. She owed her preservation to the fortunate circumstance that, as she drifted along on the tide, her hair caught in a thorny tree, to which she was thus enabled to cling. When the flood sank, she came down from the tree, and saw with sorrow that she was left all alone in the world. Beginning to feel the pangs of hunger, she wandered inland in the search for food, but finding nothing to eat, she returned disconsolately to the beach, where she hoped to catch a fish. A fish, indeed, she saw ; but when she tried to catch it, the creature glided into one of the corpses that were floating on the water or weltering on the shore. Not to be

[1] J. Freiherr von Brenner, *Besuch bei den Kannibalen Sumatras* (Wurzburg, 1894), p. 218.

[2] L. N. H. A. Chatelin, " Godsdienst en bijgeloof der Niassers," *Tijdschrift voor Indische Taal- Land- en Volkenkunde*, xxvi. (1880) p. 115 ; H. Sundermann, *Die Insel Nias* (Barmen, 1905), pp. 70 *sq.* According to the latter writer it was not Balugu Luomewona but his wife, Silewe nazarata, who caused the flood by throwing her golden comb into the sea.

balked, the woman picked up a stone and struck the corpse a smart blow therewith. But the fish leaped from its hiding-place and made off in the direction of the interior. The woman followed, but hardly had she taken a few steps when, to her great surprise, she met a living man. When she asked him what he did there, seeing that she herself was the sole survivor of the flood, he answered that somebody had knocked on his dead body, and that in consequence he had returned to life. The woman now related to him her experiences, and together they resolved to try whether they could not restore all the other dead to life in like manner by knocking on their corpses with stones. No sooner said than done. The drowned men and women revived under the knocks, and thus was the island repeopled after the great flood.[1]

Story of a
g   o d
told by the
Sea Dyaks
of Borneo.

The Ibans or Sea Dyaks of Sarawak, in Borneo, are fond of telling a story which relates how the present race of men survived a great deluge, and how their ancestress discovered the art of making fire. The story runs thus. Once upon a time some Dyak women went to gather young bamboo shoots for food. Having got them, they walked through the jungle till they came to what they took to be a great fallen tree. So they sat down on it and began to pare the bamboo shoots, when to their astonishment the trunk of the tree exuded drops of blood at every cut of their knives. Just then up came some men, who saw at once that what the women were sitting on was not a tree but a gigantic boa-constrictor in a state of torpor. They soon killed the serpent, cut it up, and carried the flesh home to eat. While they were busy frying the pieces, strange noises were heard to issue from the frying-pan, and a torrential rain began to fall and never ceased falling till all the hills, except the highest, were submerged and the world was drowned, all because these wicked men had killed and fried the serpent. Men and animals all perished in the flood, except one woman, a dog, a rat, and a few small creatures, who fled to the top of a very high mountain. There, seeking shelter from the pouring rain, the woman

---

[1] O. L. Helfrich, " Nadere bijdrage tot de kennis van het Engganeesch," *Bijdragen tot de Taal- Land- en Vol-* *kenkunde van Nederlandsch-Indie*, lxxi. (1916) pp. 543 *sq.*

noticed that the dog had found a warm place under a creeper ; How the art of making fire was c vere by the friction of against a tree.
for the creeper was swaying to and fro in the wind and was
warmed by rubbing against the trunk of the tree. She took
the hint, and rubbing the creeper hard against a piece of
wood she produced fire for the first time. That is how the
art of making fire by means of the fire-drill was discovered
after the great flood. Having no husband the woman took
the fire-drill for her mate, and by its help she gave birth to
a son called Simpang-impang, who, as his name implies,
was but half a man, since he had only one arm, one leg,
one eye, one ear, one cheek, half a body, and half a nose.
These natural defects gave great offence to his playmates the
animals, and at last he was able to supply them by striking
a bargain with the Spirit of the Wind, who had carried off
some rice which Simpang-impang had spread out to dry.
At first, when Simpang-impang demanded compensation for
this injury, the Spirit of the Wind flatly refused to pay him
a farthing ; but being vanquished in a series of contests with
Simpang-impang, he finally consented, instead of paying him
in gongs or other valuables, of which indeed he had none, to
make a whole man of him by supplying him with the missing
parts and members. Simpang-impang gladly accepted the
proposal, and that is why mankind have been provided with
the usual number of arms and legs ever since.[1]

. Another Dyak version of the story relates how, when Another Dyak stor of a great flood and e repeopling of the ьаии.
the flood began, a certain man called Trow made a boat out
of a large wooden mortar, which had hitherto served for
pounding rice. In this vessel he embarked with his wife, a
dog, a pig, a fowl, a cat, and other live creatures, and so
launched out on the deep. The crazy ship outrode the storm,
and when the flood had subsided, Trow and his wife and the
animals disembarked. How to repeople the earth after the
destruction of nearly the entire human race was now the
problem which confronted Trow ; and in order to grapple
with it he had recourse to polygamy, fashioning for him-

[1] Rev. J. Perham, in *Journal of the Straits Branch of the Royal Asiatic Society*, No. 6, December 1880 (Singapore, 1881), pp. 289-291 ; H. Ling Roth, *The Natives of Sarawak and British North Borneo* (London, 1896), i. 301 *sq.* ; Charles Hose and William McDougall, *The Pagan Tribes of Borneo* (London, 1912), ii. 144-147. This Dyak story of the flood is told more briefly by Leo Nyuak, "Religious rites and customs of the Iban or Dyaks of Sarawak," *Anthropos*, i. (1906) p. 17.

self new wives out of a stone, a log, and anything else
that came to hand. So he soon had a large and flourish-
ing' family, who learned to till the ground and became the
ancestors of various Dyak tribes.[1]   The Ot-Danoms, a tribe
of Dutch Borneo in the valley of the Barito, tell of a great
deluge which drowned many people.   Only one mountain
peak rose above the water, and the few people who were
able to escape to it in ,boats dwelt on it for three months,
till the flood subsided and the dry land appeared once
more.[2]

The Bare'e-speaking Toradjas of Central Celebes also tell
of a flood which once covered the highest mountains, all
but the summit of Mount Wawo mPebato, and in proof
of their story they point to the sea-shells which are to
be found on the tops of hills two thousand feet and more
above the level of the sea.   Nobody escaped the flood except
a pregnant woman and a pregnant mouse, who saved themselves in a pig's trough and floated about, paddling with
a pot-ladle ·instead of an oar, till the waters sank down
and the earth again became habitable.   Just then the
woman, looking about for rice to sow, spied a sheaf of rice
hanging from an uprooted tree, which drifted ashore on the
spot where she was standing.   With the help of the mouse,
who climbed up the tree and brought down the sheaf, she
was able to plant rice again.   But before she fetched down
the sheaf, the mouse stipulated that as a recompense for her
services mice should thenceforth have the right to eat up
part of the harvest.   That is why the mice come every year
to fetch the reward of their help from the fields of ripe rice ;
only they may not strip the ,fields too bare.   As for the
woman, she in due time gave birth to a son, whom she took,
for want of another, to be her husband.   By him she had a
son and daughter, who became the ancestors of the present
race of mankind.[3]   In Minahassa, a district of northern

Marginal notes:

Ot-Danom great flood

Story of a great flood told by the Bare'e-speaking Torad'as of Celebes.

[1] H. Ling Roth, *The Natives of
Sarawak and British North Borneo*
(London, 1896), i. 300, quoting C. T.
C. Grant, *A Tour amongst the Dyaks
of Sarawak,* (London, 1864), p. 68.
[2] C. A. L. M. Schwaner, *Borneo,
Beschrijving van het Stroomgebied van
den Barito* (Amsterdam, 1853–1854),

ii. 151.
[3] N. Adriani en Alb. C. Kruijt,
*De Bare'e-sprekende Toradja's van
Midden Celebes* (Batavia, 1912–1914),
i. 20, 247, ii. 258, iii. 386.   The
narrative, as told in these passages,
presents some trifling variations. Thus,
in one passage the woman is already

Celebes, there is a mountain called Lankooe, and the natives A reminis-
say that on the top of that mountain the dove which Noah e   f the
Biblical
sent out of the ark plucked the olive-branch which she story in
brought back to the patriarch.[1] The story is clearly due to Minahassa.
Mohammedan or Christian influence. In a long Malay
poem, taken down in the island of Sunda, we read how
Noah and his family were saved in the ark from the great
flood, which lasted forty days, and during the prevalence
of which all mountains were submerged except Goonoong
Padang and Goonoong Galoonggoong.[2]

The Alfoors of Ceram, a large island between Celebes Story of a
and New Guinea, relate that after a great flood, which over- great floo
and of he
whelmed the whole world, the mountain Noesakoe appeared repeopling
above the sinking tide, its sides clothed with great trees, of o t   wo
old bv the
which the leaves were shaped like the female organs of Alfoors of
generation. Only three persons survived on the top of the eram.
mountain, but the sea-eagle brought them tidings that other
mountain peaks had emerged from the waters. So the three
persons went thither, and by means of the remarkable leaves
of the trees they repeopled the world.[3] The inhabitants of Story of a
Rotti, a small island to the south-west of Timor, say that in great flood
told by the
former times the sea flooded the earth, so that all men and natives of
animals were drowned and all plants and herbs beaten down Rotti.
to the earth. Not a spot of dry ground was left. Even
the high mountains were submerged, only the peak of Lakimola, in Bilba, still rose solitary over the waves. On that
mountain a man and his wife and children had taken refuge.
After some months the tide still came creeping up and up
the mountain, and the man and his family were in great

---

a mother at the time of the flood and
saves her son along with herself in the
pig's trough. In others it seems that
the mouse did not escape with the
woman in the trough, but appeared
opportunely just at the time when its
help was wanted.

[1] J. G. F. Riedel, "De Minahasa
in 1825," *Tijdschrift voor Indische
Taal- Land- en Volkenkunde*, xviii.
(1872) p. 491.

C. M. Pleyte, " De Patapaan
Adjar soeka rĕsi, anders gezegd de

kleuzenarij op den Goenoeng Padang,"
*Tijdschrift voor Indische Taal- Land-
en Volkenkunde*, lv. (1913) pp. 332-
334.

[3] A. Bastian, *Die Culturländer des
alten America* (Berlin, 1878), i. 509
n.[1]; R. Andree, *Die Flutsagen*, p.
31 ; G. Gerland *Der Mythus von der
Sintflut*, p. 63, referring to P v. Crab,
De Moluksche Eilanden (Batavia,
1862), pp. 212 *sq.* Compare P. Four-
nier, "De zuidkust van Ceram," *Tijdschrift voor Indische Taal- Land- en
Volkenkunde*, xvi. (1866) p. 153.

fear, for they thought it would soon reach them.   So they
prayed the sea to return to his old bed.   The sea answered,
" I will do so, if you give me an animal whose hairs I cannot
count."   The man thereupon heaved first a pig, then a goat,
then a dog, and then a hen into the flood, but all in vain ;
the sea could number the hairs of every one of them, and it
still came on.   At last he threw in a cat : this was too much
for the sea, it could not do the sum, and sank abashed
accordingly.   After that the osprey appeared and sprinkled
some dry earth on the waters, and the man and his wife
and children descended the mountain to seek a new home.
Thereupon the Lord commanded the osprey to bring all
kinds of seed to the man, such as maize, millet, rice, beans,
pumpkins, and sesame, in order that he might sow them and
live with his family on the produce.   That is the reason
why in Rotti, at the end of harvest, people set up a sheaf of

Annual
festival of
thanks-
giving to
Mount
Lakimola.

rice on the open place of the village as an offering to Mount
Lakimola.   Everybody cooks rice, and brings it with betel-
nuts, coco-nuts, tobacco, bananas, and breadfruit as an oblation to the mountain ; they feast and dance all kinds of
dances to testify their gratitude, and beg him to grant a good
harvest next year also, so that the people may have plenty
to eat.[1]

Story of a
great flood
told by the
natives of
Flores.

The Nages, in the centre of the East Indian island
of Flores, say that Dooy, the forefather of their tribe,
was saved in a ship from the great flood.   His grave
is under a stone platform, which occupies the centre
of the public square at Boa Wai, the tribal capital.
The harvest festival, which is attended not only by the
villagers but also by people from far and near, takes place
round this grave of their great ancestor.   The people
dance round the grave, and sacrifices of buffaloes are offered.
The spirits of all dead members of the tribe, wherever they
may be, whether in the air, or in the mountains, or in the
caves and dens of the earth, are invited to attend the
festival and are believed to be invisibly present at it.   On
this occasion the civil chief of the tribe is gorgeously
arrayed in golden jewellery, and on his head he wears the

[1] J. Fanggidaej, " Rottineesche Verhalen," *Bijdragen tot de Taal- Land- en
Volkenkunde van Nederlandsch-Indie*, lviii. (1905) pp. 427 *sq.*

golden model of a ship with seven masts in memory of the escape of their great ancestor from the flood.[1]

Stories of a great flood are told also by some of the wild tribes of Mindanao, one of the Philippine Islands. One such tale is said to be current among the Atás of the Davao District, who are supposed to be descendants of an invading people that intermarried with the Negritoes and other aboriginal tribes. Their legend of the deluge runs thus. The greatest of all the spirits is Manama, who made the first men from blades of grass, weaving them together until they assumed the human form. In this manner he created eight persons, male and female, who later became the ancestors of the Atás and all the neighbouring tribes. Long afterwards the water covered the whole earth, and all the Atás were drowned except two men and a woman. The waters carried them far away, and they would have perished if a great eagle had not come to their aid. The bird offered to carry them on its back to their homes. One of the men refused, but the other man and the woman accepted the offer and returned to Mapula.[2] Another version of the story is told by the Mandayas, another wild tribe of the same district, who inhabit a rugged, densely wooded region, where the mountains descend almost to the water's edge, forming high sheer cliffs at their base. They say that many generations ago a great flood happened, which' drowned all the inhabitants of the world except one pregnant woman. She prayed that her child might be a boy. Her prayer was answered, and she gave birth to a boy whose name was Uacatan. When he grew up, he took his mother to wife, and from their union all the Mandayas are descended.[3]

Further, stories of a great flood are current among the wild tribes which occupy the central mountains and eastern coasts of Formosa ; and as these tribes apparently belong

Stories of a g ea ı d told by the Philippine ıslanders.

Stories of a g e ood told by the wild tribes of Formosa.

[1] G. Beker, "Het oogst- en offer-ıest bij den Nage-stam te Boa Wai (Midden-Flores)," *Bijdragen tot de Taal- Land- en Volkenkunde van Neder-landsch-Indie*, lxvii. (1913) pp. 623 *sqq.* The brief reference to the flood occurs on page 625.

[2] Fay-Cooper Cole, *The Wild Tribes of Davao District, Mindanao* (Chicago, 1913), p. 164 (*Field Museum of Natural History, Publication 170*).

[3] Fay-Cooper Cole, *op. cit.* pp. 165, 173.

by race and language to the Malayan family,[1] their traditions of a deluge may appropriately find a place here, though the large island which is their home lies off the coast of China. The stories have been recorded by a Japanese gentleman, Mr. Shinji Ishii, who resided for some years in Formosa for the sake of studying the natives. He has very kindly placed his unpublished manuscripts at my disposal for the purposes of this work.

The Ami tribe of Formosa.

One of the tribes which inhabit the eastern coast of Formosa are the Ami. They are supposed to have been the last to arrive in this part of the island. Unlike the rest of the aborigines, they trace the descent of blood and property through their mothers instead of through their fathers, and they have a peculiar system of age-grades, that is, they classify all members of the tribe in a series of ranks according to their respective ages.[2] Among these people Mr. Ishii discovered the story of a great flood in several different versions. One of them, recorded at the village of Kibi, runs as follows :—

Ami story of a great

In ancient times there existed the god Kakumodan Sappatorroku and the goddess Budaihabu. They descended to a place called Taurayan, together with two children, the boy Sura and the girl Nakao. At the same time they brought with them a pig and a chicken, which they reared. But one day it happened that two other gods, named Kabitt and Aka, were hunting near by, and seeing the pig and the chicken they coveted them. So they went up to the house and asked Kakumodan to give them the creatures, but having nothing to offer in exchange they met with a flat refusal. That angered them, and to avenge the affront they plotted to kill Kakumodan. To assist them in carrying out this nefarious design they called in a loud voice on the four sea-gods, Mahahan, Mariyaru, Marimokoshi, and Kosomatora,

[1] C. Imbault-Huart, *L'Ile Formose, Histoire et Description* (Paris, 1893), p. 255. From a comparison of the Formosan language with that of the natives about Manila, it has been suggested that the ancestors of the Formosans may have migrated from the Philippine Islands on their way from the Malay Archipelago to their present abode. See C. Imbault-Huart, *op. cit.* p. 261.

[2] Shinji Ishii, "The Island of Formosa and its Primitive Inhabitants," pp. 13, 20; reprinted from *The Transactions of the Japan Society, London*, xiv. (1916). As to age-grades, see below, vol. ii. pp. 318 *sqq.*

who readily consented to bear a hand. " In five days from now " they said, " when the round moon appears, the sea will make a booming sound : then escape to a mountain where there are stars." So on the fifth day, without waiting for the sound, Kabitt and Aka fled to the mountain where there were stars. When they reached the summit, the sea suddenly began to make the sound and rose higher and higher, till soon Kakumodan's house was flooded. But Kakumodan and his wife escaped from the swelling tide, for they climbed up a ladder to the sky. Yet so urgent was the danger and so great their haste, that they had no time to rescue their two children. Accordingly, when they had reached their place of safety up aloft, they remembered their offspring, and feeling great anxiety on their account they called them in a loud voice, but no voice answered. However, the two children, Sura and Nakao, were not drowned. For when the flood overtook them, they em-barked in a wooden mortar, which chanced to be lying in the yard of the house, and in that frail vessel they floated safely to the Ragasan mountain. The brother and sister now found themselves alone in the world ; and though they feared to offend the ancestral gods by contracting an in-cestuous marriage, they nevertheless became man and wife, and their union was blest with five children, three boys and two girls, whose names are recorded. Yet the pair sought to mitigate or avert the divine wrath by so regulating their conjugal intercourse that they came into contact with each other as little as possible ; and for that purpose they inter-posed a mat between them in the marriage bed. The first grain of millet was produced from the wife's ear during her first pregnancy, and in due time husband and wife learned the proper ritual to be observed in the cultivation of that cereal.

At the village of Baran a somewhat different version of the story was recorded by Mr. Ishii. According to this latter version the great flood was due not to a rising of the sea, but to an earthquake, followed by the bursting forth of hot subterranean waters. They say that at that time the moun-tains crumbled down, the earth gaped, and from the fissure a hot spring gushed forth, which flooded the whole face of the

Another v rs of the Ami flood story.

How two
sisters and
a brother
escaped in
a wooden
mortar.
earth.   Many people were drowned ; indeed few living things
survived the ravages of the inundation.   However, two sisters
and a brother escaped in a wooden mortar, which floated
with them southward along the coast to a place called
Rarauran.   There they landed and climbed to the top of
Mount Kaburugan to survey the country round about.   Then
they separáted, the sisters going to the south and the brother
to the west, to search for a good land ; but finding none they
returned once more to Rarauran.   Again they ascended the
mountain, and the brother and his younger sister reached the
summit, but the elder sister was so tired that she remained
behind half-way up.   When her brother and her younger
sister searched for her, they found to their sorrow that she
was turned into a stone.   After that they desired to return
to their native land, from which they had drifted in the
wooden mortar.   But when they came to examine the mortar,
they found it so rotten and leaky that they dared not venture
to put to sea in it again.   So they wandered away on foot.
One day the forlorn wanderers were alarmed by the sight of
smoke rising at a distance.   Expecting nothing less than a
second eruption and a second flood, they hurried away, the
brother taking his sister by the hand to hasten her steps.
But she was so weary with wandering that she could not go
a step farther and fell to the ground.   So there they were
forced to stay for many days.   Meantime the symptoms
which had alarmed them had ceased to threaten, and they
resolved to settle on the spot.

How the
world was
after the
great flood.
But they were now all alone in the land, and they reflected with apprehension on the misery of the childless old
age which seemed in store for them.   In this dilemma, as
there was nobody else for them to marry, they thought they
had better marry each other.   Yet they felt a natural delicacy
at doing so, and in their perplexity they resolved to submit
their scruples to the judgment of the sun.   So next morning,
when the sun was rising out of the sea, the brother inquired
of it in a loud voice whether he might marry his sister.   The
sun answered, apparently without hesitation, that he might.
The brother was very glad to hear it, and married his sister
accordingly.   A few months afterwards the wife conceived,
and, with her husband's help, gathered china-grass, spun it

into yarn, and wove the yarn into clothes for the expected baby. But when her time came, to the bitter disappointment of both parents, she was delivered of two abortions that were neither girl nor boy. In their vexation they tore up the baby-linen and threw it, with the abortions, into the river. One of the abortions swam straight down the river, and the other swam across the river ; the one became the ancestor of fish, and the other the ancestor of crabs. Next morning the brother inquired of the moon why fish and crabs should thus be born from human parents. The moon made answer, "You two are brother and sister, and marriage between you is strictly prohibited. As neither of you can find another spouse, you must place a mat between you in the marriage bed." The advice was accepted, and soon afterwards the wife gave birth to a stone. They were again painfully surprised, and said, "The moon is mocking us. Who ever heard of a woman giving birth to a stone?" In their impatience they were about to heave the stone into the river, when the moon appeared and checked them, saying, "Although it is a stone, you must take great care of it." They obeyed the injunction and kept the stone very carefully. Afterwards they descended the mountain and settled in a rich fat land called Arapanai. In time the husband died, and the wife was left with no other companion than the white stone to which she had given birth. But the moon, pitying her loneliness and grief, informed the woman that soon she would have a companion. And sure enough, only five days later, the stone swelled up, and four children came forth from it, some of them wearing shoes and others barefooted. Those that wore shoes were probably the ancestors of the Chinese.

A third version of the Ami story was recorded by Mr. Ishii at the village of Pokpok. Like the preceding versions, it relates how a brother and sister escaped in a wooden mortar from a destructive deluge, in which almost all living beings perished ; how they landed on a high mountain, married, begat offspring, and founded the village of Pokpok in a hollow of the hills, where they thought they would be secure against another deluge.

The Tsuwo, a tribe of head-hunters in the mountainous interior of Formosa, have also a story of a great flood, which

A third version of the Ami story.

Story of a
great flood
told by the
Tsuwo of
Formosa.
they told to Mr. Ishii at the village of Paichana.   When their
ancestors were living dispersed in all directions, there occurred
a mighty inundation whereby plain and mountains alike were
covered with water.   Then all the people fled and took refuge
on the top of Mount Niitaka-yama, and there they stayed
until the flood subsided, and the hills and valleys emerged
once more from the watery waste.   After that the survivors
descended in groups from the mountains and took their
several ways over the land as chance or inclination prompted
them.   They say that it was while they dwelt on the
top of the mountain, during the great flood, that they first
conceived the idea of hunting for human heads.   At first
they resorted to it simply as a pastime, cutting off the head
of a bad boy and hoisting it on the point of a bamboo, to
the great amusement of the bystanders.   But afterwards,
when they had descended from the mountain and settled in
separate villages, the young men of each village took arms
and went out to decapitate their neighbours in grim
earnest.   That, they say, was the origin of the practice of
head-hunting.

How fire
was re-
covered
after the
great flood.
        The Tsuwo of the same village also tell how they obtained
fire during the great flood.   For in their hurried retreat to the
mountain they had no time to take fire with them, and for a
while they were hard put to it by the cold.   Just then some
one spied a sparkle like the twinkling of a star on the top of
a neighbouring mountain.   So the people said, "Who will go
thither and bring fire for us?"   Then a goat came forward and
said, "I will go and bring back the fire."   So saying, the noble
animal plunged into the swelling flood and swam straight
for the mountain, guided by the starlike twinkling of the fire
on its top.   The people awaited its return in great anxiety.
After a while it reappeared from out the darkness, swimming
with a burning cord attached to its horns.   Nearer and nearer
it drew to the shore, but at the same time lower and lower
burned the fire on the cord.   Would the goat reach the
bank before the flame had burned itself out?   The excite-
ment among the people was intense, but none dared to dive
into the angry surges and swim to the rescue of the animal.
Tired with its long and strenuous exertions, the goat swam
more and more feebly, till at last it drooped its head, the

water closed over it, and the fire was out. After that the
people despatched a *taoron* (?) on the same errand, and it
succeeded in bringing the fire safe to land. So pleased were
the people at its success, that they all gathered round the
animal and patted it. That is why the creature has such a
shiny skin and so tiny a body to this day.

Further, the Tsuwo of the same village relate how the
great flood was drained by the disinterested exertions of a
wild pig, and how the natural features of the country were
artificially moulded when all the water had run away. They
say that they tried various plans for draining the water, but
all in vain, until a large wild pig came forward and said, " I
will go into the water, and by breaking a bank in a lower reach
of the river, I may cause the flood to abate. In case I should
be drowned in the river I would beg you, of your kindness, to
care for my orphan children, and to give them potatoes every
day. If you consent to this proposal, I am willing to risk
my life in your service." The people gladly closed with this
generous offer; the pig plunged into the water, and swimming
with the current, disappeared in the distance. The efforts
of the animal were crowned with success, for very soon afterwards the water of the flood suddenly sank, and the crests
of the mountains began to appear above it. Rejoiced at
their escape, the people resolved to make a river with the
help of the animals, apparently for the purpose of preventing
a recurrence of the great flood. As they descended from
Mount Niitaka-yama, where they had taken refuge, a great
snake offered to act as their guide, and by gliding straight
down the slope he hollowed out a bed for the stream. Next
thousands of little birds, at the word of command, came each
with a pebble in its beak, and by depositing the pebbles in
the channel of the river they paved it, as we see it to this
day. But the banks of the river had still to be formed, and
for this purpose the services of the animals were enlisted. By
treading with their feet and working with a will all together,
they soon fashioned the river banks and valleys. The only
bird that did not help in this great work was the eagle ;
instead of swooping down he flew high in air, and as a
punishment he has never since been allowed to drink of the
river water, but is obliged to slake his thirst at the puddles

How the
reat o
was drained
away, and
how the
country
received its
form
thereafter.

in the hollow trunks of trees. In this way the valleys and rivers were fashioned, but there was as yet no plain. Then the goddess Hipararasa came from the south and made a plain by crushing the mountains. She began in the south and worked up along the western part, levelling the mountains as she went. But when she came to the central range she was confronted by an angry bear, which said, "We are fond of the mountains. If you make them into a plain, we shall lose our dwelling-places." With that he bit and wounded the child of the goddess. Surprised by this attack, the goddess desisted from her work of destruction in order to tend her wounded child. Meantime the earth hardened, so that not even the power of God could level the mountains. That is why the central range still stands in Formosa.

Stories of a gr o told by the Bunun of ʁ ʋ (m .

The Bunun, another tribe in the interior of Formosa, whose territory borders on that of the Tsuwo to the east, tell stories of a great flood in which a gigantic snake and crab figure prominently. They say that once upon a time, in the land where their ancestors lived there fell a heavy rain for many days, and to make matters worse a huge snake lay across the river, blocking up the current, so that the whole land was flooded. The people escaped to the top of the highest mountain, but such was the strength of the rising tide that they trembled at the sight of it. Just then a crab appeared opportunely and cut the body of the snake clean through with its nippers. So the flood soon subsided ; but many people were drowned and few survived. In another version of the Bunun story the cause of the flood is related somewhat differently. A gigantic crab tried to devour a big snake, clutching it fast in its nippers. But the snake contrived to shake off its assailant and escape to the sea. At once a great flood occurred ; the waves washed the mountains, and the whole world was covered with water. The ancestors of the Bunun took refuge on Mount Usabeya (Niitaka-yama) and Mount Shinkan, where they made shift to live by hunting, till the water subsided and they returned to their former abode. There they found that their fields and gardens had been washed away ; but fortunately a stalk of millet had been preserved, the seeds were planted, and on the produce the people subsisted.   They say that many mountains and valleys were formed by the great flood, for before that time the land had been quite flat.

The primitive inhabitants of the Andaman Islands, in Story of a grea flood told b the natives Andaman Islands. the Bay of Bengal, have a legend of a great flood, which may be related here, though their islands do not strictly belong to the Indian Archipelago.   They say that some time after they had been created, men grew disobedient and regardless of the commands which the Creator had given them at their creation.   So in anger he sent a great flood which covered the whole land, except perhaps Saddle Peak where the Creator himself resided.   All living creatures, both men and animals, perished in the waters, all save two men and two women, who, having the good luck to be in a canoe at the time when the catastrophe occurred, contrived to escape with their lives.   When at last the waters sank, the little company landed, but they found themselves in a sad plight, for all other living creatures were drowned. However, the Creator, whose name was Puluga, kindly helped them by creating animals and birds afresh for their use. But the difficulty remained of lighting a fire, for the flood How mankind bt in d fire after the deluge. had extinguished the flames on every hearth, and all things were of course very damp.   Hereupon the ghost of one of their friends, who had been drowned in the deluge, opportunely came to the rescue.   Seeing their distress he flew in the form of a kingfisher to the sky, where he found the Creator seated beside his fire.   The bird made a dab at a burning brand, intending to carry it off in his beak to his fireless friends on earth, but in his haste or agitation he dropped it on the august person of the Creator himself, who, incensed at the indignity and smarting with pain, hurled the blazing brand at the bird.   It missed the mark and whizzing past him dropped plump from the sky at the very spot where the four people were seated moaning and shivering.   That is how mankind recovered the use of fire after the great flood.   When they had warmed themselves and had leisure to reflect on what had happened, the four survivors began to murmur at the Creator for his destruction of all the rest of mankind ; and their passion getting the better of them they even plotted to murder him.   From this impious attempt they were, however, dissuaded by the Creator himself, who told them, in very plain language, that they had better not try, for he was as hard as wood, their arrows could make no impression on him, and if they dared so much as to lay a finger on him, he would have the blood of every mother's son and daughter of them. This dreadful threat had its effect : they submitted to their fate, and the mollified Creator condescended to explain to them, in milder terms, that men had brought the great flood on themselves by wilful dis-obedience to his commands, and that any repetition of the offence in future would be visited by him with condign punishment. That was the last time that the Creator ever appeared to men and conversed with them face to face ; since then the Andaman Islanders have never seen him, but to this day they continue to do his will with fear and trembling.[1]

§ 11. *Stories of a Great Flood in Australia*

Story of a
g e   o
told by the
Kurnai of   The Kurnai, an aboriginal Australian tribe of Gippsland, in Victoria, say that a long time ago there was a very great flood ; all the country was under water, and all the black people were drowned except a man and two or three women, who took refuge in a mud island near Port Albert. The water was all round them. Just then the pelican, or Bunjil Borun, as the Kurnai call the bird, came sailing by in his canoe, and seeing the distress of the poor people he went to help them. One of the women was so beautiful that he fell in love with her. When she would have stepped into the canoe, he said, " Not now, next time " ; so that after he had ferried all the rest, one by one, across to the mainland, she was left to the last. Afraid of being alone with the ferry-man, she did not wait his return on his last trip, but swam ashore and escaped. However, before quitting the island, she dressed up a log in her opossum rug and laid it beside the fire, so that it looked just like herself. When the pelican

Why
pelicans
are now
black and
white.   arrived to ferry her over, he called, " Come on, now." The log made no reply, so the pelican flew into a passion, and rush-

[1] E. H. Man, *On the Aboriginal Inhabitants of the Andaman Islands* (London, N.D.), pp. 98 *sq.* Compare Sir Richard C. Temple, in *Census of India, 1901*, vol. iii. *The Andaman and Nicobar Islands* (Calcutta, 1903), p. 63.

ing up to what he took to be the woman, he lunged out with his foot at her and gave the log a tremendous kick. Naturally he only hurt his own foot, and what with the pain and the chagrin at the trick that had been played him, he was very angry indeed and began to paint himself white in order that he might fight the husband of the impudent hussy who had so deceived him. He was still engaged in these warlike preparations, and had only painted white one half of his black body, when another pelican came up, and not knowing what to make of such a strange creature, half white and half black, he pecked at him with his beak and killed him. That is why pelicans are now black and white ; before the flood they were black all over.[1]

According to the aborigines about Lake Tyers, in Victoria, the way in which the great flood came about was this. Once upon a time all the water in the world was swallowed by a huge frog, and nobody else could get a drop to drink. It was most inconvenient, especially for the fish, who flapped about and gasped on the dry land. So the animals laid their heads together and came to the conclusion that the only way of making the frog disgorge the waters was to tickle his fancy so that he should laugh. Accordingly they gathered before him and cut capers and played pranks that would have caused any ordinary person to die of laughing. But the frog did not even smile. He sat there in gloomy silence, with his great goggle eyes and his swollen cheeks, as grave as a judge. As a last resort the eel stood up on its tail and wriggled and danced about, twisting itself into the most ridiculous contortions. This was more than even the frog could bear. His features relaxed, and he laughed till the tears ran down his cheeks and the water poured out of his mouth. However, the animals had now got more than they had bargained for, since the waters disgorged by the frog swelled into a great flood in which many people perished. Indeed the whole of mankind would have been

Story of a gre ‘ told by the aborigines ol Tyers in Victoria ; w ir)g swallowed all the ...d was made to disgorge ...

---

[1] A. W. Howitt, in R. Brough Smyth's *Aborigines of Victoria* (Melbourne and London, 1878), i. 477 *sq.* ; *id.*, *Native Tribes of South-East Australia* (London, 1904), p. 486. It is said that after the deluge some of the ancestors of the Kurnai turned into animals, birds, reptiles, and fishes. See A. W. Howitt, "The Jeraeil, or Initiation Ceremonies of the Kurnai Tribe " *Journal of the Anthropological Institute*, xiv. (1885) p. 314.

drowned, if the pelican had not gone about in a canoe picking up the survivors and so saving their lives.[1]

Other stories of a flood told by the aborigines of Victoria and South Australia.

Another legend of a deluge current among the aborigines of Victoria relates how, many long ages ago, the Creator Bundjel was very angry with black people because they did evil. So he caused the ocean to swell by the same process by which Strepsiades in Aristophanes supposed that Zeus made rain to fall from the clouds ;[2] and in the rising flood all black people were drowned, except those whom Bundjel loved and catching up from the water fixed as stars in the sky. Nevertheless one man and one woman escaped the deluge by climbing a high tree on a mountain ; so they lived and became the ancestors of the present human race.[3] The Narrinyeri of South Australia say that once on a time a man's two wives ran away from him. He pursued them to Encounter Bay, and there seeing them at a distance he cried out in anger, " Let the waters arise and drown them." On that a terrible flood swept over the hills and overtaking the fugitives overwhelmed them, so that they died. To such a height did the waters rise that a certain man named Nepelle, who lived at Rauwoke, was obliged to drag his canoe to the top of the hill which is now called Point Macleay. The dense part of the Milky Way is said to be his canoe floating in the sky.[4]

Story of a great flood told by the natives of Queensland.

The natives about Mount Elliot, on the coast of Queensland, say that in the time of their forefathers there happened a great flood, which drowned most of them ; only a few were saved who contrived to escape to the top of a very high mountain, called Bibbiringda, which rises inland from the northern bay of Cape Cleveland.[5]

[1] R. Brough Smyth, *Aborigines of Victoria*, i. 429 *sq.* ; E. M. Curr, *The Australian Race* (Melbourne and London, 1886–1887), iii. 547 *sq.* Compare *The Magic Art and the Evolution of Kings*, i. 292 *sq.*, where part of the legend is given from Miss Mary E. B. Howitt's *Folklore and Legends of some Victorian Tribes* (in manuscript).

[2] Aristophanes, *Clouds*, 373.

[3] R. Brough Smyth, *Aborigines of Victoria*, i. 429.

[4] Rev. G. Taplin, "The Narrinyeri," in J. D. Woods, *Native Tribes of South Australia* (Adelaide, 1879), p. 57.

[5] E. M. Curr, *The Australian Race*, ii. 450. For some other references to floods in the traditions of the Australian aborigines, see A. Oldfield, "The Aborigines of Australia," *Transactions of the Ethnological Society of London*, New Series, iii. (London, 1865) pp. 234 *sq.* ; E. M. Curr, *The Australian Race*, iii. 420.

§ 12. *Stories of a Great Flood in New Guinea and Melanesia*

In the Kabadi district of British New Guinea the natives have a tradition that once on a time a certain man Lohero and his younger brother were angry with the people about them, and they put a human bone into a small stream. Soon the great waters came forth, forming a sea, flooding all the low land, and driving the people back to the mountains, till step by step they had to escape to the tops of the highest peaks.   There they lived till the sea receded, when some of them descended to the lowlands, while others remained on the ridges and there built houses and formed plantations.[1] The Valmans of Berlin Harbour, on the northern coast of New Guinea, tell how one day the wife of a very good man saw a great fish swimming to the bank.   She called to her husband, but at first he could not see the fish.   So his wife laughed at him and hid him behind a banana-tree, that he might peep at it through the leaves.   When he did catch sight of it at last, he was horribly afraid, and sending for his family, a son and two daughters, he forbade them to catch and eat the fish.   But the other people took bow and arrow and a cord, and they caught the fish and drew it to land. Though the good man warned them not to eat of the fish, they did it notwithstanding.   When the good man saw that, he hastily drove a pair of animals of every sort up into the trees, and then he and his family climbed up into a coco-nut tree.   Hardly had the wicked men consumed the fish than water burst from the ground with such violence that nobody had time to save himself.   Men and animals were all drowned. When the water had mounted to the top of the highest tree, it sank as rapidly as it had risen.   Then the good man came down from the tree with his family and laid out new plantations.[2]

The natives of the Mamberano River, in Dutch New Guinea, are reported to tell a story of a great flood, caused by the rising of the river, which overwhelmed Mount Vanessa,

Stories of a gre   o told by the natives of   Guinea.

[1] J. Chalmers and W. Wyatt Gill, *Work and Adventure in New Guinea* (London, 1885), p. 164.

[2] P. Chr. Schleiermacher, " Reli- giose Anschauungen und Gebrauche der Bewohner von Berlinhafen (Deutsch-Neuguinea)," *Globus*, lxxviii. (1900) p. 6.

and from which only one man and his wife escaped, together with a pig, a cassowary, a kangaroo, and a pigeon. The man and his wife became the ancestors of the present race of men ; the beasts and birds became the ancestors of the existing species. The bones of the drowned animals still lie on Mount Vanessa.[1]

R. Neuhauss on stories of a flood in New Guinea.   On the subject of deluge legends in New Guinea the following remarks of a judicious and well-informed writer deserve to be borne in mind. " New Guinea," he says, "is the classic land of earthquakes, and ten years never pass without the occurrence somewhere of a tremendous convulsion, such as the sinking of whole districts or the inroad of destructive flood-waves. Thus, for example, the sea is said to have formerly reached to the top of Saddle Mountain. Stories of a flood are therefore common in New Guinea, and have originated in the country itself under the impression of these natural phenomena. Now the Papuan hears the Biblical story of the flood, in which his fancy is particularly taken by the many great animals, of each of which a pair was saved. The terrestrial animals of his own country are hardly worth the saving, and the birds can escape from the flood without the help of man. But since in the Biblical flood large animals were saved, of which pictures are shown to the native, animals which afford much better eating than wretched rats and mice, the black man modifies his own flood legends accordingly. It cannot surprise us, therefore, that legends with a Biblical colouring already existed in New Guinea when the first mission settled there in 1886 ; for the neighbourhood of the Malay Archipelago, where missionaries had been much longer resident, facilitated the importation of the stories. Besides, a mission had been established in the island of Rook as early as about the middle of the nineteenth century ; and Rook has been in constant communication with the mainland of New Guinea by means of the neighbouring Siassi Islands. The Bismarck Archipelago also, where missionaries have long been at work, deserves to be considered with reference to the im-

---

[1] Max Moszkowski, " Die Volker-stamme am Mamberamo in Holland-ischen Neuguinea und auf vorge- lagerten Inseln," *Zeitschrift für Ethnologie*, xliii. (1911) pp. 340 *sq.*

portation of Biblical stories into Northern New Guinea
(Kaiser-Wilhelmsland) ; for a perpetual intercourse of ideas
is kept up between the two countries by the seafaring Siassi
and Tami."[1]

The Fijians have a tradition of a great deluge, which
they call Walavu-levu : some say that the flood was partial,
others that it was universal. The way in which the catastrophe came about was this. The great god Ndengei had
a monstrous bird called Turukawa, which used to wake
him punctually by its cooing every morning. One day
his two grandsons, whether by accident or design, shot
the bird dead with their bows and arrows, and buried the
carcase in order to conceal the crime. So the deity overslept
himself, and being much annoyed at the disappearance of his
favourite fowl, he sent out his messenger Uto to look for it
everywhere. The search proved fruitless. The messenger
reported that not a trace of the bird was to be found. But
a second search was more successful, and laid the guilt of the
murder at the door of the god's grandsons. To escape the
rage of their incensed grandfather the young scapegraces
fled to the mountains and there took refuge with a tribe of
carpenters, who willingly undertook to build a stockade
strong enough to keep Ndengei and all his catchpolls at
bay. They were as good as their word, and for three months
the god and his minions besieged the fortress in vain. At
last, in despair of capturing the stockade by the regular
operations of war, the baffled deity disbanded his army and
meditated a surer revenge. At his command the dark clouds
gathered and burst, pouring torrents of rain on the doomed
earth. Towns, hills, and mountains were submerged one
after the other ; yet for long the rebels, secure in the height
of their town, looked down with unconcern on the rising tide
of waters. At last when the surges lapped their wooden
walls and even washed through their fortress, they called for
help to a god, who, according to one account, instructed
them to form a float out of the fruit of the shaddock ; according to others, he sent two canoes for their use, or taught

*Fijian
tr iti n of
a great
flood.*

*How the
god
Nden ei
caused a
ug
people were
saved in
oes or
great
bowls.*

---

[1] R. Neuhauss, *Deutsch Neu-Guinea*
(Berlin, 1911), i. 414. The writer's
observations apply particularly to German New Guinea, in which he has
travelled widely.

them how to build a canoe for themselves and thus ensure their own safety. It was Rokoro, the god of carpenters, who with his foreman Rokola came to their rescue. The pair sailed about in two large double canoes, picking up the drowning people and keeping them on board till the flood subsided. Others, however, will have it that the survivors saved themselves in large bowls, in which they floated about. Whatever the minor variations may be in the Fijian legend, all agree that even the highest places were covered by the deluge, and that the remnant of the human race was saved in some kind of vessel, which was at last left high and dry by the receding tide on the island of Mbengha. The number of persons who thus survived the flood was eight. Two tribes were completely destroyed by the waters ; one of them consisted entirely of women, the members of the other had tails like those of dogs. Because the survivors of the flood landed on their island, the natives of Mbengha claimed to rank highest of all the Fijians, and their chiefs always acted a conspicuous part in Fijian history : they styled themselves " Subject to heaven alone " (*Ngali-duva-ki-langi*). It is said that formerly the Fijians always kept great canoes ready for use against another flood, and that the custom was only discontinued in modern times.[1]

Melanesian story of a it from which the hero Qat escaped in a canoe.

The Melanesians of the New Hebrides say that their great legendary hero Qat disappeared from the world in a deluge. They show the very place from which he sailed away on his last voyage. It is a broad lake in the centre of the island of Gaua. In the days of Qat the ground now occupied by the lake was a spacious plain clothed with forest. Qat felled one of the tallest trees in the wood and proceeded to build himself a canoe out of the fallen trunk. While he was at work on it, his brothers would come and jeer at him, as he sat or stood there sweating away at his

[1] Thomas Williams, *Fiji and the Fijians* (London, 1860), i. 252 ; Horatio Hale, *United States Exploring Expedition, Ethnography and Philology* (Philadelphia, 1846), p. 55 ; Charles Wilkes, *Narrative of the United States Exploring Expedition*, New Edition (New York, 1851), iii. 82 *sq.* ; J. E. Erskine, *Journal of a Cruise among* the *Islands of the Western Pacific* (London, 1853), pp. 244 *sq.* ; Berthold Seeman, *Viti, an Account of a Government Mission to the Vitian or Fijian Islands in the years 1860–1861* (Cambridge, 1862), pp. 394 *sq.* The mythical cause of the flood, namely the slaughter of the god's favourite bird, is told in detail only by the last writer.

unfinished canoe in the shadow of the dense tropical forest. "How will you ever get that huge canoe through the thick woods to the sea?" they asked him mockingly. "Wait and see," was all he deigned to answer. When the canoe was finished, he gathered into it his wife and his brothers and all the living creatures of the island, down to the smallest ants, and shut himself and them into the vessel, which he provided with a covering. Then came a deluge of rain; the great hollow of the island was filled with water, which burst through the circle of the hills at the spot where the great waterfall of Gaua still descends seaward, with a thunderous roar, in a veil of spray. There the canoe swept on the rushing water through the barrier of the hills, and driving away out to sea was lost to view. The natives say that the hero Qat took away the best of everything with him when he thus vanished from sight, and still they look forward to his joyful return. When Bishop Patteson and his companions first landed on Mota, the happy natives took him for the long-lost Qat and his brethren. And some years afterwards, when a small trading vessel was one day seen standing in for the island of Gaua and making apparently for the channel down which the water of the great cascade flows to mingle with the sea, the old people on the island cried out joyfully that Qat was come again, and that his canoe knew her own way home. But alas! the ship was cast away on the reef, and Qat has not yet come home.[1]

§ 13. *Stories of a Great Flood in Polynesia and Micronesia*

Legends of a great flood in which a multitude of people perished are told by the natives of those groups of islands which under the general names of Polynesia and Micronesia are scattered widely over the Pacific. "The principal facts," we are told, "are the same in the traditions prevailing among the inhabitants of the different groups, although they differ in several minor particulars. In one group the accounts

[1] R. H. Codrington, *The Melanesians* (Oxford, 1891), pp. 166 *sq.* The writer adds, "It is likely now that the story will be told of eight persons in the canoe; but it is certain that the story is older than any knowledge of Noah's ark among the people."

state, that in ancient times Taaroa, the principal god (according to their mythology, the creator of the world), being angry with men on account of their disobedience to his will, overturned the world into the sea, when the earth sank in the waters, excepting a few *aurus*, or projecting points, which, remaining above its surface, constituted the principal cluster of islands. The memorial preserved by the inhabitants of Eimeo states, that after the inundation of the land, when the water subsided, a man landed from a canoe near Tiataepua, in their island, and erected an altar, or *marae*, in honour of his god."[1]

Tahitian s ory f a r it fl d from which (a husband and wife), with some animals, [illegible] on a high mountain.

In Tahiti the legend ran as follows. Tahiti was destroyed by the sea . no man, nor hog, nor fowl, nor dog survived. The groves of trees and the stones were carried away by the wind. They were destroyed, and the deep was over the land. But two persons, a husband and a wife, were saved. When the flood came, the wife took up her young chicken, her young dog, and her kitten ; the husband took up his young pig. [These were all the animals formerly known to the natives; and as the term *fanaua*, 'young,' is both singular and plural, it may apply to one or more than one chicken, etc.]. The husband proposed that they should take refuge on Mount Orofena, a high mountain in Tahiti, saying that it was lofty and would not be reached by the sea. But his wife said that the sea would reach to Mount Orofena, and that they had better go to Mount O Pitohito, where they would be safe from the flood. So to Mount O Pitohito they went; and she was right, for Orofena was overwhelmed by the sea, but O Pitohito rose above the waste of waters and became their abode. There they watched ten nights, till the sea ebbed, and they saw the little heads of the mountains appearing above the waves. When the sea retired, the land remained without produce, without man, and the fish were putrid in the caves and holes of the rocks. They said, "Dig a hole for the fish in the sea." The wind also died away, and when all was calm, the stones and the trees began to fall from the heavens, to which they had been carried up by the wind. For all the trees of the land had been torn up and whirled

[1] W. Ellis, *Polynesian Researches*, Second Edition (London, 1832-1836), i. 386 *sq*.

aloft by the hurricane.   The two looked about, and the woman said, "We two are safe from the sea, but death, or hurt, comes now in these stones that are falling.   Where shall we abide?"   So the two dug a hole, lined it with grass, and covered it over with stones and earth.   Then they crept into the hole, and sitting there they heard with terror the roar and crash of the stones falling down from the sky.   By and by the rain of stones abated, till only a few stones fell at intervals, and then they dropped one by one, and finally ceased altogether.   The woman said, "Arise, go out, and see whether the stones are still falling."   But her husband said, "Nay, I go not out, lest I die."   A day and a night he waited, and in the morning he said, "The wind is truly dead, and the stones and the trunks of trees cease to fall, neither is there the sound of the stones."   They went out, and like a small mountain was the heap of fallen stones and tree trunks.   Of the land there remained the earth and the rocks, but the shrubs were destroyed by the sea.   They descended from the mountain, and gazed with astonishment: there were no houses, nor coco-nuts, nor palm-trees, nor bread-fruit, nor hibiscus, nor grass: all was destroyed by the sea.   The two dwelt together.   The woman brought forth two children; one was a son, the other a daughter.   They grieved that there was no food for their children.   Again the mother brought forth, but still there was no food; then the bread-fruit bore fruit, and the coco-nut, and every other kind of food.   In three days the land was covered with food; and in time it swarmed with men also, for from those two persons, the father and the mother, all the people are descended.[1]

In Raiatea, one of the Leeward Islands in the Tahitian group, tradition ran that shortly after the peopling of the world by the descendants of Taata, the sea-god Ruahatu was reposing among groves of coral in the depths of ocean, when his repose was rudely interrupted.   A fisherman, paddling his canoe overhead, in ignorance or forgetfulness of the divine presence, let down his hooks among the branching corals at the bottom of the clear translucent water, and they became entangled in the hair of the sleeping god.

[1] W. Ellis, *Polynesian Researches*, i. 387-389.

With great difficulty the fisherman wrenched the hooks out of the ambrosial locks and began pulling them up hand-over-hand. But the god, enraged at being disturbed in his nap, came also bubbling up to the surface, and popping his head out of the water upbraided the fisherman for his impiety, and threatened in revenge to destroy the land. The affrighted fisherman prostrated himself before the sea-god, confessed his sin, and implored his forgiveness, beseeching that the judgment denounced might be averted, or at least that, he himself might escape. Moved by his penitence and importunity, Ruahatu bade him return home for his wife and child and go with them to Toamarama, a small island situated within the reefs on the eastern side of Raiatea. There he was promised security amid the destruction of the surrounding islands. The man hastened home, and taking with him his wife and child he repaired to the little isle of refuge in the lagoon. Some say that he took with him also a friend, who was living under his roof, together with a dog, a pig, and a pair of fowls ; so that the refugees numbered four souls, together with the only domesticated animals which were then known in the islands. They reached the harbour of refuge before the close of day, and as the sun set the waters of the ocean began to rise, and the inhabitants of the adjacent shore left their dwellings and fled to the mountains. All that night the waters rose, and next morning only the tops of the high mountains appeared above the widespread sea. Even these were at last covered, and all the inhabitants of the land perished. Afterwards the waters retired, the fisherman and his companions left their retreat, took up their abode on the mainland, and became the progenitors of the present inhabitants.[1]

The coral islet in which these forefathers of the race found refuge from the great flood is not more than two feet at the highest above the level of the sea, so that it is difficult to understand how it could have escaped the inundation, while the lofty mountains which tower up thousands of feet from the adjacent shore were submerged. This difficulty, however, presents no stumbling-block to the faith of the natives ; they usually decline to discuss such sceptical doubts,

The coral isle where the ancestors of the human race found refug in the flood.

---

[1] W. Ellis, *Polynesian Researches*, i. 389-391.

and point triumphantly for confirmation of their story to the coral, shells, and other marine substances which are occasionally found near the surface of the ground on the tops of their highest mountains. These must, they insist, have been deposited there by the waters of the ocean when the islands were submerged.[1]

It is significant, as we shall see later on, that in these Tahitian legends the flood is ascribed solely to the rising of the sea, and not at all to heavy rain, which is not even mentioned. On this point the Rev. William Ellis, to whom we owe the record of these legends, makes the following observations : " I have frequently conversed with the people on the subject, both in the northern and southern groups, but could never learn that they had any accounts of the windows of heaven having been opened, or the rain having descended. In the legend of Ruahatu, the Toamarama of Tahiti, and the Kai of Kahinarii in Hawaii, the inundation is ascribed to the rising of the waters of the sea. In each account, the anger of the god is considered as the cause of the inundation of the world, and the destruction of its inhabitants." [2]

When Mr. Ellis preached in the year 1822 to the natives of Hawaii on the subject of Noah's deluge, they told him of a similar legend which had been handed down among them. " They said they were informed by their fathers, that all the land had once been overflowed by the sea, except a small peak on the top of Mouna-Kea, where two human beings were preserved from the destruction that overtook the rest, but they said they had never before heard of a ship, or of Noah, having been always accustomed to call it *kai a Kahinarii* (sea of Kahinárii)." [3]

A somewhat later version of the Hawaiian legend runs thus. " A tradition of the flood likewise exists, which states that all the land, except the summit of Mauna-kea, was overflowed by copious rains and risings of the waters. Some of the inhabitants preserved themselves in a canoe, which finally rested upon that mountain ; after which the waters fell, and the people went forth, and again dwelt in the land. This

In these Tahitian legends the flood is ascribed solely to the rising not to the fall of rain.

Hawaiian a great flood.

Another Hawaiian legend of a great flood.

---

[1] W. Ellis, *Polynesian Researches,* i. 391.

[2] W. Ellis, *op. cit.* i. 392 *sq.*

[3] W. Ellis, *op. cit.* iv. 441 *sq.*

flood is called *Kaiakahnialii*, the great deluge of *Hinalii*."[1] In this later version there are two not unimportant variations from the earlier.　First, the deluge is said to have been partly caused by rain, whereas in the earlier version there is no mention of rain, and in it the flood is attributed to the rising of the sea alone.　Second, in the later version the survivors are reported to have saved themselves in a canoe, whereas in the earlier version no canoe is mentioned, the survivors being merely said to have escaped to the mountain.　In both points the later version agrees with the Biblical legend and has probably been influenced by it.

Mangaia, one of the Hervey Islands.　　　Mangaia, one of the Hervey Group, is an island which rises from deep water as a ring of live coral.　The unbroken reef which surrounds it is covered by the sea at half tide. Inward from this ring of live coral rises a second ring of dead coral, from one to two miles wide, which falls away perpendicularly on the landward side, thus forming a sort of cyclopean wall which runs right round the island.　The interior of the island is composed of dark volcanic rock and red clay, which descend in low hills from a flat-topped centre known as the Crown of Mangaia.　There is no lagoon.　The streams, after fertilizing thousands of taro plantations, find their way to the sea by subterranean channels through the inner ring of dead coral.[2]　Such is Mangaia at the present time.　But the natives say that it was not always so. Originally, if we may believe them, the surface of the island was everywhere a gentle uniform slope from the centre to the sea without a single hollow or valley.　The process by which the island was transformed into the present shape is said to have been as follows.

Story of the transformation of Mangaia into its present shape through a contest between the gods of the sea and the rain.　　　Aokeu, a son of Echo, disputed warmly with Ake who should perform the most wonderful thing.　Ake's home is the ocean, and his constant employment is to tread down its flooring; thus he ever deepens its vast basin, and enables it to hold more of his favourite element.　Ake was confident that he could easily beat Aokeu, who was ignobly born of the continual drippings of purest water from the stalactite

[1] James Jackson Jarves, *History of the Hawaiian or Sandwich Islands* (Boston, 1843), p. 28.

[2] Rev. W Wyatt Gill, *Life in the Southern Isles* (London, N.D., preface dated 1876), pp. 7 *sq.*

roof of a narrow cavern.   His name means "Red Circle,"
and he is so called because after heavy rains the water
washes down the red clay and tinges the ocean round the
island with a crimson band.

To make sure of success Ake summoned to his help How the
Raka, the god of the winds, who drove a fearful hurricane sea
attacked
over sea and land, as if he would bury the island in the the island.
depths.   The two twin children of the blustering storm-god
also lent their aid.   One of them, Tikokura, is seen in the
line of huge curling,,foaming billows, which break in thunder
on the reef, threatening to dash the solid coral itself into shivers.
The other twin-child of the wind-god is Tane-ere-tue ; he
manifests himself in the great storm-wave, which is rarely
seen, but never without striking terror into the beholder.
On rushed these mighty monsters, secure of victory.
They swamped the rocks near the sea to the height of a
hundred feet above the level of the sea.   In proof of it you
may see to this day numberless clam and other shells, as
well as "coral-borers" (*ungakoa*) imbedded in the solid rock,
which is burrowed and worn, even at its highest points, into
a thousand fantastic shapes by the action of the sea.

Meantime, Aokeu on his side had not been idle.   He How the
caused the rain—his favourite element—to fall in sheets for rain-god
hollowed
five days and nights without intermission.   The red clay out the
and small stones were washed down into the ocean, dis- v l y
the island
colouring its waters a long way from the land.   On every
side the channels deepened until the narrow valleys were
formed ; but still the wind howled and the rain poured
incessantly, till the deep valleys, walled in on the seaward
side by perpendicular rocks, where the principal taro-grounds
may now be seen, gradually assumed their present dimensions.
The flat summit of the central hill, Rangimotia, the Crown of
Mangaia, alone rose above the water, to mark the original
height of the island.

At the outset, Rangi, the first ruler of Mangaia, had been How Rangi
warned of the desperate strife of the elements which was nd few
p ople
about to take place ; and, with his few people, awaited at escaped
Rangimotia the issue of the contest.   With deep concern he rom e
flood on the
saw on the one hand the wild ocean covering the belt of top of a
rocks which surrounds the island, and, on the other hand, mountain.

a vast lake of fresh water rising rapidly and rushing tumultuously to meet the advancing ocean. Everywhere an immense expanse of water met the eye of Rangi, save only the long narrow strip of level soil upon which he and his people tremblingly stood. Already the rising tide lapped their feet. What if it should rise a little higher? Rangi resolved to appeal to the great god Rongo to save him and his beloved island from destruction. To reach the temple (*marae*) of the god, which faced the rising sun, Rangi had to wade through the waters, which reached to his chin, along a ridge of hills to a point called Teunu, lying due east. Just there is a spot called "the standing-place of Rongo," because that god hearkened to his grandson's prayer, and looking at the war of waters—the flood from the land meeting and battling with the flood from the sea—he cried, " It is enough (*A tira*)!" The eye of Vatea, the Sun, opened at the same moment above the scene of conflict ; the god saw and pitied mankind. Then the sea sullenly sank to its former level : the rain ceased to fall : the waters of the interior were drained away ; and the island assumed its present agreeable diversity of hill and vale. Hence the proud title of the high god of Mangaia, " Rongo, the warder-off of mad billows " (*Rongo arai kea*).

Victory
rain-god.

Mankind were saved, and the land became better adapted than ever to their abode. Aokeu, lord of rain, was acknowledged victor ; for the ocean had expended its fury in vain on the rocky heights near the sea, they still stood firm, and in vain had the twin-sons of the wind-god sought to storm the heights of the island. But the turbid floods, rushing down from the hills, flowed far away into the ocean, everywhere marking their triumphant progress with the red clay of the mountains of Mangaia. So real was this war of the elements to the men of former days that they disputed as to the route which Rangi took in wading through the flood to the temple of Rongo,· some holding that he took the straight road, others that he followed a more circuitous path to avoid a dip in the hills.[1]

This story of a great flood is interesting, because it appears to be a simple myth invented to explain the peculiar physical features of the island. Had the writer who records

[1] Rev. W. Wyatt Gill, *Life in the Southern Isles*, pp. 79-83.

the tale not also described the aspect of the island, with which he was familiar, we should probably have failed to perceive the purely local origin of the story, and might have been tempted to derive it from some distant source, perhaps even to find in it a confused reminiscence of Noah and the ark. It is allowable to conjecture that many other stories of a great flood could similarly be resolved into merely local myths, if we were better acquainted with those natural features of the country which the tales were invented to explain.

A somewhat different story of a great flood is told in Rakaanga, an outlying island of the Hervey Group. They say that once on a time a certain chief named Taoiau was greatly incensed with his people for not bringing him the sacred turtle. So in his wrath he roused all the mighty sea-gods, on whose good-will the islands depend for their existence. Amongst them in particular was one who sleeps at the bottom of mid-ocean, but who on that occasion, moved by the king's prayer, stood up in anger like a vast upright stone. A dreadful hurricane burst forth ; the ocean rose and swept over the whole island of Rakaanga. The few inhabitants of those days escaped destruction by taking refuge on a mound, which was pointed out to the missionary who has recorded the tale. There was no mountain to which they could fly for safety, since the island is a low atoll covered with forests of coco-nut palms. The memorable event was long known as "the overwhelming of Taoiau." [1]

In Samoa it is, or used to be, a universal belief that of old the fish swam where the land now is ; and tradition adds that when the waters abated, many of the fish of the sea were left on the land and were afterwards changed into stones. Hence, they say, in the bush and on the mountains there are stones in plenty which were once sharks and other inhabitants of the deep. [2] According to another Samoan tradition the only survivor of the deluge was a certain Pili, who was either a man or a lizard, and by marriage with a bird, the stormy petrel, begat offspring whose names are recorded. [3] The natives of Nanumanga or Hudson's Island, in the South

[1] Rev. W. Wyatt Gill, *Life in the Southern Isles*, pp. 83 *sq.* ; as to the island, *ib.* p. 12.

[2] G. Turner, *Nineteen Years in Poly-* *nesia* (London, 1861), pp. 249 *sq.*

[3] W. v. Bülow, "Samoanische Schopfungssage und Urgeschichte," *Globus*, lxxi. (1897) p. 377.

Pacific, also tell of a deluge, and how it was dispelled by the sea-serpent, who, as a woman, married the earth as a man, and by him became the ancestress of the present race of mortals.[1]

The Maoris of New Zealand have a long legend of the deluge. They say that when men multiplied on the earth and there were many great tribes, evil prevailed everywhere, the tribes quarrelled and made war on each other. The worship of the great god Tane, who had created man and woman, was neglected and his doctrines openly denied. Two great prophets, indeed, there were who taught the true doctrine concerning the separation of heaven and earth, but men scoffed at them, saying that they were false teachers and that heaven and earth had been from the beginning just as we see them
now. The names of these two wise prophets were Para-whenua-mea and Tupu-nui-a-uta. They continued to preach till the tribes cursed them, saying, "You two can eat the words of your history as food for you, and you can eat the heads of the words of that history." That grieved the prophets, when men said the wicked words "Eat the heads," and they grew angry. So they took their stone axes and cut down trees, and dragged the trunks to the source of the Tohinga River, and bound them together with vines and ropes, and made a very wide raft. Moreover, they built a house on the raft, and put much food in it, fern-root, and sweet potatoes, and dogs. Then they recited incantations and prayed that rain might descend in such abundance as would convince men of the existence and power of the god Tane, and would teach them the need of worship for life and for peace. After that the two prophets embarked on the raft, along with two men called Tiu and Reti and a woman named Wai-puna-hau. But there were other women also on the raft. Now Tiu was the priest on the raft, and he prayed and uttered incantations for rain. So it rained in torrents for four or five days, and then the priest repeated incantations to make the rain cease, and it ceased. But still the flood rose; next day it reached the settlement, and on the following day the raft was lifted up by the waters, and floated down the River Tohinga. Great as a sea was now the inundation, and the

---

[1] G. Turner, *Samoa, a hundred years ago and long before* (London, 1884), p. 288.

raft drifted to and fro on the face of the waters. When
they had tossed about for seven moons, the priest Tiu said
to his companions, "We shall not die, we shall land on the
earth"; and in the eighth month he said moreover, "The
sea has become thin ; the flood has begun to subside." The
two prophets asked him, "By what do you know?" He
answered, "By the signs of my staff." For he had kept his
altar on one side of the deck, and there he performed his
ceremonies, and repeated his incantations, and observed his
staff. And he understood the signs of his staff, and he said
again to his companions, "The blustering winds of the past
moons have fallen, the winds of this month have died away,
and the sea is calm." In the eighth month the raft no longer
rolled as before ; it now pitched as well as rolled, so the
priest knew that the sea was shallow, and that they were
drawing near to land. He said to his companions, "This is
the moon in which we shall land on dry earth, for by the
signs of my staff I know that the sea is becoming less deep."
All the while they floated on the deep they repeated incantations and performed ceremonies in honour of the god Tane.
At last they landed on dry earth at Hawaiki. They thought
that they might find some of the inhabitants of the world still
alive, and that the earth would look as it had looked before
the flood. But all was changed. The earth was cracked and
fissured in some places, and in others it had been turned
upside down and confounded by reason of the flood. And
not one soul was left alive in the world. They who came
forth from the raft were the solitary survivors of all the tribes
of the earth. When they landed, the first thing they did was
to perform ceremonies and repeat incantations. They worshipped Tane, and the Heaven (Rangi), and Rehua, and all the
gods; and as they worshipped them they offered them seaweed,
a length of the priest's two thumbs for each god. Each god
was worshipped in a different place, and for each there was
an altar, where the incantations were recited. The altar was
a root of grass, a shrub, a tree, or a flax-bush. These were
the altars of the gods at that time ; and now, if any of the
people of the tribes go near to such altars, the food they have
eaten in their stomachs will swell and kill them. The chief
priest alone may go to such holy spots. If common folk

(marginal note:) How on landing from the raft after oo ̣ they worshipped g and made fire by fri .

were to go to these sacred places and afterwards cook food in their village, the food would kill all who ate it. It would be cursed by the sin of the people in desecrating the sanctity of the altars, and the punishment of the eaters would be death. When the persons who were saved on the raft had performed all the ceremonies needful for removing the taboo under which they laboured, they procured fire by friction at one of the sacred places. And with the fire the priest kindled bundles of grass, and he put a bundle of burning grass on each altar beside the piece destined for the god ; and the priests presented the seaweed to the gods as a thank-offering for the rescue of the people from the flood and for the preservation of their lives on the raft.[1]

Other Maori stories of a great flood associate the catastrophe with a certain legendary hero called Tawhaki. They say that once upon a time two of his brothers-in-law attacked and wounded him and left him for dead. But he recovered from his wounds and quitted the place where his wicked brothers-in-law lived. Away he went with all his own warriors and their families, and he built a fortified village upon the top of a very lofty mountain, where he could easily defend himself, and there they all dwelt secure. " Then he called aloud to the gods, his ancestors, for revenge, and they let the floods of heaven descend, and the earth was overwhelmed by the waters and all human beings perished, and the name given to that event was ' The overwhelming of the Mataaho,' and the whole of that race perished."[2] Some say that Tawhaki was a man, who went up to the top of a mountain, and, having there transfigured himself by putting off his earthly raiment and put on a garment of lightning, was worshipped as a god, and all the tribes chanted incantations and offered sacrifices to him. In his divine character he once, in a fit of anger, stamped on the floor of heaven, so that it cracked and the celestial waters burst through and flooded the earth.[3] Others say

Other
stories of a
great flood
associated
with the
name of

Tawhaki.

---

[1] John White, *The Ancient History of the Maori* (Wellington and London, 1887–1889), i. 172-178. I have much abridged the original legend. A briefer version is recorded by the same writer (*op. cit.* i. 180 *sq.*).

[2] Sir George Grey, *Polynesian Mythology* (London, 1855), pp. 60 *sq.*

[3] John White, *The Ancient History of the Maori*, i. 55 ; R. Taylor, *Te Ika A Maui, or New Zealand and its Inhabitants*, Second Edition (London, 1870), pp. 101, 115 note †.

that it was Tawhaki's mother who caused the deluge by weeping so copiously that her tears, falling on the earth, inundated it and drowned all men.[1]

In Micronesia as well as Polynesia the story of a great flood has been recorded.   The Pelew Islanders say that once on a time a man went up into the sky, whence the gods with their shining eyes, which are the stars, look down every night upon the earth.   The cunning fellow stole one of these bright eyes and brought it home with him, and all the money of the Pelew Islanders has been made out of that starry eye ever since.   But the gods were very angry at the theft, and down they came to earth to reclaim their stolen property and to punish the thief.   They disguised themselves in the likeness of ordinary men, and begged for food and lodging from door to door.   But men were churlish and turned them away without a bite or a sup.   Only one old woman received them kindly in her cottage, and set before them the best she had to eat and drink.   So when they went away they warned the old woman to make a raft of bamboo ready against the next full moon, and when the night of the full moon came she was to lie down on the raft and sleep.   She did as she was bidden.   Now with the full moon came a dreadful storm and rain, and the sea rose higher and higher, and flooded the islands, rent the mountains, and destroyed the abodes of men ; and people knew not how to save themselves, and they all perished in the rising flood.   But the good old dame, fast asleep on the raft, was borne on the face of the waters and drifted till her hair caught in the boughs of a tree on the top of Mount Armlimui.   There she lay, while the flood ebbed and the water sank lower and lower down the sides of the mountain.   Then the gods came down from the sky to seek for the good old woman whom they had taken under their protection, but they found her dead.   So they summoned one of their women-folk from heaven, and she entered into the dead body of the old woman and made her live.   After that the gods begat five children by the resuscitated old wife, and having done so they left the earth and returned to heaven ; the goddess who had kindly reanimated the corpse of the ancient dame also went back to her mansion in the

Micro-
a s y
of a great
flood told
by tne
Pelew
Islanders.

How the
gods,
disguised
as men,

old woman
and how

saved from
the flood
.. . .

[1] John White, *The Ancient History of the Maori*, i. 113 *sq.*

sky. But the five children of the divine fathers and the
human mother repeopled the Pelew Islands, and from them
the present inhabitants are descended.[1]

§ 14. *Stories of a Great Flood in South America*

At the time of their discovery the Indians of Brazil, in
the neighbourhood of what was afterwards Rio de Janeiro,
had a legend of a universal deluge in which only two
brothers with their wives were saved. According to one
account, the flood covered the whole earth and all men
perished except the ancestors of those Indians, who escaped
by climbing up into high trees ;[2] others, however, thought
that the survivors were saved in a canoe.[3]

As reported by the Frenchman André Thevet, who
travelled in Brazil about the middle of the sixteenth century,
the story related by the Indians about Cape Frio ran thus.
A certain great medicine-man, by name Sommay, had two sons
called Tamendonare and Ariconte. Tamendonare tilled the
ground and was a good father and husband, and he had a
wife and children. But his brother Ariconte cared for none
of these things. He busied himself only with war, and his
one desire was to subdue neighbouring peoples and even his
own righteous brother. One day this truculent warrior,
returning from a battle, brought to his peaceful brother the
amputated arm of a slain foe, and as he did so he said
proudly to his brother, "Away with you, coward that you
are. I'll have your wife and children, for you are not strong
enough to defend them." The good man, grieved at his
brother's pride, answered with stinging sarcasm, " If you are
as valiant as you say, why did not you bring the whole carcass of your enemy ? " Indignant at the taunt, Ariconte

[1] Karl Semper, *Die Palau-Inseln*
(Leipsic, 1873), pp. 195 *sq.* According to another version of the story the
anger of the gods was kindled, not by
the theft of one of their eyes, but by
the murder of one of their number.
The rest of the story agrees substantially
with the one given in the text. See
J. Kubary, "Die Religion der Pelauer,"
in Adolf Bastian's *Allerlei aus Volks-
und Menschenkunde* (Berlin, 1888), i.

53 *sq.*
[2] J. Lery (Lerius), *Historia Navigationis in Brasiliam, quae et America
dicitur* (1586), p. 238 [wrongly numbered 220].
[3] *The Captivity of Hans Stade of
Hesse, in A.D. 1547-1555, among the
Wild Tribes of Eastern Brazil*, translated by Albert Tootal and annotated
by (Sir) Richard F. Burton (London,
the Hakluyt Society, 1874), p. 148.

threw the arm at the door of his brother's house. At the same moment the village in which they dwelt was transported to the sky, but the two brothers remained on earth. Seeing that, in astonishment or anger Tamendonare stamped on the ground so forcibly that a great fountain of water sprang from it and rose so high that it out-topped the hills and seemed to mount above the clouds ; and the water continued to spout till it had covered the whole earth.   On perceiving their danger, the two brothers hastened to ascend the highest mountains, and there sought to save themselves by climbing the trees, along with their wives.   Tamendonare climbed one tree, called *pindona.* of which the French traveller saw two sorts, one of them with larger fruit and leaves than the other.   In his flight from the rising flood he dragged up one of his wives with him, while his brother with his wife climbed another tree called *geniper*.   While they were all perched among the boughs, Ariconte gave some of the fruit of the tree to his wife, saying, " Break off some of the fruit and let it fall."   She did so, and they perceived by the splash that the water was still high, and that it was not yet time for them to descend into the valley. The Indians believe that in this flood all men and women were drowned, except the two brothers and their wives, and that from these two pairs after the deluge there came forth two different peoples, to wit, the Tonnasseares, surnamed Tupinambo, and the Tonnaitz Hoyanans, surnamed Tominu, who are at perpetual feud and war with each other.   The Tupinambo, wishing to exalt themselves and to make themselves out better than their fellows and neighbours, say, " We are descended from Tamendonare, while you are descended from Ariconte," by which they imply that Tamendonare was a better man than Ariconte.[1]

How the o d w caused by a quarrel ween two brothers, a the brothers and their wives escaped from it by climbing trees.

A somewhat different version of the same legend was recorded by the Jesuit Simon de Vasconcellos. In it only a single family is said to have been saved, and no mention is made of the bad brother. Once upon a time, so runs the tale, there was a clever medicine-man or sorcerer named Tamanduare. To him the great god Tupi revealed the

Another version of the Brazilian story.

---

[1] Andre Thevet, *La Cosmographie Universelle* (Paris, 1575), ii. 914 *sq.* [wrongly numbered for 947 *sq.*].

coming of a great flood which would swamp the earth, so that even the high trees and mountains would be submerged. Only one lofty peak would rise above the waters, and on its top would be found a tall palm-tree with a fruit like a coco-nut. To that palm the sorcerer was warned to turn for refuge with his family in the hour of need. Without delay Tamanduare and his family betook themselves to the top of the lofty peak. When they were safely there, it began to rain, and it rained and rained till all the earth was covered. The flood even crept up the mountain and washed over the summit, and the man and his family climbed up into the palm-tree and remained in the branches so long as the inundation lasted, and they subsisted by eating the fruit of the palm. When the water subsided, they descended, and being fruitful they proceeded to repeople the drowned and devastated world.[1]

Story of a
g e o
told by the
Caingangs,

Coroados,
of Southern
~~Brazil.~~

The Caingangs, or Coroados, an Indian tribe of Rio Grande do Sul, the most southerly province of Brazil, have a tradition of a great flood which covered the whole earth inhabited by their forefathers. Only the top of the coastal range called Serra do Mar still appeared above the water. The members of three Indian tribes, namely the Caingangs, the Cayurucres, and the Cames, swam on the water of the flood toward the mountains, holding lighted torches between their teeth. But the Cayurucres and the Cames grew weary, they sank under the waves and were drowned, and their souls went to dwell in the heart of the mountain. However, the Caingangs and a few of the Curutons made shift to reach the mountain, and there they abode, some on the ground, and some on the branches of trees. Several days passed, and yet the water did not sink, and they had no food to eat. They looked for nothing but death, when they heard the song of the *saracuras*, a species of waterfowl, which flew to them with baskets of earth. This earth the birds threw into the water, which accordingly began slowly to sink. The

---

[1] Carl Teschauer, S.J., "Mythen und alte Volkssagen aus Brasilien," *Anthropos*, i. (1906) p. 738; Maximilian Prinz zu Wied-Neuwied, *Reise nach Brasilien in den Jahren 1815 bis 1817* (Frankfort, 1820–1821), ii. 59 (referring to Simam de Vasconcellos, *Noticias curiosas do Brasil*, p. 52); J. G. Müller, *Geschichte der Amerikanischen Urreligionen* (Bâle, 1867), p. 267.

people cried to the birds to hurry, so the birds called the ducks to their help, and working together they soon cleared enough room and to spare for all the people, except for such as had climbed up the trees : these latter were turned into monkeys.   When the flood subsided, the Caingangs descended and settled at the foot of the mountain.   The souls of the drowned Cayurucres and Cames contrived to burrow their way out from the bowels of the mountain in which they were imprisoned ; and when they had crept forth they kindled a fire, and out of the ashes of the fire one of the Cayurucres moulded jaguars, and tapirs, and ant-bears, and bees, and animals of many other sorts, and he made them live and told them what they should eat.   But one of the Cames imitated him by fashioning pumas, and poisonous snakes, and wasps, all in order that these creatures should fight the other animals which the Cayurucres had made, as they do to this day.[1]

A story of a great flood is told also by the Carayas, a tribe of Brazilian Indians, who inhabit the valley of the Araguaya River, which, with the Tocantins, forms the most easterly of the great southern tributaries of the Amazon. The tribe is said to differ from all its neighbours in manners and customs as well as in physical characteristics, while its language appears to be unrelated to any other known language spoken by the Indians of Brazil.[2]   The Caraya story of a deluge runs thus.   Once upon a time the Carayas were out hunting wild pigs and drove the animals into their dens.   Thereupon they began to dig them out, killing each pig as it was dragged forth.   In doing so they came upon a deer, then a tapir, and then a white deer.   Digging still deeper, they laid bare the feet of a man.   Horrified at the discovery, they fetched a mighty magician, who knew all the beasts of the forest, and he contrived to draw the man out of the earth.   The man thus unearthed was named Anatiua, and he had a thin body but a fat paunch.   He

---

[1] C. Teschauer, S.J., "Die Caingang oder Coroados-Indianer im brasilianischen Staate Rio Grande do Sol," *Anthropos*, ix. (1914) pp. 32 *sq.* The Caingangs or Coroados were formerly known as the Guayanas (*op. cit.* pp.

16 *sq.*).
[2] P. Ehrenreich, *Beiträge zur Völkerkunde Brasiliens* (Berlin, 1891), pp. 3, 9 (*Veröffentlichungen aus dem königlichen Museum fur Völkerkunde*, vol. ii. Heft 1/2).

now began to sing, " I am Anatiua. Bring me tobacco to smoke." But the Carayas did not understand what he said. They ran about the wood, and came back with all kinds of flowers and fruits, which they offered to Anatiua. But he refused them all, and pointed to a man who was smoking. Then they understood him and offered him tobacco. He took it and smoked till he fell to the ground senseless. So they carried him to the canoe and brought him to the village. There he awoke from his stupor and began to dance and sing. But his behaviour and his unintelligible speech frightened the Carayas, and they decamped, bag and baggage. That made Anatiua very angry, and he turned himself into a great *piranha* and followed them, carrying with him many calabashes full of water. He called to the Carayas to halt, but they paid no heed, and in his rage he smashed one of the calabashes which he was carrying. The water at once began to rise, but still the Carayas pursued their flight. Then he broke another calabash, and then another and another, and higher and higher rose the water, till the whole land was inundated, and only the mountains at the mouth of Tapirape River projected above the flood. The Carayas took refuge on the two peaks of that range. Anatiua now called all fish together to drag the people down into the water. The *jahu*, the *pintado*, and the *pacu* tried to do so, but none of them succeeded. At last the *bicudo* (a fish with a long beak-like snout) contrived to scale the mountain from behind and to tear the Carayas down from its summit. A great lagoon still marks the spot where they fell. Only a few persons remained on the top of the mountain, and they descended when the water of the flood had run away.[1] On this story the writer who records it remarks that "though in general regularly recurring inundations, as on the Araguaya, do not give rise to flood stories, as Andree has rightly pointed

P. Ehrenreich on the Cara a flood story.

[1] P. Ehrenreich, *Beiträge zur Volkerkunde Brasiliens* (Berlin, 1891), pp. 40 *sq.* Compare *id.*, *Die Mythen und Legenden der Südamerikanischen Urvölker* (Berlin, 1905), p. 28 (Supplement to vol. xxxvii. of the *Zeitschrift für Ethnologie*). According to another account, in their escape to the mountains the Carayas were guided by an animal ("*Maifori, o primeiro bichu, das erste oder oberste, ausgezeichnetste Tier*"). See W. Kissenberth, "Über die hauptsachlichsten Ergebnisse der Araguaya-Reise," *Zeitschrift für Ethnologie*, xliv. (1912) p. 49.

out,[1] yet the local conditions are here favourable to the creation of such a story.   The traveller, who, after a long voyage
between endless low river-banks, suddenly comes in sight of
the mighty conical mountains on the Tapirape River, towering abruptly from the plain, can easily understand how the
Carayas, who suffer much from inundations, came to tell
their story of the flood.   Perhaps on some occasion when
the inundation rose to an unusual height, these mountains
may really have served as a last refuge to the inhabitants
of the surrounding district."   And he adds, " As in most
South American legends of a flood, this particular flood is
said to have been caused, not by rain, but by the breaking
of vessels full of water." [2]

The Ipurina, a warlike tribe on the Purus River, one of Story of a
g e   o
told by the
Ipurina of
ɛɪ
Purus.
the great rivers which flow into the Upper Amazon from the
south, tell of a destructive deluge of hot water.   They say
that formerly there was a great kettle of boiling water in the
sun.   About it perched or fluttered a countless flock of
storks.   Some of the birds flew over the world collecting
everything that mouldered or decayed to throw it into the
kettle.   Only the hard, indestructible *parukuba* wood they
left alone.   The storks surrounded the kettle and waited
till something appeared on the surface of the boiling water,
whereupon they snapped it up.   Now the chief of the storks,
indeed the creator of all birds, was Mayuruberu.   When the
water in the kettle was getting low, he cast a round stone
into it.   The kettle was upset, the hot liquid poured down
on earth and burned everything up, including the woods
and even the water.   Mankind indeed survived, but of the
vegetable world nothing escaped but the cassia.   The
ancestor of the Ipurina was the sloth.   He climbed the
cassia-tree to fetch down the fruits, for men had nothing
else to subsist upon.   On earth it was very dark, for the
sun and moon were hidden.   The sloth plucked the fruit
and threw down the kernels.   The first kernel fell on hard

---

[1] R. Andree, *Die Flutsagen*, p. 146,
" A local event, such as the inundation of a river in special circumstances,
may give rise to the tradition of a
flood ; whereas regularly recurring inundations, which may be expected at
definite seasons, are no cause for the
formation of such a tradition.   The
periodical rise of the Nile, and the
mighty swelling of the Abyssinian
rivers, have never occasioned flood
legends."

[2] P. Ehrenreich, *Beiträge zur Völkerkunde Brasiliens*, p. 41.

earth, the second in water, the third in deep water, and so on. At the fall of the first kernel, the sun appeared again, but still very small, hardly an inch across ; at the fall of the second, it was larger ; at the fall of the third, it measured a span across ; and so on until it expanded to its present dimensions. Next the sloth begged Mayuruberu to give him seeds of useful fruits. So Mayuruberu appeared with a great basketful of plants, and the Ipurina began to till their fields. He who would not work was eaten by Mayuruberu. Every day Mayuruberu received a man to devour. Thus the world gradually became such as it is at the present time. The kettle still stands in the sun, but it is empty.[1]

Story of a gre flood told b other d ans of the river . Purus.

Again, the Pamarys, Abederys, and Kataushys, on the river Purus, relate that once on a time people heard a rumbling above and below the ground. The sun and moon, also, turned red, blue, and yellow, and the wild beasts mingled fearlessly with men. A month later they heard a roar and saw darkness ascending from the earth to the sky, accompanied by thunder and heavy rain, which blotted out the day and the earth. Some people lost themselves, some died, without knowing why ; for everything was in a dreadful state of confusion. The water rose very high, till the earth was sunk beneath the water and only the branches of the highest trees still stood out above the flood. Thither the people had fled for refuge, and there, perched among the boughs, they perished of cold and hunger ; for all the time it was dark and the rain fell. Then only Uassu and his wife were saved. When they came down after the flood they could not find a single corpse, no, not so much as a heap of bleached bones. After that they had many children, and they said one to the other, " Go to, let us build our houses on the river, that when the water rises, we too may rise with it." But when they saw that the land was dry and solid, they thought no more about it. Yet the Pamarys build their houses on the river to this day.[2]

Story of a great flood

Jibaros of the Upper Amazon.

The Jibaros, an Indian tribe on the upper waters of the Amazon, in the territories of Peru and Ecuador, have also a tradition, more or less confused, of a great deluge

[1] P. Ehrenreich, *Beiträge zur Volkerkunde Brasiliens*, pp. 7 1 *sq.*

[2] Carl Teschauer, S.J., " Mythen und Volkssagen aus Brasilien," *Anthropos*, i. (1906) p. 739.

which happened long ago. They say that a great cloud
fell from heaven, which turned into rain and caused the
death of all the inhabitants of the earth ; only an old man
and his two sons were saved, and it was they who repeopled the earth after the deluge, though how they contrived
to do so without the assistance of a woman is a detail about
which our authority does not deign to enlighten us. However that may be, one of the two sons who survived was
cursed by his father, and the Jibaros are descended from
him. The curse may be a reminiscence of the story of Noah
and his sons recorded in Genesis, of which the Jibaros may
have heard through missionaries. The difficulty of propa-
gating the human species without the help of the female sex
would seem to have struck the acuter minds among the
Jibaros, for according to some of them the survivors of the
deluge were a man and a woman, who took refuge in a cave
on a high mountain, together with samples of all the various
species of the animal kingdom. This version provides, with
commendable foresight, for the restoration of animals as well
as of men after the great flood. Yet another version of the
story told by the Jibaros solves the problem of population
in a more original manner. Nobody, they say, escaped the
flood but two brothers, who found refuge in a mountain which,
strange to tell, rose higher and higher with the rise of the
waters. When the flood had subsided, the two brothers
went out to search for food, and on their return to the hut
what was their surprise to find victuals set forth ready for
them ! To clear up the mystery, one of the brothers hid
himself, and from his place of concealment he saw two parrots
with the faces of women enter the hut and prepare the meal.
Darting out from his ambush he seized one of the birds and
married it or her, and from this marriage sprang three boys
and three girls, who became the ancestors of the Jibaros.[1]

The Muratos, a branch of the Jibaros in Ecuador, have
their own version of the deluge story. They say that once
on a time a Murato Indian went to fish in a lagoon of the
Pastaza River ; a small crocodile swallowed his bait, and

Story of a
g e   o
told by the
Muratos of
Ecuador.

[1] Dr. Rivet, "Les Indiens Jibaros,"
L'Anthropologie, xix. (1908) pp. 235
sq. The last of these versions is clearly
identical with the Canari story of a
flood. See below, pp. 268 sq.

the fisherman killed the young animal. The crocodile's
mother, or rather the mother of crocodiles in general, was
angry and lashed the water with her tail, till the water overflowed and flooded all the neighbourhood of the lagoon. All
the people were drowned except one man, who climbed a
palm-tree and stayed there for many days. All the time it
was as dark as night. From time to time he dropped a
fruit of the palm, but he always heard it splash in the water.
At last one day the fruit which he let fall dropped with a
simple thud on the ground ; there was no splash, so he knew
that the flood had subsided. Accordingly he descended from
the tree, built a house, and set about to till a field. He was
without a wife, but he soon provided himself with one by
cutting off a piece of his own body and planting it in the
ground ; for from the earth thus fertilized there sprang up a
woman, whom he married.[1]

Story of a
gre fl d
told b th
Arau-
ans of
Chili.

The incident of a moving mountain, which meets us
in the Jibaro story of the flood, recurs in another Indian
narrative of the great catastrophe. The Araucanians of
Chili have a tradition of a great deluge, in which only a few
persons were saved. These fortunate survivors took refuge
on a high mountain called Thegtheg, the thundering,
or the sparkling, which had three points and possessed the
property of floating on water. " From hence," says the
Spanish historian, " it is inferable that this deluge was in
consequence of some volcanic eruption, accompanied by
terrible earthquakes, and is probably very different from that
of Noah. Whenever a violent earthquake occurs, these
people fly for safety to those mountains which they fancy to
be of a similar appearance, and which of course, as they suppose, must possess the same property of floating on the
water, assigning as a reason, that they are fearful after an
earthquake that the sea will again return and deluge the
world. On these occasions, each one takes a good supply of
provisions, and wooden plates to protect their heads from
being scorched, provided the Thegtheg, when raised by the
waters, should be elevated to the sun. Whenever they are
told that plates made of earth would be much more suitable
for this purpose than those of wood, which are liable to be

[1] Dr. Rivet, "Les Indiens Jibaros," *L'Anthropologie*, xix. (1908) pp. 236 *sq.*

burned, their usual reply is, that their ancestors did so before them." [1]

The Ackawois of British Guiana tell a story of the great flood which is enriched by a variety of details. They say that in the beginning of the world the great spirit Makonaima created birds and beasts and set his son Sigu to rule over them. Moreover, he caused to spring from the earth a great and very wonderful tree, which bore a different kind of fruit on each of its branches, while round its trunk bananas, plantains, cassava, maize, and corn of all kinds grew in profusion ; yams, too, clustered round its roots ; and in short all the plants now cultivated on earth flourished in the greatest abundance on or about or under that marvellous tree. In order to diffuse the benefits of the tree all over the world, Sigu resolved to cut it down and plant slips and seeds of it everywhere, and this he did with the help of all the beasts and birds, all except the brown monkey, who, being both lazy and mischievous, refused to assist in the great work of transplantation. So to keep him out of mischief Sigu set the animal to fetch water from the stream in a basket of open-work, calculating that the task would occupy his misdirected energies for some time to come. In the meantime, proceeding with the labour of felling the miraculous tree, he discovered that the stump was hollow and full of water in which the fry of every sort of fresh-water fish was swimming about. The benevolent Sigu determined to stock all the rivers and lakes on earth with the fry on so liberal a scale that every sort of fish should swarm in every water. But this generous intention was unexpectedly frustrated. For the water in the cavity, being connected with the great reservoir somewhere in the bowels of the earth, began to overflow ; and to arrest the rising flood Sigu covered the stump with a closely woven basket. This had the desired effect. But unfortunately the brown monkey, tired of his fruitless task, stealthily returned, and his curiosity being aroused by the sight of the basket turned upside down, he imagined that it must conceal something good to eat. So he cautiously lifted it and peeped beneath, and out poured

Story of a gre   (told by the Ackawois s_ Guiana

How the flood was c   sed by the   f the brown monkey.

[1] J. Ignatius Molina, *The Geographical, Natural, and Civil History of Chili* (London, 1809), ii. 93 *sq.*

the flood, sweeping the monkey himself away and inundating the whole land.   Gathering the rest of the animals together Sigu led them to the highest point of the country, where grew some tall coco-nut palms.   Up the tallest of these trees he caused the birds and climbing animals to ascend ; and as for the animals that could not climb and were not amphibious, he shut them up in a cave with a very narrow entrance, and having sealed up the mouth of it with wax he gave the animals inside a long thorn with which to pierce the wax and so ascertain when the water had subsided.   After taking these measures for the preservation of the more helpless species, he and the rest of the creatures climbed up the palm-tree and ensconced them- selves among the branches.   During the darkness and storm which followed, they all suffered intensely from cold and hunger ; the rest bore their sufferings with stoical fortitude, but the red howling monkey uttered his anguish in such horrible yells that his throat swelled and has remained dis- tended ever since ; that, too, is the reason why to this day he has a sort of bony drum in his throat.   Meanwhile Sigu from time to time let fall seeds of the palm into the water to judge of its depth by the splash.   As the water sank, the interval between the dropping of the seed and the splash in the water grew longer ; and at last, instead of a splash, the listening Sigu heard the dull thud of the seeds striking the soft earth.   Then he knew that the flood had subsided, and he and the animals prepared to descend.   But the trumpeter- bird was in such a hurry to get down that he flopped straight into an ants' nest, and the hungry insects fastened on his legs and gnawed them to the bone.   That is why the trumpeter- bird has still such spindle shanks.   The other creatures pro- fited by this awful example and came down the tree cautiously and safely.   Sigu now rubbed two pieces of wood together to make fire, but just as he produced the first spark, he happened to look away, and the bush-turkey, mistaking the spark for a fire- fly, gobbled it up and flew off.   The spark burned the greedy bird's gullet, and that is why turkeys have red wattles on their throats to this day.   The alligator was standing by at the time, doing no harm to anybody ; but as he was for some reason an unpopular character, all the other animals accused him of having stolen and swallowed the spark.   In order to

How the sinking of the flood was d ec y the splash of seeds pp n the water.

recover the spark from the jaws of the alligator Sigu tore
out the animal's tongue, and that is why alligators have no
tongue to speak of down to this very day.[1]

The Arawaks of British Guiana believe that since its
creation the world has been twice destroyed, once by fire
and once by flood.   Both destructions were brought on it
by Aiomun Kondi, the great "Dweller on High," because of
the wickedness of mankind.   But he announced beforehand
the coming catastrophe, and men who accepted the warning
prepared to escape from the great fire by digging deep into
a sand-reef and there making for themselves a subterranean
chamber with a roof of timber supported on massive pillars
of the same material.   Over it all they spread layers of earth
and a thick upper coating of sand.   Having carefully removed
everything combustible from the neighbourhood, they retired
to this underground dwelling and there stayed quietly till the
roaring torrent of flame, which swept across the earth's surface, had passed over them.   Afterwards, when the destruction of the world by a deluge was at hand, a pious and wise
chief named Marerewana was informed of the coming flood
and saved himself and his family in a large canoe.   Fearing
to drift away out to sea or far from the home of his fathers,
he had made ready a long cable of bush-rope, with which he
tied his bark to the trunk of a great tree.   So when the
waters subsided he found himself not far from his former
abode.[2]

The Macusis of British Guiana say that in the beginning
the good spirit Makunaima, whose name means "He who
works in the night," created the heaven and the earth.
When he had stocked the earth with plants and trees, he
came down from his celestial mansion, climbed up a tall tree,
and chipped off the bark with a big stone axe.   The chips
fell into the river at the foot of the tree and were changed
into animals of all kinds.   When he had thus provided for
the creation of animals, the good spirit next created man ;
and when the man had fallen into a sound sleep he awoke to
find a woman standing at his side.   Afterwards the evil spirit

Story of the
destruction

world by
flood told
by the

of British
Guiana.

Story of a

told by the
Macusis of

Guiana.

[1] Rev. W. H. Brett, *The Indian
Tribes of Guiana* (London, 1868), pp.
378-384 ; (Sir) Everard F. im Thurn,
Among the Indians of Guiana (London,
1883), pp. 379-381.

[2] Rev. W. H. Brett, *The Indian
Tribes of Guiana*, pp. 398 *sq.*

got the upper hand on earth ; so the good spirit Makunaima sent a great flood. Only one man escaped in a canoe ; he sent out a rat to see whether the water had abated, and the rat returned with a cob of maize. When the deluge had retreated, the man repeopled the earth, like Deucalion and Pyrrha, by throwing stones behind him.[1] In this story the special creation of woman, the mention of the evil spirit, and the incident of the rat sent out to explore the depth of the flood, present suspicious resemblances to the Biblical narrative and may be due to missionary, or at all events European, influence. Further, the mode in which, after the flood, the survivors create mankind afresh by throwing stones behind them, resembles so exactly the corresponding incident in the Greek story of Deucalion and Pyrrha, that it is difficult to regard the two as independent.

Stories of a great flood current among the Indians of the Orinoco.

Legends of a great flood are current also among the Indians of the Orinoco. On this subject Humboldt observes : " I cannot quit this first chain of the mountains of Encamarada without recalling a fact which was not unknown to Father Gili, and which was often mentioned to me during our stay among the missions of the Orinoco. The aborigines of these countries have preserved a belief that at the time of the great flood, while their fathers were forced to betake themselves to canoes in order to escape the general inundation, the waves of the sea broke against the rocks of Encamarada. This belief is not found isolated among a single people, the Tamanaques ; it forms part of a system of historical traditions of which scattered notices are discovered among the Maypures of the great cataracts, among the Indians of the Rio Erevato, which falls into the Caura, and among almost all the tribes of the Upper Orinoco. When the Tamanaques are asked how the human race escaped this great cataclysm, ' the Age of Water,' as the Mexicans call it, they say that one man and one woman were saved on a high mountain called Tamanacu, situated on the banks of the Asiveru, and that on casting behind them, over their heads, the fruits of the Mauritia palm, they saw springing from the kernels of these fruits men and women, who repeopled the

[1] Richard Schomburgk, *Reisen in Britisch-Guiana* (Leipsic, 1847-1848), ii. 319, 320.

earth."[1]   This they did in obedience to a voice which they
heard speaking to them as they descended the mountain full
of sorrow at the destruction of mankind by the flood.   The
fruits which the man threw became men, and the fruits
which the woman threw became women.[2]

The Muyscas or Chibchas of Bogota, in the high Andes Story of a
of Colombia, say that long ago their ancestors offended g e   o
Chibchachum, a deity of the second rank, who had hitherto told by he
been their special patron and protector.   To punish them, Muyscas or
Chibchachum created the torrents of Sopo and Tibito, which, of Bogota.
pouring down from the hills, flooded the whole plain and
rendered cultivation impossible.   The people fled to the
mountains, but even there the rising waters of the inundation
threatened to submerge them.   In despair they prayed to
the great god Bochica, who appeared to them seated on a
rainbow and holding a golden wand in his hand.   " I have
heard your prayers," said he, " and I will punish Chibchachum.
I shall not destroy the rivers which he has created, because
they will be useful to you in time of drought, but I will open
a passage for the waters."   With these words he threw his
golden wand at the mountain, split it from top to bottom
at the spot where the river Funzha now forms the famous
waterfall of Tequendama.   So all the waters of the deluge
flowed away down this new opening in the circle of mountains which encloses the high upland tableland of Bogota,
and thus the plain became habitable again.   To punish
Chibchachum, the great god Bochica condemned him to bear
on his shoulders the whole weight of the earth, which before
that time was supported on massive pillars of wood.   When
the weary giant tries to get a little ease by shifting his burden
from one shoulder to another, he causes an earthquake.[3]

This tradition is in so far well founded as the evidence

[1] Alexandre de Humboldt, *Voyage
aux régions equinoxiales du Nouveau
Continent*, i. (Paris, 1814) pp. 238 *sq.*

[2] R.   Schomburgk,   *Reisen   in
Britisch-Guiana*, ii. 320.   The Acha-
guas of the Upper Orinoco are reported
to have a legend of a great flood, from
which one of their ancestors escaped
on a high mountain.   The authority
for the statement is a Jesuit Father
named Juan Rivero, whose work (*His-*

*toria de las Misiones de los Llanos de
Casanare y los rios Orinoco y Meta*)
was written in 1736 but not printed
till 1883 at Bogota.   See A. Ernst,
" Ueber   einige   weniger   bekannte
Sprachen aus der Gegend des Meta
und oberen Orinoco," *Zeitschrift fur
Ethnologie*, xxiii. (1891) p. 6.

[3] H.   Ternaux-Compans, *Essai sur
l'ancien Cundinamarca* (Paris, N.D.),
pp. 7 *sq.*

Geological evidence that the valley of Bogota was once occupied by a lake.

of geology appears to prove that for ages the mountain-girt plain of Bogota was occupied by a lake, and that the pent-up waters at last found vent and flowed away through a fissure suddenly cleft by a great earthquake in the sandstone rocks. The cleft in the rocky dam may be seen to this day. It is near the meeting of the rivers Bogota and Muño. Here the wall of sandstone is broken by a sort of natural gateway formed by a beetling crag on one side and a mass of shattered, crumbling rocks on the other. The scene is one well fitted to impress the mind and excite the imagination of primitive man, who sees in the sublime works of nature the handiwork of awful and mysterious beings. The sluggish current of the tawny river flows in serpentine windings towards the labyrinth of rocks and cliffs where it takes its leap into the tremendous abyss. As you near the fall, and the hollow sound of its tumbling waters grows louder and louder, a great change comes over the landscape. The bare monotonous plain of Bogota is left behind, and you seem to be entering on enchanted land. On every side rise hills of varied outline mantled to their tops with all the luxuriant vegetation of the tropics, from the grasses which carpet the ground to the thickets and tall forest trees which spread over the whole a dense veil of green. At their foot the river hurries in a series of rapids, between walls of rock, to the brink of the fall, there to vanish in a cloud of mist and spray, lit up by all the gay colours of the rainbow, into the dark and dizzy chasm below, while the thunderous roar of the cataract breaks the stillness of the lonely hills. The cascade is thrice as high as Niagara ; and by a pardonable exaggeration the river is said to fall perpendicularly from the temperate to the tropical zone.[1]

Story of a great flood told by the Cañaris of Ecuador.

The Cañaris, an Indian tribe of Ecuador, in the ancient kingdom of Quito, tell of a great flood from which two brothers escaped to a very high mountain called Huaca-ynan. As the waters rose, the hill rose with them, so that the flood never reached the two brothers on the summit. When the water sank and their store of provisions was consumed, the

[1] Fr. von Hellwald, *Die Erde und ihre Völker*, Dritte Auflage (Berlin and Stuttgart, 1884), pp. 213 *sq.* ; Élisée Reclus, *Nouvelle Géographie Universelle*, xviii. (Paris, 1893) pp. 251 *sq.*, compare pp. 274 *sq.*

brothers descended and sought their food in the hills and valleys. They built a small house, where they dwelt, eking out a miserable subsistence on herbs and roots, and suffering much from hunger and fatigue. One day, after the usual weary search, they returned home, and there found food to eat and *chicha* to drink without knowing who could have prepared or brought it. This happened for ten days, and after that they laid their heads together to find out who it was that did them so much good in their time of need. So the elder brother hid himself, and presently he saw two macaws approaching, dressed like Canaris. As soon as the birds came to the house, they began to prepare the food which they had brought with them. When the man saw that they were beautiful and had the faces of women, he came forth from his hiding-place ; but at sight of him the birds were angry and flew away, leaving nothing to eat. When the younger brother came home from his search for food, and found nothing cooked and ready as on former days, he asked his elder brother the reason, and they were both very angry. Next day the younger brother resolved to hide and watch for the coming of the birds. At the end of three days the two macaws reappeared and began to prepare the food. The two men waited till the birds had finished cooking and then shut the door on them. The birds were very angry at being thus trapped, and while the two brothers were holding the smaller bird, the larger one escaped. Then the two brothers took the smaller macaw to wife, and by her they had six sons and daughters, from whom all the Canaris are descended. Hence the hill Huaca-yñan, where the macaw lived as the wife of the brothers, is looked upon as a sacred place by the Indians, and they venerate macaws and value their feathers highly for use at their festivals.[1]

The macaw wi e.

The Indians of Huarochiri, a province of Peru in the Andes to the east of Lima, say that once on a time the world nearly

Story of a gre   o told by the Peruvian Inɑians.

[1] Christoval de Molina, "The Fables and Rites of the Yncas," in *The Rites and Laws of the Yncas*, translated and edited by (Sir) Clements R. Markham (London, Hakluyt Society, 1873), pp. 8 *sq.* Compare Pedro Sarmiento de Gamboa, *History of the Incas*, translated and edited by Sir Clements Markham (Hakluyt Society, London, 1908), pp. 30 *sq.* In this latter version of the story the mountain is called Guasano, and the two macaws are rationalized into women. With the Canari story compare the Jibaro story (above, p. 261).

came to an end altogether. It happened thus. An Indian was tethering his llama in a place where there was good pasture, but the animal resisted, showing sorrow and moaning after its manner. The master said to the llama, " Fool, why do you moan and refuse to eat ? Have I not put you where there is good food ? " The llama answered, " Madman, what do you know about it ? Learn that I am not sad without due cause ; for within five days the sea will rise and cover the whole earth, destroying all there is upon it." Wondering to hear the beast speak, the man asked whether there was any way in which they could save themselves. The llama bade him take food for five days and to follow him to the top of a high mountain called Villca-coto, between the parish of San Damian and the parish of San Geronimo de Surco. The man did as he was bid, carrying the load of food on his back and leading the llama. On reaching the top of the mountain he found many kinds of birds and animals there assembled. Hardly had he reached this place of refuge when the sea began to rise, and it rose till the water flooded all the valleys and covered the tops of the hills, all but the top of Villca-coto, and even there the waves washed so high that the animals had to crowd together in a narrow space, and some of them could hardly find foothold. The tail of the fox was dipped in the flood, and that is why the tips of foxes' tails are black to this day. At the end of five days the waters began to abate, and the sea returned to its former bounds ; but all the people in the world were drowned except that one man, and from him all the nations of the earth are descended.[1]

Another Peruvian story of a great flood.

A similar story of the flood is told by the Indians of Ancasmarca, a province five leagues from Cuzco. They say that a month before the flood came, their sheep displayed much sadness, eating no food by day and watching the stars by night. At last their shepherd asked them what ailed them, and they answered that the conjunction of stars foreshadowed the coming destruction of the world by water. So the shepherd and his six children took counsel, and gathered together all the food and sheep they could get, and with

[1] Francesco de Avila, " Narrative," in *Rites and Laws of the Yncas*, translated and edited by (Sir) Clements R. Markham, pp. 132 *sq*.

these they betook themselves to the top of an exceeding great mountain called Ancasmarca. They say that as the water rose, the mountain still rose higher, so that its top was never submerged ; and when the flood sank, the mountain sank also. Thus the six children of that shepherd returned to repeople the province after the great flood.[1]

The Incas of Peru had also a tradition of a deluge. They said that the water rose above the highest mountains in the world, so that all people and all created things perished. No living thing escaped except a man and a woman, who floated in a box on the face of the waters and so were saved. When the flood subsided, the wind drifted the box with the two in it to Tiahuanacu, about seventy leagues from Cuzco. There the Creator commanded them to dwell, and there he himself set to work to raise up the people who now inhabit that country. The way in which he did so was this. He fashioned each nation out of clay and painted on each the dresses they were to wear. Then he gave life and soul to every one of the painted clay figures and bade them pass under the earth. They did so, and then came up at the various places where the Creator had ordered the different nations to dwell. So some of them came out of caves, others issued from hills, others from fountains, and others from trunks of trees. And because they came forth from these various places, the Indians made various idols (*huacas*) and places of worship in memory of their origin ; that is why the idols (*huacas*) of the Indians are of diverse shapes.[2]

The Peruvian legends of a great flood are told more summarily by the Spanish historian Herrera as follows. "The ancient Indians reported, they had received it by tradition from their ancestors, that many years before there were any Incas, at the time when the country was very populous, there happened a great flood, the sea breaking out beyond its bounds, so that the land was covered with

Story of a great flood told by the Incas of Peru.

Herrera on the Peruvian tradition of a great flood.

---

[1] Christoval de Molina, "The Fables and Rites of the Yncas," in *The Rites and Laws of the Yncas*, translated and edited by (Sir) Clements R. Markham, pp. 9 *sq.*

[2] Christoval de Molina, *op. cit.* pp. 4 *sq.* As to the Inca tradition of the deluge compare Garcilasso de la Vega, *First Part of the Royal Commentaries of the Yncas*, translated by (Sir) Clements R. Markham (London, Hakluyt Society, 1869–1871), i. 71 ; J. de Acosta, *Natural and Moral History of the Indies* (London, Hakluyt Society, 1880), i. 70 *sq.*

water, and all the people perished.   To this the Guancas
inhabiting the vale of Xauxa, and the natives of Chiquito
in the province of Collao, add, that some persons remained
in the hollows and caves of the highest mountains, who again
peopled the land.   Others of the mountain people affirm,
that all perished in the deluge, only six persons being saved
on a float, from whom descended all the inhabitants of that
country.   That there had been some particular flood may be
credited, because all the several provinces agree in it." [1]

Story of a
great flood
told by the
Chiriguanos
of Bolivia.

The Chiriguanos, a once powerful Indian tribe of south-
eastern Bolivia, tell the following story of a great flood.
They say that a certain potent but malignant supernatural
being, named Aguara-Tunpa, declared war against the true
god Tunpaete, the Creator of the Chiriguanos.   His motive for
this declaration of war is unknown, but it is believed to have
been pure spite or the spirit of contradiction.   In order to
vex the true god, Aguara-Tunpa set fire to all the prairies
at the beginning or middle of autumn, so that along with
the plants and trees all the animals perished on which in
those days the Indians depended for their subsistence ; for
as yet they had not begun to cultivate maize and other
cereals, as they do now.   Thus deprived of food the Indians
nearly died of hunger.   However, they retreated before the
flames to the banks of the rivers, and there, while the earth
around still smoked from the great conflagration, they made
shift to live on the fish which they caught in the water.
Seeing his human prey likely to escape him, the baffled
Aguara-Tunpa had recourse to another device in order to
accomplish his infernal plot against mankind.   He caused
torrential rain to fall, hoping to drown the whole Chiriguano
tribe in the water.   He very nearly succeeded.   But happily
the Chiriguanos contrived to defeat his fell purpose.   Acting
on a hint given them by the true god Tunpaete, they looked
out for a large mate leaf, placed on it two little babies, a boy
and a girl, the children of one mother, and allowed the tiny
ark with its precious inmates to float on the face of the
water.   Still the rain continued to descend in torrents ; the

How two
. . . .
saved from
the flood
on ma e
le f.

[1] Antonio de Herrera, *The General   Indies*, translated into English by Capt.
*History of the vast Continent and Islands   John Stevens, Second Edition (London,
of America commonly called the West   1740), iv. 283.

floods rose and spread over the face of the earth to a great depth, and all the Chiriguanos were drowned ; only the two babes on the leaf of mate were saved. At last, however, the rain ceased to fall, and the flood sank, leaving a great expanse of fetid mud behind. The children now emerged from the ark, for if they had stayed there, they would have perished of cold and hunger. Naturally the fish and other creatures that live in the water were not drowned in the great flood ; on the contrary they throve on it, and were now quite ready to serve as food for the two babes. But how were the infants to cook the fish which they caught ? That was the rub, for of course all fire on earth had been extinguished by the deluge. However, a large toad came to the rescue of the two children. Before the flood had swamped the whole earth, that prudent creature had taken the precaution of secreting himself in a hole, taking with him in his mouth some live coals, which he contrived to keep alight all the time of the deluge by blowing on them with his breath. When he saw that the surface of the ground was dry again, he hopped out of his hole with the live coals in his mouth, and making straight for the two children he bestowed on them the gift of fire. Thus they were able to roast the fish they caught and so to warm their chilled bodies. In time they grew up, and from their union the whole tribe of the Chiriguanos is descended.[1]

How fire w recovered after the flood.

The natives of Tierra del Fuego, in the extreme south of South America, tell a fantastic and obscure story of a great flood. They say that the sun was sunk in the sea, that the waters rose tumultuously, and that all the earth was submerged except a single very high mountain, on which a few people found refuge.[2]

Story of a g e flo told b the Fuegians.

§ 15. *Stories of a Great Flood in Central America and Mexico*

The Indians about Panama " had some notion of Noah's flood, and said that when it happened one man escaped in a

Stories of a grea oo told by he Indians of Panama an Nicaragua.

[1] Bernardino de Nino, Misionero Franciscano, *Etnografía Chiriguana* (La Paz, Bolivia, 1912), pp. 131-133, compare p. 67.

[2] T. Bridges, " Mœurs et coutumes des Fuégiens," *Bulletins de la Société d'Anthropologie de Paris*, Troisieme Série, vii. (Paris, 1884) p. 181.

canoe with his wife and children, from whom all mankind afterwards proceeded and peopled the world."[1]   The Indians of Nicaragua believed that since its creation the world had been destroyed by a deluge, and that after its destruction the gods had created men and animals and all things afresh.[2]

Mexican tradition of a great flood.

"The Mexicans," says the Italian historian Clavigero, "with all other civilized nations, had a clear tradition, though somewhat corrupted by fable, of the creation of the world, of the universal deluge, of the confusion of tongues, and of the dispersion of the people ; and had actually all these events represented in their pictures.   They said, that when mankind were overwhelmed with the deluge, none were preserved but a man named Coxcox (to whom others give the name of Teocipactli), and a woman called Xochiquetzal, who saved themselves in a little bark, and having afterwards got to land upon a mountain called by them Colhuacan, had there a great many children ; that these children were all born dumb, until a dove from a lofty tree imparted to them languages, but differing so much that they could not understand one another.   The Tlascalans pretended that the men who survived the deluge were transformed into apes, but recovered speech and reason by degrees."[3]

Mexican tradition of a great flood contained in the Codex Chimal- popoca.

In the Mexican manuscript known as the *Codex Chimal-popoca*, which contains a history of the kingdoms of Culhuacan

[1] A. de Herrera, *The General History of the vast Continent and Islands of America*, translated by Captain John Stevens, iii. 414. Herrera's authority seems to have been Pascual de Andagoya. See Pascual de Andagoya, *Narrative of the Proceedings of Pedrarias Davila in the Provinces of Tierra Firme or Castilla del Oro* (Hakluyt Society, London, 1865), p. 14.

[2] G. F. de Oviedo y Valdes, *Histoire de Nicaragua* (Paris, 1840), pp. 21 *sq.*, in II. Ternaux - Compans's *Voyages, Relations et Mémoires originaux pour servir à l'histoire de la découverte de l'Amérique.* This tradition was elicited by François de Bobadilla, Provincial of the Order of Mercy, in an interview which he had with some Indians at the village of Teola in Nicaragua, the 28th September 1528. On being questioned, the Indian professed not to know whether all men were drowned in the flood, and whether the gods (*teotes*) had escaped on a mountain or in a canoe ; he only opined that being gods they could not be drowned.

[3] F. S. Clavigero, *The History of Mexico*, translated from the original Italian by Ch. Cullen (London, 1807), i. 244. Compare J. G. Müller, *Geschichte der Amerikanischen Urreligionen* [2] (Bâle, 1867), pp. 515 *sq.*; H. H. Bancroft, *The Native Races of the Pacific States* (London, 1875–1876), iii. 66, who says, "In most of the painted manuscripts supposed to relate to this event, a kind of boat is represented floating over the waste of water, and containing a man and a woman.   Even the Tlascaltecs, the Zapotecs, the Miztecs, and the people of Michoacan are said to have had such pictures."

and Mexico from the creation downwards, there is contained an account of the great flood. It runs thus. The world had existed for four hundred years, and two hundred years, and three score and sixteen years, when men were lost and drowned and turned into fishes. The sky drew near to the water; in a single day all was lost, and the day of Nahui-Xochitl or Fourth Flower consumed all our subsistence (all that there was of our flesh). And that year was the year of Ce-Calli or First House; and on the first day, the day of Nahui-Atl, all was lost. The mountains themselves were sunk under the water, and the water remained calm for fifty and two springs. But towards the end of the year Titlaca-huan had warned the man Nata and his wife Nena, saying, "Brew no more wine, but hollow out a great cypress and enter therein when, in the month of Toçoztli, the water shall near the sky." Then they entered into it, and when Titlacahuan had shut the door of it, he said to him, "Thou shalt eat but one sheaf of maize, and thy wife but one also." But when they had finished, they came forth from there, and the water remained calm, for the log moved no more, and opening it they began to see the fishes. Then they lit fire by rubbing pieces of wood together, and they roasted fishes. But the gods Citlallinicue and Citlallotonac at once looked down and said, "O divine Lord, what fire is that they are making there? wherefore do they thus fill the heaven with smoke?" Straightway Titlacahuan Tetzcatlipoca came down, and he grumbled, saying, "What's that fire doing here?" With that he snatched up the fishes, split their tails, modelled their heads, and turned them into dogs.[1]

In Michoacan, a province of Mexico, the legend of a deluge was also preserved. The natives said that when the flood began to rise, a man named Tezpi, with his wife and children, entered into a great vessel, taking with them animals and seeds of diverse kinds sufficient to restock the world after the deluge. When the waters abated, the man sent forth a vulture, and the bird flew away, but finding corpses to batten on, it did not return. Then the man let fly other

Michoacan legend of a great flood.

---

[1] Brasseur de Bourbourg, *Histoire des Nations Civilisées du Mexique et de l'Amérique Centrale* (Paris, 1857-1859), i. 425-427; H. H. Bancroft, *The Native Races of the Pacific States*, iii. 69 *sq.* As to the *Codex Chimal-popoca* see H. H. Bancroft, *op. cit.* v. 192 *sqq.*

birds, but they also came not back.   At last he sent forth a humming-bird, and it returned with a green bough in its beak.[1] In this story the messenger birds seem clearly to be reminiscences of the raven and the dove in the Noachian legend, of which the Indians may have heard through missionaries.

Story of a
great flood
told in the
Popol Vuh,
the sacred
book of the
Quiches of The *Popol Vuh*, a book which contains the legendary history of the Quiches of Guatemala, describes how the gods made several attempts to create mankind, fashioning them successively out of clay, out of wood, and out of maize.   But none of their attempts were successful, and the various races moulded out of these diverse materials had all, for different reasons, to be set aside.   It is true that the wooden race of men begat sons and daughters and multiplied upon the earth, but they had neither heart nor intelligence, they forgot their Creator, and they led a useless life, like that of the animals. Even regarded from the merely physical point of view, they were very poor creatures.   They had neither blood nor fat, their cheeks were wizened, their feet and hands were dry, their flesh was languid.   "So the end of this race of men was come, the ruin and destruction of these wooden puppets; they also were put to death.   Then the waters swelled by the will of the Heart of Heaven, and there was a great flood which rose over the heads of these puppets, these beings made of wood."   A rain of thick resin fell from the sky. Men ran hither and thither in despair.   They tried to climb up into the houses, but the houses crumbled away and let them fall to the ground : they essayed to mount up into the trees, but the trees shook them afar off : they sought to enter into the caves, but the caves shut them out.   Thus was accomplished the ruin of that race of men : they were all given up to destruction and contempt.   But they say that the posterity of the wooden race may still be seen in the little monkeys which live in the woods ; for these monkeys are very like men, and like their wooden ancestors their flesh is composed of nothing but wood.[2]

[1] A. de Herrera, *The General History of the vast Continent and Islands of America*, translated by Captain John Stevens (London, 1725–1726), iii. 254 *sq.* ; Brasseur de Bourbourg, *Histoire des Nations Civilisées du Mexique et de l'Amérique Centrale*, iii. 81 ; H. H. Bancroft, *The Native Races of the Pacific States*, iii. 66 *sq.*

[2] Brasseur de Bourbourg, *Popol Vuh, le Livre Sacré et les Mythes de l'Antiquité Américaine, avec les livres heroïques et historiques des Quichés* (Paris, 1861), pp. 17-31 ; H. H. Ban-

The
H   ol
Indians of
Mexico.

The Huichol Indians, who inhabit a mountainous region
near Santa Catarina in Western Mexico, have also a legend
of a deluge. By blood the tribe is related to the Aztecs,
the creators of that semi-civilized empire of Mexico which
the Spanish invaders destroyed ; but, secluded in their mountain fastnesses, the Huichols have always remained in a state
of primitive barbarism.   It was not until 1722 that the
Spaniards succeeded in subduing them, and the Franciscan
missionaries, who followed the Spanish army into the mountains, built a few churches and converted the wild Indians to
Christianity.   But the conversion was hardly more than
nominal.   It is true that the Huichols observe the principal
Christian festivals, which afford them welcome excuses for
lounging, guzzling, and swilling, and they worship the saints
as gods.   But in their hearts they cling to their ancient
beliefs, customs, and ceremonies : they jealously guard their
country against the encroachments of the whites : not a
single Catholic priest lives among them ; and all the churches
are in ruins.[1]

Huichol
story of a
great flood

The Huichol story of the deluge runs thus.   A Huichol
was felling trees to clear a field for planting.   But every
morning he found, to his chagrin, that the trees which he
had felled the day before had grown up again as tall as ever.
It was very vexatious and he grew tired of labouring in
vain.   On the fifth day he determined to try once more and
to go to the root of the matter.   Soon there rose from the
ground in the middle of the clearing an old woman with a
staff in her hand.   She was no other than Great-grandmother
Nakawe, the goddess of earth, who makes every green thing
to spring forth from the dark underworld.   But the man did

croft, *The Native Races of the Pacific
States*, iii. 44-47. The *Popol Vuh* is said
to have been discovered by a Dominican
Father, Francisco Ximenes, who was
curate of the little Indian town of
Chichicastenango, in the highlands of
Guatemala, at the end of the seventeenth or beginning of the eighteenth
century. The manuscript, containing
a Quiché text with a Spanish translation, was found by Dr. C. Scherzer
and published by him at Vienna in
1857. The edition published by the

Abbe Brasseur de Bourbourg contains
the Quiché text with a French translation, dissertation, and notes. The
original manuscript is supposed to
have been written by a Quiché Indian
in the latter part of the sixteenth
century. See F. Max Müller, *Selected
Essays on Language, Mythology and
Religion* (London, 1881), ii. 372 *sqq.*;
H. H. Bancroft, *op. cit.* iii. 42 *sqq.*

[1] Carl Lumholtz, *Unknown Mexico*
(London, 1903), ii. 22 *sq.*

not know her. With her staff she pointed to the south, north, west, and east, above and below ; and all the trees which the young man had felled immediately stood up again. Then he understood how it came to pass that in spite of all his endeavours the clearing was always covered with trees. So he said to the old woman angrily, " Is it you who are undoing my work all the time ? " " Yes," she said, " because I wish to talk to you." Then she told him that he laboured in vain. " A great flood," said she, " is coming. It is not more than five days off. There will come a wind, very bitter, and as sharp as chile, which will make you cough. Make a box from the salate (fig) tree, as long as your body, and fit it with a good cover. Take with you five grains of corn of each colour, and five beans of each colour ; also take the fire and five squash-stems to feed it, and take with you a black bitch." The man did as the woman told him. On the fifth day he had the box ready and placed in it the things she had told him to take with him. Then he entered the box with the black bitch ; and the old woman put on the cover, and caulked every crack with glue, asking the man to point out any chinks. Having made the box thoroughly water-tight and air-tight, the old woman took her seat on the top of it, with a macaw perched on her shoulder. For five years the box floated on the face of the waters. The first year it floated to the south, the second year it floated to the north, the third year it floated to the west, the fourth year it floated to the east, and in the fifth year it rose upward on the flood, and all the world was filled with water. The next year the flood began to abate, and the box settled on a mountain near Santa Cantarina, where it may still be seen. When the box grounded on the mountain, the man took off the cover and saw that all the world was still under water. But the macaws and the parrots set to work with a will : they pecked at the mountains with their beaks till they had hollowed them out into valleys, down which the water all ran away and was separated into five seas. Then the land began to dry, and trees and grass sprang up. The old woman turned into wind and so vanished away. But the man resumed the work of clearing the field which had been

Warned by a goddess, a man is saved from the flood in a box.

How the world was fashioned and repeopled after the flood.

interrupted by the flood.   He lived with the bitch in a cave,
going forth to his labour in the morning and returning home
in the evening.   But the bitch stayed at home all the time.
Every evening on his return the man found cakes baked
ready against his coming, and he was curious to know who
it was that baked them.   When five days had passed, he
hid himself behind some bushes near the cave to watch.   He
saw the bitch take off her skin, hang it up, and kneel down
in the likeness of a woman to grind the corn for the cakes.
Stealthily he drew near her from behind, snatched the skin
away, and threw it on the fire.   " Now you have burned my
tunic ! " cried the woman and began to whine like a dog.
But he took water mixed with the flour she had prepared,
and with the mixture he bathed her head.   She felt refreshed
and remained a woman ever after.   The two had a large
family, and their sons and daughters married.   So was the
world repeopled, and the inhabitants lived in caves.[1]

The Cora Indians, a tribe of nominal Christians whose
country borders that of the Huichols on the west, tell a
similar story of a great flood, in which the same incidents
occur of the woodman who was warned of the coming flood
by a woman, and who after the flood cohabited with a bitch
transformed into a human wife.   But in the Cora version of
the legend the man is bidden to take into the ark with him
the woodpecker, the sandpiper, and the parrot, as well as the
bitch.   He embarked at midnight when the flood began.
When it subsided, he waited five days and then sent out the
sandpiper to see if it were possible to walk on the ground.
The bird flew back and cried, " Ee-wee-wee ! " from which the
man understood that the earth was still too wet.   He waited
five days more, and then sent out the woodpecker to see if the
trees were hard and dry.   The woodpecker thrust his beak
deep into the tree, and waggled his head from side to side ;
but the wood was still so soft with the water that he could
hardly pull his beak out again, and when at last with a violent
tug he succeeded he lost his balance and fell to the ground.
So when he returned to the ark he said, " Chu-ee, chu-ee ! "
The man took his meaning and waited five days more, after
which he sent out the spotted sandpiper.   By this time the

Story of a
great flood
told by the
Cora
Indians
of Mexico.

[1] C. Lumholtz, *Unknown Mexico*, i. 191-193.

mud was so dry that, when the sandpiper hopped about, his legs did not sink into it ; so he came back and reported that all was well. Then the man ventured out of the ark, stepping very gingerly till he saw that the land was dry and flat.[1]

Another
rs'
the Cora
flood story.

In another fragmentary version of the deluge story, as told by the Cora Indians, the survivors of the flood would seem to have escaped in a canoe. When the waters abated, God sent the vulture out of the canoe to see whether the earth was dry enough. But the vulture did not return, because he devoured the corpses of the drowned. So God was angry with the vulture, and cursed him, and made him black instead of white, as he had been before ; only the tips of his wings he left white, that men might know what their colour had been before the flood. Next God commanded the ringdove to go out and see whether the earth was yet dry. The dove reported that the earth was dry, but that the rivers were in spate. So God ordered all the beasts to drink the rivers dry, and all the beasts and birds came and drank, save only the weeping dove (*Paloma llorona*), which would not come. Therefore she still goes every day to drink water at nightfall, because she is ashamed to be seen drinking by day ; and all day long she weeps and wails.[2] In

Biblical
infl n
on the Cora
legends.

these Cora legends the incident of the birds, especially the vulture and the raven, seems clearly to reflect the influence of missionary teaching.

Story of a
great flood
told by the
Tarahum-
ares of
Mexico.

A somewhat different story of a deluge is told by the Tarahumares, an Indian tribe who inhabit the mountains of Mexico farther to the north than the Huichols and Coras. The greater part of the Tarahumares are nominal Christians, though they seem to have learned little more from their teachers than the words Senor San Jose and Maria Santissima, and the title of Father God (*Tata Dios*), which they

---

[1] C. Lumholtz, *Unknown Mexico*, ii. 193 *sq.* ; K. Th. Preuss, *Die Nayarit-Expedition*, i. *Die Religion der Cora-Indianer* (Leipsic, 1912), pp. 277 *sqq.* In the Cora version recorded by Mr. K. Th. Preuss the man takes into the ark with him only a bitch and a *Schreivogel*, whatever species of bird that may be ; and during the preval-

ence of the flood he lets both the bird and the bitch out of the ark twice at intervals of three days, to see whether the earth is yet dry. In the text I have followed Mr. Lumholtz's version.

[2] K. Th. Preuss, *Die Nayarit-Expedition*, i. *Die Religion der Cora-Indianer*, p. 201.

apply to their ancient deity the sun-god.[1]   They say that
when all the world was water-logged, a little boy and a little
girl climbed up a mountain called Lavachi (*gourd*) to the
south of Panalachic, and when the flood subsided the two
came down again.   They brought three grains of corn and
three beans with them.   So soft were the rocks after the
flood that the feet of the little boy and girl sank into them,
and their footprints may be seen there to this day.   The two
planted corn and slept and dreamed a dream, and afterwards
they harvested, and all the Tarahumares are descended from
them.[2]   Another Tarahumare version of the deluge legend
runs thus.   The Tarahumares were fighting among themselves, and Father God (*Tata Dios*) sent much rain, and all
the people perished.   After the flood God despatched three
men and three women to repeople the earth.   They planted
corn of three kinds, soft corn, hard corn, and yellow corn,
and these three sorts still grow in the country.[3]

The Caribs of the Antilles had a tradition that the
Master of Spirits, being angry with their forefathers for not
presenting to him the offerings which were his due, caused
such a heavy rain to fall for several days that all the people
were drowned : only a few contrived to save their lives by
escaping in canoes to a solitary mountain.   It was this
deluge, they say, which separated their islands from the
mainland and formed the hills and pointed rocks or sugar-
loaf mountains of their country.[4]

Story of a
grea   flo
told b   he
Caribs of
Antilles.

§ 16. *Stories of a Great Flood in North America*

The Papagos of south-western Arizona say that the
Great Spirit made the earth and all living creatures before

Story of a
gre   o
told by the
Papagos of
Arizona.

[1] C. Lumholtz, *Unknown Mexico*,
i. 295 *sq.*   However, we learn from
Mr. Lumholtz that the Tarahumares
celebrate the Christian feasts in their
own way, and have some knowledge
of the devil.   According to them the
enemy of mankind is a one-eyed man
with a big beard, who plays the guitar
and would like very much to go to
heaven, but is prevented from doing
so by the shamans.   In heaven the
Father God (*Tata Dios*) has nothing
better to do than to run foot-races with

the angels.

[2] C. Lumholtz, *Unknown Mexico*,
i. 298.

[3] C. Lumholtz, *Unknown Mexico*,
i. 298 *sq.*

[4] De la Borde, "Relation de
l'Origine, Mœurs, Coustumes, Religion, Guerres et Voyages des Caraibes
sauvages des Isles Antilles de l'Amérique," p. 7, in *Recueil de divers Voyages faits en Afrique et en l'Amerique
qui n'ont point esté encore publiez* (Paris,
1684).

he made man. Then he came down to earth, and digging in the ground found some potter's clay. This he took back with him to the sky, and from there let it fall into the hole which he had dug. Immediately there came out the hero Montezuma, and with his help there also issued forth all the Indian tribes in order. Last of all appeared the wild Apaches, who ran away as fast as they were created. Those first days of the world were happy and peaceful. The sun was then nearer the earth than he is now : his rays made all the seasons equable and clothing superfluous. Men and animals talked together : a common language united them in the bonds of brotherhood. But a terrible catastrophe put an end to those golden days. A great flood destroyed all flesh wherein was the breath of life : Montezuma and his friend the coyote alone escaped. For before 'the waters began to rise, the coyote prophesied the coming of the flood, and Montezuma took warning, and hollowed out a boat for himself, and kept it ready on the top of Santa Rosa. The coyote also prepared an ark for himself; for he gnawed down a great cane by the river bank, entered it, and caulked it with gum. So when the waters rose, Montezuma and the coyote floated on them and were saved ; and when the flood retired, the man and the animal met on dry land. Anxious to discover how much dry land was left, the man sent out the coyote to explore, and the animal reported that to the west, the south, and the east there was sea, but that to the north he could find no sea, though he had journeyed till he was weary. Meanwhile the Great Spirit, with the help of Montezuma, had restocked the earth with men and animals.[1]

Story of a great flood told by the Pimas.

The Pimas, a neighbouring tribe, related to the Papagos, s , that the earth and mankind were made by a certain Chiowotmahke, that is to say Earth-prophet. Now the Creator had a son called Szeukha, who, when the earth began to be tolerably peopled, lived in the Gila valley. In the same valley there dwelt at that time a great prophet, whose name has been forgotten. One night, as the prophet slept, he was wakened by a noise at the door. When he opened, who should stand there but a great eagle? And

[1] H. H. Bancroft, *The Native Races of the Pacific States*, iii. 75 *sq.*

the eagle said, "Arise, for behold, a deluge is at hand." But the prophet laughed the eagle to scorn, wrapt his robe about him, and slept again. Again, the eagle came and warned him, but again he would pay no heed. A third time the long-suffering bird warned the prophet that all the valley of the Gila would be laid waste with water, but still the foolish man turned a deaf ear to the warning. That same night came the flood, and next morning there was nothing alive to be seen but one man, if man indeed he was ; for it was Szeukha, the son of the Creator, who had saved himself by floating on a ball of gum or resin. When the waters of the flood sank, he landed near the mouth of the Salt River and dwelt there in a cave on the mountain ; the cave is there to this day, and so are the tools which Szeukha used when he lived in it. For some reason or other Szeukha was very angry with the great eagle, though that bird had warned the prophet to escape for his life from the flood. So with the help of a rope-ladder he climbed up the face of the cliff where the eagle resided, and finding him at home in his eyrie he killed him. In and about the nest he discovered the mangled and rotting bodies of a great multitude of people whom the eagle had carried off and devoured. These he raised to life and sent them away to repeople the earth.[1]

Another version of the Pima legend runs as follows. In the early days of the world the Creator, whom the Indians call Earth Doctor, made the earth habitable by fashioning the mountains, the water, the trees, the grass, and the weeds ; he made the sun also and the moon, and caused them to pursue their regular courses in the sky. When he had thus prepared the world for habitation, the Creator fashioned all manner of birds and creeping things ; and he moulded images of clay, and commanded them to become animated human beings, and they obeyed him, and they increased and multiplied, and spread over the earth. But in time the increase of population outran the means of subsistence ; food and even water became scarce, and as sickness and death were as yet unknown, the steady multiplication of the species was attended by ever growing famine and distress. In these circumstances

Another
ve s
the Pima
legend.
T   P ma
story of
creation.

---

[1] H. H. Bancroft, *The Native Races of the Pacific States*, iii. 78 *sq.*

the Creator saw nothing for it but to destroy the creatures
he had made, and this he did by pulling down the sky on
the earth and crushing to death the people and all other
living things. After that he restored the broken fabric of
the world and created mankind afresh, and once more the
human race increased and multiplied.

How Elder   It was during this second period of the world that the
Brother
resolved   earth gave birth to one who has since been known as *Siuuhù*
to destroy   or Elder Brother. He came to Earth Doctor, that is, to the
mankind   Creator, and spoke roughly to him, and the Creator trembled
by a great
flood.   before him. The population was now increasing, but Elder
Brother shortened the lives of the people, and they did not
overrun the earth as they had done before. However, not
content with abridging the natural term of human existence, he resolved to destroy mankind for the second time
altogether by means of a great flood. So he began to fashion
a jar, in which he intended to save himself from the deluge,
and when the jar should be finished, the flood would come.
He announced his purpose of destruction to the Creator, and
the Creator called his people together and warned them of
the coming deluge. After describing the calamity that would
befall them, he chanted the following staves :—

> " *Weep, my unfortunate people !*
>   *All this you will see take place.*
> *Weep, my unfortunate people !*
>   *For the waters will overwhelm the land.*
> *Weep, my unhappy relatives !*
>   *You will learn all.*
> *The waters will overwhelm the mountains.*"

How the   Also he thrust his staff into the ground, and with it bored a
e
saved from   hole right through to the other side of the earth. Some
the flood on people took refuge in the hole for fear of the coming flood,
a log, and
Elder   and others appealed for help to Elder Brother, but their
Brother in   appeal was unheeded. Yet the assistance which Elder
a jar.
Brother refused to mankind he vouchsafed to the coyote or
prairie wolf ; for he told that animal to find a big log and
sit on it, and so sitting he would float safely on the surface
of the water along with the driftwood. The time of the
deluge was now come, and accordingly Elder Brother got
into the jar which he had been making against the great

day ; and as he closed the opening of the jar behind him he
sang—

> *" Black house ! Black house ! hold me safely in ;*
> *Black house ! Black house ! hold me safely in,*
> *As I journey to and fro, to and fro."*

And as he was borne along on the flood he sang—

> *" Running water, running water, herein resounding,*
> *As on the clouds I am carried to the sky.*
> *Running water, running water, herein roaring,*
> *As on the clouds I am carried to the sky."*

The jar in which Elder Brother ensconced himself is
called by him in the song the Black House, because it was
made of black gum.   It bobbed up and down on the face of
the waters and drifted along till it came to rest beyond
Sonoita, near the mouth of the Colorado River.   There the
jar may be seen to this day ; it is called the Black Mountain, after the colour of the gum out of which the jar was
moulded.   On emerging from the jar Elder Brother sang—

How Elder
Brot er
landed
after the
ood on
B ck
Mountain.

> *" Here I come forth !   Here I come forth !*
> *With magic powers I emerge.*
> *Here I come forth !   Here I come forth !*
> *With magic powers I emerge.*
>
> *I stand alone !   Alone !*
> *Who will accompany me ?*
> *My staff and my crystal*
> *They shall bide with me "*

The Creator himself, or Earth Doctor, as the Indians call
him, also escaped destruction by enclosing himself in his
reed staff, which floated on the surface of the water.   The
coyote, too, survived the great flood ; for the log on which
he had taken refuge floated southward with him to the place
where all the driftwood of the deluge was gathered together.
Of all the birds that had been before the flood only five of
different sorts survived ; they clung with their beaks to the
sky till a god took pity on them and enabled them to make
nests of down from their own breasts, and in these nests they
floated on the waters till the flood went down.   Among the
birds thus saved from the deluge were the flicker and the

How the
C eator
escat d
from the
flood in a
reed, and
some
e
were saved
in holes in

vulture.   As for the human race, some people were saved in the deep hole which the Creator had bored with his staff, and others were saved in a similar hole which a powerful person- age, called the South Doctor, had in like manner made by thrusting his cane into the earth.   Yet others in their distress resorted to the Creator, but he told them that they came too late, for he had already sent all whom he could save down the deep hole and through to the other side of the earth.

How others
were turned
to stone on
the top of
ᵈ
Mountain
However, he held out a hope to them that they might still be saved if they would climb to the top of Crooked Moun- tain, and he directed South Doctor to assist the people in their flight to this haven of refuge.   So South Doctor led the people to the summit of the mountain, but the flood rose apace behind them.   Yet by his enchantments did South Doctor raise the mountain and set bounds to the angry water ; for he traced a line round the hill and chanted an incantation, which checked the rising flood.   Four times by his incanta- tions did he raise the mountain above the waters ; four times did he arrest the swelling tide.   At last his power was exhausted ; he could do no more, and he threw his staff into the water, where it cracked with a loud noise.   Then turning, he saw a dog near him, and sent the animal to see how high the tide had risen.   The dog turned towards the people and said, " It is very near the top."   At these words the anxious watchers were transformed into stone ; and there to this day you may see them standing in groups, just as they were at the moment of transformation, some of the men talking, some of the women cooking, and some crying.[1]

Pima story
ᵒᶠ ᵗʰᵉ
marvellous
youth who
consɯr eᴅ
with
human
wives
and had
children by
them before
the flood.
This Pima legend of the flood contains, moreover, an episode which bears a certain reminiscence to an episode in the Biblical narrative of the great catastrophe.   In Genesis we read how in the days immediately preceding the flood, " the sons of God came in unto the daughters of men, and they bare children to them ; the same were the mighty men which were of old, the men of renown." [2]   In like manner the Pimas relate that when Elder Brother had determined to destroy mankind, he began by creating a handsome youth,

[1] Frank Russell, " The Pima In- dians," *Twenty-Sixth Annual Report of the Bureau of American Ethnology* (Washington, 1908), pp. 206-213.   In the text I have considerably abridged the story.

[2] Genesis vi. 4.

whom he directed to go among the Pimas, to wed their women, and to beget children by them. He was to live with his first wife "until his first child was born, then leave her and go to another, and so on until his purpose was accomplished. His first wife gave birth to a child four months after marriage and conception. The youth then went and took a second wife, to whom a child was born in less time than the first. The period was yet shorter in the case of the third wife, and with her successors it grew shorter still, until at last the child was born from the young man at the time of the marriage. This was the child that caused the flood which destroyed the people and fulfilled the plans of Elder Brother. Several years were necessary to accomplish these things, and during this time the people were amazed and frightened at the signs of Elder Brother's power and at the deeds of his agent."[1] How the child of the young man's last wife caused the flood is not clearly explained in the story, though we are told that the screams of the sturdy infant shook the earth and could be heard at a great distance.[2] Indeed, the episode of the handsome youth and his many wives is, like the corresponding episode in the Biblical narrative, fitted very loosely into the story of the flood. It may be that both episodes were originally independent of the diluvial tradition, and that in its Indian form the tale of the fair youth and his human spouses is a distorted reminiscence of missionary teaching.

The Indians of Zuni, a pueblo village of New Mexico, relate that once upon a time a great flood compelled them to quit their village in the valley and take refuge on a lofty and conspicuous tableland, which towers like an island from the flat, with steep or precipitous sides of red and white sandstone. But the waters rose nearly to the summit of the tableland, and the Indians, fearing to be swept off the face of the earth, resolved to offer a human sacrifice in order to appease the angry waters. So a youth and a maiden, the children of two Priests of the Rain, were dressed in their finest robes, decked with many precious beads, and thrown into the swelling flood. Immediately the waters began to recede, and the youth and maiden were turned into stone.

Story of a g e told by the Indians of New Mexico.

---

[1] Frank Russell, *op. cit.* p. 209.   [2] Frank Russell, *op. cit.* p. 210.

You may still see them in the form of two great pinnacles of rock rising from the tableland.[1]

Story of a gre o told by the Acag- Indians of California.

The Acagchemem Indians, near St. Juan Capistrano in California, "were not entirely destitute of a knowledge of the universal deluge, but how, or from whence, they received the same, I could never understand. Some of their songs refer to it ; and they have a tradition that, at a time very remote, the sea began to swell and roll in upon the plains and fill the valleys, until it had covered the mountains ; and thus nearly all the human race and animals were destroyed, excepting a few, who had resorted to a very high mountain which the waters did not reach. But the songs give a more distinct relation of the same, and they state that the descendants of Captain Ouiot asked of Chinigchinich venge-ance upon their chief—that he appeared unto them, and said to those endowed with the power, 'Ye are the ones to achieve vengeance—ye who cause it to rain ! Do this, and so inundate the earth, that every living being will be destroyed.' The rains commenced, the sea was troubled, and swelled in upon the earth, covering the plains, and rising until it had overspread the highest land, excepting a high mountain, where the few had gone with the one who had caused it to rain, and thus every other animal was destroyed upon the face of the earth. These songs were supplications to Chinigchinich to drown their enemies. If their opponents heard them, they sang others in opposition, which in sub-stance ran thus : ' We are not afraid, because Chinigchinich does not wish to, neither will he destroy the world by another inundation.' Without doubt this account has reference to the universal deluge, and the promise God made, that there should not be another." [2]

Story of a gre flo told b the Luiseño f California

The Luiseño Indians of Southern California also tell of a great flood which covered all the high mountains and drowned most of the people. But a few were saved, who took refuge on a little knoll near Bonsall. The place was

[1] Mrs. Matilda Coxe Stevenson, "The Religious Life of the Zuni Child," *Fifth Annual Report of the Bureau of Ethnology* (Washington, 1887), p. 539 ; *id.*, "The Zuni In-dians," *Twenty-Third Annual Report of the Bureau of American Ethnology* (Washington, 1904), p. 61.

[2] Father Friar Geronimo Boscana, "Chinigchinich, an Historical Ac-count, etc., of the Acagchemem Nation," appended to [A. Robinson's] *Life in California* (New York, 1846), pp. 300 *sq.*

called Mora by the Spaniards, but the Indians call it Katuta.
Only the knoll remained above water when all the rest of the
country was inundated.   The survivors stayed there till the
flood went down.   To this day you may see on the top of
the little hill heaps of sea-shells and seaweed, and ashes, and
stones set together, marking the spot where the Indians
cooked their food.   The shells are those of the shell-fish
which they ate, and the ashes and stones are the remains of
their fire-places.   The writer who relates this tradition adds
that "the hills near Del Mar and other places along the coast
have many such heaps of sea-shells, of the species still found
on the beaches, piled in quantities."   The Luisenos still
sing a Song of the Flood, in which mention is made of the
knoll of Katuta.[1]

An Indian woman of the Smith River tribe in California Story of a
gave the following account of the deluge.   At one time g e   o
told by the
there came a great rain.   It lasted a long time and the Smith
water kept rising till all the valleys were submerged, and the e
Indians of
Indians retired to the high land.   At last they were all swept California.
away and drowned except one pair, who escaped to the
highest peak and were saved.   They subsisted on fish, which
they cooked by placing them under their arms.   They had
no fire and could not get any, as everything was far too wet.
At last the water sank, and from that solitary pair all the
Indians of the present day are descended.   As the Indians
died, their spirits took the forms of deer, elks, bears, snakes,
insects, and so forth, and in this way the earth was repeopled
by the various kinds of animals as well as men.   But still
the Indians had no fire, and they looked with envious
eyes on the moon, whose fire shone so brightly in the
sky.   So the Spider Indians and the Snake Indians laid
their heads together and resolved to steal fire from the
moon.   Accordingly the Spider Indians started off for the
moon in a gossamer balloon, but they took the precaution to
fasten the balloon to the earth by a rope which they paid
out as they ascended.   When they arrived at the moon, the
Indians who inhabited the lunar orb looked askance at the

Constance Goddard du Bois, *The
Religion of the Luiseno Indians of
Southern California* (Berkeley, 1908),
pp. 116, 157 (*University of California
Publications in American Archaeology
and Ethnology*, vol. viii. No. 3).

newcomers, divining their errand. To lull their suspicions
the Spider Indians assured them that they had come only to
gamble, so the Moon Indians were pleased and proposed to
begin playing at once. As they sat by the fire deep in the
game, a Snake Indian dexterously climbed up the rope by
which the balloon was tethered, and before the Moon Indians
knew what he was about he had darted through the fire and
escaped down the rope again. When he reached the earth,
he had to travel over every rock, stick, and tree ; everything
he touched from that time forth contained fire, and the hearts
of the Indians were glad. But the Spider Indians were long
'kept prisoners in the moon, and when they were at last
released and had returned to earth, expecting to be welcomed
as the benefactors of the human race, ungrateful men killed
them lest the Moon Indians should wish to take vengeance
for the deceit that had been practised on them.[1]

Story of a
g e flo
told b the
Ashochimi
California.

The Ashochimi Indians of California say that long ago
there was a mighty flood which prevailed over all the land
and drowned every living creature save the coyote alone.
He set himself to restore the population of the world as
follows. He collected the tail-feathers of owls, hawks, eagles,
and buzzards, tied them up in a bundle, and journeyed with
them over the face of the earth. He sought out the sites of
all the Indian villages, and wherever a wigwam had stood
before the flood, he planted a feather. In due time the
feathers sprouted, took root, and flourished greatly, at last
turning into men and women ; and thus the world was
repeopled.[2]

Story of a
great flood
told by the
Maidu
f
C lif rnia

The Maidu Indians of California say that of old the
Indians abode tranquilly in the Sacramento Valley, and were
happy. All on a sudden there was a mighty and swift
rushing of waters, so that the whole valley became like the
Big Water, which no man can measure. The Indians fled
for their lives, but many were overtaken by the waters and
drowned. Also, the frogs and the salmon pursued swiftly
after them, and they ate many Indians. Thus all the Indians
perished but two, who escaped to the hills. But the Great
Man made them fruitful and blessed them, so that the world

---

[1] Stephen Powers, *Tribes of California* (Washington, 1877), pp. 70 *sq.*
[2] S. Powers, *Tribes of California*, p. 200.

was soon repeopled.   From these two there sprang many tribes, even a mighty nation, and one man was chief over all this nation—a chief of great renown.   Then he went out on a knoll, overlooking the wide waters, and he knew that they covered fertile plains once inhabited by his ancestors.   Nine sleeps he lay on the knoll without food, revolving in his mind the question, 'How did this deep water cover the face of the world?'   And at the end of nine sleeps he was changed, for now no arrow could wound him.   Though a thousand Indians should shoot at him, not one flint-pointed arrow would pierce his skin.   He was like the Great Man in heaven, for none could slay him henceforth.   Then he spoke to the Great Man, and commanded him to let the water flow off from the plains which his ancestors had inhabited.   The Great Man obeyed ; he rent open the side of the mountain, and the water flowed away into the Big Water.[1]

According to Du Pratz, the early French historian of Louisiana, the tradition of a great flood was current among the Natchez, an Indian tribe of the Lower Mississippi.   He tells us that on this subject he questioned the guardian of the temple, in which the sacred and perpetual fire was kept with religious care.   The guardian replied that "the ancient word taught all the red men that almost all men were destroyed by the waters except a very small number, who had saved themselves on a very high mountain ; that he knew nothing more regarding this subject except that these few people had repeopled the earth."   And Du Pratz adds, "As the other nations had told me the same thing, I was assured that all the natives thought the same regarding this event, and that they had not preserved any memory of Noah's ark, which did not surprise me very much, since the Greeks, with all their knowledge, were no better informed, and we ourselves, were it not for the Holy Scriptures, might perhaps know no more than they."[2]   Elsewhere he reports the tradition somewhat more fully as follows.   "They said that a great rain fell on the earth so abundantly and during such a long time that it was completely covered except a very high mountain where some men saved themselves ; that

Tradition of a great flood among the Natchez.

---

[1] S. Powers, *Tribes of California*, p. 290.
[2] Le Page du Pratz, *Histoire de la Louisiane* (Paris, 1758), iii. 27 *sq*.

all fire being extinguished on the earth, a little bird named
Couy-oüy, which is entirely red (it is that which is called in
Louisiana the cardinal bird), brought it from heaven. I
understood by that that they had forgotten almost all the
history of the deluge."[1]

Story of a
gre flo
told b the
Mandan
In ians.

The Mandan Indians had a tradition of a great deluge
in which the human race perished except one man, who
escaped in a large canoe to a mountain in the west.   Hence
the Mandans celebrated every year certain rites in memory
of the subsidence of the flood, which they called *Mee-nee-ro-
ka-ha-sha*, " the sinking down or settling of the waters." The
time for the ceremony was determined by the full expansion
of the willow leaves on the banks of the river, for according
to their tradition " the twig that the bird brought home was
a willow bough and had full-grown leaves on it " ; and the
bird which brought the willow bough was the mourning- or
turtle-dove.   These doves often fed on the sides of their
earth-covered huts, and none of the Indians would destroy
or harm them ; even their dogs were trained not to molest
the birds.   In the Mandan village a wooden structure was
carefully preserved to represent the canoe in which the only
man was saved from the flood.   " In the centre of the Mandan
village," says the painter Catlin, " is an open, circular area of
a hundred and fifty feet diameter, kept always clear, as a
public ground, for the display of all their feasts, parades, etc.,
and around it are their wigwams placed as near to each other
as they can well stand, their doors facing the centre of this
public area.   In the middle of this ground, which is trodden
like a hard pavement, is a curb (somewhat like a large hogs-
head standing on its end) made of planks and bound with
hoops, some eight or nine feet high, which they religiously preserve and protect from year to year, free from mark or scratch,
and which they call the ' big canoe ' : it is undoubtedly a
symbolic representation of a part of their traditional history of the Flood ; which it is very evident, from this and
numerous other features of this grand ceremony, they have
in some way or other received, and are here endeavouring to

[1] John R. Swanton, *Indian Tribes
of the Lower Mississippi Valley and Adjacent Coast of the Gulf of Mexico* (Washington, 1911), p. 177 (*Smithsonian
Institution, Bureau of American Ethnology, Bulletin 43*), quoting Dumont,
Mém. sur la Louisiane, 1. 163-164.

perpetuate by vividly impressing it on the minds of the whole nation. This object of superstition, from its position as the very centre of the village, is the rallying-point of the whole nation. To it their devotions are paid on various occasions of feasts and religious exercises during the year."

On the occasion when Catlin witnessed the annual cere-mony commemorative of the flood, the first or only man (*Nu-mohk-muck-a-nah*) who escaped the flood was personated by a mummer dressed in a robe of white wolf-skins, which fell back over his shoulders, while on his head he wore a splendid covering of two ravens' skins and in his left hand he carried a large pipe. Entering the village from the prairie he approached the medicine or mystery lodge, which he had the means of opening, and which had been strictly closed during the year except for the performance of these religious rites. All day long this mummer went through the village, stopping in front of every hut and crying, till the owner of the hut came out and asked him who he was and what was the matter. To this the mummer replied by relating the sad catastrophe which had happened on the earth's surface through the overflowing of the waters, saying that " he was the only person saved from the universal calamity ; that he landed his big canoe on a high mountain in the west, where he now resides ; that he had come to open the medicine-lodge, which must needs receive a present of some edged tool from the owner of every wigwam, that it may be sacrificed to the water ; for he says, ' If this is not done, there will be another flood, and no one will be saved, as it was with such tools that the big canoe was made.' " Having visited every wigwam in the village during the day, and having received from each a hatchet, a knife, or other edged tool, he deposited them at evening in the medicine lodge, where they remained till the afternoon of the last day of the ceremony. Then as the final rite they were thrown into a deep pool in the river from a bank thirty feet high in presence of the whole village ; " from whence they can never be recovered, and where they were, undoubtedly, *sacrificed* to the Spirit of the Water." Amongst the ceremonies observed at this spring festival of the Mandans was a bull dance danced by men disguised as buffaloes and intended to procure

Annual re ony of the Mandan commemo-rative of the flood.

Bull dance for the multiplication of buffaloes.

a plentiful supply of buffaloes in the ensuing season; further, the young men underwent voluntarily a series of excruciating tortures in the medicine lodge for the purpose of commending themselves to the Great Spirit. But how far these quaint and ghastly rites were connected with the commemoration of the Great Flood does not appear from the accounts of our authorities.[1]

Importance ascribed by the Mandans to the celebration of the festival.

This Mandan festival went by the name of *O-kee-pa* and was "an annual religious ceremony, to the strict observance of which those ignorant and superstitious people attributed not only their enjoyment in life, but their very existence; for traditions, their only history, instructed them in the belief that the singular forms of this ceremony produced the buffaloes for their supply of food, and that the omission of this annual ceremony, with its sacrifices made to the waters, would bring upon them a repetition of the calamity which their traditions say once befell them, destroying the whole human race, excepting one man, who landed from his canoe

The tradition of a great flood widely spread among the Indians of North, South, and Central America.

on a high mountain in the West. This tradition, however, was not peculiar to the Mandan tribe, for amongst one hundred and twenty different tribes that I have visited in North and South and Central America, not a tribe exists that has not related to me distinct or vague traditions of such a calamity, in which one, or three, or eight persons were saved above the waters, on the top of a high mountain. Some of these, at the base of the Rocky Mountains and in the plains of Venezuela, and the Pampa del Sacramento in South America, make annual pilgrimages to the fancied summits where the antediluvian species were saved in canoes or otherwise, and, under the mysterious regulations of their *medicine* (mystery) men, tender their prayers and sacrifices to the Great Spirit, to ensure their exemption from a similar catastrophe."[2]

Cherokee story of a great flood.

The Cherokee Indians are reported to have a tradition that the water once prevailed over the land until all mankind

[1] Geo. Catlin, *Letters and Notes on the Manners, Customs, and Condition of the North American Indians*, Fourth Edition (London, 1844), i. 155 *sqq.*, Letter 22; Maximilian Prinz zu Wied, *Reise in das Innere Nord-America* (Coblenz, 1839–1841), ii. 159 *sq.*, 172 *sqq.*

[2] George Catlin, *O Kee-Pa, a Religious Ceremony; and other Customs of the Mandans* (London, 1867), pp. 1 *sq.*

were drowned except a single family. The coming of the calamity was revealed by a dog to his master. For the sagacious animal went day after day to the banks of a river, where he stood gazing at the water and howling piteously. Being rebuked by his master and ordered home, the dog opened his mouth and warned the man of the danger in which he stood. "You must build a boat," said he, "and put in it all that you would save ; for a great rain is coming that will flood the land." The animal concluded his prediction by informing his master that his salvation depended on throwing him, the dog, into the water ; and for a sign of the truth of what he said he bade him look at the back of his neck. The man did so, and sure enough, the back of the dog's neck was raw and bare, the flesh and bone appearing. So the man believed, and following the directions of the faithful animal he and his family were saved, and from them the whole of the present population of the globe is lineally descended.[1]

Stories of a great flood are widely spread among Indians of the great Algonquin stock, and they resemble each other in some details. Thus the Delawares, an Algonquin tribe whose home was about Delaware Bay, told of a deluge which submerged the whole earth, and from which few persons escaped alive. They saved themselves by taking refuge on the back of a turtle, which was so old that his shell was mossy like the bank of a rivulet. As they were floating thus forlorn, a loon flew their way, and they begged him to dive and bring up land from the depth of the waters. The bird dived accordingly, but could find no bottom. Then he flew far away and came back with a little earth in his bill. Guided by him, the turtle swam to the place, where some dry land was found. There they settled and repeopled the country.[2]

The Montagnais, a group of Indian tribes in Canada who

[1] Henry R. Schoolcraft, *Notes on the Iroquois* (Albany, 1847), pp. 358 *sq.* The tradition purports to have been obtained in the summer of 1846 from " Mr. Stand Watie, a respectable and intelligent chief of that tribe, who was attending at the seat of government, as one of the delegates of his people, to compromise certain difficulties which had arisen between separate parts of the Cherokee nation and the government."

[2] D. G Brinton, *The Lenâpé and their Legends* (Philadelphia, 1885), p. 134.

Story of a
g e   o
told by the
Montagnais
~~~~~~~ ~~
Canada.

also belong to the great Algonquin stock,[1] told an early Jesuit missionary that a certain mighty being, whom they called Messou, repaired the world after it had been ruined by the great flood. They said that one day Messou went out to hunt, and that the wolves which he used instead of hounds entered into a lake and were there detained. Messou sought them everywhere, till a bird told him that he saw the lost wolves in the middle of the lake. So he waded into the water to rescue them, but the lake overflowed, covered the earth, and overwhelmed the world. Greatly astonished, Messou sent the raven to search for a clod of earth out of which he might rebuild that element, but no earth could the raven find. Next Messou sent an otter, which plunged into the deep water, but brought back nothing. Lastly, Messou despatched a musk-rat, and the rat brought back a little soil, which Messou used to refashion the earth on which we live. He shot arrows at the trunks of trees, and the arrows were changed into branches: he took vengeance on those who had detained his wolves in the lake; and he married a musk-rat, by which he had children, who repeopled the world.[2]

Another
rs n
of the
Montagnais
s ory.

In this legend there is no mention of men; and but for the part played in it by the animals we might have supposed that the deluge took place in the early ages of the world before the appearance of life on the earth. However, some two centuries later, another Catholic missionary tells us that the Montagnais of the Hudson Bay Territory have a tradition of a great flood which covered the world, and from which four persons, along with animals and birds, escaped alive on a floating island.[3] Yet another Catholic missionary reports the Montagnais legend more fully as follows. God, being angry with the giants, commanded a man to build a large canoe. The man did so, and when he had embarked in it, the water rose on all sides, and the canoe with it, till no land was anywhere to be seen. Weary of beholding nothing but a heaving mass of water, the man threw an otter into the

[1] F. W. Hodge, *Handbook of American Indians North of Mexico* (Washington, 1907-1910), i. 933, *s.v.* "Montagnais."

[2] *Relations des Jésuites*, 1643, p. 13 (Canadian reprint, Quebec, 1858).

This story is repeated, somewhat more briefly, by the Jesuit Charlevoix in his *Histoire de la Nouvelle France* (Paris, 1744), vi. 147.

[3] Mgr. Tache, in *Annales de la Propagation de la Foi*, xxiv. (1852) p. 336.

flood, and the animal dived and brought up a little earth. The man took the earth or mud in his hand and breathed on it, and at once it began to grow. So he laid it on the surface of the water and prevented it from sinking. As it continued to grow into an island, he desired to know whether it was large enough to support him. Accordingly he placed a reindeer upon it, but the animal soon made the circuit of the island and returned to him, from which he concluded that the island was not yet large enough. So he continued to blow on it till the mountains, the lakes, and the rivers were formed. Then he disembarked.[1] The same missionary reports a deluge legend current among the Crees, another tribe of the Algonquin stock in Canada; but this Cree story bears clear traces of Christian influence, for in it the man is said to have sent forth from the canoe, first a raven, and second a wood-pigeon. The raven did not return, and as a punishment for his disobedience the bird was changed from white to black; the pigeon returned with his claws full of mud, from which the man inferred that the earth was dried up; so he landed.[2]

The genuine old Algonquin legend of the flood appears to have been first recorded at full length by a Mr. H. E. MacKenzie, who passed much of his early life with the Salteaux or Chippeway Indians, a large and powerful branch of the Algonquin stock. He communicated the tradition to Lieutenant W. H. Hooper, R.N., at Fort Norman, near Bear Lake, about the middle of the nineteenth century. In substance the legend runs as follows.

Once upon a time there were certain Indians and among them a great medicine-man named Wis-kay-tchach. With them also were a wolf and his two sons, who lived on a footing of intimacy with the human beings. Wis-kay-tchach called the old wolf his brother and the young ones his nephews; for he recognized all animals as his relations. In the winter time the whole party began to starve; so in order to find food the parent wolf announced his intention of separating with his children from the band. Wis-kay-tchach offered to bear him company, so off they set together. Soon

[1] Mgr. Faraud, in *Annales de la Propagation de la Foi*, xxxvi. (1864)   pp. 388 *sq.*
[2] Mgr. Faraud, *op. cit.* p. 387.

they came to the track of a moose.   The old Wolf and the medicine-man Wis (as we may call him for short) stopped to smoke, while the young wolves pursued the moose. After a time, the young ones not returning, Wis and the old Wolf set off after them, and soon found blood on the snow, whereby they knew that the moose was killed.   Soon they came up with the young wolves, but no moose was to be seen, for the young wolves had eaten it up.   They bade Wis make a fire, and when he had done so, he found the whole of the moose restored and already quartered and cut up.   The young wolves divided the spoil into four portions ; but one of them retained the tongue and the other the mouffle (upper lip), which are the chief delicacies of the animal.   Wis grumbled, and the young wolves gave up these dainties to him.   When they had devoured the whole, one of the young wolves said he would make marrow fat, which is done by breaking up the bones very small and boiling them.   Soon this resource was also exhausted, and they all began to hunger again. So they agreed to separate once more.   This time Old Wolf went off with one of his sons, leaving Wis and the other young wolf to hunt together.

How the gwⁱ f, the friend of Wis-kay- a was killed and ev bv water- lynxes.
The story now leaves the Old Wolf and follows the fortunes of Wis and his nephew, one of the two young wolves. The young wolf killed some deer and brought them home in his stomach, disgorging them as before on his arrival.   At last he told his uncle that he could catch no more, so Wis sat up all night making medicine or usingⁱ enchantments.   In the morning he bade his nephew go a-hunting, but warned him to be careful at every valley and hollow place to throw a stick over before he ventured to jump himself, or else some evil would certainly befall him. So away went the young wolf, but in pursuing a deer he forgot to follow his uncle's directions, and in attempting to leap a hollow he fell plump into a river and was there killed and devoured by water-lynxes.   What kind of a beast a water-lynx is, the narrator did not know.   But let that be. Enough that the young wolf was killed and devoured by these creatures.   After waiting long for his nephew, Wis set off to look for him, and coming to the spot where the young wolf had leaped, he guessed rightly that the animal had

neglected his warning and fallen into the stream.   He saw a
kingfisher sitting on a tree and gazing fixedly at the water.
Asked what he was looking at so earnestly, the bird replied
that he was looking at the skin of Wis's nephew, the young
wolf, which served as a door-mat to the house of the water-
lynxes ; for not content with killing and devouring the
nephew, these ferocious animals had added insult to injury
by putting his skin to this ignoble use.   Grateful for the information, Wis called the kingfisher to him, combed the
bird's head, and began to put a ruff round his neck ; but
before he had finished his task, the bird flew away, and that
is why down to this day kingfishers have only part of a ruff
at the back of their head.   Before the kingfisher flew away,
he gave Wis a parting hint, that the water-lynxes often came
ashore to lie on the sand, and that if he wished to be revenged
on them he must turn himself into a stump close by, but
must be most careful to keep perfectly rigid and on no
account to let himself be pulled down by the frogs and snakes,
which the water-lynxes would be sure to send to dislodge
him.   On receiving these directions Wis returned to his
camp and resorted to enchantments ; also he provided all
things necessary, among others a large canoe to hold all the
animals that could not swim.

Before daylight broke, he had completed his preparations
and embarked all the aforesaid animals in the big canoe.
He then paddled quietly to the neighbourhood of the lynxes,
and having secured the canoe behind a promontory, he landed,
transformed himself into a stump, and awaited, in that
assumed character, the appearance of the water-lynxes.
Soon the black one crawled out and lay down on the sand ;
and then the grey one did the same.   Last of all the white
one, which had killed the young wolf, popped his head out
of the water, but espying the stump, he grew suspicious, and
called out to his brethren that he had never seen that stump
before.   They answered carelessly that it must have been
always there ; but the wary white lynx, still suspicious, sent
frogs and snakes to pull it down.   Wis had a severe struggle
to keep himself upright, but he succeeded, and the white
lynx, his suspicions now quite lulled to rest, lay down to
sleep on the sand.   Wis waited a little, then resuming his

How Wis-
ay c
killed the
water-lynx,
a
the great
flood rose

natural shape he took his spear and crept softly to the white lynx. He had been warned by the kingfisher to strike at the animal's shadow or he would assuredly be balked; but in his eagerness he forgot the injunction, and striking full at his adversary's body he missed his mark. The creature rushed towards the water, but Wis had one more chance and aiming this time at the lynx's shadow he wounded grievously the beast itself. However, the creature contrived to escape into the river, and the other lynxes with it. Instantly the water began to boil and rise, and Wis made for his canoe as fast as he could run. The water continued flowing, until land, trees, and hills were all covered. The canoe floated about on the surface, and Wis, having before taken on board all animals that could not swim, now busied himself in picking up all that could swim only for a short time and were now struggling for life in'the water around him.

How with the aid of a rat, which dived into the water, Wis-kay-tchach restored the earth after the great flood.

But in his enchantments to meet the great emergency, Wis had overlooked a necessary condition for the restoration of the world after the flood. He had no earth, not even a particle, which might serve as a nucleus for the new lands which were to rise from the waste of waters. He now set about obtaining it. Tying a string to the leg of a loon he ordered the bird to try for soundings and to persevere in its descent even if it should perish in the attempt; for, said he, "If you are drowned, it is no matter: I can easily restore you to life." Encouraged by this assurance, the bird dropped like a stone into the water, and the line ran out fast. When it ceased to run, Wis hauled it up, and at the end of the line was the loon dead. Being duly restored to life, the bird informed Wis that he had found no bottom. So Wis next despatched an otter on the same errand, but he fared no better than the loon. After that Wis tried a beaver, which after being drowned and resuscitated in the usual way, reported that he had seen the tops of trees, but could sink no deeper. Last of all Wis let down a rat fastened to a stone; down went the rat and the stone, and presently the line slackened. Wis hauled it up and at the end of it he found the rat dead but clutching a little earth in its paws. Wis had now all that he wanted. He restored the rat to life and spread out the earth to dry; then he blew upon it till it swelled and grew to a great extent. When he thought it large enough, he sent out a wolf to explore, but the animal soon returned, saying that the world was small. Thereupon Wis again blew on the earth for a long time, and then sent forth a crow. When the bird did not return, Wis concluded that the world was now large enough for all ; so he and the animals disembarked from the canoe.[1]

A few years later, in September 1855, a German traveller obtained another version of the same legend from an old Ojibway woman, the mother of a half-caste. In this Ojibway version the story turns on the doings of Menaboshu, a great primeval hero, who, if he did not create the world, is generally believed by the Ojibways to have given to the earth its present form, directing the flow of the rivers, moulding the beds of the lakes, and cleaving the mountains into deep glens and ravines. He lived on very friendly terms with the animals, whom he regarded as his kinsfolk and with whom he could converse in their own language. Once he pitched his camp in the middle of a solitary wood. The times were bad ; he had no luck in the chase, though he fasted and hungered. In his dire distress he went to the wolves and said to them, "My dear little brothers, will you give me something to eat ?" The wolves said, "That we will," and they gave him of their food. He found it so good that he begged to be allowed to join them in the chase, and they gave him leave. So Menaboshu hunted with the wolves, camped with them, and shared their booty.

This they did for ten days, but on the tenth day they came to a cross-road. The wolves wished to go one way, and Menaboshu wished to go another, and as neither would give way, it was resolved to part company. But Menaboshu said that at least the youngest wolf must go with him, for he loved the animal dearly and called him his little brother. The little wolf also would not part from him, so the two went one way, while all the rest of the wolves went the other. Menaboshu and the little wolf camped in the middle of the wood and hunted together, but sometimes the little wolf hunted alone. Now Menaboshu was anxious for the

Another version of the story told by an Ojibway woman

How the Menaboshu made the wolves.

How the little wolf the friend of Menaboshu was drowned.

[1] Lieut. W. H. Hooper, R.N., *Ten Months among the Tents of the Tuski* (London, 1853), pp. 285-292. In the text I have somewhat abridged the legend.

safety of the little wolf, and he said to him, " My dear little brother, have you seen that lake which lies near our camp to the west ? Go not thither, never tread the ice on it ! Do you hear ? " This he said because he knew that his worst enemy, the serpent-king, dwelt in the lake and would do anything to vex him. The little wolf promised to do as Menaboshu told him, but he thought within himself, " Why does Menaboshu forbid me to go on the lake ? Perhaps he thinks I might meet my brothers the wolves there ! After all I love my brothers ! " Thus he thought for two days, but on the third day he went on the lake and roamed about on the ice to see whether he could find his brothers. But just as he came to the middle of the lake, the ice broke, and he fell in and was drowned.

How Menabo u visi ed he lake, where wolf had been killed by the serpent- king.

All that evening Menaboshu waited for his little brother, but he never came. Menaboshu waited for him the next day, but still he came not. So he waited five days and five nights. Then he began to weep and wail, and he cried so loud after his little brother, that his cries could be heard at the end of the wood. All the rest of the melancholy winter he passed in loneliness and sorrow. Well he knew who had killed his brother ; it was the serpent-king, but Menaboshu could not get at him in the winter. When spring came at last, he went one bright warm day to the lake in which his little brother had perished. All the long winter he could not bear to visit the fatal spot. But now on the sand, where the snow had melted, he saw the footprints of his lost brother, and when he saw them he broke into lamentations so loud that they were heard far and near.

How f b hu deceived the serpent- king.

The serpent-king heard them also, and curious to know what was the matter, he popped his head out of the water. " Ah, there you are," said Menaboshu to himself, wiping away the tears with the sleeve of his coat, " you shall pay for your misdeed." He turned himself at once into a tree-stump and stood in that likeness stiff and stark on the water's edge. The serpent-king and all the other serpents, who popped out after him, looked about very curiously to discover who had been raising this loud lament, but they could discover nothing but the tree-stump, which they had never seen there before. As they were sniffing about it, " Take care," said one of them, "there's more there than meets the eye. Maybe it is our foe, the sly Menaboshu, in disguise." So the serpent-king commanded one of his attendants to go and search the matter out. The gigantic serpent at once coiled itself round the tree-stump and squeezed it so hard, that the bones in Menaboshu's body cracked, but he bore the agony with stoical fortitude, not betraying his anguish by a single sound. So the serpents were easy in their minds and said, "No, it is not he. We can sleep safe. It is only wood!" And the day being warm, they all lay down on the sandy beach of the lake and fell fast asleep.

Scarcely had the last snake closed his eyes, when Mena- How
boshu slipped from his ambush, seized his bow and arrows, Me b shu killed the
and shot the serpent-king dead. Three also of the serpent- serpent-
king's sons he despatched with his arrows. At that the other king ow the floo l
serpents awoke, and glided back into the water, crying, rose, and
"Woe! woe! Menaboshu is among us! Menaboshu is kill- escaped
ing us!" They made a horrible noise all over the lake and from it to a
lashed the water with their long tails. Those of them who ....
had the most powerful magic brought forth their medicine-
bags, opened them, and scattered the contents all around on
the banks and the wood and in the air. Then the water
began to run in whirlpools and to swell. The sky was over-
cast with clouds, and torrents of rain fell. First the neighbourhood, then half the earth, then the whole world was flooded.
Frightened to death, Menaboshu fled away, hopping from
mountain to mountain like a squirrel, but finding no rest for
the soles of his feet, for the swelling waves followed him
everywhere. At last he escaped to a very high mountain,
but soon the water rose even over its summit. On the top
of the mountain grew a tall fir-tree, and Menaboshu climbed
up it to its topmost bough. Even there the flood pursued
him and had risen to his mouth, when it suddenly stood still.

In this painful position, perched on the tree-top and How with
surrounded by the heaving waters of the flood, Menaboshu the help of
remained five days and five nights, wondering how he could a musk-rat, which
escape. At last he saw a solitary bird, a loon, swimming on d ed in o the water
the face of the water. He called the bird and said, "Brother Menaboshu
loon, thou skilful diver, be so good as to dive into the depths es e he earth after
and see whether thou canst find any earth, without which I the flood.

cannot live." Again and again the loon dived, but no earth could he find. Menaboshu was almost in despair. But next day he saw the dead body of a drowned musk-rat drifting towards him. He caught it, took it in his hand, breathed on it, and brought it to life again. Then he said to the rat, "Little brother rat, neither you nor I can live without earth. Dive into the water and bring me up a little earth. If it be only three grains of sand, yet will I make something out of it for you and me." The rat dived and after a long time, reappeared on the surface. It was dead, but Menaboshu caught it and examined its paws. On one of the fore-paws he found two grains of sand or dust. So he took them, dried them on his hand in the sun, and blew them away over the water. Where they fell they grew into little islands, and these united into larger ones, till at last Menaboshu was able to jump down from the tree-top on one of them. On it he floated about as on a raft, and helped the other islands to grow together, until at last they formed lands and continents. Then Menaboshu walked from place to place, restoring nature to its former beauty and variety. He found little roots and tiny plants which he planted, and they grew into meadows, shrubs, and forests. Many of the dead bodies of animals had drifted ashore. Menaboshu gathered them and blew on them, and they came to life. Then he said, "Go each of you to his own place." So they went all of them to their places. The birds nested in the trees. The fishes and beavers chose for themselves the little lakes and rivers, and the bears and other four-footed beasts roamed about on the dry land. Moreover, Menaboshu walked to and fro with a measuring-line, determining the length of the rivers, the depth of the lakes, the height of the mountains, and the form of the lands. The earth thus restored by Menaboshu was the first land in the world to be inhabited by the Indians ; the earlier earth which was overwhelmed by the flood was inhabited only by Menaboshu and the wolves and the serpent-king and his satellites. So at least said the old Ojibway woman who told the story of the flood to the German traveller.[1]

[1] J. G. Kohl, *Kitschi-Gami oder Erzählungen vom Obern See* (Bremen, 1859), i. 321-328. The Chippeway (Ojibway) story of the deluge is given by an old traveller in a very concise form as follows : " They describe a

Another version of the same story has been recorded more briefly, with minor variations, among the Ojibways of south-eastern Ontario. It runs thus. Nenebojo was living with his brother in the woods. Every day he went out hunting, while his brother stayed at home. One evening when he returned he noticed that his brother was not at home; so he went out to look for him. But he could find him nowhere. Next morning he again started in search of his brother. As he walked by the shore of a lake, what should he see but a kingfisher sitting on a branch of a tree that drooped over the water. The bird was looking at something intently in the water below him. "What are you looking at?" asked Nenebojo. But the kingfisher pretended not to hear him. Then Nenebojo said again, " If you will tell me what you are looking at, I will make you fair to see. I will paint your feathers." The bird gladly accepted the offer, and as soon as Nenebojo had painted his feathers, the kingfisher said, " I am looking at Nenebojo's brother, whom the water-spirits have killed and whose skin they are using as a door-flap." Then Nenebojo asked again, " Where do these water-spirits come to the shore to sun themselves? " The kingfisher answered, " They always sun themselves over there at one of the bays, where the sand is quite dry."

Then Nenebojo left the kingfisher. He resolved to go over to the sandy beach indicated to him by the bird, and there to wait for the first chance of killing the water-spirits. He first pondered what disguise he should assume in order to approach them unawares. Said he to himself, " I will change myself into an old rotten stump." No sooner said than done ; the transformation was effected by a long rod, which Nenebojo always carried with him. When the lions came out of the water to sun themselves, one of them noticed the stump and said to one of his fellows, " I never saw that old stump there before. Surely it can't be Nenebojo." But the lion he spoke to said, " Indeed, I have seen that stump before." Then a third lion came over to peer and make

Another versions of the same story told among Ojibways of south-eastern Ontario. In this version the hero is called Nenebojo.

How Nenebojo killed the water-lions before the flood rose

deluge, when the waters spread over the whole earth, except the highest mountains, on the tops of which they preserved themselves " (Alexander Mac-kenzie, *Voyages from Montreal through the Continent of North America*, London, 1801, p. cxviii).

sure. He broke a piece off and saw that it was rotten. So all the lions were easy in their minds and lay down to sleep. When Nenebojo thought they were fast asleep he struck them on their heads with his stick. As he struck them the water rose from the lake. He ran away, but the waves pursued him. As he ran he met a woodpecker, who showed him the way to a mountain where grew a tall pine-tree. Nenebojo climbed up the tree and began to build a raft. By the time he had finished the raft the water reached to his neck. Then he put on the raft two animals of all the kinds that existed, and with them he floated about.

How, with
ᴛe p
of the
musk-rat,
Nᴇ──ʙ──
restored the
earth after
ᴛʜᴇ ʜᴏᴏᴅ.

When they had drifted for a while, Nenebojo said, "I believe that the water will never subside, so I had better make land again." Then he sent an otter to dive to the bottom of the water and fetch up some earth ; but the otter came back without any. Next he sent the beaver on the same errand, but again in vain. After that Nenebojo despatched the musk-rat to bring up earth out of the water. When the musk-rat returned to the surface his paws were tightly closed. On opening them Nenebojo found some little grains of sand, and he discovered other grains in the mouth of the musk-rat. So he put all the grains together, dried them, and then blew them into the lake with the horn which he used for calling the animals. In the lake the grains of sand formed an island. Nenebojo enlarged the island, and sent out a raven to find out how large it was. But the raven never returned. So Nenebojo decided to send out the hawk, the fleetest of all birds on the wing. After a while the hawk returned, and being asked whether he had seen the raven anywhere, he said he had seen him eating dead bodies by the shore of the lake. Then Nenebojo said, "Henceforth the raven will never have anything to eat but what he steals." Yet another interval, and Nenebojo sent out the caribou to explore the size of the island. The animal soon returned, saying that the island was not large enough. So Nenebojo blew more sand into the water, and when he had done so he ceased to make the earth.[1]

[1] Paul Radin, *Some Myths and Tales of the Ojibwa of South-eastern Ontario* (Ottawa, 1914), pp. 19-21 (*Canada, Department of Mines, Geological Sur-* *vey, Memoir 48*). Compare *id.* pp. 22 *sq.* The lions of this tale are clearly mythical animals, like the water-lynxes and the serpents of the preceding tales.

The same story is told, with variations, by the Timagami
Ojibways of Canada.   They speak of a certain hero named
Nenebuc, who was the son of the Sun by a mortal woman.
One day, going about with his bow and arrows, he came to a
great lake with a beautiful sandy shore, and in the lake he saw
lions.   They were too far off to shoot at, so he waited till,
feeling cold in the water, the lions came ashore to sun and dry
themselves on the sandy beach.   In order to get near them
unseen, he took some birch-bark from a rotten stump, rolled
it into a hollow cylinder and set it, like a wigwam, near the
shore.   Then he ensconced himself in it, making a little loophole in the bark, through which he could see and shoot the
lions.   The lions were curious as to this new thing on the
shore, and they sent a great snake to spy it out.   The snake
coiled itself round the cylinder of bark and tried to upset it,
but it could not, for Nenebuc inside of it stood firm.   Then
the lions themselves approached, and Nenebuc shot an arrow
and wounded a lioness, the wife of the lion chief.   She
was badly hurt, but contrived to crawl away to the cave in
which she lived.   The cave may be seen to this day.   It is
in a high bluff on the west shore of Smoothwater Lake.
Disguised in the skin of a toad, and pretending to be a
medicine-woman, Nenebuc was admitted to the presence of
the wounded lioness in the cave ; but instead of healing
her, as he professed to do, he thrust the point of the arrow
still deeper into the wound, so that she died.   No sooner did
she expire than a great torrent of water poured out of the
cave, and the lake began to rise.   " That is going to flood
the world and be the end of all things," said Nenebuc.   So
he cut down trees and made a raft.   And hardly was the
raft ready, when the flood was upon him.   It rose above the
trees, bearing the raft with it, and wherever he looked he
could see nothing but water everywhere.   All kinds of
animals were swimming about in it ; they made for his raft,
and he took them in.   For he wished to save them in order
that, when the flood subsided, the earth should be stocked
with the same kinds of animals as before.   They stayed
with him on the raft for a long while.   After a time he made
a rope of roots, and tying it to the beaver's tail, he bade him
dive down to the land below the water.   The beaver dived,

but came up again, saying that he could find no bottom. Seven days afterwards Nenebuc let the musk-rat try whether he could not bring up some earth. The musk-rat plunged into the water and remained down a long time. At last he came up dead, but holding a little earth in his paws. Nenebuc dried the earth, but not entirely. That is why in some places there are swamps to this day. So the animals again roamed over the earth, and the world was remade.[1]

Another version of the same story told by the Blackfoot Indians

The Blackfoot Indians, another Algonquin tribe, who used to range over the eastern slopes of the Rocky Mountains and the prairies at their foot, tell a similar tale of the great primeval deluge. "In the beginning," they say, "all the land was covered with water, and Old Man and all the animals were floating around on a large raft. One day Old Man told the beaver to dive and try to bring up a little mud. The beaver went down, and was gone a long time, but could not reach the bottom. Then the loon tried, and the otter, but the water was too deep for them. At last the musk-rat dived, and he was gone so long that they thought he had been drowned, but he finally came up, almost dead, and when they pulled him on to the raft, they found, in one of his paws, a little mud. With this, Old Man formed the world, and afterwards he made the people."[2]

An Ottawa version of the story of the great flood.

The Ottawa Indians, another branch of the Algonquin stock,[3] tell a long fabulous story, which they say has been handed down to them from their ancestors. It contains an account of a deluge which overwhelmed the whole earth, and from which a single man, by name Nanaboujou, escaped by floating on a piece of bark.[4] The missionary who reports this tradition gives us no further particulars concerning it, but from the similarity of the name Nanaboujou to the names Nenebojo, Nenebuc, and Mena-

[1] F. G. Speck, *Myths and Folk-lore of the Timiskaming Algonquin and Timagami Ojibwa* (Ottawa, 1915), pp. 28 *sq.*, 34-37 (*Canada, Department of Mines, Geological Survey, Memoir 71*). The name Nenebuc is clearly equivalent to Nenebojo and Menaboshu in the preceding versions of the tale. The word which Mr. Speck renders by "lion" is explained by him to mean "giant-lynx."

It is therefore the equivalent of the "water-lynxes" in another version of the story (above, pp. 298 *sqq.*).

[2] G. B. Grinnell, *Blackfoot Lodge Tales* (London, 1893), p. 272.

[3] F. W. Hodge, *Handbook of American Indians North of Mexico* (Washington, 1907-1910), ii. 167 *sq.*

[4] Clicteur, in *Annales de l'Association de la Propagation de la Foi*, iv. (1830), pp. 477 *sq.*

boshu, we may surmise that the Ottawa version of the deluge legend closely resembled the Ojibway versions which have already been narrated.[1]

Certainly similar stories appear to be widely current among the Indian tribes of North-Western Canada. They are not confined to tribes of the Algonquin stock, but occur also among their northern neighbours, the Tinnehs or Dénés, who belong to the great Athapascan family, the most widely distributed of all Indian linguistic families in North America, stretching as it does from the Arctic coast far into Mexico, and extending from the Pacific to Hudson's Bay, and from the Rio Colorado to the mouth of the Rio Grande.[2] Thus the Crees, who are an Algonquin tribe,[3] relate that in the beginning there lived an old magician named Wissaketchak, who wrought marvels by his enchantments. However, a certain sea monster hated the old man and sought to destroy him. So when the magician was paddling in his canoe, the monster lashed the sea with his tail till the waves rose and engulfed the land. But Wissaketchak built a great raft and gathered upon it pairs of all animals and all birds, and in that way he saved his own life and the lives of the other creatures. Nevertheless the great fish continued to lash his tail and the water continued to rise, till it had covered not only the earth but the highest mountains, and not a scrap of dry land was to be seen. Then Wissaketchak sent the diver duck to plunge into the water and bring up the sunken earth ; but the bird could not dive to the bottom and was drowned. Thereupon Wissaketchak sent the musk-rat, which, after remaining long under water, reappeared with its throat full of slime. Wissaketchak took the slime, moulded it into a small disk, and placed it on the water, where it floated. It resembled the nests which the musk-rats make for themselves on the ice. By and by the disk swelled into a hillock. Then Wissaketchak blew on it, and the more he blew on it the more it swelled, and being baked by the sun it became a solid mass. As it grew and hardened, Wissaketchak sent forth the

[1] See above, pp. 301 *sqq.*
[2] F. W. Hodge, *Handbook of American Indians North of Mexico,* i. 108 *sqq.*, ii. 754 *sq.*
[3] F. W. Hodge, *Handbook of American Indians North of Mexico,* i. 359.

animals to lodge upon it, and at last he himself disembarked and took possession of the land thus created, which is the

Dogrib
and Slave
version of
the story
of the great
flood.

world we now inhabit.[1] A similar tale is told by the Dogrib and Slave Indians, two Tinneh tribes,[2] except that they give the name of Tchapewi to the man who was saved from the great flood ; and they say that when he was floating on the raft with couples of all sorts of animals, which he had rescued, he caused all the amphibious animals, one after the other, including the otter and the beaver, to dive into the water, but none of them could bring up any earth except the musk-rat, who dived last of all and came up panting with a little mud in his paw. That mud Tchapewi breathed on till it grew into the earth as we now see it. So Tchapewi replaced the animals on it, and they lived there as before ; and he propped the earth on a stout stay, making it firm and solid.[3]

The Hareskin Indians, another Tinneh tribe,[4] say that a certain Kunyan, which means Wise Man, once upon a time resolved to build a great raft. When his sister, who was also his wife, asked him why he would build it, he said, "If there comes a flood, as I foresee, we shall take refuge on the raft." He told his plan to other men on the earth, but they laughed at him, saying, "If there is a flood, we shall take refuge on the trees." Nevertheless the Wise Man made a great raft, joining the logs together by ropes made of roots. All of a sudden there

[1] Émile Petitot, *Traditions Indiennes du Canada Nord-ouest* (Paris, 1886), pp. 472-476. In this tale the wizard's name Wissaketchak seems clearly identical with the name Wiskay-tchach of the Chippeway legend (above, p. 297). A similar tale is told by the Assiniboins, a tribe of the Siouan or Dacotan stock, who are closely associated with the Crees. They say that formerly, when all the earth was flooded with water, the Trickster, whom they call Inktonmi, sent animals to dive for dirt at the bottom of the sea, but no creature could bring up any. At last he sent the musk-rat, and the rat came up dead, but with dirt in its claws. So the Trickster took the dirt and made the earth out of it. Afterwards he

created men and horses out of dirt. See Robert H. Lowie, *The Assiniboine* (New York, 1909), p. 101 (*Anthropological Papers of the American Museum of Natural History*, vol. iv. Part i.). According to this account, the flood preceded the creation of mankind. But as the story is apparently much abridged, we may perhaps suppose that in the full version the human species were said to have been drowned in the flood and afterwards created afresh out of mud by the Trickster.

[2] F. W. Hodge, *Handbook of American Indians North of Mexico*, i. 108 *sq.*, ii. 754.

[3] E. Petitot, *op. cit.* pp. 317-319.

[4] F. W. Hodge, *Handbook of American Indians North of Mexico*, ii. 754.

came a flood such that the like of it had never been seen before. The water seemed to gush forth on every side. Men climbed up in the trees, but the water rose after them, and all were drowned. But the Wise Man floated safely on his strong and well-corded raft. As he floated he thought of the future, and he gathered by twos all the herbivorous animals, and all the birds, and even all the beasts of prey he met with on his passage. "Come up on my raft," he said to them, "for soon there will be no more earth." Indeed, the earth disappeared under the water, and for a long time nobody thought of going to look for it. The first to plunge into the depth was the musk-rat, but he could find no bottom, and when he bobbed up on the surface again he was half drowned. "There is no earth!" said he. A second time he dived, and when he came up, he said, "I smelt the smell of the earth, but I could not reach it." Next it came to the turn of the beaver. He dived and remained a long time under water. At last he reappeared, floating on his back, breathless and unconscious. But in his paw he had a little mud, which he gave to the Wise Man. The Wise Man placed the mud on the water, breathed on it, and said, "I would there were an earth again!" At the same time he breathed on the handful of mud, and lo! it began to grow. He put a small bird on it, and the patch of mud grew still bigger. So he breathed, and breathed, and the mud grew and grew. Then the man put a fox on the floating island of mud, and the fox ran round it in a single day. Round and round the island ran the fox, and bigger and bigger grew the island. Six times did the fox make the circuit of the island, but when he made it for the seventh time, the land was complete even as it was before the flood. Then the Wise Man caused all the animals to disembark and landed them on the dry ground. Afterwards he himself disembarked with his wife and son, saying, "It is for us that this earth shall be repeopled." And repeopled it was, sure enough. Only one difficulty remained with which the Wise Man had to grapple. The floods were still out, and how to reduce them was the question. The bittern saw the difficulty and came to the rescue. He swallowed the whole of the water, and then lay like a log on the bank, with his belly

How the ... e an with the help of the which dived into ... restored the earth after destroyed in he great flood

swollen to a frightful size.   This was more than the Wise
Man had bargained for ; if there had been too much water
before, there was now too little.   In his embarrassment the
Wise Man had recourse to the plover.   " The bittern," he
said, " is lying yonder in the sun with his belly full of water.
Pierce it."   So the artful plover made up to the unsuspecting bittern.   " My grandmother," said he, in a sympathizing
tone, " has no doubt a pain in her stomach."   And he passed
his hand softly over the ailing part of the bittern as if to
soothe it.   But all of a sudden he put out his claws and
clawed the swollen stomach of the bittern.   Such a scratch
he gave it !   There was a gurgling, guggling sound, and out
came the water from the stomach bubbling and foaming.   It
flowed away into rivers and lakes, and thus the world became
habitable once more.[1]

Some Tinneh Indians affirm that the deluge was caused
by a heavy fall of snow in the month of September.   One
old man alone foresaw the catastrophe and warned his
fellows, but all in vain.   " We will escape to the mountains,"
said they.   But they were all drowned.   Now the old man
had built a canoe, and when the flood came, he sailed about
in it, rescuing from the water all the animals he fell in with.
Unable long to support this manner of life, he caused the
beaver, the otter, the musk-rat, and the arctic duck to dive
into the water in search of the drowned earth.   Only the
arctic duck came back with a little slime on its claws ; and
the man spread the slime on the water, caused it to grow by
his breath, and for six days disembarked the animals upon
it.   After that, when the ground had grown to the size of a
great island, he himself stepped ashore.   Other Tinnehs say
that the old man first sent forth a raven, which gorged itself
on the floating corpses and came not back.   Next he sent
forth a turtle-dove, which flew twice round the world and
returned.   The third time she came back at evening, very
tired, with a budding twig of fir in her mouth.[2]   The influence of Christian teaching on this last version of the story is
manifest.

[1] E. Petitot, *Traditions Indiennes
du Canada Nord-ouest*, pp. 146-149.
Compare *id.*, *Monographie des Dèné-*
Dindjié (Paris, 1876), p. 80.
   [2] É Petitot, *Monographie des Dèné-*
Dindjié (Paris, 1876), p. 74.

The Tinneh Indians in the neighbourhood of Nulato tell a story of a great flood which happened thus. In a populous settlement there lived a rich youth and his four nephews. Far away across the sea there dwelt a fair damsel, whom many men had wooed in vain. The rich young man resolved to seek her hand, and for that purpose he sailed to her village across the sea with his nephews in their canoes. But she would not have him. So next morning he was preparing to return home. He was already in his canoe down on the beach ; his nephews had packed up everything, and were about to shove off from the shore. Many of the villagers had come out of their houses to witness the departure of the strangers, and among them was a woman with her baby in her arms, an infant not yet weaned. Speaking to her baby, the fond mother said, "And what of this little girl? If they want a little girl, why not take this one of mine?" The rich young man heard the words, and holding out his paddle to the woman, he said, " Put her upon this, the little one you speak of." The woman put the baby on the paddle, and the young man drew the child in and placed it behind him in the canoe. Then he paddled away and his nephews after him. Meanwhile the girl whom he had asked to marry him came down to get water. But as she stepped on the soft mud at the water's edge she began to sink into it. " Oh ! " she cried, " here I am sinking up to my knees." But the young man answered, " It is your own fault." She sank still deeper and cried, "Oh! now I am in up to my waist!" But he said again, " It is your own fault." Deeper yet she sank and cried, " Oh! I am in up to my neck!" And again he answered, " It is your own fault." Then she sank down altogether and disappeared.

But the girl's mother saw what happened, and angry at the death of her daughter, she brought down some tame brown bears to the edge of the water, and laying hold of their tails she said to them, " Raise a strong wind " ; for thus she hoped to drown the young man who had left her daughter to perish. The bears now began to dig the bottom in a fury, making huge waves. At the same time the water rose exceedingly and the billows ran high. The young man's four nephews were drowned in the storm, and all the inhabitants of that village perished in the waters, all except the mother of the baby and her husband ; these two were the only people that survived. But the young man himself escaped, for he possessed a magical white stone, and when he threw it ahead it clove a smooth passage for his canoe through the angry water ; so he rode out the storm in safety. Still all around him was·nothing but the raging sea. Then he took a harpoon and threw it and hit the crest of a wave. Soon after he found himself in a forest of spruce-trees. The land had been formed again. The wave he struck with his harpoon had become a mountain, and rebounding from the rock the harpoon had shot up into the sky and there stuck fast. The harpoon is there to this day, though only the medicine-men can see it. After that the young man turned to the baby girl behind him in the canoe. But he found her grown into a beautiful woman with a face as bright as the sun. So 'he married her, and their offspring repeopled the drowned earth. But the man and the woman who had been saved from the waters in his wife's village became the ancestors of the people beyond the sea.[1]

Sarcee version of of the great flood. The Sarcees, another Indian tribe belonging to the great Tinneh stock, were formerly a powerful nation, but are now reduced to a few hundreds. Their reserve, a fine tract of prairie land, adjoins that of the Blackfeet in Alberta, a little south of the Canadian Pacific Railway. They have a tradition of a deluge which agrees in its main features with that of the Ojibways, Crees, and other Canadian tribes. They say that when the world was flooded, only one man and woman were left alive, being saved on a raft, on which they also collected animals and birds of all sorts. The man sent a beaver down to dive to the bottom. The creature did so and brought up a little mud, which the man moulded in his hands to form a new world. At first the world was so small that a little bird could walk round it, but it kept growing bigger and bigger. " First," said the narrator, " our father took up his abode on it, then there were men, then women, then animals, and then birds. Our father next created the

[1] Rev. J. Jetté, ''On Ten'a Folk-lore '' *Journal of the Royal Anthropological Institute*, xxxviii. (1908) pp.

312 *sq.* In the text I have slightly abridged the story.

rivers, the mountains, the trees, and all the things as we now see them." At the conclusion of the story the white man, who reports it, observed to the Sarcees that the Ojibway tradition was very like their, except that in the Ojibway tradition it was not a beaver but a musk-rat that brought up the earth from the water. The remark elicited a shout of approval from five or six of the tribe, who were squatting around in the tent. "Yes! yes!" they cried in chorus. "The man has told you lies. It was a musk-rat! it was a musk-rat!"[1]

A different story of a great flood is told by the Loucheux or Dindjies, the most northerly Indian tribe of the great Tinneh family which stretches from Alaska to the borders of Arizona. They say that a certain man, whom they call the Mariner (*Etroetchokren*), was the first person to build a canoe. One day, rocking his canoe from side to side, he sent forth such waves on all sides that the earth was flooded and his canoe foundered. Just then a gigantic hollow straw came floating past, and the man contrived to scramble into it and caulk up the ends. In it he floated about safely till the flood dried up. Then he landed on a high mountain, where the hollow straw had come to rest. There he abode many days, wherefore they call it the Place of the Old Man to this day. It is the rocky peak which you see to the right of Fort MacPherson in the Rocky Mountains. Farther down the Yukon River the channel contracts, and the water rushes rapidly between two high cliffs. There the Mariner took his stand, straddlewise, with one foot planted on each cliff, and with his hands dipping in the water he caught the dead bodies of men as they floated past on the current, just as you might catch fish in a bag-net. But of living men he could find not one. The only live thing within sight was a raven, who, gorged with food, sat perched on the top of a lofty rock fast asleep. The Mariner climbed up the rock, surprised the raven in his nap, and thrust him without more ado into a bag, intending to make short work of Master Raven. But

Story of a g ea flo told b he Loucheux r es a tribe of Tinneh Indians.

The Mariner and the raven.

---

[1] Rev. E. F. Wilson, "Report on the Sarcee Indians," in "Fourth Report of the Committee on the North-Western Tribes of Canada," in *Report of the Fifty-eighth Meeting of the* *British Association for the Advancement of Science, held at Bath in September 1888* (London, 1889), p. 244.

the raven said, " I beg and entreat that you will not cast me down from this rock. For if you do, be sure that I will cause all the men who yet survive to disappear, and you will find yourself all alone in the world." Undeterred by this threat, the man let the raven in the bag drop, and the bird was dashed to pieces at the foot of the mountain. However, the words of the raven came true, for though the man travelled far and wide, not a single living wight could he anywhere discover. Only a loach and a pike did he see sprawling on the mud and warming themselves in the sun. So he bethought him of the raven, and returned to the spot where the mangled body, or rather the bones, of the bird lay bleaching at the foot of the mountain. For he thought within himself, " Maybe the raven will help me to repeople the earth." So he gathered the scattered bones, fitted them together as well as he could, and by blowing on them caused the flesh and the life to return to them. Then the man and the raven went together to the beach, where the loach and the pike were still sleeping in the sun. " Bore a hole in the stomach of the pike," said the raven to the man, " and I will do the same by the loach." The man did bore a hole in the pike's stomach, and out of it came a crowd of men. The raven did likewise to the loach, and a multitude of women came forth from the belly of the fish. That is how the world was repeopled after the great flood.[1]

Story of a great flood told by the Tlingit Indians of Alaska.

In the religion and mythology of the Tlingits or Thlinkeets, an important Indian tribe of Alaska, Yehl or the Raven plays a great part. He was not only the ancestor of the Raven clan but the creator of men ; he caused the plants to grow, and he set the sun, moon, and stars in their places.

How Yehl or the raven had a wicked uncle who caused the flood, and how the raven escaped from it.

But he had a wicked uncle, who had murdered Yehl's ten elder brothers either by drowning them or, according to others, by stretching them on a board and sawing off their heads with a knife. To the commission of these atrocious crimes he was instigated by the passion of jealousy, for he had a young wife of whom he was very fond, and he knew that according to Tlingit law his nephews, the sons of his sister, would inherit his widow whenever he himself should

---

[1] É. Petitot, *Traditions Indiennes du Canada Nord-ouest*, pp. 13, 34-38. Compare *id., Monographie des Dènè-Dindjié* (Paris, 1876), pp. 88 *sq.*

depart from this vale of tears. So when Yehl grew up to manhood, his affectionate uncle endeavoured to dispose of him as he had disposed of his ten elder brothers, but all in vain. For Yehl was not a common child. His mother had conceived him through swallowing a round pebble which she found on the shore at ebb tide ; and by means of another stone she contrived to render the infant invulnerable. So when his uncle tried to saw off his head in the usual way, the knife made no impression at all on Yehl. Not discouraged by this failure, the old villain attempted the life of his virtuous nephew in other ways. In his fury he said, " Let there be a flood," and a flood there was which covered all the mountains. But Yehl assumed his wings and feathers, which he could put off and on at pleasure, and spreading his pinions he flew up to the sky, and there remained hanging by his beak for ten days, while the water of the flood rose so high that it lapped his wings. When the water sank, he let go and dropped like an arrow into the sea, where he fell soft on a bank of seaweed and was rescued from his perilous position by a sea otter, which brought him safe to land. What happened to mankind during the flood is not mentioned in this version of the Tlingit legend.[1]

Another Tlingit legend tells how Raven caused a great flood in a different way. He had put a woman under the world to attend to the rising and falling of the tides. Once he wished to learn about all that goes on under the sea, so he caused the woman to raise the water, in order that he might go there dry-shod. But he thoughtfully directed her to heave the ocean up slowly, so that when the flood came people might have time to load their canoes with the necessary provisions and get on board. So the ocean rose gradually, bearing on its surface the people in their canoes. As they rose up and up the sides of the mountains, they could see the bears and other wild beasts walking about on the still unsubmerged tops. Many of the bears swam out to the canoes, wishing to scramble on board ; then the people

Another ring story of a flood. Raven caused the flood restored men to life afterwards.

---

[1] H. J. Holmberg, "Ethnographische Skizzen über die Völker des Russischen Amerika," *Acta Societatis Scientiarum Fennicae*, iv. (Helsingfors, 1856) pp. 332-336 ; Aurel Krause, *Die Tlinkit-Indianer* (Jena, 1885), pp. 253-257. The versions recorded by these two writers are independent and differ in some details from each other.

who had been wise enough to take their dogs with them were very glad of it, for the noble animals kept off the bears. Some people landed on the tops of the mountains, built walls round them to dam out the water, and tied their canoes on the inside. They could not take much firewood up with them; there was not room for it in the canoes. It was a very anxious and dangerous time. The survivors could see trees torn up by the roots and swept along on the rush of the waters; large devil-fish, too, and other strange creatures floated past on the tide-race. When the water subsided, the people followed the ebbing tide down the sides of the mountains; but the trees were all gone, and having no firewood they perished of cold. When Raven came back from under the sea, and saw the fish lying high and dry on the mountains and in the creeks, he said to them, "Stay there and be turned to stones." So stones they became. And when he saw people coming down he would say in like manner, "Turn to stones just where you are." And turned to stones they were. After all mankind had been destroyed in this way, Raven created them afresh out of leaves. Because he made this new generation out of leaves, people know that he must have turned into stone all the men and women who survived the great flood. And that, too, is why to this day so many people die in autumn with the fall of the leaf; when flowers and leaves are fading and falling, we also pass away like them.[1]

Another Tlingit story of a great flood.　　According to yet another account, the Tlingits or Kolosh, as the Russians used to call them, speak of a universal deluge, during which men were saved in a great floating ark which, when the water sank, grounded on a rock and split in two; and that, in their opinion, is the cause of the diversity of languages. The Tlingits represent one-half of the population, which was shut up in the ark, and all the remaining peoples of the earth represent the other half.[2] This last legend may be of Christian origin, for it exhibits a sort of blend of Noah's ark with the tower of Babel.

[1] John R. Swanton, *Tlingit Myths and Texts* (Washington, 1909), pp. 16 *sq.*, 18, 418 (*Bureau of American Ethnology, Bulletin 39*).

[2] H. J. Holmberg, "Ethnographische Skizzen uber die Volker des Russischen Amerika," *Acta Societatis Scientiarum Fennicae*, iv. (Helsingfors, 1856), pp. 345 *sq.*; T. de Pauly, *Description Ethnographique des peuples de la Russie* (St. Petersburg, 1862), *Peuples de l'Amérique Russe*, p. 14.

The Haida Indians of Queen Charlotte Islands say that "very long ago there was a great flood by which all men and animals were destroyed, with the exception of a single raven. This creature was not, however, exactly an ordinary bird, but—as with all animals in the old Indian stories— possessed the attributes of a human being to a great extent. His coat of feathers, for instance, could be put on or taken off at will, like a garment. It is even related in one version of the story that he was born of a woman who had no husband, and that she made bows and arrows for him. When old enough, with these he killed birds, and of their skins she sewed a cape or blanket. The birds were the little snow-bird with black head and neck, the large black and red, and the Mexican woodpeckers. The name of this being was Ne-kil-stlas. When the flood had gone down Ne-kil-stlas looked about, but could find neither companions nor a mate, and became very lonely. At last he took a cockle (*Cardium Nuttalli*) from the beach, and marrying it, he constantly continued to brood and think earnestly of his wish for a companion. By and by in the shell he heard a very faint cry, like that of a newly born child, which gradually became louder, and at last a little female child was seen, which growing by degrees larger and larger, was finally married by the raven, and from this union all the Indians were produced and the country peopled." [1]

The Tsimshians, an Indian tribe who inhabit the coast of British Columbia, opposite to the Queen Charlotte Islands, have a tradition of a great flood which was sent by heaven as a punishment for the ill-behaviour of man. First, all people, except a few, were destroyed by a flood, and afterwards they were destroyed by fire. Before the flood the earth was not as it is now, for there were no mountains and no trees. These were created by a certain Leqa after the deluge.[2] Once when a clergyman, in a sermon preached at Observatory Inlet, referred to the great flood, a Tsimshian

Story of a great flood told by the Haida of Queen Charlotte Islands.

Story of a great flood told by the Tsimshian Indians of British Columbia.

[1] G. M. Dawson, *Report on the Queen Charlotte Islands, 1878* (Montreal, 1880), pp. 149B *sq.* (*Geological Survey of Canada*).

[2] F. Boas, in "Fourth Report of the Committee on the North-Western Tribes of the Dominion of Canada," *Report of the Fifty-eighth Meeting of the British Association for the Advancement of Science, held at Bath in September 1888* (London, 1889), p. 239.

chief among his hearers told him the following story. "We have a tradition about the swelling of the water a long time ago. As you are going up the river you will see the high mountain to the top of which a few of our forefathers escaped when the waters rose, and thus were saved. But many more were saved in their canoes, and were drifted about and scattered in every direction. The waters went down again; the canoes rested on the land, and the people settled themselves in the various spots whither they had been driven. Thus it is the Indians are found spread all over the country; but they all understand the same songs and have the same customs, which shows that they are one people."[1]

Story of a great flood told by the Bella Coola as of British Columbia.

The Bella Coola Indians of British Columbia tell a different story of the flood. They say that the great Masmasalanich, who made men, fastened the earth to the sun by a long rope in order to keep the two at a proper distance from each other and to prevent the earth from sinking into the sea. But one day he began to stretch the rope, and the consequence naturally was that the earth sank deeper and deeper, and the water rose higher and higher, till it had covered the whole earth and even the tops of the mountains. A terrible storm broke out at the same time, and many men, who had sought safety in boats, were drowned, while others were driven far away. At last Masmasalanich hauled in the rope, the earth rose from the waves, and mankind spread over it once more. It was then that the diversity of tongues arose, for before the flood all men had been of one speech.[2]

Story of a great flood told by the Kwakiutl dians of British Columbia.

The Kwakiutl, who inhabit the coast of British Columbia to the south of the Bella Coola, have also their legend of a deluge. "Very long ago," they say, "there occurred a great flood, during which the sea rose so as to cover everything with the exception of three mountains. Two of these are very high, one near Bella-Bella, the other apparently to the north-east of that place. The third is a low but prominent hill on Don Island, named Ko-Kwus by the Indians; this they say rose at the time of the flood so as to remain above

---

[1] R. C. Mayne, *Four Years in British Columbia* (London, 1862), pp. 273 *sq.*

[2] F. Boas, "Mittheilungen über die Vilχula-Indianer," *Original-Mittheilungen aus der Ethnologischen Abtheilung der Königlichen Museen zu Berlin*, i. (Berlin, 1885–1886) pp. 178 *sq.*

the water. Nearly all the people floated away in various directions on logs and trees. The people living where Kit-Katla now is, for instance, drifted to Fort Rupert, while the Fort Ruperts drifted to Kit-Katla. Some of the people had small canoes, and by anchoring them managed to come down near home when the water subsided. Of the Hailtzuk there remained only three individuals : two men and a woman, with a dog. One of the men landed at Ka-pa, a second at another village site, not far from Bella-Bella, and the woman and dog at Bella-Bella. From the marriage of the woman with the dog, the Bella-Bella Indians originated. When the flood had subsided there was no fresh water to be found, and the people were very thirsty. The raven, however, showed them how, after eating, to chew fragments of cedar (*Thuya*) wood, when water came into the mouth. The raven also advised them where, by digging in the ground, they could get a little water ; but soon a great rain came on, very heavy and very long, which filled all the lakes and rivers so that they have never been dry since. The water is still, however, in some way understood to be connected with the cedar, and the Indians say if there were no cedar trees there would be no water. The converse would certainly hold good." [1]

The Lillooet Indians of British Columbia say that in former times, while they lived together around Green Lake and below it on the Green River, there came a great and continuous rain, which made all the lakes and rivers overflow their banks and deluge the surrounding country. A man called Ntcinemkin had a very large canoe, in which he took refuge with his family. The other people fled to the mountains, but the water soon covered them too ; and in their distress the people begged Ntcinemkin to save at least their children in his canoe. But the canoe was too small to hold all the children, so Ntcinemkin took one child from each family, a male from one, a female from the next, and so on.

Story of a great flood told by the Lillooet of British Columbia.

[1] George M. Dawson, " Notes and Observations on the Kwakiool People of the Northern Part of Vancouver Island and adjacent Coasts, made during the Summer of 1885," *Proceedings and Transactions of the Royal Society of Canada for the Year 1887*, vol. v. (Montreal, 1888), Section ii. pp. 84 *sq.* This legend was obtained by Mr. Dawson in 1878 from Hnmtshit, a chief of the Hailtzuk division of the Kwakiool (Kwakiutl), at Ka-pa (Kilkite, village of charts), Yeo Island, Milbank Sound.

But still the rain fell and the water rose till all the land was submerged, except the peak of the high mountain called Split (*Ncikato*), which rises on the west side of the Lower Lillooet Lake, its pinnacle consisting of a huge precipice cleft in two from top to bottom.   The canoe drifted about on the flood until the waters sank and it grounded on Smimelc Mountain. Each stage in the sinking of the water is marked by a flat terrace on the side of the mountain, which can be seen there to this day.[1]

Story of a great flood told by the Thompson Indians of British Columbia.

The Thompson Indians of British Columbia say that once there was a great flood which covered the whole country, except the tops of some of the highest mountains.   The Indians think, though they are not quite sure, that the flood was caused by three brothers called Qoaqlqal, who in those days travelled all over the country working miracles and transforming things, till the transformers were themselves transformed into stones.   Be that as it may, everybody was drowned in the great flood except the coyote and three men ; the coyote survived because he turned himself into a piece of wood and so floated on the water, and the men escaped with their lives by embarking in a canoe, in which they drifted to the Nzukeski Mountains.   There they were afterwards, with their canoe, transformed into stones, and there you may see them sitting in the shape of stones down to this day. As for the coyote, when the flood subsided, he was left high and dry on the shore in the likeness of the piece of wood into which, at the nick of time, he had cleverly transformed himself.   So he now resumed his natural shape and looked about him.   He found he was in the Thompson River country.   He took trees to him to be his wives, and from him and the trees together the Indians of the present day are descended.   Before the flood there were neither lakes nor streams in the mountains, and therefore there were no fish.   When the waters of the deluge receded, they left lakes in the hollows of the mountains, and streams began to flow down from them towards the sea.   That is why we now find lakes in the mountains, and fish in the lakes.[2]

[1] James Teit, "Traditions of the Lillooet Indians of British Columbia," *Journal of American Folk-lore*, xxv. (1912) p. 342.

[2] James Teit, *Traditions of the Thompson River Indians of British Columbia* (Boston and New York, 1898), pp. 19, 20. Compare *id.*, "The

Thus the deluge story of the Thompson River Indians appears to have been invented to explain the presence of lakes in the mountains ; the primitive philosopher accounted for them by a great flood which, as it retired, left the lakes behind it in the hollows of the hills, just as the ebbing tide leaves pools behind it in the hollows of the rocks on the sea-shore.

The Kootenay Indians, who inhabit the south-eastern part of British Columbia, say that once upon a time a chicken-hawk (*Accipiter Cooperi*) forbade his wife, a small grey bird, to bathe in a certain lake. One day, after picking berries on the mountain in the hot sun, she was warm and weary, and seeing the lake so cool and tempting she plunged into it, heedless of her husband's warning. But the water rose, a giant rushed forth, and ravished the bird, or rather the woman ; for in these Indian tales no sharp line of distinction is drawn between the animal and the human personages. Her angry husband came to the rescue and discharged an arrow which struck the giant in the breast. To be revenged, the monster swallowed all the waters, so that none remained for the Indians to drink. But the injured wife plucked the arrow from the giant's breast, and the pent-up waters gushed forth and caused a flood. The husband and his wife took refuge on a mountain, and remained there till the flood subsided. In another version of this Kootenay story, a big fish takes the place of the giant and is killed by the injured husband ; the spouting blood of the fish causes the deluge, and the man, or the hawk, escapes from it by climbing up a tree. The scene of the story is laid on the Kootenay River near Fort Steele.[1]

Legends of a great flood appear to have been current among the Indian tribes of Washington State. Thus the

Marginal notes: Story of a great flood told by the Kootenay Indians of British Columbia.

Stories of a great flood told by the Indians of Washington State. The Twana version of the story.

Thompson Indians of British Columbia," p. 338 (*Memoirs of the American Museum of Natural History, The Jesup North Pacific Expedition*, April, 1900).

[1] A. F. Chamberlain, "Report on the Kootenay Indians of South-eastern British Columbia," in *Eighth Report of the Committee on the North-Western Tribes of Canada*, pp. 31 sq. (separate reprint from the *Report of the British Association for the Advancement of Science, Edinburgh meeting, 1892*). The chicken-hawk (*Accipiter Cooperi*) is a very important character in the tales of the Kootenay Indians. He accompanies the coyote in his search for the sun, and in a rage he throws that animal into the fire. See A. F. Chamberlain, *op. cit.* p. 33.

Twanas, on Puget Sound, say that once on a time the people were wicked and to punish them a great flood came, which overflowed all the land except one mountain. The people fled in their canoes to the highest mountain in their country —a peak of the Olympic range—and as the water rose above it they tied their canoes with long ropes to the highest tree, but still the water rose above it. Then some of the canoes broke from their moorings and drifted away to the west, where the descendants of the persons saved in them now live, a tribe who speak a language like that of the Twanas. That, too, they say, is why the present number of the tribe is so small. In their language this mountain is called by a name which means "Fastener," because they fastened their canoes to it at that time. They also speak of a pigeon which went out to view the dead.[1]

The *a m* version of the story. The Clallam Indians of Washington State, whose country adjoins that of the Twanas, also have a tradition of a flood, but some of them believe that it happened not more than a few generations ago. Indeed about the year 1878 an old man asserted that his grandfather had seen the man who was saved from the flood, and that he was a Clallam Indian. Their Ararat, too, is a different mountain from that on which the Twana Noah and his fellows found refuge. The Lummi Indians, who live near the northern boundary of Washington State, also speak of a great flood, but no particulars of their tradition are reported. The Puyallop Indians, near Tacoma, say that the deluge overspread all the country except one high mound near Steilacoom, and this mound is still called by the Indians "The Old Land," because it was not submerged.[2]

Story of a great flood Cascade Mountains. "Do you see that high mountain over there?" said an old Indian to a mountaineer about the year 1860, as they were riding across the Cascade Mountains. "I do," was the reply. "Do you see that grove to the right?" the Indian next asked. "Yes," answered the white man. "Well," said

[1] Rev. Myron Eels (Shokomish, Washington Territory), "Traditions of the Deluge among the Tribes of the North-West," *The American Antiquarian*, i. (1878-1879) p. 70 ; *id.*, "The Twana, Chemakum, and Klallam Indians of Washington Territory,"

Report of the Smithsonian Institution for 1887, p. 674.

[2] Rev. M. Eels, "Traditions of the Deluge among the Tribes of the North-West," *The American Antiquarian*, i. (1878-1879) p. 70.

the Indian, "a long time ago there was a flood, and all the country was overflowed. There was an old man and his family on a boat or raft, and he floated about, and the wind blew him to that mountain, where he touched bottom. He stayed there for some time, and then sent a crow to hunt for land, but it came back without finding any. After some time it brought a leaf from that grove, and the old man was glad, for he knew that the water was abating."[1]

When the earliest missionaries came among the Spokanas, Nez Perces, and Cayuses, who, with the Yakimas, used to inhabit the eastern part of Washington State, they found that these Indians had their own tradition of a great flood, in which one man and his wife were saved on a raft. Each of these three tribes, together with the Flathead tribes, had its own separate Ararat on which the survivors found refuge.[2]

Story of a g o among he Spokanas, rerces, and Cayuses.

The story of a great flood is also told by the Indians of Washington State who used to inhabit the lower course of the Columbia River and speak the Kathlamet dialect of Chinook.[3] In one respect their tale resembles the Algonquin legend. They say that a certain maiden was advised by the blue-jay to marry the panther, who was an elk-hunter and the chief of his town to boot. So away she hied to the panther's town, but when she came there she married the beaver by mistake instead of the panther. When her husband the beaver came back from the fishing, she went down to the beach to meet him, and he told her to take up the trout he had caught. But she found that they were not really trout at all, but only willow branches. Disgusted at the discovery, she ran away from him, and finally married the panther, whom she ought to have married at first. Thus deserted by the wife of his bosom, the beaver wept for five days, till all the land was flooded with his tears. The houses were overwhelmed, and the animals took to their canoes. When the flood reached nearly to the sky, they bethought them of fetching up earth from the depths, so they said to the blue-jay, "Now dive, blue-jay!" So the blue-jay dived,

Story of a g o told by the Kathlamet- a g Indians of the Lower River.

---

[1] Rev. M. Eels, *op. cit.* p. 71.

[2] Rev. M. Eels, *op. cit.* p. 71.

[3] Franz Boas, *Handbook of American Indian Languages*, i. (Washington, 1911) p. 563.

but he did not go very deep, for his tail remained sticking out of the water. After that, all the animals tried to dive. First the mink and next the otter plunged into the vasty deep, but came up again without having found the bottom. Then it came to the turn of the musk-rat. He said, " Tie the canoes together." So they tied the canoes together and laid planks across them. Thereupon the musk-rat threw off his blanket, sang his song five times over, and without more ado dived into the water, and disappeared. He was down a long while. At last flags came up to the surface of the water. Then it became summer, the flood sank, and the canoes with it, till they landed on dry ground. All the animals jumped out of the canoes, but as they did so, they knocked their tails against the gunwale and broke them off short. That is why the grizzly bears and the black bears have stumpy tails down to this day. But the otter, the mink, the musk-rat, and the panther returned to the canoe, picked up their missing tails, and fastened them on the stumps. That is why these animals have still tails of a decent length, though they were broken off short at the flood.[1] In this story little is said of the human race, and how it escaped from the deluge. But the tale clearly belongs to that primitive type of story in which no clear distinction is drawn between man and beast, the lower creatures being supposed to think, speak, and act like human beings, and to live on terms of practical equality with them. This community of nature is implicitly indicated in the Kathlamet story by the marriage of a girl, first to a beaver, and then to a panther ; and it appears also in the incidental description of the beaver as a man with a big belly.[2] Thus in describing how the animals survived the deluge, the narrator may have assumed that he had sufficiently explained the survival of mankind also.

Stories of a great flood among the Eskimo of Alaska.

In North America legends of a great flood are not confined to the Indian tribes ; they are found also among the Eskimo and their kinsfolk the Greenlanders. At Oro-wignarak, in Alaska, Captain Jacobsen was told that the

[1] Franz Boas, *Kathlamet Texts* (Washington, 1901) pp. 20-25, 252 sq. (*Bureau of American Ethnology,* Bulletin 26).

[2] Franz Boas, *Kathlamet Texts,* p. 20.

Eskimo have a tradition of a mighty inundation which, simultaneously with an earthquake, swept over the land so rapidly that only a few persons were able to escape in their skin canoes to the tops of the highest mountains.[1] Again, the Eskimo of Norton Sound, in Alaska, say that in the first days the earth was flooded, all but a very high mountain in the middle. The water came up from the sea and covered the whole land except the top of this mountain. Only a few animals escaped to the mountain and were saved ; and a few people made a shift to survive by floating about in a boat and subsisting on the fish they caught till the water subsided. As the flood sank and the mountains emerged from the water, the people landed from the canoe on these heights, and gradually followed the retreating flood to the coast. The animals which had escaped to the mountains also descended and replenished the earth after their kinds.[2]

Again, the Tchiglit Eskimo, who inhabit the coast of the Arctic Ocean from Point Barrow on the west to Cape Bathurst on the east, tell of a great flood which broke over the face of the earth and, driven by the wind, submerged the dwellings of men. The Eskimo tied several boats together so as to form a great raft, and on it they floated about on the face of the great waters, huddling together for warmth under a tent which they had pitched, but shivering in the icy blast and watching the uprooted trees drifting past on the waves. At last a magician named An-odjium, that is, Son of the Owl, threw his bow into the sea, saying, " Enough, wind, be calm ! " After that he threw in his ear-rings ; and that sufficed to cause the flood to subside.[3]

The Central Eskimo say that long ago the ocean suddenly began to rise and continued rising until it had inundated the whole land. The water even covered the tops of the mountains, and the ice drifted over them. When the flood had subsided, the ice stranded and ever since forms an ice-cap on the top of the mountains. Many shell-fish, fish,

---

[1] A. Woldt, *Captain Jacobsen's Reise an der Nordwestkuste Amerika's 1881– 1883* (Leipsic, 1884), p. 252.

[2] E. W. Nelson, "The Eskimo about Bering Strait," *Eighteenth Annual Report of the Bureau of Ameri-* can *Ethnology*, Part i. (Washington, 1899) p. 452.

[3] É. Petitot, *Traditions Indiennes du Canada Nord-ouest* (Paris, 1886), pp. 6 *sq.*

seals, and whales were left high and dry, and their shells and bones may be seen there to this day. Many Eskimo were then drowned, but many others, who had taken to their boats when the flood began to rise, were saved.[1]

Story of a
g   o
told by the
Green-
landers.

With regard to the Greenlanders their historian Crantz tells us that "almost all heathen nations know something of Noah's Flood, and the first missionaries found also some pretty plain traditions among the Greenlanders ; namely, that the world once overset, and all mankind, except one, were drowned ; but some were turned into fiery spirits. The only man that escaped alive, afterwards smote the ground with his stick, and out sprang a woman, and these two re-peopled the world. As a proof that the deluge once over-flowed the whole earth, they say that many shells, and relics of fishes, have been found far within the land where men could never have lived, yea that bones of whales have been found upon a high mountain."[2] Similar evidence in support of the legend was adduced to the traveller C. F. Hall by the Innuits or Eskimo with whom he lived. He tells us that "they have a tradition of a deluge which they attribute to an unusually high tide. On one occasion when I was speak-ing with Tookoolito concerning her people, she said, 'Innuits all think this earth once covered with water.' I asked her why they thought so. She answered, 'Did you never see little stones, like clams and such things as live in the sea, away up on mountains?'"[3]

An Eskimo man once informed a traveller, that he had often wondered why all the mammoths are extinct. He added that he had learned the cause from Mr. Whittaker, the missionary at Herschel Island. The truth is, he explained, that when Noah entered into the ark and invited all the animals to save themselves from the flood by following his example, the sceptical mammoths declined to accept the kind invitation, on the ground that they did not believe there would be much of a flood, and that even if there were, they thought their legs long enough to keep their heads above water. So they stayed outside and perished in

[1] Franz Boas, "The Central Es-kimo," in *Sixth Annual Report of the Bureau of Ethnology* (Washington, 1888), pp. 637 *sq.*

[2] David Crantz, *History of Green-land* (London, 1767), i. 204 *sq.*

[3] C. F. Hall, *Life with the Esqui-maux* (London, 1864), ii. 318.

their blind unbelief, but the caribou and the foxes and the wolves are alive to this day, because they believed and were saved.[1]

§ 17. *Stories of a Great Flood in Africa*

It is curious, that while legends of a universal flood are widely spread over many parts of the world, they are hardly to be found at all in Africa. Indeed, it may be doubted whether throughout that vast continent a single genuinely native tradition of a great flood has been recorded. Even traces of such traditions are rare. None have as yet been discovered in the literature of ancient Egypt.[2] In Northern Guinea, we are told, there is " a tradition of a great deluge which once overspread the face of the whole earth ; but it is coupled with so much that is marvellous and imaginative, that it can scarcely be identified with the same event recorded in the Bible." [3] As the missionary who reports this gives no details, we cannot judge how far the tradition is native and how far borrowed from Europeans. Another missionary has met with a reference to a great flood in the traditions of the natives of the Lower Congo. " The sun and moon once met together, they say, and the sun plastered some mud over a part of the moon, and thus covered up some of the light, and that is why a portion of the moon is often in shadow. When this meeting took place there was a flood, and the ancient people put their porridge (*luku*) sticks to their backs and turned into monkeys. The present race of people is a new creation. Another statement is that when the flood came the men turned into monkeys, and the women into lizards : and the monkey's tail is the man's gun. One would think from this that the transformation took place, in their opinion, in very recent times ; but the Congo native has no legend concerning the introduction of the gun into their country, nor any rumours of the time when hunting and fighting were carried on with spears, shields, bows and arrows, and knives." [4] The Bapedi, a Basuto tribe of South

Absence of es a great flood in Africa.

Reported are such stories in Guinea the Congo.

[1] V. Stefansson, *My Life with the Eskimo* (London, 1913), p. 422.
[2] So I am informed by Professor W. M. Flinders Petrie.
[3] Rev. J. L. Wilson, *Western Africa* (London, 1856), pp. 229 *sq.*
[4] John H. Weeks, *Among the Primitive Bakongo* (London, 1914), p. 286.

Africa, are said to have a legend of a great flood which
destroyed nearly all mankind.[1]   The experienced missionary
Dr. Robert Moffat made fruitless inquiries concerning legends
of a deluge among the natives of South Africa ; one native
who professed to have received such a legend from his forefathers was discovered to have learned it from a missionary
named Schmelen.   "Stories of a similar kind," adds Dr.
Moffat, "originally obtained at a missionary station, or from
some godly traveller, get, in course of time, so mixed up and
metamorphosed by heathen ideas, that they look exceedingly
like native traditions."[2]   After recording a legend as to the
formation of Lake Dilolo in Angola, in which a whole village
with its inhabitants, its fowls, and its dogs is said to have
perished, Dr. Livingstone remarks, "This may be a faint
tradition of the Deluge, and it is remarkable as the only one
I have met with in this country."[3]   My experienced missionary friend, the Rev. John Roscoe, who spent about twenty-
five years in intimate converse with the natives of Central
Africa, particularly the Uganda Protectorate, tells me that
he has found no native legend of a flood among the tribes
with which he is acquainted.

Traditions of a great flood have, however, been discovered
by German writers among the natives of East Africa, but the
stories are plainly mere variations of the Biblical narrative,
which has penetrated to these savages through Christian or
possibly Mohammedan influence.   One such tradition has
been recorded by a German officer among the Masai.   It
runs as follows :—

Tumbainot was a righteous man whom God loved.   He
married a wife Naipande, who bore him three sons, Oshomo,
Bartimaro, and Barmao.   When his brother Lengerni died,
Tumbainot, in accordance with Masai custom, married the
widow Nahaba-logunja, whose name is derived from her high
narrow head, that being a mark of beauty among the Masai.
She bore her second husband three sons ; but in consequence
of a domestic jar, arising from her refusal to give her husband

[1] A. Merensky, *Beiträge zur Kenntniss Sud-Afrikas* (Berlin, 1875), p.
124.
[2] Robert Moffat, *Missionary Labours
and Scenes in Southern Africa* (London,

1842), pp. 126 *sq*.

[3] David Livingstone, *Missionary
Travels and Researches in South Africa*
(London, 1857), p. 327.

a drink of milk in the evening, she withdrew from his home-stead and set up one of her own, fortifying it with a hedge of thorn-bushes against the attacks of wild beasts. In those days the world was thickly peopled, but men were not good. On the contrary they were sinful and did not obey God's commands. However, bad as they were, they refrained from murder. But at last, one unlucky day, a certain man named Nambija knocked another man named Suage on the head. This was more than God could bear, and he resolved to destroy the whole race of mankind. Only the pious Tum-bainot found grace in the eyes of God, who commanded him to build an ark of wood, and go into it, with his two wives, his six sons, and their wives, taking with him some animals of every sort. When they were all safely aboard, and Tum-bainot had laid in a great stock of provisions, God caused it to rain so heavily and so long that a great flood took place, and all men and beasts were drowned, except those which were in the ark ; for the ark floated on the face of the waters. Tumbainot longed for the end of the rain, for the provisions in the ark began to run short. At last the rain stopped. Anxious to ascertain the state of the flood, Tumbainot let a dove fly out of the ark. In the evening she came back tired, so Tumbainot knew that the flood must still be high, and that the dove could have found no place to rest. Several days later he let a vulture fly out of the ark, but before doing so he took the precaution to fasten an arrow to one of its tail-feathers, calculating that if the bird perched to eat, it would trail the arrow behind it, and that the arrow, hitching on to something as it was dragged over the ground, would stick fast and be lost. The event answered his expectation, for in the evening the vulture returned to the ark without the arrow and the tail-feather. So Tumbainot inferred that the bird had lighted on carrion, and that the flood must be abating. When the water had all run away, the ark grounded on the steppe, and men and animals disembarked. As he stepped out of the ark, Tumbainot saw no less than four rainbows, one in each of the four quarters of the sky, and he took them as a sign that the wrath of God was over.[1]

Another version of the flood story is reported by a

[1] M. Merker, *Die Masai* (Berlin, 1904), pp. 265-267.

Another
rs
the Hebrew
story of a
o
reported
from East
.... German missionary from the same region. He obtained it at the mission-station of Mkulwe, on the Saisi or Momba river, about twenty miles from where the river flows into Lake Rukwa. His informant professed to have had it from his grandfather, and stoutly asserted that it was a genuine old tradition of the country and not borrowed from foreigners. His statement was corroborated by another truth-loving native, who only differed from his fellow in opining that the African Noah sent out two doves instead of one. The story runs thus :—

Long ago, the rivers came down in flood. God said to the two men, " Go into the ship. Also take into it seeds of all sorts and all animals, male and female." They did so. The flood rose high, it overtopped the mountains, the ship floated on it. All animals and all men died. When the water dried up, the man said, " Let us see. Perhaps the water is not yet dried up." He sent out a dove, she came back to the ship. He waited and sent out a hawk, but she did not return, because the water was dried up. The men went out of the ship, they also let out all animals and all seeds.[1]

§ 18. *The Geographical Diffusion of Flood Stories*

Geogra-
...
diffusion of
stories of a
grea   oo . The foregoing survey of diluvial traditions suffices to prove that this type of story, whether we call it legendary or mythical, has been widely diffused throughout the world. Before we inquire into the relation in which the traditions stand to each other, and the cause or causes which have given rise to them, it may be well to recapitulate briefly the regions in which they have been found. To begin with Asia, we have found examples of them in Babylonia, Palestine, Syria, Phrygia, ancient and modern India, Burma, Cochin China, the Malay Peninsula, and Kamtchatka. Roughly speaking, therefore, the traditions prevail in Southern Asia,
Absence of
flo dst   s
in Eastern
Central,
and
Northern
Asia. and are conspicuously absent from Eastern, Central, and Northern Asia. It is particularly remarkable that neither of the great civilized peoples of Eastern Asia, the Chinese

[1] Alois Hamberger, " Religiose Überlieferungen und Gebrauche der Landschaft Mkulwe (Deutsch-Ost-Afrika)," *Anthropos*, iv. (1909) p. 304.

and the Japanese, should, so far as I know, have preserved in their voluminous and ancient literatures any native legends of a great flood of the sort we are here considering, that is, of a universal inundation in which the whole or the greater part of the human race is said to have perished.

In Europe native diluvial traditions are much rarer than in Asia, but they occurred in ancient Greece, and have been reported in Wales, and among the Lithuanians, the gipsies of Transylvania, and the Voguls of Eastern Russia. The Icelandic story of an inundation of giant's blood hardly conforms to the general type. Rarity of fl es in Europe.

In Africa, including Egypt, native legends of a great flood are conspicuously absent ; indeed no single clear case of one has yet been reported. Africa.

In the Indian Archipelago we find legends of a great flood in the large islands of Sumatra, Borneo, and Celebes, and among the lesser islands in Nias, Engano, Ceram, Rotti, and Flores. Stories of the same sort are told by the native tribes of the Philippine Islands and Formosa, and by the isolated Andaman Islanders in the Bay of Bengal. The Indian ipe - ago.

In the vast islands, or continents, of New Guinea and Australia, we meet with some stories of a great flood, and legends of the same sort occur in the fringe of smaller islands known as Melanesia, which sweeps in a great arc of a circle round New Guinea and Australia on the north and east. New Australia and e anesia.

Passing still eastward out into the Pacific, we discover diluvial traditions widely spread among the Polynesians who occupy the scattered and for the most part small islands of that great ocean, from Hawaii on the north to New Zealand on the south. Among the Micronesians a flood legend has been recorded in the Pelew Islands. Polynesia and Micronesia

In America, South, Central, and North, diluvial traditions are very widespread. They have been found from Tierra del Fuego in the south to Alaska in the north, and in both continents from east to west. Nor do they occur only among the Indian tribes ; examples of them have been reported among the Eskimo from Alaska on the west to Greenland on the east. America, Central, and North.

Such being in general the geographical diffusion of the traditions we have next to ask, how are they related to each

How are
the various
flood stories
related to
each other?

All the
stories of a
great flood
cannot be
derived
from the
Hebrew
story, which
was itself
derived
from a
Babylon-
ian, or
rather
Sumerian
original.

But may
the Baby-
lonian, or
rather
Sumerian,
story be
the source
of all the
others?

other?   Are they all genetically connected with each other, or are they distinct and independent?   In other words, are they all descended from one common original, or have they originated independently in different parts of the world? Formerly, under the influence of the Biblical tradition, inquirers were disposed to identify legends of a great flood, wherever found, with the familiar Noachian deluge, and to suppose that in them we had more or less corrupt and apocryphal versions of that great catastrophe, of which the only true and authentic record is preserved in the Book of Genesis.   Such a view can hardly be maintained any longer. Even when we have allowed for the numerous corruptions and changes of all kinds which oral tradition necessarily suffers in passing from generation to generation and from land to land through countless ages, we shall still find it difficult to recognize in the diverse, often quaint, childish, or grotesque stories of a great flood, the human copies of a single divine original.   And the difficulty has been greatly increased since modern research has proved the supposed divine original in Genesis to be not an original at all, but a comparatively late copy, of a much older Baby- lonian or rather Sumerian version.   No Christian apologist is likely to treat the Babylonian story, with its strongly polytheistic colouring, as a primitive revelation of God to man ; and if the theory of inspiration is inapplicable to the original, it can hardly be invoked to account for the copy.

Dismissing, therefore, the theory of revelation or inspira- tion as irreconcilable with the known facts, we have still to inquire, whether the Babylonian or Sumerian legend, which is certainly by far the oldest of all diluvial traditions, may not be the one from which all the rest have been derived. The question is one to which a positive answer can hardly be given, since demonstration in such matters is impossible, and our conclusion must be formed from the consideration of a variety of probabilities which different minds will estimate differently.   It is no doubt possible to analyse all the stories into their elements, to classify these elements, to count up the number of them which the various versions have in common, and from the sum of the common elements found in any one narrative to calculate the probability of its being a derivative or original version.   This, in fact, has been done by one of my predecessors in this department of research,[1] but I do not propose to repeat his calculations : readers with a statistical and mathematical turn of mind may either consult them in his work or repeat them for themselves from the data submitted to them in the foregoing pages.   Here I shall content myself with stating my general conclusion, leaving the reader to verify, correct, or reject it by reference to the evidence with which I have furnished him.   Apart, then, from the Hebrew legend, which is unquestionably derived from the Babylonian, and from modern instances which exhibit clear traces of late missionary or at all events Christian influence, I do not think that we have decisive grounds for tracing any of the diluvial traditions to the Babylonian as their original.   Scholars of repute have, indeed, maintained that both the ancient Greek and the ancient Indian legends are derived from the Babylonian ; they may be right, but to me it does not seem that the resemblances between the three are sufficient to justify us in assuming identity of origin.   No doubt in the later ages of antiquity the Greeks were acquainted both with the Babylonian and the Hebrew versions of the deluge legend, but their own traditions of a great flood are much older than the conquests of Alexander, which first unlocked the treasuries of Oriental learning to western scholars ; and in their earliest forms the Greek traditions exhibit no clear marks of borrowing from Asiatic sources.   In the Deucalion legend, for example, which comes nearest to the Babylonian, only Deucalion and his wife are saved from the flood, and after it has subsided they are reduced to the necessity of miraculously creating mankind afresh out of stones, while nothing at all is said about the restoration of animals, which must presumably have perished in the waters.   This is very different from the Babylonian and Hebrew legend, which provides for the regular propagation both of the human and the animal species after the flood by taking a sufficient number of passengers of both sorts on board the ark.

Similarly a comparison of the ancient Indian with the Babylonian version of the legend brings out serious dis-

Apart rom e tr ces of missionary ng, there seems to be ....od ground for tracing any h flood stories, t ɔ Hebrew o a Babylonian or rian original.

The ancient Greek stories of a flood p ar o be independent of t y lonian.

---

[1] M. Winternitz, *Die Flutsagen*, pp. 312-333.

Discrep-·
cie
between the
ancient
▼ ·'
the ancient
Babylonian
ıe
great flood.

crepancies between them.   The miraculous fish which figures
so prominently in all the ancient Indian versions has no
obvious parallel in the Babylonian ; though some scholars
have ingeniously argued that the deity, incarnate in a fish, who
warns Manu of the coming deluge in the Indian legend, is a
duplicate of Ea, the god who similarly warns Ut-napishtim in
the Babylonian legend, for there seems to be no doubt that
Ea was a water deity, conceived and represented partly in
human and partly in fish form.[1] If this suggested parallel
between the two legends could be made out, it would certainly
forge a strong link between them.   On the other hand, in the
oldest Indian form of the story, that in the *Satapatha Brahmana*, Manu is represented as the solitary survivor of the
great flood, and after the catastrophe a woman has to be
miraculously created out of the butter, sour milk, whey and
curds of his sacrifice, in order to enable him to continue the
species.   It is only in the later versions of the story that
Manu takes a large assortment of animals and plants with
him into the ship ; and even in them, though the sage
appears on shipboard surrounded by a band of brother sages
whom he had rescued from a watery grave, nothing whatever
is said about rescuing his wife and children.   The omission
betrays a lack not only of domestic affection but of common
prudence on the part of the philosopher, and contrasts forcibly
with the practical foresight of his Babylonian counterpart, who
under the like distressing circumstances has at least the consolation of being surrounded by the family circle on the
stormy waters, and of knowing that as soon as the flood has
subsided he will be able, with their assistance, to provide for

[1] Fr. Lenormant, *Les Origines de
l'Histoire d'après la Bible : De la
Création de l'Homme au Déluge* (Paris,
1880), pp. 424 *sqq.* ; M. Winternitz,
Die Flutsagen, p. 328. As to the
aqueous and fishy nature of Ea in
Babylonian mythology, see M. Jastrow,
Religion of Babylonia and Assyria,
pp. 136 *sq.* ; P. Dhorme, *La Religion
Assyro-Babylonienne* (Paris, 1910), pp.
73 *sq.* ; and especially Alfred Jeremias,
"Oannes-Ea," in W. H. Roscher's
*Ausführliches Lexikon der Griechischen
und Romischen Mythologie*, iii. 577
sqq., where the half-human, half-fish

character of the god is illustrated from
Babylonian monuments. Berosus speaks
of this deity under the name of Oannes,
and describes his amphibious form
nearly as it is figured in Babylonian
art ; he tells us that Oannes appeared
from the Red Sea, that is, from the
Persian Gulf, and after passing the day
in conversation with men, whom he
taught the elements of civilization, retired at sunset to the sea. See Berosus,
in *Fragmenta Historicorum Graecorum*,
ed. C. Müller, ii. 496 *sq.* ; Eusebius,
Chronic., ed. A. Schoene, vol. i. col.
14.

the continuance of the human race by the ordinary processes of nature. In this curious difference between the two tales is it fanciful to detect the contrast between the worldly prudence of the Semitic mind and the dreamy asceticism of the Indian ? [1]

On the whole, then, there is little evidence to prove that the ancient Indian and Greek legends of a flood are derived from the corresponding Babylonian tradition. When we remember that the Babylonians, so far as we know, never succeeded in handing on their story of a deluge to the Egyptians, with whom they were in direct communication for centuries, we need not wonder if they failed to transmit it to the more distant Greeks and Indians, with whom down to the days of Alexander the Great they had but little intercourse. In later ages, through the medium of Christian literature, the Babylonian legend has indeed gone the round of the world and been echoed in tales told under the palms of coral islands, in Indian wigwams, and amid the Arctic ice and snow ; [2] but in itself, apart from Christian or Mohammedan agencies, it would seem to have travelled little beyond the limits of its native land and the adjoining Semitic regions.

On the whole, the Babylonian story seems . . . . . been widely spread through Christian and . . . . medan influence.

If, among the many other diluvial traditions which we have passed in review, we look about for evidence of derivation from a common source, and therefore of diffusion from a single centre, we cannot fail to be struck by the manifest tokens of such derivation and diffusion in the Algonquin stories of North America.[3] The many flood legends recorded among different tribes of that widely spread stock resemble each other so closely that we cannot but regard them as mere variations of one and the same tradition. Whether

Wide . . . . . on . . . . . of the Algonquin story in North America.

[1] The theory of the dependence of the Indian on the Babylonian legend was maintained by Eugène Bournouf and François Lenormant (*Les Origines de l'Histoire d'après la Bible : De la Création de l'Homme au Déluge*, Paris, 1880, pp. 423 *sqq.*) and more recently by M. Winternitz (*Die Flutsagen*, pp. 327 *sq.*). Professor H. Oldenberg also inclines to it (*Die Literatur des Alten Indien*, Stuttgart and Berlin, 1903, p. 47). On the other hand the theory was rejected by F. Max Muller (*India, what can it teach us ?* London, 1892,

pp. 133 *sqq.*) and more hesitatingly by R. Andree (*Die Flutsagen*, pp. 17 *sqq.*).

[2] For traces of the legend, in its Christian form, among barbarous and savage tribes see above, p. 195 (Kamars), p. 223 (Minahassans), pp. 245 *sq.* (Hawaiians), pp. 265 *sq.* (Macusis), pp. 275 *sq.* (Michoacan Indians), p. 280 (Cora Indians), p. 297 (Cree Indians), p. 312 (Tinneh Indians), pp. 328 *sq.* (Eskimo), pp. 330 *sq.* (Masai).

[3] Above, pp. 295 *sqq.*

in the original story the incident of the various animals
diving into the water to fetch up earth is native or based
on a reminiscence of the birds in the Noachian story, which
has reached the Indians through white men, may be open to
question,

Evidence of
ffus
in South
America

Polynesia

Further, we have seen that according to Humboldt a
general resemblance may be traced between the diluvial
traditions among the Indians of the Orinoco,[1] and that
according to William Ellis a like resemblance prevails among
the Polynesian legends.[2]   It may be that in both these regions
the traditions have spread from local centres, in other words,
that they are variations of a common original.

Independ-
e t   uge
legends.

But when we have made allowance for all such cases of
diffusion from local centres, it seems probable that there still
remain deluge legends which have originated independently.

§ 19. *The Origin of Stories of a Great Flood*

The old
 e   a
universal
deluge was
 p   te1
by the
evidence
of marine
fossils
found
inland.

We have still to ask, What was the origin of diluvial
traditions ? how did men come so commonly to believe that
at some time or other the earth, or at all events the whole
inhabited portion of it, had been submerged under the waters
of a mighty flood in which almost the entire human race
perished ?   The old answer to the question was that such a
catastrophe actually occurred, that we have a full and authentic
record of it in the Book of Genesis, and that the many
legends of a great flood which we find scattered so widely
among mankind embody the more or less imperfect, confused
and distorted reminiscences of that tremendous cataclysm.[8]
A favourite argument in support of this view was drawn from
marine shells and fossils, which were supposed to have been
left high and dry in deserts and on mountain-tops by the
retiring waters of the Noachian deluge.   Sea-shells found
on mountains were adduced by Tertullian as evidence that
the waters had once covered the earth, though he did

---

[1] Above, p. 266.

[2] Above, pp. 241 *sq*.

[3] This, for example, was the view
of the Scotch geologist Hugh Miller,
though he rejected the theory of a

universal deluge, preferring to suppose
that the flood covered the limited area
to wh'ch the human race had then
spread.   See his book, *The Testimony
of the Rocks* (Edinburgh, 1857), pp.
267 *sqq*.

not expressly associate them with the flood recorded in Genesis.[1] When excavations made in 1517, for repairing the city of Verona, brought to light a multitude of curious petrifactions, the discovery gave rise to much speculation, in which Noah and the ark of course figured conspicuously. Yet they were not allowed to pass unchallenged; for a philosophical Italian naturalist, Fracastoro, was bold enough to point out difficulties in the popular hypothesis. "That inundation, he observed, was too transient: it consisted principally of fluviatile waters; and if it had transported shells to great distances, must have strewed them over the surface, not buried them at vast depths in the interior of mountains. His clear exposition of the evidence would have terminated the discussion for ever, if the passions of mankind had not been enlisted in the dispute."[2] Towards the end of the seventeenth century the field of geology was invaded by an army of theologians, recruited in Italy, Germany, France, and England, who darkened counsel and left confusion worse confounded. "Henceforward, they who refused to subscribe to the position, that all marine organic remains were proofs of the Mosaic deluge, were exposed to the imputation of disbelieving the whole of the sacred writings. Scarcely any step had been made in approximating to sound theories since the time of Fracastoro, more than a hundred years having been lost, in writing down the dogma that organised fossils were mere sports of nature. An additional period of a century and a half was now destined to be consumed in exploding the hypothesis, that organised fossils had all been buried in the solid strata by Noah's flood. Never did a theoretical fallacy, in any branch of science, interfere more seriously with accurate observation and the systematic classification of facts. In recent times, we may attribute our rapid progress chiefly to the careful determination of the order of succession in mineral masses, by means of their different organic contents, and their regular superposition. But the old diluvialists were induced by their

The theory propounded by the Italian naturalist Fracastoro.

Long prevalence of the diluvial theory of fossil deposits.

---

[1] Tertullian, *De Pallio*, 2, "*Mutavit et totus orbis aliquando, aquis omnibus obsitus: adhuc maris conchae et buccinae peregrinantur in montibus, cupientes Platoni probare etiam ardua fluitasse.*"

[2] Sir Charles Lyell, *The Principles of Geology*, Twelfth Edition (London, 1875), i. 31.

system to confound all the groups of strata together, referring all appearances to one cause and to one brief period, not to a variety of causes acting throughout a long succession of epochs. They saw the phenomena only, as they desired to see them, sometimes misrepresenting facts, and at other times deducing false conclusions from correct data. In short, a sketch of the progress of geology, from the close of the seventeenth to the end of the eighteenth century, is the history of a constant and violent struggle of new opinions against doctrines sanctioned by the implicit faith of many generations, and supposed to rest on scriptural authority."[1]

Survivals of the theory of a universal deluge among geologists in the nineteenth century.

The error thus stigmatized by Sir Charles Lyell died hard. Less than a century ago, when William Buckland was appointed Reader in Geology at Oxford, he could still assure his hearers, in his inaugural address to the University, that "the grand fact of an universal deluge at no very remote period is proved on grounds so decisive and incontrovertible, that had we never heard of such an event from Scripture or any other Authority, Geology of itself must have called in the assistance of some such catastrophe to explain the phenomena of diluvial action."[2] And within our own lifetime another eminent geologist wrote and published as follows : " I have long thought that the narrative in Genesis vii. and viii. can be understood only on the supposition that it is a contemporary journal or log of an eye-witness incorporated by the author of Genesis in his work. The dates of the rising and fall of the water, the note of soundings over the hill-tops when the maximum was attained, and many other details, as well as the whole tone of the narrative, seem to require this supposition, which also removes all the difficulties of interpretation which have been so much felt."[3] But if the story of the flood in Genesis is the contemporary log-book of an eye-witness, how are we to explain the remarkable discrepancies it contains with regard to the duration of the flood and the number of the animals admitted to the ark ? Such a theory, far from solving the difficulties that beset the narrative, would on

[1] Sir Charles Lyell, *Principles of Geology*, Twelfth Edition, i. 37 *sq.*

[2] Quoted by W. J. Sollas, *The Age of the Earth* (London, 1905), p. 244.

[3] (Sir) John William Dawson, *The Story of the Earth and Man*, Sixth Edition (London, 1880), p. 290 note *.

the contrary render them altogether inexplicable, except on a supposition alike injurious and unjust either to the veracity or to the sobriety of the narrator.[1]

Nor need we linger long over another explanation of flood stories which has of late years enjoyed a good deal of popularity in Germany. On this view the story of the flood has really nothing to do with water or an ark ; it is a myth relating to the sun or the moon or the stars, or all three of

---

[1] In a later work (*The Meeting Place of Geology and History*, Second Edition, London, 1895, pp. 121 *sqq.*) Sir J. W. Dawson still attempted to maintain the literal accuracy of the narrative in Genesis, supporting it by what he represented as the testimony of geology. On this it may suffice to quote the observations of the late Professor S. R. Driver (*The Book of Genesis*, Tenth Edition, p. 103 note [1]) : " Sir J. W. Dawson, in his *Meeting Place of Geology and History* (1894), extending, as it seems, this theory of Professor Prestwich, speaks very confidently (pp. 88 f., 130, 148 f., 154 f., 204, 205) of a great submergence, and accompanying ' diluvial catastrophe,' which took place shortly after the close of the glacial period, and destroyed palaeolithic man, and which is identified by him (pp. 155, 205) with the Deluge of Noah. An eminent English geologist, Canon T. G. Bonney, Emeritus Professor of Geology at University College, London, and an ex-President of the Geological Society, who has examined Sir J. W. Dawson's arguments, permits me, however, to say that he considers this identification to be altogether untenable : he is aware of no evidence showing that ' a vast region ' of either Europe or Asia was submerged at the age spoken of ; and even supposing that it were so submerged, the flood thus produced would be many thousand years before the time at which, according to the Biblical chronology, the Deluge will have taken place. He adds that he is acquainted with no geological indications favouring the supposition that a submergence, embracing certainly Asia, and including in particular Armenia (the ' mountains of Ararat '), and causing great destruc-

tion of animal life, took place at *c.* B.C. 2500 or 3000." The theory of Sir Joseph Prestwich, to which Professor S. R. Driver here refers, was that long after the appearance of palaeolithic man a great part of western, central, and southern Europe, and portions of northern Africa were temporarily submerged, and that in the vast inundation, which he supposes to have been of short duration, some species of animals (as the hippopotamus in Sicily) became extinct in the regions which they formerly inhabited. The geological evidence on which Sir Joseph Prestwich based his theory consisted of the wide diffusion of what he called " rubble drift " and the deposit of fine earth known as loess, together with the discovery of many bones of heterogeneous animals accumulated on heights or in caves and crevices, to which, on his view, the animals either fled for refuge from the rising flood or were swept after death by the retiring waters. To this temporary submergence of a considerable part of the Old World he would refer the Biblical story of the flood and similar traditions. See (Sir) Joseph Prestwich, *On Certain Phenomena belonging to the Close of the Last Geological Period and on their Bearing upon the Tradition of the Flood* (London, 1895). The theory has been examined and rejected by the Rev. Professor T. G. Bonney, who concludes his examination with the words : " The idea of a universal deluge, or even of closely connected but local deluges on a large scale, cannot, I think, claim any real support from geology." See T. G. Bonney, "Science and the Flood," *The Expositor*, June 1903, pp. 456-472.

them together ; for the learned men who have made this surprising discovery, while they are united in rejecting the vulgar terrestrial interpretation, are by no means agreed among themselves as to all the niceties of their high celestial theory.   Some of them will have it that the ark is the sun ; [1] another thinks that the ark was the moon, that the pitch with which it was caulked is a figurative expression for a lunar eclipse ; and that by the three stories in which the vessel was built we must understand the phases of the lunar orb.[2]   The latest advocate of the lunar theory seeks to reconcile all contradictions in a higher unity by embarking the human passengers on board the moon, while he leaves the animals to do the best they can for themselves among the stars.[3]   It would be doing such learned absurdities too much honour to discuss them seriously.   I have noticed them only for the sake of the hilarity with which they are calculated to relieve the tedium of a grave and prolonged discussion.

The testimony of geology is opposed to the theory that our planet has ever been covered with water during the period of man's residence on earth.

But when we have dismissed these fancies to their appropriate limbo, we are still confronted with the question of the origin of diluvial traditions.   Are they true or false? Did the flood, which the stories so persistently describe, really happen or did it not ?   Now so far as the narratives speak of floods which covered the whole world, submerging even the highest mountains and drowning almost all men and

[1] H. Usener, *Die Sintflutsagen* (Bonn, 1899); *id.*, "Zu den Sintflutsagen," *Kleine Schriften*, iv. (1913) pp. 382-398 ; H. Zimmern and T. K. Cheyne, in *Encyclopaedia Biblica, s.v.* "Deluge," vol. i. coll. 1058 *sq.*, 1063 *sq.* ; H. Zimmern, in E. Schrader's *Die Keilinschriften und das Alte Testament* (Berlin, 1902), pp. 555 *sq.*   The solar theory of diluvial traditions appears to have been first broached by a German scholar Schirren in a work called *Wanderungen der Neuseelander*, published in 1856, which I have not seen.   Compare G. Gerland, in Th. Waitz's *Anthropologie der Naturvölker*, vi. (Lei 1872), pp. 270 *sqq.*   So far as I am aware, the late Professor T. K. Cheyne is the only English scholar who has interpreted the deluge legend as a solar

myth.
[2] E. Boklen, "Die Sintflutsage," *Archiv fur Religionswissenschaft*, vi. (1903) pp. 1-61, 97-150.
[3] G. Gerland, *Der Mythus von der Sintflut* (Bonn, 1912), pp. 117 *sqq.* This work contains the ripe result of the author's reflection after many years of incubation.   In an earlier and less mature work he seems to have shipped Noah on board the sun and his wife on board the moon, while he distributed Shem, Ham, and Japhet and their wives, somewhat at haphazard, among the stars.   See his exposition in Th. Waitz's *Anthropologie der Naturvölker*, vi. (Leipsic, 1872) pp. 269 *sqq.*   But Professor Gerland expresses himself in both his works so indistinctly that I cannot feel sure of having grasped his meaning correctly.

animals, we may pronounce with some confidence that they are false ; for, if the best accredited testimony of modern geology can be trusted, no such cataclysm has befallen the earth during the period of man's abode on it. Whether, as some philosophers suppose, a universal ocean covered the whole surface of our planet long before man had appeared upon it, is quite a different question. Leibnitz, for example, imagined the earth " to have been originally a burning luminous mass, which ever since its creation has been undergoing refrigeration. When the outer crust had cooled down sufficiently to allow the vapours to be condensed, they fell, and formed a universal ocean, covering the loftiest mountains, and investing the whole globe." [1] A similar view of a universal primeval ocean, formed by the condensation of aqueous vapour .while the originally molten matter of the planet gradually lost its heat, follows almost necessarily from the celebrated Nebular Hypothesis as to the origin of the stellar universe, which was first propounded by Kant and afterwards developed by Laplace.[2] Lamarck, too, " was deeply impressed with a belief prevalent amongst the older naturalists that the primeval ocean invested the whole planet long after it became the habitation of living beings." [3] But such speculations, even if they might have occurred to primitive man, are to be clearly distinguished from stories of a deluge which destroyed the majority of mankind, for these stories presuppose the existence of the human race on the earth and therefore can hardly refer to a time earlier than the Pleistocene period.[4]

But though stories of such tremendous cataclysms are almost certainly fabulous, it is possible and indeed probable that under a mythical husk many of them may hide a kernel of truth ; that is, they may contain reminiscences of inundations which really overtook particular districts, but which in passing through the medium of popular tradition have been

Philosophical theories

universal primeval ocean before the appearance of man.

Many of these floods may contain reminiscences of real, but not universal, inundations.

---

[1] Sir Charles Lyell, *Principles of Geology*, Twelfth Edition, i. 39.

[2] T. H. Huxley, " Geological form," *Collected Essays*, iv. 320 *sqq.* ; (Sir) J. W. Dawson, *The Story of the Earth and Man* [6] (London, 1880), pp. 4, 8, 12, 14 *sq.*, 17. On this hypothesis, the universal ocean of water would seem to have been preceded by a universal ocean of boiling lava. See W. J. Sollas, *The Age of the Earth* (London, 1905), pp. 5 *sq.*

[3] Sir Charles Lyell' *Principles of Geology*, Twelfth Edition, ii. 256.

[4] See above, p. 169.

Many
ns n es
of memor-
able floods
in Holland.

The origin
Zuyder Zee

magnified into world-wide catastrophes. The records of the past abound in instances of great floods which have spread havoc far and wide ; and it would be strange indeed if the memory of some of them did not long persist among the descendants of the generation which experienced them. For examples of such disastrous deluges we need go no farther than the neighbouring country of Holland, which has suffered from them again and again. In the thirteenth century "the low lands along the Vlie, often threatened, at last sank in the waves. The German Ocean rolled in upon the inland Lake of Flevo. The stormy Zuyder Zee began its existence by engulfing thousands of Frisian villages, with all their population, and by spreading a chasm between kindred peoples. The political, as well as the geographical, continuity of the land was obliterated by this tremendous deluge. The Hollanders were cut off from their relatives in the east by as dangerous a sea as that which divided them from their Anglo-Saxon brethren in Britain."[1] Again, early in the sixteenth century, a tempest blowing from the north, drove the waters of the ocean on the low coast of Zealand more rapidly than they could be carried off through the Straits of Dover. The dykes of South Beveland burst, the sea swept over the land, hundreds of villages were overwhelmed, and a tract of country, torn from the province, was buried beneath the waves. South Beveland became an island, and the stretch of water which divides it from the continent has ever since been known as "the Drowned Land." Yet at low tide the estuary so formed can be forded by seafaring men who know the ground. During the rebellion which won for Holland its national independence, a column of Spanish troops, led by a daring officer, Colonel Mondragon, waded across the ford by night, with the water breast high, and relieved a garrison which was beleagured by the rebels in the city of Tergoes.[2]

The great
flood of
1570 in
Holland.

Again, "towards the end of the year 1570, still another and a terrible misfortune descended upon the Netherlands. An inundation, more tremendous than any which had yet

[1] J. L. Motley, *The Rise of the Dutch Republic, Historical Introduction*, vi. vol. i. p. 35 (London, 1913).

[2] J. L. Motley, *The Rise of the Dutch Republic*, Part iii. chap. viii. vol. ii. pp. 374 *sqq.* (London, 1913).

been recorded in those annals so prolific in such catastrophes, now swept the whole coast from Flanders to Friesland. Not the memorable deluge of the thirteenth century, out of which the Zuyder Zee was born ; not that in which the waters of the Dollart had closed for ever over the villages and churches of Groningen ; not one of those perpetually recurring floods by which the inhabitants of the Netherlands, year after year, were recalled to an anxious remembrance of the watery chaos out of which their fatherland had been created, and into which it was in daily danger of resolving itself again, had excited so much terror and caused so much destruction. A continued and violent gale from the north-west had long been sweeping the Atlantic waters into the North Sea, and had now piled them upon the fragile coasts of the provinces. The dykes, tasked beyond their strength, burst in every direction. The cities of Flanders, to a considerable distance inland, were suddenly invaded by the waters of the ocean. The whole narrow peninsula of North Holland was in imminent danger of being swept away for ever. Between Amsterdam and Meyden, the great Diemer dyke was broken through in twelve places. The Hand-bos, a bulwark formed of oaken piles, fastened with metal clamps, moored with iron anchors, and secured by gravel and granite, was snapped to pieces like packthread. The 'Sleeper,' a dyke thus called, because it was usually left in repose by the elements, except in great emergencies, alone held firm, and prevented the consummation of the catastrophe. Still the ocean poured in upon the land with terrible fury. Dort, Rotterdam, and many other cities were, for a time, almost submerged. Along the coast, fishing vessels, and even ships of larger size, were floated up into the country, where they entangled themselves in groves and orchards, or beat to pieces the roofs and walls of houses. The destruction of life and of property was enormous throughout the maritime provinces, but in Friesland the desolation was complete. There nearly all the dykes and sluices were dashed to fragments ; the country, far and wide, converted into an angry sea. The steeples and towers of inland cities became islands of the ocean. Thousands of human beings were swept out of existence in a few hours. Whole districts of territory, with all their villages, farms and churches, were rent from their places, borne along by the force of the waves, sometimes to be lodged in another part of the country, sometimes to be entirely engulfed. Multitudes of men, women, children, of horses, oxen, sheep, and every domestic animal, were struggling in the waves in every direction. Every boat, and every article which could serve as a boat, were eagerly seized upon. Every house was inundated ; even the graveyards gave up their dead. The living infant in his cradle, and the long-buried corpse in his coffin, floated side by side. The ancient flood seemed about to be renewed. Everywhere, upon the tops of trees, upon the steeples of churches, human beings were clustered, praying to God for mercy, and to their fellow-men for assistance. As the storm at last was subsiding, boats began to ply in every direction, saving those who were still struggling in the water, picking fugitives from roofs and tree-tops, and collecting the bodies of those already drowned. Colonel Robles, Seigneur de Billy, formerly much hated for his Spanish or Portuguese blood, made himself very active in this humane work. By his exertions, and those of the troops belonging to Groningen, many lives were rescued, and gratitude replaced the ancient animosity. It was estimated that at least twenty thousand persons were destroyed in the province of Friesland alone. Throughout the Netherlands, one hundred thousand persons perished. The damage done to property, the number of animals engulfed in the sea, were almost incalculable." [1]

In many ste flood is said to have bee ause by the rising of the sea. Such tales are common in the Pacific, where earthquake-waves are wn to be very destructive

On these and other occasions the floods which have laid great tracts of Holland under water have been caused, not by heavy rains, but by risings of the sea. Now it is to be observed that in not a few diluvial traditions the cause alleged for the deluge is in like manner not the fall of rain but an incursion of the ocean. Thus we have found a rising of the sea assigned as the cause of the flood by the natives of the islands of Nias,[2] Engano,[3] Rotti,[4] Formosa,[5] Tahiti,[6] Hawaii,[7]

[1] J. L. Motley, *The Rise of the Dutch Republic*, Part iii. chap. v. vol. II. pp. 285-287. These events took place on the first and second of November 1570. So short a time sufficed to cause so great a ruin.

[2] Above, p. 219.
[3] Above, p. 219.
[4] Above, p. 223.
[5] Above, p. 227.
[6] Above, pp. 242 *sqq.*
[7] Above, p. 245.

Rakaanga,[1] and the Pelew Islands,[2] by Indian tribes on the west coast of America from Tierra del Fuego in the south to Alaska in the north,[3] and by Eskimo on the shores of the Arctic Ocean.[4] The occurrence of such stories far and wide on the coasts and among the islands of the Pacific is very significant, for that ocean is subject from time to time to great earthquake-waves, which have often inundated the very coasts and islands where stories of great floods caused by the rising of the sea are told. Are we not allowed, nay compelled, to trace some at least of these stories to these inundations as their true cause? All the probabilities seem to be in favour of a causal rather than of an accidental connexion between the two things.

To take instances of such earthquake-waves in the Pacific, we may notice the dreadful calamities which have repeatedly overtaken Callao, the seaport of Lima in Peru. One of the most fearful of which we have any account happened on the 20th of October 1687. The earthquake "began at four in the morning, with the destruction of several publick edifices and houses, whereby great numbers of persons perished; but this was little more than a presage of what was to follow, and preserved the greatest part of the inhabitants from being buried under the ruins of the city. The shock was repeated at six in the morning with such impetuous concussions, that whatever had withstood the first, was now laid in ruins; and the inhabitants thought themselves very fortunate in being only spectators of the general devastation from the streets and squares, to which they had directed their flight on the first warning. During this second concussion the sea retired considerably from its bounds, and returning in mountainous waves, totally overwhelmed Callao, and the neighbouring parts, together with the miserable inhabitants."[5] The same wave which submerged the city carried ships a league into the country, and drowned man and beast for fifty leagues along the shore.[6]

Great ke waves at Callao in 1687.

---

[1] Above, p. 249.
[2] Above, p. 253.
[3] Above, pp. 262, 270, 271, 273, 288, 313 *sq.*, 317 *sq.*, 320, 327.
[4] Above, p. 327.
[5] Don George Juan and Don Antonio de Ulloa, *Voyage to South America*, translated from the original Spanish by John Adams, Fifth Edition (London, 1807), ii. 82.

[6] Sir Charles Lyell, *The Principles of Geology*, Twelfth Edition (London, 1875), ii. 157.

Again, on the 28th of October 1746, Callao was over-whelmed by another earthquake and another sea-wave. " At half an hour after ten at night, five hours and three quarters before the full of the moon, the concussions began with such violence, that in little more than three minutes, the greatest part, if not all the buildings, great and small, in the whole city, were destroyed, burying under their ruins those inhabit-ants who had not made sufficient haste into the streets and squares; the only places of safety in these terrible con-vulsions of nature. At length the horrible effects of this shock ceased : but the tranquillity was of short duration ; concussions returning with such frequent repetitions, that the inhabitants, according to the account sent of it, computed two hundred in the first twenty-four hours. . . . The fort of Callao, at the very same hour, sunk into the like ruins ; but what it suffered from the earthquake in its buildings, was inconsiderable, when compared with the terrible catastrophe which followed ; for the sea, as is usual on such occasions, receding to a considerable distance, returned in mountainous waves foaming with the violence of the agitation, and sud-denly turned Callao, and the neighbouring country, into a sea. This was not, however, totally performed by the first swell of the waves ; for the sea retiring further, returned with still more impetuosity ; the stupendous water covering both the walls and other buildings of the place ; so that whatever had escaped the first, was now totally overwhelmed by those terrible mountains of waves ; and nothing remained except a piece of the wall of the fort of Santa Cruz, as a memorial of this terrible devastation. There were then twenty-three ships and vessels, great and small, in the harbour, of which nineteen were absolutely sunk, and the other four, among which was a frigate called *St. Fermin*, carried by the force of the waves to a great distance up the country. This terrible inundation extended to other ports on the coast, as Cavallos and Guanape ; and the towns of Chancay, Guara, and the valleys della Baranca, Sape, and Pativilca, underwent the same fate as the city of Lima. The number of persons who perished in the ruin of that city, before the 31st of the same month of October, according to the bodies found, amounted to 1300, besides the maimed and wounded, many of which lived only a short time in torture. At Callao, where the number of inhabitants amounted to about 4000, two hundred only escaped ; and twenty-two of these by means of the above-mentioned fragment of a wall. According to an account sent to Lima after this accident, a volcano in Lucanas burst forth the same night and ejected such quantities of water, that the whole country was overflowed ; and in the mountain near Patas, called Conversiones de Caxamarquilla, three other volcanoes burst, discharging frightful torrents of water."[1] From the last part of the foregoing account it appears that a flood of water may be caused by the eruption of a volcano alone.

More recent observations have proved that the oceanic disturbances set up by great earthquakes are not necessarily limited to a short stretch of coast, but that they may be propagated in the form of huge waves across the whole breadth of the Pacific. For example, on the 23rd of December 1854, Simoda in Japan was devastated by an earthquake, and the waves to which it gave rise crossed the North Pacific Ocean and broke on the coast of California. Again, a violent shock of earthquake occurred near Arica, on the coast of Peru, on the 13th of August 1868, and the agitation which it created in the sea was felt north and south along the west coast of America ; the waves rose in wild turmoil for several days about the Sandwich Islands, and broke on the Samoan Islands, the east coast of Australia, New Zealand, and the Chatham Islands. The French frigate *Neréide*, bound at the time for Cape Horn, encountered in latitude 51° S. great packs of jagged icebergs, freshly broken off, which the mighty flood had set free as it penetrated beneath the Antarctic ice. Again, during the earthquake which befell Iquique in Peru on the 9th of May 1877, the Pacific Ocean rose in great waves on the opposite coast from Kamtchatka and Japan in the north to New Zealand and the Chatham Islands in the south. At the Samoan Islands the waves were from six to twelve feet high ; in Japan the sea rose and fell from five to ten feet ; in New Zealand the waves varied from three to

These earthquake waves are sometimes propagated over very wide areas Pacific.

---

[1] Ulloa, *Voyage to South America*, translated by John Adams, Fifth Edition (London, 1807), ii. 83 *sq.*

twenty feet in height.[1]   Indeed, on the coasts of South America and Japan these earthquake waves are often more destructive and therefore more dreaded than the earthquakes themselves.[2]   In Japan, which is subject to very frequent movements of the earth, regular calendars of earthquakes are kept, and from them we learn that the eastern coasts of the country have often been devastated by sea waves which have carried off from one thousand to one hundred thousand of the people.   On the night of 15th June 1896, for example, such a wave swept over the north-west coast of Nipon for a length of seventy miles, causing a loss of nearly thirty thousand lives.   At one place four steamers were carried inland, whilst a hundred and seventy-six vessels of various sorts lined the foot of the hills.   Indeed, the ancient capital of Japan, which once numbered a million of inhabitants and included the palace of a Shogun, had to be abandoned in consequence of the inundations which broke over it from the sea in the years 1369 and 1494.   The site is now occupied by the quiet village of Kamakura, sheltered by sand dunes and crooked pines.   Only a gigantic bronze image of Buddha, fifty feet high, cast more than six centuries ago, rises in solemn majesty and peace to attest the grandeur that has passed away.[3]

In the Pacific native traditions of floods may often embody reminiscences of the devas- caused by earthquake waves.

On coasts where the shock of an earthquake is commonly accompanied or followed by an inroad of the sea, it is natural that the first impulse of the natives, on feeling the concussion, should be to take refuge on a height where they may be safe from the dreaded rush of the water.[4]   Now we have seen that the Araucanian Indians of Chili, who have a tradition of a great deluge and fear a repetition of the disaster, fly for safety to a mountain when they feel a violent shock of earthquake ;[5] and that the Fijians, who have likewise a tradition

[1] Eduard Suess, *The Face of the Earth*, translated by Hertha B. Sollas, i. (Oxford, 1904) pp. 18 *sq.* ; John Milne, *Earthquakes and other Earth Movements* (London, 1886), pp. 168-170.

[2] J. Milne, *Earthquakes and other Earth Movements*, p. 166 ; *id.*, *Seismology* (London, 1898), p. 191.

[3] J. Milne, *Seismology*, pp. 191-193.

[4] "The first movement which is usually observed is a drawing back of the waters, and this is so well known to precede the inrush of large waves, that many of the inhabitants in South America have used it as a timely warning to escape towards the hills and save themselves from the terrible reaction which, on more than one occasion, has so quickly followed" (J. Milne, *Earthquakes and other Earth Movements*, p. 166).

[5] Above, p. 262.

of a calamitous flood, used to keep canoes in readiness against the recurrence of a similar inundation.[1] Taking all these facts into account we may accept as reasonable and probable the explanation which the distinguished American ethnologist, Horatio Hale, gave of the Fijian tradition of a deluge. Commenting on the statement that the Fijians formerly kept canoes ready against a repetition of the flood, he writes as follows :—

"This statement (which we heard from others in the same terms) may induce us to inquire whether there might not have been some occurrence in the actual history of the islands to give rise to this tradition, and the custom here mentioned. On the 7th of November 1837, the Pacific Ocean was traversed from east to west by an immense wave, which, taking its rise with the shock of an earthquake in Chili, was felt as far as the Bonin Islands. At the Sandwich Islands, according to the account given by Mr. Jarvis in his History, p. 21, the water rose, on the east coast of Hawaii, twenty feet above high-water mark, inundated the low lands, swept away several villages, and destroyed many lives. Similar undulations have been experienced at these islands on several occasions. If we suppose (what is no way improbable) that, at some time within the last three or four thousand years, a wave of twice this height crossed the ocean, and swept over the Vitian [Fijian] Islands, it must have submerged the whole alluvial plain on the east side of Viti-levu, the most populous part of the group. Multitudes would no doubt be destroyed. Others would escape in their canoes, and as Mbengga is a mountainous island, in the neighbourhood of this district, it would naturally be the place of refuge for many."[2]

A similar explanation would obviously apply to the other legends of a great flood recorded in the islands of the Pacific, for all these islands have probably suffered in like manner from the invasion of huge earthquake-waves.[3] At

(margin) A similar explanation may apply to other flood stories in the Pacific.

---

[1] Above, p. 240. However, it is to be observed that the cause assigned by the Fijians for the flood seems to have been heavy rain rather than a rising of the sea.

[2] Horatio Hale, *United States Exploring Expedition, Ethnography and Philology* (Philadelphia, 1846), p. 55.

[3] This is the view also of the eminent Austrian geologist, Professor E. Suess. He says, "That accounts of great floods should be met with even in the most remote islands is, I think, rendered easily intelligible by the information concerning seismic sea-waves which has been collected within the last

least, in the present state of our knowledge, it seems safer to accept provisionally the view of the eminent American ethnologist than to adopt the theory of an eminent German ethnologist, who would explain all these Polynesian traditions as solar, lunar, and stellar myths.[1]

Other flood   If some of the traditions of a great flood caused by a
may
embody   rising of the sea may thus rest on an historical basis, there
reminis-   can be no reason why some of the traditions of a great flood
of real   caused by heavy rain should not be equally well founded.
inundations   Here in England we who live in flat parts of the country
y
heavy rain.   are familiar with local floods produced by this cause; not
many years ago, for example, large tracts of Norfolk, including the city of Norwich, were laid under water by a sudden
and violent fall of rain, resembling a cloudburst.   A similar
cause inundated the low-lying parts of Paris a few years ago,
creating anxiety and alarm not only among the inhabitants,
but among the friends of the beautiful city in all parts of
the world.   It is easy to understand how among an ignorant
and unlettered population, whose intellectual horizon hardly
extends beyond the limits of their vision, the memory of a
similar catastrophe, orally transmitted, might in the course
of a few generations grow into the legend of a universal
deluge, from which only a handful of favoured individuals
had contrived in one way or another to escape.   Even the
tradition of a purely local flood, in which many people had
been drowned, might unconsciously be exaggerated into vast
dimensions by a European settler or traveller, who received
it from savages and interpreted it in the light of the Noachian
deluge, with which he himself had been familiar from childhood.   For instance, we have seen that stories of a great
flood are reported to be told by the Indians of Guiana.   On
this subject it is well to bear in mind the caution given us
by Sir Everard F. Im Thurn, who knows these Indians well.
" The calamity to which an Indian is perhaps most exposed
is to be driven from his home by a sudden rise in the river

decade or so. In some of these traditions it is expressly stated that the flood
was produced by the sea. Such seismic
floods are, according to our present
knowledge, only likely to occur in the
case of islands, of low-lying coast-land,

and of the lower parts of great river
valleys " (*The Face of the Earth*, i.
20).
    [1] G. Gerland, in Th. Waitz's *Anthro-
pologie der Naturvölker*, vi. (Leipsic,
1872) pp. 269 *sqq.*

and consequent flooding of the whole forest. His way to escape is to get into his canoe with his family and his live stock, and to seek temporarily some higher ground, or, as sometimes happens, if none such can be found, the whole party lives as best they may in the canoe until the waters disappear from the face of the earth. It is well known how in all countries the proverbial ' oldest inhabitant ' remembers and tells of the highest flood that ever happened. When therefore the Indian tells in his simple language the tradition of the highest flood which covered all the small world known to him, and tells how the Indians escaped it, it is not difficult to realise that the European hearer, theologically prejudiced in favour of Noah, his flood, and his ark, is apt to identify the two stories with each other, and with many similar stories from many parts of the world." [1]

In this manner it has been proposed to explain the Babylonian and Hebrew traditions of a great flood by the inundations to which the lower valley of the Euphrates and Tigris is annually exposed by the heavy rains and melting snows in the mountains of Armenia. " The basis of the story," we are told, " is the yearly phenomenon of the rainy and stormy season which lasts in Babylonia for several months and during which time whole districts in the Euphrates Valley are submerged. Great havoc was caused by the rains and storms until the perfection of canal systems regulated the overflow of the Euphrates and Tigris, when what had been a curse was converted into a blessing and brought about that astonishing fertility for which Babylonia became famous. The Hebrew story of the Deluge recalls a particularly destructive season that had made a profound impression, and the comparison with the parallel story found on clay tablets of Ashurbanapal's library confirms this view of the local setting of the tale." [2]

On this hypothesis, the great flood was brought about, by an unusually heavy fall of rain and snow ; [3] it was only

The Babylonian and Hebrew traditions of a great flood have been thus explained

This view accords with the alleged cause of the flood.

---

[1] (Sir) Everard F. Im Thurn, *Among the Indians of Guiana* (London, 1883), p. 375.

M. Jastrow, *Hebrew and Babylonian Traditions* (London, 1914), pp. 37 *sq.* ; compare *id.*, pp. 322 *sq.*

[3] Sir Francis Younghusband has, from personal observation, suggested to me that the regularly recurring effects of rain and snow may have been accidentally aggravated by the bursting of a dam which had been

an extraordinary case, of an ordinary occurrence, and the widespread devastation which it wrought in the valley imprinted it indelibly on the memory of the survivors and of their descendants. In favour of this view it may be said that in the Babylonian and the oldest form of the Hebrew tradition the only alleged cause of the deluge is heavy rain.[1]

The theory is also supported by the annual inundations to which the valleys of the Euphrates and Tigris are still subject. The theory may also be supported by the dangerous inundations to which the country is still yearly liable through the action of the same natural causes. When Loftus, the first excavator of the ancient city of Erech, arrived in Baghdad, on the 5th of May 1849, he found the whole population in a state of the utmost apprehension and alarm. In consequence of the rapid melting of the snows on the Kurdish mountains, and the enormous influx of water from the Euphrates through the Seglawiyya canal, the Tigris had risen that spring to the unprecedented height of twenty-two and a half feet ; which was about five feet above its highest level in ordinary years and exceeded the great rise of 1831, when the river broke down the walls and destroyed no less than seven thousand dwellings in a single night, at a time when the plague was committing the most fearful ravages among the inhabitants. A few days before the arrival of the English party, the Turkish pasha of Baghdad had summoned the whole population, as one man, to guard against the general danger by raising a strong high mound completely round the walls. Mats of reeds were placed outside to bind the earth compactly together. The water was thus prevented from devastating the interior of the city, though it filtered through the fine alluvial soil and stood several feet deep in the cellars. Outside the city it reached to within two feet of the top of the bank. On the side of

---

formed by a landslip in the mountains. He writes : " In the Himalayas there is often a mountain slide which blocks up a river for some time and forms a lake till this temporary dam suddenly gives way and the pent-up waters rush down and cause a flood in the plains below. I have known the Indus rise 40 feet near Gilgit, at the back of Kashmir, through one of its tributaries having been blocked in this way, and then the plains of the Punjab were flooded. I thought a big mountain slip of this kind in the Armenian ranges might have caused the Flood, and the bursting of the dam might have coincided with heavy rains." His letter is dated Mill Cottage, Wimbledon Common, S.W., January 7th, 1917.

[1] Above, p. 139, and below, pp. 357 *sq.*

the river the houses alone, many of them very old and frail, prevented the ingress of the flood. It was a critical juncture. Men were stationed night and day to watch the barriers. If the dam or any of the foundations had failed, Baghdad must have been bodily washed away. Happily the pressure was withstood, and the inundation gradually subsided. The country on all sides for miles was under water, so that there was no possibility of proceeding beyond the dyke, except in the boats which were established as ferries to keep up communication across the flood. The city was for a time an island in a vast inland sea, and it was a full month before the inhabitants could ride beyond the walls. As the summer advanced, the evaporation from the stagnant water caused malaria to such an extent that, out of a population of seventy thousand, no less than twelve thousand died of fever.[1]

Similar inundations probably occurred in antiquity.

If the floods caused by the melting of the snow in the Armenian mountains can thus endanger the cities in the river valley down to modern times, it is reasonable to suppose that they did so in antiquity also, and that the Babylonian tradition of the destruction of the city of Shurippak in such an inundation may be well founded. It is true that the city appears to have ultimately perished by fire rather than by water;[2] but this is quite consistent with the supposition that at some earlier time it had been destroyed by a flood and afterwards rebuilt.

Yet Egypt, which similarly flooded every year, has no tradition of flood.

However, the theory which would explain the Babylonian and Hebrew tradition of a great flood by the inundations to which the country is annually exposed, may be combated by an argument drawn from the analogy of Egypt. For Egypt from time immemorial has been similarly subject to yearly inundations; yet it has never, so far as we know, either evolved a flood legend of its own or accepted the flood legend of its great Oriental rival. If annual floods sufficed to produce the legend in Babylonia, why, it may be asked, did not the same cause produce the same effect in Egypt?

To meet this difficulty a different explanation of the

[1] W. K. Loftus, *Travels and Researches in Chaldaea and Susiana* (London, 1857), pp. 7 *sq.*
[2] Above, p. 125.

Babylonian story has been put forward in recent years by an eminent geologist, Professor Eduard Suess of Vienna. Regarding the regular annual changes in the basin of the Euphrates as insufficient to account for the legend, he has recourse to irregular or catastrophic causes. He points out that "there are other peculiarities of the Euphrates valley which may occasionally tend to exacerbate the evils attendant on the inundations. It is very subject to seismic disturbances; and the ordinary consequences of a sharp earthquake shock might be seriously complicated by its effect on a broad sheet of water. Moreover the Indian Ocean lies within the region of typhoons; and if, at the height of an inundation, a hurricane from the south-east swept up the Persian Gulf, driving its shallow waters upon the delta and damming back the outflow, perhaps for hundreds of miles up-stream, a diluvial catastrophe, fairly up to the mark of Hasisadra's, might easily result."[1]

Thus Professor Suess would supplement and reinforce the comparatively slow and gentle pressure of rain by the sudden and violent shock of an earthquake and the bursting of a typhoon; and in support of these two catastrophic causes he appeals to two features in the Hebrew version of the flood story; or rather to one feature which actually occurs in that version, and to another which he would import into it by altering the text so as to suit his hypothesis. We will consider each of his arguments separately.

First, in regard to the earthquake, Professor Suess points out that in the Hebrew narrative one cause alleged for the deluge is the breaking out of subterranean waters.[2] "This rising of great quantities of water from the deep," he says, "is a phenomenon which is a characteristic accompaniment of earthquakes in the alluvial districts of great rivers. The subterranean water is contained in the recent deposits of the great plains on both sides of the stream, and its upper limit rises to right and left above the mean level of the river, its elevation increasing in proportion to the distance from the

Side notes: Suess's theory that the Babylonian ... caused or aggravated earthquake and a typhoon. / In support ... theory he appeals to ... tradition. / He ... that an earthquake caused sub- ter anean water to burst forth.

[1] T. H. Huxley, "Hasisadra's Adventure," *Collected Essays*, iv. 246 *sq.* Thus clearly and concisely does Huxley sum up the theory which Professor E. Suess expounds at great length in his work, *The Face of the Earth*, vol. i. (Oxford, 1904) pp. 17-72.

[2] Genesis vii. 11, viii. 2.

river. What lies beneath this limit is saturated and mobile ; the ground above it is dry and friable. When seismic oscillations occur in a district of this kind the brittle upper layer of the ground splits open in long clefts, and from these fissures the underground water, either clear or as a muddy mass, is violently ejected, sometimes in great volumes, sometimes in isolated jets several yards high."[1] For example, the young alluvial land about the Danube in Wallachia was rent by an earthquake in 1838, and from the fissures water spouted out in many places fathoms high. The same thing happened when the alluvial plain of the Mississippi, a little below the confluence of the Ohio, was convulsed by an earthquake in January 1812 : the water that had filled the subterranean cavities forced a passage for itself and blew up the earth with loud explosions, throwing up an enormous quantity of carbonized wood in jets from ten to fifteen feet high, while at the same time the surface of the ground sank, and a black liquid rose as high as a horse's belly. Again, in January 1862 a violent shock of earthquake affected the whole region south of Lake Baikal, and in particular the delta of the river Selenga which flows into the lake. In the town of Kudara the wooden lids of the fountains were shot into the air like corks from champagne bottles, and springs of tepid water rose in places to a height of more than twenty feet. So terrified were the Mongols that they caused the Lamas to perform ceremonies to appease the evil spirits which, as they imagined, were shaking the earth.[2]

Instances s cr outbursts of sub- n water during quakes.

On this it is to be observed that the reference to subterranean waters as one cause of the deluge occurs only in the Hebrew version of the legend, and even there it is found only in the later Priestly narrative : it does not occur in the earlier Jehovistic narrative, nor in the still earlier Babylonian version ;[3] nor, finally, is it found in the original Sumerian

But the to subterranean the Hebrew tradition seems to be a late addition.

[1] L. Suess, *The Face of the Earth*, i. 31.
[2] E. Suess, *The Face of the Earth*, i. 31 *sq.*
[3] Professor Suess, indeed, discovers a reference to subterranean waters in a passage of the Babylonian legend which, following Professor Paul Haupt, he translates "the Anunnaki caused floods to rise," supposing the Anunnaki to be "the spirits of the deep, of the great subterranean waters" (*The Face of the Earth*, i. 31). But the better translation of that passage seems to be "the Anunnaki lifted up flaming torches" (so P. Jensen, A. Jeremias, L. W.

legend from which both the Babylonian and the Hebrew stories are derived.   Accordingly it may be dismissed as a late addition to the legend on which it would be unsafe to build any hypothesis.

So much for the earthquake ; next for the typhoon, which Professor Suess would also extract from the Biblical narrative.   He supposes that while the valley of the Euphrates was still rocking under an earthquake, a great sea-wave, driven by a hurricane up the Persian Gulf, suddenly swept over the land, completing the destruction of the doomed cities and their miserable inhabitants.   This tremendous effect he produces very simply by altering the vowel-points of the Hebrew text in two passages so as to read " the flood from the sea " instead of " the flood of waters." [1]   The textual change, it is true, is very slight, for it extends only to the vowel-points and leaves the consonants unaffected.   But though the vowel-points form no part of the original text of the Scriptures, having been introduced into it not earlier than the sixth century of our era, they are not to be lightly altered, since they represent the traditional pronunciation of the sacred words, as it had been handed down with scrupulous care, generation after generation, by a guild of technically trained scholars, the Massorets, as they were called, who " devoted themselves to preserving not only the exact writing of the received consonantal text, but the exact pronunciation and even the musical cadence proper to every word of the sacred text, according to the rules of the synagogal chanting." [2]   Hence the proposed emendation in the two verses of Genesis has been rightly rejected by the

Suess's theory that the flood was ... ly caused by a typhoon

alteration of the Hebrew text, which is not accepted by scholars.

King, W. Muss-Arnolt, M. Jastrow, P. Dhorme, A. Ungnad, R. W. Rogers). See above, p. 115. Hence the reference must be to some phenomena not of water but of light, perhaps to flashes of lightning, as Jensen and Dhorme suggest. See P. Jensen, *Assyrisch-Babylonische Mythen und Epen*, p. 580 ; P. Dhorme, *Choix de Textes Religieux Assyro-Babyloniens*, p. 110.

[1] Genesis vi. 17 and vii. 6 reading םיִ for םִיַ (*miyam* for *mayim*).

[2] W. Robertson Smith, *The Old*

Testament in the Jewish Church, Second Edition (London and Edinburgh, 1892), p. 58.   As to the Massorets and their work, see W. R. Smith, *op. cit.* pp. 58-60.   On the other hand Renan, while he agreed as to the date of the introduction of the vowel-points, inclined to attribute their invention, not to the Massorets, but to a class of doctors called Saboreans, who resided in Babylonia rather than in Palestine. See E. R ., *Histoire Générale des Langues Sémitiques*, Première Partie [6] (Paris, 1878), pp. 170 *sq.*

best recent scholars,[1] and with it the appeal to the Hebrew text for evidence of the marine origin of the great flood must be dismissed as unfounded.

It does not of course follow that Professor Suess's theory is false because the arguments by which he supports it are feeble. Fortunately for the world many a sound conclusion is reached from inadequate or even totally irrelevant premises, otherwise it is to be feared that for most men the chances of ever arriving at the truth would be infinitesimal. If the Biblical narrative rests, as seems probable, on a basis of fact, it is quite possible that the great flood which it describes may actually have been produced by an earthquake or a typhoon, or by both combined. But the theory that it was so produced derives extremely little support from the only authorities open to us, the Hebrew, Babylonian, and Sumerian traditions ; hence it hardly amounts to more than a plausible conjecture. On a simple calculation of chances, it seems likely that the catastrophe was brought about by forces which are known to act regularly every year on the Euphrates valley, and to be quite capable of producing widespread inundations, rather than by assumed forces which, though certainly capable of causing disastrous floods, are not historically known to have ever done so in that region ; for, apart from the supposed references in Semitic tradition, I am aware of no record of a Babylonian deluge caused either by an earthquake-wave or by a typhoon.

On the whole, then, there seems to be good reason for thinking that some and probably many diluvial traditions are merely exaggerated reports of floods which actually occurred, whether as the result of heavy rain, earthquake-waves, or other causes. All such traditions, therefore, are partly legendary and partly mythical : so far as they preserve reminiscences of floods which really happened, they are legendary ; so far as they describe universal deluges which never happened, they are mythical. But in our survey of diluvial traditions we found some stories which appear to be

[marginal notes:] It seems more probable that the — ian flood was caused by — than by irregular and catastrophic causes.

Many diluv l traditions are exagger-ated reports a floods ; but others seem mythical.

---

[1] A. Dillmann, H. Gunkel, and J. Skinner, in their commentaries, explicitly ; S. R. Driver, W. H. Bennett, and H. E. Ryle, in their commentaries, implicitly. In his critical edition of the Hebrew text (*Biblia Hebraica*, Part i., Leipsic, 1905, p. 8) R. Kittel cuts the knot by rejecting the words מים as a gloss, thus eradicating the last trace of an argument for a typhoon.

purely mythical, that is, to describe inundations which never took place. Such, for example, are the Samothracian and Thessalian stories of great floods which the Greeks associated with the names of Dardanus and Deucalion. The Samothracian story is probably nothing but a false inference from the physical geography of the Black Sea and its outlets, the Bosphorus and Dardanelles : the Thessalian story is probably nothing but a false inference from the physical geography of the mountain-ringed Thessalian basin and its outlet, the gorge of Tempe.[1] In like manner the stories which describe the miraculous desiccation of the upland valleys of Cashmeer and Bogota are probably nothing but false inferences from the natural configuration of these mountain-girt basins.[2] Such stories, therefore, are not legendary but purely mythical : they describe catastrophes which never occurred. They are examples of that class of mythical tales which, with Sir Edward Tylor, we may call myths of observation, since they are suggested by a true observation of nature, but err in their interpretation of it.[3]

Among the
m ...
storie of
floods may
as:
those which
originate
... ...
observation
of marine
fossils in
inland
regions.

Another set of diluvial traditions, of which we have found examples, also falls into the class of myths of observation. These are the stories of a great flood which rest on the observation of marine fossils found on mountains or in other places remote from the sea. Such tales, as we saw, are told by the Mongolians, the Bare'e-speaking people of Celebes, the Tahitians, and the Eskimo and Greenlanders.[4] Being based on the false assumption that the sea must formerly have risen above the heights where the fossils are now found, they are mistaken inferences, or myths of observation ; whereas if they had assumed the former depression of these heights under the level of the sea, they would have been true inferences, or anticipations of science.

No reason
to think
that any
diluvial
it s
older than
a few
thousand
years.

Thus, while there is reason to believe that many diluvial traditions dispersed throughout the world are based on re-miniscences of catastrophes which actually occurred, there is no good ground for holding that any such traditions are older than a few thousand years at most ; wherever they

---

[1] See above, pp. 167 *sqq.*, 171 *sqq.*

[2] See above, pp. 205 *sqq.*, 268.

[3] (Sir) Edward B. Tylor, *Researches*

into the Early History of Mankind, Third Edition (London, 1878), pp. 306 *sqq.*

[4] Above, pp. 217, 222, 245, 327 *sq.*

appear to describe vast changes in the physical configuration of the globe, which must be referred to more or less remote epochs of geologic time, they probably embody, not the record of contemporary witnesses, but the speculation of much later thinkers. Compared with the great natural features of our planet, man is but a thing of yesterday, and his memory a dream of the night.

CHAPTER V

THE TOWER OF BABEL

AMONG the problems which beset any inquiry into the early history of mankind the question of the origin of language is at the same time one of the most fascinating and one of the most difficult. The writers whose crude speculations on human origins are embodied in the early chapters of Genesis have given us no hint as to the mode in which they supposed man to have acquired the most important of all the endowments which mark him off from the beasts—the gift of articulate speech. On the contrary they seem to have assumed that this priceless faculty was possessed by him from the beginning, nay that it was shared with him by the animals, if we may judge by the example of the talking serpent in Eden. However, the diversity of languages spoken by the various races of men naturally attracted the attention of the ancient Hebrews, and they explained it by the following tale.

In the early days of the world all mankind spoke the same language. Journeying from the east [1] as nomads in one huge caravan, they came to the great plains of Shinar or Babylonia, and there they settled. They built their houses of bricks, bound together with a mortar of slime, because stone is rare in the alluvial soil of these vast swampy flats. But not content with building themselves a city, they proposed to construct out of the same materials a tower so high that its top should reach to heaven ; this they did in order to make a name for themselves, and also to prevent the

[1] Genesis xl. 2, מקדם, literally, "from the east." The words are sometimes translated "eastward" or "in the east." But see Principal J. Skinner, *Commentary on Genesis*, p. 225.

citizens from being scattered over the face of the whole earth. For when any had wandered from the city and lost his way on the boundless plain, he would look back westward and see afar off the outline of the tall tower standing up dark against the bright evening sky, or he would look eastward and behold the top of the tower lit up by the last rays of the setting sun. So he would find his bearings, and guided by the landmark would retrace his steps homeward. Their scheme was good, but they failed to reckon with the jealousy and power of the Almighty. For while they were building away with all their might and main, God came down from heaven to see the city and the tower which men were raising so fast. The sight displeased him, for he said, "Behold, they are one people, and they have all one language; and this is what they begin to do: and now nothing will be withholden from them, which they purpose to do." Apparently he feared that when the tower reached the sky, men would swarm up it and beard him in his den, a thing not to be thought of. So he resolved to nip the great project in the bud. "Go to," said he to himself, or to his heavenly counsellors, "let us go down, and there confound their language, that they may not understand one another's speech." Down he went accordingly and confounded their language and scattered them over the face of all the earth. Therefore they left off to build the city and the tower; and the name of the place was called Babel, that is, Confusion, because God did there confound the language of all the earth.[1]

---

[1] Genesis xi. 1-9. Compare Josephus, *Antiquit. Jud.* i. 4. 3, ὁ δὲ τόπος ἐν ᾧ τὸν πύργον ᾠκοδόμησαν, νῦν Βαβυλὼν καλεῖται διὰ τὴν σύγχυσιν τοῦ περὶ τὴν διάλεκτον πρῶτον ἐναργοῦς. Ἑβραῖοι γὰρ τὴν σύγχυσιν Βαβὲλ καλοῦσιν. In this passage the awkward and scarcely grammatical words τοῦ περὶ τὴν διάλεκτον πρωτον ἐναργοῦς have the appearance of a gloss added by a scribe to define τὴν σύγχυσιν. The plural verbs in Genesis xi. 7 ("Let us go down and confound" נֵרְדָה וְנָבְלָה) suggest that God was conceived to be not alone but surrounded by inferior gods or angels. It has been argued by B. Stade that in the original narrative the deity, or his messenger, first went down to earth and after inspecting the city and tower returned to heaven and reported what he had seen to the celestial council. The council then deliberated on his report, and, the case being deemed serious, the deity as chairman moved that they should go down in a body and confound the language of men. The resolution was carried unanimously and executed on the spot. On this theory, the polytheistic colouring of the story in its original form was toned down by the Hebrew narrator, who

Later
Jewish
legends as
to the
Tower of
Babel.

On the plain stuff of this narrative later Jewish tradition has embroidered a rich band of picturesque details.
From them we learn that the enterprise of the tower
was flat rebellion against God, though the rebels were not
at one in their aims. Some wished to scale heaven and
there wage war with the Almighty in person, or set up
their idols to be worshipped in his stead ; others limited
their ambition to the more modest scheme of damaging the
celestial vault by showers of spears and arrows. Many,
many years was the tower in building. It reached so high
that at last a bricklayer took a whole year to ascend to the
top with his hod on his back. If he fell down and broke
his neck, nobody minded for the man, but everybody wept
for the brick, because it would take a whole year to replace
it on the top of the tower. So eagerly did they work, that
a woman would not interrupt her task of brickmaking even
to give birth to a child ; she would merely tie the baby in
a sheet round her body and go on moulding bricks as if
nothing had happened. Day and night the work never
slackened ; and from their dizzy height they shot heaven-
ward arrows, which returned to them dabbled with blood ;
so they cried, " We have slain all who are in heaven." At
last the long-suffering deity lost patience, and turning to the
seventy angels who encompass his throne, he proposed that
they should all go down and confound the language of men.
No sooner said than done. The misunderstandings which
consequently arose were frequent and painful. One man,
for example, would ask for mortar, and the other would hand
him a brick, whereupon the first, in a rage, would hurl the
brick at his mate's head and kill him. Many perished in
this manner, and the rest were punished by God according
to the acts of rebellion which they had meditated. As for
the unfinished tower, a part of it sank into the earth, and
another part was consumed by fire ; only one-third of it
remained standing. The place of the tower has never lost
its peculiar quality. Whoever passes it forgets all he knows.

struck out the express mention of the
council of gods or angels, though he
inadvertently left a trace of them in
the plural verbs of verse 7. See B.
Stade, "Der Thurm zu Babel," *Zeit-*
schrift fur die alttestamentliche Wissen-
schaft, xv. (1895) pp. 157 *sqq.*
[1] Louis Ginzberg, *The Legends of*
the Jews, i. (Philadelphia, 1909) pp.
179 *sq.*

The scene of the legend was laid at Babylon, for Babel is only the Hebrew form of the name of the city. The popular derivation from a Hebrew verb *balal* (Aramaic *balbel*) " to confuse" is erroneous; the true meaning, as shown by the form in which the name is written in inscriptions, seems to be " Gate of God " (*Bāb-il* or *Bāb-ilu*).[1] The commentators are probably right in tracing the origin of the story to the deep impression produced by the great city on the simple minds of Semitic nomads, who, fresh from the solitude and silence of the desert, were bewildered by the hubbub of the streets and bazaars, dazzled by the shifting kaleidoscope of colour in the bustling crowd, stunned by the din of voices jabbering in strange unknown tongues, and overawed by the height of the buildings, above all by the prodigious altitude of the temples towering up, terrace upon terrace, till their glistering tops of enamelled brick seemed to touch the blue sky. No wonder that dwellers in tents should imagine, that they who scaled the pinnacle of such a stupendous pile by the long winding ramp, and appeared at last like moving specks on the summit, must indeed be near the gods.[2]

Of two such gigantic temples the huge mouldering remains are to be seen at Babylon to this day, and it is probable that to one or other of them the legend of the Tower of Babel was attached. One of them rises among the ruins of Babylon itself, and still bears the name of Babil ; the other is situated across the river at Borsippa, some eight or nine miles away to the south-west, and is

The Tower
f   e
probably a
reminis-
c   o
one of the
temple-
Babylonia.

Two such
ruined
towers at
Babylon.

[1] E. Schrader, *The Cuneiform Inscriptions and the Old Testament* (London and Edinburgh, 1885-1888), i. 112 *sqq.* ; S. R. Driver, *The Book of Genesis*, Tenth Edition, p. 136, on Genesis xi. 9 ; J. Skinner, *Commentary on Genesis*, pp. 210, 227, on Genesis x. 10, xi. 9 ; H. E. Ryle, *The Book of Genesis*, p. 148, on Genesis, xi. 9 ; Fr. Brown, S. R. Driver, and Ch. Briggs, *Hebrew and English Lexicon* (Oxford, 1906), p. 93.

[2] These temples were built in solid quadrangular blocks of bricks, one on the top of the other, each block smaller

than the one below it, so as to present the appearance of a gigantic staircase on all four sides. A ramp wound round the whole building, leading up to the comparatively small flat summit, on which stood the shrine of the god. The native Babylonian name for such a structure was *zikkurat* or *ziggurat*. See G. Perrot et Ch. Chipiez, *Histoire de l'Art dans l'Antiquité*, ii. (Paris, 1884) pp. 379 *sqq.* ; M. Jastrow, *The Religion of Babylonia and Assyria* (Boston, 1898), pp. 613 *sqq.* ; (Sir) Gaston Maspero, *Histoire Ancienne des peuples de l'Orient Classique, Les Origines* (Paris, 1895), pp. 627 *sqq.*

known as Birs-Nimrud. The ancient name of the temple in the city of Babylon was E-sagil : it was dedicated to Marduk. The ancient name of the temple at Borsippa was E-zida : it was dedicated to Nebo. Scholars are not agreed as to which of these ancient edifices was the original Tower of Babel · local and Jewish tradition identifies the legendary tower with the ruins of Birs-Nimrud at Borsippa.[1]

The mound of Babil formerly the temple Marduk.

The mound of Babil, once the temple of the chief Baby-lonian god Bel or Marduk, is now merely an oblong mass composed chiefly of unbaked brick, measuring about two hundred yards in length on the longer northern and southern faces, and rising to a height of at least one hundred and ten feet above the plain. The top is broad and flat, but uneven and broken with heaps of rubbish. While the solid core of the structure was built of crude or sun-dried bricks, its outer faces were apparently coated with walls of burnt bricks, some of which, inscribed with the name of King Nebuchadnezzar, have been found on the spot.[2] From Herodotus we learn that the temple rose in a series of eight terraces or solid towers, one on the top of the other, with a ramp winding up on the outside, but broken about half-way up by a landing-place, where there were seats for the rest and refreshment of persons ascending to the summit.[3] In the ancient Sumerian

[1] George Rawlinson, The History of Herodotus, Fourth Edition (London, 1880), ii. 573 sqq. ; E. Schrader, Cuneiform Inscriptions and the Old Testament, i. 106 sqq. ; Principal J. Skinner, Commentary on Genesis, pp. 228 sq. ; H. Gunkel, Genesis übersetzt und erklärt³ (Gottingen, 1910), pp. 96 sq.

[2] George Rawlinson, The History of Herodotus, Fourth Edition (London, 1880), ii. 576 sq · G. Perrot et Ch. Chipiez Histoire de l Art dans l Anti-quité, ii. 399 sq.

[3] Herodotus i. 181. As to the remains of the temple, see R. Kolde-wey, The Excavations at Babylon, translated by Agnes S. Johns (London, 1914), pp. 183 sqq. ; L. W. King, History of Babylon (London, 1915), pp. 73 sqq. By the beginning of our era the building seems to have been almost as ruinous as it is now. See

Diodorus Siculus ii. 9 ; Strabo xvi. i. 5. p. 738, ed. Casaubon. Herodotus's description of the temple-tower, rising in terraces, one above the other, is confirmed by a boundary-stone of the time of Merodach-baladan I., on which is figured just such a temple-tower, built in stories, or stepped stages, set one upon the other, with the emblem of Nabu at the foot of the tower. See L. W. King, History of Babylon (London, 1915), pp. 78 sq. The German excavator of Babylon, Mr. R. Koldewey, would set the evidence of Herodotus and of the monuments at defiance by reconstructing the temple on a single stage (op. cit. pp. 194 sq. with Fig. 119), but his view is rightly set aside by Mr. L. W. King, who observes that "there is no reason to reject the interpretation that has so long been accepted of the famous description of the tower that is given by Herodotus" (op. cit. p. 81).

language the temple was called E-temen-an-ki or "The House of the Foundation of Heaven and Earth."[1] Towards the end of the seventh century before our era the temple had fallen into disrepair, if not into ruins, but it was then restored by King Nabopolassar, who reigned 625–604 B.C. In an inscription, which has been preserved, the king describes himself as "the restorer of Esagila and Ezida," and records the restoration of Esagila or Etemenanki as follows :—

"As for Etemenanki, the temple-tower of Babylon, which before my time had become weakened and had fallen in, Marduk the lord commanded me to lay its foundation in the heart of the earth (and) to raise its turrets to heaven. Baskets, spades (?), and U.RU. I made out of ivory, *ushu* and *mismakanna* wood ; I caused the numerous workmen assembled in my land to carry them. I set to work (?) ; I made bricks, I manufactured burnt bricks. Like the down-pour of heaven, which cannot be measured, like the massive flood, I caused the Arahtu to carry bitumen and pitch. With the co-operation of Ea, with the insight of Marduk, with the wisdom of Nabu and Nisaba, in the broad under-standing with which the god, my creator, had endowed me, with my great ingenuity (?), I came to a decision ; I gave orders to the skilled workmen. With a *nindanaku* measure I measured the measurements of the *aba ash-lam* (?). The architects at first made a survey of the ground plot (?). Afterwards I consulted Shamash, Ramman, and Marduk ; to my heart they gave decision, they sanctioned the measure-ments, the great gods by decree indicated the later stages of the work. By means of exorcism, in the wisdom of Ea and Marduk, I cleared away that place, (and) on the original site I laid its platform-foundation ; gold, silver, stones from mountain and sea in its foundation I set * * * goodly oil, sweet-smelling herbs, and * * * I placed underneath the bricks. An image of my royalty carrying a *dupshikku* I constructed ; in the platform-foundation I placed it. Unto Marduk, my lord, I bowed my neck ; I arrayed myself in my gown, the robe of my royalty. Bricks and mortar I

Inscription a polassar, King of recording the restoration of Ete-menanki, e-tower of Babylon.

[1] R. F. Harper, *Assyrian and Babylonian Literature* (New York, 1901), p. 137 ; Principal J. Skinner, `Commentary on Genesis, p. 228 ; H. Gunkel, *Genesis übersetzt und erklärt*,[3] p. 97.

carried on my head, a *dupshikku* of gold and silver I wore ·
and Nebuchadrezzar, the first-born, the chief son, beloved of
my heart, I caused to carry mortar mixed with wine, oil, and
(other) products along with my workmen.   Nabushumlisher,
his twin brother, the offspring of my own flesh, the junior,
my darling, I ordered to take a basket and spade (?) ; a
dupshikku of gold and silver I placed (on him).   Unto
Marduk, my lord, as a gift, I dedicated him.   I built the
temple in front of Esharra with joy and rejoicing, and like
a mountain I raised its tower aloft; to Marduk, my lord,
as in days of old, I dedicated it for a sight to be gazed at.

"O Marduk, my lord, look with favour upon my goodly
deeds!   At thy exalted command, which cannot be altered,
let the performance of my hands endure for ever!   Like the
bricks of Etemenanki, which are to remain firm for ever, do
thou establish the foundation of my throne for all time!
O Etemenanki, grant blessing to the king who has restored
thee!   When Marduk with joy takes up his abode in
thee, O temple, recall to Marduk, my lord, my gracious
deeds!"[1]

Inscrip-
tions of
Nebuchad-
nezzar,
King of
Babylon,
recording
the
restoration
of the
temple-
tower of
Babylon.

Again, the temple was further repaired and adorned by
Nabopolassar's son and successor, Nebuchadrezzar the Second,
the Nebuchadnezzar of the Bible.   To these restorations the
great king repeatedly refers in his inscriptions.   Thus he
says :—

"The temples of Babylon I rebuilt and restored.   As
for E-temen-an-ki (house of the foundation of heaven and
earth) with burnt brick and bright *ugnu*-stone I raised on
high its turrets.   To the rebuilding of Esagila my heart
incited me ; I held it constantly in mind.   I selected the
best of my cedar trees, which I had brought from Mount
Lebanon, the snow-capped forest, for the roofing of E-kua,
the shrine of his lordship, and I decorated with brilliant gold
the inner sides of the mighty cedar trunks, used in the roofing of E-kua.   I adorned the under side of the roof of cedar
with gold and precious stones.   Concerning the rebuilding
of Esagila I prayed every morning to the king of the gods,

[1] R. F. Harper, *Assyrian and
Babylonian Literature* (New York,
1901), pp. 131-133.   Compare   *Keilinschriftliche Bibliothek*, herausgegeben von Eberhard Schrader, vol.
iii. 2. Halfte (Berlin, 1890), pp. 2 *sqq.*

the lord of lords." [1]   Again, in another Babylonian inscription King Nebuchadrezzar II. says : " In Esagila, the majestic shrine, the temple of heaven and earth, the dwelling-place of royalty, I decorated with shining gold E-kua, the shrine of the lord of the gods, Marduk, Bab-Hili-shud, the home of Çarpanit, (and) Ezida in Esagila, the shrine called 'the king of the gods of heaven and earth,' and I made (them) to shine like the day. E-temen-an-ki, the temple-tower of Babylon, I made anew." [2]   Again, in another inscription the king declares : " Esagila, the temple of heaven and earth, the dwelling-place of the lord of the gods Marduk, and E-kua, his shrine, I adorned with shining gold like a wall. Ezida I built anew, and with silver, gold, precious stones, bronze, palm-wood, cedar-wood I completed its construction. E-temen-an-ki, the temple-tower of Babylon, I built and completed, and with burnt brick and shining *ugnu*-stone I raised on high its turrets." [3]

The huge pyramidal mound, to which the Arabs give the name of Birs-Nimrud, is a solitary pile rising abruptly from the vast expanse of the desert some eight or nine miles from the ruins of Babylon. Roughly speaking, the mound forms a rectangular oblong, measuring about six hundred and fifty feet on the long sides and four hundred feet on the short sides. The height of its summit above the plain is about one hundred and fifty-three feet. To the ordinary observer at the present time it presents the appearance rather of a natural hill crowned by a ruin than of a structure reared by the hand of man. Yet there appears to be no doubt that the great mound is wholly artificial, being built entirely of bricks, which have to some extent solidified into a single mass. Thirty-seven feet of solid brickwork, looking like a tower, stand exposed at the top, while below this the original building is almost hidden under the masses of rubbish which have crumbled down from the upper portion.

The mound of Birs-Nimrud, near BabΙl, with the ruins of a e-tower dedicated to Nebo.

R. F. Harper, *Assyrian and Babylonian Literature*, p. 137. Compare *Keilinschriftliche Bibliothek*, herausgegeben von E. Schrader, iii. 2. Halfte (Berlin, 1890), pp. 14 *sqq.*
" *Keilinschriftliche Bibliothek*, herausgegeben von E. Schrader, iii. 2. Halfte (Berlin, 1890), p. 47 ; R. F.

Harper, *Assyrian and Babylonian Literature*, p. 144.

[3] *Keilinschriftliche Bibliothek*, herausgegeben von E. Schrader, iii. 2. Halfte (Berlin, 1890), p. 53 ; R. F. Harper, *Assyrian and Babylonian Literature*, p. 151.

The whole structure, however, is deeply channelled by exposure to the rain, and in places the original brickwork is sufficiently exposed to reveal the true character and plan of the edifice. From the researches carried on by Sir Henry Rawlinson in the year 1854 it appears that the temple, like that of Bel or Marduk in Babylon, was built in a series of receding stages, seven in number, which rose one above the other in a sort of oblique pyramid to a height of about one hundred and fifty-six feet above the plain. The grand entrance was on the north-east, where stood the vestibule, a separate building, of which the remains prolong the mound very considerably in this direction. Such are the mouldering ruins of E-zida, the great temple of Nebo (Nabu), whose shrine probably occupied the summit of the pyramidal or tower-like structure. In its present form the edifice is chiefly the work of King Nebuchadnezzar (Nebuchadrezzar the Second), whose name appears exclusively on the bricks composing it, and on the cylinders deposited at its angles.[1] The modern name of Birs-Nimrud preserves in a slightly altered form the first syllable of Borsippa, the ancient name of the city which stood here.[2]

Inscription
N b h d
nezzar,
King of
Bab lon.
recording
tne
restoration
of the
-e-
tower at
Birs-
Nimrud

On two of the cylinders found by Sir Henry Rawlinson at the angles of the temple is engraved an inscription, in which King Nebuchadnezzar (Nebuchadrezzar II.) records his restoration of the edifice, which had fallen into ruins before his time. The inscription runs thus :—

"Behold now the building named 'the Stages of the Seven Spheres,' which was the wonder of Borsippa, had been built by a former king. He had completed forty-two *ammas* (of the height), but he did not finish its head. From the lapse of time it had become ruined ; they had not taken care of the exits of the waters, so the rain and wet had penetrated into the brickwork : the casing of burnt bricks had bulged out, and the terraces of crude brick lay scattered in heaps ; (then) Merodach, my great lord, inclined my heart to repair the building. I did not change its site, nor did I destroy its foundation platform ; but in a fortunate month, and on an

---

[1] George Rawlinson, *The History of Herodotus*, Fourth Edition (London, 1880), ii. 581-586.

[2] H. V. Hilprecht, *Explorations in Bible Lands during the Nineteenth Century* (Edinburgh, 1903), p. 43.

auspicious day, I undertook the rebuilding of the crude-brick terraces, and the burnt-brick casing (of the temple). I strengthened its foundation, and I placed a titular record in the part that I had rebuilt. I set my hand to build it up and to finish its summit. As it had been in ancient times, so I built up its structure ; as it had been in former days, thus I exalted its head. Nebo, the strengthener of his children, he who ministers to the gods (?), and Merodach, the supporter of sovereignty, may they cause my work to be established for ever ! May it last through the seven ages ! May the stability of my throne and the antiquity of my empire, secure against strangers and triumphant over many foes, continue to the end of time ! " [1]

From this record we learn that the ancient Babylonian king, who began to build the great temple-tower at Borsippa, had left it incomplete, wanting its top. It may have been the sight of the huge edifice in its unfinished state which gave rise to the legend of the Tower of Babel.

However, there were many more such temple-towers in ancient Babylonia, and the legend in question may have been attached to any one of them. For example, the remains of such a temple still exist at Uru, the Ur of the Chaldees, from which Abraham is said to have migrated to Canaan.[2] The place is now known as Mukayyar or Muge-yer ; it is situated on the right bank of the Euphrates about a hundred and thirty-five miles south-east of Babylon.[3] A series of low mounds, forming an oval, marks the site of the ancient city. The country all around is so flat that often . during the annual flood of the Euphrates, from March till June or July, the ruins form an island in a great marsh and can only be approached by boat. Groves of date-palms here line the banks of the river and extend in unbroken succession along its course till it loses itself in the waters of the Persian Gulf. Near the northern end of the site rise the remains of the temple-tower to a height of about seventy

Ruined temple-t

Uru (Ur Chaldees)

---

[1] George Rawlinson, *The History of Herodotus*, Fourth Edition (London, 1o8o), ii. 586. Merodach is another way of spelling the name of Marduk, the great god of Babylon. For other translations of the inscription, see *Keilinschriftliche Bibliothek*, iii. 2 Halfte (Berlin, 1890), pp. 53, 55 ; R. F. Harper, *Assyrian and Babylonian Literature*, pp. 150 *sqq*.

[2] Genesis xi. 31.

[3] *Encyclopaedia Biblica*, iv. coll. 5231 *sqq*., *s.v.* " Ur of the Chaldees."

feet. The edifice is a rectangular parallelogram, in two stories, with the larger sides facing north-east and south-west, each of them measuring about two hundred feet in length, while the shorter sides measure only one hundred and thirty-three feet. As in all similar Babylonian build-ings, one angle points almost due north. The lower story, twenty-seven feet high, is supported by strong buttresses; the upper story, receding from thirty to forty-seven feet from the edge of the first, is fourteen feet high, surmounted by about five feet of brick rubbish. The ascent was on the north-east. A tunnel driven into the mound proved that the entire edifice was built of sun-dried bricks in the centre, with a thick coating of massive, partially burnt bricks of a light red colour with layers of reeds between them, the whole, to a thickness of ten feet, being cased with a wall of inscribed kiln-burnt bricks. Inscribed cylinders were discovered at the four corners of the building, each standing in a niche formed by the omission of a single brick in the layer. Sub-sequent excavations seem to prove that commemorative inscriptions, inscribed on cylinders, were regularly deposited by the builders or restorers of Babylonian temples and palaces at the four corners of the edifices.[1]

Inscription of Nabonidus, King of Babylon, recording restoration of the temple-tower of Ur.

The inscriptions on the cylinders found at Ur record the restoration of the temple-tower by Nabonidus, the last king of Babylon (555–538 B.C.), and give us in outline a history of the ancient edifice. One of them runs as follows :—

" Nabonidus, King of Babylon, patron of Esagila and Ezida, who fears the great gods, am I.

" As for E-lugal-(?)-si-di, the temple-tower of E-gish-shir-gal, which is in Ur, which Ur-uk, a former king, had built, but had not completed—Dun-gi, his son, completed its construction. From the inscriptions of Ur-uk and Dun-gi, his son, I learned that Ur-uk had built this temple-tower, without completing it, and that Dun-gi, his son, had com-pleted its construction. This temple-tower was now old, and upon the old platform-foundation which Ur-uk and Dun-gi, his son, had built, I undertook the reconstruction of

[1] W. K. Loftus, *Travels and Researches in Chaldaea and Susiana* (London, 1857), pp. 127 sqq.; H. V. Hilprecht, *Explorations of Bible Lands during the Nineteenth Century* (Edin-burgh, 1903), pp. 171 sqq.

this temple-tower, as of old, with bitumen and burnt brick, and for Sin, the lord of the gods of heaven and earth, the king of the gods, the god of gods, who inhabit the great heavens, the lord of E-gish-shir-gal, which is in Ur, my lord, I founded and built (it).

"O Sin, lord of the gods, king of the gods of heaven and earth, the god of gods, who inhabit the great heavens, upon thy joyful entrance into that temple may the good done to Esagila, Ezida (and) E-gish-shir-gal, the temples of thy great divinity, be established on thy lips!

"And do thou implant the fear of thy great divinity in the heart of its people, that they may not sin against thy great divinity, (and) like the heavens may their foundations stand fast!

"As for me, Nabonidus, King of Babylon, save me from sinning against thy great divinity! A life of far-distant days grant me as a present! And as regards Belshazzar, the first-born son, my offspring, do thou implant in his heart the fear of thy great divinity! May he not fall into sin! May he be satisfied with fulness of life!"[1]

From this inscription we learn that the name of the city was Ur, and that the temple was dedicated to Sin, the Babylonian moon-god. Further we are informed that King Ur-uk or Urengur, as his name should rather be spelt, who built the temple-tower, left it unfinished, and that the edifice was completed by his son, King Dungi. The reign of King Ur-uk or Urengur is variously dated about 2700 B.C. or 2300 B.C.[2] In either case the foundation of the temple preceded, perhaps by hundreds of years, the date which is usually

[1] R. F. Harper, *Assyrian and Babylonian Literature*, pp. 157 sq. Compare *Keilinschriftliche Bibliothek*, herausgegeben von E. Schrader, iii. 2. Halfte (Berlin, 1890), pp. 95, 97. Belshazzar, the king's son, is no doubt the Belshazzar spoken of in the Book of Daniel (chapter v.), though the writer of that book appears to have been mistaken in representing Belshazzar as a son of Nebuchadnezzar. See S. R. Driver, *The Book of Daniel* (Cambridge, 1905), pp. xxviii, 1-lii, 60 sq. Till lately it was supposed that the author of the Book of Daniel committed

another mistake in speaking of Belshazzar as king. However, a cuneiform inscription, recently deciphered by Dr. T. G. Pinches, seems to show that, in the twelfth year of the reign of King Nabonidus, his son Belshazzar was associated with him in the royal power. See *The Athenæum*, May 1916, p. 255.

[2] H. V. Hilprecht, *Explorations in Bible Lands*, p. 174 (who dates the foundation of the temple about 2700 B.C.); Ed. Meyer, *Geschichte des Altertums*,[2] i. 2 (Stuttgart and Berlin, 1909), p. 495 (who dates the king's reign 2304-2287 B.C.).

assigned to the birth of Abraham ;[1] so that if the patriarch
really migrated from Ur to Canaan, as Hebrew tradition
relates, this very building, whose venerable ruins exist on the
spot to this day, dominating by their superior height the
flat landscape through which the Euphrates winds seaward,
must have been familiar to Abraham from childhood, and
may have been the last object on which his eyes rested
when, setting out in search of the Promised Land, he took a
farewell look backward at his native city disappearing behind
its palm groves in the distance.   It is possible that in the
minds of his descendants, the conspicuous pile, looming dim
and vast through the mists of time and of distance, may have
assumed the gigantic proportions of a heaven-reaching
tower, from which in days of old the various nations of
the earth set out on their wanderings.

Theories
1
primitive
language
mankind.

The authors of Genesis say nothing as to the nature of
the common language which all mankind spoke before the
confusion of tongues, and in which our first parents may be
supposed to have conversed with each other, with the serpent, and with the deity in the garden of Eden.   Later
ages took it for granted that Hebrew was the primitive
language of mankind.   The fathers of the Church appear to
have entertained no doubt on the subject ; and in modern
times, when the science of philology was in its infancy,
strenuous, but necessarily abortive, efforts were made to
deduce all forms of human speech from Hebrew as their
original.   In this naïve assumption Christian scholars did
not differ from the learned men of other religions, who have
seen in the language of their sacred writings the tongue not
only of our first forefathers but of the gods themselves.   The
first in modern times to prick the bubble effectively was
Leibnitz, who observed that " there is as much reason for
supposing Hebrew to have been the primitive language of
mankind, as there is for adopting the view of Goropius, who
published a work at Antwerp, in 1580, to prove that Dutch

---

[1] On the strength of the identification
of Amraphel, King of Shinar (Genesis
xiv. 1) with Hammurabi, King of Babylon, some modern scholars are disposed
to make Abraham a contemporary of
Hammurabi, and therefore to date him
about 2100 B.C.   See S. R. Driver,
The Book of Genesis, Tenth Edition,
pp. xxviii *sq.* ; Principal J. Skinner,
Commentary on Genesis, pp. xiv *sq.*
Mr. L. W. King dates Hammurabi's
reign 2123-2083 B.C. (*History of
Babylon*, London, 1915, p. 320).   See
above, p. 121 note [2].

was the language spoken in Paradise."[1]   Another writer
maintained that the language spoken by Adam was Basque ;
while others, flying clean in the face of Scripture, introduced
the diversity of tongues into Eden itself, by holding that
Adam and Eve spoke Persian, that the language of the
serpent was Arabic, and that the affable archangel Gabriel
discoursed with our first parents in Turkish.   Yet another
eccentric scholar seriously argued that the Almighty addressed Adam in Swedish, that Adam answered his Maker
in Danish, and that the serpent conversed with Eve in
French.[2]   We may suspect that all such philological theories
were biassed by the national prejudices and antipathies of
the philologers who propounded them.

Attempts have been made to arrive at the primitive
language of mankind by the experimental method.   The
first recorded experiment of this nature is said to have been
made by Psammetichus, King of Egypt.   Desirous of learning what race of man was first created or evolved, he had
recourse to the following device.   He took two newborn
babes, selected at haphazard, and gave them in charge to a
goatherd with strict injunctions to rear them in a lonely hut,
where they were to be fed on goat's milk and never to hear
a word of human speech ; for the sagacious monarch calculated that, left to themselves, uncontaminated · by oral
intercourse with others, the children would in due time yield
to the promptings of nature and break out into the primeval
language of our first forefathers.   The result seemed to
justify his prevision.   For when two years had passed, it
chanced that one day the goatherd opened the door of the
solitary hut as usual to give the two children their daily meal
of goat's milk, and no sooner did he do so than the two
little ones ran at him, holding out their hands and crying
"*Bekos*"!   At first he said nothing, but when the same
thing happened day after day, he reported the matter to the
king, who on making inquiries discovered that *bekos* was the
Phrygian word for bread.   On the strength of that discovery,
King Psammetichus concluded that the Phrygians were the

Attempts
eter
mine the
primitive
language
of
mankind
ment.
The experi-
Psamme-
tichus,
King of
Egypt.

[1] Quoted by F. Max Müller, *Lectures on the Science of Language*, Sixth
Edition (London, 1871), i. 149.   As
to the theory that Hebrew was the
primitive language of mankind, see F.
Max Müller, *op. cit.* i. 145 *sqq.*

[2] F. Max Müller, *op. cit.* i. 149.

most ancient race of mankind, and that the Egyptians must accordingly yield to them the coveted palm of antiquity. Such is the tale as told by the Greek historian Herodotus. We may suspect that it is not an Egyptian but a Greek story, invented to flatter Greek vanity by humbling the pride of the Egyptians and transferring the crown of remotest eld from their brows to those of a race akin to the Grecian.[2] A later rationalism, accepting the truth of the anecdote, disputed the conclusion drawn from it, by arguing that *bekos* was nothing but a natural imitation of the bleating of the goats, whose voices the children heard and whose milk they imbibed daily.[3] The experiment is said to have been repeated in later ages by several monarchs, including the German emperor Frederick the Second[4] and the Mogul emperor Akbar Khan. Of the latter potentate it is told that, anxious to discover the true religion, and perplexed by the contradictory claims of the rival systems, hê hit upon the following device for solving the problem. He took thirty young children and caused them to be brought up by persons who were strictly forbidden to converse with their youthful charges; for he was resolved to adopt the religious faith of that people whose language the infants should spontaneously speak, being apparently satisfied in his own mind that the religion thus authenticated by the voice of nature could be none other than the true one. The result of the experiment was to confirm the philosophic Mogul in his scepticism ; for the children, we are informed, spoke no particular language, and the emperor accordingly continued to be of no particular religion.[5] · In our own country James IV. of Scotland is reported to have shut up two children with a dumb woman in the island of Inchkeith, desiring to know what language the children would speak when they came to the age of perfect speech. Some say that they spoke good

Experi-
ments of
Frederick
the Second,
Khan, and
James IV.
Scotland.

---

[1] Herodotus ii. 2.

[2] See A. Wiedemann, *Herodots Zweites Buch* (Leipsic, 1890), p. 45, who points out that even if the anecdote had been historical, the Egyptians might still have claimed the prize of superior antiquity, since *bek* is an Egyptian word meaning "oil," and is also a late name for the land of Egypt itself.

[3] Scholiast on Apollonius Rhodius, *Argonaut.* iv. 262.

[4] J. C. F. Baehr, in his edition of Herodotus (Leipsic, 1856–1861), vol. ii. pp. 431 *sq.*

[5] Samuel Purchas, *Purchas His Pilgrimes* (London, 1625–1626), v. 516.

Hebrew, but the chronicler seems to have had doubts on the subject.[1]

Stories which bear a certain resemblance to the legend of the Tower of Babel are reported among several African tribes. Thus, some of the natives of the Zambesi, apparently in the neighbourhood of the Victoria Falls, " have a tradition which may refer to the building of the Tower of Babel, but it ends in the bold builders getting their crowns cracked by the fall of the scaffolding." [2] The story thus briefly referred to by Dr. Livingstone has been more fully recorded by a Swiss missionary. The A-Louyi, a tribe of the Upper Zambesi, say that formerly their god Nyambe, whom they identify with the sun, used to dwell on earth, but that he afterwards ascended up to heaven on a spider's web. From his post up aloft he said to men, " Worship me." But men said, " Come, let us kill Nyambe." Alarmed at this impious threat, the deity fled to the sky, from which it would seem that he had temporarily descended. So men said, " Come, let us make masts to reach up to heaven." They set up masts and added more masts, joining them one to the other, and they clambered up them. But when they had climbed far up, the masts fell down, and all the men on the masts were killed by the fall. That was the end of them.[3] The Bambala of the Congo say " that the Wan- gongo once wanted to know what the moon was, so they started to go and see. They planted a big pole in the ground, and a man climbed up it with a second pole which he fastened to the end ; to this a third was fixed, and so on. When their Tower of Babel had reached a considerable height, so high in fact that the whole population of the village was carrying poles up, the erection suddenly collapsed, and they fell victims to their ill-advised curiosity. Since that time no one has tried to find out what the moon is." [4] The natives of Mkulwe, in German East Africa, tell a similar tale. According to them, men one day

Stories like the legend of the Tower of Babel told in Africa about people who tried to climb up to heaven.

Louyi story.

Bambala story.

Mkulwe story.

---

[1] Robert Lindsay of Pitscottie, *The Chronicles of Scotland* (Edinburgh, 1814), i. 249 *sq.*

David Livingstone, *Missionary Travels and Researches in South Africa* (London, 1857), p. 528.

[3] E. Jacottet, *Études sur les langues du Haut-Zambèze*, Troisieme Partie, *Textes Louyi* (Paris, 1901), p. 118.

[4] E. Torday, *Camp and Tramp in African Wilds* (London, 1913), pp. 242 *sq.*

said to each other, "Let us build high, let us reach the moon!" So they rammed a great tree into the earth, and fixed another tree on the top of it, and another on the top of that, and so on, till the trees fell down and the men were killed. But other men said, "Let us not give up this undertaking," and they piled trees one on the top of the other, till one day the trees again fell down and the men were killed. Then the people gave up trying to
Ashantee story. climb aloft to the moon.[1] The Ashantees have a tradition that God of old dwelt among men, but that, resenting an affront put on him by an old woman, he withdrew in high dudgeon to his mansion in the sky. Disconsolate at his departure, mankind resolved to seek and find him. For that purpose they collected all the porridge pestles they could find and piled them up, one on the top of the other. When the tower thus built had nearly reached the sky, they found to their dismay that the supply of pestles ran short. What were they to do? In this dilemma a wise man stood up and said, "The matter is quite simple. Take the lowest pestle of all, and put it on the top, and go on doing so till we arrive at God." The proposal was carried, but when they came to put it in practice, down fell the tower, as indeed you might have expected. However, others say that the collapse of the tower was caused by the white ants, which gnawed away the lowest of the pestles. In whichever way it happened, the communication with heaven was not completed, and men were never able to ascend up to God.[2]

Anal story of a man who tried to climb up to heaven. The Anal clan of the Kuki tribe, in Assam, tell of an attempt made by a man to climb up into the sky, in order to recover his stolen property. The story is as follows. Once upon a time there was a very pious man who devoted much time to worshipping God, and he had a pet bitch. Envious of his noble qualities, the sun and moon resolved to rob him of his virtue. In pursuit of this nefarious design, they promised to give him their virtue, if only he would first entrust them with his. The unsuspecting saint fell into the trap,

[1] Alois Hamberger, "Religiose Überlieferungen und Gebräuche der Landschaft Mkulwe," *Anthropos*, iv. (1909) p. 304.
[2] E. Perregaux, *Chez les Achanti* (Neuchâtel, 1906); p. 200.

and the two celestial rogues made off with his virtue.   Thus
defrauded, the holy man ordered his dog to pursue and catch
the thieves.   The intelligent animal brought a long pole and
climbed up it to reach the fugitives, and the saint swarmed
up the pole behind his dumb friend.   Unfortunately he
ascended so slowly that, before he reached the sky, the white
ants had eaten away the lower end of the pole, so he fell
down and broke his neck.   But the bitch was more agile ;
before the white ants had gnawed through the wood, she
had got a footing in the sky, and there the faithful animal
is to this day, chasing the sun and moon round and round
the celestial vault.   Sometimes she catches them, and when
she does so, the sun or moon is darkened, which Europeans
call an eclipse.   At such times the Anals shout to the bitch,
"Release! Release!" meaning, of course, that she is to let
go the sun or moon.[1]

A story like the Biblical narrative of the Tower of
Babel is told of the great pyramid of Cholula in Mexico,
the vastest work of aboriginal man in all America.   This
colossal fabric, on which the modern traveller still gazes
with admiration, stands near the handsome modern city of
Puebla, on the way from Vera Cruz to the capital.   In form
it resembles, and in dimensions it rivals, the pyramids of
Egypt.   Its perpendicular height is nearly two hundred feet,
and its base is twice as long as that of the great pyramid of
Cheops.   It had the shape common to the Mexican *teocallis*,
that of a truncated pyramid, facing with its four sides the
cardinal points and divided into four terraces.   Its original
outlines, however, have been effaced by time and the weather,
while its surface is now covered by an exuberant growth of
shrubs and trees, so that the huge pile presents the aspect of
a natural hill rather than of a mound reared by human labour.
The edifice is built of rows of bricks baked in the sun and
cemented together with mortar, in which are stuck quantities
of small stones, potsherds, and fragments of obsidian knives
and weapons.   Layers of clay are interposed between the
courses of brick.   The flat summit, which comprises more
than an acre of ground, commands a superb prospect over

The py mi temple of Cholula in Mexico.

[1] Lieut.-Colonel J. Shakespear, *The Lushei Kuki Clans* (London, 1912),
pp. 183 *sq.*

the broad fertile valley away to the huge volcanic mountains which encircle it, their lower slopes covered with grand forests, their pinnacles of porphyry bare and arid, the highest of them crowned with eternal snow.[1]

Story of the foundation of the pyramidal temple of Cholula.

A legend concerning the foundation of this huge monument is recorded by the Dominican friar Pedro de los Rios. It runs as follows. Before the great flood, which took place four thousand years after the creation of the world, this country was inhabited by giants. All who did not perish in the inundation were turned into fishes, except seven who took refuge in caves. When the waters had retired, one of the seven, by name Xelhua, surnamed the Architect, came to Cholula, where, in memory of the mountain of Tlaloc, on which he and his six brothers had found safety, he built an artificial hill in the shape of a pyramid. He caused the bricks to be made in the province of Tlalmanalco, at the foot of Mount Cocotl, and in order to transport them to Cholula he set a line of men on the road, who passed the bricks from hand to hand. It was his purpose to raise the mighty edifice to the clouds, but the gods, offended at his presumption, hurled the fire of heaven down on the pyramid, many of the workmen perished, and the building remained unfinished. Afterwards it was dedicated to the great god Quetzalcoatl.[2] It is said that at the time of the Spanish conquest the inhabitants of Cholula preserved with great veneration a large aerolite, which according to them was the very thunderbolt that fell on the pyramid and set it on fire.[3]

Another version of the story told by Duran, a Spanish historian.

A similar tradition, differing somewhat in details, is related by the Spanish historian Duran, who wrote in 1579. "In the beginning," says he, "before the light and sun were created, the earth was in darkness and gloom, void of all created things, quite flat, without hill or dale, encircled by water on every side, without trees and without any other created thing. As soon as the sun and the light were born in the east, some men appeared there, ungainly giants who

[1] W. H. Prescott, *History of the Conquest of Mexico* (London, 1901), ii. 5 *sqq.*; Brasseur de Bourbourg, *Histoire des Nations civilisées du Mexique et de l'Amérique-Centrale* (Paris, 1857–1859), i. 299 *sqq.*; (Sir) Edward B. Tylor, *Anahuac* (London, 1861), pp. 274 *sq.*

[2] Brasseur de Bourbourg, *op. cit.* i. 301 *sq.* Compare W. H. Prescott, *op. cit.* iii. 365; (Sir) Edward B. Tylor, *Anahuac*, pp. 276 *sq.*; H. H. Bancroft, *The Native Races of the Pacific States*, iii. 67 *sq.*, v. 200.

[3] (Sir) E. B. Tylor, *Anahuac*, p. 277.

possessed the land.   Wishing to see the rising and the setting
of the sun, they agreed to go in search of it ; so dividing into
two bands they journeyed, the one band toward the west, and
the other toward the east.   So they journeyed till they were
stopped by the sea.   Thence they resolved to return to the
place from which they had set out : so they came back to
the place called *Iztacçulin ineminian*.   Not knowing how
to reach the sun, and charmed with its light and beauty, they
decided to build a tower so high that its top should reach the
sky.   In their search for materials with which to carry out
their design they found a clay and a very sticky bitumen with
which they began in a great hurry to build the tower.
When they had reared it as high as they could, so high that
it is said to have seemed to reach the sky, the lord of the
heights was angry and said to the inhabitants of heaven,
'Have you seen how the inhabitants of the earth have built
a tower so high and so proud to climb up here, charmed
as they are with the light and beauty of the sun ?   Come,
let us confound them ; for it is not meet that the people of
the earth, who live in bodies of flesh, should mix with us.'
In a moment, the inhabitants of heaven, setting out towards
the four quarters of the world, overthrew as by a thunderbolt
the edifice which the men had built.   After that, the giants,
scared and filled with terror, separated and scattered in all
directions over the earth."[1]

In this latter tradition the traces of Biblical influence
appear not only in the dispersal of the builders over the face
of the earth, but also in the construction of the tower out of
clay and bitumen ; for while these are the materials out of
which the Tower of Babel is said to have been built, bitumen
seems never to have been used by the Mexicans for such a
purpose and is not found anywhere near Cholula.[2]   "The
history of the confusion of tongues seems also to have existed
in the country, not long after the Conquest, having very probably been learnt from the missionaries ; but it does not seem

The story
of the
foundation
of the
temple of
Cholula
betrays
Biblical
influence.

[1] Diego Duran, *Historia de las Indias
de Nueva-Espana y Islas de Tierra
Firme*, i. (Mexico, 1867) pp. 6 *sq*.
With the accidental omission of a line
("*los unos caminaron hácia Ponente,
los otros fiácia Oriente*"), the passage
has been extracted and translated into
French by Brasseur de Bourbourg,
*Histoire des Nations civilisées du
Mexique et de l'Amérique-Centrale*, i.
433 *sq*.

[2] (Sir) Edward B. Tylor, *Anahuac*,
p. 277.

to have been connected with the Tower-of-Babel legend of
Cholula.   Something like it at least appears in the Gemelli
table of Mexican migrations, reproduced in Humboldt, where
a bird in a tree is sending down a number of tongues to a
crowd of men standing below."[1]   On the strength of these
suspicious resemblances Tylor may be right in condemning
the legend of Cholula "as not genuine, or at least as partly
of late fabrication."[2]

Story like
Tower of
Babel
as r···
the Toltecs
of Mexico.

A like suspicion of spuriousness, or at all events of
assimilation to Biblical traditions, must apparently rest on
a legend ascribed to the Toltecs of Mexico.   "Ixtlil-xochitl
writes of this tradition as follows : They say that the world
was created in the year Ce Tecpatl, and this time until the
deluge they call Atonatiuh, which means the age of the sun
of water, because the world was destroyed by the deluge.
It is found in the histories of the Toltecs that this age and
first world, as they term it, lasted seven hundred and sixteen years ; that man and all the earth were destroyed by
great showers and by lightnings from heaven, so that
nothing remained, and the most lofty mountains were
covered up and submerged to the depth of *caxtolmoletltli*,
or fifteen cubits, and here they add other fables of how men
came to multiply again from the few who escaped the
destruction in a *toptlipetlacali* ; which word very nearly
signifies a closed chest ; and how, after multiplying, the
men built a *zacuali* of great height, and by this is meant a
very high tower, in which to take refuge when the world
should be a second time destroyed.   After this their tongue
became confused, and, not understanding each other, they
went to different parts of the world."[3]   In this legend the
coincidences with the Biblical narratives of the flood, the
ark, the tower of Babel, and the confusion of tongues seem
too numerous to be accidental.

---

[1] (Sir) Edward B. Tylor, *Anahuac*,
p. 277.   As to this Mexican picture,
see further H. H. Bancroft, *Native
Races of the Pacific States*, iii. 68 note,
who strongly suspects the genuineness
of the legend based on certain Aztec
paintings.   The authenticity of these
traditions is questioned also by Prescott, *History of the Conquest of Mexico*

(London, 1901), iii. 365 note[18]

[2] (Sir) Edward B. Tylor, *Anahuac*,
p. 71.

[3] H. H. Bancroft, *The Native Races
of the Pacific States*, v. 19-21, referring to " Relaciones " in Lord Kings-
borough's *Antiquities of Mexico*, vol.
ix. pp. 321 *sq.*

A similar verdict may be pronounced, with even less hesitation, on a tale told by the Karens of Burma, a tribe who display a peculiar aptitude for borrowing Christian legends and disguising them with a thin coat of local colour. Their edition of the Tower of Babel story, as told by the Gaikho section of the tribe, runs as follows. " The Gaikhos trace their genealogy to Adam, and make thirty generations from Adam, to the building of the Tower of Babel, at which time they say they separated from the Red Karens. . . . In the days of Pan-dan-man, the people determined to build a pagoda that should reach up to heaven. The place they suppose to be somewhere in the country of the Red Karens, with whom they represent themselves as associated until this event. When the pagoda was half way up to heaven, God came down and confounded the language of the people, so that they could not understand each other. Then the people scattered, and Than-mau-rai, the father of the Gaikho tribe, came west, with eight chiefs, and settled in the valley of the Sitang." [1]

Karen vers the story of the Tower of Babel.

The Biblical story of the Tower of Babel and the confusion of tongues reappears also among the Mikirs, one of the many Tibeto-Burman tribes of Assam. They say that in days of old the descendants of Ram were mighty men, and growing dissatisfied with the mastery of the earth they aspired to conquer heaven. So they began to build a tower which should reach up to the skies. Higher and higher rose the building, till at last the gods and demons feared lest these giants should become the masters of heaven, as they already were of earth. So they confounded their speech, and scattered them to the four corners of the world. Hence arose all the various tongues of mankind. [2] Again, we find the same old story, in a slightly disguised form, among the Admiralty Islanders. They say that the tribe or family of the Lohi numbered one hundred and thirty souls and had for their chief a certain Muikiu. This Muikiu said to his people, " Let us build a house as high as heaven." So they built it, and when it nearly reached the sky, there came to them from

Mikir ver ion o the stor of the Tower of Babel.

Version of the story of the Tower of by the Admiralty Islanders.

---

[1] F. Mason, D.D., " On dwellings, works of art, laws, etc. of the Karens," *Journal of the Asiatic Society of Bengal*, New Series, xxxvii. (1868) pp. 163, 164.

[2] Edward Stack, *The Mikirs*, edited, arranged, and supplemented by Sir Charles Lyall (London, 1908), p. 72.

Kali a man named Po Awi, who forbade them to go on with the building. Said he to Muikiu, " Who told you to build so high a house ? " Muikiu answered, " I am master of our people the Lohi. I said, ' Let us build a house as high as heaven.' If I had had my way, our houses should have been as high as heaven. But now, thy will is done, our houses will be low." So saying he took water and sprinkled it on the bodies of his people. Then was their language confounded ; they understood not each other and dispersed into different lands. Thus every land has now its own speech.[1] There can be little doubt that this story is merely an echo of missionary teaching.

Greek and African traditions as to the origin of the diversity of tongues.

Not a few peoples have attempted to explain the diversities of human speech without reference to a Tower of Babel or similar structures. Thus the Greeks had a tradition that for many ages men lived at peace, without cities and without laws, speaking one language, and ruled by Zeus alone. At last Hermes introduced diversities of speech and divided mankind into separate nations. So discord first arose among mortals, and Zeus, offended at their quarrels, resigned the sovereignty and committed it to the hands of the Argive hero Phoroneus, the first king of men.[2] The Wa-Sania of British East Africa say that of old all the tribes of the earth knew only one language, but that during a severe famine the people went mad and wandered in all directions, jabbering strange words, and so the different languages arose.[3] A different explanation of the diversities of language is given by the Kachcha Nagas, a hill tribe of Assam. According to them, at the creation all men were of one race, but they were destined soon afterwards to be broken up into different nations. The king of the men then on earth had a daughter named Sitoylê. She was wondrous fleet of foot, and loved to roam the jungle the

Explanation of the diversities of language given by the Kachcha Nagas of Assam.
·

---

[1] Josef Meier, " Mythen und Sagen der Admiralitatsinsulaner," *Anthropos*, ii. (1907) pp. 933 *sq*. The legend is reported in the original language, with a literal interlineal translation into German, which is not very clear. I have tried to represent the general sense, but do not feel sure that I have grasped the exact meaning.

[2] Hyginus, *Fabul.* 143. The legend appears not to be mentioned by any extant Greek author.

[3] Captain W. E. H. Barrett, " Notes on the Customs of the Wa-Giriama, etc., of British East Africa " *Journal of the Royal Anthropological Institute*, xli. (1911) p. 37.

livelong day, far from home, thereby causing much anxiety to her parents, who feared lest she should be devoured by wild beasts. One day her father conceived a plan for keeping her at home. He sent for a basket of linseed, and upsetting it on the ground he ordered his daughter to put the seeds back, one by one, into the basket, counting them as she did so. Then thinking that the task he had set her would occupy the maiden the whole day, he withdrew. But by sunset his daughter had counted all the seeds and put them back in the basket, and no sooner had she done so than away she hurried to the jungle. So when her parents returned, they could find no trace of their missing daughter. After searching for days and days, however, they at last came across a monster python lying gorged in the shade of the trees. All the men being assembled, they attacked the huge reptile with spear and sword. But even as they struck at the snake, their appearance changed, and they found themselves speaking various dialects. The men of the same speech now drew apart from the rest and formed a separate band, and the various bands thus created became the ancestors of the different nations now existing on earth.[1] But what became of the princess, whether she was restored to her sorrowing parents, or whether she had been swallowed by the python, the story does not relate.

The Kukis of Manipur, another hill race of Assam, account for the diversity of languages in their tribes by saying, that once on a time the three grandsons of a certain chief were all playing together in the house, when their father bade them catch a rat. But while they were busy hunting the animal, they were suddenly smitten with a confusion of tongues and could not understand each other, so the rat escaped. The eldest of the three sons now spoke the Lamyang language ; the second spoke the Thado language ; and as for the third, some say that he spoke the Waiphie language, but others think it was the Manipur tongue which he spoke. At all events the three lads became the ancestors of three distinct tribes.[2] The En-

Other
attempts to
explain the
diversity of
languages
told by the
Kukis of
and the
Encounter
Bay tribe
of South
Australia.

---

[1] C. A. Soppitt, *A Short Account of the Kachcha Nâga (Empêo) tribe in the North Cachar Hills* (Shillong, 1885), pp. 15 *sq.*

[2] Major W. McCulloch, *Account of the Valley of Munnipore and of the Hill Tribes* (Calcutta, 1859), p. 56 (*Selections from the Records of the Government of India*, No. xxvii.).

counter Bay tribe of South Australia trace the origin of languages to an ill-tempered old woman, who died long ago. Her name was Wurruri, she lived towards the east, and generally walked about with a big stick in her hand to scatter the fires round which other people were sleeping. When at last she died, her people were so glad to be rid of her, that they sent messengers in all directions to announce the good news of her death. Men, women, and children accordingly assembled, not to mourn but to rejoice over the decease and to celebrate it by a cannibal banquet. The Raminjerar were the first who fell upon the corpse and commenced to devour the flesh ; and no sooner did they do so than they began to speak intelligibly. The other tribes to the eastward, arriving later, ate the contents of the intestines, which caused them to speak a language slightly different. Last of all came the northern tribes, and having consumed the intestines and all that remained of the corpse, they spoke a language which differed still more from that of the Raminjerar.[1]

Stories to
x   t
diversit of
tongues
told by
some
tribes of
e can
Indians.

The Maidu Indians of California say that down to a certain time everybody spoke the same language. But once, when the people were having a burning, and everything was ready for the next day, suddenly in the night everybody began to speak in a different tongue, except that each husband and wife talked the same language. That night the Creator, whom they call Earth-Initiate, appeared to a certain man named Kuksu, told him what had happened, and instructed him how to proceed next day when the Babel of tongues would commence. Thus prepared, Kuksu summoned all the people together, for he could speak all the languages. He taught them the names of the different animals and so forth in their various dialects, showed them how to cook and to hunt, gave them their laws, and appointed the times for their dances and festivals. Then he called each tribe by name, and sent them off in different directions, telling them where they were to dwell.[2] We

---

[1] H. E. A. Meyer, "Manners and Customs of the Aborigines of the Encounter Bay Tribe, South Australia," in *The Native Tribes of South Australia,* with an Introductory Chapter by J. D. Woods (Adelaide, 1879), pp.

204 *sq.*

[2] Roland B. Dixon, "Maidu Myths," *Bulletin of the American Museum of Natural History,* xvii. Part ii. (New York, 1902) pp. 44 *sq.* The "burning" alluded to in the text, of which

have seen that the Tlingits of Alaska explain the diversity
of tongues by the story of a great flood, which they may
have borrowed from Christian missionaries or traders.[1]   The
Quiches of Guatemala told of a time, in the early ages of
the world, when men lived together and spoke but one language, when they invoked as yet neither wood nor stone,
and remembered naught but the word of the Creator, the
Heart of heaven and of earth.   However, as years went on
the tribes multiplied, and leaving their old home came to
a place called Tulan.   It was there, according to Quiché
tradition, that the language of the tribes changed and the
diversity of tongues originated ; the people ceased to understand each other's speech and dispersed to seek new homes
in different parts of the world.[2]

These last stories, in attempting to account for the
diversities of language, make no reference to a Tower of
Babel, and accordingly they may, with the possible exception
of the Tlingit tale, be accepted as independent efforts of the
human mind to grapple with that difficult problem, however little they succeed in solving it.

These stories are independente Hebrew tradition.

---

the writer gives no explanation, would
seem to have been a performance of the
shamans, who danced to the light of a
fire kindled by the friction of wood,
and who professed to walk through fire
unscathed.   See Roland B. Dixon,
"The Northern Maidu," *Bulletin of
the American Museum of Natural*

History, vol. xvii. Part iii. (New York,
1905) pp. 273, 275, 279, 283.
[1] Above, p. 318.

[2] Brasseur de Bourbourg, *Popul
Vuh, le Livre Sacré et les Mythes de
l'Antiquité Américaine* (Paris, 1861),
pp. 211-217.

PART II

THE PATRIARCHAL AGE

CHAPTER I

THE COVENANT OF ABRAHAM

WITH the story of the Tower of Babel, and the dispersion of the peoples from that centre, the authors of Genesis conclude their general history of mankind in the early ages of the world. They now narrow the scope of their narrative and concentrate it on the Hebrew people alone. The history takes the form of a series of biographies, in which the fortunes of the nation are set forth, not in vague general outlines, but in a series of brilliantly coloured pictures recording the adventures of individual men, the forefathers of the race.[1] The unity which runs through the lives of the patriarchs is not merely genealogical ; a community of occupation as well as of blood binds these ancestors of Israel together ; all are nomadic shepherds and herdsmen, roaming from place to place with their flocks and herds in search of fresh pasture ; they have not yet settled down to the humdrum life of the peasant, who repeats, year after year, the same monotonous round of labour on the same fields on which his father and his father's father had laboured all their days before him. In short, it is the pastoral age which the writers of Genesis have depicted with a clearness of outline and a vividness of colouring which time has not dimmed, and which, under all the changed conditions of modern life, still hold the reader spellbound by their ineffable charm. In this gallery of

---

[1] I see no sufficient reason to question, with some modern writers, the historical reality of the great Hebrew patriarchs, though doubtless some of the incidents and details which tradition has recorded concerning them are unhistorical. On this subject I am in substantial agreement with the recent English commentators on Genesis, S. R. Driver (*The Book of Genesis*, Tenth Edition, pp. xliii *sqq.*), Principal Skinner (*Commentary on Genesis*, pp. xxiii *sqq.*), and Bishop Ryle (*The Book of Genesis*, pp. xxxix *sqq.*).

portraits, painted against a background of quiet landscape, the first place is occupied by the majestic figure of Abraham. After quitting Babylonia, the land of his birth, he is said to have migrated to Canaan and there to have received from God in person the assurance of the future grandeur and glory of his race. To confirm his promise the deity, we are told, condescended to enter into a regular covenant with the patriarch, observing all the legal formalities which were customary on such occasions among men. The narrative of this important transaction affords us an interesting glimpse into the means adopted by covenanters in primitive society for the purpose of creating a binding obligation on both sides.

God's covenant with Abraham.

We read in Genesis that God commanded Abraham, saying to him, " Take me an heifer of three years old, and a she-goat of three years old, and a ram of three years old, and a turtledove, and a young pigeon." So Abraham took the heifer, the she-goat, and the ram, cut them in two, and laid each half of the animal over against the other ; but the birds he did not divide. And when the birds of prey came down on the carcasses, Abraham drove them away. When the sun was going down, Abraham sank into a deep sleep, and a horror of great darkness fell upon him. And it came to pass that when the sun had set, and it was dark, behold a smoking furnace and a flaming torch passed between the pieces of the sacrificial victims, and God proclaimed his covenant with Abraham.[1]

Hebrew mode of ratifying a covenant by cutting a sacrificial victim in two.

In this description the horror of great darkness which falls on Abraham at sunset is a premonition of the coming of God, who in the darkness of night passes between the pieces of the slaughtered animals in the likeness of a smoking furnace and a flaming torch. In doing so the deity only complied with the legal formalities required by ancient Hebrew law at the ratification of a covenant ; for we know from Jeremiah that it was the custom of the contracting parties to cut a calf in twain and pass between the pieces.[2] That this was the regular form observed on such occasions is strongly suggested by the Hebrew phrase for making a covenant, which is literally to " cut a

[1] Genesis xv. 9-21.   [2] Jeremiah xxxiv. 18.

covenant,"[1] and the inference is confirmed by analogies in the Greek language and ritual; for the Greeks used similar phrases and practised similar rites. Thus they spoke of *cutting* oaths in the sense of swearing them,[2] and of *cutting* a treaty instead of making one.[3] Such expressions, like the corresponding phrases in Hebrew and Latin,[4] are undoubtedly derived from a custom of sacrificing victims and cutting them in pieces as a mode of adding solemnity to an oath or a treaty. For example, we are told that when Agamemnon was about to lead the Greeks to Troy, the soothsayer. Calchas brought a boar into the market-place, and divided it into two parts, one on the west, and one on the east. Then each man, with a drawn sword in his hand, passed between the pieces of the boar, and the blade of his sword was smeared with the blood. Thus they swore enmity to Priam.[5] But sometimes, and perhaps more commonly, in Greek ritual, instead of passing between the pieces of the victims, the person who made an oath stood upon them. So in trials before the court of the Areopagus at Athens the accuser made oath standing on the pieces of a boar, a ram, and a bull, which had been sacrificed by special persons on special days.[6] Again, when the fair Helen was wooed by many suitors, her father Tyndareus, fearful of the revenge which the rejected lovers might take, made them all swear to defend her and the man of her choice, whoever he might be; and to give solemnity to the oath he sacrificed a horse, cut it up, and caused the suitors to swear standing on the pieces.[7] Again, in the council-chamber at Olympia there was an image of Zeus surnamed the God of Oaths; and before the Olympian games began, it was customary for the athletes, their fathers and brothers, and also the trainers, to swear on the cut pieces of a boar that they would be guilty of no foul play.[8] In Messenia

Similar practice in ancient Greece and Rome.

Greek form of oath by standing on pieces of a sacrificial victim.

---

[1] כָּרַת בְּרִית, W. Robertson Smith, *Religion of the Semites*, New Edition, (London, 1894), pp. 480 *sq.*

[2] ὅρκια τέμνειν. See, for example, Homer, *Iliad*, ii. 124, *Odyssey*, xxiv. 483; Herodotus vii. 132.

[3] Euripides, *Helena*, 1235, σπονδὰς τέμωμεν καὶ διαλλάχθητί μοι. But the phrase is unusual and perhaps only poetical. The ordinary expression is σπονδὰς ποιεῖσθαι, "to make a treaty."

[4] See below, p. 401, note [2].

[5] Dictys Cretensis, *Bellum Trojanum*, i. 15.

[6] Demosthenes, *Or.* xxiii. p. 642.

[7] Pausanias iii. 20. 9.

[8] Pausanias v. 24. 9.

there was a place called the Boar's Grave, because Hercules
was there said to have exchanged oaths with the sons of
Neleus over the pieces of a boar.[1]

*Similar
ceremonies
at taking
an oath
observed
by
barbarous
tribes in
antiquity.*   Similar ceremonies at taking an oath or making peace
were observed also by barbarous tribes in antiquity. Thus
the Molossians used to cut up oxen into small pieces when
they made a treaty and swore to observe it ;[2] however, we
are not told what use precisely they made of the pieces in
the ceremony.   Among the Scythians, when a man conceived that he was wronged by another, against whom single-
handed he was powerless, he appealed to his friends for help
in the following manner.   He sacrificed an ox, cut up and
boiled the flesh, and having spread out the reeking hide on
the ground he sat down on it, with his arms doubled up
behind him, as if they were pinioned.   This was the most
urgent form of supplication known to the Scythians.   While
the man sat thus on the hide, with the slices of boiled beef
beside him, his friends and relations and any one else who
chose to help him, would take each of them a slice of the
beef, and planting every man his right foot on the hide
would promise to furnish so many soldiers, horse or foot,
all found and free of charge, to assist the suppliant in
avenging himself on his enemy.   Some would promise to
bring five men, some ten, and some more ; while the poorest
would offer only their personal services.   In this way sometimes a large force would be mustered, and so levied it was
deemed very formidable, because every man in it was bound
by his oath to stand by his fellow.[3]   In Tibetan law-courts to
*Tibetan
form of
oath.*   this day, "when the great oath is taken, which is seldom,
it is done by the person placing a holy scripture on his head,
and sitting on the reeking hide of an ox and eating a part
of the ox's heart.   The expense of this ceremony is borne
by the party who challenges the accused."[4]

*Similar
ceremonies
observed
at peace-
making by
the
Kavirondo,
Nandi, and
Bagesu of
East
Africa.*   Ceremonies of a like kind are still observed at peace-
making by savage tribes in Africa and India.   Thus among
the Kavirondo, of British East Africa, in making peace after

[1] Pausanias iv. 15. 8.
[2] Zenobius, *Cent.* ii. 83, in *Paroemio-
graphi Graeci*, ed. E. L. Leutsch et
F. G. Schneidewin (Göttingen, 1839-
1851), i. 53 ; Suidas, *s.v.* Βοῦς ὁ
Μολοττῶν.
[3] Lucian, *Toxaris*, 48.
[4] L. Austine Waddell, *The Buddhism of Tibet* (London, 1895), p. 569
note [7].

a war, the vanquished side takes a dog and cuts it in halves. The delegates from each side then hold respectively the forequarters and the hindquarters of the divided dog, and swear peace and friendship over the half dog which they hold in their hands.[1]   A similar ceremony is used to seal a covenant of peace among the Nandi, another tribe of the same region.   They cut a dog in halves : the two halves are held by men representing the two sides who have been at war ; and a third man says, " May the man who breaks this peace be killed like this dog."   Others kill a tortoise with blows of a club, or smash a calabash full.of water and flies, and say, " May the man who breaks this peace be killed like these things."   Others again castrate a goat, and after one man of each party has taken one of the testicles in his hand they say : " May God castrate the man who breaks this peace." [2]   Among the Bagesu, a Bantu tribe of Mount Elgon, in British East Africa, when two clans have been at war and wish to make peace, the representatives of the clans hold a dog, one by the head and the other by the hind legs, while a third man cuts the dog through with a large knife at one stroke.   The body is then thrown away in the bush and left, and thereafter the members of the two clans may freely intermingle without any fear of trouble or danger.[3]

Among the Masai of East Africa, " in settling serious disputes by oath, each disputant takes hold of a goat or sheep, which is then cut in two.   This is done in presence of witnesses, and the matter thus settled is not supposed to be reopened." [4]   Among the Karamojo, another tribe of East Africa, " a solemn oath is taken in the following way : a black ox is selected and speared, the interested parties then take hold of a leg each and these are cut from the body ; each then partakes of the marrow from the leg he has thus received." [5]   In the Wachaga tribe of the same

Similar ratifying oaths to g among Masai and Karamojo Africa.

[1] Sir Harry Johnston, *The Uganda Protectorate* [2] (London, 1904), ii. 752 *sq.* ; C. W. Hobley, *Eastern Uganda* (London, 1902), p. 25.
[2] A. C. Hollis, *The Nandi, their Language and Folk - Lore* (Oxford, 1909), p. 84.   Compare Sir Harry Johnston, *The Uganda Protectorate*, ii. 884.

[3] John Roscoe, *The Northern Bantu* (Cambridge, 1915), pp. 170 *sq.*
[4] J. R. L. Macdonald, " Notes on the Ethnology of Tribes met with during progress of the Juba Expedition," *Journal of the Anthropological Institute*, xxix. (1899) p. 233.
[5] J. R. L. Macdonald, *op. cit.* pp. 235 *sq.*

At making
Wachaga
of East
Africa cut
a kid and
a rope in
two.

region, when two districts have resolved to form a solemn league and covenant of peace, the ceremony observed at the ratification of the treaty is as follows. The warriors of the two districts assemble and sit down crowded together in a circle on some piece of open ground. A long rope is stretched round the assembly and its free ends are knotted together on one side, so that the whole body of warriors from both sides is enclosed within the rope. But before the knot is tied, the rope is moved thrice or seven times round the circle and a kid is carried with it. Finally, on the side of the circle where the ends are knotted together, the rope is passed over the body of the kid, which is held stretched at full length by two men, so that the rope and the kid form parallel lines, the rope being over the kid. These motions of the rope and of the kid round the sitting warriors are carried out by two uncircumcised and therefore childless lads ; and the circumstance is significant, because the lads symbolize that infertility or death without offspring which the Wachaga regard as the greatest of curses, and which they commonly refer to the action of the higher powers. In most of their treaties they imprecate this dreaded curse on perjurers, and on the contrary call down the blessing of numerous progeny on him who shall keep his oath. In the ceremony under discussion the employment of uncircumcised youths is intended not merely to symbolize the fate of the perjurer but to effect it by sympathetic magic. For a similar reason the curses and the blessings are recited by old men, because they are past the age of begetting children. The recitation runs as follows, "If after the making of this covenant I do anything to harm thee or devise devices against thee without giving thee warning, may I be split in two like this rope and this kid!" Chorus, "Amen!" "May I split in two like a boy who dies without begetting children!" Chorus, "Amen!" "May my cattle perish, every one!" Chorus, "Amen!" "But if I do not that; if I be true to thee, so may I fare well!" Chorus, "Amen!" "May my children be like the bees in number!" Chorus, "Amen!" And so forth and so forth. When the representatives of the two covenanting districts have sworn the oath, the rope and the kid are cut in two at one stroke, and the spouting blood is sprinkled on the covenanters, while the old men in a comprehensive formula call down curses and blessings impartially on both sides. Afterwards the flesh of the goat is eaten by old men who are past the age of begetting children, and the rope is divided between the two districts, each of which keeps its portion carefully. If epidemics should break out and be attributed by the diviners, who interpret the will of the higher powers, to some breach of the treaty committed wittingly or unwittingly by the inhabitants of the afflicted country, the rope must be expiated or, as the native phrase goes, "cooled." For the magical power with which the covenant invested the rope is now believed to be actively engaged in avenging its violation. The expiation consists . in sacrificing a lamb and smearing its blood and dung on the rope, while the following words are spoken : " Those people have done wrong without knowing it. Rope, to-day I expiate thee, that thou mayst harm them no more! Be expiated ! Be expiated ! Be expiated !" The persons who have committed the breach of faith are expiated by a medicine-man, who sprinkles them with a magical mixture compounded out of the blood of tortoises, rock-badgers, and antelopes, together with portions of certain plants, the whole being administered by means of a bunch of herbs of definite sorts and accompanied by appropriate words.[1]

Wachaga
m d
expiating a
breach of
trea y.

Somewhat different, though conforming to the same general type, are the ceremonies observed at peace-making among some tribes of South Africa. Thus, in the Barolong tribe, when the chief wished to make a covenant of peace with another chief who had fled to him for protection, he took the paunch of a large ox, and bored a hole through it, and the two chiefs crawled through the hole, the one after the other, in order to intimate by this ceremony that their tribes would thenceforth be one.[2] Similarly among the Bechuanas "in making a public covenant or agreement with one another, two chiefs *tshwaragana moshwang*; that is to say, an animal is slaughtered, and some of the contents of its

Cere-
monies at
making
mo
some tribes
of South
rica.

[1] J. Raum, " Blut- und Speichel-bünde bei den Wadschagga," *Archiv für Religionswissenschaft*, x. (1907) pp. 285-288.

[2] Robert Moffat, *Missionary Labours and Scenes in Southern Africa* (London, 1842), p. 278.

stomach are laid hold of by both covenanting parties, their hands meeting together and laying hold of each other, while covered over with the contents of the sacrificed animal's stomach.   This would seem to be the most solemn form of public agreement known in the country.   It was performed more than once at Shoshong while I was there, in the case of chiefs who, with their people, placed themselves under Sekhome's protection." [1]

Similar
m   es
observed at
peace-
. . g
among the
Nagas and
ei
Kukis of
Assam.

Equivalent ceremonies are observed at peace-making among some of the hill tribes of Assam.   Thus the Nagas " have several ways of taking an oath.   The commonest and most sacred is for the two parties to the oath to lay hold of a dog or fowl, one by its head the other by its tail or feet, whilst the animal or bird is cut in two with a *dâo*, emblematic of the perjurer's fate." [2]   According to another authority, among the forms of oaths taken by the Nagas are the following : " When they swear to keep the peace, or to perform any promise, they place the barrel of a gun or a spear between their teeth, signifying by this ceremony that, if they do not act up to their agreement, they are prepared to fall by either of the two weapons.   Another simple but equally binding oath is, for two parties to take hold of the ends of a piece of spear-iron, and to have it cut into two pieces, leaving a bit in the hand of each party ; but the most sacred oath, it is said, is for each party to take a fowl, one by the head and the other by the legs, and in this manner to pull it asunder, intimating that treachery or breach of agreement would merit the same treatment." [3] Other Naga tribes of Assam have a somewhat different way of settling disputes.   " A representative of each of the

---

[1] John Mackenzie, *Ten Years North of the Orange River* (Edinburgh, 1871), p. 393.   Compare W. C. Willoughby, " Notes on the Totemism of the Becwana," *Journal of the Anthropological Institute*, xxxv. (1905) p. 306.

[2] Lieut.-Col. R. G. Woodthorpe, " Notes on the Wild Tribes inhabiting the so-called Naga Hills," *Journal of the Anthropological Institute*, xi. (1882) p. 71 ;   W. W. Hunter, *Statistical Account of Assam* (London, 1879), ii. 184.   The *dâo* is a long

knife or sword, narrow at the haft, square, broad, and pointless at the tip, with only one edge sharpened.   The ordinary *dâo* is used for many purposes, such as felling trees and cutting timber; the fighting *dâo*, long and heavy, is a weapon of war.   See Colonel Lewin, quoted by T. C. Hodson, *The Nāga Tribes of Manipur* (London, 1911), p. 36.

[3] Major John Butler, *Travels and Adventures in the Province of Assam* (London, 1855), p. 154.

litigant parties holds an end of a cane basket inside which a cat, alive, is placed, and at a signal a third man hacks the cat in two, and both sides then cut it up with their daos, taking care to stain the weapon with blood. On the occasion when I saw this ceremony I was told that the ceremony was a form of peace-making or treaty, and that therefore the slaughter of the cat bound them in a kind of covenant."[1] Among the Lushei Kuki clans of Assam " an oath of friendship between chiefs is a serious matter. A mithan is tied up to a post and the parties to the oath, grasping a spear with their right hands, stab it behind the shoulder with sufficient force to draw blood, repeating a formula to the effect that until the rivers run backwards into the earth again they will be friends. The animal is then killed and a little of the blood is smeared on the feet and forehead of the oath takers. To make this oath more binding they both eat a small piece of the liver raw."[2]

We have now to ask, what is the meaning of these sacrifices at making a covenant or swearing an oath? Why should the parties to a covenant or an oath ratify it by killing an animal, cutting it in pieces, standing on the pieces or passing between them, and smearing the blood on their persons? Two different theories have been suggested. The one may be called the *retributive* theory and the other the *sacramental* or purificatory. We will consider the retributive theory first. According to it, the killing and cutting up of the victim is symbolic of the retribution which will overtake the man who breaks the covenant or violates the oath ; he, like the animal, will perish by a violent death. This certainly appears to be the interpretation put upon the ceremony by some of the peoples who observe it. Thus the Wachaga say, "May I split in two like this rope and this kid!" and in cutting a dog in two the Nandi say, "May the man who breaks this peace be killed like this dog."[3]

Two theories to explain ceremonies, the retributive theory, and the mental or purificatory theor

The r t ve theory is in harmony tne view of some of the peoples who observe the ceremonies.

---

[1] T. C. Hodson, *The Naga Tribes of Manipur* (London, 1911), p. 111.
[2] Lieut.-Col. J. Shakespear, *The Lushei Kuki Clans* (London, 1912), p. 56. A mithan is a species of bison. These animals are allowed to wander at will in the jungle round the village ; towards dusk they return of themselves, each to his owner's house. They are only used for slaughter. The tame mithan interbreed freely with the wild mithan. See J. Shakespear, *op. cit.* pp. 31 *sq.*
[3] Above, pp. 395, 396.

A similar ceremony, accompanied by similar imprecations, used to solemnize the making of peace among the
Awome, a people of the Niger delta who are better known
to Europeans as New Calabars.   When two towns or sub-
tribes grew weary of fighting, they would send to the ancient
village of Ke, situated near the ·coast, to the east of the
Sombreiro River, where was a fetish or ju-ju called Ke-ni
Opu-So.   On such occasions the fetish priest was invited
to come and preside over the ratification of peace between
the belligerents.   Accordingly he came in his canoe decked
with young palm leaves, and arranged with the former foes
to meet on an appointed day and swear to the covenant.
When the day came, the people gathered together, and the inhabitants of Ke also came, bringing with them the necessary
offerings, which consisted of a sheep, a length of black or
dark blue cloth, gunpowder, and grass or grass seed.   Over
these offerings the old enemies swore peace and friendship,
the priest first saying, " To-day we Ke people bring peace
to your town.   From now on neither of you may have evil
mind against the other."   With these words he drew forward the sheep and cleft it in two, saying, " Should either
town fight again, may it be cleft asunder like this sheep."
Then, lifting up the piece of dark cloth, he said, " As this
cloth is dark, so may the offending town be darkened."
Next, setting fire to the gunpowder, he said, " As this powder
is burnt, so may fire burn the guilty town."   Lastly, holding
out the grass, he said, " Should either town fight again, may
that town be covered with grass."   On account of the
services which the people of Ke rendered as peace-makers,
an ancient law of Calabar forbade any other town to wage
war on Ke under pain of banishment to be inflicted on the
transgressors by all the other members of the tribe in con-
cert.[1]   In these Calabar rites the retributive intention of
cleaving the sheep in two is expressed without ambiguity,
and it is corroborated by the imprecations by which the
other symbolic ceremonies are accompanied.

The same explanation is given of the similar rite

---

[1] For this account of the peace-mak-·
ing ceremony of the Awome I am in-
debted to my friend Mr. P. Amaury   Talbot, District Commissioner in South
Nigeria.   His letter is dated Degema,
S. Nigeria, December 7th, 1916.

among the Nagas, and is confirmed by the variations in the form of the oath, which seem best explained as signifying the retribution that will befall the perjurer.[1] The retributive theory can be also supported by evidence drawn from classical antiquity. Thus when the Romans and the Albans made a treaty, which, according to Livy, was the most ancient treaty on record, the representative of the Roman people prayed to Jupiter, saying, " If the Roman people shall knowingly and of set purpose depart from the terms of this treaty, then smite thou them, O Jupiter, on that day, as I smite this boar-pig to-day." So saying, he smote and killed the pig with a flint knife.[2] Again, we read in Homer that at the making of a truce between the Greeks and the Trojans, lambs were slaughtered, and while they lay gasping out their life on the ground, Agamemnon poured a libation of wine, and as he did so, both Greeks and Trojans prayed that whichever side violated their oath, their brains might be dashed out, even as the wine was poured on the ground.[3]

The retributive intention of the sacrifice in such cases comes out very clearly in an Assyrian inscription, which records the solemn oath of fealty taken by Mati'-ilu, prince of Bit-Agusi, to Ashur-nirari, king of Assyria. Part of the inscription runs thus : " This he-goat has not been brought up from its flock for sacrifice, neither to the brave war-like (goddess Ishtar), nor to the peaceful (goddess Ishtar), neither for sickness nor for slaughter, but it has been brought up that Mati'-ilu may swear fealty by it to Ashur-nirari, king of Assyria. If Mati'-ilu sins against his oath, just as this he-goat has been brought up from his flock, so that he returns not to his flock and sets himself no more at the head of his flock, so shall Mati'-ilu be brought up from his land, with his sons, his daughters, and the people of his land, and he shall not return to his land, neither set himself at the head of his land. This head is not the head of the he-goat, it is the head of Mati'-ilu, it is the head of his children, of his nobles, of the people of his land. If Mati'-ilu

The retributive theory of the sacrifice in such cases confirmed practice of the Nagas and of the ancient Romans and Greeks.

The ... theory of the sacrifice ceremonies illustrated Assyrian oath of fealt...

---

[1] Above, pp. 398 *sq.*

Livy i. 24. Hence the Latin phrase "to *strike* a treaty" (*foedus ferire* and *foedus ictum*, Livy *l.c.*) in the sense of *making* a treaty, like the Greek ὅρκια τέμνειν.

[3] Homer, *Iliad*, iii. 292 *sqq.*

breaks this oath, as the head of this he-goat is cut off, so shall the head of Mati'-ilu be cut off.   This right foot is not the right foot of the he-goat, it is the right hand of Mati'-ilu, the right hand of his sons, of his nobles, of the people of his land.   If Mati'-ilu (breaks this covenant), just as the right foot (of this he-goat) is torn off (so shall the right hand of Mati'-ilu, the right hand of) his sons (of his nobles, and of the people of his land), be torn off."   Here there is a long gap in the inscription.   We may conjecture that in the missing portion the dismemberment of the victim was further described, and that as each limb was lopped off, the sacrificer proclaimed that it was not the limb of the goat that was severed, but the limb of Mati'-ilu, of his sons, his daughters, his nobles, and the people of his land, if they should prove traitors to their liege lord, the king of Assyria.[1]

Similar sacrifices, interpreted by similar imprecations, occur in the ritual of barbarous peoples. Examples from the Indian Archipelago.

Similar sacrifices, accompanied and interpreted by similar imprecations, meet us in the ritual of barbarous peoples at the present time.   Thus in the island of Nias, by way of ratifying a solemn oath or covenant, a man will cut the throat of a sucking-pig, while at the same time he calls down on his own head a like death if he forswears himself or breaks his engagement.[2]   Int he island of Timor a common form of giving evidence on oath is this : the witness takes a fowl in one hand and a sword in the other, and says, " Lord God, who art in heaven and on earth, look upon me! If I bear false witness to harm my fellow-men, may I be punished!   This day I make my oath, and if I am not speaking the truth, may my head be cut off like the head of this fowl !"   So saying, he chops off the bird's head on a wooden block.[3]   Among the Battas of Sumatra when chiefs are assembled to make peace or enter into a solemn covenant, a pig or a cow is brought forth, and the chiefs stand round it, each with his spear in his hand.   Then the

<hr/>

[1] F. E. Peiser, *Studien zur orie talischen Altertumskunde*, pp. 3 *sqq.* (*Mitteilungen der Vorderasiatisch Gesellschaft*, Berlin, 1898).   The words enclosed in brackets are wanting in the inscription.

[2] J. T. Nieuwenhuisen en H. C. B. von Rosenberg, "Verslag omtrent het

eiland Nias en deszelfs Bewoners," *Verhandelingen van het Bataviaasch Genootschap van Kunsten en Weten- schappen*, xxx. (Batavia, 1863) p. 105.

[3] H. D. Wiggers, "Gewone eid der Timoreezen en Rottineezen," *Tijd- schrift voor Indische Taal-, Land- en Volkenkunde*, xxxvi. (1893) p. 279.

gongs are beaten, and the oldest or most respected chief cuts the animal's throat with his knife ; afterwards the beast's body is opened, and the still palpitating heart torn out and chopped into as many bits as there are chiefs present. Each chief thereupon puts his morsel on a spit, roasts or warms it at a fire, and holding it up says, " If ever I break my oath, may I be slain like this beast that lies bleeding before me, and may I be eaten as its heart is now eaten." So saying he swallows the morsel. When all the chiefs have observed this rite, the still reeking carcass is divided among the people present and serves them for a feast.[1]

The Malagasy had a solemn form of swearing allegiance to a new sovereign, which was called " spearing the calf." A young bullock was killed and dismembered, the head and tail being cut off and reversed in their position at each end of the animal, while the hind-feet and the fore-feet were similarly transposed ; moreover the carcass was cut open, and a spear thrust into the bowels. Then a number of the chiefs or other principal men who were to be sworn, took hold of the spear, as many as could conveniently grasp it, and standing round the mangled animal listened, while the senior judge pronounced the oath, calling down many terrible curses on all who should perjure themselves, and winding up with these words, " If any of you ever retract, if any of you ever refuse allegiance to the sovereign appointed to reign, whether all has been specifically named or not, whether present or absent, great or small, old or young, male or female, newly brought to life or still unborn, whether holding the spear or not holding it, behold this glittering spear ! behold this young bullock ! and let the perjurer be as this bullock ; let him be speared of god ; let him not be favoured in any thing, but let him be wholly accursed ! "[2]

Among the Gallas of East Africa, when a man is accused of a crime, a common form of clearing himself from the accusation is this. A cock and a rusty knife are handed to him ; he kills the bird, cuts it limb from limb,

(marginal notes:) Similar sacrifices and imprecations in gascar.

Similar cri and imprecations in East Africa

---

[1] Franz Junghuhn, *Die Battaländer auf Sumatra* (Berlin, 1847), ii. 142 sq.

[2] William Ellis, *History of Madagascar* (London and Paris, preface dated 1838) i. 368 sq.

then hacks the body in pieces till he has made mince meat of it down to the last feather, which he throws away with an imprecation, praying that, if he is guilty, it may be done unto him as he has done unto the fowl.[1] Among the Akikuyu of East Africa the most solemn form of oath is administered by beating a goat to death with a stone and imprecating at the same time a like fate on all who should forswear themselves. The ceremony may only be performed by an elder of a particular clan. Mr. C. W. Hobley has described how the oath was administered to the tribe on a particular occasion, when the head chief desired to bind his people to the discharge of certain obligations which they had of late neglected. "A male goat of not less than two or three colours had its four legs tied together in a bunch by means of a green withy, a number of twigs of certain plants were gathered and then packed in between the legs and the body of the animal. . . . These preparations being complete all the participators in the oath moved to the windward of the animal—all except the elder who conducted the ceremony. The elder in question then took a large stone and beat the legs of the animal until he considered they were broken, all the time calling out that any who broke the oath would have their legs broken in a similar way. He then enumerated the obligations which it was essential they should fulfil. Next he hammered the spine of the animal, and finally beat in the skull with a stone, continually haranguing the assembly and condemning them to a similar fate if they broke the oath by omitting to fulfil the duties he enumerated. It is considered very deadly to stand down wind from the goat while this ceremony is going on. The assembled crowd then marched off chanting, and about half a mile down the road another speckled male goat had been slaughtered and the blood and contents of the stomach were spread on the path ; each member of the assembly had to tread in this with his bare feet, and on every one who did this the oath was considered binding. The second goat was killed by its stomach being opened. Neither of the sacrificial animals was eaten but left in the

Kikuyu
~~~~~ ~~ ~~~~
ceremony.
</div>

---

[1] Ph. Paulitschke, *Ethnographie Nordost-Afrikas, die geistige Cultur der Danâkil, Galla und Somâl* (Berlin, 1896), p. 52.

bush to be devoured by hyaenas." [1]   Among the Atheraka,
another tribe of British East Africa, the blood-feud which
arises from a murder may be settled by the payment of a
fine and the performance of the following ceremony.   The
murderer and the representative of the injured family are
taken by the elders to a river.   A sheep and a goat are
produced, of which the sheep is killed first and its fat
smeared over the eyes of both men, so that they cannot
see.   Thus blindfolded they are led to a hole which has
been dug in the ground, and between them the goat is
placed.   The two men must then between them force the
goat's head into the hole, which is afterwards filled up, and
the men hold the goat with its head in the ground till it is
suffocated.   Finally, they must break the animal's legs with
their hands, and as they do so, an elder addresses them in
these words, "You are now as brothers, if you quarrel you
shall be broken as these bones." [2]

Again, among the Chins, who inhabit the hills on the
borders of Assam and Burma, when two tribes take an oath
of friendship, they meet and produce a tame bison.   The
wise men of each village pour liquors over it and mutter to
their respective spirits to note the agreement which is now
to be made over blood.   The chiefs of either side each
take a spear and standing on opposite sides of the bison
drive their spears into its heart.   If guns and not spears
are used, the two chiefs simultaneously fire into the animal's
brain or heart.   As the bison falls its throat is cut and
the blood collected in bowls ; the tail of the animal is then
cut off and dipped in the blood, and with it the chiefs and
elders of the two parties daub the blood on each other's
faces, whilst the wise men mutter, "May the party who
breaks this agreement die even as this animal has died,
and may he be buried outside the village and his spirit
never rest ; may his family also die and may every bad
fortune attend his village." [3]

[1] C. W. Hobley, *Ethnology of A-
Kamba and other East African tribes*
(Cambridge, 1910), pp. 142 *sq.*   See
also Hon. C. Dundas, "The Organization and Laws of some Bantu tribes in
East Africa," *Journal of the Royal Anthropological Institute*, xlv. (1915) p.

255, who tells us that this oath is commonly used in all Kikuyu districts.

[2] Hon. C. Dundas, *op. cit.* p. 271.

[3] Bertram S. Carey and H. N. Tuck,
The Chin Hills, i. (Rangoon, 1896)
p. 195.   Compare Major W. Gwynne
Hughes, *The Hill Tracts of Arakan*

Similar
sacrifices
and
impreca-
tions
among the
ai ns of
Burma.

In the old days, when the Karens of Burma desired to make peace with their enemies, the representatives of the two sides met and proceeded as follows.   Filings made from a sword, a spear, a musket barrel, and a stone were mixed in a cup of water with the blood of a dog, a hog, and a fowl, which were killed for the purpose.   This mixture of blood, water, and filings was called the " peace-making water." Next the skull of the slaughtered dog was chopped in two, and the representative of one side took the lower jaw of the animal and hung it by a string round his neck, while the representative of the other hung the dog's skull, including the upper jaw, round his neck in like manner.   Thereafter the representatives solemnly promised that their people would thenceforth live at peace with each other, and in confirmation of the promise they drank the " peace-making water," and having drunk it they said, " Now that we have made peace, if any one breaks the engagement, if he does not act truly, but goes to war again and stirs up the feud again, may the spear eat his breast, the musket his bowels, the sword his

(Rangoon, 1881), p. 44. A good example of a symbolic oath, without the sacrifice of an animal, is furnished by the one which some Kuki-Lushai tribes of Assam take on the occasion when two villages make a covenant of peace. The symbolic objects on which the oath is sworn are an egg, a tiger's tooth, a lump of earth, a red thread, a black thread, a spear, a sword, and the leaf of a very sharp-stinging nettle. The swearer prays that, if he forswears himself he may be like the egg which has neither hands nor feet, neither ears nor head ; that he may be devoured by a tiger like the one on whose tooth he swears ; that he may be washed away by the rain like the lump of earth ; that his red blood may be shed in war like the red thread ; that his sight may fail and the world be dark to him like the black thread ; that he may be wounded by spear and sword ; and that his body may be continually sub- jected to tortures like those inflicted by the stinging nettle.   See C. A. Soppitt, A Short Account of the Kachcha Nâga (Empêo) Tribe in the North Cachar Hills (Shillong, 1885), p. 13. In

the East Indian Island of Buru people who swear an oath drink water mixed with salt, earth, and gunpowder from a bowl in which are placed a knife and a pair of scissors.   The meaning is that the perjurer will waste away like salt in water ; that the earth will gape and swallow him ; that, like gunpowder in the fire, he will be consumed ; and that the knife and the scissors will cut his throat.   See J. H. W. van der Miesen, "Een en ander over Boeroe," Mededeel- ingen van wege het Nederlandsche Zen- delinggenootschap, xlvi. (1902) pp. 449 sq.   Compare J. G. F. Riedel, De sluik-en kroesharige rassen tusschen Selebes en Papua (The Hague, 1886), p. 11.   In the Mentawei Islands, to the west of Sumatra, a man who is taking an oath will whittle away a stick with his knife, praying that, if he breaks his oath, the spirits may cut him to pieces just as he does to the stick. See J. F. K. Hansen, " De groep Noord- en Zuid-Pageh van de Mentawei-eilanden," Bijdragen tot de Taal-Land- en Volken- kunde van Nederlandsche-Indië, lxx. (1915) p. 217.

head; may the dog devour him, may the hog devour him, may the stone devour him!"[1]   Here the sword, the spear, the musket, and the stone, as well as the slain dog, hog, and fowl, are supposed to assist in bringing down vengeance on the perjurer, who has imbibed portions of them all in the " peace-making water."

In these examples the retributive virtue ascribed to the sacrifice is rendered unmistakable by the accompanying words: the slaughter of the animal symbolizes the slaughter of the perjurer, or rather it is a piece of imitative magic designed to bring down on the transgressor the death which he deserves.   A retributive effect is also ascribed to the slaughter of an animal in the following instances, though in them apparently the efficient cause is believed to be the ghost of the slain animal rather than the magical virtue of the ceremony.   Thus the Kayans or Bahaus of Central Borneo swear in ordinary cases on the tooth of a royal tiger; but in serious cases they put a dog slowly to death by stabbing it repeatedly with a sword, while the man who takes the oath smears his body with the streaming blood. They believe that if he forswears himself the ghost of the dog will haunt, bite, and kill him.[2]   Similarly, among the Ossetes of the Caucasus, a man who swears will sometimes cut off a cat's head or hang a dog, praying that if he swears falsely or breaks his oath, the cat or dog may bite or scratch him.[3]   Here again it seems obvious that it is the ghost of the hanged dog or decapitated cat which is charged with the duty of avenging perjury.

In these ceremonies the slaughter animal symbolizes slaughter of the perjurer. But me 'm the host of the slain an [1] thought to haunt the perjurer.

---

[1] Rev. F. Mason, D.D., " On Dwellings, Works of Art, Laws, etc., of the Karens " *Journal of the Asiatic Society of Bengal*, New Series, xxxvii. (Calcutta, 1868) pp. 160 *sq.*

[2] A. W. Nieuwenhuis, *Quer .durch Borneo* (Leyden, 1904–1907), i. 62. The Malanaus of Central Borneo " use a dog in taking a very solemn oath, and sometimes the dog is killed in the course of this ceremony. Or instead of the dog being killed, its tail may be cut off, and the man taking the oath licks the blood from the stump; this is considered a most binding and solemn form of oath.   The ceremony

is spoken of as *Koman asu, i.e.* 'the eating of the dog'" (Ch. Hose and W. McDougall, *The Pagan Tribes of Borneo*, London, 1912, ii. 80).   However, in this case we are not told that vengeance is wreaked on the perjurer by the ghost of the dog.

[3] Julius von Klaproth, *Reise in den Kaukasus und nach Georgien* (Halle and Berlin, 1812–1814, ii. 603).   For more examples of the symbolical or magical sacrifice of animals at taking oaths, see R. Lasch, *Der Eid* (Stuttgart, 1908), pp. 51 *sq.*, 84-88, where many of the preceding instances are cited.

But it may be questioned whether the retributive function
of the sacrifice suffices to explain the remarkable feature in
the Hebrew and Greek rite which consists in passing between
the pieces of the slain animal or standing upon them.
Accordingly W. Robertson Smith suggested what we may
call the sacramental or purificatory interpretation of the
rite.   He supposed that "the parties stood between the
pieces, as a symbol that they were taken within the mystical
life of the victim";[1] and in confirmation of this view he
pointed to the use of the very same rite in other cases to
which the idea of punishment or retribution appears to be
inapplicable, but of which some at least can be explained as

modes of ceremonial purification.   Thus in Boeotia a form
of public purification was to cut a dog in two and pass
between the pieces.[2]   A similar rite was observed at purifying
a Macedonian army.   A dog was cut in two : the head and
fore part were placed on the right, the hinder part, with the
entrails, was placed on the left, and the troops in arms
marched between the pieces.   On the conclusion of the rite
the army used to divide into two and engage in a sham

fight.[3]   Again, it is said that when Peleus sacked Iolcus, he
slew the king's wife Astydamia, cut her in pieces, and caused
the army to march between the pieces into the city.[4]   The
ceremony was probably regarded as a form of purification
to which a high degree of solemnity was imparted by the
use of a human victim.   This interpretation is confirmed by the ritual which the Albanians of the Caucasus
observed at the temple of the Moon ; from time to
time they used to sacrifice a sacred slave by stabbing him
with a spear, after which the body was carried to a certain

place and all the people stepped on it as a purificatory
rite.[5]   Among the Basutos of South Africa a form of
ceremonial purification is this.   They slaughter an animal,
pierce it through and through, and then cause the person
who is to be purified to pass through the hole in the car-

[1] W. Robertson Smith, *Religion of
the Semites* [2] (London, 1894), p. 481.
[2] Plutarch, *Quaestiones Romanae*,
111.   In the same treatise (*Quaest.
Rom.* 68) Plutarch tells us that almost
all the Greeks used dogs as victims in
purificatory rites, but he does not describe the ritual.
[3] Livy xl. 6 ; Quintus Curtius, *De
gestis Alexandri Magni*, x. 9. 28.
[4] Apollodorus, *Bibliotheca*, iii. 13. 7.
[5] Strabo xi. 4.7,p.503, ed. Casaubon.

cass.[1] We have seen that among the Barolong of South Africa a similar rite is observed at making a covenant: the covenanters force themselves through a hole in the stomach of the slaughtered animal.[2] Together, these South African customs suggest that the passage between the pieces of a sacrificial victim is a substitute for passing through the carcass itself.

The purificatory, or better, perhaps, the protective, interpretation of such rites is strongly confirmed by the practice of the Arabs of Moab, who still observe similar ceremonies in times of public calamity, such as drought or epidemic, and explain them as intended to deliver the people from the evil which afflicts or threatens them. If, for example, the tribe is suffering from the ravages of cholera, the sheikh will stand up in the middle of the camp and cry out, " Redeem yourselves, O people, redeem yourselves ! " Thereupon every family takes a sheep, sacrifices it, and, having divided it in two, hangs the pieces under the tent or on two posts in front of the door. All the members of the family then pass between the two pieces of the victim ; children too young to walk are carried by their parents. Often they pass several times between the bleeding fragments of the sheep, because these are thought to possess the virtue of driving away the evil or the jinn who would injure the tribe. A similar remedy is resorted to in seasons of drought, when the pastures are withered and the cattle dying for lack of rain. The sacrifice is regarded as a ransom for man and beast. The Arabs say, " This is our ransom, for us and for our flocks." Questioned as to the mode in which the ceremony produces this salutary effect, they say that the sacrifice meets and combats the calamity. The epidemic, or drought, or whatever it may be, is conceived as a wind blowing across the plains and sweeping all before it, till it encounters the sacrifice which, like a lion, bestrides the path. A terrific combat ensues ; the disease or drought is beaten and retires discomfited, while the victorious sacrifice remains in possession of the field.[3] Here certainly there is

The purificatory or protective interpretation of the rites confirmed by a ceremony which the Arabs of Moab for in times of public calamity.

---

[1] E. Casalis, *Les Bassoutos* (Paris, 1860), pp. 270 *sq.* In the English translation of this work, usually very correct, the present passage is wrongly rendered.

[2] Above, p. 397.

[3] Antonin Jaussen, *Coutumes des Arabes au pays de Moab* (Paris, 1908), pp. 361-363 ; *id.*, "Coutumes Arabes," *Revue Biblique*, April 1903, p. 248.

no idea of retribution : neither symbolically nor magically is the death of the sheep supposed to entail the death of the people who pass between the joints of mutton ; on the contrary, it is believed to save their lives by protecting them against the evil which, in one way or another, threatens their existence.

Similar rites observed by the Chins, the ̄ѵ૦ɹуаᴋꜱ, and the gipsies of Transyl-vania.

In the like circumstances a precisely similar custom is observed and similarly explained by the Chins, who inhabit the hill country bordering on Assam and Burma. Among these people, "when a person believes that he is followed by an enraged spirit, such as the spirit of cholera, it is a common practice to cut a dog in half without severing the entrails and to place the fore-quarters on one side of the road and the hind-quarters on the other side and connected by the intestines stretched across the road; this is to appease the spirit and to dissuade him from following any further." [1] So strictly do the Chins personify cholera as a dangerous spirit, that when a party of them visited Rangoon in time of the epidemic, they carried their swords drawn, wherever they went, to scare away the demon, and they spent the day hiding under bushes that he might not find them. [2] Similar means of averting a plague or pestilence used to be employed by the Koryaks of north-eastern Siberia. They slaughtered a dog, wound the guts about two posts, and passed under them. [3] No doubt they also thought in this way to give the slip to the spirit of disease, who would find an insurmountable barrier in dog's guts. Again, women after childbirth are commonly supposed to be·unclean and to be exposed to the attacks of malignant supernatural beings. Hence among the gipsies of Transylvania, when a woman in such circumstances leaves her bed of sickness, she is made to pass between the pieces of a cock which has been cut in two, if her child is a boy, but

[1] Bertram S. Carey and H. N. Tuck, *The Chin Hills*, i. (Rangoon, 1896) p. 200 ; H. W. Read, *Hand Book of Haka Chin Customs* (Rangoon, 1917), p. 40.

[2] Bertram S. Carey and H. N. Tuck, *The Chin Hills*, i. 198.

[3] S. Krascheninnikow, *Beschreibung aes Landes Kamtschatka* (Lemgo, 1766), pp. 277 *sq.* This particular form of

sacrifice would seem to be now obsolete among the Koryaks ; at least it is not mentioned by Mr. W. Jochelson in his account of Koryak sacrifices, though he describes the sacrifice of dogs as still common in the tribe. See Walde-mar Jochelson, " The Koryak, Religion and Myths," *The Jesup North Pacific Expedition*, vol. vi. Part i. (Leyden and New York, 1905), pp. 90 *sqq.*

between the pieces of a hen, if her child is a girl ; after
which the cock is eaten by men, or the hen by women.[1]

In all these cases the passage between the severed pieces
of the animal is clearly protective, not retributive, in intention : the flesh and blood of the victim are thought somehow or other to present an obstacle to the powers of evil,
and so to prevent them from pursuing and injuring the
person who has passed through the narrow way. All such
ceremonies may therefore be called purificatory in the wide
sense of the word, since they purify or deliver the sufferer
from malignant influences. The same purpose apparently
is effected in a slightly different way by the Khonds of
India. The death of any person in one of their villages
requires a purification, which is usually carried out by the
sacrifice of a buffalo. But if a man has been killed by a
tiger, his death requires an extraordinary ceremony to
expiate it. For this purpose the men of the village are
drawn up in a line with their legs astraddle : a pig is
brought forward, its head is chopped off with an axe by a
hill weaver, and then, all dripping with blood, it is passed
between the legs of all the men. But it would be a bad
omen if the head touched any of the straddling legs.[2] In
this case, instead of the men passing between the animal,
the animal is made to pass between the legs of the men ;
but the intention of the ceremony is probably the same,
and its effect is without doubt equally salutary.

Returning to the point from which we started, we may
now ask whether the ancient Hebrew form of making a
covenant, by passing between the severed pieces of a
sacrificial victim, was retributive or purificatory in its intention ; in other words, was it a symbolic mode of imprecating death on the perjurer? or was it a magical mode of
purifying the covenanters from evil influences and so guarding them against certain dangers to which both parties alike
were exposed? The other instances which I have cited of
passing between the severed pieces of a sacrificial victim
seem to support the purificatory or protective explanation

[1] H. von Wlislocki, *Vom wandernden Zigeunervolke* (Hamburg, 1890),
p. 92.

[2] Edgar Thurston, *Ethnographic
Notes in Southern India* (Madras,
1906), pp. 165 *sq.*

of the Hebrew rite ; for while none of them require the retributive interpretation, some positively exclude it ; and on the other hand some are only explicable on the purificatory or protective hypothesis, which is in fact expressly alleged by certain of the peoples, such as the Arabs and the Chins, who observe the custom.   Certainly, in any attempt to explain the ancient Hebrew rite, much weight must be given to the analogy of the modern Arab ceremony ; for the two customs are identical in form, and the peoples who practise or have practised them are both members of the Semitic family, speaking kindred Semitic languages and inhabiting the same country ; since the land of Moab, where the Arabs still observe the ancient custom, formed part of the land of Israel, where Abraham of old sojourned and covenanted with God in like manner.   The inference seems almost inevitable, that the ancient Hebrew and the modern Arab rite are both derived from a common Semitic original, the purificatory or protective intention of which is still clearly borne in mind by the Arabs of Moab.

Robertson Smith's sacramental interpretation of the Hebrew custom as a form of blood covenant.

One question still remains to be asked.   In what did the purificatory or protective virtue of such an act consist ? why should the passage between the pieces of a slaughtered animal be thought to protect a man against danger ? Robertson Smith's answer is given in what may be called the sacramental interpretation of the custom.   He supposed that the persons who stood or passed between the pieces of the victim were thought to be thereby united with the animal and with each other by the bond of a common blood ; in fact, he held that such a covenant is only a variant of the widespread custom known as the blood covenant, in which the covenanters artificially create a tie of consanguinity between themselves by actually mixing a little of their own blood.[1]   On this hypothesis the only material difference between the two forms of covenant is, that the blood of an animal is substituted in the one for the human blood of the covenanters themselves in the other. Much is to be said for this theory.   In the first place, as

[1] W. Robertson Smith, *The Religion of the Semites*[2] (London, 1894), pp. 480 *sq*.   As to the blood covenant, see C. H. Trumbull, *The Blood Cove-* *nant* (London, 1887).   Many more examples of the custom could be added to those collected by the latter writer.

we saw,[1] the South African evidence clearly points to the conclusion that the passage between the severed pieces of a sacrificial victim is merely a substitute for the passage through the carcass of the animal. This conclusion is confirmed by observing that the Chins, in cutting the sacrificial dog in two, do not absolutely divide it, but keep the fore-quarters connected with the hind-quarters· by the string of the animal's guts, under which the people pass ; and the same appears, though less clearly, to have been the practice of the Koryaks.[2] The retention of the string of guts as a bond uniting the otherwise severed halves of the victim seems clearly to be an attempt to combine the theoretical unity of the slain animal with the practical convenience of dividing it, so as to admit of the passage of people through its carcass. But what could be the sense of thus putting people, as it were, into the body of the animal unless it were for the purpose of investing them with some qualities which the animal is believed to possess, and which, it is assumed, can be transferred to anybody who physically identifies himself with the animal by actually entering into it?

That this is indeed the conception at the base of the rite is suggested by the analogy of a custom observed by the Patagonian Indians. Among these people, " in some cases when a child is born, a cow or mare is killed, the stomach taken out and cut open, and into this receptacle while still warm the child is laid. Upon the remainder of the animal the tribe feast. . . . A variation of the foregoing birth-ceremony is yet more savage. If a boy is born, his tribe catch a mare or a colt—if the father be rich and a great man among his people, the former; if not, the latter— a lasso is placed round each leg, a couple round the neck, and a couple round the body. The tribe distribute them-selves at the various ends of these lassos and take hold. The animal being thus supported cannot fall. The father of the child now advances and cuts the mare or colt open from the neck downwards, the heart, etc., is torn out, and the baby placed in the cavity. The desire is to keep the animal quivering until the child is put inside. By this means they believe that they ensure the child's becoming a

The inter-
n
confirmed
by the
na gy of
various
savage
ıtuaıs.

The
sacra-
........l
inter-
pretation
confirmed
by a custom
t
Patagonian
Indians.

---

[1] Above, pp. 408 *sq.*   [2] Above, p. 410.

fine horseman in the future."[1] The custom and the reason
alleged for it are both significant. If you wish to make a
child a good horseman, these Indians argue, the best
possible way is to identify him at birth with a horse by
putting him into the body of a living mare or colt;
surrounded by the flesh and blood of the animal he will be
one with it corporeally, he will have the hunting seat of a
Centaur, whose human body is actually of a piece with the
body of his horse. In short, the placing of the child in the
body of the mare or colt is neither more nor less than a
piece of sympathetic magic intended to endue a human
being with equine properties.

The
Scythian
rite
similarly
explained.
On the same principle, as Robertson Smith pointed out,[2]
we can explain the Scythian form of covenant by treading
on the hide of a slaughtered ox.[3] All who put their right
feet on the hide thereby made themselves one with the
animal and with each other, so that all were united by a tie
of common blood which ensured their fidelity to each other.
For the placing of one foot on the hide was probably an
abridged form of wrapping up the man completely in it; as
a worshipper at the shrine of the Syrian goddess at Hierapolis used to kneel on the skin of the sheep he had sacrificed, and drawing the sheep's head and trotters over his
own head and shoulders prayed, as a sheep, to the goddess
to accept his sacrifice of a sheep.[4]

Robertson
Smith's
explanation
of the
Scythian
rite
confirmed
by an
African
parallel.
This interpretation of the Scythian custom, proposed by
Robertson Smith, is strikingly confirmed by an African
parallel. Among the Wachaga of East Africa it is
customary for lads to receive what may be called their war-
baptism two years after they have been circumcised. They
assemble with their fathers and all the grown men at the
chief's village. Two oxen and two goats are killed, and
their blood is caught in an ox-hide, which is held by several
men. The lads strip themselves and go in long rows four
times round the blood-filled hide. Then they stand in a
row. An old man makes a small cut in each of their
lower arms. Thereupon each boy, stepping up to the blood-

[1] H. Hesketh Pritchard, *Through
the Heart of Patagonia* (London, 1902),
p. 96.
[2] *Religion of the Semites*,[2] p. 402

note[3].
[3] Above, p. 394.
[4] Lucian, *De dea Syria*, 55.

filled hide, allows some drops of blood from his arm to fall
into it, takes up a handful of the mixed blood, swallows it,
and puts on his clothes.   Then they crouch down round
the chief, and after many speeches each lad receives a war-
name from his father or, if his father is dead, from an
old man who acts in place of his father.   Next the
chief harangues them, declaring that they are no longer
children but soldiers, and instructing them in their new
duties.   He also gives them all a common scutcheon for
their shields, which marks them out as belonging to one
and the same company.[1]   Here the lads who are to fight
shoulder to shoulder in the same company knit themselves
together by a double bond of blood, their own and the
blood of the sacrificed animals, which are mixed together in
the ox-hide and drunk together from the hide by each of
the future warriors.   Nothing could well demonstrate more
clearly the truth of Robertson Smith's view that the intention of the ox-hide in the Scythian rite was similarly to
unite the warriors by the tie of a common blood.

With regard to the pieces of the sacrificial victim which
is cut in two at some of those rites, Robertson Smith conjectured that they may formerly have been eaten by the
covenanters as a mode of further cementing the bond
between them by participation in the flesh and blood of
the slaughtered animal.[2]   The conjecture is supported by
the Wachaga custom of drinking the blood of the sacrificial victims, and it is also to some extent confirmed by
the practice of the Transylvanian gipsies, who, as we saw,
eat the pieces of the fowl through which a woman after
childbirth has to pass on leaving her bed.[3]   However,
in the latter case the rite, to all appearance, is a purely
protective measure : it is in no sense a covenant.   The
identification of a man with an animal, by eating of its
flesh and surrounding himself with its fragments, may have
been the intention of a curious ceremony which Giraldus
Cambrensis, writing towards the end of the twelfth century,
reports to have been observed at the inauguration of a king

Further illustrations from gipsy and ancient customs[1]

[1] M. Merker, *Rechtsverhältnisse und Sitten der Wadschagga* (Gotha, 1902), p. 16 (*Petermanns Mitteilungen*, *Ergänzungsheft*, No. 138).
[2] *Religion of the Semites*,[2] p. 481.
[3] Above, p. 411.

in Ireland. "There is," he tells us, "in the northern and most remote part of Ulster, namely at Kenel Cunil, a nation which practises a most barbarous and abominable rite in creating their king. The whole people of that country being gathered in one place, a white mare is led into the midst of them, and he who is to be inaugurated, not as a prince but as a brute, not as a king but as an outlaw, comes before the people on all fours, confessing himself a beast with no less impudence than imprudence. The mare being immediately killed, and cut in pieces and boiled, a bath is prepared for him from the broth. Sitting in this, he eats of the flesh which is brought to him, the people standing round and partaking of it also. He is also required to drink of the broth in which he is bathed, not drawing it in any vessel, nor even in his hand, but lapping it with his mouth. These unrighteous rites being duly accomplished, his royal authority and dominion are ratified."[1]

Discovery a skeleton of a bisected human body at Gezer in Palestine.

Perhaps this discussion of Abraham's covenant may help to throw light on a very dark spot of Canaanite history. In his excavations at Gezer, in Palestine, Professor Stewart Macalister discovered a burial-place of a very remarkable kind. It is simply a cylindrical chamber about twenty feet deep and fifteen feet wide, which has been hewn out of the rock and is entered from the top by a circular hole cut in the roof. The chamber appears to have been originally a water-cistern and to have been used for that purpose before it was converted into a tomb. On the floor of the chamber were found fifteen skeletons of human beings, or rather fourteen and a half skeletons; for of one body only the upper part was discovered, the lower part was wanting. The half skeleton was that of a girl about fourteen years of age; she had been cut or sawn through the middle "at the eighth thoracic vertebra, and as the front ends of the ribs had been divided at this level, it is plain that the section had been made while as yet the

---

[1] Giraldus Cambrensis, *Topography of Ireland*, ch. 25 (*The Historical Works of Giraldus Cambrensis*, revised and edited by Thomas Wright, London, 1887, p. 138). In a note the translator tells us that Kenel Cunil is Tir-connell, now the county of Donegal; and he adds, "Irish antiquaries utterly repudiate the disgusting account here given by Giraldus of the inauguration of the kings of this territory."

bones were supported by the soft parts." The fourteen other skeletons were all males, two of them immature, aged about eighteen and nineteen years respectively ; all the rest were full-grown adults, of fair stature and strongly built. The position of the bodies showed that they had not been thrown in through the hole in the roof but deposited by persons who descended with them into the cave ; and a large quantity of charcoal found among the bones is thought to indicate that a funeral feast, sacrifice, or other solemn rite had been observed within the sepulchral chamber. Some fine bronze weapons — spear-heads, an axe and a knife — deposited with the bodies may be regarded as evidence that the burial took place before the advent of the Israelites, and accordingly that the men belonged to a race who preceded the Hebrews in Palestine. Judged by the shape of their bones, their large capacious skulls, their arched noses, and other anatomical peculiarities, the males are believed to be representative specimens of a race not unlike the Palestinian Arab of to-day.[1] If the corporeal resemblance between these ancient men and the present inhabitants of the country is sufficient to justify us in con- sidering them as members of the same stock, we may perhaps conclude that both belong to that Canaanite race whom the Hebrew invaders found in occupation of Palestine, and whom, though they reduced to bondage, they never succeeded in exterminating. For it is the opinion of competent judges that the modern Fellaheen or Arabic- speaking peasants of Palestine are descendants of the pagan tribes which dwelt there before the Israelite invasion and have clung to the soil ever since, being submerged but never destroyed by each successive wave of conquest which has swept over the land.[2] If that is so, it seems reasonable to suppose that in the half-skeleton of the girl at Gezer we have a relic of that custom of human sacrifice which, as we know alike from the Hebrew prophets and classical writers of antiquity, played a prominent part in Canaanite religion. The supposition is strengthened by the discovery of many

The half-skeleton probably a relic of sacrifice.

[1] R. A. Stewart Macalister, *Reports on the Excavation of Gezer* (London, N.D.), pp. 66-73, 103 *sq.*; *id.*, *The Excavation of Gezer* (London, 1912),

ii. 429-431.

[2] C. T. Wilson, *Peasant Life in the Holy Land* (London, 1906), p. 3, quot- ing Conder.

skeletons of infants, which were found at Gezer buried in large jars under the floor of the temple area ; for these remains are commonly believed to attest a practice of sacrificing firstborn children at birth in honour of the local deity.   Similar burials of infants in jars have been discovered round a rock-hewn altar at Taanach in Palestine, and they have been similarly interpreted.[1]

Why was the human victim bisected? To effect a purification or to ratify a covenant?

But if the half-skeleton of the girl discovered in the cistern at Gezer is indeed a relic of human sacrifice, we have still to ask, why was she hewn or sawn asunder? The analogy of the covenant of Abraham and the similar rites which we have examined suggests that the bisection of the victim may have been intended either to effect a public purification or to ratify a covenant ; or, to be more explicit, we may suppose that the girl was cut in two and that the people passed between the pieces either by way of averting some present or threatened evil, or by way of cementing a solemn treaty of peace.   We will consider the purificatory or protective interpretation first.

The purificatory theory of the rite may explain the Greek tradition of Peleus and Astydamia.

We have seen that when Peleus captured the city of Iolcus, he is said to have taken the king's wife, cut her in two, and then led his army between the pieces into the city.[2] The tradition is not likely to be a pure invention ; it may well embody the reminiscence of a barbarous custom formerly observed by conquerors on entering a conquered city.   We know that early man stands in great fear of the magic of strangers, and that he resorts to a variety of ceremonies in order to protect himself against it, either when he admits strangers to his own country, or when he enters the territory of another tribe.[3]   A traveller in Central Africa, for instance, tells us that magical ceremonies are performed there on innumerable occasions to avert trouble and misfortune from the country, to prevent the entrance of

---

[1] R. A. Stewart Macalister, *Reports on the Excavation of Gezer*, pp. 85-88 ; *id.*, *The Excavation of Gezer* (London, 1912), ii. 405 *sq.*; H. Vincent, *Canaan d'après l'Exploration Récente* (Paris, 1914), pp. 188 *sqq.*; E. Sellin, "Tell Ta'annek," *Denkschriften der Kaiser. Akademie der Wissenschaften, Philosophisch-historische Klasse*, l. (Vienna, 1904), No. iv. pp. 32-37, 97 *sq.* However, these infant burials are susceptible of a different interpretation, which I have suggested elsewhere (*Adonis, Attis, Osiris*,[3] i. 108 *sq.*).

[2] Above, p. 408.

[3] For examples see *Taboo and the Perils of the Soul*, pp. 102 *sqq.* (*The Golden Bough*, Third Edition, Part ii,).

inconvenient strangers, to ensure success in war, and so on ; and he describes, by way of example, how when he and his party entered the land of the Wanyamwesi, the chief of that tribe caused a white cock to be killed and buried under an old earthenware pot at the boundary of his territory, just in the path of the strangers.[1]   A similar dread of hostile magic may induce a conqueror to adopt extraordinary precautions for the purpose of safeguarding himself and his troops against the machinations of their enemies, before he ventures to enter the city which he has won from them by the sword.   Such an extraordinary precaution might consist in taking a captive, hewing him or her in two, and then causing the·army to defile between the pieces into the city.   On the sacramental interpretation of this rite the effect of the passage between the pieces of the victim would be to form a blood covenant between the conquerors and the conquered, and thus to secure the victors from all hostile attempts on the part of the vanquished. This would explain the tradition as to the treatment which Peleus meted out to the captive queen of Iolcus : it was a solemn mode of effecting a union between the invaders and the invaded.   If this explanation be accepted, it seems to follow that the purificatory or protective and the covenantal aspects of the rite practically coincide : the invaders purify or protect themselves from the malign influence of their foes by implicitly entering into a blood covenant with them.

It is possible that a similar Semitic custom may explain the severed skeleton of the girl at Gezer.   To judge from the human remains that have been found on the site, the city was occupied by different races at different times : in the earliest ages it was the seat of a short, slenderly built, yet muscular people, with long oval heads, who did not belong to the Semitic stock and have not yet been correlated with any known Mediterranean race.[2]   If the city was conquered by the Canaanites who afterwards possessed it, these barbarous conquerors may have inaugurated their entrance into the city by putting the queen or another

The purificatory or protective theory may a o in the bisection of the victim at Gezer.

[1] Fr. Stuhlmann, *Mit Emin Pascha ins Herz von Afrika* (Berlin, 1894), p. 94. In *Taboo and the Perils of the Soul*, p. 111, I have reported this incident incorrectly.

[2] Professor Alexander Macalister, in R. A. Stewart Macalister's *Reports on the Excavation of Gezer*, p. 37.

female captive to death, sawing her body in two and march-
ing between the pieces into the city.[1]   But in that case,
how are we to explain the absence of the lower half of the
body?   We need not suppose, as the discoverer suggested,
that it was either burnt or devoured at a cannibal banquet ;[2]
it may have been buried elsewhere, perhaps on the opposite
side of the town, for the purpose of extending the magical
influence of the sacrifice over all the intermediate space, so
as to render the whole city secure for the conquerors and at
the same time impregnable to the assaults of their enemies.
In like manner an ancient king of Burma is said to have
rendered his capital impregnable by cutting the body of a
traitor into four pieces and burying the quarters at the four
corners of the city.   In vain did the traitor's brother besiege
the capital with an army ; all his assaults were fruitless, till
the widow of the slain man informed him that he could
never take the city so long as her dead husband guarded
the walls.   So the besieger contrived to dig up the mouldering quarters of his dismembered brother, and after that he
captured the city without resistance.[3]   Similarly among the
Lushais of Assam, when a woman is in hard labour, her
friends, in order to facilitate the birth, will take a fowl, kill
it, and cut the carcass in two equal parts.   The portion
with the head is then put at the upper end of the village
with seven pieces of cane rolled into bundles, and the lower
portion of the fowl is put at the lower end of the village
with five rolls of cane.   Moreover, the woman is given a
little water to drink.   This ceremony is called *arte-pum-
phelna*, "to open the stomach with a fowl," because it is
supposed to enable the sufferer to bring forth.[4]   The mode
in which the rite is believed to produce this salutary effect

[1] On this hypothesis the body of
the girl must have belonged to the pre-
Canaanite race, and therefore must
have differed in physical type from the
male skeletons which were discovered
with her in the cistern.   However, the
remains of the skeleton appear to leave
the question open.   Professor Alexander
Macalister says, "There was not any
characteristic sufficiently   distinctive
whereby it could be ascertained
whether she belonged to the same race
or not.   My general impression, however, is that she did" (quoted by R.
A. Stewart Macalister, *Reports on the
Excavation of Gezer*, p. 104).

[2] R. A. Stewart Macalister, *Reports
on the Excavation of Gezer*, pp. 70, 72.

[3] A. Bastian, *Die Voelker des Oest-
lichen Asien*, i. (Leipsic, 1866) p. 47,
compare p. 214.

[4] Lieut.-Colonel J. Shakespear, *The
Lushei Kuki Clans* (London, 1912),
p. 81.

is not mentioned, but we may conjecture that the severed pieces of the fowl placed at the two ends of the village are thought to guard the intermediate space from the incursion of those evil and especially demoniacal powers which had hitherto prevented the birth of the child.

This theory of a purificatory or protective intention of the sacrifice of the girl at Gezer may perhaps be confirmed by another discovery made at the same place. Later excavations brought to light the half-skeleton of a boy about seventeen years of age, who, like the girl in the cistern, had been cut or sawn through the middle between the ribs and the pelvis ; and, just as in the case of the girl, only the upper half of the body was found, the lower half was missing. Along with it were found the complete skeletons of two men lying at full length, with a number of earthenware vessels above and around them. These remains were discovered under, though not directly below, the foundations of a building. Hence Professor Stewart Macalister plausibly inferred that the skeletons are the remains of human victims who, in accordance with a widespread custom, had been sacrificed and buried under the foundations in order to give strength and stability to the edifice or to guard against enemies.[1] The custom has been so amply illustrated by examples drawn from many lands that it would be superfluous to dwell on it. I will cite only a single instance recorded by an eye-witness, because it clearly shows the train of thought which led to the institution of the practice. Between seventy and eighty years ago a runaway English sailor, by name John Jackson, lived alone for nearly two years among the still heathen and barbarous Fijians, and he has left us an artless, but valuable, account of his experiences. While he was with the savages, it happened that the house of the local chief or king was rebuilt. One day, being near the place where the work was going on, Jackson saw men led along and buried alive in the holes in which the posts of the house were set up. The natives tried to divert his attention from the scene, but in order not to be

Discovery
of a
skeleton of
another
human
victim at
Gezer.

Theory that
the half-
skeleton is
a relic of a
foundation
sacrifice

Example
of a
foundation
sacrifice
among the
Fijians

---

[1] R. A. Stewart Macalister, "Report on the Excavation of Gezer," *Palestine Exploration Fund, Quarterly Statement for 1908*, p. 206 ; *id.*, *The Excavation of Gezer* (London, 1912), ii. 428 *sq.*

deceived he ran up to one of the holes and saw a man standing in it with his arms round the post and his head still clear of the soil.   When he asked the Fijians why they buried men alive at the foot of the posts, they answered that the house could not stand long if men did not sit down and continually hold the posts up.   When he further inquired how they could hold up the posts after they were dead, the Fijians answered, that if the men sacrificed their lives in endeavouring to keep the posts in position, the virtue of the sacrifice would induce the gods to uphold the house after the men were dead.[1]

The theory of a foundation sacrifice hardly explains the half-skeleton at
Such a train of thought might well explain the position of the two male skeletons under the foundations at Gezer; for one of them was discovered with his bony hand in a bowl, as if helping himself to food and thereby fortifying himself for the weary task of holding up the walls.   But it is less easy to understand the half-skeleton of the boy in the same place, and the half-skeleton of the girl in the cistern.   If the object was indeed to bear up the foundations, it seems obvious that stalwart men would naturally be selected for so fatiguing a duty; of what use would half a boy and half a girl be for such a purpose?   How could walls stand firm on lads and lasses who had no legs?   Hence the theory that these victims were slain and bisected as foundation sacrifices can hardly be accepted as satisfactory.

The ~~covenantal~~ theory of the half-skeletons at Gezer is confirmed by the practice of the Wachaga of East Africa, who bisect a kid or a human victim at making a solemn covenant.
Thus far we have considered the purificatory or protective theory of these mysterious sacrifices at Gezer.   Let us now turn to the covenantal theory, and try whether it will not fit the facts better.   The theory is that the boy and girl were slain and cut in two, not as a form of purification or mode of protecting the site, but as a ratification of a covenant, and that the covenanters passed between the

[1] " Jackson's Narrative," in J. E. Erskine's *Journal of a Cruise among the Islands of the Western Pacific* (London, 1853), pp. 464 *sq.*   Compare Mrs. Leslie Milne, *Shans at Home* (London, 1910), pp. 178 *sq.*, " In old times it was the custom in the Shan States, as in Burma, to bury alive a man or woman under the palace or gate of a new city, so that the spirits of the dead, in guarding the place from human enemies, should also keep evil spirits, that bring sickness, at a distance."   For collections of evidence on the subject, see (Sir) E. B. Tylor, *Primitive Culture*,[2] i. 104 *sqq.*; P. Sartori, " Über das Bauopfer," *Zeitschrift für Ethnologie*, xxx. (1898) pp. 1-54 ; *Taboo and the Perils of the Soul*, pp. 90 *sq.*, with the references.

pieces of the human victims, just as in making a covenant the ancient Hebrews passed between the halves of a slaughtered calf. This view may be confirmed by the following analogy. We have seen that the Wachaga of East Africa solemnize a covenant and league of peace between two districts by cutting a kid and a rope in two at one stroke, while they pray that, if they break their oath, they also may be split in two, like the kid and the rope. But they have another mode of concluding an alliance which is said to have the sanction of great antiquity. They take a boy and a girl and lead them three or seven times round the assembled covenanters, while solemn curses or blessings are pronounced on such as shall break or keep their oath. Then the boy and girl are cut in two through the middle, the four halves are buried at the boundary of the two districts, and the representatives of the two peoples who have made the covenant walk over the grave, and disperse to their homes. The notion, we are told, is an implied curse that the life of such as forswear themselves may be cut in two, like the young victims, and that, like them, they may perish without offspring. In order, it is said, that we may understand the full depth and significance of this curse, it is necessary to know that the religion of the Wachaga consists in the worship of ancestral spirits ; so that a man who dies without offspring has no one to offer the sacrifices which alone can ensure him a favourable reception and a continued maintenance among the dead ; a childless man must lead for ever a lonely life in the far country, with no one to stay his hunger for beef and to quench his thirst for beer ; for beer and beef, or mutton, are the things which the spirits of the departed chiefly desire to receive at the hands of their surviving relatives.[1]

If this comparison of Wachaga with Semitic ritual is well founded, we can readily understand both why the victims at Gezer were cut in two, and why they were a boy and girl, not a full - grown man and woman. We need only suppose that they were killed and cleft in two at the making of a solemn covenant ; that the covenanters passed

The Wachaga parallel explains human victims at Gezer were a boy and a girl.

[1] J. Raum, "Blut- und Speichel- bünde bei den Wadschagga," *Archiv*   *für Religionswissenschaft*, x. (1907) pp. 289 *sq.*

between the pieces, and that each side took half a boy or half a girl home with them as a guarantee of the good faith of the other side, exactly as among the Wachaga each side takes home one half of the cut rope as a guarantee of the good faith of the other party. At Gezer we have one half of the girl and one half of the boy, in both cases the upper half. It seems not wholly impossible that further excavations in Palestine may yet bring to light the lower halves of the same bodies which had been carried away and buried at home by the other parties to the covenant. Further, we can now understand why the victims chosen for the sacrifice were a boy and a girl, not a grown man and woman. If the Wachaga parallel holds good, the motive was an implied curse, that if either side broke their oath they might perish without offspring, like the child through whose mangled remains they had passed. When we remember the passionate desire of the Semite for offspring, we can appreciate the full gravity for him of such a curse, and can estimate the strength of the bond which it knit between the covenanters.

The parallel confirms the retributive explanation of the Hebrew ritual.

Lastly, it is to be observed that the analogy of the Wachaga ritual at making a covenant, whether the victim cut in two is a kid or a human being, strongly supports the retributive explanation of the Hebrew ritual on similar occasions; since in both the Wachaga cases we are given to understand that the cutting of the victim in two symbolizes the fate of the perjurer. Nevertheless it may still be open to us to interpret the passage between the pieces of the victim in the sense advocated by Robertson Smith, namely, as a mode of identifying the persons with the victim for the purpose of endowing them with certain properties which the victim is supposed to possess, and which, it is believed, can be imparted to all who enter into communion with the animal, either by passing through its body or in other ways, such as by smearing themselves with its blood or wearing pieces of its skin.[1] In the making of a covenant the motive for identifying the covenanters with the victim is apparently to ensure, by

---

[1] As to the custom of wearing pieces of the skin of a sacrificial victim, see below, vol. ii. pp. 7 *sqq.*

means of sympathetic magic, that if any of the covenanters forswear themselves they shall share the fate of the victim : it is the magical sympathy thus created between the covenanters and the victim which gives a binding force to the covenant and furnishes the best guarantee of its fulfilment.

Thus if my analysis of the Covenant of Abraham is correct, the rite is composed of two distinct but correlated elements, namely, first, the cutting of the victim in two, and, second, the passing of the covenanters between the pieces. Of these two elements the first is to be explained by the retributive, and the second by the sacramental theory. The two theories are complementary to each other, and together furnish a complete explanation of the rite.

The b ve and the sacra- menta⁻ theories are comple- men ary.

Before leaving the subject of Abraham's covenant, it may be well to return for a little to the practice of the Arabs of Moab.[1] The name which they give to the sacrifice in question is *fedou*, and the term is defined as " the immola- tion of a victim sacrificed generally in the face of Allah to deliver man or beast from some malady or impending destruction."[2] In short, the sacrifice appears to be a ransom offered to God for the people or their flocks : it is a sub- stitute which the deity deigns to accept instead of human and animal life. Hence the words with which the sheikh commands the offering : " Redeem yourselves, O people ! Redeem yourselves ! " Hence, too, the saying of the Arabs that the sacrifice is a ransom for themselves and their flocks.[3]

The modern Arab theory of *fedou* o vica i us sacrifice.

This vicarious theory of sacrifice as a substitute offered for the life of a man or animal appears to be widely spread, not only among the Arabs of Moab, but among the Fella- heen or peasantry of Palestine generally. The evidence has been collected by the late Professor S. I. Curtiss of Chicago, whose researches into the living folk-lore of the Holy Land have shed much light on primitive Semitic religion, and whose too early death was a grievous loss to Biblical studies. From him we learn that in Syria the term

The theory ous sacrifice widely held modern peasantry o ausume.

[1] See above, pp. 409 *sq.*
[2] A. Jaussen. *Coutumes des Arabes* *au pays de Moab*, p. 361.
[3] A. Jaussen, *op. cit.* pp. 362, 363.

fedou is commonly applied to the vicarious sacrifice of an animal in a general sense, without any necessary implication that the sacrificer cuts the victim in two and passes between the pieces. The following definition of *fedou* was given to Professor Curtiss by Derwish Hatib, of Der Atiyeh, in the Syrian Desert, who is a lecturer and leads the service in the mosque of his village : "*Fedou* means that it redeems the other, in place of the other, substitute for the other. Something is going to happen to a man, and the sacrifice is a substitute for him. It prevents disease, sufferings, robbery and enmity." [1] Again, a Moslem at Nebk in the Syrian Desert told Professor Curtiss that "the *fedou* is commonly for the future to ward off evil. When they lay the foundation of a house, they slaughter with the idea that (*Khuddr*) St. George, will preserve the workmen. Every house must be redeemed. If not redeemed by the sacrifice of some animal, it must be redeemed by a human life." [2] Similarly, an orthodox Moslem, servant of a shrine at Homs, informed Professor Curtiss that he was familiar with the *fedou*. He said, "In moving from house to house, or in occupying a new building ; the first night he sleeps in the house he kills the *fedou*. The object is the bursting forth of blood unto the face of God. It is for himself and family, a redemption. It keeps off disease and the jinn." [3] To the same effect the minister of the "Chair" on the mountain-side of Zebedani said, "When a man finishes a house, he makes a sacrifice on the doorstep. It is redemption for the building. Every house must have its death, a man, woman, child, or animal. God has appointed a *fedou* for every building through sacrifice. If God has accepted the sacrifice he has redeemed the house." [4]

An animal still sacrificed in parts of Syria as a substitute for a child.

These statements clearly prove that the *fedou* or sacrifice of an animal at occupying a new house is vicarious : it is a substitute for the human life, which otherwise God or a saint would require at the hands of the occupants. Similarly the sacrifice which in some parts of Syria is still offered for a child appears to be regarded as a substitute accepted by

[1] S. I. Curtiss, *Primitive Semitic Religion To-day* (Chicago, New York, Toronto, 1902), pp. 195 *sq.*

[2] S. I. Curtiss, *op. cit.* pp. 196 *sq.*
[3] S. I. Curtiss, *op. cit.* p. 197.
[4] S. I. Curtiss, *op. cit.* p. 196.

God or a saint for the life of the child. Thus, speaking of the custom of sacrificing for children, one of the Ismailiyeh of northern Syria said, " When they make a sacrifice for a child they slaughter the victim in the courtyard where he lives, and put a few drops of blood on his forehead and on his nose, to indicate that the sacrifice is on his behalf. The breaking forth of blood is *fedou*. It redeems the child. They vow to the saint that blood shall flow for the child if he redeems it." The sacrifice offered for a son is usually a goat or a sheep, but if the family is poor, a cock will be accepted for a baby boy, and a hen for a baby girl.[1]

Thus it appears that the essence of all these sacrifices consists in its vicarious character : the animal is a substitute for the man. The principle of substitution in sacrifice is brought out with unmistakeable clearness in a custom observed by Indian Moslems at the largest mosque in Baghdad, to which they go on pilgrimage : " They vow that An animal if a man who is ill begins to recover he shall go to the a substitute shrine. He is stripped to the waist. Then two men lift a for a man at lamb or a kid above his head, and bathe his face, shoulders, Baghdad. and the upper part of his body with the blood. While the butcher kills the animal the sheikh repeats the first sura of the Koran. They also wrap him in the skin of the animal."[2] Here the pouring of the animal's blood on the man, and the wrapping of him in the skin, are very instructive. In order to perfect the substitution of the animal for the man, the ritual requires that the man should as far as possible be identified with the animal, being drenched with its blood and clothed with its skin. How could the pretended identification be represented more graphically ?

The same principle of substitution is still followed in The same Syria not only in the relation of man to God, but in the prin i o substitution relation of man to man. " In the neighbourhood of Nablus followed it is customary, when a reconciliation has been made of murder. between the murderer and the avenger of blood, for the murderer to kill a goat or a sheep. He then kneels before the avenger with a red handkerchief tied about his neck. Some of the blood of the animal slain is put on the palms of his hands. The avenger draws his sword and intimates

[1] S. I. Curtiss, *op. cit.* pp. 202 *sq.*   [2] S. I. Curtiss, *op. cit.* pp. 205 *sq.*

that he could take his life from him, but that he gives it back to him." [1]   Here the identification of the man with the animal is carried out by smearing him with the blood of the slaughtered sheep or goat, and tying a red handkerchief round his neck to simulate the severance of his head from his body.

Vicarious sacrifice in ancient Syrian ritual.

We can now fully understand the sacrificial ritual at the temple of the great Syrian goddess in antiquity, in accordance with which the worshipper clothed himself in the skin of the sheep which he offered to the deity. [2]   The life of the sheep was a substitute for his own, and to perfect the substitution he pretended to be a sheep.

Vicarious aspect of bisected victims in the rituals reviewed.

Now, too, we can understand why in certain solemn sacrifices, to avert or mitigate calamity, the sacrificer cuts the victim in two and passes between the parts.   The passage between the parts, as we saw, is probably a modification of an older practice of passing through the carcass ; and that in its turn can hardly have any other meaning than that the man identifies himself with the animal into whose body he forces himself, and that he offers it to the higher powers as a substitute for himself.   The principle of vicarious sacrifice, which has played so great a part in the history of religion, could hardly be carried out more perspicuously than in these savage and bloody rites.

[1] S. I. Curtiss, *op. cit.* p. 191.   [2] Above, p. 414.

CHAPTER II

THE HEIRSHIP OF JACOB OR ULTIMOGENITURE

§ 1. *Traces of Ultimogeniture in Israel*

THE traditions concerning the patriarch Jacob are fuller
than those which relate to his father Isaac and his grandfather Abraham, and they are correspondingly richer in
folk-lore, that is, in reminiscences of archaic belief and
custom.   It was natural that memories or fancies should
gather thick about the ancestral hero from whom the people
of Israel derived their name as well as their blood.

The
J co
tradition.

Yet the character of this great ancestor, as it is por-
trayed for us in Genesis, has little to attract or please a
modern reader, and it contrasts unfavourably both with the
calm dignity of his grandfather Abraham and with the
meditative piety of his father Isaac.   If Abraham is the
type of the Semitic sheikh, brave and hospitable, dignified
and courteous, Jacob is the type of the Semitic trader,
supple and acute, fertile in expedients, with a keen eye to
gain, compassing his ends not by force but by craft, and
not too scrupulous in the choice of means by which to
outwit and overreach his rivals and competitors.   This
unamiable combination of cupidity and cunning reveals
itself in the earliest recorded incidents of the patriarch's
life, the devices by which he contrived to cheat his elder
brother Esau out of his birthright and his father's blessing.
For Esau and Jacob were twins, and as the elder of the
two [1] Esau was entitled, according to the ordinary rule, to
receive the paternal benediction and to succeed to the

Jacob the
e
the sharp
Semitic
trader.

---

[1] Genesis xxv. 21-26.

429

The frauds practised on his ⸱ ⸱ ⸱ ⸱r an father.

paternal inheritance.[1] The means by which Jacob managed to supplant his elder brother were, to put it mildly, pieces of very sharp practice : he first took advantage of Esau's hunger to buy from him his birthright for a mess of pottage ;[2] and afterwards, by dressing in his brother's clothes and simulating the hairiness of his brother's skin, he palmed himself off as Esau on his blind old father, and so intercepted the blessing which was meant for his twin brother.[3] It is true that in the second of these transactions the trick which the young hopeful played his doddered parent was not of his own devising ; he was instigated to it by his mother Rebekah, whose maiden name might have been Sharp, to judge by the skill with which she choused her husband. Yet the readiness with which Jacob lent himself to the hoax proves that it was not the goodwill, but only the quick wit, that was wanting on his part to gull his father.

At a certain f moralit such frauds condoned or even adm'r ⸱.

At a certain stage of moral evolution such frauds excite little or no reprobation except among those who immediately suffer by them ; the impartial spectator indeed is apt to applaud them as exhibitions of superior intelligence and dexterity triumphing over mere honest stupidity. However, a time comes when public opinion ranges itself on the side of the honest dullard and against the clever sharper, because experience proves that every fraud, however admirable the ingenuity and foresight it displays, directly injures not only individuals but society as a whole by loosening that bond of mutual confidence by which alone any corporate body of men is held together. When this truth has been generally recognized, the historian comes to judge the doings of men in the past by a moral standard which neither the men themselves nor their contemporaries ever dreamed of applying to their actions ; and if the heroic figures of the past seem to fall far below that standard, the charitable critic, instead of frankly acknowledging the gulf which moral progress has created between himself and them, attempts to bridge it over by finding excuses or even justifications for

---

[1] Under the Deuteronomic law the eldest son received the largest part of the family property (Deuteronomy xxi. 15-17).

[2] Genesis xxv. 29-34.

[3] Genesis xxvii.

deeds which his own ethical judgment leads him to condemn. The process of whitewashing moral blackamoors, when it is prompted by the charity of a kindly heart and not by the empty vanity of maintaining a paradox, is creditable to the whitewasher and perhaps harmless to other people, therein differing from the contrary practice, which consists in blackening the whitest characters; for that execrable, though popular, practice not merely wounds the innocent by a stab in the back, but inflicts a public wrong by lowering the moral standard, since it robs us of those too rare models of virtue, the contemplation of which is better fitted to touch the heart with the admiration and love of goodness than any number of abstract treatises on moral philosophy.

In recent years the defence of Jacob's moral character has been undertaken by a compatriot and namesake, Mr. Joseph Jacobs, who has essayed to wipe out the blot on the ancestral scutcheon by demonstrating that in virtue of an ancient law Jacob, as the younger son, was really entitled to the inheritance, and that the chicane to which, in the Biblical narrative, he resorts in order to obtain it is merely a gloss put by the historian on a transaction he did not understand.[1] Whether this ingenious apology is sound or not, I will not venture to say; but certain it is that such an ancient law of inheritance as his apologist supposes has prevailed among many peoples, and there seems to be no reason why it should not have obtained at a remote time among the ancestors of Israel. The law or custom in question is known as junior-right or ultimogeniture in contrast to primogeniture, because it gives the inheritance to the youngest son instead of to the eldest. In this chapter I propose to illustrate the custom by examples and to inquire into its origin.

Let us begin by looking at other possible traces of junior-right or ultimogeniture which may be detected in the Old Testament. In the first place, then, if Jacob supplanted his elder brother, he only did what his father Isaac had done before him. For Isaac also was a younger son

[Marginal notes: Joseph Jacobs's view that Jacob, younger son, was entitled to the inheritance. Other custom of junior-ultimogeniture in the patriarchal history.]

[1] Joseph Jacobs, "Junior-Right in Genesis," *Studies in Biblical Archaeology* (London, 1894), pp. 46-63.

and displaced his elder brother Ishmael in the inheritance of their father Abraham.[1] And the principle, if principle it was, on which Jacob acted in dealing with his father and brother, he appears to have followed in dealing with his own sons and grandsons. For we are told that he loved his son Joseph more than his elder sons "because he was the son of his old age"; and he showed his preference so decidedly that the jealousy of Joseph's elder brothers was aroused, and they plotted against his life.[2] It is true that according to the narrative, as it now stands, Joseph was not the youngest son, he was only the youngest but one, since Benjamin was born after him.[3] But we may surmise that in the original narrative Joseph was actually the youngest; the great affection which his father lavished on him, the coat of many colours, or rather the coat with long sleeves, by which he was distinguished among his brethren, and the position of superiority to them which he attained in the sequel, all point in this direction.[4] Again, the name of Benjamin, the youngest of Jacob's sons, means "the son of the right hand";[5] and that this title marks him out as the lawful heir appears to be indicated by the remarkable account of the way in which Jacob, in blessing his two grandsons, the sons of Joseph, deliberately preferred the younger to the elder by laying his right hand on the head of the younger (Ephraim) and his left hand on the head of the elder (Manasseh), in spite of the protest of their father Joseph, who had placed his sons before their grandfather in such a position that he would naturally lay his right hand on the elder and his left hand on the younger; so that the old man was obliged to cross his hands over his breast in order to reach the head of the younger with his right hand, and the head of the elder with his left.[6] Thus an apologist for Jacob may say with truth that he was at least consistent through life in his preference for younger over elder sons,

'Benjamin,
t
of the right
hand."

---

[1] Genesis xvi., xxi. 1-7.

[2] Genesis xxxvii. 3 *sqq.* As to the birth of Joseph, see Genesis xxx. 22-24.

[3] Genesis xxxv. 18.

[4] So Mr. Joseph Jacobs argued, *Studies in Biblical Archaeology*, p. 58.

[5] F. Brown, S. R. Driver, and Ch. A. Briggs, *Hebrew and English Lexicon of the Old Testament* (Oxford, 1906), p. 122, *s.v.* בִּנְיָמִין.

[6] Genesis xlviii. Note particularly Jacob's words in *v.* 19, "His younger brother shall be greater than he." Compare Joseph Jacobs, *Studies in Biblical Archaeology*, p. 57.

and that he did not merely resort to that principle when it suited his own selfish interests to do so.

But other witnesses may be called to speak in his favour, in other words, to testify to an ancient custom of junior-right or ultimogeniture in Israel. We read in Genesis that Tamar, the daughter of Judah, brought forth twin sons, named Perez and Zerah, and though Perez was born first, a curious detail as to the birth of the children is related, of which the intention seems to be to prove that Perez was really, like Jacob himself, the younger of the twins, and not, as might have been thought, the elder.[1] The motive for proving Perez to be the younger son is not obvious on the face of the narrative, but it becomes intelligible when we remember that Perez was the direct ancestor of King David,[2] that David himself was the youngest son of his father, and that he was deliberately promoted by Samuel to the kingdom in preference to all his elder brothers.[3] Thus the purpose of the narrator in giving what might seem needless, if not indecent, details as to the birth of the twins in Genesis, may have been to prove that King David was not only himself a youngest son, but that he was also descended from the younger of Judah's twin grandsons. And David in his turn transmitted the kingdom to one of his younger sons, Solomon, deliberately setting aside one of his elder sons, Adonijah, who claimed the crown.[4] All these facts taken together may be held to raise a presumption that in Israel the custom of primogeniture, or preference for the eldest son, had been preceded by an older custom of ultimogeniture or preference for the youngest son as heir to his father. And the presumption is strengthened when we observe that a similar custom of junior-right or ultimogeniture has prevailed in other parts of the world.

§ 2. *Ultimogeniture in Europe*

One of the countries in which the custom of ultimogeniture has been observed, and is still observed, is England. Under the title of Borough English this ancient usage is

[1] Genesis xxxviii. 27-30. Compare Joseph Jacobs, *Studies in Biblical Archaeology*, p. 56.

[2] 1 Chronicles ii. 4-15.

[3] 1 Samuel xvi. 1-13.

[4] 1 Kings i.

still, or was till lately, the law of the land in many parts of
the country.[1]   The English name for the custom is taken
from a local word used in a trial of the time of Edward the
Third.   It appears from a report in the Yearbook for the
first year of that reign that in Nottingham there were then
two tenures of land, called respectively Borough English
and Borough French ; and that under Borough English all
the tenements descended to the youngest son, and that
under Borough French all the tenements descended to the
eldest son, as at the common law.   It is said that as late
as 1713 Nottingham remained divided into the English
Borough and the French Borough, the customs of descent
continuing distinct in each ; and even at the present time
similar customs are observed in that neighbourhood.[2]

Local
distribution
of Borough
English.

The distribution of Borough English or ultimogeniture
in England was roughly as follows.   The custom extended
along the whole line of the " Saxon Shore " from the Wash
to the neighbourhood of the Solent, including the whole of
the south-eastern counties.   To be more precise, it was
most prevalent in Kent, Sussex, and Surrey, in a ring of
manors encircling ancient London, and to a less extent in
Essex and the East Anglian kingdom.   In Sussex it prevails so generally on copyhold lands that it has often been
called the common law of the county ; and in the Rape of
Lewes the custom indeed is almost universal.   There are
few examples in Hampshire, but farther west a great part
of Somerset in one continuous tract was under the rule of
ultimogeniture.   In the Midland Counties the usage was
comparatively rare, at the rate of two or three manors to
a county ; but it occurred in four out of the five great
Danish towns, namely in Derby, Stamford, Leicester, and
Nottingham, as well as in other important boroughs, as
Stafford and Gloucester.   To the north of a line drawn
between the Humber and the Mersey the custom appears
to have been unknown.[3]

[1] The evidence is adduced and discussed at length by Charles Elton,
Origins of English History (London,
1882), chapter viii. pp. 183-221.
[2] Ch. Elton, *Origins of English
History*, p. 184.

[3] Ch. Elton, *Origins of English
History*, pp. 188, 191, 194.   Among
the boroughs round London in which
Borough English prevails, or used to
prevail, are Islington and Edmonton
(*op. cit.* p. 193).

However, the usage was not confined to the Saxon parts of the country ; it existed also in Celtic regions, such as Cornwall, Devon, and Wales.   In the ancient laws of Wales it is ordained that, "when brothers share their patrimony the youngest is to have the principal messuage (*tyddyn*), and all the buildings and eight acres of land, and the hatchet, the boiler, and the ploughshare, because a father cannot give these three to any one but his youngest son, and though they are pledged, yet they can never become forfeited."   But the Welsh rule applied only to estates comprising at least one inhabited house ; when property of any other kind was divided, the youngest son could claim no exceptional privilege.[1]   In Scotland there seems to be no evidence that ultimogeniture anywhere prevailed ; but in the Shetland Islands it was the practice that the youngest child of either sex should have the dwelling-house, when the property came to be divided.[2]

In old English law ultimogeniture appears to have been commonly associated with servile tenure.   On this subject the late Professor F. W. Maitland wrote to me as follows : "As to the prevalence of ultimogeniture, I have seen a great deal of it in English documents of the thirteenth century, and rightly or wrongly it is always regarded as evidence, though not conclusive proof, of servile tenure—the theory being, apparently, that in strictness there is no *inheritance* of servile tenements, but that custom requires the lord to accept one of the family of the dead tenant as a new tenant.   Here the choice of the youngest seems not unnatural : there being no inheritance to transmit, the children are sent into the world as they come of age ; the youngest is the one most likely to be found at the hearth when the father dies.   In several customs which divide the inheritance equally among sons, the youngest keeps the homestead, the *astre* or hearth.   I am far from saying that the servile origin of ultimogeniture is proved, but certainly the succession of the youngest was regarded as servile in the thirteenth century. I could give you ample proof of that.   It is thus brought

Borough Engl sh in C ltic regions.

Borough Englis commonly associated w ervi e tenure

---

[1] Ch. Elton, *op. cit.* pp. 186 *sq.* Compare Sir Henry Sumner Maine, *Lectures on the Early History oj*

Institutions (London, 1875), pp. 223 *sq.*

[2] Ch. Elton, *op. cit.* p. 186.

into connection with the *merchetum*.[1] Very commonly they are mentioned together: 'You are my villains, for I have talliged you, you paid fine for your daughter's marriage, you were your father's youngest son and succeeded to his tenement.'"[2]

Succession igest daughters.
It deserves to be noticed that in England the right of ultimogeniture is not limited to males. There are scores, if not hundreds, of little districts, where the right is extended to females, the youngest of the daughters, or the youngest sister or aunt, being preferred above the other coheiresses.[3]

Ultimoge ge in France particularly in Brittany.
The custom of ultimogeniture, or the succession of the youngest to the inheritance, also obtained in some parts of France. Thus "in some districts of the county of Cornouailles, in Brittany, the youngest child enjoyed an exclusive right, which is exactly the counterpart of the right of the eldest: the last born, whether son or daughter, succeeded to all the tenure called *quevaise*, to the exclusion of his or her brothers and sisters." This is the right known in French law as *maineté*.[4] Though the custom existed in several extensive lordships of Brittany, we cannot estimate its original prevalence in that country; for when the customs of the province were codified by the feudal lawyers the nobles set their faces against the abnormal usage; and we learn that in the seventeenth century the area within which it survived was almost daily diminishing. The districts where the custom was in vogue included the Duchy of Rohan, the Commandery of Pallacrec, and the domains of the Abbeys of Rellec and Begare. In Brittany, as in England, ultimogeniture was an incident of servile tenure; and in Brittany, as in many parts of England, when a man left no sons, the inheritance went to the youngest daughter. Further, under the names of *Maineté* and *Madelstad*, the custom existed in Picardy, Artois, and Hainault, in Ponthieu and Vivier, in the districts around Arras, Douai, Amiens,

---

[1] *Merchetum, mercheta* or *marcheta*, the fine which on the marriage of his daughter a tenant paid to his feudal lord. See below, pp. 486 *sqq.*
[2] Letter of F. W. Maitland to me, dated 15 Brookside, Cambridge, 1st November, 1887.

[3] Ch. Elton, *Origins of English History*, pp. 184 *sq.*
[4] Paul Viol H.'sto're du Droit Civile Français, Seconde Édition (Paris, 1893), 1. 84 .
[5] Ch. Elton, *op. cit.* pp. 187 *sq.*

Lille, and Cassel, and in the neighbourhood of St. Omer. In all these districts the right of ultimogeniture ranged between the descent of the whole inheritance and the privileged succession to articles of household furniture.[1] The same rule of inheritance was also followed at Grimbergthe in Brabant.[2]

Similar customs prevailed in many parts of Friesland. The most notable of these was the *Jus Theelacticum*, or custom of the "Theel-lands," doles or allottable lands, at Norden in East Friesland, not far from the mouth of the Ems. The "Theel-boors" of that district continued down to the nineteenth century to hold their allotments under a complicated system of rules designed to prevent an unprofitable subdivision of estates. An inherited allotment was indivisible : on the death of the father it passed intact to the youngest son, and on his death without issue it became the possession of the whole community.[3]

Other examples of ultimogeniture may be drawn from local customs, now superseded by the Civil Code, in Westphalia and those parts of the Rhine provinces which were under the "Saxon Law," and in the Department of Herford near Minden, the natives of which claim to belong to the purest Saxon race. So strong, we are informed, is the hold of the custom on the peasants that "until quite recently no elder child ever demanded his legal obligatory share : the children acquiesced in the succession of the youngest, even if no portions were left to them, and never dreamed of claiming under the law of indefeasible inheritance ; and even if the peasant die without making the usual will the children acquiesce in the passing of the undivided inheritance to the youngest son."[4] A similar practice has grown up in Silesia and in certain parts of Würtemberg, where the modern laws of succession have failed to break down the time-honoured privilege of the youngest, whose rights are

Marginal notes: Ultimogeniture in Friesland. Ultimogeniture in Germany.

---

[1] Ch. Elton, *op. cit.* p. 195. Compare P. Viollet, *Histoire du Droit Civile Français*, Seconde Édition (Paris, 1893), pp. 842 *sq.*

[2] Adolf Bastian, *Die Rechtsverhaltnisse bei verschiedenen Volkern der Erde* (Berlin, 1872), p. 185 *n.*[1].

[3] Ch. Elton, *Origins of English History*, p. 196, quoting Wenckebach, *Jus Theelachticum Redivivum* (1759), p. 69.

[4] Ch. Elton, *Origins of English History*, pp. 196 *sq.*

guarded by a secret settlement or by the force of the local opinion.[1] Again, in the Forest of the Odenwald, and the thinly peopled district to the north of the Lake of Constance, there are properties called *Hofgüter*, which cannot be divided, but descend to the youngest son or, in default of sons, to the eldest daughter.[2] And many more examples, we are told, might be found in Swabia, in the Grisons of Switzerland, in Alsace and other German or partly German countries, where old customs of this sort have existed and still influence the feelings of the peasantry, though they have ceased to be legally binding.[3]

No evidence of ultimogeniture in Scandinavia. No evidence of ultimogeniture appears to have been discovered in Denmark, Norway, or Sweden. But the youngest son has his privilege in the Island (once the Kingdom) of Bornholm, an outlying appendage of the Danish Crown ; and traces of a like custom have been recorded in the territory of the old Republic of Lubeck.[4]

Ultimogeniture in Russia. In the south and west of Russia it is becoming the practice to break up the old joint families and to establish the children in houses of their own ; and it is said that in such cases the youngest son is regarded as the proper successor to the family dwelling-house.[5] On this subject I am indebted to Miss M. A. Czaplicka, the distinguished Polish ethnologist, for the following information : "Junior or Minor right is known to have been the custom of the Russian peasants as early as the time of *Russkaya Pravda*, the first Russian code at the time of Yaroslav the Great. It is even now a very widespread practice in the peasants' customary law, which makes it possible to trace the origin of this law of inheritance. The 'minor right' is not a privilege but a natural course, owing to the fact that the elder sons usually separate from the father and from their own households, while the younger, or youngest, 'never severs from the father's root.' If in addition to the father's house the younger son inherits other property to the dis-

[1] Ch. Elton, *op. cit.* p. 197.
[2] Ch. Elton, *op. cit.* p. 197.
[3] Ch. Elton, *op. cit.* p. 197 ; A. Bastian, *Die Rechtsverhältnisse bei verschiedenen Volkern der Erde*, p. 185 n.[1]. For traces of ultimogeniture in old German law see also J. Grimm, *Deutsche Rechtsalterthumer*[3] (Gottingen, 1881), p. 475.
[4] Ch. Elton, *Origins of English History*, pp. 197 sq.
[5] Ch. Elton, *op. cit.* p. 198.

advantage of the elder sons, he also inherits certain duties : to take care of his enfeebled father and mother, and often also of unmarried sisters. If the elder sons have not separated from the father before his death, the house goes to the youngest son, but it is his duty to help the elder brothers in starting new households for themselves."[1] Further, Miss Czaplicka tells me that "there is no trace of junior right among any other class than that of peasants in Russia, and among the peasants it is restricted to the house, or the house and a piece of personal, not communal land."[2]

Thus far we have considered the prevalence of ultimogeniture among the Aryan peoples of Europe. Passing now to the European peoples who do not belong to the Aryan stock we learn that "in Hungary it was the law of the country districts that the youngest son should inherit the father's house, making a proper compensation to the other coheirs for the privilege. Among the Northern Tchuds, although the chief of the family can delegate his power to the eldest or youngest son, or even to a stranger if he so pleases, yet the house in which he lives must go to the youngest son at his death."[3]

Ultimogeniture in — —

§ 3. *The Question of the Origin of Ultimogeniture*

So much for the distribution of ultimogeniture or the preference for youngest sons in Europe. We have now to ask, What was the origin of a custom which nowadays strikes us as so strange and indeed unjust? On this subject speculation has been rife. It may be well to begin by quoting the opinion which the learned and judicious Sir William Blackstone has expressed in his celebrated Commentaries on English Law. Speaking of the tenure of

Sir William Blackstone on the origin of English

---

[1] Andreevsky's *Encyclopaedia*, vol. xix. (1896) p. 385, article by V. N., quoted and translated by Miss M. A. Czaplicka in a letter to me, dated 58 Torrington Square, W.C., July 25th, 1916. In the same letter Miss Czaplicka refers me to a bibliographical work, *Obychnoye Pravo*, by Y. Yakushkin, Second Edition (Yaroslav,

1896), pp. 39, 41, 47, 173, 221, 231, 387, for references to seven authorities for "junior right" among the Russian peasants, as far as the house is concerned.

[2] Miss M. A. Czaplicka, in the letter cited in the preceding note.

[3] Ch. Elton, *Origins of English History*, p. 218.

property in boroughs, or towns which had the right of sending
members to parliament, he opposes it to military tenure or
knight-service, and regards it as a relic of Saxon liberty
retained by such persons as had neither forfeited it to the king
nor been obliged to exchange it " for the more honourable,
as it was called, but, at the same time, more burthensome
tenure of knight-service." Saxon liberty, in his opinion
" may also account for the great variety of customs, affect
ing many of these tenements so held in antient burgage
the principal and most remarkable of which is that called
Borough English ; so named in contradistinction as it were
to the Norman customs, and which is taken notice of by
Glanvil, and by Littleton ; viz. that the youngest son, and
not the eldest, succeeds to the burgage tenement on the
death of his father. For which Littleton gives this reason :
because the younger son, by reason of his tender age, is
not so capable as the rest of his brethren to help himself.
Other authors have indeed given a much stranger reason
for this custom, as if the lord of the fee had antiently a
right of concubinage with his tenant's wife on her wedding-
night ; and that therefore the tenement descended not to
the eldest, but the youngest son, who was more certainly
the offspring of the tenant. But I cannot learn that ever
this custom prevailed in England, though it certainly did
in Scotland (under the name of *mercheta* or *marcheta*), till

Ultimo-
g n
re orted
among the
Tartars.

abolished by Malcolm III. And perhaps a more rational
account than either may be fetched (though at a sufficient
distance) from the practice of the Tartars ; among whom,
according to Father Duhalde, this custom of descent to the
youngest son also prevails. That nation is composed totally
of shepherds and herdsmen ; and the eldest sons, as soon as
they are capable of leading a pastoral life, migrate from
their father with a certain allotment of cattle ; and go to
seek a new habitation. The youngest son, therefore, who
continues latest with his father, is naturally the heir of his
house, the rest being already provided for. And thus we
find that, among many other northern nations, it was the
custom for all the sons but one to migrate from the father,
which one became his heir. So that possibly this custom,
wherever it prevails, may be the remnant of that pastoral

state of our British and German ancestors, which Caesar and Tacitus describe."[1]

I have not found the passage of Du Halde to which Blackstone refers, but his statement is confirmed by a modern historian, who tells us that " a still more characteristic feature of ancient law among the Turks and Mongols, and one which sheds a vivid light on their history, is the custom which, for want of another term, I shall call 'inverse adoption.' Turkish custom regulates succession in a very peculiar manner ; the permanent heir, who is in a manner attached to his native soil, is the youngest of the sons ; it is he who is called the *Ot-dzékine*, as thé Mongols say, or the *Tékine*, as the Turks say, ' the guardian of the hearth ' ; it is to him that the invariable portion of land reverts which is mentioned by Chinese annalists and western travellers. The elder brothers divide among themselves the moveables, above all the principal one, the *mal*, or capital, that is, the flocks and herds."[2] Further, I find the custom of ultimogeniture common in a group of Mongoloid tribes in south-western China and the adjoining parts of Burma and India. An inquiry into their social state may throw light on the problem before us. But at the outset of the inquiry I would observe that, contrary to what we should expect if Blackstone's theory is correct, none of these tribes is pastoral : all are agricultural, depending almost wholly for their subsistence on the produce which they extract from the earth by tillage.

Ultimogen ture among the Turks and ongo s.

Ultimogeniture fo Mongoloid es of South Eastern Asia.

[1] Sir William Blackstone, *Commentaries on the Laws of England*, Eighteenth Edition (London, 1829), ii. 81-84. The statement as to the rule of ultimogeniture among the Tartars is repeated by Letourneau, but he does not cite his authority. See Charles Letourneau, *La Sociologie d'apres l'Ethnographie*, Deuxieme Édition (Paris, 1884), p. 417 ; *id.*, *Property, its Origin and Development* (London, 1892), p. 325.

[2] Leon Cahun, *Introduction a l'Histoire de l'Asie, Turcs et Mongols* (Paris, 1896), pp. 61 *sq.* However, Miss M. A. Czaplicka writes to me (July 25th, 1916), as follows : " As I am now tracing the Tungus in Mongolian history, I have come across this note which may be of some use to you as a proof that junior right is not recognised among the Mongols. ' Tomair(?) —Shaniuy, sent away by the Chinese from Southern Mongolia, moved with his people to Khalka, in 225 B.C., or thereabouts. He wanted to pass over his elder son Mods and leave the throne to his younger son. But Mods, offended at this, killed his father and his stepmother and his younger brother, and ascended the throne ' (Father Jakiuth Bichurin, ' Notes on Mongolia,' *Zapiski o Mongolia*, iii. pp. 9-10)."

§ 4. *Ultimogeniture in Southern Asia*

The
Lushais of
Assam.   We begin with the Lushais, a tribe who inhabit a large
tract of hills in Assam.   They are a short, sturdy, muscular
people, with broad and almost hairless faces, prominent
cheek-bones, short flat noses, small almond-shaped eyes, and
a complexion that varies between different shades of yellow
and brown.   Their Mongolian origin is therefore unmistakeable.[1]   And the evidence furnished by their physical
appearance is confirmed by their language, which belongs to
the Tibeto-Burman branch of the Tibeto-Chinese family of
speech.[2]   They are an agricultural people and their staple
Their
migratory
system of
cultivation. food is rice.[3]   Yet in virtue of the mode of cultivation
which they follow they are compelled to be migratory,
seldom residing many years in any one district.   Their
system of farming is commonly known to English writers
on India as *jhuming* or *jooming*.   They fell the timber or
bamboos in a piece of the forest or jungle ; and when the
fallen trees or bamboos have dried, they are burnt, and the
ashes serve to manure the ground.   The surface of the field
thus obtained is lightly hoed, and when the gathering clouds
warn the husbandmen that the dry season is nearly over
and that the rains are about to begin, every one sallies out
with a basket of seed over his shoulder and a long broad-
ended knife (*dao*) in his hand.   Thus equipped, the whole
family sows the field, digging shallow holes in the ground
with their knives and dropping a few seeds into each hole.
The chief crop is rice, but maize, millet, Job's tears, peas,
beans, tobacco, and cotton are also grown.   This mode of
cultivation is very wasteful, for seldom more than two crops
are taken off the same piece of ground in successive years,
and the land is then allowed to lie fallow till it is again
overgrown with jungle or underwood.   If the clearing has
been made in a bamboo jungle, three or four years will
elapse before the land is again fit for cultivation ; but if the
clearing was made in a forest, a period of from seven to ten
years will pass before the process of felling the trees is

[1] Lieut.-Colonel J. Shakespear, *The
Lushei Kuki Clans* (London, 1912),
pp. 1 *sq*.
[2] *The Imperial Gazetteer of India*,

The Indian Empire (Oxford, 1909),
i. 393.
[3] J. Shakespear, *The Lushei Kuki
Clans*, pp. 17, 36.

repeated.   Forest land is said to yield better crops than
jungle land, but the labour of clearing and weeding it is
much greater.   In this way all the arable land within reach of
a large village is in time used up, and a migration to another
home becomes necessary.   The choice of a new site is a
matter of anxious concern ; a deputation of elders is sent
to sleep on the ground, and they draw omens from the
crowing of a cock which they take with them for the
purpose.   If the fowl crows lustily an hour before daybreak,
the site is adopted.   A village may be occupied for four or
five years, and in the old days the new village might be
distant two or three days' journey from the old one.   The
inhabitants must carry all their worldly goods on their backs
from one place to the other ; and the prospect of frequent
and laborious transportations naturally deters men from
multiplying their possessions, and so checks the growth of
wealth and industry.[1]   Under such a system of shifting
cultivation, which is common to most of the hill tribes of
this region, the peasants acquire no rights in the soil, and
even the chiefs claim no property in the land and the
forests.   A chief asserts his authority only over the men of
his tribe, wherever they may wander, and wherever they
may temporarily settle.   Among some of the wilder tribes
the labour of reclaiming and tilling the ground used to be
performed in great part by slaves, whom the tribesmen
had captured on raids mainly undertaken for the purpose
of procuring bondmen to relieve them of such servile
toil.[2]

Under this system there is no property in land.

The villages of the Lushais are generally perched on the
tops of ridges and extend down the steep sides of the hills.
They are large, often comprising hundreds of houses ; but
under the security for life and property which the British
Government has brought to the country, the need for con-
gregating in large fortified villages has passed away, and
accordingly the size of the villages is steadily decreasing,
and the people are scattering more and more into hamlets
and even into lonely houses in the jungle far from other

The Lushai villages.

[1] J. Shakespear, *The Lushei Kuki Clans*, pp. 23 *sq.*, 32 *sq.*

[2] Alexander Mackenzie, *History of the Relations of the Government with the Hill Tribes of the North-East Frontier of Bengal* (Calcutta, 1884), pp. 331 *sq.*

habitations.[1]   A notable feature in a Lushai village is regularly the *zawlbuk* or bachelors' hall, in which the unmarried
men and lads from the age of puberty upwards pass the night;
for they are not allowed to sleep in the houses of their parents.
Travellers from other villages also lodge in these halls, of which
in a large village there will be several.   The institution is a
common one among the hill tribes of Assam.[2]

Among the
Lushais the
youngest
son of a
chief
succeds to
his father's
office and
property.
Among the Lushais, each village is a separate state,
ruled over by its own chief.   " Each son of a chief, as he
attained a marriageable age, was provided with a wife at
his father's expense, and given a certain number of households from his father's village, and sent forth to a village of
his own.   Henceforth he ruled as an independent chief,
and his success or failure depended on his own talents for
ruling.   He paid no tribute to his father, but was expected
to help him in his quarrels with neighbouring chiefs ; but
when fathers lived long it was not unusual to find their
sons disowning even this amount of subordination.   The
youngest son remained in his father's village and succeeded
not only to the village, but also to all the property." [3]   Thus
the practice of the Lushais strongly confirms the theoretical
explanation of ultimogeniture which was suggested by
Blackstone ; for among them it would seem that the
youngest son inherits simply because he remains at his
father's home when all his elder brothers have left it and
gone forth into the world to form new homes of their own.

But
through a
change of
circum-
ultimogeni-
ture seems
to be now
passing into
primogeni-
ture among
the Lushais.
If further confirmation of this view were needed it appears
to be furnished by a change which is taking place in the
tribe at the present day.   In the last Census Report on
Assam we read that among the Lushais, " the decrease in
the size of villages has led to an important modification of
the custom under which the youngest son inherits his father's
village and property.   The *raison d'etre* of this system of
inheritance is that elder sons established villages of their own
on their marriage.   In order to enable them to do so, a
certain number of headmen or Upas and also of the
common people were told off to accompany the young

---

[1] J. Shakespear, *The Lushei Kuki
Clans*, pp. 20 *sq.*

[2] J. Shakespear, *op. cit.* pp. 21 *sq.*

[3] J. Shakespear, *op. cit.* p. 43, compare *id.* p. 54.

chief and form the nucleus of his new village. When all the elder sons had been established in this way, it is not unnatural that the youngest should inherit his father's village and property, and on him rested the responsibility for his mother's support. But while there has been no tendency for chiefs' families to decrease, the average size of villages has been decreased by half and there are not enough houses to go round among the sons. Indeed, in some cases none of the sons have been able to start a separate village, and it is obvious that under these circumstances inheritance should pass to the eldest son, and this change has been readily accepted by the people." [1]

Thus it would seem that among these people ultimogeniture is actually passing into primogeniture, because the social causes which led to the adoption of ultimogeniture are ceasing to exist. It is true that so far only the rule of inheritance in chiefs' families has been referred to ; but substantially the same rule obtains as to the inheritance of private property among ordinary people. According to one account "property is divided amongst the sons ; the youngest, however, gets the largest share ; the rest in equal portions." [2]   According to a later account, "the general rule is for the youngest son to inherit, but occasionally the eldest also claims a share." [3]   And the reason for the custom in the families of commoners is probably the same as in the families of chiefs ; for we have seen that when a chief's son is sent forth to found another village he takes with him a certain number of commoners to be his retainers and subjects in the new home. It is reasonable to suppose that in all such cases the colonists are drawn from the elder sons of families, while the youngest sons remain with their fathers in the old home and inherit the family property.

Among the Angamis, another Mongoloid tribe of Assam, the custom of ultimogeniture is found in a limited form.

Ultimogeniture in private families of Lushais.

Ultimogeniture among the Angamis of Assam.

---

[1] *Census of India, 1911*, vol. iii. *Assam*, Part I. *Report* by J. McSwiney (Shillong, 1912), p. 138.

[2] Capt. T. H. Lewin, *Wild Races of South - Eastern India* (London, 187), p. 53.

[3] J. Shakespear, *The Lushei Kuki Clans*, p. 54. Among the Anals and Purums, two clans of Manipur who are related to the Lushais, "the sons of the deceased divide the property, but the youngest son takes the house and supports the widow, thus approximating to the Lushai custom " (J. Shakespear, *op. cit.* pp. 155 *sq.*).

"During a man's life his sons, as they marry, receive their share of his landed property. Should, however, a man die, leaving several unmarried sons, these will all receive equal shares. As the sons marry, they leave the paternal mansion, and build houses of their own. The youngest son, therefore, in practice nearly always inherits his father's house."[1] Here again, therefore, the inheritance of the paternal mansion by the youngest son depends simply on the accident of his being left last at home after his elder brothers have married and set up separate establishments of their own. If, at the time of their father's death, it should happen that there are several unmarried sons at home, the youngest will have no advantage over his elder brothers.

The
s
practise a
permanent
m
agriculture. It deserves to be noted that the Angamis, who are the largest of the Naga tribes of Assam, are not migratory and do not cultivate the soil in the primitive and wasteful manner common to most hill tribes of this region, namely by clearing patches in the forest or jungle, cultivating them for a few years, and then suffering them to relapse into their former state of wild nature. On the contrary, the Angamis raise their crops on permanent terraces excavated with great labour and skill from the hillsides, and these terraces they irrigate by means of artificial channels carried along the slope of the hills for long distances at easy gradients. Their large fortified villages are also permanent, for the Angamis are strongly attached to their homes and reluctant to change them.[2]

Ultimo-
g t e
among the
Naga tribes
of Manipur. Ultimogeniture is reported to prevail to a certain extent among some of the Naga tribes of Manipur, though the rules of inheritance appear to vary from tribe to tribe, and even within the same tribe. Thus in the Mao group of tribes, for example, at Jessami the youngest son gets the house and the best of the moveable property, while the other brothers take equal shares ; at Laiyi, on the other hand, the eldest son inherits half the property, and the other sons divide the other half between them ; and at Mao the eldest son gets a special

[1] *Census of India, 1891, Assam*, by (Sir) E. A. Gait, vol. i. *Report* (Shillong, 1892), p. 240.

[2] *Census of India, 1891, Assam*, by (Sir) E. A. Gait, vol. i. *Report* (Shillong, 1892), pp. 237 *sq.* As to the permanence of the Naga villages and the attachment of the people to the sites, see J. Shakespear, *The Lushei Kuki Clans*, pp. 20, 21.

share, but the house is reserved for the youngest son. Among the Kabuis, again, the property is divided among the sons, but the share of the youngest is larger than those of his elder brothers. Similarly among the Quoirengs, another Naga tribe of Manipur, it is said that in one village the youngest son takes all the property, but that in another village the eldest son inherits the whole, but is charged with the maintenance of all his brothers and sisters; while in yet a third village the rule is, that if all the sons are grown up at the time of their father's death, the property is divided equally among them, but if they are too young to look after it themselves, their eldest surviving paternal uncle enjoys the estate and maintains his nephews out of it until they are old enough to take the management of the property into their own hands. On this seeming diversity of usage our informant, Mr. T. C. Hodson, observes: "I think the variations are perhaps more apparent than real, because the eldest son would be the natural 'manager' of the property if he were grown up and the younger sons still children, and that the paternal uncle is the manager failing the sons, while the custom of giving the youngest son the lion's share may be associated with the custom of making provision for the others as they grow to maturity and marry." [1] Like the rest of the Mongoloid tribes with whom we are here concerned, these Nagas of Manipur subsist chiefly by husbandry; they inhabit fortified villages built on heights, to which paths, overgrown with jungle, lead steeply up from the valleys. Within the stockade or rampart of stones, which usually surrounds a village, the large, substantially built houses are irregularly disposed in groups according to the clans which occupy them. [2] Some of the tribes migrate periodically when the land in their neighbourhood is exhausted; others cling to their villages tenaciously, but are compelled to shift the area of cultivation year by year according to a fixed rotation. [3]

[1] T. C. Hodson, *The Nāga Tribes of Manipur* (London, 1911), pp. 103-105.

[2] T. C. Hodson, *The Naga Tribes of Manipur*, pp. 39, 41, 43.

[3] T. C. Hodson, *The Nāga Tribes of Manipur*, p. 50. As to the agricultural system of these tribes, see Major W. McCulloch, *Account of the Valley of Munnipore and of the Hill Tribes* (Calcutta, 1859), pp. 44-47 (*Selections from the Records of the Government of India, Foreign Department*, No. xxvii.). The passage is quoted also by T. C. Hodson, *op. cit.* pp. 51 *sqq.*

The
M... .
of Assam.

The Meitheis, who constitute the dominant race of Manipur, in Assam, are a Mongoloid people speaking a Tibeto-Burman tongue. Although by blood and language they are akin to the wild hill tribes which surround them, they have advanced to a higher degree of social culture, so as to form a singular oasis of comparative civilization and organized society in the midst of a wilderness of barbarism.[1] They live in settled villages, and subsist chiefly by the rice which they cultivate in permanent fields.[2] They have thus passed beyond the stage of periodical migrations caused by the exhaustion of the arable lands in their neighbourhood. As to the rules of inheritance among the Meitheis, we are told that " the Chronicles of Manipur do not afford us much aid in ascertaining the rules of inheritance for private property, and at the present time the economics of the State are in flux under pressure of new ideas political and social.

Ultimo-
·
among the
Meitheis.

Land is regarded as held at the will of the ruling power of the State. As regards moveable property the general practice seems to be to provide for the sons during the lifetime of the father, and to regard the youngest son as the heir general if at the time of the father's death he is still living in the ancestral home. If he had separated and was living apart from his father, the property should be equally divided among the sons. Marriage is of course the cause of the separation of the sons from the home, and is the occasion of finding provision for them as well as for the daughters." [3] Thus among the Meitheis, as among the Angamis, of Assam, the heirship of the youngest son depends solely on the accident of his being left last at the paternal home, after his elder brothers have married and settled elsewhere. If like them he should have married and set up house for himself, he will have no preference in the inheritance, but will divide the property equally with his brothers. Further, we see that in Assam, as in England, the custom of ultimogeniture survives in a limited form after the population has ceased to be migratory and has settled

[1] T. C. Hodson, *The Meitheis* (London, 1908), pp. xvii. 10 *sq.*
[2] Compare T. C. Hodson, *The Meitheis*, pp. 26 *sq.*, 39 *sq.*, whose evidence, however, as to the perman-

ence of the Meithei villages and cultivation is only implicit.

[3] T. C. Hodson, *The Meitheis*, pp. 77 *sq.*

down in permanent villages surrounded by fields which remain the same from generation to generation.

The Kachins or, as they call themselves, the Chingpaws or Singphos, are a Mongoloid race who inhabit the northern parts of Upper Burma. Their old settlements were on the head waters of the Irrawaddy River, but they have spread eastward into the Chinese province of Yunnan, and westward into the Indian province of Assam. The name of Chingpaws or Singphos, which they give themselves, means simply "men." The Burmese call them Kachins or Kakhyens. They are wild and savage mountaineers, broken up into a number of small communities or petty tribes, each under its own chief; their raids were much dreaded by the more pacific Burmese and Shans before the English occupation of the country. Yet they cultivate the soil, and indeed are expert at tillage; their fields are often deep down in the valleys, while their villages stand far above them on the hills.[1] Of the Tartar origin of the Kachins, we are told, there cannot be much doubt. Their traditions point to a first home somewhere south of the desert of Gobi, and their movements have always been towards the south. But the diversity of complexion and features which prevails even in tracts where Shan and Burmese influences have apparently never penetrated, seems to point to admixture with aboriginal races whom the Kachins supplanted.[2]

The law of inheritance among the Kachins, as it is often stated, combines the principles of primogeniture and ultimogeniture; for we are told that "the patrimony is divided between the eldest and the youngest son; while any children that may intervene, are left to push their own fortunes as they best can. The eldest son succeeds to the

[1] E. T. Dalton, *Descriptive Ethnology of Bengal* (Calcutta, 1872), pp. 9 *sq.*; J. Anderson, *Mandalay to Momien* (London, 1876), pp. 125 *sq.*; (Sir) J. George Scott and J. P. Hardiman, *Gazetteer of Upper Burma and the Shan States* (Rangoon, 1900-1901), Part I. vol. i. pp. 331 *sq.*, 369 *sqq.*; O. Hanson, "The Kachin Tribes and Dialects," *Journal of the Royal Asiatic Society for 1907* (London, 1907), pp. 381 *sqq.*; Ch. Gilhodes, "Mythologie et Religion des Katchins," *Anthropos*, iii. (1908) p. 672.

[2] (Sir) J. George Scott and J. P. Hardiman, *Gazetteer of Upper Burma and the Shan States*, Part I. vol. i. p. 396; Ch. Gilhodes, "La Culture matérielle des Katchins," *Anthropos*, v. (1910) pp. 617 *sq.*

title and estate, while the youngest, carrying away all the personal and moveable property, goes in quest of a settlement for himself." [1]   According to this account, which has been substantially repeated by several writers on the Kachins, the eldest son remains at home in possession of the paternal estate, while the youngest son takes the personal property and goes out to push his way in the world.   This is just the contrary of what is commonly said to happen among the kindred Mongoloid tribes of this region, and we may suspect that the account, which appears to have originated with Captain J. B. Neufville in 1828, rests on a misunderstanding.   At all events Sir George Scott, who had ample means of acquainting himself with the customs of the Kachins, has given a different account of their law of inheritance.   He says, " There has been a constant tendency to disintegration among the Kachins just as there has been among the Tai, and the hillier character of their country has made the subdivisions very much more minute. This disintegration was also in past times due, no doubt, chiefly to the necessity for migration caused by over-population and the wasteful character of the hill cultivation.   It became the custom, on the death of a chief, for the youngest son to succeed : while the elder brothers set out with such following as they could muster and founded fresh settlements, which, if they were successful, in time came to be distinct tribes named after their own founder.   The Kentish law of Borough English no doubt is a reminiscence of a similar custom among the Anglian tribes." [2]

Different ownership in the hills n respectively, depending on different systems of agriculture.

Elsewhere Sir George Scott gives us an instructive account of the different systems of ownership, communal and individual, which prevail in the hills and the valleys respectively, the difference in the ownership depending on the difference between the migratory and the permanent systems of

[1] W Robinson, *A Descriptive Account of Assam* (Calcutta and London, 1841), p. 378.   To the same effect Capt. J. B. Neufville, "On the Geography and Population of Assam," *Asiatic Researches*, xvi. (Calcutta, 1828) p. 341 ; J. McCosh, "Account of the Mountain Tribes on the Extreme N. - E. Frontier of Bengal,"
Journal of the Asiatic Society of Bengal v. (1836) p. 202 ; R. G. Latham, *Descriptive Ethnology* (London, 1859), i. 135 ; E. T. Dalton, *Descriptive Ethnology of Bengal*, p. 13.

[2] (Sir) J. George Scott and J. P. Hardiman, *Gazetteer of Upper Burma and the Shan States*, Part I. vol. i. p. 373.

agriculture practised in the hills and valleys.   He says,
"With regard to *taungya* or hill cultivation, individual
property is not recognized ; the land is regarded as belonging to the whole community as represented by their *Duwa*
[chief], and the system of cultivation does not permit of a
constant use of the same plot of ground.   Where land is
owned in the valleys and wet-weather paddy is cultivated,
the case is different, and individual ownership is admitted
with this restriction, that the land cannot be parted with to
an alien.   It is as a recognition of his theoretical ownership
of all the land that the *Duwa* gets·one or two baskets of
paddy per house annually.   Land descends to a household
as a whole, and is worked in common for the benefit of all.
Those who leave the household lose all right to participate.
When the household breaks up voluntarily, a division is
made according to no fixed rules, except that the youngest
son gets Benjamin's share, as well as the ancestral home-
stead." [1]

In this account a sharp distinction appears to be drawn
between the uplands, where the cultivation is migratory,
and the lowlands, where the cultivation is permanent : on
the hills the rice is grown on the dry system, in the valleys
it is grown on the wet system.   The coincidence of the dry
system with migratory cultivation, and of the wet system
with permanent cultivation, is not accidental ; for while the
dry system is compatible with a temporary occupation of
the ground, the wet system necessitates its permanent
occupation.   In Java, for example, where the cultivation of
rice is carried to a high pitch of excellence by means of
artificial irrigation, there are lands which have produced
two crops every year beyond the memory of living man.[2]
Now it is very significant that among the Kachins the lands
which are under temporary cultivation are held in common,
whereas the lands which are under permanent cultivation are
owned by individuals.   Similarly we saw that among the
Lushais, who follow the migratory system of agriculture,

(margin note:) Permanent associated with ̱ ̱ ̱ ownership; migratory associated with communal ownership.

[1] (Sir) J. George Scott and J. P.
Hardiman, *Gazetteer of Upper Burma
and the Shan States*, Part I. vol. i.
p. 416.
[2] John Crawford, *History of the*
Indian Archipelago (Edinburgh, 1820),
i. 363.   As to the different modes of
cultivating rice, the dry and the wet,
see *id.* pp. 360 *sqq.*

there is no private property in the soil.[1] The reason is obvious. Permanent occupation is essential to individual ownership ; it is not essential to communal or tribal owner-ship. And as in human history the nomadic life of the hunter, the herdsman, and the migratory husbandman pre-cedes the settled life of the farmer under the more advanced systems of tillage, it seems to follow that individual owner-ship of land has been developed later than communal or tribal ownership, and that it cannot be recognized by law until the ground is under permanent cultivation. In short, common lands are older than private lands, and the transition from communal to private ownership of the soil is associated with a greatly improved mode of tillage, which in its turn, like all economic improve-ments, contributes powerfully to the general advance of society.[2]

The Kachins of China, like those of Burma, practise both the migratory and the permanent system of agriculture.

Like their brethren of Burma, the Kachins of China practise both the migratory and the permanent modes of agriculture. Viewed from the top of a lofty mountain, their country stretches away on every side like a sea of hills, far as the eye can range, their summits and slopes in great part clothed with forest, except where little clearings mark the sites of villages, or where an opening in the mountains reveals a river winding through a narrow valley far below. The villages are always situated near a perennial mountain

[1] Above, p. 443.

[2] The truth, that private rights of property in land only come to be re-cognized after the amount of land at the disposal of a tribe has ceased to be practically unlimited, is clearly brought out by Mr. A. W. Davis in his re-marks on landed property among the tribes of the Naga Hills in Assam (*Census of India, 1891, Assam*, by E. A. Gait, vol. i. *Report*, Shillong, 1892, p. 250). He says, ",Private rights of property in land are the rule amongst all the tribes in this district, except the Kukis, Mikirs, and plains Rengmas, *i.e.* the migratory tribes. That private rights of property in land are not recognised amongst these tribes is due to the fact that they are in no way pressed for land, the villages being small and uncut jungles extensive.

When, however, we come to tribes like the Angamis, Lhotas, and Aos, who live in permanent and large villages, and amongst whom land is none too plentiful, we find that the rights of individuals to property in land are well known and well recognised, and the rules as to inheritance and partition of such property settled by strict customary law. Amongst the Angamis land, especially permanent terraced cultivation, is freely sold and bought, there being no more difficulty in selling a terraced field than in selling a pig or a cow. Amongst the other tribes the custom of letting out land is largely practised, a rent varying from Rs. 3 to Rs. 5 for a field (*jhum*) large enough for the support of a household being the usual amount charged for the use of land for two years." .

stream, generally in a sheltered glen, or straggling with their enclosures up a gentle slope, and covering perhaps a mile of ground. The houses, which usually face eastward, are all built on the same plan. They are constructed of bamboo and usually measure from one hundred and fifty to two hundred feet in length, by forty to fifty feet in breadth. The first room of one of these large communal dwellings is reserved for the reception of strangers ; the others are the apartments of several families, connected with each other by blood or marriage, which compose the household community. The projecting eaves, supported by posts, form a verandah, where men and women work or lounge by day, and where the buffaloes, mules, ponies, pigs, and fowls lodge by night.

Near the houses are small enclosures, where white-flowered poppies, plantains, and indigo are cultivated ; rice and maize are grown together on the adjacent slopes and knolls, which are carefully scarped in terraces, often presenting the appearance of an amphitheatre. The stream is dammed near the highest point, and directed so as to overflow the terraces and rejoin its bed in the valley below. Sometimes the water is led in bamboo conduits to rice fields or distant houses. Fresh clearings are made every year by felling and burning the forests on the hillsides. Near every village disused paths may be seen, which have been cut to former clearings, and along which little canals have been carried. The cleared ground is broken up with a rude hoe, but in the cultivated terraces wooden ploughs are used. Excessive rain rather than drought is the evil most dreaded by these rude husbandmen. But generally the natural fertility of the soil more than repays their labours with bountiful crops of rice, maize, cotton, and tobacco, all of excellent quality. Near the villages are orchards, where peaches, pomegranates, and guavas are grown ; and the forest abounds with chestnuts, plums, cherries, and various wild brambleberries. On the higher slopes, oaks and birches flourish, and large tracts are covered with *Cinnamomum caudatum* and *C. cassia*, of which the oil is commonly sold as oil of cinnamon. Thousands of these trees are felled annually to clear new ground for cultivation, and their fallen trunks and branches are burned where they lie.[1]

The
Kachins
are
ngo an
in o igin.

The Mongolian origin of these Chinese Kachins is apparent from their physical features, though two types may be distinguished among them. By far the commoner of the two comprises a short, round face, low forehead, prominent cheek-bones, broad nose, thick protruding lips, broad square chin, and slightly oblique eyes set far apart. The ugliness of the face is only redeemed by its good-humoured expression. The hair and eyes are usually dark brown, the complexion a dirty buff. The other type shows finer cut features, which recall the womanly faces of the Kacharis and Lepchas of Sikhim. In it the obliqueness of the eyes is very marked, and the face is a longish, rather compressed oval, with pointed chin, aquiline nose, prominent cheek-bones, and a complexion so fair that in some cases it might almost pass for European. This type may point to admixture with Shan or Burmese blood. The stature of the Kachins is rather low ; the limbs are slight, but well formed, the legs, however, being disproportionately short. Though not muscular, they are athletic and agile. They bring down from the hills loads of firewood and deal planks, which the ordinary European has much ado in lifting ; and the young girls bound like deer along the hill-paths, their loose dark locks streaming behind them on the wind.[2]

Ultimo-
es
among the
Chinese
Kachins.

Among these mountaineers the patriarchal system of government has hitherto universally prevailed. Each clan is governed by an hereditary chief assisted by lieutenants, whose office is also hereditary ; but curiously enough, while the office of lieutenant should in strictness be held only by the eldest son of the family, "the chieftainship descends to the youngest son, or, failing sons, to the youngest surviving brother. The land also follows this law of inheritance, the younger sons in all cases inheriting, while the elder go forth and clear wild land for themselves."[3] Thus among the Kachins, as among the Lushais, the right of ultimogeniture appears to be founded on a custom of sending out

[1] John Anderson, M.D., *Mandalay to Momien* (London, 1876), pp. 125, 128-130.

[2] J. Anderson, *Mandalay to Momien*, p. 127.

pp. 130 *sq.*

[3] J. Anderson, *Mandalay to Momien*,

the elder sons into the world to fend for themselves, while the youngest remains with his parents in the old home.

A similar rule of succession, based on a similar custom, was found by Dr. John Anderson to prevail among the Shans of China, the neighbours of the Kachins in the province of Yunnan. Among them, he tells us, the chiefs, assisted by a council of headmen, exercise full patriarchal authority in their states, adjudicating on all cases, civil and criminal. The chief (*tsawbwa*) "is the nominal owner of all land, but each family holds a certain extent, which they cultivate, paying a tithe of the produce to the chief. These settlements are seldom disturbed, and the land passes in succession, the youngest son inheriting, while the elder brothers, if the farm is too small, look out for another plot, or turn traders ; hence the Shans are willing to emigrate and settle on fertile lands, as in British Burma."[1]   Most of these Chinese Shans are engaged in agriculture, and as farmers they may rank with the Belgians. Every inch of ground is cultivated ; the principal crop is rice, which is grown in small square fields, shut in by low embankments, with passages and floodgates for irrigation. During the dry weather, the water of the nearest stream is led off and conducted in innumerable channels, so that each field can be irrigated at will. At the beginning of May, the valley, from one end to the other, presents the appearance of an immense watery tract of rice plantations glistening in the sunshine, while the bed of the river is left half bare by the withdrawal of the water.[2]

The Shans or Tai, as they should rather be called, are the most numerous and widely spread race of the Indo-Chinese peninsula, extending from Assam far into the Chinese province of Kwang-si, and from Bangkok to the interior of Yunnan. Siam is now the only independent Shan state. The people are closely akin to the Chinese both in physical appearance and in speech ; indeed in grammatical structure as well as vocabulary the Chinese and Shan are sister languages, differing widely from the

Ultimogeniture among the Chinese Shans.

Distribution of the Shans · their affinity to the Chinese.

---

[1] J. Anderson, *Mandalay to Momien*, p. 302.

[2] J. Anderson, *Mandalay to Momien*, pp. 299 *sq.*

Burmese and Tibetan, which nevertheless belong to the
same general family of speech, now called by philologers
the Tibeto-Chinese. Though much of their territory is
mountainous, the Shans do not profess to be a hill people,
preferring to cling to the flat alluvial valleys or wide
straths, which are interposed between the mountains.
Everywhere they are diligent cultivators of the soil ; the
larger plains are intersected with irrigation canals, while in
the smaller the streams are diverted by dams into channels
which water the slopes, or bamboo wheels are used to raise
the water to the fields, where the river-banks are high and
there is enough flat land to repay the expense and trouble.[1]
However, when holdings are not to be obtained in the plain,
young men will sometimes apply for jungle land at a
distance from the village on the hillside. Of such jungle
land there is no lack, but it is useless for the cultivation of
rice and has to be laid out in orchards or banana-gardens.[2]
It is interesting to observe the ancient custom of ultimogeniture surviving among a people so comparatively advanced as the Shans.

The custom of ultimogeniture is also said to be observed
by the Chins, who inhabit the hills on the borders of
Burma and Assam. Their racial affinities have not yet been
exactly determined, but apparently they belong to the great
Mongolian family and speak dialects of the Tibeto-Burman
speech.[3] Most of the Chins are still in a very wild state,
living at enmity with all their neighbours. They are
divided into numerous small clans, which make frequent
raids on each other or on neighbouring Burmese villages.
For their subsistence they depend chiefly on agriculture,
raising crops of rice, millet, peas, beans, sessamum, and
tobacco. But their country does not lend itself well to

*Their
agriculture.*

*Ultimo-
geniture
among tne
Chins, a
race
on the
borders of
Assam and
Burma.*

[1] (Sir) J. George Scott and J. P.
Hardiman, *Gazetteer of Upper Burma
and the Shan States* (Rangoon, 1900–
1901), Part I. vol. i. pp. 187 *sqq.*, 272
sqq. The identity of the Shan race is
obscured by a bewildering variety of
local names, such as Pai-i, Moi, Muong,
Tho or Do, and Hkamti (Khamtee),
with many more. As to the Tibeto-
Chinese family of languages see Sir G.
A. Grierson, in *The Imperial Gazetteer*
of India, The Indian Empire (Oxford,
1909), i. 384 *sqq.*; *Census of India,
1911*, vol. i. *Report* by (Sir) E. A.
Gait (Calcutta, 1913), pp. 329 *sq.*,
336.

[2] Mrs. Leslie Milne, *Shans at Home*
(London, 1910), p. 98.

[3] (Sir) J. George Scott and J. P.
Hardiman, *Gazetteer of Upper Burma
and the Shan States*, Part I. vol. i.
pp. 451 *sqq.*

tillage, for the hills are overgrown with jungle and under-wood and broken up by ravines. Small patches, however, are cleared for cultivation in the neighbourhood of the villages. Among their remarkable laws of marriage and inheritance are the custom which gives a man prior right to marry his cousin, and the rule that "the younger son is the heir of a Chin family, and he is bound to stay at home and take care of his parents and sisters."[1] However, among the Haka Chins at the present time the custom of ultimo-geniture seems to have passed, or to be passing, into primo-geniture, though in two at least of the families or clans, the Kenlawt and the Klarseowsung, the youngest son still regularly succeeds to the family dwelling, unless he waives his claim, or has quarrelled with his father, or is a leper or insane. Formerly it was the invariable rule in all the Haka clans that the youngest son should inherit the family dwell-ing; but a certain Lyen Non, of Sangte, bequeathed his house to his eldest instead of to his youngest son, and since his time the change of descent has been adopted by most of the clans. "As regards landed property (*lai ram*), situated within the Haka Tracts, two-thirds is apportioned to the eldest and one-third to the youngest son."[2]

Among the Kamees or Hkamies, a hill tribe of Arakan, on the borders of Burma, the rule of inheritance is that "if a man die leaving two or more sons, the property is divided as follows:—two divide equally; if there be more than two, the eldest and youngest take two shares each, and the others one share each."[3] This rule of inheritance is apparently a compromise between the principles of primogeniture and ultimogeniture, the eldest and the youngest sons being both

Compromise between primogeniture and ultimogeniture of Hkamies of Arakan.

[1] (Sir) J. George Scott and J. P. Hardiman, *op. cit.* Part II. vol. ii. pp. 302 *sqq.*

[2] W. R. Head, *Hand Book on the Haka Chin Customs* (Rangoon, 1917), pp. 20 *sq.*

[3] Major W. Gwynne Hughes, *The Hill Tracts of Arakan* (Rangoon, 1881), p. 27. See also R. F. St. Andrew St. John, "A short account of the Hill Tribes of North Aracan," *Journal of the Anthropological Institute*, ii. (1873) p. 241. Mr. St. John, who

was Assistant Commissioner of British Burma, and lived among these tribes for eighteen months, reports the rule of inheritance as if it applied alike to all the hill tribes of North Arakan. But this is apparently incorrect, for among the Chins of Arakan, "if a man die leaving two sons, the younger is en-titled to nothing; his elder brother is bound however to provide for his mar-riage, the expenses of which he must pay" (Major W. Gwynne Hughes, *The Hill Tracts of Arakan*, p. 30).

preferred in equal degrees to their intermediate brothers. Perhaps the compromise marks a transition from ultimogeniture to primogeniture.

Ultimo-
geniture
among the
Lolos.

The practice of ultimogeniture is reported also to prevail among the Lolos, an important and widespread aboriginal race in the Chinese province of Yunnan, who belong to the Mongolian family and speak a branch of the Tibeto-Burman language.[1] Among them, according to an English traveller, "the order of succession to property and chieftainship is curious ; the youngest son generally succeeds and after him the eldest." [2]

Heirship
of the
youngest
daughter
among the
Khasis and
Garos of
Assam.
The
Khasis,
their
language.

Thus far we have dealt with Mongoloid tribes in which the principal heir to property is the youngest son. We have now to consider two tribes in which the principal heir is the youngest daughter. These are the Khasis and Garos of Assam. The origin and racial connexions of the Khasis are still matters of discussion.[3] They certainly speak a language which, unlike that of all the tribes around them, does not belong to the Mongolian family and is apparently related to the Mon-Kmer languages of Indo-China, which in their turn are now believed to constitute a branch of a great Austric family of languages spoken from Madagascar in the west to Easter island in the east, and from New Zealand in the south to the Punjab in the north.[4] However, their possession of a non-Mongolian language is no proof that the Khasis belong to a non-Mongolian race ; for when a language has not been fixed by being committed to writing the people who speak it are very ready to drop it and replace it by another borrowed from a dominant race with which they have been brought into contact. Instructive instances of such easy and rapid transitions from one language to another have been observed and recorded in modern times among the tribes of Burma, who speak a

[1] See above, vol. i. pp. 212 sq.
[2] E. Colborne Baber, " Travels and Researches in the Interior of China," Royal Geographical Society, Supplementary Papers, vol. i. (1886) p. 70. However, a somewhat different account of the rule of inheritance among the Lolos is given by a French writer. See below, p. 531.

[3] Lieut.-Colonel P. R. T. Gurdon, The Khasis, Second Edition (London, 1914), pp. 10 sqq.
[4] Census of India, 1911, vol. i. India, Part I. Report by (Sir) E. A. Gait (Calcutta, 1913), pp. 324, 327, 336. Compare (Sir) G. A. Grierson, in The Imperial Gazetteer of India, The Indian Empire (Oxford, 1909), i. 382, 386.

variety of languages and dialects.[1] The physical appearance and character of the Khasis seem to point to a Mongolian origin; indeed, according to Sir William Hunter, their Mongolian physiognomy is unmistakeable.[2] They are a short, muscular people, with well-developed calves, broad high cheek-bones, flat noses, little beard, black straight hair, black or brown eyes, eyelids set obliquely, though not so acutely as in the Chinese and some other Mongols, and a complexion, according to locality, varying from a light yellowish - brown to a dark brown. In disposition they are cheerful, light-hearted, good-natured, and thoroughly appreciate a joke.[3] These characteristics certainly favour the view that the Khasis belong to the Mongolian stock rather than to the southern and chiefly tropical family of peoples, with whom they are allied by language.

Be that as it may, in their manner of life and the general level of their culture the Khasis do not differ markedly from the Mongoloid tribes of south-eastern Asia who practise ultimogeniture. They live in settled villages, which they seldom shift,[4] and they subsist chiefly by agriculture, being industrious cultivators, though their modes of tillage are somewhat primitive. Like most hill tribes of this region, they obtain fresh land for tillage by clearing the forest, felling the trees, and burning the fallen timber.[5] Their staple food is rice and dried fish.[6]

The social system of the Khasis is based on mother-kin, that is, on the custom of tracing descent exclusively through women. Each clan claims to be sprung from a common ancestress, not from a common ancestor; and each man reckons his genealogy through his mother, grandmother, and so on, not through his father, grandfather, and so on.[7] And as with blood, so with inheritance, it passes through

Margin notes: The Khasis apparently a Mongolian people. Mode of life and agriculture of the Khasis. Mother-kin of the Khasis.

[1] *Census of India, 1911*, vol. i. *India*, Part I. *Report* by (Sir) E. A. Gait (Calcutta, 1913), p. 328.
[2] (Sir) W. W. Hunter, *A Statistical Account of Assam* (London, 1879), ii. 216. Similarly, Sir Joseph Hooker says, "The Khasia people are of the Indo-Chinese race" (*Himalayan Journals*, London, 1891, p. 485).
[3] Sir Joseph Hooker, *Himalayan Journals* (London, 1891), p. 485; P. R. T. Gurdon, *The Khasis*,[2] pp. 2 *sqq.* Unlike Lieut.-Col. Gurdon, Hooker describes the Khasis as "sulky, intractable fellows."
[4] P. R. T. Gurdon, *The Khasis*,[2] p. 33.
[5] P. R. T. Gurdon, *op. cit.* p. 39.
[6] P. R. T. Gurdon, *op. cit.* p. 51.
[7] P. R. T. Gurdon, *op. cit.* pp. 63, 82 *sq.*

The
youngest
daughter
the heir
among the
Khasis.
women only, not through men, and it is the youngest, not
the eldest, daughter who inherits ; if she dies in her mother's
lifetime, she is succeeded by the next youngest daughter,
and so on. Failing daughters, a woman's property goes to
her sister's youngest daughter, who in her turn is succeeded
by her youngest daughter, and so on. It is true that on
the mother's death, the other daughters are entitled to a
share in her property ; but the youngest daughter gets the
largest share, including the family jewellery and the family
house, together with the greater part of the contents. Still
she may not dispose of the house without the unanimous
consent of all her elder sisters, who, on the other hand, are
bound to repair the dwelling for her at their own charges.[1]
As for the landed estate, it belongs to the youngest daughter
only, but her elder sisters are entitled to maintenance from
the produce.[2] Almost invariably the grandmother, her
daughters, and her daughters' daughters live together under
one roof or in adjoining houses within the same enclosure ;
and during her lifetime the grandmother is head of the

Insignifi-
cance of
men in a
Khasi
household.
house.[3] In such a household of women a mere man is
nobody. If he is a son or brother, he is of no account,
because, when he marries, he will leave the house and go
and live with his wife's family. If he is the husband of one
of the women, he is still of no account, not being a member
of the family, and having no share in the inheritance. He
is looked upon as a mere begetter. Any property he may
earn by his own exertions will go at his death to his wife,
and after her to her children, the youngest daughter as
usual getting the largest share. So long as he lives, he is
a stranger in his wife's house ; and when he dies, even his
ashes may not rest beside hers in the family tomb.[4]

The custom of tracing descent and transmitting property

---

[1] P. R. T. Gurdon, *The Khasis*,[2]
p. 83.

[2] P. R. T. Gurdon, *op. cit.* p. 88.

[3] P. R. T. Gurdon, *op. cit.* pp. 31,
63. That the mother and daughters
do not always live in the same
house appears from the former of
these passages (p. 31), where we
read that "when a daughter leaves
her mother's house and builds a house
in the mother's compound, it is con-

sidered *sang* or taboo for the daughter's
house to be built on the right-hand
side of the mother's house, it should
be built either on the left hand or at
the back of the mother's house."

[4] P. R. T. Gurdon, *The Khasis*,[2]
pp. 76, 82, 83 *sq.*; E. T. Dalton,
Descriptive Ethnology of Bengal, pp.
56 *sq.*; (Sir) W. W. Hunter, *Statistical
Account of Assam* (London, 1879), ii.
217 *sq.*

through women instead of through men is common among
uncivilized races, and may in its origin have been based
on the certainty of motherhood compared with the uncertainty of fatherhood in a state of society which allowed
great freedom of intercourse between the sexes. But that is
a large and difficult problem, the discussion of which would
lead us too far. Among the Khasis at the present time,
whatever its remote origin may have been, the custom is
clearly bound up with the rule which keeps all the daughters
at home and sends out all the sons to live with their wives'
families. For under such a rule the women are the only
lifelong members of the household, and it is therefore
natural that the house and its contents should be in their
hands rather than in the hands of the males, who leave or
enter the house only at marriage, and hence spend only a
portion of their life within its walls ; and the same reasoning
would apply also to landed property, if the lands are near the
houses, and the sons on marrying take up their abode with
their wives' people in distant villages. Under such circumstances it is easy to understand why daughters rather than sons
should succeed to the family property, both real and personal.

But if the preference of daughters to sons as heirs is
thus explained, the reason for preferring the youngest
daughter, as heiress, to all her elder sisters is still to seek.
The Khasis themselves account for the favoured position of
the youngest daughter by the religious duties which she is
bound to discharge. She holds the religion, as their phrase
is ; that is, she is bound to perform the family ceremonies
and propitiate the family ancestors ; hence it is right that,
incurring such heavy obligations to the family, she should
receive the largest share of the property. For the same
reason, if she changes her religion or commits an act of
sacrilege by violating a taboo, she forfeits her privileges and
is succeeded in them by her next youngest sister, just as if
she had died.[1] This explanation of the privileged position
accorded to the youngest daughter is hardly satisfactory ;
for we have still to ask, why should the youngest daughter
be deemed better fitted than her elder sisters to discharge
the duty of worshipping the ancestors ? To this question

*Why
daughters
rather than
sons
succee to
property
among the
Khasis.*

*Reason
assigned by
the Khasis
for the
succession
of the
youngest
daughter.*

[1] P. R. T. Gurdon, *The Khasis,*[2] pp. 82 *sq.*

no answer seems to be forthcoming. And the reason assigned in other tribes for preferring the youngest son as heir, because he stays at home in the parental house after his elder brothers have gone out into the world, seems inapplicable to the youngest daughter among the Khasis; since in that tribe all the daughters apparently remain all their lives at home in the parental house and there receive their husbands. Yet we should naturally expect the reason for preferring the youngest daughter to be analogous to the reason for preferring the youngest son; and accordingly a theory which explains the one case but not the other, can hardly be regarded as adequate.

The other tribe of Assam who follow the customs of mother-kin and ultimogeniture in favour of the youngest daughter are the Garos, who inhabit the thickly wooded but not lofty hills which take their name from the tribe. They undoubtedly belong to the Mongolian race, for they are a short, stout-limbed, active people, with strongly marked Chinese countenances,[1] and they speak a Tibeto-Burman language of the Tibeto-Chinese family.[2] Indeed, they have a very distinct " story of their migration from Thibet; of their arrival in the plains at the foot of the Himalayas; of their wanderings eastward up the Brahmaputra valley, and of the subsequent retracing of their steps until 'they came to the plains which lie between that river and the hills they now inhabit. Here they seem to have settled for a time before making the last move into the mountainous country that now forms the home of the tribe." [3] Most of the great virgin forests which formerly covered the Garo Hills have been destroyed to make room for tillage, and their place has been taken by bamboos and small trees; for, fostered by the heavy rainfall, a dense jungle has overspread almost the whole face of the country except where patches of land have been cleared for cultivation.[4] The Garo is essentially a husbandman. To till the soil is the beginning and the

[1] Buchanan, quoted by E. T. Dalton, *Descriptive Ethnology of Bengal*, p. 66. According to Major A. Playfair, the Garos are darker than the Khasis " and they possess the Mongolian type of feature in a more marked degree " (*The Garos*, London, 1909, p. 1).

[2] (Sir) G. A. Grierson, in *The Imperial Gazetteer of India, The Indian Empire* (Oxford, 1909), i. 387, 393.

[3] M ɟ A. Playfair, *The Garos* ,London, 2 ɔ, ɛ· 8.

[4] A. Playfair, *The Garos*, pp. 5 *sq.*

end of his life's work, and the occupation to which he devotes all the energy he can muster.[1]   His mode of cultivation is rude.   A piece of land, generally on a hillside, is chosen and the jungle on it cut down in the cold weather, which lasts from December to February.   The felled trees or bamboos—for in many parts of the hills the jungle consists of bamboos only—cumber the ground till the end of March, when they are burnt as they lie.   The crops are sown in April and May as soon as the first showers have fallen.   The land is not hoed, much less ploughed ; but holes are made in it with a pointed stick and a few seeds of rice dropped into each.   Millet is simply sown broadcast in the ashes of the burnt jungle.   Land thus reclaimed is kept under cultivation for two years ; then it is abandoned and lies fallow for at least seven years.[2]   The villages are usually built in valleys or in hollows on the hillsides, where there is plenty of running water.   Around, on all sides, stretches the limitless jungle.   The houses are raised on piles and are very long, often more than a hundred feet in length ; being destitute of windows, the interiors are dark and gloomy.   The public room of the family occupies the greater part of the building, and there the unmarried women sleep on the floor ; but spaces are portioned off in it for married daughters and their husbands, and the householder and his wife have a bedroom to themselves.   The bachelors do not sleep in their parents' house, but in a house set apart for the use of all the unmarried men of the village.   In this bachelors' hall strangers are lodged, and the village elders hold their meetings.[3]   Such dormitories for the unmarried men are a regular institution with the Naga tribes of Assam, but they are not found among the Khasi Uplanders.[4]

The and houses of the Garos.

Amongst the Garos, as amongst the Khasis, the system of mother-kin prevails.   The wife is the head of the family, and through her all the family property descends.[5]

Mother-kin among the Garos.

[1] A. Playfair, *The Garos*, p. 33.

[2] A. Playfair, *The Garos*, pp. 34 *sq.*, 45.   Compare E. T. Dalton, *Descriptive Ethnology of Bengal*, p. 65.

[3] A. Playfair, *The Garos*, pp. 35 *sqq.*; E. T. Dalton, *Descriptive Ethnology of Bengal*, pp. 61 *sq.*; John Eliot, "Observations on the Inhabitants of the Garrow Hills," *Asiatick Researches*, iii. (London, 1807) pp. 23 *sq.*

[4] P. R. T. Gurdon, *The Khasis*,[2] p. 32.

[5] Sir W. W. Hunter, *Statistical Account of Assam* (London, 1879), ii. 154.

The tribe is divided into a great many family groups or "motherhoods," called *machongs*. All the members of a "motherhood" claim to be descended from a common ancestress; and all the children of a family belong to their mother's "motherhood," not to that of their father, whose family is barely recognized. Inheritance also follows the same course and is restricted to the female line. No man may possess property except what he earns by his own exertions; no man may inherit property under any circum-

Among the Garos, women nominally hold property, but men really control it.

stances whatever.[1] "The law of inheritance may be briefly stated to be, that property once in a motherhood, cannot pass out of it. A woman's children are all of her *machong* [motherhood], and therefore it might at first appear that her son would satisfy the rule; but he must marry a woman of another clan, and his children would be of their mother's sept, so that, if he inherited his mother's property, it would pass out of her *machong* [motherhood] in the second generation. The daughter must therefore inherit, and her daughter after her, or, failing issue, another woman of the clan appointed by some of its members."[2]   However, although in the eyes of the law the family estate and property belong to the woman, in practice her husband has full use of both during her lifetime, and while he cannot will it away, his authority otherwise over it is unquestioned. For example, the lands of a village belong, strictly speaking, to the wife of the village headman, yet he is always thought of and spoken of as the proprietor; and although he derives his rights exclusively through his wife, she is never considered, unless it is convenient to mention her name in a lawsuit. Practically, therefore, a woman is merely the vehicle by which property descends from generation to generation for the benefit principally of males.[3]

Heirship of youngest daughters among the Garos.

So far we have heard of the legal preference of daughters to sons among the Garos, but nothing has yet been said as to a preference of the youngest daughter to all the rest. Indeed, Major Playfair, who has given us a valuable monograph on the tribe, drops no hint of such a preference; from which we may perhaps infer that the practice of

[1] A. Playfair, *The Garos*, pp. 65, 71.

[2] A. Playfair, *op. cit.* pp. 71 *sq.*

[3] A. Playfair, *op. cit.* pp. 72, 73.

ultimogeniture is obsolete or obsolescent among the Garos
at the present day.   However, it appears to have existed in
the tribe down at least to nearly the end of the eighteenth·
century ; for an Englishman who visited and studied the
Garos in 1788 has recorded the custom among them.
After describing a Garo marriage which he witnessed, he J. Eliot's
goes on as follows : " I discovered these circumstances of evi ence.
the marriage ceremony of the Garrows, from being present
at the marriage of Lungree, youngest daughter of the chief
Oodassey, seven years of age, and Buglun, twenty-three
years old, the son of a common Garrow : and I may here
observe, that this marriage, disproportionate as to age and
rank, is a very happy one for Buglun, as he will succeed to
the *Booneahship* [chieftainship] and estate ; for among all
the Garrows, the youngest daughter is always heiress ; and
if there be any other children who were born before her,
they would get nothing on the death of the *Booneah* [chief].
What is more strange, if Buglun were to die, Lungree would
marry one of his brothers ; and if all his brothers were
dead, she would then marry the father : and if the father
afterwards should prove too old, she would put him aside,
and take any one else whom she might chuse." [1]

Thus we have found the custom of ultimogeniture These
observed by a number of tribes of South-Western China M ngolian
and the adjoining regions of Burma and Assam.   With the tribs,
doubtful exception of the Khasis, all these tribes are of the practising
Mongolian family.   Their original home is believed to have geniture,
been North-Western China, between the upper courses of seem to
the Yang-tse-kiang and the Ho-ang-ho, from which they migrated
spread out in all directions.   Following the river valleys in to their
their migrations, they passed down the Chindwin, Irrawaddy, homes
and Salween into Burma, and down the Brahmaputra into from
Assam.   Three successive waves of migration of these N t-
Mongoloid peoples have been traced ; the latest of them Western
was that of the Kachins or Singphos, which was actually in Crina.

[1] John Eliot, "Observations on
the Inhabitants of the Garrow Hills,"
Asiatick Researches, iii. (London, 1807)
pp. 27 *sq.* Similarly, speaking of the
Garos, R. G. Latham says, "The
youngest daughter inherits. The
widow marries the brother of the
deceased ; if he die, the next ; if all,
the father" (*Descriptive Ethnology*,
London, 1859, vol. i. p. 109).   His
authority seems to be Eliot, whom he
cites.

progress when it was stopped by the British conquest of
Upper Burma.[1]   The valleys of the great rivers Brahmaputra and Irrawaddy are indeed the gateways through
which the hardy northern invaders have poured from
their colder, bleaker homes in Central Asia to-invade the
warmer, richer regions of the South.   By means of this
natural highway they were able to turn the flank of the
long, almost impenetrable barrier which the Himalayas

Their halt present to a direct invasion of India from the north.   Yet
highlands in their southward march their hordes would seem never to
of Assam. have advanced beyond the rugged, wooded, rain-drenched
mountains of Assam ; there they halted, and there they
remain to this day, like the vanguard of a great army looking out from their breezy hill-tops and the edge of their
high tablelands over the hot valleys and sultry plains,
carpeted as with green velvet, which stretch away thousands
of feet below, till they melt into the sky-line or are bounded
by blue mountains in the far distance.   The heat of India
probably served on this side as a better shield against the
northern invader than the feeble arms of its unwarlike
inhabitants.   He could breath freely among the oaks, the
chestnuts, and the firs of these mountains: he feared to
descend among the palms, the rattans, and the tree-ferns of
the vales below.[2]

Ultimo-
e
among the
Mrus. However, the custom of ultimogeniture, or the preference
for the youngest child, whether son or daughter, is not
restricted in these regions to Mongoloid tribes.   Thus
among the Mrus, a small tribe who inhabit the hills between
Arakan and Chittagong, "if a man has sons and daughters,
and they marry, he will live with his youngest child, who

[1] (Sir) G. A. Grierson, in *The
Imperial Gazetteer of India, The Indian
Empire* (Oxford, 1909), i. 384 sq. .
[2] Compare *The Imperial Gazetteer
of India, The Empire of India* (Oxford, 1909), i. 295 sq.   The view
from the edge of the Khasi tableland
is finely described by Sir Joseph
Hooker, *Himalayan Journals* (London, 1891), pp. 488 sqq.   As to the
forests of the Khasi hills (oaks, firs,
birches, chestnuts, rhododendrons), see
P. R. T. Gurdon, *The Khasis*,[2] p. 8.
At the southern foot of the Khasi

mountains grow luxuriant orange
groves, which supply all Bengal with
oranges.   The fruit appears to be indigenous to the country, and from it,
according to Sir George Birdwood,
the orange may have been first carried
by the Arabs to Syria, whence the
Crusaders helped to propagate the tree
over southern Europe.   See P. R. T.
Gurdon, *The Khasis*,[2] pp. 41 sq.;
Alexander Mackenzie, *History of the
Relations of the Government with the
Hill Tribes of the North-East Frontier
of India* (Calcutta, 1884), p. 235.

also inherits all property on the death of the father."[1]   The
Mrus are tall, powerful, dark men, with no traces of the
Mongol in their faces.   They cultivate rice and drink milk,
and eat the flesh of the cow or any other animal.   In
character they are a peaceable, timid, simple folk, who settle
their disputes by an appeal to the spirits rather than by
fighting.   Among them a young man serves three years for
his wife in her father's house, but if he is wealthy, he can
compound for this period of servitude by paying two
hundred or three hundred rupees down.[2]

Further, the custom of ultimogeniture prevails among
the Hos or Larka Kols (Lurka Coles), who inhabit the
district of Singbhum in south-western Bengal.   The Hos
belong to the dark aboriginal race of India, resembling the
Dravidians in physical type, though they speak a totally
different language believed to be a branch of that great
Southern or Austric family of speech to which the Khasi
language in Assam also belongs.   The race of which the
Kols (Coles) are members, used to be called Kolarian, but
it is now generally named Munda after the tribe of that
name.[3]   The Hos or Larka Kols are a purely agricultural
people, and have advanced so far as to use wooden ploughs
.tipped with iron.[4]   Their original home appears to have
been Chota Nagpur, the great and isolated tableland to the
north of their present country, where their kindred the
Mundas still dwell.   The Hos admit their kinship with the

*Ultimo-
gen u e
among the
Hos or
r҄ a
Coles of
Bengal.*

*Racial
ın anḋ
original
home of
ᴜ��ᴇ ᴀᴀᴏꜱ.*

---

[1] Capt. T. H. Lewin, *Wild Races
of South - Eastern India* (London,
1870), pp. 234 *sq.* As to the Mrus,
compare E. T. Dalton, *Descriptive
Ethnology of Bengal*, p. 113.

[2] T. H. Lewin, *op. cit.* pp. 232,
234, 235.

[3] E. T. Dalton, *Descriptive Ethnology of Bengal*, pp. 177 *sq.*, 184 *sqq.*;
*The Imperial Gazetteer of India, The
Indian Empire* (Oxford, 1909), i. 298
sq., 382 *sqq.*; *Census of India, 1911*,
vol. i. *India*, Part I. *Report* by (Sir) E.
A. Gait (Calcutta, 1913), pp. 322 *sqq.*
The main physical characteristics of
this aboriginal Indian stock are "a
broad nose, a long head, plentiful and
sometimes curly (but not frizzly or
woolly) hair, a black or nearly black

skin, and a rather low stature " (E. A.
Gait, *op. cit.* p. 325).   However,
Dalton writes (*op. cit.* p. 190), " In
features the Hos exhibit much variety,
and I think in a great many families
there is considerable admixture of
Aryan blood.   Many have high noses
and oval faces, and young girls are
sometimes met with who have delicate,
and regular features, finely chiselled
straight noses, and perfectly formed
mouths and chins.   The eyes, however, are seldom so large, so bright
and gazelle-like as those of pure Hindu
maidens, but I have met strongly
marked Mongolian features, and some
are dark and coarse like the Santáls."

[4] E. T. Dalton, *Descriptive Ethnology of Bengal*, pp. 195, 196.

Mundas, and preserve a tradition of their migration from Chota Nagpur. According to the Oraons, a still more primitive tribe who inhabit Chota Nagpur, it was their invasion of the plateau which drove the Hos from it to seek a new home in the south ; but it is difficult to believe that the Hos should have given way to so inferior and so un-warlike a race as the Oraons. Whatever the cause of the migration may have been, the Hos now inhabit a country still more wild and mountainous than the romantic hills and valleys of Chota Nagpur which their forefathers abandoned long ago.[1] Their territory, known as Kolhan or Kolehan, is everywhere undulating, traversed by dykes of trap which rise in rugged masses of broken rock ; and the views are bounded on all sides by ranges of mountains about three thousand feet high. The most fertile, populous, and highly cultivated parts of the country are the lowlands surrounding the station of Chaibasa. To the west stretches a region of hills and vast jungles interspersed with some fruitful valleys ; while the extreme south-west is occupied by a mass of rugged, forest-clad mountains known as " Saranda of the Seven Hundred Hills," where the miserable inhabitants of a few poor solitary hamlets, nestling in deep glens, can hardly struggle for mastery with the tigers which prowl the thick jungle. The Hos of these secluded high-lands are more savage and turbulent than their brethren of the lowlands,[2] and their agriculture is primitive. They clear a few patches in the forest or jungle which surrounds their hamlets ; and though the rich black soil yields at first an abundant harvest, it is soon exhausted by the rude mode of cultivation which the Hos practise, and in three or four years they are obliged to make fresh clearings, and build for themselves fresh lodges in another part of the great wilder-ness. When even these resources failed them in time of famine, the wild highlanders used to raid their neighbours and bring back to their mountain fastnesses such plunder as

The mode of life of the Hos.

---

[1] Lieut. Tickell, "Memoir on the Hodésum (improperly called Kole-han)," *Journal of the Asiatic Society of Bengal*, vol. ix. Part II. (Calcutta, 1840), pp. 694 *sqq.*; Dr. William Dunbar, "Some observations on the manners, customs, and religious opinions of the Lurka Coles," *Journal of the Royal Asiatic Society*, xviii. (London, 1861) pp. 370 *sq.*; E. T. Dalton, *Descriptive Ethnology of Bengal*, pp. 177 *sq.*

[2] Lieut. Tickell, *op. cit.* pp. 699 *sqq.*; E. T. Dalton, *op. cit.* pp. 177 *sq.*

they could lay hands on.[1]   Things are better with their kinsfolk who inhabit the more open and fertile districts in the north.   There the villages are often prettily situated on hills overlooking the flat terraced rice-fields and undulating uplands.   Very ancient and noble tamarind trees mark the sites, and, mingled with mango and jack trees and bamboos, add a pleasing feature to an agreeable landscape.   The roomy, substantially built houses, with their thatched roofs and neat verandahs, stand each in its own plot of ground, and each is so arranged with outhouses as to form a square with a large pigeon-house in the centre.   The village green, carpeted with turf and shaded by grand tamarind trees, contains the great slabs of stone under which " the rude forefathers of the hamlet sleep."   There, under the solemn shade of the trees, when the work and heat of the day are over, the elders love to gather, and sitting on the stones to enjoy a gossip and smoke ; there, too, in due time they will be laid to their last long rest with their fathers under the stones.[2]

Each Ho village is under the authority of a headman called a *Munda* ; and a group of villages, numbering from six to twelve, is governed by a chief called a *Mankie*.[3] Curiously enough, the rule of inheritance for the chieftain-ship differs from the rule of inheritance for private property ; for while the descent of the· chieftainship is regulated by primogeniture, the descent of property is regulated by ultimogeniture.   The distinction was ascertained by Dr. William Dunbar, who tells us that " the custom of the Coles regarding the inheritance of property is singular, and was first explained to me in the case ·of a *Mankie,* as he is termed, whose villages are contiguous to the cantonments of Chaibassa.   Although he ruled over a considerable number of these, and was reckoned a powerful man among his class, I was surprised to find that his house was a small and poor one, and that his younger brother resided in the largest building in the place, which had formerly belonged to the deceased *Mankie,* his father.   On enquiry, I found that on the death of the parent, the youngest son uniformly

---

[1] Lieut. Tickell, *op. cit.* p. 784 ;   E. T. Dalton, *op. cit.* p. 189.
Dr. W. Dunbar, *op. cit.* p. 372.
[2] Lieut. Tickell, *op. cit.* p. 783 ;   [3] Dr. W. Dunbar, *op. cit.* p. 371.

receives the largest share of the property strictly personal ; and hence the *Mankie*, though he succeeded to his father's authority and station as a patriarchal ruler, was obliged to resign all the goods and chattels to his younger brother." [1] Although Dr. Dunbar was not aware of it, the same rule of succession to private property among the Hos or Larka Kols (Lurka Coles) had been recorded many years before by Lieutenant Tickell in the following terms : " The youngest born male is heir to the father's property, on the plea of his being less able to help himself on the death of the parents than his elder brethren, who have had their father's assistance in settling themselves in the world, during his lifetime." [2] The reason for the distinction between the two rules of succession is perhaps not far to seek ; for while on the death of a chief the enjoyment of his private possessions might safely enough be left to his youngest son, even should he be a minor, prudence would generally pre- scribe that the exercise of his public authority should be committed to the more experienced hands of his eldest son.

The Bhils, wi ce of Central India.

Again, ultimogeniture in a limited form is reported to be practised by the Bhils, a wild indigenous race of Central India. They are a short dark people, wiry and often thick- set, with great powers of endurance. Their name is said to be derived from the Dravidian word for bow, the charac- teristic weapon of the tribe. [3] They have lost their original language, but it probably belonged either to the Munda

Their mode of life.

(Kolarian) or to the Dravidian family. [4] Formerly they roved as huntsmen through the forests of their native mountains, but they have now had to abandon the indiscriminate slaughter of game and the free use of the woods, in which they committed destructive ravages. At present many of them live in the open country and have become farm servants and field labourers. Some of them are tenants, but very few own villages. [5] In the Barwani district of

[1] Dr. W. Dunbar, *op. cit.* p. 374.
[2] Lieut. Tickell, *op. cit.* p. 794 note*.
[3] *The Ethnographical Survey of the Central India Agency*, Monograph No. II., *The Jungle Tribes of Malwa*, by Captain C. E. Luard (Lucknow, 1909), p. 17.
[4] R. V. Russell, *The Tribes and*

Castes of the Central Provinces of India (London, 1916), ii. 279.
[5] R. V. Russell, *op. cit.* ii. 292. Compare *The Ethnographical Survey of the Central India Agency*, Mono- graph No. II., *The Jungle Tribes of Malwa*, by Captain C. E. Luard (Luck- now, 1909), p. 33.

Central India, for example, they are said to be as yet little affected by civilization and to lead a most primitive life. They have no fixed villages. The collections of huts, which pass for villages, are abandoned at the least alarm ; the report that a white man is coming often suffices to put the whole population to flight. Even within what may be called a village the huts are commonly far apart, for each man fears the treachery of his neighbours and their designs upon his wife.[1] The Bhil is an excellent woodsman. He knows the shortest cuts over the hills, and can walk the roughest paths and climb the steepest crags without slipping or feeling distressed. In old Sanscrit works he is often called *Venaputra*, that is " child of the forest," or *Pal Indra*, "lord of the pass." These names well describe his character. For his country is approached through narrow defiles (*pál*), and through these in the olden time none could pass without his permission. On travellers he used always to levy blackmail, and even now natives on a journey find him ready to assert what he deems his just rights. As a huntsman the Bhil is skilful and bold. He knows all the haunts of tigers, panthers, and bears, and will track them down and kill them. ´Armed only with swords a party of Bhils will attack a leopard and cut him in pieces.[2]

Among the Bhils of Western Malwa and the Vindhyan-Satpura region along the Narbada Valley, in Central India, tribal custom determines inheritance. Of the property half goes to the youngest son, who is bound to defray all the expenses of the funeral feast held usually on the twelfth day after his father's death. He has also to make provision for his sisters. The other half of the property is divided between the elder sons. But if all the sons live together, which very rarely happens, they share the property equally between them.[3] Here again, therefore, the preference for the youngest son in the inheritance apparently depends on his being left alone with his father at the time of his father's

Ultimo-geniture among the Bhils.

[1] *Census of India, 1901*, vol. xix. *Central India*, Part I. *Report*, by Captain C. E. Luard (Lucknow, 1902), p. 197.
[2] R. V. Russell, *The Tribes and Castes of the Central Provinces of India*, ii. 292, quoting Major Hendley's *Account of the Mewar Bhils*, pp. 357, 358.
[3] *The Ethnographical Survey of the Central India Agency*, Monograph No. II., *The Jungle Tribes of Malwa*, by Captain C. E. Luard (Lucknow, 1909), p. 26.

death; if all the sons chance to be living together with their father at the time of his death, the youngest enjoys no special privilege, but merely receives an equal share with the rest.

Ultimo-
among the Badagas of Southern India.

Further, it appears that ultimogeniture in a limited form prevails among the Badagas, an agricultural people who, along with the agricultural Kotas and the purely pastoral Todas, inhabit the Neilgherry Hills of Southern India. On this subject Dr. Rivers reports as follows: "Breeks has stated that the Toda custom is that the house shall pass to the youngest son. It seems quite clear that this is wrong, and that this custom is absolutely unknown among the Todas. It is, however, a Badaga custom, and among them I was told that it is due to the fact that as the sons of a family grow up and marry, they leave the house of the parents and build houses elsewhere. It is the duty of the youngest son to dwell with his parents and support them as long as they live, and when they die he continues to live in the parental home, of which he becomes the owner." [1]

Traces of ultimo-geniture in the Malay region and Georgia.

Very few traces of ultimogeniture appear to be reported from the Malay region. In Rembau, one of the States of the Malay Peninsula, all ancestral property vests in women. When there are several daughters in a family, the mother's house is normally inherited by the youngest daughter, who undertakes, in return for the prospective inheritance, to support her mother in old age.[2] The Battas of Sumatra are an agricultural people living in settled villages. Among them, when a man dies and leaves several sons or brothers, the custom is to divide the inheritance among them, giving the eldest and the youngest a larger share than the rest, generally double the other shares.[3] In the Transcaucasian province of Georgia, according to the provisions of a written but apparently unpublished code, it is the rule that, on the death of a prince or nobleman, the

[1] W. H. D. Rivers, *The Todas* (London, 1906), pp. 559 *sq.* As to the Badagas and the Kotas, see Edgar Thurston, *Castes and Tribes of Southern India* (Madras, 1909), i. 63 *sqq.*, iv. 3 *sqq.*

[2] C. W. C. Parr and W. H. Mackray, "Rembau," *Journal of the Straits Branch of the Royal Asiatic Society,* No. 56 (Singapore, December 1910), pp. 65, 68.

[3] G. A. Wilken, "Over de verwantschap en het huwelijks-en erfrecht bij de volken van het maleische ras," *De verspreide Geschriften* (The Hague, 1912), i. 332.

youngest son should get his father's house, with the adjoining buildings and garden ; if there is a church tower, the youngest son keeps it also, but it is valued, and he pays his elder brothers a portion of the value.   On the death of a peasant his house and meadows go to his eldest son, but his granary to the youngest.[1]

§ 5. *Ultimogeniture in North-Eastern Asia*

So far the peoples amongst whom we have found the practice of ultimogeniture are all agricultural.   The custom however prevails to some extent among tribes in the hunting and pastoral stages of society.   Thus it is reported to obtain among the Yukaghirs, a Mongolian tribe of north-eastern Siberia, who live partly by hunting and fishing, and partly by their herds of reindeer.   The possibility of agriculture is excluded by the extreme rigour of the climate, which is the coldest in all Siberia, indeed one of the coldest on earth.[2]   "The Yukaghir who subsist by hunting and fishing near river-banks are so poor, and their mode of life is so primitive, that the private possession in the family of any article, not to speak of food-products, is almost entirely beyond their conception.   Whatever is procured through hunting or fishing is turned over by the hunters and the fishermen to the women, the oldest of whom looks after its distribution. . . . Individual ownership is recognized to some extent with reference to articles of clothing, and hunting-implements, such as the gun, the bow, etc.   Each member of the family has what he calls *his* clothing, and the hunter has *his* gun. . . . The principle of private property holds also in regard to women's ornaments, and to such utensils as needles, thimbles, scissors, and thread.   Here also belong the smoking utensils —the pipe, the strike-a-light, the tobacco-pouch, and the tinder—and the canoe.   But boats, fishing-nets, house and all household implements are the common property of the whole family. . . . With regard to inheritance of family property, the principle of minority is

The Yukaghirs of north-eastern Siberia.

Ultimogeniture among the Yukaghirs.

[1] A. von Haxthausen, *Transkaukasia* (Leipsic, 1856), ii. 207, 215.
[2] Waldemar Jochelson, *The Yukaghir and the Yukaghirized Tungus* (Leyden and New York, 1910), p. 7 (*The Jesup North Pacific Expedition, Memoir of the American Museum of Natural History, New York*).

generally applied. When the older brothers separate from
the family, or, after their parents' death, go to live in the
families of their wives' parents, the family property remains
in the hands of the youngest brother. He also becomes the
owner of the father's gun, after the death of the latter, while
all the dresses and trinkets of the mother become the property of the youngest daughter. As already stated, the
youngest son does not leave the house of his parents to go
to live with his father-in-law. He serves for the latter a
certain time, in requital for his bride, and then she goes to
live with his parents. The Yukaghir explain the custom of
minority right to inheritance by saying that the youngest
child loves its parents more than do the other children, and
is more attached to them than they are." [1]

Among the
Yukaghirs
ultimo-
geniture
is based
on the
principle
that the
child who
remains at
home after
the others
have left it
is the heir.

In spite of the sentimental reason alleged by the
Yukaghirs for preferring younger children in the inheritance,
we may suspect that among them, as among the other tribes
considered above, the preference is really based on the
custom of keeping the youngest son at home, after his
elder brothers have married and quitted the parental house
to live in the houses of their wives' parents. The suspicion
is raised to something like certainty when we observe in
that branch of the tribe which depends for its subsistence on
herds of reindeer, that the sons " do not leave their father's
house after marriage, but remain in the family, and share
the property in common. The brothers are kept together,
on the one hand by ties of kinship, and on the other by the
scarcity of reindeer, which makes divided households im-
practicable." [2]   Nothing could well set the true origin of
ultimogeniture in a clearer light than the observation that
within the narrow limits of the same small tribe—for the
Yukaghirs number only a few hundreds all told [3] — the
youngest son only succeeds to the whole of the property in
that branch of the tribe where he remains alone in his
father's house, whereas, in that branch of the tribe where all
the sons alike remain in their father's house, the youngest
son has no special privilege, but all the sons share alike in
the property at the death of their father. On the other

[1] W. Jochelson, *The Yukaghir*, pp. 107-109.
[2] W. Jochelson, *op. cit.* p. 109.   [3] W. Jochelson, *op. cit.* p. 2.

hand among these reindeer-breeding Yukaghirs a married daughter leaves the house of her parents and goes to live in the house of her parents - in - law. Hence she gets no part of the family property on the death of her parents ; the mother's personal property, such as clothes, trinkets, and working utensils, pass at her death to her unmarried daughters.[1] Thus among these reindeer-breeding Yukaghirs the social conditions are to some extent directly the reverse of those which prevail among the Khasis. Among the Yukaghirs the sons remain at the parental home all their lives and inherit the parental property, whereas daughters quit the parental home at marriage and inherit nothing. Among the Khasis, on the other hand, daughters remain at the parental home all their lives and inherit the parental property, whereas sons quit the parental home at marriage and inherit nothing.[2] In both cases the inheritance passes, as is natural, to the children who stay at home, whether they are sons or daughters.

Among the reindeer-breeding Chukchee, who inhabit the north-eastern extremity of Asia, great importance is attached to the fire-board, which is a rude figure carved out of wood in human form and used in the kindling of fire by friction. These fire-boards are personified and held sacred : they are supposed to protect the herds of reindeer, and actually to keep watch over them. Many families have several fire-boards, some of them comparatively new, others inherited from preceding generations. In every case the oldest fire-board, as a precious heirloom, descends, with the house and its belongings, to the principal heir, who is usually either the eldest or the youngest son.[3] Apparently the question whether the eldest or the youngest son is to be the principal heir is decided in favour of the one who remains last at home ; for we are told that "when the elder brother leaves, the house is then given over to a younger brother, who becomes the principal heir."[4]

[1] W. Jochelson, *The Yukaghir*, p. 109.

[2] Above, pp. 459 *sqq.*

[3] Waldemar Bogoras, *The Chukchee* (Leyden and New York, 1904–1909), pp. 349 *sqq.*, compare p. 677

(*The Jesup North Pacific Expedition, Memoir of the American Museum of Natural History, New York*).

[4] W. Bogoras, *The Chukchee*, p. 359.

Ultimo-
⁝ e
among the
Koryaks
of north-
eastern
Siberia.

The Koryaks of north-eastern Siberia entertain a similar superstitious reverence for their fire - boards, which they regard as the deities of the household fire, the guardians of the family hearth, and to which they ascribe the magical functions of protecting the herds of reindeer and helping the men to hunt and kill the sea-mammals. "Among the Maritime group, as well as among the Reindeer Koryak, the sacred fire-board is connected with the family welfare, and therefore it must not be carried into a strange house. But if two families join for the winter and live in one house, in order to obviate the necessity of procuring fuel for two houses, both take their own charms along into the common house, without risk to their effectiveness by so doing. The sacred fire - board is usually transmitted to the younger son,—or to the younger daughter, provided her husband remains in his father - in - law's house and the brothers establish new houses for themselves or raise separate herds."[1] Here again, therefore, ultimogeniture seems to be determined solely by the residence of the youngest child in the paternal home after the elder children have quitted it : the right is not affected by sex, for the heir may be either the youngest son or the youngest daughter, whichever happens to remain last in the house.

Primo-
g it re
in other
Siberian
tribes.

Among the other principal races of Siberia, including the Voguls, Ostyaks, Samoyeds, Tungus, Buriats, and Yakuts, it is said to be always the elder son who inherits, but he is bound to make a certain provision for the younger son, even though his younger brother should be richer than himself.[2]

§ 6. *Ultimogeniture in Africa*

Ultimo-
geniture
rare in
Africa.

Among the pastoral tribes of Africa the custom of ultimogeniture seems to be exceedingly rare. It is practised in a limited form by the Bogos, a tribe who subsist chiefly by their herds of cattle, though they also till the ground to

---

[1] W. Jochelson, *The Koryak* (Leyden and New York, 1908), pp. 34-36 (*The Jesup North Pacific Expedition, Memoir of the American Museum of Natural History, New York*).

[2] This I learn from a letter written to me by Miss M. A. Czaplicka (dated 58 Torrington Square, W.C., July 25th, 1916), in which she refers for her authority to a work on the customary law of the Siberian natives by D. Y. Samokvasov, *Sbornik Obychnavo prava sibirskikh inorodtsev* (Warsaw, 1876), pp. 20, 28, 29, 49, 183, 233.

a certain extent.   They inhabit the outlying spurs of the
Abyssinian mountains towards the north ; their country
lacks woods and flowing water, but enjoys a temperate and
healthy climate.   Almost the whole year the cattle roam
the mountains in search of fresh pastures, and about a third
of the population migrates with them, dwelling in tents of
palm-mats, which, when the camp shifts, are transported on
the backs of oxen.   The rest of the people live in more or
less permanent villages of straw huts; but in case of need
they can burn down these frail habitations and decamp
with the herds in a night, for land is to be had in plenty
everywhere.[1]   Among the Bogos the rule of primogeniture
prevails.   The firstborn is the head of the family ; and
the chieftainship also descends through the firstborn from
generation to generation.   Indeed, the firstborn of a great
family is regarded as something holy and inviolable ; he is
a king without the kingly power.[2]   On the death of a man
his property is divided, and the firstborn gets the best share,
including the highly valued white cows and all the furniture
and other domestic goods in the house.   But the empty
house itself belongs of right to the youngest son.[3]   Among
the Nuers, a pastoral people on the White Nile, when the
king dies he is succeeded by his youngest son.[']   Among
the Suk, a tribe of British East Africa, the eldest son inherits most of his father's property, and the youngest son
inherits most of his mother's.   The Suk appear to have
been originally a purely agricultural people, but for some
time past they have been divided into two sections, the one
agricultural and the other pastoral.   The rule of inheritance
just mentioned obtains in both sections of the tribe, and
also among the Turkanas, another tribe of the same district.[5]

   The custom of ultimogeniture or junior right is observed
by some of the Ibos, a settled agricultural people of Southern
Nigeria ; but among them, curiously enough, the rule applies
only to property inherited from women, it does not extend

[1] Werner Munzinger, *Sitten und Recht der Bogos* (Winterthur, 1859), pp. 25, 77-79.

[2] W. Munzinger, *op. cit.* p. 29.

[3] W. Munzinger, *op. cit.* p. 74.

[4] Brun-Rollet, *Le Nil Blanc et le Soudan* (Paris, 1855), p. 241.   As to the Nuers, see J. Deniker, *The Races of Man* (London, 1900), p. 445.

[6] M. W. H. Beech, *The Suk, their Language and Folklore* (Oxford, 1911), pp. 4, 35.

to property inherited from men, and even in this limited form
the custom appears to be exceptional rather than general.
On this subject Mr. N. W. Thomas, who has reported the
practice, observes that " with regard to a woman's property
there are two currents of custom—(*a*) primogeniture or equal
division among sons and daughters of the classes of property
heritable by either ; and (*b*) junior right or borough English,
as it is known in this country, in certain exceptional areas.
Junior right is undoubtedly the original custom at Aguku
and its sister town Enugu, if we may judge by the fact that
it applies to inheritance both by sons and daughters.   At
Nofia and Nise, their nearest neighbours on either side, it
applies only in the case of sons, and it is reasonable to
suppose that it is an imported custom due to intermarriage
with Enugu or Aguku, the more so as both at Nofia and Nise
we also find that the custom of primogeniture, or rather a
preferential share for the firstborn, is combined with that of
giving a preferential share to the lastborn." [1]   To come to
details, at Mbwaku the youngest son buries his mother and
inherits her property.   At Aguku the youngest son gets the
house of his dead mother, though in theory the husband
of the deceased is the owner ; and the youngest daughter
inherits her mother's pots, grinding-stones, and ivory anklets.
At Enugu the youngest son is heir to his mother's trees, and
the youngest daughter is heir to her mother's pots and household property.   At Nise the eldest son and the youngest
son both get preferential shares of their dead mother's property, but a daughter, whether married or single, gets nothing
but pots and the like.   The house goes to the youngest son,
unless he has a house of his own.   At Nofia sons inherit
their mother's property, the eldest and the youngest getting
preferential shares.   If the mother had land, the youngest
son will get three shares, the eldest two, and the others one
each.   " *Okwa* trees would be equally divided, with an extra
one to the youngest ; yams the same, with a double portion
for the youngest ; fowls and goats the same ; after the
youngest had taken his extra ones, any that remained over

[1] Northcote W. Thomas, *Anthropological Report on the Ibo-speaking
Peoples of Nigeria*, Part i. (London,
1913) p. 93. 'Mr. Thomas's observations refer particularly to the Ibos in
the neighbourhood of Awka.

would be killed and shared. The house would go to the youngest son till he got his own house, when the eldest would become entitled to it. The camwood stone and market basket would go to the youngest daughter ; the wife of the youngest son would get the pots and household stuff ; and if he were, unmarried, the youngest son would take them over till such time as he got a wife."[1] From this diversity of usage in the inheritance of women's property Mr. N. W. Thomas infers that the custom of allowing women to own property is of comparatively recent origin among these people.[2]

Among the Namaquas, a Hottentot tribe of South Africa, the presumptive heir to the chieftainship, according to one account, is usually the chief's youngest son.[3] But this report is probably incorrect ; for a good authority on the Namaquas, Sir James E. Alexander, tells us that, according to information given to him personally by old men of the tribe, the custom is to choose the eldest son of the last chief to succeed him in office.[4] The Thonga, a Bantu tribe of Mozambique, have a curious notion that a reigning chief ought not to see his grandson ; hence among them a chief's heir may not wed his official wife during his father's lifetime, lest she should give birth to a son, and consequently the reigning chief should have the misfortune of beholding his grandson. In the neighbouring district of Gaza, which is part of Mozambique, the Ba - Ngoni of Gungunyane, another Bantu tribe, entertain a similar objection to allowing a chief to see the grandson who is ultimately, after his son, to succeed him on the throne ; but they evade the difficulty in a different way. Among them "the eldest son of the chief's principal wife, when at the age requisite for marriage, takes a wife and loses the right of succession ; it is the youngest son, still young at the time of his father's death,

Ultimo-
gen u e
orted
among the
Namaquas.

Ultimo-
geniture

Ba-Ngoni
f M zam-
bi ue

---

[1] N. W. Thomas, *op. cit.* i. 94 *sq.*

[2] N. W. Thomas, *op. cit.* i. 86.

[3] Gustav Fritsch, *Die Eingeborenen Sud-Afrika's* (Breslau, 1872), p. 365, "*Der präsumptive Erbe der Hauptlingswürde soll gewohnlich der jungste Sohn sein.*" The form of the statement ("*soll*") seems to imply a doubt as to its accuracy. I do not know who

was Fritsch's authority. It appears not to be Theophilus Hahn, a good witness, to whom Fritsch repeatedly refers. See Th. Hahn, "Die Nama-Hottentoten," *Globus,* xii. (1870) pp. 238-242, 275-279, 304-307, 332-336.

[4] Sir James Edward Alexander, *An Expedition of Discovery into the Interior of Africa* (London, 1838), i. 171.

who inherits the throne, because he has no children of his own. This leads to jealousy, civil war between brothers · it has brought numberless misfortunes to the royal family of Gaza, and it was one of the causes of the downfall of Gungunyane. The Thonga custom is much the more simple and less dangerous to the maintenance of peace · the chief must not see his grandson, therefore his son will not be officially married until after his father's death. Any wives he may previously have taken will be morganatic, and their children not entitled to inherit." [1]   From this account we gather that among the Ba-Ngoni of Gungunyane the youngest son succeeds to the chieftainship only if his elder brothers are married at the time of their father's death, but that, if all the sons remain unmarried during their father's lifetime, the eldest son will succeed him on the throne in accordance with the usual rule of succession among Bantu tribes.   Thus even among the Ba-Ngoni it would seem that succession to the throne is regulated by the rule of primogeniture, though under certain definite circumstances that rule is superseded by the rule of ultimogeniture.

The reluctance of an African chief in certain tribes to see his grandchild may be derived from an old custom of killing either the chief himself or his grandchild.

Why in these tribes a chief should be so reluctant to see his grandson is not explained by the writer who reports the reluctance. But when we remember that in some parts of south-eastern Africa it appears to have been customary to put a chief to death on the first symptoms of old age,[2] we may conjecture that in certain tribes the fatal symptom was the birth of a grandson, and that in order to avert it the chief forbade his sons to marry during his lifetime. Of such a prohibition the rule which permitted the eldest son to marry on condition of losing the right of succession may have been a mitigation. Or possibly the rule that a chief should not see his grandson may have been an alleviation of an older custom of putting the grandson to death. The practice of killing the firstborn of a family seems to have been widespread, and there are some grounds for thinking that it is based on a theory of transmigration. The soul of a parent or grandparent is supposed to be born again in

---

[1] Henri A. Junod, *The Life of a South African Tribe* (Neuchatel, 1912–1913), i. 343.

[2] For the evidence, see *The Dying God*, pp. 36 *sqq.* (*The Golden Bough*, Third Edition, Part iii.).

the person of his or her child or grandchild.   But if the person whose soul is thus born again should chance to be still alive at the time of the rebirth, it seems clear that he runs a risk of dying in his own person at the same moment that he comes to life again in his child or grandchild ; and such a risk may be obviated either by preventing the child or grandchild from being born or by killing it immediately after birth in order to restore to its original owner the soul which the infant had temporarily abstracted from him or her.[1]   Thus the unwillingness of an African chief to see his grandson may possibly be derived from an old custom of killing either the grandson or the grandfather himself, a custom which in later times, through the growth of humane feeling, has been softened into a simple rule that the grandfather may not look upon his grandchild, as if, by a sort of legal fiction, he refused to recognize the infant's existence.

§ 7. *The Origin of Ultimogeniture*

Surveying the instances of ultimogeniture as they meet us among the tribes of Asia and Africa, we may conclude, that the custom is compatible with an agricultural as well as with a pastoral life.   Indeed, the great majority of peoples who are known to observe ultimogeniture at the present day subsist mainly by agriculture.   But the migratory system of agriculture which many of them follow is wasteful, and requires an extent of territory large out of all proportion to the population which it supports.   As the sons of a family grow up, they successively quit the parental abode and clear for themselves fresh fields in the forest or jungle, till only the youngest is left at home with his parents ; he is therefore the natural support and guardian of his parents in their old age.   This seems to be the simplest and most probable explanation of ultimogeniture, so far at least as it relates to the rights of youngest sons. It is confirmed by the present practice of the Russian peasants, among whom both the custom and the reason for it survive to the present time.[2]   Further, it is corroborated

The re e ence for the youngest son a h ir is a natural quence of his remaining longest with his parents.

[1] See *The Dying God*, pp. 179-193, and below, pp. 562 *sq.*
[2] See above, pp. 438 *sq.*

by the observation that the parental house is the part of the inheritance which oftenest goes to the youngest son; it is his rightful share, even if he gets nothing else.[1] The rule is natural and equitable, if the youngest son is the only child left in the parental house at the time of his parent's death.[2]

The same explanation may apply to the preference for the youngest daughter as heir.

Perhaps among tribes like the Khasis and the Garos, who observe the custom of mother-kin, the succession of the youngest daughter can be explained on similar principles. The youngest daughter is naturally the last to marry; indeed in some peoples, including the Garos, she is actually forbidden to marry before her elder sisters.[3] She therefore naturally remains at home longest with her parents and becomes their stay and comfort in life and their heir after death. Even when, as appears to be the custom with the Khasis, the married daughters also remain at home in the old parental dwelling or in adjoining houses, the care of their families will necessarily absorb most of their time and energy, leaving them comparatively little leisure to spare for attending to their parents. In this case also, therefore, the preference for the youngest daughter in the inheritance seems not unnatural.

The preference for youngest sons is particularly natural among pastoral peoples.

Among pastoral peoples, as Blackstone long ago perceived, the preference for youngest sons is still more easily intelligible. The wide extent of territory needed to support a tribe of nomadic shepherds or herdsmen leaves ample room for the sons, as they grow up, to go out into the world and push their fortunes with wandering flocks or

---

[1] See above, pp. 435 (Wales), 435 (Shetland), 438 *sq.* (Russia), 439 (Hungary), 439 (Northern Tchuds), 457 (Chins), 472 (Badagas), 472 *sq.* (Georgia), 477 (Bogos).

[2] A similar view is taken of the origin of ultimogeniture or *maineté*, as it is called in French law, by the historian of French civil law, Paul Viollet. He says, " *Ce droit que je retrouve en Angleterre, en Frise, en Saxe, chez les Slaves, etc., n'est particulier a aucune race: on s'est quelquefois égaré a la recherche de ses origines. C'est tout simplement la consolidation d'un usage que la nécessité a rendu fré-*

quent chez les petites gens: a la mort du père, les aînés sont souvent pourvus; le plus jeune resté dans la famille prend donc naturellement la place du père. Que ce fait se répète à plusieurs reprises et il deviendra le droit, alors même que les circonstances qui l'expliquaient et le justifiaient ne se rencontreraient plus: telle est, à mes yeux, l'une des origines du droit de maineté" (L. Viollet, *Histoire du Droit Civil Français*, Seconde Edition, Paris, 1893, p. 842).

[3] Major A. Playfair, *The Garos* (London, 1909), p. 69. For examples of a similar prohibition among other peoples see below, vol. ii. pp. 264 *sqq.*

herds, while the youngest remains to the last with the old
folks, to nourish and protect them in the decline of life,
and to succeed to their property when in due time they are
gathered to their fathers.   Among the Bedouins the rela- Among the
tion between a father and his sons are such as might easily Bedouins a
result in a preference for the youngest son over his elder often on
brothers.   On this subject Burckhardt, who was familiar bad terms
with Bedouin life, writes as follows : "The daily quarrels elder sons.
between parents and children in the desert constitute the
worst feature of the Bedouin character.   The son, arrived
at manhood, is too proud to ask his father for any cattle, as
his own arm can procure for him whatever he desires ; yet
he thinks that his father ought to offer it to him : on the
other hand, the father is hurt at finding that his son behaves
with haughtiness towards him ; and thus a breach is often
made, which generally becomes so wide that it never can be
closed.   The young man, as soon as it is in his power,
emancipates himself from the father's authority, still paying
him some deference as long as he continues in his tent :
but whenever he can become master of a tent himself (to
obtain which is his constant endeavour), he listens to no
advice, nor obeys any earthly command but that of his own
will.   A boy, not yet arrived at puberty, shows respect for
his father by never presuming to eat out of the same dish
with him, nor even before him.   It would be reckoned
scandalous were any one to say, ' Look at that boy, he
satisfied his appetite in the presence of his father.'   The
youngest male children, till four or five years of age, are
often invited to eat by the side of their parents, and out of
the same dish."[1]   Here again, as in so many other cases,
the turning-point in the relations between a father and his
sons appears to come at the moment when the sons quit
the paternal abode to set up dwellings of their own.   The
haughty spirit of independence, which a Bedouin manifests
to his father from the time when he ceases to dwell with
his parent in the same tent, might easily alienate the father's
affections and lead him, in disposing of his property, to pass
over the proud headstrong elder son, who has gone forth

[1] John Lewis Burckhardt, *Notes on the Bedouins and Wahabys* (London,

from him, and to leave everything to the obsequious deferential youngest son, who has remained with him in the tent. It is true that, under the influence of Mohammedan law, the Arabs now divide the property equally among their sons ;[1] but in old days, before the rise of Islam, they may often have yielded to the natural impulse to disinherit their elder in favour of their younger sons.

With a change of social conditions ultimogeniture tends to pass into primogeniture.

Thus, whether at the pastoral or the agricultural stage of society, the conditions requisite for the rise and prevalence of ultimogeniture seem to be a wide territory and a sparse population. When through the growth of population or other causes it ceases to be easy for the sons to hive off from the old stock and scatter far and wide, the right of the youngest to the exclusive inheritance is apt to be disputed by his elder brothers, and to fall into abeyance or even to be replaced by primogeniture, as is happening at the present time among the Lushais of Assam. Nevertheless, through sheer force of inherited custom, the old rule may continue to be observed even when the conditions of life in which it originated have passed away. Hence it comes about that ultimogeniture still exists, or existed till lately, side by side with primogeniture in not a few parts of England.

Among the Hebrews primogeniture may have been preceded by ultimogeniture.

Hence, too, to return to the point from which we started, we can understand why among the ancient Hebrews some traces of ultimogeniture should have survived long after the people generally had abandoned it for primogeniture, having exchanged the nomadic life of herdsmen in the desert for the settled life of peasants in Palestine. The historian of a later age, when the old custom of ultimogeniture had long been forgotten, was surprised to find traditions of younger sons inheriting to the exclusion of their elder brothers, and, in order to explain cases of succession which violated all his own notions of propriety, he represented them as exceptions due to a variety of fortuitous causes, such as an accident at birth, the arbitrary preference of the father, or the cupidity and cunning of the younger son. On this view, therefore, Jacob did no wrong

---

[1] J. L. Burckhardt, *Notes on the Bedouins and Wahabys*, i. 131, "The laws of inheritance among the Arabs are those prescribed by the Koran, and the property is divided among the male children in equal shares."

to his elder brother Esau ; he merely vindicated for himself
that right of succession which the ancient law had universally conferred on younger sons, though in his own day
a new fashion had crept in of transferring the inheritance
from the youngest to the eldest son.

§ 8. *Ultimogeniture and Jus primae Noctis*[1]

Having found what seems to be the true cause, or at
least one of the true causes, of ultimogeniture, we may consider some other theories which have been put forward to
account for the succession of the youngest. One of these
theories, as we have seen,[2] would base the preference for the
youngest son on a doubt as to the legitimacy of his elder
brothers, or at least of his eldest brother, " as if the lord of
the fee had antiently a right of concubinage with his
tenant's wife on her wedding-night ; and that therefore the
tenement descended, not to the eldest, but the youngest
son, who was more certainly the offspring of the tenant."
The first writer to give this explanation of Borough English
or ultimogeniture in England appears to have been Robert
Plot, Keeper of the Ashmolean Museum and professor of
chemistry at Oxford in the latter part of the seventeenth
century, who, in his history of Staffordshire, after noticing
the existence of Borow-English (Borough English) at two
places in the county, proceeds to discuss the origin of the
custom. He first notices the opinion of Littleton that the
youngest children are preferred " for that in law they are
presumed the least able to shift for themselves." This
simple solution of the problem does not satisfy the learned
Keeper of the Ashmolean, and he discards it for a much

Supposed derivation of Itim geniture o so-called jus primae noctis.

Robert Plot e origin of Borough ng is .

---

[1] The so-called *jus primae noctis* or
seignorial right is well handled in the
following works : Lord Hailes (Sir
David Dalrymple), *Annals of Scotland*
(Edinburgh, 1797), vol. iii. Appendix
I., " Of the Law of Evenus and the
Mercheta mulierum," pp. 1-21 ; L.
Veuillot, *Le Droit du Seigneur* (Paris,
1854) ; K. Schmidt, *Jus primae Noctis*
(Freiburg im Breisgau, 1881). Of
these works, the first is concerned
chiefly with Scotland ; the second is a

passionate, but just, defence of the
Catholic Church against a false and
ridiculous accusation which has been
brought against it by ignorant and
prejudiced writers ; the third is a comprehensive and dispassionate discussion
of the whole evidence. All three
writers, Scotch, French, and German,
agree substantially in their conclusion,
which I believe to be correct.

[2] Above, p. 440.

more recondite one, which he propounds as follows : " Which
are reasons that appear plausible enough, but I guess the
more substantial cause of this custom may rather be, that
the places where now Borow-English obtains, were anciently
lyable to the same ungodly custom granted to the Lords of
Manors in Scotland by King Evenus or Eugenius, whereby
they had the privilege of enjoying the first night's lodging
with their tenants' brides,[1] so that the eldest son being presumed to be the lord's they usually setled their lands (and
not without reason) upon the youngest son, whome they
thought their owne ; which being practised a long time,
grew at length to a custom.   Now that this custom obtained
as well in England as Scotland, we may rationally conclude
from the *Marcheta mulierum* (which King Malcolm ordered
the tenants to give their lords in liewe of it when he took it
away[2]) that was anciently paid here as well as there : for
which we have the express testimony of Bracton : *Tranavit*
(says he) *totam Angliam Marcheti hujus pecuniarii consuetudo in mancipiorum filiabus maritandis*,[3] *i.e.* that this
custom was spread all over the nation, etc."[4]

Plot's
erroneous
interpreta-
tion of the
marcheta
mulierum.

From Plot's own words it appears that the discreditable
origin which he assigns to Borough English was no more
than a guess of his own, which he founded, first, on an
alleged custom of this sort said to have been practised
many ages ago in Scotland but long since abolished, and
second, on the former exaction both in Scotland and
England of a tax or fine, called *marchet* or *merchet* (*Marcheta mulierum*), which tenants had to pay to their lord
whenever they gave their daughters in marriage, and which
Dr. Plot, following older writers,[5] believed to be a substitute
for a right of concubinage formerly exercised by a lord
over his tenants' daughters on their marriage night.   As
Plot plainly admits that not only the custom itself, but even
the fine which he regarded as a pecuniary substitute for it,
had long been obsolete, it is clear that, if ever[1] the custom

---

[1] *Hect. Boetii Hist. Soc. Lib.* 3.
cap. 12.

[2] *Geo. Buchanani Rer. Scot. Hist.
Lib.* 7, *Fol.* 64.

[3] *Bracton de Legib. et Consuetud.*

Angl. Lib. 2. *tit.* i. *cap.* 8. *num.* 2.

[4] Robert Plot, *The Natural History
of Staffordshire* (Oxford, 1686), p.
278.

[5] Sir John Skene and Sir Henry
Spelman. See below, pp. 490 *sq.*

was practised at all, it must be referred to some period of more or less remote antiquity. Leaving out of account for the present the positive tradition that a licentious custom of this sort once prevailed in Scotland, we may ask what is the value of Plot's inference from the *marchet* or *merchet* to the former observance of a similar custom in England? Was that tax or fine for the marriage of a tenant's daughter really, as he supposed, a commutation for an older and grosser privilege enjoyed by the landlord over the woman's person on her wedding night?

On that point Dr. Plot's opinion is in direct conflict with the views of the best modern historians of English law, who seem to be unanimous in affirming that they know of no evidence for the recognition of any such right or privilege at any time in England. Blackstone, as we saw, writes,[1] "I cannot learn that ever this custom prevailed in England, though it certainly did in Scotland (under the name of *mercheta* or *marcheta*), till abolished by Malcolm III." On this subject of Borough English I consulted, many years ago, the great historian of English law, F. W. Maitland, and in a letter to me he wrote as follows: "I have great doubt about the *jus primae noctis*—I have never seen the slightest proof that it existed or was supposed to exist in England ; on the other hand I have seen thousands of entries about the *marchetum*, *e.g.* temp. Edw. i. almost all tenants who were not freeholders paid *merchet* in this part of England. It may be worth your notice that the *merchet* was often higher for marriage out of the manor than for marriage within the manor. I have just seen some tenants of the Abbey of Ramsey who paid an arbitrary (*i.e.* unfixed) fine for marrying their daughters *extra villam*, but only five shillings *intra villam*. Also fines for marrying *sons* out of the manor are not unknown, and the *merchet* is often mentioned in close connection with a prohibition against giving sons a clerical education—an education which would enable them to take orders and so escape from bondage :—the context often gives the lord a right of pre-emption over the beasts of the villainors. The idea at the root of the *merchetum* seems to me much rather that of preserving the

Plot's theory of the origin of Borough ig rejected by modern of English law.

[1] Above, p. 440.

live stock on the manor than that of a *jus primae noctis*—
of which even in legends I have seen no trace whatever.
However, there certainly was talk of it in France (how
about Scotland?), and where there was so much smoke
there may have been some fire.   I may add that in England
the *merchet* was regarded as very servile—at least as a
general rule to pay it argues not merely base tenure but
personal unfreedom : such at any rate was the view of the
lawyers."[1]   Again, I consulted Professor Paul Vinogradoff
on the subject of Borough English, and in his reply, after
referring me to passages of his books[2] in which he had
touched on that theme, he adds, "You will see that I did
not even allude to the fanciful explanation from *jus primae
noctis.*   I do not know of any evidence in support of it."[3]
Similarly in conversation with me Sir Frederick Pollock
expressed complete scepticism as to such a right of concubinage (the so-called *jus primae noctis*) having ever been
claimed or exercised in England ; and he writes to me
that "the supposed *jus primae noctis* - or *droit du seigneur*
has long been exploded among scholars," and "certainly
there is no trace of such a thing in any authentic record
of English or Scottish customs."[4]   But where Blackstone,
Maitland, Vinogradoff, and Pollock have looked in vain for
evidence of an alleged rule of English law, it is not likely
that any one else will ever find it ; and accordingly we may
safely dismiss the alleged rule as a fable.   Hence the theory
which would explain Borough English from such a supposed
seignorial privilege derives no support from English law.

In Scotland the so-called *jus primae noctis* is said to have been legalized by the legendary King Evenus.

But we have seen that, while Blackstone knew of no
evidence for such a privilege in England, he confidently
affirmed that it had existed in Scotland down to the reign
of Malcolm III.   What was his authority for saying so?
He appears to have derived his information, directly or
indirectly, from the old Scottish historian Hector Boece, the
friend of Erasmus and first Principal of the University of

[1] F. W. Maitland, in a letter to me, dated 15 Brookside, Cambridge, 1st November 1887.

[2] *The Growth of the English Manor* (London, 1905), pp. 314 *sq.*; *Villain-age in England* (Oxford, 1892), pp. 82, 157, 185.

[3] Professor Paul Vinogradoff, in a letter to me dated Court Place, Iffley, Oxford, 9th May 1916.

[4] Sir Frederick Pollock's letter is dated 13 Old Square, Lincoln's Inn, 27th November 1917.

Aberdeen, the earliest writer known to have definitely asserted the existence of such a custom in Scotland. In his *History of Scotland*, published in the year 1527, Boece tells of a certain early king of Scotland, by name ·Evenus, who introduced a number of wicked laws, allowing his sub- jects to marry any number of wives up to ten, according to the degree of their wealth, placing the wives of commoners at the disposal of nobles, and permitting a feudal lord to deflower the daughters of his vassals at their marriage. While the former laws, continues Boece, were abolished not long afterwards by the authority of the kings, the last law, which permitted a landlord to deflower the virgin brides of his tenants, remained in force down to the reign of Malcolm Canmore ('1057–1093 A.D.), who at the advice of good Queen Margaret abolished it entirely and decreed that a gold coin, called in the historian's time *marcheta*, should be paid to the landlord as the price of redemption of the bride's chastity at her marriage. "And that custom," adds the historian, " is observed by our 'countrymen even at the present time." [1] Elsewhere, in treating of the reign of Malcolm Canmore, Boece repeats the statement in more explicit terms. He says that the tyrant Evenus had established a wicked and pestilent custom, in accordance with which lords or feudal superiors had the right of deflowering all the virgin brides in their territory, but that this custom was abrogated by King Malcolm Canmore, who permitted a bride to redeem her chastity by the pay- ment of half a silver mark, "which they are still compelled to pay, and which is commonly called *mulierum marketa*." [2]

The es of the early Scottish Boece. [1]

---

[1] Boece, lib. iii. 35*a*, quoted by Lord Hailes (Sir David Dalrymple), *Annals of Scotland* (Edinburgh, 1797), iii. 1 *sq.*, "*Fecit ad haec plura relatu indigna, leges tulit improbas omnem olentes spurcitiam : Ut liceret singulis suae gentis plures uxores, aliis sex, aliis decem, pro opibus, ducere ; nobilibus plebeiorum uxores communes essent, ac virginis novae nuptae, loci dominus primam libandi pudicitiam potestatem haberet. Haec lex tametsi reliquae duae regum authoritate haud multo post penitus sublatae fuerunt, nullo labore longa post secula potuit abrogari,* adeo ea pestis magnatum adolescentum animos infecerat ; eam tandem Mal- colmus Canmor Rex, diva Margareta Regina suadente, ut opportuniori re- feretur loco, velut in Deum et homines injuriam, prorsus submovit, sanciens nummum aureum (Marchetam *nostra* vocat aetas), in nuptiis sponsae pudoris redimendi causa, loci domino penden- dum : Idque populares nostri vel hoc aevo observant.*"

[2] Boece, xii. 260*a*, quoted by Lord Hailes (Sir David Dalrymple), *Annals of Scotland* (Edinburgh, 1797), iii. 2, "*Illud vero inter caetera haud indig.*

On this it is to be observed that King Evenus III., the alleged author of the wicked law, appears to be a purely mythical monarch ; for he is said to have reigned as sixteenth king of Scotland at a time before the Christian era as to which all genuine historical documents are totally wanting.[1] Sober modern historians disdain to mention even his name. But if the king himself is mythical, the iniquitous legislation fathered on him must be equally fabulous. The repetition of Boece's statement in other words by later authors, such as the historian Buchanan[2] and the legal antiquaries Sir John Skene[3] and Sir Henry Spelman,[4] adds nothing to its authority. Apart from that

num memoria existimem, abrogatam pessimam eam ac pestilentem consuetudinem, olim ab Eveno tyranno inductam, ut domini praefectivi in suo territorio sponsarum omnium virginitatem praelibarent, dimidiata argenti marca unam [l. primam] noctem a praefectorum uxoribus redimente sponsa, quam etiamnum pendere coguntur, vocantqne vulgo mulierum marketam."

[1] Some say that he reigned about 60 B.C. ; others, with a show of chronological accuracy, would date his reign from 12 B.C. to 8 B.C. See L. Veuillot, *Le Droit du Seigneur au Moyen Age* (Paris, 1854), pp. 266 sq.; K. Schmidt, *Jus primae Noctis* (Freiburg im Breisgau, 1881), p. 204. Buchanan, who solemnly catalogues these mythical kings, says that Evenus III. was strangled in prison after a reign of seven years (*Rerum Scoticarum Historia*, lib. iv. cap. 16).

[2] George Buchanan, *Rerum Scoticarum Historia*, lib. iv. cap. 21 (*Opera Omnia*, Leyden, 1725, vol. i. p. 110), "*Huic successit Evenus Tertius, indignus optimo patre filius : qui non contentus centum e nobilitate concubinis, ni suam spurcitiem latis legibus in vulgus proderet. Tulit enim, Ut cuivis liceret, pro opibus, quot alere posset, uxores ducere : ut Rex ante nuptias sponsarum nobilium, nobiles plebeiarum praelibarent pudicitiam : ut plebeiorum uxores cum nobilitate communes essent*" : *id.*, lib. vii. cap. 21 (*Opera Omnia*, Leyden, 1725, vol.

i. p. 206), speaking of Malcolm Canmore, who succeeded to the crown in 1057 A.D., "*Uxoris etiam precibus dedisse fertur, ut primam novae nuptae noctem, quae proceribus per gradus quosdam lege Regis Eveni debebatur, sponsus dimidiata argenti marca redimere posset : quam pensionem adhuc* Marchetas mulierum *vocant*" (where for *Eveni* all the MSS. read *Eugenii*).

[3] (Sir) John Skene, *De Verborum Significatione, The Exposition of the Termes and Difficill Wordes, contained in the foure buikes of Regiam Majestatem* (Edinburgh, 1797), s.v. "Marcheta," "King *Evenus* did wickedlie ordaine, that the Lord or maister of the ground, or Land, suld have the first nicht of ilk maried woman within the samin. The quhilk ordinance, was after abrogate be King Malcome the Thrid ; quha ordained, that the Bridegroome sulde have the use of his awin wife. And therefore suld pay ane peece of money, called *Marca*. *Hector Boetius, lib.* 3, *c.* 12. For the quhilk, certaine Kye, was used to be payed. *Lib.* 4, *cap. Sciendum* 63. . . I think that *Marcheta mulieris* is the raide of the woman, or the first carnall copulation and conjunction with her : quhilk in respect of her virginitie is maist esteemed be men. Quhilk interpretation is confirmed alswa bee *Cuiac. Lib. I. de feudis.*"

[4] Sir Henry Spelman, *Glossarium Archaiologicum*, Editio Tertia (London, 1687), p. 397, s.v. "*Marchet, Marcheta, et Marchetum :* aliis *Mer-*

statement and its echo by later authors there seems to be no evidence at all of the exercise in Scotland of a licentious privilege of the sort commonly designated by the phrase *jus primae noctis* ; and we may reasonably suppose that the fable of such a- privilege originated in Scotland, as in England, partly at least through a simple misinterpretation of the *marchet* or *merchet*, the fine paid by a vassal to his lord on the marriage of his, the tenant's, daughter. Certainly the notion, to which Sir John Skene gave currency, in the sixteenth century, that the *marchet* or *merchet* was a pecuniary commutation for a former right claimed by a feudal lord of sleeping with his vassals' daughters on their wedding night,[1] derives no support from the account of the *marchet* or *merchet* given in the most ancient code of Scottish laws, the so-called *Regiam Majestatem*,[2] which is popularly referred to the reign of King David I. in the twelfth century, but was probably compiled at a somewhat later period, perhaps early in the fourteenth century.[3]

The fable seems to have originated in a misinterpretation of marchet or merchet, the fine paid by a tenant on the marriage of his daughter.

---

chet, et Bractono *Merchetum*," " *Turpis Scotorum veterum consuetudo, quâ territorii dominus vassalli sponsam primâ nocte comprimeret, floremque carperet pudicitiae. Hanc instituisse fertur Rex Evenus, planè Ethnicus, sub Augusti seculo, sustulisse verò Rex Malcolmus 3 Christianus qui floruit Annum circiter gratiae* 1080 *redemptionisque nomine domino statuisse impendendum (ut ait Hector Boetius lib.* 3. *cap.* 12.) *marcam argenti, marchetamque inde suggerit appellatam*." After which Spelman quotes Buchanan, Sir John Skene, and *Regiam Majestatem*,.lib. iv. cap. 31.

[1] See the passage of Sir John Skene quoted above, p. 490, note [3].

[2] The following is Sir John Skene's own translation of the passage of the *Regiam Majestatem* (Book IV. chapter 31) which bears on the *marchet* or *merchet*, " *On the Marchet of Wemen*. It is to wit, that conforme to the law of Scotland, the *marchet* of ane woman, noble, or servant, or hyreling, is ane young kow or thrie schillings : and the richt dewtie to the sergent thrie pennies. 2. And she be the dochter of ane frie man, and not of the Lord of the village,

her *marchet* sall be ane kow, or sax schillings ; and for the sergents dewtie, sax pennies. 3. *Item*, The *marchet* of the dochter of ane Thane, or Ochiern, twa kye, or twelve schillings ; or the dewtie to the sergent, twelve pennies. 4. *Item*, The *marchet* of the dochter of ane Earl perteines to the Queene, and is twelve kye." See *Regiam Majestatem, The Auld Laws and Constitutions of Scotland, faithfullie collected furth of the Register . . . and translated out of Latine in Scottish Language . . . be* Sir John Skene of Curriehill, Clerk of our Soveraigne Lordis Register, Counsell, and Rollis (Edinburgh, 1774), p. 137. In all this there is no hint that the *marchet* or *merchet* was a pecuniary commutation for an infamous right formerly exercised by lords over their vassals' daughters.

[3] It seems to be now generally agreed that the *Regiam Majestatem* was based on the *Tractatus de legibus et consuetudinibus regni Angliae* which was composed by Ranulph de Glanville, Chief Justiciary of England in the reign of Henry II. (died 1190). Indeed references to Glanville by name occur

Modern
eg
authorities
on the
marchet or
merchet.

This view of the true nature of the *marchet* or *merchet* in Scots Law has the sanction of high legal authorities. Thus Lord Bankton writes, " Charters from the crown, and even those from subjects, frequently contain a grant of *Merchetae Mulierum*, the Merchets of women. We have this described in our old law book;[1] and it is a consideration due to the over-lord, by his vassals, upon the marriage of any of their daughters, taxed according to their quality. There is not the least insinuation of the infamous original assigned to it by some of our historians and lawyers, and therefore I must doubt the truth of it ; for since there was due to the superior the casuality of marriage, upon the heir's marrying, it was thought reasonable that he should have a consideration on the marriage of his vassals' daughters : the conveying it in the charter imports a discharge of the same, and having gone into disuse some ages since, it is only matter of style."[2] And in his lectures on Scottish legal antiquities Mr. Cosmo Innes makes the following observations : " Some learning has been brought to show that on the Continent this tax— *mercheta mulierum*—represented an ancient seignorial right —the *jus primae noctis.* I have not looked carefully into the French authorities ; but I think there is no evidence of a custom so odious existing in England ; and in Scotland

in all the seven manuscripts of the *Regiam Majestatem* which are preserved in Scotland. The historian of Scotland, John Hill Burton, was of opinion that the *Regiam Majestatem* was put together by some unknown person soon after the War of Independence. See Lord Hailes (Sir David Dalrymple), *Annals of Scotland* (Edinburgh, 1797), vol. iii. Appendix Second, No. 10, " An Examination of some of the Arguments for the high Antiquity of *Regiam Majestatem*," pp. 278-336 ; John Hill Burton, *History of Scotland* (Edinburgh, 1876), ii. 58 *sqq.* In his dissertation on the subject Lord Hailes has shown that the testimony borne to the antiquity of the *Regiam Majestatem* in the *Chronicle of the Abbey of Kinlos* is of little or no value, since the *Chronicle of Kinlos* was drawn up about 1537, from very scanty and untrustworthy materials,

by a Piedmontese named Johannes Ferrerius, who came to Scotland in 1528 and earned his bread as a literary hack by compiling unhistorical histories of the land which gave him hospitality.

[1] *Regiam Majestatem*, lib. iv. cap. 31.

[2] Andrew McDouall [Lord Bankton], *An Institute of the Laws of Scotland* (Edinburgh, 1751-1753), i. 395 *sq.* In Scots law "casualities of superiority are certain emoluments arising to the superior, which, as they depend on uncertain events, are termed *casualities.*" See Bell's *Dictionary and Digest of the Law of Scotland,* adapted by George Watson (Edinburgh, 1882), p. 123. I have to thank my old friend Lord Strathclyde, President of the Court of Session, for kindly referring me to these and other works on Scots Law.

I venture to say that there is nothing to ground a suspicion of such a right. The *merchet* of women with us was simply the tax paid by the different classes of bondmen and tenants and vassals, when they gave their daughters in marriage, and thus deprived the lord of their services, to which he was entitled, *jure sanguinis.*" [1]

A similar view as to the real meaning of the *marchet* or *merchet* in old Scots law was expressed more fully by the eminent Scottish lawyer and historian, Lord Hailes. After carefully examining the evidence on the subject he concludes as follows : " The probable reason of the custom appears to have been this : Persons of low rank, residing on an estate, were generally either *ascripti glebae,* or were subjected to some species of servitude similar to that of the *ascripti glebae.* On that estate they were bound to reside, and to perform certain services to the lord. As women necessarily followed the residence of their husbands, the consequence was, that when a woman of that rank married a stranger, the lord was deprived of that part of his *live stock.* He would not submit to this loss, without requiring indemnification ; at first, the sum paid by the father of the young woman would nearly amount to an estimated indemnification ; and as the *villains* were grievously under the power of their lord, it would be often exorbitant and oppressive. In process of time, the lord would discover, that as the young women of his estate were exported, the young men of his estate would import others ; so that, upon the whole, no great prejudice could arise from *extra-territorial marriages.* Hence the indemnification would be converted into a small pecuniary composition, acknowledging the old usage, and the right of the master. As the intrinsic and marketable value of money decreased, this stated composition would be gradually omitted out of terriers and rent-rolls, or would be thrown into the aggregate sum of rent." [2]

A similar explanation probably holds good of the *marchet* or *merchet* in English law : there too, we may reasonably suppose, the *merchet* was in substance a compensation paid to the lord of the manor for the loss of a

Lord Hailes the marchet *or* merchet.

F. W. Maitland on the marchet *or* merchet.

---

[1] Cosmo Innes, *Lectures on Legal Antiquities* (Edinburgh, 1872), p. 52.
[2] Lord Hailes, *Annals of Scotland* (Edinburgh, 1797), iii. 12 *sq.*

woman's services on her marriage. We have seen that this was the opinion of the learned and acute historian of English law, F. W. Maitland,[1] and he confirmed it by pointing out first, that the *merchet* was often higher for marriage out of the manor than for marriage within the manor ; second that fines for marrying *sons* out of the manor were not unknown ; and, third, that the *merchet* is often coupled with a prohibition against giving the sons of tenants or bondsmen a clerical education, which, by enabling them to take orders might deliver them from bondage and so deprive the lord of their services. All these facts point clearly to the true nature of *merchet* as a compensation paid to the lord of the manor for that loss of services which he incurred, or was supposed to incur, through the marriage of his bondsmen's or tenants' daughters, especially when they married men who did not belong to the manor.

Professor
P. Vinogradoff
on the
merchet.

A like view is taken of the meaning of the *merchet* by another distinguished historian of English law, Professor Paul Vinogradoff. He writes as follows : " The same observations hold good in regard to other customs which come to be considered as implying personal servitude. *Merchet* was the most striking consequence of unfreedom, but manorial documents are wont to connect it with several others. It is a common thing to say that a villain by birth cannot marry his daughter without paying a fine, or permit his son to take holy orders, or sell his calf or horse, that he is bound to serve as a reeve, and that his youngest son succeeds to the holding after his death.[2] This would be a more or less complete enumeration, and I need not say that in particular cases sometimes one and sometimes another item gets omitted. The various pieces do not fit well together : the prohibition against selling animals is connected with disabilities as to property, and not derived directly from the personal tie ; as for the rule of succession, it testifies merely to the fact that the so-called custom of Borough English was most widely spread among the unfree class. The obligation of serving as a reeve or in any other capacity is certainly derived from the power of a lord over the person of his subject ; he had it always at his discretion

---

[1] See above, pp. 487 *sq.*   [2] " *Notebook of Bracton*, pl. 1230."

to take his man away from the field and to employ him at pleasure in his service. Lastly, the provision that the villain may not allow his son to receive holy orders stands on the same level as the provision that he may not give his daughter in marriage outside the manor : either of these prohibited transactions would have involved the loss of a subject." [1]

On the whole we may conclude that neither in England nor in Scotland is there any evidence worth speaking of for the view that the lord of a manor formerly enjoyed a customary right of concubinage with his tenants' daughters on the first night of their marriage. That view appears to spring largely, perhaps mainly, from a simple misunderstanding of the true meaning of *merchet*.

No real evidence for the so-called jus primae noctis in Britain.

In the secluded highlands of Scotland the *merchet*, and the uncharitable construction put upon it by popular prejudice, appear to have lingered down to the latter half of the eighteenth century. When Dr. Johnson visited the small island of Ulva, to the west of Mull, in the year 1773, he stayed in the house of the chief, M'Quarrie, who claimed that his family had owned the island for nine hundred years. In conversation with his English visitor, M'Quarrie "insisted that the *Mercheta Mulierum* mentioned in our old charters, did really mean the privilege which a lord of a manor, or a baron, had, to have the first night of all his vassals' wives. Dr. Johnson said, the belief of such a custom having existed was also held in England, where there is a tenure called *Borough English*, by which the eldest child does not inherit, from a doubt of his being the son of the tenant. M'Quarrie told us, that still, on the marriage of each of his tenants, a sheep is due to him ; for which the composition is fixed at five shillings. I suppose, Ulva is the only place where this custom remains." [2] In the light of the foregoing discussion we may say with some confidence that both the highland chief and his learned guest misunderstood the true meaning and history of the *mercheta mulierum*. It is instructive to observe that to this day every man of a certain African tribe

Survival of the mercheta mulierum in the highlands of Scotland.

An African parallel to the mercheta mulierum.

---

[1] Paul Vinogradoff, *Villainage in England* (Oxford, 1892), pp. 156 *sq.*
[2] James Boswell, *Journal of a Tour in the Hebrides*, under "Saturday, 16th October" (p. 312 in *The Temple Classics* Edition, London, 1898).

in the valley of the Congo is obliged, on the marriage of his
daughter, to give his chief a goat, precisely as every M'Quarrie
in the island of Ulva had to give his chief a sheep on a similar
occasion. "Marriage with the Bayaka," we are told, "is
always by purchase, and the price is 10,000 *djimbu*; the
father of the bride must pay a goat to his chief, because the
bride goes out of the village. The woman follows her
husband, and he has absolute power over her."[1] The reason
here assigned for the custom ("because the bride goes out
of the village") is doubtless the true one ; the chief loses a
subject when a woman marries out of his village, and he
accepts a goat as compensation for the loss.

The so-called *jus primae noctis* equally fabulous on the Continent.
On the Continent of Europe, for example in France and
Germany, a similar misunderstanding has originated, or served
to support, a similar fable ; there, too, the fine which
vassals paid to their feudal superior on the marriage of their
daughters has been erroneously represented as a pecuniary
commutation for the right which the superior, whether
civil or ecclesiastical, could legally claim of lying with his
vassals' daughters on their wedding night. Writers who have
made careful search in the archives, where the supposed
right or traces of it might be expected to be recorded,
have wholly failed to find any such records.[2] The story
of the right may therefore safely be dismissed as unfounded.

But the belief in this fabulous right of a lord over his
vassals' wives was strengthened by another misapprehension

[1] E. Torday, *Camp and Tramp in African Wilds* (London, 1913), p. 134.

[2] L. Veuillot, *Le Droit du Seigneur* (Paris, 1854), pp. 276 *sqq.*; L'Abbé Hanauer, *Les Paysans de l'Alsace au Moyen - Age* (Paris and Strasburg, 1865), pp. 135 *sq.*; K. Schmidt, *Jus primae Noctis*, pp. 91 *sqq.* Bayle has given currency to a story that the house of Rovere in Piedmont possessed the privilege of deflowering the brides whom their vassals married. The story is told on the authority of an Italian writer Bonifacio Vannozzi, who lived at the beginning of the seventeenth century, and who, after retailing the familiar fable about King Evenus and King Malcolm, asserted vaguely that such a custom formerly existed in Piedmont, and that Cardinal Hieronimo della Rovere told him how he himself had burned a charter conveying the privilege in question to his house. See P. Bayle, *Dictionnaire Historique et Critique* (Amsterdam and Leyden, 1730), iv. 224, *s.v.* "Sixte IV." No weight can be given to such a hearsay report in the absence of the charter on which the supposed right was alleged to be founded. If the charter ever existed, it probably conferred on the house of Rovere only the usual right to the payment of fines on the marriage of their vassals' daughters. Compare Lord Hailes (Sir David Dalrymple), *Annals of Scotland* (Edinburgh, 1797), iii. 20 *sq.*; K. Schmidt, *Jus primae Noctis*, pp. 239, 372.

of a similar kind. During the middle ages there prevailed in various parts of Europe a custom generally termed the *jus primae noctis*, the true nature of which, like the true nature of the *merchet*, has been misunderstood and consequently perverted into a proof of a licentious seignorial privilege, with which in reality it had nothing to do. Indeed the custom, far from originating in licence, appears on the contrary to have taken its rise in an austere practice of chastity which was inculcated by the early Christian Church, as we learn from a decree of the fourth Council of Carthage, held in the year 398 A.D., which enacted that "When the bridegroom and bride have received the benediction, let them remain that same night in a state of virginity out of reverence for the benediction."[1] This enactment was received into the canon law and was twice repeated in the decretals.[2]

By subsequent enactments the period of chastity which bride and bridegroom were required or recommended to observe after marriage was extended from one to two or three nights. Thus in the capitularies of Charlemagne it is written, "Let the bride at the proper time, according to custom, be blessed in priestly fashion by the priest with prayers and oblations, and after she has been guarded by bridesmaids, as usage demands, and attended by her relations, let her, at the proper time, be legally asked and given and solemnly received ; and let them for two or three days devote themselves to prayer and the observation of chastity, in order that good offspring may be begotten, and that they may please the Lord in their actions."[3] The biographer of

---

[1] "*Sponsus et sponsa cum benedicendi sunt a sacerdote, a parentibus suis vel a paranymphis offerantur, qui cum benedictionem acceperint, eadem nocte, pro reverentia ipsius benedictionis, in virginitate permaneant,*" J. P. Migne, *Patrologia Latina,* lxxxiv. (Paris, 1850) col. 201. Compare Lord Hailes (Sir David Dalrymple), *Annals of Scotland* (Edinburgh, 1797), iii. 15; L. Veuillot, *Le Droit du Seigneur* (Paris, 1854), pp. 190 *sq.*; K. Schmidt, *Jus primae Noctis,* p. 152.

[2] Lord Hailes (Sir David Dal-

rymple), *Annals of Scotland* (Edinburgh, 1797), iii. 15. Compare L. Veuillot, *Le Droit du Seigneur* (Paris, 1854), pp. 191 *sq.*

[3] "*Et a quibus custoditur, uxor petatur, et a parentibus propinquioribus sponsetur et legibus dotetur, et suo tempore, sacerdotaliter, ut mos est, cum praecibus et oblationibus a sacerdote benedicatur, et a paranimphis, ut consuetudo docet, custodita et sociata a proximis, et tempore congruo petita legibus detur et solemniter accipiatur. Et biduo vel triduo orationibus vacent et castitatem custodiant, ut bonae*

2 K

St. Louis tells us that when that pious king married in the year 1234 A.D., he and his wife observed continence and devoted themselves to prayer for three nights after marriage, "which was taught by the counsel of the Blessed Son of God and confirmed by the example of Tobias."[1]   Several rituals of the fifteenth century, particularly those of Liége, Limoges, and Bordeaux, lay down the same rule in regard to the first three nights of marriage.[2]   In the sixteenth century the sainted Carlo Borromeo, at a synod held in Milan, enjoined the priests of his diocese to inculcate the observance of the same rule on all married couples.[3]   A provincial council, held at Cologne in 1538, went no farther than to advise that the example of Tobias and his wife should be earnestly recommended to the imitation of newly wedded pairs.[4]   And similarly in a religious manual of the eighteenth century we read, "When a curate perceives that bride and bridegroom are persons of piety who enter into marriage only from Christian views and can follow the most perfect maxims of Christianity, he may advise them, first, to practise what Tobias and Sarah, and all the righteous persons of the Old Testament, practised, according to the account of Saint Augustine ; what Saint Louis and many other saints in the New Testament exactly observed ; that is to say, to live in continence the first days of their marriage, in order to employ them in prayer and good works."[5]

The story of Tobias and his wife Sarah in of Tobit.   Thus we see that the practice of chastity for some days after marriage was commended to the faithful by the Catholic Church with special reference to the good example set by Tobias and his wife Sarah.   The story of that pious couple, as related in the apocryphal *Book of Tobit*, runs as

suboles generentur et Domino suis in actionibus placeant " J. P. Migne, *Patrologia Latina*, xcvii. (Paris, 1851) col. 859. Compare Lord Hailes (Sir David Dalrymple), *Annals of Scotland* (Edinburgh, 1797), iii. 15 *sq.*; L. Veuillot, *Le Droit du Seigneur* (Paris, 1854), p. 192.

[1] Geoffroy de Beaulieu, *Vie de Saint Louis*, ch. xvi°. *qui est de saintée con-tinence,* quoted by L. Veuillot, *Le*

Droit du Seigneur (Paris, 1854), p. 196.

[2] L. Veuillot, *l.c.*

[3] L. Veuillot, *Le Droit du Seigneur* (Paris, 1854), p. 197.

[4] K. Schmidt, *Jus primae Noctis*, p. 153.

[5] L. Veuillot, *op. cit.* pp. 197 *sq.*, quoting Mangin, *Introduction au saint ministère* (1750), p. 403.

follows. A certain Jewess of Ecbatana in Persia, named Sarah had been married to no less than seven husbands, but all of them had perished as soon as they had gone in to her ; for a wicked demon, named Asmodeus, loved Sarah, and out of spite and jealousy he slew her seven bridegrooms in the bridal chamber on the wedding night. On this account Sarah was exposed to the painful suspicion of having murdered her seven husbands ; and one day when she chanced to chide her handmaid for some fault, the hussy turned on her and said, " Would you kill me as you have already killed seven men, you murderess of your husbands ? Go after them ! Let us never see son or daughter of yours ! " The reproach touched the sensitive widow to the quick ; a thought of suicide crossed her mind, but out of consideration for her father Raguel, whom such an act would have covered with shame, she nobly resolved to live for his sake, and retiring to an upper chamber she devoted herself to prayer and fasting for three days and nights, consoling herself in her affliction by the thought that perhaps her seven husbands had not been worthy of her, and that it might yet be God's good pleasure to reserve her for an eighth. The prayers, perhaps we may add the wishes, of the widow were heard. An eighth bridegroom was even then on his way to her under the safe-conduct of the archangel Raphael, disguised as a courier. The bold suitor was no other than her cousin Tobias, to whom his angelic conductor had explained the whole situation with perfect frankness. " You are her father's heir," said the angel, " his whole property is yours, but you must marry his daughter." Tobias was in a painful dilemma. The prospect of the property was sweet, but the prospect of marrying a widow, who had laid out seven husbands in rapid succession, was dubious. The ardour of the lover was damped by the caution of the man. He hesitated. But the archangel reassured him, " Take my advice," said he, " and I will show thee how to prevail over the demon. They who on entering into marriage shut out God from their thoughts and give themselves up to their own lusts, like the horse and mule which have no understanding, over such has the demon power.

How a m w the seven husbands on their wedding nights.

How, w rne l by e archangel ae Tobias put the demon s... and marrying

Sarah,
continence
with her
for three
nights.

But thou, when thou hast received thy wife and hast entered into the chamber, abstain from carnal intercourse with her for three days and give thyself up to nothing but prayer with her. On the first night, burn the heart and liver of the fish, and make a smoke with it, and the demon will be put to flight.[1] On the second night thou wilt be admitted to communion with the holy patriarchs ; on the third night thou wilt obtain the blessing that sons shall be begotten of thee safe and sound. But when the third night is passed, thou shalt receive the virgin with the fear of God, moved by a love of offspring rather than by lust, that thou mayest obtain a blessing in respect of sons in the seed of Abraham." Emboldened by these words, Tobias plucked up courage and married the widow. Having taken the plunge, he carried out the angel's instructions to the letter and with the happiest results. On the first night, when he entered the bridal chamber, he burned the heart and liver of the fish on a coal fire ; and the demon Asmodeus no sooner smelled the ill-savour than he fled away into the utmost parts of Egypt, and there the angel bound him fast. Thus rid of his ghostly rival, Tobias said to his bride, "Sarah, arise, and let us pray God to-day and to-morrow and the day after to-morrow, because in these three nights we are joined to God, but when the third night is passed we shall be joined to each other in matrimony." So they prayed that night, and after they had prayed they laid them down and slept. Now the father of the bride had been so accustomed to bury his sons-in-law on the morning after the wedding night, that on that particular morning, from mere force of habit, he got up at cock-crow, and, summoning his servants, went out and dug the usual grave. When it was ready, he said to his wife, "Send one of thy handmaids to see if he is dead, that I may bury him before daybreak." So the maid went, and on entering the room she saw bride and bridegoom both fast asleep.

---

[1] On the way to Ecbatana, as he crossed the Tigris, Tobias had been attacked by a fish, which by the advice of the angel he caught and killed, and having done so he extracted the fish's heart, liver, and gall. His angelic companion thereupon informed him that the smoke made by burning the fish's heart and liver would drive away a devil, and that the gall dropped on blind eyes would restore their sight, See the *Book of Tobit*, vi. 1-8.

When she returned and reported the good news, Raguel blessed God, and commanded his servants to fill up the grave, and instead of burying his son-in-law he prepared to celebrate his wedding-feast.[1]

An abstinence like that which the pious Tobias practised by the advice of the angel was long observed, with the approval of the Church, by newly married couples in France and other parts' of ·Europe ; but in time the clergy judged it expedient to mitigate the rigour of the canon, and accordingly they granted husbands the right of lying with their own wives on the first night of marriage, provided that they paid a moderate fee for the privilege to the proper ecclesiastical authority.   This was the true *jus primae noctis*, a right accorded, not to a licentious feudal superior, but to a woman's lawful husband.   For example, the Bishops of Amiens were wont to grant such dispensations or indulgences to married couples on receiving payment of certain dues.   In course of time, however, the flock growing restive under these exactions of their shepherds, husbands refused to pay the bishop a fee for the privilege of cohabiting with their own wives on the wedding night.   The bishop, on the other hand, stood stiffly on what he conceived to be his legal rights, and accordingly the mayor and aldermen of Abbeville brought the case before the parliament of Paris. They alleged that " although by common law husbands are freely allowed to be with their wives on the first night of marriage, nevertheless the said bishop, of himself or through his officials, did exact of the said husbands, of some ten, of others twelve, and of some as much as twenty or thirty francs, before he would grant them a licence to lie on the

In time the Church allowed h ban s the right of lying with on the first night of on payment of a fee.

permission was the real .... noctis.

Lawsuit wee the Bishop of Amiens town of Abbeville about the jus primae noctis.

---

[1] Tobit iii.-viii. (following the Vulgate chiefly).   There are serious discrepancies between the Greek text of the Septuagint and the Latin text of the Vulgate ; in particular the injunction and the practice of continence for three nights are not mentioned in the Septuagint, hence they are omitted in the English version. See below, pp. 517 *sqq.* In an Armenian tale, which presents some points of similarity to the story of Tobias and to other incidents in the *Book of Tobit*, a woman had been married to five husbands, all of whom were killed on the wedding night by a serpent, which crept out of the bride's mouth and stung them.   The hero marries her, but is saved from death by his servant, who keeps watch in the bridal chamber and cuts off the serpent's head with a sword.   It turns out that the servant is really the grateful ghost of a debtor, whose debts the hero had paid after the man's death. See A. von Haxthausen, *Transkaukasia* (Leipsic, 1856), i. 333 *sq.*

said first night with their own newly wedded wives; otherwise he compelled them to abstain from their wives for three nights." On the other hand the Bishop pleaded in reply that " in the town, deanery, and banlieue of the said Abbeville it was an ancient custom that no one might lie with his wife until the third night of marriage, without a dispensation granted by himself or his official, and that this custom was agreeable to canon law, to reâson, and to the opinion of the Church Fathers; and that for the payment of the clerk who wrote the dispensation, for the seal and signature of the official, he, the bishop, might ask and receive sometimes ten, sometimes twelve, sometimes sixteen, and sometimes twenty Parisian sous; and that if he received more than the said sum of twenty sous, it was and had been as a consideration for an absolution from a sentence of excommunication or a dispensation from a ban, in accordance with custom and synodical statutes." Notwithstanding this plea of ancient custom, judgment was given by the parliament against the bishop and in favour of husbands, represented by the mayor and aldermen of Abbeville. The judgment, dated 19th March 1409, is still preserved in the National Archives at Paris. In it we read that " by the same judgment it was declared that any inhabitant of the said town of Abbeville may lie with his wife on the first day of their marriage without the licence or dispensation of the said bishop." [1] The official report of

---

[1] L. Veuillot, *Le Droit du Seigneur* (Paris, 1854), pp. 232-243, 451-459; K. Schmidt, *Jus primae Noctis*, pp. 273-282. Compare Lord Hailes (Sir David Dalrymple), *Annals of Scotland* (Edinburgh, 1797), iii. 16. Extracts from the judgment are printed by K. Schmidt; the whole judgment is printed by L. Veuillot, *op. cit.* pp. 451-459. The most important passages, which I have translated in the text, are as follows. The plaintiffs urged, " *Et quamvis, de jure communi, maritis cum uxoribus suis prima nocte nuptiarum cubare libere concedatur, dictus tamen episcopus, per se aut suos officiarios, dictos conjuges, quosdam ad decem, alios ad duodecim, nonnullos ad viginti vel triginta francos, priusquam* ipsis de cubando dicta prima nocte cum suis de novo uxoribus licentiam impertiri vellet, exigebat, aut aliter [sic Schmidt; alios Veuillot] ipsos a suis uxoribus per tres noctes abstinere compellebat.*" The plea of the bishop ran thus: " *Dicto vero episcopo ex adverso separatim proponente, quod in villa, decanatu et banleuca de predicta Abbatisvilla, ex consuetudine, sacro canoni, rationi et sanctis patribus consona, ab antiquis observatum fuerat, ne cui usque ad tertiam nuptiarum noctem cum uxore sua cubare sine sua aut officialis sui dispensatione, absque emenda, liceret; quodque tam pro salario clerici litteram dispensationis scribendi quam pro sigillo et officialis signeto, interdum decem, nonnunquam*

the case, from which the foregoing extracts are translated, sets the true nature of the *jus primae noctis*, and of the fee paid for it to the bishop, in the clearest light ; it shows that the fee was paid to the bishop for an ecclesiastical dispensation allowing the husband to sleep with his wife on the first three nights of their marriage ; it lends not a shadow of support to the fantastic supposition, that the fee was paid to the bishop to compensate him for his self-denial in not lying himself with the bride before turning her over to the bridegroom.

Though the payment formerly exacted by the Church from a husband for the immediate exercise of his marital rights has long been abolished, nevertheless, through the force of habit and tradition the old custom of observing chastity for three nights after marriage is still voluntarily observed, or was observed till lately, by the common people in many parts of Europe. Thus in several communes of Brittany "the bride is entrusted, during the first night of marriage, to the supervision of the best man and the bridesmaid, so that the spouses still remain strangers to each other." [1]   At Scaer, in Brittany, "out of respect for certain canonical rules, the first night of the marriage belongs to God, the second to the Virgin, and the third to the husband's patron saint." [2]   At Sachelay, in the department of Seine-et-Oise, the marriage night is dedicated to the Holy Virgin ; the newly married pair do not meet in the bridal chamber till the second night.[3]   Down to the second half of the nineteenth century the custom of practising continence for three nights after marriage was still observed in some districts of Alsace.[4]   In various parts of

Survival of the practice of the "Tobias Night" in modern Europe.

---

duodecim, et aliquando sexdecim et quandoque viginti solidos parisienses [*sic* Schmidt ; *parisisiensium* Veuillot], *secundum personarum facultates, petere et recipere poterat. Et si ultra dictam viginti solidorum summam receperat, illud ratione absolutionis a sententia excommunicationis sive bannorum dispensationis erat et fuerat, ex consuetudine etiam et sinodalibus statutis, observatum.*" Part of the judgment given by the parliament of Paris ran as follows ; *"Et per idem judicium dictum fuit quod quilibet habitanitum*

dicte ville de Abbatisvilla, prima die suarum nuptiarum poterit cum sua uxore, absque congedio seu dispensatione predicti episcopi, cubare."

[1] A. de Nore, *Coutumes, Mythes et Traditions des Provinces de France* (Paris and Lyons, 1846), p. 195.

[2] A. de Nore, *op. cit.* p. 194.

[3] Ida von Düringsfeld und Otto Freiherr von Reinsberg-Düringsfeld, *Hochzeitsbuch* (Leipsic, 1871), p. 250.

[4] L'Abbé Hanauer, *Les paysans d'Alsace au Moyen-Age* (Paris and Strasburg, 1865), p. 137 note [2].

Switzerland and Germany, including the Bohmerwald and the Upper Palatinate, bride and bridegroom practise continence for three nights after marriage, because they believe that otherwise their wedded life would be unlucky.[1] " A beautiful custom, based on the Bible, was observed in the Allgau, for example at Christatzhofen and Egloffs ; whether it is still observed I do not know. It was the custom of keeping the ' Tobias nights.' In the *Book of Tobit* vi. 22 it is written, ' When the third night is passed, take to thee the virgin in the fear of the Lord ' ; and accordingly the newly wedded pairs pass the first three nights after marriage in like manner without exercising their conjugal rights. The marriage will be all the more fortunate, because in consequence of this abstinence the devil will not be able to do any harm." [2]   At Bettringen, near Gmund, " the ' Tobias nights ' are here and there observed ; that is, the bridegroom does not touch his bride for three successive nights. Through this abstinence people hope to secure the release of·a poor soul from purgatory." [3]

Survival of e ustom of the "Tobias. ... .." among the South Slavs.

A similar custom of continence after marriage is still practised by some of the South Slavs.   Thus in Herzegovina and Montenegro the newly wedded pair do not sleep together on the marriage night.   The bride sleeps, fully dressed, with the bridesman, who is commonly chosen from among the husband's brothers ; she passes the following nights with her sisters-in-law.   This separation of husband and wife may last a long time.   The husband's mother alone has the right to decide when it shall end.[4]   " Neither on the first nor on the following nights does the bridegroom sleep with the bride ; it is the bridesman who sleeps with her, but so as if she were his sister." [5]   On the Bocche de Cattaro, in Dalmatia, the bride sleeps the first night with two bridesmen, between whom she is also seated at the wedding feast.   It is not till the second night that the bridegroom is allowed access to her in her bridal chamber.[6]   At Risano, on the Bocche de

[1] A. Wuttke, *Der deutsche Volks-aberglaube*[2] (Berlin, 1869), p. 352, § 569.

[2] Anton Birlinger, *Volksthümliches aus Schwaben* (Freiburg im Breisgau, 1861–1862), ii. 334.

[3] A. Birlinger, *op. cit.* ii. 354.

[4] F. Demelić, *Le Droit Coutumier des Slaves Méridionaux d'après les Recherches de M. V. Bogisić* (Paris, 1877), pp. 109 *sq.*

[5] F. S. Krauss, *Sitte und Brauch der Sudslaven* (Vienna, 1885), p. 456.

[6] F. Demelic, *op. cit.* pp. 108 *sq.*

Cattaro, the bride formerly had to sleep the first three nights with two bridesmen, who were fully dressed. But this custom has now been changed.[1]   In some parts of Croatia it is believed that a married pair will beget children for as many years as are the nights during which they practise continence immediately after marriage.[2]   Among the Esthonians it used to be the rule that a husband might not unloose his wife's girdle nor take any other liberty with her on the wedding night.[3]   Writing in the latter part of the eighteenth century Lord Hailes observes, "I am informed that the superstitious abstinence sanctified by the Council of Carthage is still observed by the vulgar in some parts of Scotland."[4]

It is natural enough to suppose, as some writers appear to have done, that such customs are founded on the teaching of the Christian Church, exemplified and confirmed by the case of Tobias in the *Book of Tobit*.   But in point of fact the practice of deferring the consummation of marriage for a certain time after the nuptial ceremony is older than Christianity, and has been observed by heathen tribes in many parts of the world ; from which we may reasonably infer that, far from instituting the rule and imposing it on the pagans, the Church on the contrary borrowed it from the heathen and sought to give it a scriptural sanction by appealing to the authority of the archangel Raphael.   Certainly the archangel's advice to Tobias has its exact counterpart in the rule which ancient Indian law laid down for the guidance of a Vedic householder.   In the *Grihya-Sutras*, a series of codes regulating domestic ritual, the practice of continence for three nights after marriage is repeatedly enjoined.[5]   Thus in the code which passes under the name of Apastamba

The practice of continence for some time r marriage is older than anity, and has been by many heathen ....

Continence o r nights after marriage en ii Vedic India.

[1] F. S. Krauss, *l.c.*
[2] Baron Rajacsich, *Das Leben, die Sitten und Gebräuche der im Kaiserthume Oesterreich lebenden Südslaven* (Vienna, 1873), p. 147.
[3] Boecler-Kreutzwald, *Der Ehsten abergläubische Gebräuche, Weisen und Gewohnheiten* (St. Petersburg, 1854), p. 25.
[4] Lord Hailes, *Annals of Scotland* (Edinburgh, 1797), iii. 15 note*.
[5] The *Sutras*, the latest product of Vedic literature, may roughly be dated between 500 and 200 B.C.   See Professor A. A. Macdonell, "Sanskrit Literature," in *The Imperial Gazetteer of India, The Indian Empire*, ii. (Oxford, 1909) p. 232.   The date of the *Book of Tobit*, which appears to be a composite work, is uncertain ; in its original form the book is thought by W. Erbt to have been written about 200 B.C.   See *Encyclopædia Biblica*, iv. col. 5126, *s.v.* "Tobit."

we read, " Let him notice the day on which he brings his wife home.   (From that day) through three nights they should both sleep on the ground, they should be chaste, and should avoid salt and pungent food.   Between their sleeping-places a staff is interposed, which is anointed with perfumes and wrapped round with a garment or a thread." [1]   Similarly in another of these codes, which is attributed to Gobhila, we read, " From that time through a period of three nights they should both avoid eating saline or pungent food, and should sleep together on the ground without having con-jugal intercourse." [2]   In another of these codes, ascribed to Khadirakarya, abstinence from milk as well as from salted food is enjoined on the newly married pair during the three nights when they observe the rule of continence.[3]   But, in other codes drawn up for the guidance of householders in the Vedic age, the period of continence imposed on bride and bridegroom is extended to six or twelve nights or even a year.   Thus in one of them we read, " Through a period of three nights they shall eat no saline food ; they shall sleep on the ground ; through one year they shall refrain from conjugal intercourse, or through a period of twelve nights, or of six nights, or at least of three nights." [4]   As an inducement to observe continence for a whole year after marriage, another of these codes holds out to the wedded pair the prospect of having a saint *(Rishi)* born to them.[5]   Yet another ancient Indian lawgiver refines on the rule still further by offering five different periods of con-tinence to the choice of the newly married couple, and promising them a son of rank exactly proportioned to the

Sometimes India the period of continence after marriage was extended to six or twelve nights or a whole year.

[1] *The Grihya-Sutras,* translated by H. Oldenberg, Part II. (Oxford, 1892) p. 267 (*Sacred Books of the East,* vol. xxx.) ; M. Winternitz, *Das altindische Hochzeitsrituell nach dem Apastambiya-Grihyasutra* (Vienna, 1892), p. 25 (*Denkschriften der Kaiserlichen Aka-demie der Wissenschaften in Wien, Philosophisch-Historische Classe,* vol. x'.`.
[2] *The Grihya-Sutras,* translated by H. Oldenberg, Part II. p. 48.   A similar injunction is contained in the *Grihya-Sutra* ascribed to Sankhayana. See *The Grihya-Sutras,* translated by

H. Oldenberg, Part I. (Oxford, 1886) p. 43 (*Sacred Books of the East,* vol. xxix.), " Through a period of three nights let them refrain from conjugal intercourse.   Let them sleep on the ground."
[3] *The Grihya-Sutras,* translated by H. Oldenberg, Part I. p. 384.
[4] *The Grihya-Sutras,* translated by H. Oldenberg, Part I. p. 286.   This *Sutra* is attributed to Paraskara.
[5] *The Grihya-Sutras,* translated by H. Oldenberg, Part I. p. 171.   This *Sutra* is ascribed to Asvalayana.

longer or shorter time during which they had abstained from the exercise of their conjugal rights. An abstinence of three nights, he tells us, would be recompensed with the birth of a Vedic scholar of the ordinary type ; an abstinence of twelve nights would be blessed with a really first-class Vedic scholar ; an abstinence of four months would produce a Brahman of a still more exalted rank ; an abstinence of six months would be rewarded by the birth of a saint (*Rishi*) ; and an abstinence of a whole year would be crowned by the nativity of a god.[1]

In India the custom of deferring the consummation of marriage until some time after the nuptials has not been confined to the Aryan race. Among the Kammas, a Telugu caste of Southern India, "consummation does not take place till three months after the marriage ceremony, as it is considered unlucky to have three heads of a family in a household during the first year of marriage. By the delay, the birth of a child should take place only in the second year, so that, during the first year, there will be only two heads, husband and wife. In like manner, it is noted by Mr. Francis,[2] that, among the Gangimakkulu and Madigas, the marriage is not consummated till three months after its celebration."[3] Among the Variyars, Pisharotis, and Nambuthiris of Cochin, in Southern India, the consummation of marriage is deferred until the night of the fourth day.[4] Among the Rajjhars, a mixed Hindoo and aboriginal caste of the Central Provinces, bride and bridegroom sleep on their wedding night with a woman lying between them.[5] The Wazirs of Bannu, in the Punjab, say that formerly it was their practice not to consummate the marriage for a long time after the wedding ceremony.[6] In Baluchistan, even after the marriage has been solemnized, the bride " often continues to share her bed with a kinswoman

Continence time after marriage by various non-Aryan India and Baluchi-

---

[1] M. Winternitz, *Das altindische Hochzeitsrituell nach dem Apastambīya-Grihyasutra* (Vienna, 1892), pp. 86 *sq.*

[2] *Gazetteer of the Bellary District.*

[3] Edgar Thurston, *Castes and Tribes of Southern India* (Madras, 1909), iii. 103 *sq.*

[4] L. K. Anantha Krishna Iyer, *The*

Cochin Tribes and Castes (Madras, 1909–1912), ii. 139, 143, 192.

[5] R. V. Russell, *Tribes and Castes of the Central Provinces of India* (London, 1916), iv. 407.

[6] H. A. Rose, *Glossary of the Tribes and Castes of the Punjab and North-West Frontier Province*, iii. (Lahore, (1914) p. 507.

for three nights more ; and when her husband eventually joins her, he is expected in some tribes to defer consummation for a considerable period." [1]

Again, the practice of deferring consummation is observed by some of the wild hill tribes of Assam. Thus we are told that among these tribes "marriage has a curious prohibition attached to it. In some groups the young couple are forbidden to come together until they have slept under the same roof at least three nights without intercourse. The prohibition is relaxed in the case of the marriage of widows." [2] Amongst the Naga tribes of Manipur "marital intercourse within the dwelling house is prohibited for the initial nights of the married life. This prohibition extends in some cases over a period of a month, but is always less in cases of re-marriage." [3] In the Angami tribe of Nagas, a bride is conducted on the wedding day to the house of the bridegroom's parents. She is escorted by a large number of persons of her own clan (*khel*), of whom two women and one man sleep with her that night in the house, while the bridegroom returns to the bachelors' hall (*deka chang*), where he sleeps with the other unmarried men of the village. Next day the bride and bridegroom meet and eat together, but at night the bridegroom again returns to the bachelors' hall, while his bride remains in his father's house. On the morning of the third day after the wedding the young couple go together to the husband's field where they both do a little work and eat and drink together. They then wait for another seven or eight days. At the end of that time the high priest of the clan is called in ; he sacrifices a chicken, and the ceremony of marriage is complete. Till then the bride and bridegroom do not sleep together, but after the completion of the ceremony they are allowed to cohabit. [4] Among the Aos, another Naga tribe of Assam, for six

[1] *Census of India, 1911*, vol. iv. *Baluchistan*, by Denys Bray (Calcutta, 1913), p. 113.

[2] T. C. Hodson, "The *Genna* amongst the tribes of Assam," *Journal of the Anthropological Institute*, xxxvi. (1906) p. 97.

[3] T. C. Hodson, *The Naga Tribes of Manipur* (London, 1911), p. 87.

[4] *Census of Assam, 1891, Assam*, by (Sir) E. A. Gait, vol. i. *Report* (Shillong, 1892), p. 239. As to the bachelors' hall (*deka chang*) in a Naga village, see Miss G. M. Godden, "Naga and other frontier tribes of North - East India," *Journal of the Anthropological Institute*, xxvi. (1897) pp. 179 *sqq.*

nights after marriage six men and six women sleep in the house of the newly wedded pair ; the men and women keep apart from each other, the bridegroom sleeping with the men, and the bride sleeping with the women.[1] Among the Kacharis, another tribe of Assam, it is said that "custom sanctions a certain interval of time, sometimes amounting to five days, between the bride's entering her husband's house and the consummation of the marriage."[2] Similarly among the Meches, a cognate tribe of the same region, it is reported that "matrimonial etiquette requires postponement of consummation of the marriage for a week or so after the completion of the wedding ceremonial."[3] Among the Khyoungtha, a hill tribe of Chittagong, it is the rule that a bridegroom "does not consummate his marriage until he and his wife (sleeping apart) have for seven days eaten together seven times a day."[4] So among the Kachins or Chingpaws of Upper Burma, "as a rule, cohabitation does not take place for some days after marriage, the only reason given being that the parties are ashamed."[5]

A like custom of observing continence for some time after the celebration of the marriage ceremony is practised by various peoples of the Indian Archipelago. Thus in Central Sumatra a husband is not always allowed to sleep with his wife on the wedding night ; in many villages the young couple are prevented from enjoying each other for three nights by old women of the family, who keep watch over them.[6] In Achin, at marriages between persons of the higher classes, bride and bridegroom sleep apart from each other for several nights in the same room, which is kept constantly illuminated ; and they are further watched by old women, who do not leave the pair alone till the seventh day.[7] Among the inhabitants of the Teng'ger

Continence for om t me after marriage se by various peoples of and Java.

---

[1] *Census of India, 1891, Assam,* by (Sir) E. A. Gait, vol. i. *Report* (Shillong, 1892), p. 245.

[2] Rev. S. Endle, *The Kacharis* (London, 1911), p. 46.

[3] Rev. S. Endle, *The Kacharis,* p. 95.

[4] Capt. T. H. Lewin, *Wild Races of South - Eastern India* (London, 1870), p. 130.

[6] (Sir) J. George Scott and J. P. Hardiman, *Gazetteer of Upper Burma and the Shan States* (Rangoon, 1900–1901), Part I. vol. i. p. 407.

[6] A. L. van Hasselt, *Volkesbeschrijving van Midden-Sumatra* (Leyden, 1882), p. 280.

[7] J. A. Kruijt, *Atjeh en de Atjehers* (Leyden, 1877), pp. 192 *sq.*

Mountains in Java the marriage is not consummated till the fifth day after the nuptial ceremony. "This interval between the solemnities and the consummation of marriage is termed by them *úndang mántu*, and is in some cases still observed by the Javans in other parts of the island, under the name of *unduh mántu*."[1] "I questioned Drahman concerning Javanese weddings and courtings, and was surprised to learn that the man and woman we had just seen were not yet married, though, according to the rites of the Mohammedan creed, they had been legally allied for nearly a whole week. The young couple were as yet only passing through a probationary period, during which they live apart. Among the princes and the wealthy this separation sometimes continues three months, during which time the bridegroom meets his bride every afternoon, in the presence of a number of friends invited on such occasions, for whose entertainment music is provided." When food is set before them, it is the duty of the bridegroom to feed his bride with rice before all the people. At midnight the bridegroom conducts his bride to bed, draws the curtains, and leaves her; he may not see her again till the middle of the next day.[2] Among the Sundaneeze of Java the bridegroom does not cohabit with the bride until the fourth day after marriage; during the first three nights she sits beside him like a waxen doll, with downcast eyes, not answering a word to his whispered remarks.[3] Among the Madureeze and in some parts of Eastern Java cohabitation takes place for the first time on the third night after the celebration of the wedding.[4]

Continence for some marriage d in Flores the Babar   In Endeh, a district of the East Indian island of Flores, eight women sleep with the bride and bridegroom for the first four nights after marriage, and two of them must always keep awake to prevent the young couple from approaching too near each other.[5] In the Babar Archi-

[1] T. S. Raffles, *History of Java* (London, 1817), i. 331.

[2] W. Barrington d'Almeida, *Life in Java* (London, 1864), i. 315 *sq.*

[3] G. A. Wilken, "Plechtigheden en Gebruiken bij Verlovingen en Huwelyken bei de Volken van den Indischen Archipel," *De verspreide Geschriften* (The Hague, 1912), i. 500, referring to Ritter, *Java*, p. 29.

[4] P. J. Veth, *Java, Geographisch, Ethnologisch, Historisch* (Haarlem, 1875–1884), i. 635 *sq.*

[5] S. Roos, "Iets over Endeh," *Tijdschrift voor Indische Taal- Land- en Volkenkunde*, xxiv. (1878) p. 525.

pelago, after the marriage ceremony has been performed Archi-
p ago,
the K i
Islands,
Celebes,
New

and the
Philippine
the newly wedded pair are at liberty to sleep near each
other, but the bridegroom must be surrounded by his male
relations and the bride by her female relations. Should the
two, in spite of these precautions, contrive to come together
in the dark, the watchers return home on the fourth or fifth
day, or even earlier.[1] So in the Kei Islands, to the south-
west of New Guinea, after the celebration of the marriage,
the young couple sleep for three nights with an old woman,
a relation of the bride, between them. Sometimes a child,
too young to run about, is introduced by the bride into the
bridal chamber to sleep between her and her husband.[2]
Among some of the Dyaks of Dutch Borneo a husband and
wife are on no account allowed to come together on the
first night of marriage ; the bride spends the night in the
house of her mother or of some other kinswoman.[3] Among
the tribes of the Barito valley in Dutch Borneo a bridegroom
usually abstains from cohabiting with his bride during the
first three nights of their wedded life ; he passes the interval
drinking in the company of his friends, but he visits his wife
from time to time to eat and drink with her and overcome
her shyness.[4] In families of high rank among the Macassars
and Bugineeze of Southern Celebes the marriage ceremonies
are elaborate and sometimes last for a month. During this
time the bride is attended by eight old women, whose duty it is
to sleep at night with the newly wedded pair and to prevent a
too close intimacy between them.[5] Among the Tinguianes,
of the Philippine Islands, the marriage may not be consummated on the wedding night, and to prevent an infringement of the rule a boy, six or eight years old, sleeps
between the young couple, who are forbidden even to speak
to each other.[6] Among the Nufors of Geelvinks Bay, in
Dutch New Guinea, bride and bridegroom are obliged to

[1] J. G. F. Riedel, *De sluik- en
kroesharige rassen tusschen Selebes en
Papua* (The Hague, 1886), p. 351.

[2] J. G. F. Riedel, *op. cit.* p. 236.

[3] M. T. H. Perelaer, *Ethnographische Beschrijving der Dajaks* (Zalt-
Bommel, 1870), p. 53.

[4] C. A. L. M. Schwaner, *Beschrijv-*

ing van het Stroomgebied van den Barito
(Amsterdam, 1853-1854), i. 197.

[5] B. F. Matthes, *Bijdragen tot de
Ethnologie van Zuid - Celebes* (The
Hague, 1875), pp. 29, 35.

[6] F. Blumentritt, *Versuch einer
Ethnographie der Philippinen* (Gotha,
1882), p. 38 (*Petermann's Mittheilungen, Ergänzungsheft*, No. 67).

pass the first night, or according to another account, the first four nights, after marriage sitting with their backs turned to each other ; they may not fall asleep, and if they grow drowsy, their friends wake them. They believe that to keep awake on the wedding night is a means of ensuring a long life.[1]

Continence <br> for some <br> time after <br> marriage <br> observed <br> by the <br> aborigines <br> of
 Australia.

The custom of deferring the consummation of marriage for some time after the completion of the wedding ceremony was observed even by some of the savage aborigines of Australia. Thus in the Narrinyeri tribe of South Australia, " it is a point of decency for the couple not to sleep close to each other for the first two or three nights ; on the third or fourth night the man and his wife sleep together under the same rug. This arrangement is for the sake of decency. At the marriage many persons are present, sleeping in the same camp ; so the newly-married couple wait till they have moved off, and only a few relatives are left with them. They then often make a little hut for themselves." [2] Among the natives of Fraser Island (Great Sandy Island), Queensland, it is said that bride and bridegroom do not come together for nearly two months after marriage.[3] Among the aboriginal tribes of Western Victoria, a marriage used to be observed with somewhat elaborate ceremonies and attended by a large number, perhaps two hundred, of the friends and relations of the couple. A new hut was erected for the bridegroom by his friends, and here he and his bride had to sleep on opposite sides of the fire for two months. During all this time they were not allowed to speak to or look at each other. Hence the bride was called a *tiirok meetnya*, " not look round." She kept her head and face covered with her opossum rug, while her husband was present, and he in like manner turned his face away from her. Their mutual avoidance of each other during these months was a source of much

[1] J. B. Van Hasselt, " Die Noeforezen," *Zeitschrift fur Ethnologie*, viii. (1876) pp. 181 *sq.*; A. Goudswaard, *De Papoewa's van de Geelvinksbaai* (Schiedam, 1863), p. 67 ; Otto Finsch, *Neu-Guinea und seine Bewohner* (Bremen, 1865), p. 103 ; Carl Hager, *Kaiser Wilhelms-Land*

und *der Bismarck-Archipel* (Leipsic, N.D.), p. 26.

[2] Rev. George Taplin, in E. M. Curr, *The Australian Race* (Melbourne and London, 1886–1887), ii. 245.

[3] R. Brough Smyth, *The Aborigines of Victoria* (Melbourne and London, 1887), i. 84 note*.

amusement to young people, who would peep into the hut
and laugh at the abashed pair. If the two needed to
communicate with each other, they must do so indirectly
through friends. The observance of these rules was ensured
by the attendance of a bridesman and a bridesmaid, who
waited on the bridegroom and bride respectively both by
day and by night. At night the bridesman, who was a
bachelor friend, slept with the bridegroom on one side of
the fire ; while the bridesmaid, who must be the nearest
unmarried relative of the bridegroom, slept with the bride
on the other side of it.[1]

In Usambara, a district of East Africa, the "marriage
ceremonies are peculiar. The young people meet at the
house of a friend ; two native bedsteads are placed one on
either side of the room, with a big fire between. On these
the bride and bridegroom recline in the sight of each other
for four days without food. Lukewarm water is allowed
them when they are thirsty. On the fifth day one basin of
thin porridge is given them before the bridal procession
commences to the house of the bride's mother." [2] Among
the Wataveta, a people of mixed Hamitic and Bantu race at
the foot of Mount·Kilimanjaro, in British East Africa, a bride
sleeps with four little bridesmaids for five nights after marriage,
and it is not until about a week afterwards that the bridegroom is at length allowed to take possession of her.[3] Among
the Zulus, according to one account, marriage may not be
consummated until the third night after the ceremony.[4]
Among the Baganda of Central Africa a bride was attended
to her husband's house by a girl who slept with her for
the first two nights. Not till the third night did the bridegroom consummate the marriage.[5] So among the Ban-

Continence
for om
t me after
marriage
s rvec
by various
tribes in
Africa.

[1] James Dawson, *Australian Aborigines* (Melbourne, Sydney, and Adelaide, 1881), pp. 31 *sq.*
[2] J. P. Farler, "The Usambara
Country in East Africa," *Proceedings
of the Royal Geographical Society*, N.S.
I. 18 9) 9 e ce m y s
similarly described by O. Baumann,
Usambara und seine Nachbargebiete
(Berlin, 1891), pp. 133 *sq.*, from
whose account we learn that the tribe
who practise the custom are the

Wabondei.
[3] C. Hollis, "Notes on the History
and Customs of the People of Taveta,
East Africa," *Journal of the African
Society*, No. 1 (October, 1901), pp.
115-117.
[4] A. Delegorgue, *Voyage dans
l'Afrique Australe* (Paris, 1847), ii.
231.
[5] John Roscoe, *The Baganda* (London, 1911), pp. 90 *sq.*

yankole or Bahima, another tribe of Central Africa, a bride is accompanied to her new home by an aunt, her father's sister, who remains with her for three nights. On the third night the marriage is consummated, and the aunt returns to her home.[1] Among the Banyoro, another tribe of Central Africa, marriage was consummated in the evening of the second day after the wedding ceremony, when the guests had departed.[2] In Darfur " it must be observed that the marriage is seldom considered as completely cele- brated until the seventh day, and never until the third. A husband always shuns the insulting epithet of the impatient man. Each day of temperance is dedicated to some parti- cular person : the first to the father of the bride, the second to the mother, and so on." [3] Among the Ait Tameldu of Morocco a bridegroom has not intercourse with his bride until the third day after she has been brought to his house, when all the guests have gone away.[4]

Continence for some time after marriage observed by various tribes of American Indians.

Similar customs have been observed by various tribes of American Indians. · Thus among the Musos and Colimas of New Granada "at sixteen or seventeen years of age parents disposed of their daughters in marriage, the relations making up the match without the knowledge of the bride ; which done the bridegroom went to the place where she was and spent three days caressing her, she in the mean- time scolding, striking him with her fist, or cudgelling him. When the three days were over, she grew good-humoured, dressed the meat, sent it him by her mother or some kins- woman, and then he lay by her all that moon without con- summating the marriage, sowed a piece of ground with Indian wheat for the bride and her mother, gave the string of beads which was the portion, and if he were a rich man presented clouts to wrap about them with hawksbells after their fashion, which made a dull noise as they moved. But if the matrimony happened to be consummated during the first three days, they looked upon the woman as lewd and

[1] John Roscoe, *The Northern Bantu* (Cambridge, 1915), p. 120.
[2] John Roscoe, *The Northern Bantu*, p. 40.
[3] *Travels of an Arab Merchant* [Mohammed Ibn-Omar El Tounsy] *in*

Soudan, abridged from the French by Bayle St. John (London, 1854), p. 107.
[4] Edward Westermarck, *Marriage Ceremonies in Morocco* (London, 1914), pp. 252 *sq.*

wicked."[1] Among the Karayas on the Rio Araguaya, in Brazil, bride and bridegroom sleep for the first four nights on a mat with a wide interval between them ; custom forbids them to approach each other on these nights, and the marriage is not consummated till several days later.[2] Among the ancient Mexicans, when the guests who had been invited to a marriage were flushed with wine, "they went out to dance in the yard of the house, while the married pair remained in the chamber, from which, during four days, they never stirred, except to obey the calls of nature, or to go to the oratory at midnight to burn incense to the idols, and to make oblations of eatables. They passed these four days in prayer and fasting, dressed in new habits, and adorned with certain ensigns of the gods of their devotion, without proceeding to any act of less decency, fearing that otherwise the punishment of heaven would fall upon them. Their beds on these nights were two mats of rushes, covered with small sheets, with certain feathers, and a gem of *Chalchihuitl* in the middle of them. At the four corners of the bed, green canes and spines of the aloe were laid, with which they were to draw blood from their tongues and their ears in honour of their gods. The priests were the persons who adjusted the bed to sanctify the marriage ; but we know nothing of the mystery of the canes, the feathers, and the gem. Until the fourth night the marriage was not consummated ; they believed it would have proved unlucky, if they had anticipated the period of consummation."[3] " The Mazatec bridegroom abstained for the first fifteen days of his wedded life from carnal knowledge of his wife, and both spent the time in fasting and penance."[4] Among the Nootka Indians of Vancouver Island there used to be no intercourse between a newly married pair for a

[1] Antonio de Herrera, *The General History of the Vast Continent and Islands of America*, translated into English by Captain John Stevens (London, 1725-1726), vi. 184.

[2] P. Ehrenreich, *Beiträge zur Völkerkunde Brasiliens* (Berlin, 1891), p. 29 (*Veröffentlichungen aus dem Königlichen Museum fur Volkerkunde*, vol. ii. Heft 1/2).

[3] F. S. Clavigero, *The History of*

Mexico, translated by Charles Cullen (London, 1807), i. 320 *sq.* Compare Brasseur de Bourbourg, *Histoire des Nations civilisées du Mexique et de l'Amérique - Centrale* (Paris, 1857–1859), iii. 565 *sq.*; H. H. Bancroft, *Native Races of the Pacific States* (London, 1875-1876), ii. 258 *sq.*

[4] H. H. Bancroft, *Native Races of the Pacific States*, ii. 261.

period of ten days after marriage.[1]   Of the Thompson Indians in British Columbia we read that " a newly married couple, although sleeping under the same robe, were not supposed to have connubial connection until from two to seven nights —generally four nights—after coming together.   The young wife slept with her husband, but still wore her maiden's breech-cloth."[2]   Among the Thlinkeets or Tlingits of Alaska bride and bridegroom had to fast severely for four days at marriage ; after the fast they were allowed to live together but not to consummate the marriage for four weeks.[3]   Speaking of the Indian tribes of Canada and the United States, a writer of the eighteenth century, who knew them well, observes, " What is almost incredible and is nevertheless attested by good authors is, that in several places the newly married spouses are together for a whole year, living in perfect continence, for the purpose, as they say, of showing that they have married out of friendship and not in order to satisfy their passions.   They would even point the finger at any young woman who might be found with child within a year of marriage."[4]

The function of bridesmen and brides- maids.

In these customs it deserves to be noticed that men and women are often employed as attendants on the bride and bridegroom for the express purpose of preventing the speedy consummation of marriage.   The frequency of the practice suggests that this may have been the original function of bridesmen and bridesmaids in Europe generally, as it is still among some of the South Slavs.

The precept of observing the "Tobias nights" was probably borrowed by the Church from paganism.

Finding the custom of continence for a certain time, especially for three nights, after marriage observed so widely throughout the world by races who can hardly have learned it from Jewish or Christian teachers, we may reasonably suspect that in Europe the Church did not institute the practice, but merely borrowed it, like so many other cus-

[1] H. H. Bancroft, *op. cit.* i. 198.

[2] James Teit, *The Thompson Indians of British Columbia*, p. 326 (*The Jesup North Pacific Expedition, Memoir of the American Museum of Natural History, New York*, April, 1900).

[3] H. J. Holmberg, " Ueber die Volker des Russischen Amerika," *Acta*

Societatis Scientiarum Fennicae, iv. (Helsingfors, 1856) pp. 314 *sq.*; T. de Pauly, *Description Ethnographique des Peuples de Russie* (St. Petersburg, 1862), *Peuples de l'Amérique Russe*, p. 12 ; H. H. Bancroft, *Native Races of the Pacific States*, i. 111.

[4] Charlevoix, *Histoire de la Nouvelle France* (Paris, 1744), v. 422.

toms, from paganism, and attempted to give it a Christian, or at all events a Biblical colour, by citing the pious example of Tobias and his wife Sarah. Curiously enough, the three nights of continence, which these personages are said to have observed for the sake of defeating the nefarious designs of a demon, are not so much as mentioned in most of the extant versions of the *Book of Tobit*, including the Greek, the Old Latin (the *Itala*), and the Aramaic ;[1] they appear only, so far as I am aware, in the Latin of the Vulgate and in a Hebrew version, which agrees closely with the Vulgate and may perhaps represent the original text from which the Vulgate was derived through the medium of an Aramaic translation.[2] For Jerome, the author of the

Though it occurs in the Vulgate, it is wanting in most of the ancient versions of The Book of Tobit.

[1] The Aramaic version was first published and translated into English, from a unique manuscript in the Bodleian, by A. Neubauer, who reprinted along with it the old Latin (*Itala*) version and the Hebrew version, which is commonly called the Münster text. This Münster text was first printed at Constantinople in 1516 and was reprinted by Sebastian Münster in 1542. It is believed to have been made from the Aramaic at some time between the fifth and the seventh century of our area. See Ad. Neubauer *The Book of Tobit* (Oxford, 1878), pp. ix *sqq.* The incident of the " Tobias nights " is not mentioned in it. The Aramaic version has been translated into German. See Prof. Dr. Adalbert Schulte, " Die aramäische Bearbeitung des Büchleins Tobias verglichen mit dem Vulgatatext," *Theologische Quartalschrift*, xc. (Tübingen, 1908) pp. 182-204. The German translator professes to compare the Aramaic text with the Vulgate, but omits to notice the presence of the remarkable incident of the " Tobias nights " in the Vulgate and its absence from the Aramaic.

[2] This Hebrew version (which is not to be confounded with the so-called Münster text, see the preceding note) was first described and translated into English from a manuscript (Add. 11639) in the British Museum, by Dr. M. Gaster. See M. Gaster, " Two unknown Hebrew versions of the Tobit legend," *Proceedings of the Society of*

Biblical Archaeology, xviii. (1896) pp. 208 *sqq.*, 259 *sqq.* The manuscript, according to Dr. Gaster, is not later than the thirteenth century, and is probably copied from a manuscript of the eleventh century. The language of the version is closely akin to Biblical Hebrew ; indeed, so close is the resemblance that Jerome could easily have understood it without an interpreter. Hence we cannot identify this Hebrew version with the Aramaic version which Jerome, with the help of an interpreter, turned into Latin. And while there is a general agreement between the Hebrew and the Vulgate, the discrepancies between them are, in Dr. Gaster's opinion, sufficient in number and kind to forbid the supposition that the Hebrew is a mere translation from the Vulgate. On the whole he concludes that, " looking now upon our newly-recovered Hebrew text in the light which I have tried to throw upon it, we may confidently assert that we have here undoubtedly the oldest Semitic text extant—older than Jerome and Vetus Latin, and coming nearest to the lost Hebrew original, if it does not faithfully represent it " (*op. cit.* pp. 217 *sq.*). For the mention of the " Tobias nights " in this Hebrew version, see Dr. Gaster's translation, pp. 267 *sq.*, 269. I am indebted to my learned friend Dr. J. Sutherland Black for calling my attention to the Hebrew and Aramaic versions of *The Book of Tobit.*

Vulgate, tells us that he translated the book into Latin from a Chaldee, that is an Aramaic, text with the help of a man who was a master both of Aramaic and of Hebrew; the interpreter rendered the Aramaic into Hebrew, and Jerome turned the Hebrew into Latin, dictating his translation to a secretary, who wrote it down. In this way the Latin version of the *Book of Tobit*, as we have it in the Vulgate, was completed in a single day.[1] Now in the Greek version the demon Asmodeus is overcome and put to flight, not by the continence of the newly wedded pair, but simply by the smell of the fish's liver, which Tobias, by the advice of the archangel Raphael, burned on entering the marriage chamber.[2] The Vulgate preserves the incident of the fumigation and the consequent flight of the demon; but it adds the injunction and the practice of continence for three nights as a further means of vanquishing the foul fiend. It seems unlikely that both incidents—the fumigation and the continence—were contained in the original version of the story; and since the incident of the fumigation is interwoven much more closely into the texture of the tale[3] than the incident of the continence, which can be omitted without affecting the rest of the narrative, it seems probable that the latter incident is an interpolation which has been at some time foisted into the story for the pious purpose of inculcating a temporary practice of continence on all married couples at the commencement of their wedded life. Whether the interpolation was found in the Aramaic text from which Jerome made his Latin translation; whether it was inserted by Jerome himself or by the Jew whom he employed as interpreter; or, finally, whether it has been introduced into the Vulgate at some later time, are questions which apparently we have no means of definitely deciding. If the

The incident of the "Tobias nights" seems to have been interpolated in The Book of Tobit for the sake of inculcating temporary continence after marriage.

---

[1] See Jerome's Preface, *Biblia Sacra Vulgatae Editionis* (Tornaci Nerviorum, 1901), p. xix, " *Et quia vicina est Chaldaeorum lingua sermoni Hebraico, utriusque linguae peritissimum loquacem reperiens, unius diei laborem arripui: et quidquid ille mihi Hebraicis verbis expressit, hoc ego accito notario, sermonibus Latinis exposui.*"

[2] *Book of Tobit*, viii. 2 *sqq.* The English translation follows the Greek, omitting all mention of the nights of continence.

[3] The gall of the same fish is used by Tobias to heal the eyes of his father Tobit, who had lost his sight through an accident consequent on his charity in burying the body of a Jew who had been executed. See the *Book of Tobit*, ii. 1-10, vi. 1-8, xi. 11-13.

Hebrew version, which contains the incident of the "Tobias nights," really represents, as Dr. Gaster believes, the original text which was known to Jerome through the medium of an Aramaic translation, it will follow that the interpolation of that incident in the narrative is older than the time of Jerome ; but if it should turn out that, contrary to the view of Dr. Gaster, the Hebrew version is merely a translation from the Vulgate, the question of the date at which the episode of the "Tobias nights" was worked into the story would have to remain open, and we should consequently be unable to pronounce with any confidence whether the interpolator was a Jew or a Christian. But, Jew or Christian, his motive for making this addition to the story seems clearly to have been the practical one of recommending chastity as the best prelude to married life ; and the same motive probably led the Church to dwell on the three "Tobias nights" as the model to which all virtuous and God-fearing couples should conform their behaviour at marriage.

At first sight it is natural to suppose that this injunction of continence for three nights after marriage flowed simply from an exalted conception of the virtue of chastity and a corresponding depreciation of the only means which nature has vouchsafed for the continuance of our species; in other words, it might be thought that the injunction was merely one manifestation or effect of that ascetic ideal which has profoundly influenced Oriental religion and has stamped itself deep on Christianity. But the discovery of a similar counsel and a similar practice among many barbarous and even savage races, whom neither their admirers nor their detractors can tax with a propensity to asceticism, suffices to prove that the origin of the custom must be sought in some other direction ; and the story of Tobias, as it is related in the Vulgate, may perhaps furnish us with a clue in the search. For in that story the practice of continence is enjoined, not primarily as a means of pleasing God, but for the purpose of defeating the jealous devil, who had already massacred Sarah's seven husbands, and would have killed her eighth, if that bold man had not received timely warning and prudently abstained from exercising his conjugal rights for three nights after marriage. The inference suggested by the narrative is

The practice of continence after m rriage was probably ase o a fear of he demons, ... commonly supposed wait for the newly married.

that by this abstinence Tobias left the field open to his spiritual rival, who, after enjoying the bride undisturbed for three nights, was content to pass her on to her lawful husband for the term of his natural life. The temporary restraint which the bridegroom imposed on his passions was, in short, an accommodation, not with heaven but with hell, in virtue of which the demon lover resigned his cast-off mistress to the arms of her human spouse. At all events, if this explanation does not fit all the facts, it is more on a level with the ideas of the peoples who have practised the custom than the theory which would derive it from a glorified asceticism. A kindred explanation has been proposed, with special reference to the Vedic practice, by a learned and acute Vedic scholar, Professor Hermann Oldenberg. He says, " If after marriage the young couple are enjoined to practise continence for a time, whether for three nights or a longer period, the original meaning of this ancient custom, though it was obviously no longer understood by the Vedic Indians, must, in my opinion, undoubtedly be sought in the fear of spirits who, in the act of copulation, might slip into the woman and endanger her offspring, or might even themselves beget offspring on her, for spirits are well known to lust after such intercourse ; they are misled by a pretence of omitting the consummation of marriage." [1]   On this I would only observe that the intention of the custom is perhaps not so much to deceive the demons by pretending that the marriage is not to be consummated, as to leave them free scope for making love to the bride in the absence of the bridegroom. But in which ever way the custom is supposed to protect bride and bridegroom at marriage, the danger apprehended is probably believed, at least in many cases, to spring from demons ; for it is a common belief that evil spirits lie in wait for newly married couples, and many are the superstitious devices resorted to for the sake of cheating them out of their prey. To illustrate this topic fully would lead us too far. It must suffice to cite a few typical instances.

A traveller in Java tells us that " among other apartments we saw the ' family bridal chamber,' in which we noticed two painted wooden figures, one of a man and the other of a

[1] H. Oldenberg, *Die Religion des Veda* (Berlin, 1894), p. 271.

woman, standing at the foot of the 'family nuptial couch.' Precau-
n   cen
against
demons at
marriage
in Java,
Borneo,
Celebes,
and India.
These figures, as we were told, are called Lorobonyhoyo, or
the youth and maiden, and are placed there to cheat the
devil, who, according to their belief, during the wedding-night
hovers round the bed, with the view of carrying off one of the
happy pair.   These figures, however, are their protection, for,
deceived by their resemblance, he carries them off instead of
the sleeping lovers."[1]   The Javanese of Surakarta similarly
believe that newly wedded pairs are exposed on the first night
of their marriage to the injuries and outrages of evil spirits, who
try to turn their love to hate.   Hence when the young couple
have been in the bridal chamber for about an hour, their
friends enter with burning torches and poke about the room
with them, as if they were looking for something.   This they
do to frighten away the demons by the glare of the torches,
or at least to disturb and thwart them in their hellish design.[2]
Among some of the Dyaks of Dutch Borneo bride and bridegroom are not allowed to sleep on the wedding night, lest
evil spirits should avail themselves of their slumber to make
them sick.[3]   At a marriage between persons of high rank in
Southern Celebes the bridegroom's nails, both on his hands
and feet, together with the palms of his hands and the instep
of his feet, are dyed red with the juice of *Lawsonia alba* L.,
because this is believed to be a good protection against the
envy of evil spirits.[4]   It is said that among high-caste
Hindoos of the Punjab a bridegroom, on entering the bridal
chamber, always carries an iron weapon with him to drive
away the evil spirits that haunt him at the marriage ceremony.[5]   Similarly we are told that in Bombay the bridegroom, from the beginning to the end of the marriage rites,
keeps a dagger in his hand day and night for the purpose of
averting evil spirits.[6]   Among the Naoda, a caste of ferrymen

[1] W. B. d'Almeida, *Life in Java* (London, 1864). ii. 160 *sq.*
[2] C. F. Winter, "Instellingen, Ge-woonten en Gebruiken der Javanen te Soerakarta," *Tijdschrift voor Neêrlands Indie*, Batavia, 1843, Eerste Deel, p. 485; P. J. Veth, *Java, Geographisch, Ethnologisch, Historisch* (Haarlem, 1875–1884), i. 635.
[3] M. T. H. Perelaer, *Ethnograph-ische Beschrijving der Dajaks* (Zalt-

Bommel, 1870), p. 53.
[4] B. F. Matthes, *Bijdragen tot de Ethnologie van Zuid-Celebes* (The Hague 1875) p 30.
[5] Maya Das, in *Panjab Notes and Queries*, vol. 1. p. 98, § 759 (June 1004).
[6] Munshi, in *Panjab Notes and Queries*, vol. i. p. 125, § 940 (August 1884).

in the Central Provinces of India, " before the bridegroom starts for his wedding his mother takes and passes in front of him, successively from his head to his feet, a pestle, some stalks of *rusa* grass, a churning-rod and a winnowing-fan. This is done with the object of keeping off evil spirits, and it is said that by her action she threatens to pound the spirits with the pestle, to tie them up with the grass, to churn and mash them with the churning-rod, and to scatter them to the winds with the winnowing-fan." [1]   Among the Rajjhars, another caste of the Central Provinces, when bride and bridegroom arrive for the first time after marriage at the bridegroom's house, the bridegroom's mother meets him at the door " and touches his head, breast and knees with a churning-stick, a winnowing-fan and a pestle, with the object of exorcising any evil spirits who may be accompanying the bridal couple." [2]   Among the Savars of the Central Provinces of India, " on the return of the bridal pair seven lines are drawn in front of the entrance to the bridegroom's house. Some relative takes rice and throws it at the persons returning with the marriage procession, and then pushes the pair hastily across the lines and into the house. They are thus freed from the evil spirits who might have accompanied them home, and who are kept back by the rice and the seven lines." [3]   Among the Oraons of Bengal a screen is held round bride and bridegroom while the marriage rite is being performed, in order to protect them from the gaze of demons and of strangers who may have the evil eye.[4]   The custom of veiling the bride, which is common to many peoples, was probably in origin intended to serve the same purpose.

Precautions taken against demons at marriage in Armenia, Morocco, and Normandy.   In Armenia bride and bridegroom are believed to be exposed to the machinations of demons both before and after the wedding ceremony ; hence they carry as talismans a locked door-lock and a closed clasp-knife. Further, they are constantly attended by a man armed with a sword for their protection. Whenever they pass through a door their guardian makes a cross with the sword over the lintel,

---

[1] R. V. Russell, *The Tribes and Castes of the Central Provinces of India* (London, 1916), iv. 284.

[2] R. V. Russell, *op. cit.* iv. 407.

[3] R. V. Russell, *op. cit.* iv. 506.

[4] Sarat Chandra Roy, *The Oraons of Chota-Nagpur* (Ranchi, 1915), p. 363.

because doorways are thought to be the abode of spirits.[1] At marriages in Morocco "the constant firing of guns, the loud music, and the quivering noise of women, especially of the one who keeps hold of the bridegroom's hood, obviously serve the purpose of purifying the atmosphere and frightening away evil spirits by the noise and, in the case of the powder-play, also by the smell of powder, of which the jinn are believed to be much afraid. For a similar reason the bridegroom carries a sword, dagger, or pistol ; and the crossing of swords over his head or in front of him is likewise intended to ward off jinn, who are afraid of steel and, especially, of weapons of this metal. The same is the case with his wearing of various charms and the use of salt, which is also a common safeguard against evil spirits." [2] At weddings in Normandy, when the bridegroom joined the bride in the marriage chamber, it was customary for a friend to crack a whip in order to drive away the evil spirits who, but for this precaution, might molest the newly wedded pair.[3]

The precautions against spirits at marriage are peculiarly stringent whenever one of the couple happens to be a widow or a widower, because in that case the usual demons are powerfully reinforced by the jealous ghost of the deceased husband or wife, whose tenderest feelings are wounded by the sight of his or her relict in the arms of a living rival. Common prudence suggests the desirability of averting the threatened danger by appeasing the anger of the injured ghost, eluding his inconvenient attentions, or forcibly driving him away. The last of these measures is adopted by the Nufors of Dutch New Guinea. When a widow walks for the first time with her second husband into the forest, the couple are followed by widows or married women, who throw sticks at the ghost of the bride's first husband to hasten his departure.[4]

Precautions against the ghost husband or wife at the marriage of a widow or widower.

[1] Manuk Abeghian, *Der armenische Volksglaube* (Leipsic, 1899), p. 91.

[2] Edward Westermarck, *Marriage Ceremonies in Morocco* (London, 1914), pp. 122 *sq.* In quoting Dr. Westmarck I have altered his spelling *jnun* into the usual English *jinn.*

[3] Alfred de Nore, *Coutumes, Mythes, et Traditions des Provinces de France*

(Paris and Lyons, 1846), p. 240.

[4] J. B. van Hasselt, " Die Noeforezen," *Zeitschrift für Ethnologie,* viii. 8   182 s . J. L. van Hasselt, " Eenige aanteekingen aangaande de bewoners der N. Westkust van Nieuw Guï   meer bepaaldelijk de stam Noefoorezen," *Tijdschrift voor Indische Taal- Land- en Volkenkunde,* xxxi. (1886) p. 585.

The Baganda of Central Africa adopted a more conciliatory attitude towards the departed spirit. "When a man wished to marry a widow, he first paid the deceased husband a barkcloth and a fowl, which he put into the little shrine at the grave; in this way he imagined he could pacify the ghost."[1] The Savaras of Southern India in like manner seek to propitiate the jealous spirits of deceased husbands. Whenever one of them marries a widow, he kills a pig and offers the flesh of the animal, with some liquor, to the ghost of the bride's late husband, while a priest prays the ghost not to spoil the wedded bliss of his widow and her second spouse. "Oh! man," says the priest, addressing the deceased by name, "here is an animal sacrificed to you, and with this all connexion between this woman and you ceases. She has taken with her no property belonging to you or your children. So do not torment her within the house or outside the house, in the jungle or on the hill, when she is asleep or when she wakes. Do not send sickness on her children. Her second husband has done no harm to you. She chose him for her husband, and he consented. Oh! man, be appeased; oh! unseen ones; oh! ancestors, be you witnesses."[2] Among the Somavansi Kshatriyas in Bombay "there is a strong belief that when a woman marries another husband, her first husband becomes a ghost and troubles her. This fear is so strongly rooted in their minds, that whenever a woman of this caste sickens, she attributes her sickness to the ghost of her former husband, and consults an exorcist as to how she can get rid of him. The exorcist gives her some charmed rice, flowers, and basil leaves, and tells her to enclose them in a small copper box and wear it round her neck. Sometimes the exorcist gives her a charmed cocoa-nut, which he tells her to worship daily, and in some cases he advises the woman to make a copper or silver image of the dead and worship it every day."[3] "So in Northern India, people who marry again after the death of the first wife wear what is known as the Saukan Maura, or second wife's crown. This is a little

---

[1] John Roscoe, *The Baganda* (London, 1911), p. 97.

[2] Edgar Thurston, *Castes and Tribes of Southern India* (Madras, 1909), vi. 321.

[3] W. Crooke, *Popular Religion and Folk-lore of Northern India* (Westminster, 1896), i. 235 *sq.*, quoting J. M. Campbell's *Notes on the Spirit Basis of Belief and Custom*, p. 171.

silver amulet, generally with an image of Devi engraved on it. This is hung round the husband's neck, and all presents made to the second wife are first dedicated to it. The idea is that the new wife recognizes the superiority of her predecessor, and thus appeases her malignity. The illness or death of the second wife or of her husband soon after marriage is attributed to the jealousy of the ghost of the first wife, which has not been suitably propitiated." [1] In the Punjab, for a similar reason, "if a man has lost two or three wives in succession, he gets a woman to catch a bird and adopt it as her daughter. He then pays the dower, marries his bird bride, and immediate divorces her. By this means the malignant influence is diverted to the bird, and the real wife is safe." [2]

Nor is this the only kind of mock marriage which is celebrated in the Punjab for the purpose of appeasing or eluding the wrath of a dead wife when the widower marries again. " The custom of mock marriage, *i.e.*, going through a form of marriage with an animal, tree or other inanimate object, which prevails among certain castes of the Hindus more or less throughout the Province, is based upon fear of ill luck. Mock marriages take place (1) when a widower wishes to marry a third wife, and (2) when the horoscope of a girl shows that the influence of certain stars is likely to lead to early widowhood. In cases of the former kind, the mock marriage is celebrated in the western Punjab with a sheep, in the central Punjab with the Ber (*Zizyphus jujuba*) tree or sometimes with the Pipal (*Ficus religiosa*) and in the eastern Punjab with the Ak (*Calotropis procera*) bush. The fear of ill luck is due partly to the suspicion, caused by the death of the two former wives, viz., that the wife of the man whosoever she might be, is destined to die, and particularly the wife taken by the third marriage, which is considered to be peculiarly inauspicious. . . . But it is also due partly to the belief that the, jealousy of the spirit of the first wife is instrumental in causing the death of the subsequent wives. It is for this latter reason that when a widower has to marry a second time, a miniature picture of the first wife, either

Mock marriages widowers widows in the Punjab.

---

[1] W. Crooke, *op. cit.* i. 236.   [2] W. Crooke, *l.c.*

cased in silver or gold or engraved on a silver or gold plate,
is hung round the neck of the bride at the wedding ceremonies.   When a picture cannot be obtained or engraved,
the name of the deceased wife is substituted for the picture.
The idea seems to be to humour the spirit of the first wife,
by proving the fidelity of the husband, who in marrying the
second wife pretends to really marry the picture or name of
the deceased wife, thus identifying the second wife with the
first.   In the central Punjab, at a second marriage, the bride
is dressed like a milk-maid (*Gujri*) or a flower-seller (*Málan*)
and given a servile nickname such as *Gujri, Málan, Jatto,
Mehri*, etc.   The object of this apparently is to convince
the spirit of the deceased wife, that the female being
married is not a real *patni* (wife) but a *dási* (slave-girl).
But when the death of the second wife shows that the
device was unsuccessful, a mock marriage is resorted to, at
the third occasion.   The bridegroom is sometimes taken out
to a tree of the above-mentioned variety, which is bedecked
with clothes and jewelry, and he is made to go round it,
with the usual incantations, as if he were going through the
Láván ceremony.   After completing this preliminary step,
he proceeds to the bride's house, to celebrate the formal
marriage with the bride, which is supposed to be a nominal
one or equivalent to a fourth.   But in most cases, a twig or
(in the Western Punjab) a sheep is taken to the bride's
house, where it is anointed and bedecked with clothes and
ornaments to represent a wife, and at every stage of the
ceremony the bridegroom goes through the forms, first with
this mock-wife and then with the real bride.   It is interesting to watch the bedecked sheep sitting on the *khárás*
(reversed baskets) with a bridegroom and being led by him
round the sacrificial fire while the real bride sits by.   All
these formalities are peculiar to the third marriage, and if
the third wife also dies and a fourth one has to be married,
no mock marriage is usually deemed necessary, as the evil
influence of the first wife is believed to have spent itself." [1]
•   Similar pretences are enacted for similar purposes in
other parts of India at the marriages of widowers or widows.

[1] *Census of India*, 1911, vol. xiv. Harikishan Kaul (Lahore, 1912), pp.
Punjab, Part i. *Report*, by Pandit   283 *sq.*

Thus in the Konkan, a province on the coast of the Bombay Presidency, when a man has lost two wives and wishes to marry a third, he is married to a *Rui* plant before he weds the real bride, because people believe that the third wife would be sure to die if the spirit of the deceased wife were not made to enter the *Rui* plant.[1] Among the Barais, a caste of growers and sellers of the betel-vine leaf in the Central Provinces of India, " a bachelor espousing a widow must first go through the ceremony of marriage with a swallow-wort plant. When a widower marries a girl a silver impression representing the deceased first wife is made and worshipped daily with the family gods."[2] In the latter case the intention of worshipping the portrait of a deceased wife at marriage with a second is no doubt to propitiate the jealous ghost of the dead woman and induce her to spare her living rival. Among the Kawars, a primitive tribe of the Central Provinces of India, " if a widower marries a girl for his third wife it is considered unlucky for her. An earthen image of a woman is therefore made, and he goes through the marriage ceremony with it ; he then throws the image to the ground so that it is broken, when it is considered to be dead and its funeral ceremony is performed. After this the widower may marry the girl, who becomes his fourth wife."[3] Here apparently the ghost of the first wife is thought to be contented with the breaking of the earthen image, which perhaps she is supposed to mistake for the real bride. In some parts of Bastar, which is one of the Central Provinces of India, the Gonds view with particular apprehension marriage with a widow whose husband has been killed by a tiger, because they believe that the ghost of the deceased has entered into the tiger and in that form will seek to devour the rash man who marries his widow. In order to prevent that catastrophe the widow is formally married, not to her new husband, but either to a

[1] R. E. Enthoven, *Folk-lore of the Konkan*, p. 73 (Supplement to *The Indian Antiquary*, vol. xliv. Bombay, 1915). '

[2] R. V. Russell, *Tribes and Castes of the Central Provinces* (London, 1916), ii. 195. In like manner among the Kunbis of the Central Provinces of India a bachelor who marries a widow must first be married to an *ákra* or swallow-wort (*Calotropis gigantea*), a very common plant with mauve or purple flowers, which grows on waste land. See R. V. Russell, *op. cit.* iv. 28.

[3] R. V. Russell, *op. cit.* iii. 395.

dog or to a lance, axe, or sword, because they calculate that
the ghost, mistaking apparently the fictitious for the real
bridegroom, will either carry off the dog or perish by one of
these lethal weapons.[1]

Still more elaborate are the precautions which the
Kunbis, a great agricultural class of the Central Provinces
of India, adopt for the purpose of protecting a man who
marries a widow against the assaults of her late husband's
ghost. Among these people, we are told, " the ceremony of
widow-marriage is largely governed by the idea of escaping
or placating the wrath of the first husband's ghost, and also
of its being something to be ashamed of and contrary to
orthodox Hinduism. It always takes place in the dark
fortnight of the month and always at night. Sometimes no
women are present, and if any do attend they must be
widows, as it would be the worst of omens for a married
woman or unmarried girl to witness the ceremony. This, it
is thought, would lead to her shortly becoming a widow
herself. The bridegroom goes to the widow's house with
his male friends, and two wooden seats are set side by side.
On one of these a betel-nut is placed which represents the
deceased husband of the widow. The new bridegroom
advances with a small wooden sword, touches the nut with
its tip, and then kicks it off the seat with his right toe.
The barber picks up the nut and burns it. This is supposed
to lay the deceased husband's spirit and prevent his interference with the new union. The bridegroom then takes
the seat from which the nut has been displaced and the
woman sits on the other side to his left   He puts a neck-
lace of beads round her neck and the couple leave the house

[1] R. V. Russell, *Tribes and Castes of the Central Provinces of India* (London, 1916), iii. 81. Mock marriages with plants or inanimate objects, less frequently with animals, are common in India, and apparently they cannot all be explained on the same principle. The fear of the ghost of a dead wife or husband is only one of the motives which has contributed to the observance of these quaint ceremonies. Generally the mock marriage appears to be contracted for the sake of averting some ill-luck or misfortune which would otherwise attend the union. See R. V. Russell, *op. cit.* iii. 188 *sq.*, iv. 506 ; W. Crooke, *Popular Religion and Folk-lore of Northern India* (Westminster, 1896), ii. 115-128 ; *id.*, " The Hill Tribes of the Central Indian Hills," *Journal of the Anthropological Institute*, xxviii. (1899) pp. 242 *sq.* ; *Totemism and Exogamy*, iv. 210 *sqq.* ; *The Magic Art and the Evolution of Kings*, ii. 57 *sq.* (*The Golden Bough*, Third Edition, Part i.).

in a stealthy fashion and go to the husband's village.   It is considered unlucky to see them as they go away, because the second husband is regarded in the light of a robber. Sometimes they stop by a stream on the way home, and, taking off the woman's clothes and bangles, bury them by the side of the stream.   An exorcist may also be called in, who will confine the late husband's spirit in a horn by putting in some grains of wheat, and after sealing up the horn deposit it with the clothes.   When a widower or widow marries a second time and is afterwards attacked by illness, it is ascribed to the ill-will of their former partner's spirit. The metal image of the first husband or wife is then made and worn as an amulet on the arm or round the neck." [1] Again, among the Manas, a Dravidian caste of cultivators and labourers in the Central Provinces of India, " when a widow is to be remarried, she stops on the way by the banks of a stream as she is proceeding to her new husband's house, and here her clothes are taken off and buried by an exorcist with a view to laying the first husband's spirit and preventing it from troubling the new household." [2]   In this practice of burying a widow's clothes on the bank of a river, which, as we have just seen, is observed also by the Kunbis of the same region, we may probably detect an effort to disguise the woman from her husband's ghost, like the attempt of a criminal to evade the pursuit of justice by shaving his whiskers and donning a strange attire.   The circumstance of burying the cast-off garments by the side of a stream is perhaps a further refinement of the subterfuge, designed to take advantage of a spirit's well-known inability to cross water.

The foregoing instances may serve to illustrate some of the spiritual dangers which, in the opinion of many peoples, attend the entrance into the married state, and

No real
that in
Europe
lords ever
possessed
ht of
concubin-
age with
their
tenants'
brides at
marriage.

[1] R. V. Russell, *Tribes and Castes of the Central Provinces of India*, iv. 27 *sq.*

[2] R. V. Russell, *The Tribes and Castes of the Central Provinces of India*, iv. 175.   The belief that a widow is haunted by the jealous and dangerous ghost of her deceased husband is illustrated by Mr. E. S. Hartland in a learned essay ("The Haunted Widow," *Ritual and Belief*, London, 1914, pp. 194-234).   In Madagascar it is admitted that a dead man sometimes begets a child on his widow, and the infant is acknowledged as legitimate.   See A. et G. Grandidier, *Ethnographie de Madagascar*, ii. (Paris, 1914) p. 246 note [2].

they perhaps account, at least in some measure, for the delay in consummating the marriage. Certainly, however we may explain it, the practice of continence for a certain time, especially for three nights, after marriage has been widespread over the world among heathen as well as Christian peoples, and its persistence in Europe down to our own day combines with the historical evidence to prove that the *jus primae noctis* was no more than an ecclesiastical dispensation granted by the Church to free newly married couples from the obligation of complying with an ancient custom, which, through a change in public opinion, had come to be felt superfluous and burdensome. The notion that the *jus primae noctis* in Europe was a right which a feudal lord or ecclesiastical dignitary claimed of sleeping with the wives of his tenants or subordinates on their marriage night appears to be destitute alike of historical proof and of intrinsic probability; it is a monstrous fable born of ignorance, prejudice, and confusion of ideas. The sources of the fable appear to be mainly twofold, a misapprehension of the nature of the *merchet*, and a misapprehension of the nature of the *jus primae noctis*. These two things were perfectly distinct and had no connexion with each other. The *merchet* was the fine which a tenant or vassal paid to his feudal lord for the right of giving his daughter in marriage ; the *jus primae noctis* was the right of sleeping with his own wife on the wedding night, which a husband received from his bishop or other ecclesiastical authority on the payment of a fee for the licence. Neither the one nor the other had anything to do with a practice of sacrificing the virginity of brides to men other than their husbands. Yet these two things, totally different in nature and in origin, were popularly confounded together and perverted into a baseless calumny on two classes of men—feudal lords and the higher clergy— who, whatever other faults and failings may be laid to their charge, appear to have been perfectly innocent of such a systematic outrage on the domestic affections of their civil and ecclesiastical inferiors.

To return to the question from which we started, we conclude that in Europe the rule of ultimogeniture, or the preference for the youngest son in the inheritance, cannot be founded on a custom which allowed a man other than the husband to cohabit with the bride at marriage, since no such custom is known ever to have been practised in Europe.

But since ultimogeniture has prevailed among other races in various parts of the world, it may be asked whether among these races, some of which stand at a comparatively low level of culture, the rule of ultimogeniture may not have arisen through a doubt as to the legitimacy of the firstborn consequent on a right of concubinage exercised with the mother at marriage by men other than the husband ? To this question the reply is like that which has been given for Europe. There seems to be no positive proof that such a right has ever been recognized in any of the tribes which are known to practise ultimogeniture. Only in one of the tribes, so far as I know, is there a slight ground for suspecting such an origin of the custom. Among the Lolos of South-Western China, as we saw,[1] the youngest son is said to inherit in preference to the eldest. However, a French writer gives a somewhat different account of the rule of inheritance in the tribe. He tells us that " the first child of the marriage, though reared with the same care and attention as those that come afterwards, is nevertheless not recognized by the husband, who considers it in some sort as a stranger. It is to the second child, whether boy or girl, that the title of eldest is given."[2] If this account is correct, it sets the custom of junior right (for it could not strictly be called ultimogeniture) among the Lolos in a very different light ; for it suggests that the firstborn is excluded from the heritage on the ground of illegitimacy, and consistently with that supposition it apparently assigns the inheritance, not to the youngest, but to the second child, whether male or female. All this would be a natural consequence of a practice of submitting brides at marriage to the embraces of men other than their husbands. Now in Tibet, the natives of which are racially akin to the Lolos and speak a language of the same family, a practice of the defloration of virgins by strangers before marriage is reported by Marco Polo to

Marginal notes: Ultimogeniture in Europe not derived fabulous right. No proof that ultimogeniture has anywhere been based on the illegitimacy of the firstborn. Some slight ground for suspecting such an origin of ultimogeniture among the Lolos.

[1] See above, p. 458.
[2] Emile Rocher, *La Province chinoise* *Yun-nan*, Deuxieme Partie (Paris, 1880), p 17.

Marco Polo
on a
practice
of the
d-fl----:--
of virgins by
strangers
in Tibet. have actually prevailed at the time when he travelled through
the land. "No man of that country," he tells us, "would
on any consideration take to wife a girl who was a maid;
for they say a wife is nothing worth unless she has been
used to consort with men. And their custom is this, that
when travellers come that way, the old women of the place
get ready, and take their unmarried daughters or other girls
related to them, and go to the strangers who are passing,
and make over the young women to whomsoever will accept
them ; and the travellers take them accordingly and do
their pleasure ; after which the girls are restored to the old
women who brought them, for they are not allowed to follow
the strangers away from their home. In this manner people
travelling that way, when they reach a village or hamlet or
other inhabited place, shall find perhaps twenty or thirty
girls at their disposal. And if the travellers lodge with
those people they shall have as many young women as they
could wish coming to court them. You must know, too,
that the traveller is expected to give the girl who has been
with him a ring or some other trifle, something in fact that
she can show as a lover's token, when she comes to be
married. And it is for this in truth and for this alone that
they follow that custom ; for every girl is expected to obtain
at least twenty such tokens in the way I have described
before she can be married, and those who have most tokens,
and so can show that they have been most run after, are in
the highest esteem, and most sought in marriage, because
they say the charms of such are greatest. But after marriage these people hold their wives very dear, and would
consider it a great villainy for a man to meddle with another's
wife ; and thus though the wives have before marriage acted
as you have heard, they are kept with great care from light
conduct afterwards."[1]

It may be that the people of whom Marco Polo here
speaks were no other than the Lolos ;[2] but it is highly im-

---

[1] *The Book of Ser Marco Polo*, newly
translated and edited by Colonel (Sir)
Henry Yule, Second Edition (London,
1875), 11. 35, 37.

[2] Commenting on the preceding passage of Marco Polo, Sir Henry Yule

observes, " All this is clearly meant
to apply only to the rude people towards the Chinese frontier ; nor would
the Chinese (says Richthofen) at this
day think the description at all exaggerated, as applied to the Lolo who

probable that any such usage prevails among them at the present time. However, the French writer, whose account of their rule of inheritance I have quoted, mentions a Lolo custom observed at marriage which might perhaps be inter- preted as a relic of a former licence accorded to women before marriage. He says, " An old custom requires that on the day after marriage the bride should quit her husband's roof at sunrise and return to the house of her parents with- out any consideration for her husband or her new family ; she has not the right to return to her spouse till she feels the first symptoms of motherhood. During the whole time of this separation, she enjoys complete liberty and makes no scruple of running about the neighbouring villages or taking part in the festivals and amusements of the young people. If at the end of a certain time, which varies from a year to eighteen months, she experiences no sign of maternity, her husband, convinced that he has no hope of offspring by her, takes back his word, as he has a right to do by virtue of ancient custom, and looks out elsewhere for another wife. On the contrary when, after some months, his wife returns to his roof to become a mother, from that time the husband, assured of having a numerous posterity, calls her to no account for her conduct and treats her with the regard due to her fecundity. She on her side bids farewell to the pleasures of youth and begins the active and laborious life of housekeeping." [1]

However, the custom which permits or requires a bride soon after marriage to return for a time to the house of her parents, appears to be not uncommon ; [2] it need not have any connexion with leave granted to the woman to cohabit with men other than her husband. On the whole, if we may judge from the custom of ultimogeniture as it is actually observed by Mongoloid tribes akin to the Lolos, it seems

(marginal notes) Liberty of brides after marriage among the Lolo. / The Lolo rule of inheritance probably not a case of a profligate practice.

occupy the mountains to the south of Yachaufu" (*The Book of Ser Marco Polo*, newly translated and edited by Colonel Henry Yule, Second Edition, London, 1875, vol. ii. p. 40).

[1] Emile Rocher, *La Province chinoise Yün-nan*, Deuxième Partie (Paris, 1880), pp. 16 *sq.*

[2] For examples see E. Westermarck, *Marriage Ceremonies in Morocco* (London, 1914), pp. 300 *sqq.* ; R. V. Russell, *The Tribes and Castes of the Central Provinces of India* (London, 1916), iii. 193, iv. 187. Similar in- stances could, I believe, be multiplied.

more probable that the French writer has unwittingly mis‑ represented and misinterpreted the Lolo rule of inheritance than that it is based on a profligate practice, of the existence of which there is no evidence in this group of tribes.

It is true that a custom of entrusting the defloration of brides at marriage to men other than their husbands has undoubtedly been observed among not a few peoples,[1] and that wherever such a usage prevails it must necessarily throw doubt on the legitimacy of the eldest child born after marriage. But this custom cannot be accepted as the true or probable explanation of ultimogeniture, and that for two reasons: first, because the custom is not known to be observed by any of the peoples who practise ultimogeniture; and, second, because such a custom, though it might supply a plausible reason for preferring the second child to the first‑ born, could not explain the preference of the youngest to all his elder brothers and sisters, which is the characteristic feature of ultimogeniture. Thus even if we granted the existence of a practice like that which is commonly, though incorrectly, understood to be indicated by the phrase *jus primae noctis*, it would not account for the very facts which it is adduced to explain.

§ 9. *Ultimogeniture and Polygamy.*

Yet another theory has been proposed to account for the origin of ultimogeniture. It has been said that among polygamous peoples the last wife whom a man marries is generally the principal wife and the mother of the heir, who

[1] For evidence see W. Hertz, " Die Sage vom Giftmadchen," *Gesammelte Abhandlungen* (Stuttgart and Berlin, 1905), pp. 195 *sqq.*; and for references to the authorities who have recorded the custom, see *Adonis, Attis, Osiris,* Third Edition, i. 57 *sqq.* The custom is reported to be observed in some parts of Morocco. See Ed. Wester- marck, *Marriage Ceremonies in Morocco* (London, 1914), pp. 269 *sq.* In the Banaro tribe of northern New Guinea a woman's first child after marriage is regularly begotten on her, not by her husband, but by a friend of her hus- band's father. The intercourse between the two takes place in the spirit or goblin house of the village; the man personates a spirit or goblin; and the child which he has by the woman is called the spirit-child or goblin-child. See Richard Thurnwald, " Banaro Society," *Memoirs of the American Anthropological Association,* vol. iii. No. 4 (October–December, 1916), pp. 261 *sqq.* Yet it does not appear that among the Banaro this custom has led to a preference for younger sons over the firstborn.

is, or may be, the youngest son of the father.   On this view, ultimogeniture rests, or may rest, in polygamous society on a preference for the youngest son of the last wife.   This theory was independently suggested by the late Sir Laurence Gomme and Dr. Br. Nicholson ; and both of them appealed in confirmation of it to the customs of the Kafir tribes of South Africa, among whom they apparently supposed the practice of ultimogeniture to prevail.[1]   The facts, so far as I am acquainted with them, seem rather to refute than to confirm the theory that has been built upon them.   For, in the first place, among the polygamous peoples of Africa the principal or great wife is generally the first, not the last, to be married by the husband ; and, in the second place, whether she is the first, or the last, or an intermediate wife, it is not her youngest but her eldest son who regularly succeeds to the inheritance.   In short, the principle which regulates the succession both of property and of power in the great majority of polygamous African tribes is not ultimogeniture but primogeniture ; which is just the contrary of what we should expect if ultimogeniture were a natural consequence of polygamy.   All the evidence that I have been able to discover for the practice of ultimogeniture in Africa has already been laid before the reader.[2] It is meagre in quantity and to some extent doubtful in quality.   The evidence for the practice of primogeniture in Africa, on the contrary, is both abundant and trustworthy. To deal with it at large would be out of place here.   I shall content myself with citing such facts as bear directly on the

But the evidence, to which the advocates of this appeal, seems rather to refute than to support i

---

[1] G. Laurence Gomme, "On archaic conceptions of property in relation to the Laws of Succession, and their survival in England," *Archaeologia, or Miscellaneous Tracts relating to Antiquity, published by the Society of Antiquaries of London*, vol. l. (London, 1887) pp. 212 *sq.* (referring to Maclean's *Kafir Laws and Customs*, p. 26) ; *id., Folklore as an Historical Science* (London, 1908), pp. 171-174 ; Br. Nicholson, M.D., "Heirship of the Youngest among the Kafirs," *The Archaeological Review*, ii. (London, 1889), pp. 163-166.   Sir Laurence Gomme is careful to state that he does not put this theory forward as the only

one which can account for the origin of ultimogeniture ; on the contrary he accepts the ordinary and (as I believe) the correct explanation of ultimogeniture in Europe, namely, that "it originated in the tribal practice of the elder sons going out of the tribal household to found tribal households of their own, thus leaving the youngest to inherit the original homestead " (*Folk-lore as an Historical Science*, pp. 171 *sq.*). But he thinks that among savages who practice polygamy the rule of ultimogeniture arises through a preference for the son of the last wife.

[2] Above, pp. 476-481.

questions raised by the theory under discussion. These questions are two. First, what is the position of the principal or "great" wife, the mother of the heir, in a polygamous family? Is she generally the last wife married, as the theory supposes, or is she not? Second, what is the position of the heir among the children of the principal or "great" wife? Is he generally the youngest son, as 'the theory supposes, or is he not? The following facts appear to answer both these questions in the negative.

Superiority
e rs
wife in
Sene-
a
Sierra
Leone, and
Guinea

In Senegambia "polygamy is admitted in principle and exists in practice among the Wolofs, as among all the Mohammedans. The husband may take as many as three legitimate wives and as many concubines as he can afford. The first legitimate wife, who bears the title of *awho*, has extensive prerogatives in the household, owns the finest house, and has the right of first choice of presents offered to the family." [1] In regard to the tribes of Sierra Leone we are told that "polygamy is universally practised upon this coast, which tends still more to debase the female sex. Every man may have as many wives as his circumstances will allow him to maintain; his wealth is therefore estimated according to this criterion, and he rises in the esteem of his neighbours in proportion to the number of his women. . . . The first wife a man takes enjoys a greater share of respect than the others, and retains the title of head woman, with a degree of enviable authority, long after her personal charms have ceased to enslave her husband's affections." [2] At Great Bassam, on the Ivory Coast, "as in the Gaboon, so here the wife first married is almost always the favourite. She possesses the full confidence of her husband, prepares him his food, rules the whole household, and has besides the right to cohabit with the head of the family oftener than the other wives." [3] To the same effect another writer informs us that on the Ivory Coast "the first wife enjoys a special authority. She commands the others, she has often

[1] L. J. B. Berenger-Féraud, *Les peuplades de la Sénégambie* (Paris, 1879), p. 40.
[2] Thomas Winterbottom, *Account of the Native Africans in the neighbour-hood of Sierra Leone* (London, 1803), pp. 145-147.
[3] Hyacinth Hecquard, *Reise an die Küste und in das Innere von West-Afrika* (Leipsic, 1854), p. 44.

authority over all the children of the house, especially over the daughters. The husband who desires to take another wife must obtain the consent of the first, to whom all the wives owe a certain deference."[1]   Speaking of the natives of the coast of Guinea in general, an old writer observes, " Those who are rich, have two wives perpetually exempted from labour ; the first of which is the oldest and principal wife, here called *La Muliere Grande*, or the chief woman ; to whom the house-keeping and command over all the rest is entrusted. The second is she who is consecrated to his god, and thence called Bossum, of whom he is very jealous, and so much enraged if any man kisses her, that if he could do it privately, he would so severely punish her that she would not be able to serve him so again ; but as for the remainder of his wives, he doth not watch them so narrowly, especially if he can get any money by them."[2]   On the Slave Coast, "one of the wives, usually the first, has the name of *iya'lle*, ' mistress of the house.'   That does not mean that the master allows her to stand on a footing of equality with him.   She approaches the master more nearly than the others ; she prepares and serves the meals ; she manages everything in the interior of the house and looks after its good administration ; she has a real precedence over the other wives, and up to a certain point she enters into the secrets and the plans of the master whose immediate and habitual servant she is."[3]

The Ewe-speaking peoples of Togoland believe that their souls lived in another world before they were born upon earth. Further, it is an article of their creed that in that other world every man had but one wife, and it is tacitly assumed that the first wife whom he marries here on earth is the same woman to whom he was married in the spiritual realm. She is the only true and proper wife given by God and the Mother of Spirits to him. If he fails to find her here below, and marries another, his spirit-wife will continually disturb his domestic bliss, and she

Superiority of life among the Ewe-speaking peoples of the Slave and among the Hausas of North Africa.

---

[1] G. Joseph, "Condition de la femme en Côte d'Ivoire," *Bulletins et Mémoires de la Société d'Anthropologie de Paris*, vi[e] Serie, iv. (1913) p. 589.

[2] William Bosman, "The Coast of Guinea," in J. Pinkerton's *General Collection of Voyages and Travels* (London, 1808-1814), xvi. 419 *sq.*

[3] Pierre Bouche, *La Côte des Esclaves* (Paris, 1885), p. 147.

must be appeased with sacrifices and gifts.[1]   Polygamy
prevails among the Ewe-speaking peoples of the Slave
Coast.   Each wife has her own separate dwelling in the
enclosure in which her husband's house stands, and her
children and slaves reside with her.   "The first wife is
termed the 'head-wife'; she supervises the internal arrangements of the entire household, is consulted by her husband,
and sometimes her opinion has weight.   The second wife
acts as the assistant of the head-wife; those married later
are all classed together.   It is unusual, except amongst
chiefs, for a man to have more than four or five wives."[2]
Among the Yoruba-speaking people of the Slave Coast in
like manner "each wife has her own house, situated in the
'compound' of the husband, and her own slaves and
dependents.   The wife first married is the head wife, and is
charged with the preservation of order among the women.
She is styled *Iyale* (*Iya ile*), 'Mistress of the house.'   The
junior wives are called *Iyawo* (*Iya owo*), 'Trade-wives' or
'Wives of commerce,' probably because they sell in the
markets."[3]   In Dahomey "the subject is allowed as many
concubines as he can maintain; but the first wife is alone
considered the legitimate one.   She superintends and directs
all the domestic duties, and all must be subject to her
control."[4]   Among the Hausas of North Africa "the firstborn son of any wife is the eldest son, and ranks accordingly, but the first wife is the chief, or Uwar-Gida (Mother
of the House) and is in charge of the others."[5]

Among the Ekoi of Southern Nigeria, on the border of

[1] Jakob Spieth, *Die Ewe-Stämme*
(Berlin, 1906), pp. 63 *sq.*   On the
other hand another German writer,
speaking of Togoland, affirms that
"among the Ewe negroes a man who
is in a position to keep several wives
generally has two or three.   In that
case for the most part the favourite
wife is the younger, who ornaments
herself, serves only for the husband's
pleasure, and bears rule over the other
wives" (H. Klose, *Togo unter deutscher
Flagge*, Berlin, 1899, p. 254).   But
the authority of this latter writer, whose
work is partly a compilation from previous publications, is not equal to that
of the missionary Jakob Spieth, who

wrote throughout from personal observation, and whose book on the Ewe
tribes is one of the most thorough
monographs ever published on an
African people.

[2] (Sir) A. B. Ellis, *The Ewe-speaking peoples of the Slave Coast of West
Africa* (London, 1890), pp. 204 *sq.*

[3] (Sir) A. B. Ellis, *The Yoruba-
speaking peoples of the Slave Coast of
West Africa* (London, 1894), pp. 182 *sq.*

[4] F. T. Valdez, *Six Years of a
Traveller's Life in Western Africa*
(London, 1861), i. 346.

[5] A. J. N. Tremearne, *The Ban of
the Bori* (London, preface dated 1914),
p. 122.

the Cameroons, " on marriage the wife becomes a member
of her husband's family, and goes to live in his compound.
A man's first wife is always the head of the house.   The
younger wives obey her and consider her in everything.
Therefore a wife likes her husband to marry plenty of other
women.   The chief complaint of cruelty brought by the
wife of Njabong of Oban before the Native Court was that
her husband refused to marry anyone but herself." [1]   Among
the M'Pongos of the Gaboon " polygamy is permitted, and
every man takes as many wives as he believes he can
support.   However, the wife whom he married first bears
rule over all his other wives.   She alone has the
keys to everything, knows where the money is hidden,
generally tastes first all the foods and drinks offered to
her husband, lest they should be poisoned, and is named
the Great Wife." [2]   In the Shekiani tribe, to the south of
the Gaboon River, " each man has generally a head or chief
wife—mostly the woman he married first ; and for any one
to have criminal intercourse with this woman ranks as a
most heinous crime, for which the offender is at least sold
into slavery.   When the husband forms new marriage connexions, and, as often happens, his new bride is but a child,
she is then put under the care and guardianship of the head
wife, who brings her up to the proper age." [3]   In Angola
" the men take as many wives as they can maintain, but the
first has some authority over the others, if her marriage was
celebrated with Christian rites." [4]   Among the Bayas, who
inhabit the right bank of the Kadei River in French Congo,
on the border of the Cameroons, " with the exception of the
first and oldest of a man's wives, who always keeps her
priority over the others, there is perfect equality among all
the wives of the household.   Each of the other wives
flatters the oldest by presents, so as to be distinguished by
her and to be appointed to succeed her at her death in the
domestic command." [5]

Superiority
of the first
wife in
Southern
Nigeria,
the
Gaboon,
and French
Congo.

[1] P. Amaury Talbot, *In the Shadow of the Bush* (London, 1912), p. 109.
[2] H. Hecquard, *Reise an die Kuste und in das Innere von West-Afrika* (Leipsic, 1854), p. 8.
[3] Paul B. du Chaillu, *Explorations and Adventures in Equatorial Africa*
(London, 1861), p. 162.
[4] O. Dapper, *Description de l'Afrique* (Amsterdam, 1686), p. 367.
[5] A. Poupon, "Etude ethnographique des Baya de la circonscription du M'bimou," *L'Anthropologie*, xxvi. (1915) p. 125.

Superiority
tl
first wife
among the
a o
Central
Africa.
Among the Baganda of Central Africa "there were no restrictions as to the number of wives that a man might take from one clan ; he might even marry two or three sisters, if he wished to do so.   When a man married more than one wife, he built a separate house for each ; the houses were generally side by side, and were enclosed by a fence.   He had his own house in front of the women's quarters, and the wives visited him, and slept in his house, when he invited them to do so."[1]   With regard to the order of precedence among Baganda wives, and the rule of inheritance among their children, my experienced friend, Mr. John Roscoe, our principal authority on the tribe, writes to me, "My African knowledge leads me to agree fully with you about the first wife being the principal wife.   In Uganda she was called *Kadulubare* (the little guardian of the *Lubare*), because she took charge of all her husband's fetishes and directed all worship and offerings during his absence.   She also had chief authority over his wives and was responsible for their moral conduct, especially during her husband's absence.   So far as I can remember, she was never divorced.   The ultimogeniture theory does not at present commend itself to me for any solution of African law of inheritance.   All children in Uganda belonged to the clan, and a man's property belonged to the clan ; hence any member might be chosen to inherit a certain property, though he was not a son. . . . I have no theory to offer as to how a man is chosen from a clan to inherit.   I cannot remember any special rule having ever been suggested."[2]   From this account, which may be regarded as authoritative, we gather that among the Baganda inheritance was regulated neither by primogeniture nor by ultimogeniture.

Superiority
of the first

East
Africa.
Among the Nandi of British East Africa "a man may marry as many wives as he can support, and rich men have

[1] Rev. John Roscoe, *The Baganda* (London, 1911), p. 83.

[2] Rev. John Roscoe, in a letter to me, dated "Ovington Rectory, Thetford, 14th July 1916." Compare J. Roscoe, *The Baganda* (London, 1911), p. 83, from which we learn that it was with his first wife that a man was bound to fulfil the taboos of journeying or going to war ; further that a man was compelled to take his second wife from his paternal grandmother's clan, and that this second wife, whom he called *Nasaza*, " had her special duties, such as shaving him, cutting his nails, and so disposing of the hair and nail-chips that they should not fall into an enemy's hands."

had as many as forty wives.   Each wife has her own house,
and with her children attends to a portion of her husband's
property, both live-stock and plantations.   The first wife is
always the chief wife, and her eldest son is considered the
eldest son of the family, even if one of the other wives
bears a son first."[1]   "In Masai families the first wife
remains the chief wife, even if she ceases to be a favourite,
and the arrangement of the affairs of the household is in
her hands."[2]   Among the Wanyamwesi of German East
Africa "polygamy of course exists, but the first wife is
considered the principal one," and "at a man's death the
eldest son of his principal wife inherits the larger portion
of the property, including the other wives of his father."[3]
Similarly among the Sangos of German East Africa
"the wife first married is the chief wife.   She takes precedence of all others.   The husband must build her house
for her first, and so on.   The other wives occupy a subordinate position in regard to her.   Nevertheless her
children, in the matter of inheritance, are only on an
equality with the children of the other wives.   An exception is made among chiefs.   The eldest son of this wife is
the ruler, but gets no more of the inheritance than the
other children."[4]   Among the tribes on the south-eastern

[1] A. C. Hollis, *The Nandi, their Language and Folk-lore* (Oxford, 1909), p. 64.

[2] S. L. Hinde and H. Hinde, *The Last of the Masai* (London, 1901), p. 76.

[3] Lionel Decle, *Three Years in Savage Africa* (London, 1898), p. 348. In many other African tribes it is similarly customary for the eldest son, as principal heir, to inherit all his father's wives except his own mother. For examples see L. Decle, *op. cit.* p. 486 ; *Emin Pasha in Central Africa* (London, 1888), pp. 86, 209, 230 ; Franz Stuhlmann, *Mit Emin Pascha ins Herz von Afrika* (Berlin, 1894), pp. 93, 525 ; E. Nigmann, *Die Wahehe* (Berlin, 1908), p. 61 ; John Roscoe, *The Northern Bantu* (Cambridge, 1915), pp. 261, 263 ; John H. Weeks, *Among Congo Cannibals* (London, 1913), p. 111 ; C. T. Wilson and R.

W. Felkin, *Uganda and the Egyptian Soudan* (London, 1882), i. 187, 188, ii. 49 ; W. Bosman, "The Coast of Guinea," in John Pinkerton's *Voyages and Travels* (London, 1808–1814), xvi. 480, 528 ; H. Ling Roth, *Great Benin* (Halifax, 1903), p. 97 ; N. W. Thomas, *Anthropological Report on the Edo-Speaking Peoples of Nigeria*, Part i. (London, 1910) pp. 69, 74, 75, 76, 78, 79, 86, 87 ; Theodor Waitz, *Anthropologie der Naturvölker* (Leipsic, 1860–1877), ii. 115 ; A. H. Post, *Afrikanische Jurisprudenz* (Oldenburg and Leipsic, 1887), i. 419 *sqq.* Absalom's treatment of his father's concubines (2 Samuel xvi. 21 *sq.*) suggests that a similar custom formerly obtained in Israel.

[4] Missionar Heese, "Sitte und Brauch der Sango," *Archiv für Anthropologie*, Neue Folge, xii. (1913) p. 137.

banks of Lake Tanganyika "when the father of a family
is polygamous, he must build a different house for each
of his wives. The first in date has always ᐟ the first
rank, and generally lives in the principal house. The
secondary wives have all therefore their separate establishments and receive the husband at their table according to his good pleasure, but in a rotation of a sort ;
for customary law obliges him to hold the balance
nearly even." [1]   "We have said that the first wife kept
a superior position in the family. She is dressed more
elegantly and stylishly. It is she who distributes to the
secondary wives the meat, fish, beans, and everything that,
with *ougali*, makes up the ordinary fare. In this distribution she naturally reserves for herself a share proportionate
to her rank. She has also the special right of enjoying,
for herself and her children, the property of her husband,
when he at his death leaves no surviving brother. This
peculiar position is not subject to the caprice of the husband.
It cannot be infringed unless the first wife chooses to quit
the family hearth." [2]   Moreover, in these tribes "the children
of the first wife are regarded as the eldest of the family
and take precedence over the children of later wives." [3]

Superiority
h first
wife in
North-

Rhodesia
and British
Central
Africa.   Among the Ainamwanga and Awiwa of North-Eastern
Rhodesia "the first wife married by law and custom is
treated as superior to the second wife, who may have had
only a proxy-*Bwinga* marriage or even no ceremony at
all. But an inherited wife carries with her her previous
status. Thus the widow of an elder brother, on being
inherited, ranks officially before the first wife of her in-
heritor (the deceased man's brother) ; she has the privilege
of joining in the prayers and assisting in the other rites of
family worship. The husband may still show his private
preference for the wife of his choice, though to neglect an
inherited wife would be considered very wrong if done in
public." [4]   Among the Angoni ᐟ of British Central Africa

[1] Mgr. Lechaptois, *Aux Rives du
Tanganika* (Algiers, 1913), p. 125.
[2] Mgr. Lechaptois, *Aux Rives du
Tanganika*, pp. 126 *sq.*
[3] Mgr. Lechaptois, *Aux Rives du
Tanganika*, p. 123.

[4] J. C. C. Coxhead, *The Native Tribes
of North-Eastern Rhodesia, their Laws
and Customs* (London, 1914), p. 52.
(*The Royal Anthropological Institute,
Occasional Papers*, No. 5). *Bwinga*
is the native name for the marriage

"the woman a man first marries is looked upon as his head wife ; " and the law of succession is "that the eldest son of the chief, by his first wife (should she have been secured by purchase), shall succeed the father. Should he have only female issue, a daughter will succeed, should the chief have no brother."[1] Among the Anyanjas, at the southern end of Lake Nyasa, "the first wife is the head wife, she does no cleaning nor cooking ; a man may change his head wife, but must sleep equally with each wife, otherwise she may bring a case against him ; each wife lives in a separate house, occasionally in a room of a large one."[2] Among the tribes of British Central Africa, "the chief wife is generally the woman that was married first.   There may be exceptions.   For instance, if the principal wife be betrothed in infancy to a full-grown man, this man will take a female ' to fill the place of the betrothed infant.'   After being married for a year or two the husband is almost expected to get junior wives.   These the chief wife, as a matter of courtesy, calls her younger sisters (*apwao*).   We have seen instances, however, when a great strife arose on the introduction of the other wives, and where the chief wife would threaten a separation, and carry it out too.   But these were instances rather of self-will than of conformity to the customs of the country.   It is an object of common aspiration to be possessed of five wives. The chief wife has the superintendence of the domestic and agricultural establishment.   She keeps the others at their work, and has power to exercise discipline upon them. The punishment she inflicts for laziness is to banish junior wives from meals until hunger bring them to their senses. When a junior wife is very obstreperous her superior may put her in a slave stick.   The authority of the chief wife is not a matter to jest with.   I know of a case of a junior wife that had her infant child promptly put upon the fire

---

ceremony, "The *Bwinga* was performed by the husband in person for the first wife, but for a second wife the husband was represented by a young boy who went through the ceremony as bis proxy" (J. C. C. Coxhead, *op. cit.* p. 50).

[1] R. Sutherland Rattray, *Some Folklore Stories and Songs in Chinyanja* (London, 1907), pp. 188 *sq.*, 202.
[2] H. S. Stannus, "Notes on some Tribes of British Central Africa," *Journal of the Royal Anthropological Institute*, xl. (1910) p. 309.

by this terrible overseer.   When a man is severely pressed by some legal action and has to pay heavy fines, he begins by selling off his junior wives.   When reduced to one wife he has reached the highest point of distress.   His free wife he cannot sell as she is under the protection of her surety." [1] In the old native kingdom of Monomotapa, which bordered on Sofala in Portuguese East Africa, " a man is allowed to take as many wives as he can keep, but the first remains the mistress ; her children are the heirs, and the other wives are regarded as little better than servants.   The king has more than a thousand wives, who are all daughters of his vassals ; but the first is the queen, and the eldest of her children is the heir to the throne." [2]

Superiority of the first wife in Western, Central, and Eastern Africa.

The preceding examples, drawn from widely separated tribes of Western, Central, and Eastern Africa, appear to raise a presumption that in these regions the principal wife of a polygamous family is generally she whom the husband first married.   It remains to consider the Bantu or, as they are commonly called, the Kafir tribes of South Africa, on whose marriage customs the particular theory of ultimo-geniture, which we are now discussing, has been especially founded.

Superiority of the first wife among the Herero of South-Western Africa.

Among the Herero, a tribe of nomadic herdsmen in South-Western Africa, it is the custom for chiefs or men rich in cattle to marry a number of wives in proportion to their wealth.   "The first wife gets the title of *omunene*, the 'great wife.'   Her hut is distinguished from those of the other wives by its size, by the number of hides which form the roof, and by the large quantity of firewood lying on the roof or stacked round about.   But the owner of the kraal does not live in the hut of the 'great wife' ; he inhabits a

[1] Duff Macdonald, *Africana* (London, Edinburgh, and Aberdeen, 1882), i. 134 *sq.*   As usual, this writer gives no indication of the particular tribes to which his description applies.   Miss Alice Werner's account of the marriage customs of these tribes is also somewhat vague, but in the course of it she mentions the Yaos, Anyanjas, and Angonis (*The Natives of British Central Africa*, London, 1906, pp. 132 *sq.*).   Perhaps Mr. Duff Macdonald's descrip- tion holds good of one or all of these tribes.

[2] O. Dapper, *Description de l'Afrique* (Amsterdam, 1686), p. 391.   For more evidence as to the superiority of the first wife in polygamous marriages in Africa, see A. H. Post, *Afrikanische Jurisprudenz* (Oldenburg and Leipsic, 1887), i. 312, by whom many of the foregoing instances have already been cited.

hut of his own. The other wives are called *ovombanda*, that is, 'the women taken afterwards.' Their huts stand round about in the kraal or at a distance on the larger cattle stations."[1]   The rules of inheritance among the Herero are complicated by the existence of a curious double system of clans, one set hereditary in the paternal and the other hereditary in the maternal line ;[2] but it may be said broadly that in the tribe descent both of power and of property is traced in the female line and is regulated by the principle of primogeniture. Thus the chieftainship descends, not to the chief's own eldest son, but to the eldest son of his eldest sister ;[3] in the paternal clans the property descends, not to a man's own eldest son, but to the eldest son of his eldest sister ;[4] and in the maternal clans property descends to the eldest sister of the deceased, whether man or woman.[5]   Thus in every case primogeniture, not ultimogeniture, controls the inheritance.

Among the Ovambo, another Bantu tribe of South-Western Africa, polygamy also prevails ; the richer a man is, the more wives he has ; chiefs often have ten or fifteen or even more. Among the wives there is always one who ranks as the principal wife, and generally she is the one whom the husband first married.[6]   The descent of power and property is regulated among the Ovambo, as among the Herero, by the principles of mother-kin and primogeniture ; hence the chieftainship descends, not to the late chief's eldest son, but to his eldest surviving brother, or, failing a brother, to the eldest son of his eldest sister.[7]   Here again there is no hint of ultimogeniture.

Superiority he first wife among the South-Western Africa.

Among the Basutos also polygamy is customary, and "the marriage of all the wives is contracted in a similar manner ; but a very marked distinction exists between the first and those who succeed her. The choice of the *great* wife (as she is always called) is generally made by the father, and is an event in which all the relations are

Superiority f the first wife among the asu os.

[1] J. Irle, *Die Herero* (Gütersloh, 1906), p. 109.

[2] J. Irle, *Die Herero*, pp. 144 *sqq*. As to this double system of clans, namely the *otuzo* (paternal clans) and the *omaanda* (maternal clans), see *Totemism and Exogamy*, ii. 357 *sqq*.

[3] J. Irle, *Die Herero*, p. 137.

[4] J. Irle, *Die Herero*, p. 146.

[5] J. Irle, *D'e Herero*, p. 145.

[6] H. Tonjes, *Ovamboland Land, Leute, Mission* (Berlin, 1911), p. 132.

[7] H. Tonjes, *op. cit.* pp. 130 *sq*.

interested. The others, who are designated by the name of *serete* (heels), because they must on all occasions hold an inferior position to the mistress of the house, are articles of luxury, to which the parents are not obliged to contribute. These wives of a second order are exactly what Bilhah and Zilpah were to Jacob. In the reigning families, only the children of the great wife have the right of succeeding their father. The chief of the Basutos can hardly keep an account of the children that are born to him; still, when asked by foreigners how many he has, he answers 'Five,' only alluding to those of his first wife. He says sometimes that he is a widower, which means that he has lost his real wife, and has not raised one of his sixty concubines to the rank she occupied. She has been dead for more than twenty years, and her dwelling is kept in perfect order, and still bears her name. The chief would have thought he was offering an insult to the memory of the deceased by introducing another partner to this retreat, where the sons of Mamohato take up their abode when they visit their native village. . . . The inheritance of the father belongs of right to the sons of the first wife; and these, with the eldest at their head, give what they choose to the other offspring of their father. . . . The idea of that which is improper and anomalous In polygamy is so inherent in every human conscience, that many natives dread dying near a wife of second order; that is called, in the language of the Basutos, 'making a bad death.' The wives of the first rank consider their rights so firmly established, that, in certain cases, they themselves encourage their husbands to become polygamists. They are prompted by motives. of interest and idleness, as they intend to put off upon others the most laborious of their occupations." [1]

These facts lend no countenance to the view of those who look for ultimogeniture among the Kafirs, and who find the origin of the custom in a preference for the last over the first wife of a polygamous family. However, it is true that in a certain group of Kafir tribes in South-Eastern Africa the principal wife of a chief and the mother of his heir is often not his first wife, and that she

[1] E. Casalis, *The Basutos* (London, 1861), pp. 186-188.

may be even his last wife. But it is to be carefully observed, first, that even in tribes where the principal wife of a chief is usually one of his later wives, the principal wife of a commoner is still as a rule the first married ; and, second, even where the principal wife of a chief is a later wife or the last wife, it is still not her youngest but her eldest son who inherits the chieftainship, so that here also, as in most African tribes, succession is regulated by primogeniture and not by ultimogeniture.

Amongst the Bantu tribes in which the principal wife is commonly either the first or a later wife according as her husband is a commoner or a chief, are the Thonga, who inhabit the southern part of Mozambique, about Delagoa Bay. In this tribe, so far as the families of commoners are concerned, "the first wife is certainly the most respected ; she is called the 'great one' (*nsati liwe' nkulu*) ; those who are taken in marriage afterwards being the 'little wives.' She is the true wife and acts as such in some old rites, those which accompany widowhood and the foundation of the village."[1] "There are amongst the Thonga some striking customs, giving to the 'first' or 'great' wife a special position, which seem to confirm the hypothesis of a primitive monogamy. The first of these is the ritual incision made by the first wife in the inguinal region after the death of the husband ; it is not performed by the other widows. In the same way the widower accomplishes this rite only after the death of the first wife and not when 'little wives' die. The second one is met with, in the rite of the foundation of the village ; . . . the first wife has a special part to play in these significant customs. When I asked Magingi, an old Rikatla heathen, why such a difference was made between the first wife and her co-wives, he told me : 'The first one is the true one and the others are but thieves. That is why it is said at the death of the first wife : "the house of the husband has been crushed" (*a tjhobekelwi hi yindlu ya kwe*). When another dies, it is only said : "he has lost a wife (*a felwi hi nsati*)."" [2]

In some Kafi tribes of South-Africa a chief's wife and the mother of his heir is often not his first wife. Superiority of the . . . ; among commoners in th Thonga tribe.

[1] Henri A. Junod, *The Life of a South African Tribe* (Neuchatel, 1912–1913), i. 186 *sq.*

[2] Henri A. Junod, *The Life of a South African Tribe*, i. 272 *sq.*

But while among Thonga commoners the first wife is the principal wife and occupies a position of strongly marked superiority over the wives whom the husband marries afterwards, among Thonga chiefs the principal wife, the mother of the heir to the throne, is usually not the first but a later wife. She is called "the wife of the country," perhaps because the lord of the land is to be born from her, or perhaps rather because it is a rule that she must be bought with money collected from all the people. Yet though she is in a sense the principal wife, she does not rank as the equal of the first wife in certain respects; for at her death the chief does not have an incision made in his groin, as he does at the death of his first wife: in short, on a comparison between these two wives "the first in date remains the first from the ritual point of view." [1]

If we ask why, in contrast to the wives of Thonga commoners, the principal wife of a Thonga chief should not be the one whom he married first, the answer appears to be that the custom rests on a curious aversion which the chief entertains to seeing his grandchild; "there is a saying, a precept of the royal code, as follows: *Hosi a yi faneli ku bona ntukulu*, a chief must never see his grandson, *i.e.* the one who will eventually succeed his son in the royal line." Hence in order to satisfy his father in this respect the heir does not marry his official wife, the "wife of the country," until after his father's death, and thus he spares the old man the pain of looking on the face of the grandchild who will be his next successor but one on the throne. But the heir, if he is of mature age, is at liberty to marry other wives in his father's lifetime; and the first of these, though she cannot give birth to the heir, will always possess the usual superiority in religious ritual over all the subsequent wives, including the "wife of the country," the mother of the heir. [2]

The writer who records these customs does not assign any motive for a chief's reluctance to behold the grandchild who will ultimately reign after him. It may be that the reluctance springs merely from a natural unwillingness

[1] Henri A. Junod, *op. cit.* i. 273, 341, 348, compare p. 198.   [2] Henri A. Junod, *op. cit.* i. 273, 342 *sq.*

on the part of the chief to be reminded of the lapse of time
and the approach of the hour when he must quit the stage
to make room for another.   Yet it is difficult to suppose
that a sentiment so contrary to the instinctive love of
offspring could suffice to originate the custom in question ;
and accordingly I have conjectured that the aversion to
beholding a son's son dates from a time when the birth of a
grandson was the signal for deposing or even putting to
death the chief, his grandsire, on the plea that a grandfather
must be too old and feeble to handle the reins of power.[1]
The conjecture is confirmed by the observation that in
these tribes the chief apparently entertains a similar objection
to looking on the face even of the infant son, his own offspring, who will afterwards reign in his stead.   For when his
principal wife, she who is called " the wife of the country,"
perceives that she will in due course present her lord with an
heir, she is sent away, under pretext of illness, from the
capital into one of the provinces.   It may not be whispered
abroad that she is with child, for, from this moment, every
precaution must be taken to hide the future chief.   If the
infant should prove to be a boy, the knowledge of it is kept
secret.   Only the most renowned doctors of the country,
whose loyalty to the chief is beyond reproach, assemble to
watch the birth and to prepare the precious fluid, which,
drunk by the infant daily, is believed to promote its growth
even better than its mother's milk.   When the queen walks
about carrying the baby on her back, she covers it with
a cloth to prevent any one from seeing whether it be a boy
or a girl.   She will even dress the boy in girl's clothing, because it is dangerous to say in a loud voice, " This
child will be a chief."   Such an imprudent declaration would
bring bad luck on the little one, and to dress him in boy's
clothes would be equally disastrous.[2]   All these precautions
to conceal the birth of an heir may be intended to soothe
the jealousy of the child's father, by removing from his sight
the youthful rival who is one day to supplant him.

Unnatural as such paternal jealousy may seem to us, it

formerly rr a e chief may have been pet . . . or killed on the birth of a grandson. This explanation is confirmed by a similar eluct nce on the art of a chief o se s o vn son

[1] See above, pp. 480 *sq.*

[2] Henri A. Junod, *The Life of a* *South African Tribe*, i. 341.   As to the medicine administered to infants to make them grow, see *id.* i. 46 *sq.*

might easily have originated under an old rule of succession like that which prevailed in Polynesia and particularly in Tahiti, where as soon as a king had a son born to him he was compelled by custom to abdicate the throne in favour of the infant;[1] for even when the custom had been abolished or had fallen into desuetude, the feelings which it engendered might easily survive and find expression in a practice of concealing the royal infant from the eyes of his jealous parent. On this hypothesis the declared reluctance of a Thonga chief to see his grandson, and his apparent reluctance to behold his own son, are both to be explained as relics of an ancient usage of deposing, if not of killing, the ruler as soon as he came to be regarded as super-annuated, the signal for his deposition or death being given by the birth either of a son or of a grandson. If that was so, it seems probable that the more stringent practice, which superseded a chief the moment he became a father, was afterwards relaxed and replaced by a milder practice, which suffered him to rule until he attained to the rank of a grandfather. However, it is possible that the curious veil of secrecy thrown over the birth and childhood of a Thonga chief's son is to be explained on a totally different principle as designed to protect the infant from the baneful influence of envious demons who lie in wait for children. The practice of dressing the boy as a girl favours the latter interpretation ; for such a change of costume is known to be adopted else-where as a protection against the evil eye.[2]

Among the tribes which occupy what used to be called

---

[1] See The Dying God, p. 190 (The Golden Bough, Third Edition, Part iii.). To the authorities there cited I would now add John Turnbull, Voyage round the World (London, 1813), pp. 134, 137, 188 sq., 344, who says, "By the laws of Otaheite the son, immediately on his birth, succeeds to the dignity of his father, the father from that instant becoming only administrator for his child" (p. 134); and again, "The custom of the son disinheriting his father exists here [in the island of Ulitea] as at Otaheite, accompanied by circumstances still more degrading and unnatural. From the birth, or at least the manhood of the son, the whole authority of the father vanishes ; and, however great or powerful he might have been before, he now becomes a petty chief. The father of this king made us a visit, but with so little appearance of rank or influence, that had he not been pointed out to us as such, we should not have known him ; he had absolutely nothing about him which could lead to any suspicion that he was above the meanest of his countrymen" (pp. 188 sq.).

[2] Evidence of this has been cited by me in a note, "The Youth of Achilles," in The Classical Review, vii. (1893) pp. 292 sq., and in a note on Pausanias, i, 22, 6 (vol. ii. p. 266).

Kaffraria in South-Eastern Africa, a chief's principal or "great" wife. the mother of his heir, is also frequently, perhaps generally, not the first but a later wife.   The reason why in this group of tribes the "great" wife of a chief is seldom his first wife, has been explained as follows : "The first wife of a Kafir chief, 'the wife of his youth,' is not unfrequently taken from amongst the families of his own councillors.   He is as yet unknown to fame ; his wealth is not so considerable as it is to be.   After a while his alliance becomes more worthy the attention of those of other tribes, whose daughters demand a higher dowry than was required by the humbler parents of his first wife.   Another and another are sent to him ; for it must be borne in mind that a Kafir chief does not choose his own wives.   He is surprised from time to time by the arrival of a bridal party, bringing with them as his offered bride some chief's daughter whom he has never seen before.   The danger of refusing her is according to the rank and power of the family to which she belongs, for to decline such an alliance is to offer a public insult to the whole tribe.   The usual order of things, then, is, that as a chief grows older and richer, wives of higher rank are sent to him, and the reasons which operate against their refusal operate also against their having an inferior rank allotted to them in the successional distribution.   The mother of him who is to be the 'great son' may thus be the last wife the chief has taken, which is, in fact, sometimes the case." [1]

In these tribes a chief commonly has three wives who rank above all the rest, and bear respectively the titles of the "great wife," the "right-hand wife," and the "left-hand wife," or "the wife of the ancestors."   The "right-hand wife" is usually the first wife whom the chief marries, but it is not always so ; sometimes both the "great wife" and the "right-hand wife" are chosen and invested with their dignity by the chief in council.   In the kraal the hut of the "right-hand wife" stands to the right of the hut of the "great wife"; and we may conjecture, though this does not appear to be expressly affirmed, that the hut of the "left-hand wife"

Among the Kaffraria a chief's ... a wife, the mother of frequently not his ... ... a later wife.

The "great ... he "right-hand wife," an the "left-hand wife" of a ... chief.

[1] Rev. H. H. Dugmore, in Col. John Maclean's *Compendium of Kafir Laws and Customs* (Cape Town, 1866), pp. 25 *sq.*   Compare Rev. James Mac- donald, "Bantu Customs and Legends," *Folk-lore*, iii. (1892) pp. 338 *sq.* · G. M'Call Theal, *Records of South-Eastern Africa*, vii. (1901) pp. 396 *sq.*

stands to the left of the hut of the "great wife." Of the
three wives, the "great wife" ranks highest, the "right-hand
wife" next, and the "left-hand wife" lowest. With the
"left-hand wife" rests the responsibility of providing an heir,
in case the "great wife" has no son. The son of the "left-
hand wife" is called the "representative of the ancestors."
The office of "left-hand wife" is a comparatively modern
institution, having been created by the chief Graika some six
generations ago. On the other hand, the distinction between
the "great wife" and the "right-hand wife" is of great
antiquity. These three wives form three main "houses," and
however many wives a chief may have, they are all added as
"rafters" to one or other of the three main "houses," which
they are supposed to support. The eldest son of the "great
wife" is the heir, and succeeds to the chieftainship on the
death of his father. The eldest son of the "right-hand wife"
cannot succeed to the chieftainship till all the other wives
have failed to supply a son. On the other hand, this eldest
son of the "right-hand wife" is constituted the head of a
certain allotted portion of the tribe, and on the death of his
father he assumes the separate jurisdiction of that portion.
He thus becomes the originator of a new tribe, acknowledging the precedency in rank of his brother, the son of the
"great wife," but independent of him except in matters
involving the general relations of the tribes at large. Moreover, if the old chief dies while his heir, the eldest son of the
"great wife," is still a minor, which he may often do, since
the "great wife" is not uncommonly married by him comparatively late in life, the "right-hand" house assumes the
regency. Thus a conflict of interest between the two brothers
may easily arise, and the elder brother, the son of the "right-
hand wife," may become a dangerous rival of his younger
brother, the rightful heir to the throne. Accordingly there
are numberless legends, most of them marvellous, but some
of them probably historical, of the perfidy of the "right-hand
wife's" son and the ultimate triumph of the true heir.[1]

[1] Col. John Maclean, *Compendium of Kafir Laws and Customs* (Cape Town, 1866), pp. 11 sq., 25 sq., 45, 69 sq., 113 sq.; Rev. James Macdonald, "Bantu Customs and Legends," *Folk-lore*, iii. (1892) pp. 338 sq.; G. M'Call Theal, *Records of South-Eastern Africa*, vii. (1901) pp. 396 sq.; Dudley Kidd, *The Essential Kaffir* (London, 1904), pp. 13 sq., 360 sq.

It is this possible or even general succession of a younger in preference to an elder half-brother among these tribes, which has created a specious but illusive appearance of junior right or ultimogeniture in Kafir law.   The writers who have been imposed upon by this appearance have failed to observe that the chief, though possibly younger than many of his half-brothers, the sons of other wives, is, nevertheless, invariably the eldest son of his mother ; [1] so that even in these tribes the succession to the throne is regulated by the principle of primogeniture, not of ultimogeniture.

When we quit the sphere of public law, regulating the succession to the chieftainship, and turn to private law, regulating the succession to property, the prevalence of primogeniture as opposed to ultimogeniture in Kafir law is still more clearly manifest ; for in ordinary families, not related to the chief, the first wife married is usually the " great wife," [2] and since the heir is always the eldest son of the "great wife," it follows that among commoners the heir is generally the eldest son not only of his mother but of his father also, and therefore that he is older than all his half-brothers, the sons of his father's other wives ; in short, he is the eldest male of the whole family.   However, it need not be so.   The " great wife " is not necessarily the wife first married ; a commoner, like a chief, may have three principal wives, to wit, the " great wife," the " right-hand wife," and the " left-hand wife " ; and in that case each of these three women is at the head of a separate house or establishment.   The eldest son of each house inherits all the property which has been allotted by his father in his lifetime to that house ; but if the father has neglected in his life to declare in a formal and public manner what portion of his property he has assigned to his several establishments, he may be said to die intestate, and in that case the eldest son of the " great house " takes possession, as heir-at-law, of the whole of his father's estate,

---

[1] Col. John Maclean, *Compendium of Kafir Laws and Customs*, p. 11, " The eldest son of the 'great' wife is presumptive heir to his father's dignity, and succeeds him in his general government " ; G. M'Call Theal, *Records of South-Eastern Africa*, vii. (1901) p.

396, " It generally happened that his consort of highest rank was taken when he was of advanced age. . . . She was termed the great wife, and her eldest son was the principal heir."

[2] Dudley Kidd, *The Essential Kafir*, p. 14.

though he is bound at the same time to care and provide for all his father's establishments.[1] Thus in private as in public law the succession of Kafir tribes is determined by primogeniture.

We conclude that the theory which would derive ultimogeniture from a preference for the youngest wife in a polygamous family, derives no support from Kafir law and custom.

Relative
o of
wives in
polygam-
outside of
Africa.

The relative position of wives in polygamous families outside of Africa has not yet, so far as I know, been fully examined ; but a considerable body of evidence on the subject has been collected by Dr. Edward Westermarck,[2] and it tends to show that elsewhere, as in Africa, the woman who is first married usually ranks above the later wives and enjoys a position of dignity and authority in her husband's household. As this superiority of the first wife bears directly on the theory of ultimogeniture which is now under discussion, I propose to illustrate it by examples drawn from races in many parts of the world.

In India
the first
wife of a
polygam-
u
is generally
the chief
wife.

In ancient India "a peculiar sanctity," we are told, "seems to have been attributed to the first marriage, as being that which was contracted from a sense of duty, and not merely for personal gratification. The first married wife had precedence over the others, and her firstborn son over his half-brothers. It is probable that originally the secondary wives were considered as merely a superior class of concubines, like the handmaids of the Jewish patriarchs."[3] To the same effect another authority on ancient Hindu law observes that in the literature "there is frequently mention of the privileges of the eldest, that is, the first married wife ; for even among several wives, who were equal in respect of birth, she as a rule ranked first."[4] Among the Chuhras, the sweeper or scavenger caste of the Punjab, "two wives are allowed ;

[1] Col. John Maclean, *Compendium of Kafir Laws and Customs*, pp. 45, 69, 113 ; Dudley Kidd, *The Essential Kafir*, pp. 360 *sq.*

[2] Edward Westermarck, *The History of Human Marriage* (London, 1891), pp. 441-448.

[3] John D. Mayne, *A Treatise of Hindu Law and Usage*, Third Edition (Madras and London, 1883), p. 82, § 85.

[4] Julius Jolly, *Recht und Sitte* (Strasburg, 1896), p. 64, § 19 (in G. Bühler's *Grundriss der Indo-Arischen Philologie und Altertumskunde*, vol. ii.).

the former of whom is considered the head, and has peculiar rites and privileges. The wives live together in the same house." [1]   Among the Bhots or Bhotiyas, a tribe apparently of Tibetan origin in North-Western India, "the wife of the first marriage is the head wife, and she receives by inheritance a share one-tenth in excess of that given to the other wives. [2]   Among the Kharwars, a Dravidian tribe of land-owners and cultivators in South Mirzapur, "a man may marry as many wives as he can afford to purchase and maintain. They live in separate rooms in the same house. The senior wife is head of the household, and is treated with respect at social meetings." [3]   Similarly among the Parahiyas, another Dravidian tribe of Mirzapur, "polygamy is recognized, but as a rule a man does not take a second wife unless the first is barren. The senior wife rules the household and shares in the family worship ; if she is not treated with respect, they believe that the family goes to ruin. The wives live apart in separate huts." [4]   Among the Kadirs, a people of short stature and dark skins, who lead an isolated life in the jungles and forests of Southern India, "in the code of polygynous etiquette, the first wife takes precedence over the others, and each wife has her own cooking utensils." [5]   The Khamtis, a people of the Shan or Tai stock in north-eastern Assam, "are not restricted to one wife. I do not, however, recollect having met with more than two to one husband, and though the second wife may be the favorite companion of her lord, the supremacy of the first wife is always maintained." [6]   In the Old Kuki clans, as they are called, of Manipur, "polygamy is, as a rule, permitted. Among the Anal and Lamgang, the first wife is entitled to the company of her husband for five nights, the second for four, and the third for three." [7] With regard to the Meitheis of Manipur we are told that "in polygamous households the husband's attentions to the several wives are strictly regulated by precedence, the eldest

---

[1] H. A. Rose, *Glossary of the Tribes and Castes of the Punjab and North-West Frontier Provinces*, ii. (Lahore, 1911) p. 190.

[2] W. Crooke, *Tribes and Castes of the North-Western Provinces and Oudh* (Calcutta, 1896), ii. 62.

[3] W. Crooke, *op. cit.* iii. 241.

[4] W. Crooke, *op. cit.* iv. 127.

[5] Edgar Thurston, *Castes and Tribes of Southern India* (Madras, 1909), iii. 19.

[6] E. T. Dalton, *Descriptive Ethnology of Bengal* (Calcutta, 1872), p. 8.

[7] J. Shakespear, *The Lushei Kuki Clans* (London, 1912), p. 155.

getting twice the nominal share, of the wife next below her. In actual practice, I am given to understand that these rules are often broken."[1] Speaking of the Naga tribes of Manipur the same writer observes that "polygamy is permitted among the Tangkhuls, who have a knowledge of the practice of the Manipuris in this respect. It is not very common, as separate establishments must be maintained, and custom demands that, as in Manipur, the greater attentions should still be paid to the elder wife."[2]

In other pa s Asia the first wife of ous family is generally the chief wife.

In Burma "polygamy is legal, but except among officials and the wealthy, is seldom practised. . . . Though all the wives are equally legitimate, there is always one chief wife, generally the first married, whose house is the family home; the lesser wives being provided each with her own house, perhaps living in another town or village, but never under the same roof as the head wife."[3] In Siam "the rich and the great take several wives ; but the first, with whom they have performed the ceremony of the *khan mak*, is always regarded as the only legitimate spouse. They call her 'the great wife,' whereas the others go by the name of 'little wives.' She is the true mistress of the house ; she and her children inherit all the husband's property, whereas the 'little wives' and their children have no right to anything except what their husband gives them personally, or what the heir may be pleased to bestow on them."[4] Among the Koryaks of north-eastern Siberia, "in a household with more than one wife, the first is considered the mistress of the house. The second wife consults the first in everything, and carries out her instructions."[5] Among the Chukchees, at the north-eastern extremity of Asia, who practise polygamy, "the position of the several wives is different in different families. The first wife is generally much older, and has had several children when the young wife makes her first appearance in the family. In such cases the first wife is the mistress, while the second

[1] T. C. Hodson, *The Meitheis* (London, 1908), p. 77.

[2] T. C. Hodson, *The Naga Tribes of Manipur* (London, 1911), p. 94.

[3] C. J. F. S. Forbes, *British Burma and its People* (London, 1878), pp. 64, 65.

[4] Mgr. Pallegorix, *Description du* *Royaume Thai ou Siam* (Paris, 1854), i. 231.

[5] Waldemar Jochelson, *The Koryak* (Leyden and New York, 1908), p. 754 (*The Jesup North Pacific Expedition*, vol. vi., *Memoir of the American Museum of Natural History, New York*).

is treated almost like a maid. The first wife sits with the husband in the warm sleeping-room, while the second works outside in the cold, prepares the food, and serves it." [1]

Among the Kirghiz of Semipalatinsk, a province of south-western Siberia, polygamy has been customary with the richer nomads ever since the conversion of the people to Islam, which, while it diminished the number of their gods, increased the number of their wives. As Kirghiz wives are expected to work hard for their living, it is in the interest of the first wife that her husband should marry others, who will relieve her, to some extent, of her laborious duties ; nor has she much reason to be jealous of her younger rivals, since women age rapidly and soon lose their youthful bloom under the severe conditions of nomadic life. With regard to the relative position of the wives, we are told that, " as the bride-price *(kalym)* is regarded as earnest-money, and the wife as an article that has been bought, the first thing expected of her is submission, like that of a female slave ; the only exception is made in favour of the first wife, on whom age confers a privilege. The second, third, or fourth wife may never appear uninvited in the tent of the master of the family ; she must always remain in the lower part *(eden)* of the tent ; she may never sit down by the fire, and still less take a place at the common table, and she must content herself with the leavings of the meal. In accordance with customary law the first wife, if she is energetic enough, need brook no infringement of her privilege as mistress supreme. By her intrigues, or sometimes even by violence, she can hinder her husband from marrying a second wife, who is called *Takal-kadin* (' concubine') or *Kirnak* (' young wench ') ; and if she fails to do so, her faithless spouse must find a place for his new flame at a distance from the principal tent ; nay, even from that bower of love the first wife may chase her husband with a whip, and drive him to her own tent, whither, fretting and fuming, he must follow her amid the laughter and jeers of the spectators." [2]

In the Indian Archipelago " the wife of the first marriage

[1] Waldemar Bogoras, *The Chukchee* (Leyden and New York, 1904–1909), p. 600 (*The Jesup North Pacific Expedition*, vol. vii., *Memoir of the American Museum of Natural History, New York*).

[2] Hermann Vambery, *Das Türkenvolk* (Leipsic, 1885), p. 248.

is always the real mistress of the family, and the rest often little better than her handmaids. No man will give his daughter for a second or third wife to a man of his own rank, so that, generally, no wife but the first is of equal rank with the husband."[1] In Lampong, the most southernly district of Sumatra, "whoever can contrive to do so, marries several, not uncommonly four wives, and maintains besides a number of concubines. The third wife is subject to the first wife, and the fourth to the second, while the concubines have to obey all four. The first wife is the highest in rank, and has also the best room in the house. . . . The eldest son of the eldest wife is his father's successor ; but he does not inherit the whole property, only the half, while the other sons get the remaining half."[2] Among the Battas or Bataks of Central Sumatra " polygamy is allowed, but as the price of a wife is high, being about seven buffaloes or forty-five piasters, it follows that hardly any common villager possesses more than one, and monogamy is predominant in the country. To this rule the solitary exception is made by the Rajahs, who are almost the only opulent persons among the people ; they have always more wives than one, usually three, often five, but seldom more, and never more than eight, who all possess equal rights among themselves, except that the eldest, that is, the one who was first married, exercises a certain authority over the others."[3] Among the Bagobos of Mindanao, one of the Philippine Islands, " a man may have as many wives as he desires and can afford, but he may not take a second mate until a child has been born to the first union, or the wife has been proved beyond doubt to be barren. . . . The first wife is generally the lady of the house, and does not particularly object to having other girls added to the family, provided they are willing to obey her."[4] In New Zealand every Maori chief was at liberty to take as many wives as he pleased, but "the first wife was generally a lady of rank, and always viewed as the head, however many there might be, and of whatever

[1] John Crawford, *History of the Indian Archipelago* (London, 1820), i. 77.

[2] G. A. Wilken, "Over het huwe-lijks- en erfrecht bij de volken van Zuid-Sumatra," *De verspreide Geschriften* (The Hague, 1912), ii. 281 *sq.*

[3] Franz Junghuhn, *Die Battaländer auf Sumatra* (Berlin, 1847), ii. 133.

[4] Fay-Cooper Cole, *The Wild Tribes of Davao District, Mindanao* (Chicago, 1913), p. 103 (*Field Museum of Natural History, Publication 170*).

rank ; some were regarded as only servile ones." [1]   Among the Narrinyeri, an aboriginal tribe of South Australia, "polygamy is practised ; but there are seldom more than two wives. The eldest wife is the chief. An elderly wife has little objection to her husband having a younger one, as she is subordinate to her." [2]

Polygamy prevails among some but not all the Indian tribes of British Guiana, but "even when there is more than one wife, the first is almost always chiefly regarded and favoured ; those that are married afterwards seem to be taken more as domestic helpers of the first and real wife." [3] The Uaupes Indians of Brazil "generally have but one wife, but there is no special limit, and many have two or three, and some of the chiefs more ; the elder one is never turned away, but remains the mistress of the house." [4]   Among the Juris, Passes, Uainumas, Miranhas, and many other Indian tribes of Brazil, "the wife whom a man first married is regarded as the head-wife. Her hammock hangs next to that of her husband. Power, influence over the community, ambition, and temperament are the motives which lead the husband afterwards to take several subordinate wives or concubines to the number of five or six, but seldom more. To possess several wives is deemed a matter of luxury and vanity. Each of them gets her own hammock, and usually also a separate hearth, especially as soon as she has children. Despite frequent jealousy and quarrels, the eldest or head-wife exerts her influence in household affairs to such a pitch that on the decline of her personal charms she will herself introduce younger wives to her consort." [5]   The Araucanians of Chili may marry as many wives as they can pay for, but "the first wife, who is called *unendomo*, is always respected

Among the Indians of South America the first wife of a polygamous generally the chief wife

[1] Rev. Richard Taylor, *Te Ika A Maui, or New Zealand and its Inhabitants*, Second Edition (London, 1870), pp. 337 *sq.*
[2] Rev. George Taplin, in E. M. Curr's *The Australian Race* (Melbourne and London, 1886-1887), ii. 246. Compare *id.* "The Narrinyeri," in J. D. Wood's *The Native Tribes of South Australia* (Adelaide, 1879), p. 12, "In case of a man having two wives, the elder is always regarded as

the mistress of the hut or wurley."
[3] (Sir) Everard F. im Thurn, *Among the Indians of Guiana* (London, 1883), p. 223.
[4] Alfred Russel Wallace, *Narrative of Travels on the Amazon and Rio Negro* (London 1889), p. 346 (*The Minerva Library*).
[5] C. Fr. Phil. v. Martius, *Zur Ethnographie Amerika's, zumal Brasiliens* (Leipsic, 1867), pp. 105 *sq.*

as the real and legitimate one by all the others, who are called *inandomo*, or secondary wives. She has the management of the domestic concerns, and regulates the interior of the house." [1]

Among the Indians of Central and North America the first wife of a ygamous family is generally the chief wife.

Among the Mosquito Indians of Central America "polygamy obtains, some men having six wives each, and the king yet more. The first wife, who as a rule is betrothed from early infancy, is mistress commanding; her marriage is attended with festivities, and later additions to the harem are subject to her." [2] Concerning the Indian tribes who inhabit, or rather used to inhabit, Western Washington and North-Western Oregon, we are told that "the condition of the woman is that of slavery under any circumstances. She is the property of her father, of her nearest relative, or of her tribe, until she becomes that of her husband. She digs the roots and prepares them for winter, digs and dries clams, cures the fish which he catches, packs the horses, assists in paddling the canoe, and performs all the menial offices. The more wives a man possesses, therefore, the richer he is; and it is an object for him to purchase others as his means increase. The accession of a new wife in the lodge very naturally produces jealousy and discord, and the first often returns for a time in dudgeon to her friends, to be reclaimed by her husband when he chooses, perhaps after propitiating her by some presents. The first wife almost always retains a sort of predominance in the lodge; and the man, at least after his appetite for a subsequent one is satisfied, usually lives with her. Wives, particularly the later ones, are often sold or traded off." [3] Among the Tlingits or Thlinkeets of Alaska "polygamy is general, especially among the richer men, but the first wife always preserves a certain authority over the others." [4] Similarly among the Koniags of Alaska

[1] J. Ignatius Molina, *The Geographical, Natural, and Civil History of Chili* (London, 1809), ii. 115 *sq.*

[2] H. H. Bancroft, *Native Races of the Pacific States* (London, 1875-1876), i. , 29.

[3] George Gibbs, "Tribes of Western Washington and Northwestern Oregon," in *Contributions to North American Ethnology*, i. (Washington, 1877),

pp. 198 *sq.*

[4] H. J. Holmberg, "Ueber die Volker des Russischen Amerika," *Acta Societatis Scientiarum Fennicae*. iv. (Helsingfors, 1856) p. 313. To the same effect writes D Au el Krause, *Die Tlinkit-Indianer* (Jena, 1885), p. 220, "Rich men may have several wives, as many as they can maintain, but the first always ranks above the rest."

polygamy used to be prevalent ; rich men would have as many as five wives, but "the first wife always ranked above the rest."[1]   Of the Eskimo about Bering Strait we read that "men who are able to provide for them frequently take two or even more wives.   In such cases the first wife is regarded as the head of the family and has charge of the food."[2]   Among the Eskimo of Hudson's Bay, " when the family is prosperous the husband often takes a second wife, either with or without the approval of the first, who knows that her household duties will be lessened, but knows also that the favors of her husband will have to be divided with the second wife.   The second wife is often the cause of the first wife's leaving, though sometimes she is sent away herself. . . .   The sons of the first wife, if there be more than one wife, take precedence over those of the second or third wife. . . .   When the father becomes superannuated or his sons are old enough to enable him to live without exertion, the management of affairs devolves on the eldest son, and to the second is delegated the second place."[3]   Here the superiority of the first wife to the later wives, though it is not directly affirmed by the writer, may be inferred from the acknowledged superiority of her sons to the sons of the second or third wife.   Among the Greenlanders, before the arrival of Christian missionaries, polygamy was lawful, but few men had more than one wife, and in polygamous families "the first wife was reckoned the mistress."[4]

These examples, drawn from many different races in many different parts of the world, seem to show that where polygamy prevails the first wife generally occupies the principal place in the household, ranking above the other wives, exercising authority over them, and continuing to maintain her hold on the affections of her husband even when age and infirmity have robbed her of youthful grace and beauty.   And

[marginal notes: Among the and Greenlanders the first wife of a polygamist is generally the chief ..... In polygamous families generally the first wife is the chief wife, the heir is her eldest son.]

[1] H. J. Holmberg, *op. cit.* pp. 398 *sq.*

[2] E. W. Nelson, " The Eskimo about Bering Strait," *Eighteenth Annual Report of the Bureau of American Ethnology*, Part i. (Washington, 1899) p. 292.

[3] Lucien M. Turner, " Ethnology of the Ungava District, Hudson Bay Territory," *Eleventh Annual Report of the Bureau of Ethnology* (Washington, 1894), pp. 189, 190.

[4] Hans Egede, *Description of Greenland* (London, 1818), p. 140.

On the whole polygamy seems to favour primo-

rather than ultimo-geniture.

so far as the question of inheritance is raised in the foregoing instances, it seems to be always the eldest, not the youngest, son of the eldest wife who succeeds to his father's rank and property. Thus the evidence tells decidedly against the theory that ultimogeniture, or the preference for the youngest child in the inheritance, arises naturally through the favour accorded by the husband to the youngest wife in a polygamous family. On the contrary, the tendency of polygamy is apparently to promote primogeniture rather than ultimogeniture.

§ 10. *Ultimogeniture and Infanticide*

Possible connexion of ultimo-geniture with the custom of killing the firstborn.

In considering the causes which may have operated to produce a custom of ultimogeniture, the practice of infanticide should not, perhaps, be left wholly out of account. Many races in different parts of the world are reported to have been in the habit of putting all their firstborn children to death.[1] The motives for this barbarous custom are obscure, but among them in certain cases appears to have been a superstitious fear, that the birth of a firstborn son was in some way a menace to the life of the father. For example, among the Baganda "in most clans the first child born to a chief was awaited with considerable anxiety, because it was thought that the birth of a boy indicated that his father would die ; hence, if a male was born, the midwife strangled it, and gave out that it was born dead ; in this way the chief's life was ensured, otherwise, it was thought, he would die."[2] This practice of putting a chief's firstborn son to death, out of regard for the father's life, fits in with one of the alternative explanations which I have suggested for the remarkable precautions taken to conceal the birth of a chief's heir among the Thonga,[3] a tribe which belongs to the same Bantu stock as the Baganda ; the concealment of the infant may have been a substitute for an older practice of putting it to death. In fact, we are informed that down to comparatively recent times among the Kafir tribes of South Africa only

---

[1] The evidence has been collected by me in *The Dying God*, pp. 171 *sqq.* (*The Golden Bough*, Third Edition, Part iii.).

[2] John Roscoe, *The Baganda* (London, 1911), p. 54.

[3] See above, pp. 480 *sq.*, 549 *sq.*

one son of a chief was allowed to live.[1]   Which of the sons was spared, we are not told ; if it was the youngest, then certainly the practice of ultimogeniture existed in the utmost rigour among the chiefly families of Kafir tribes in South Africa ; but in the absence of definite and authentic evidence it would be rash to make any affirmation on the subject.   The Greek story how Zeus, the youngest of his brothers and sisters, succeeded his father Cronus on the throne of heaven, may perhaps contain a reminiscence of a practice of ultimogeniture carried out with the same ruthless severity ; for it is said that Cronus, having learned that he was destined to be vanquished by his son, took the precaution of swallowing his children as soon as they were born, and that Zeus, the youngest, was only saved from the fate of all his elder brothers and sisters by the cunning of his mother Rhea, who hid him in a cave and gave his cruel father a stone wrapt in swaddling bands to swallow instead of the babe.[2]

However, it seems unlikely that infanticide has had any share in establishing a custom of ultimogeniture.   For, in the first place, a practice of putting the firstborn to death, while it might explain a preference for second sons, could hardly account for the preference for youngest sons in the inheritance ; and, in the second place, a practice of killing all children except the youngest, if it ever existed, has probably been so rare that it can hardly have originated the widespread custom of ultimogeniture.

Nevertheless it may not be irrelevant to remark on the coincidence in ancient Israel of traces of ultimogeniture with almost indubitable traces of a systematic practice of putting firstborn children to death.[3]   The coincidence may

But a connexion of u timogeniture infanticide is improbable.

Traces in Israel both f geniture a practice of killing the firstborn

---

[1] Dudley Kidd, *The Essential Kafir*, p. 14.   According to Mr. Kidd, this rule was observed down to the time, six generations ago, when the custom of the "left-hand wife," or "wife of the ancestors" was instituted.   See above, pp. 551 *sq.*, 553.

[2] Hesiod, *Theogon.* 453-491.   In Finnish mythology we hear of a god named Mir-Susne-Khum, who was the youngest of his family, yet was appointed ruler of his elder brothers and

of men.   This pre-eminence, however, he attained, not by knocking his elder brothers on the head, but simply by anticipating them in tying his bridle to a silver post in front of his father's house.   See Miss M. A. Czaplicka, *Aboriginal Siberia* (Oxford, 1914), p. 289.

[3] For the evidence see *The Dying God*, pp. 166 *sqq.* (*The Golden Bough*, Third Edition, Part iii.).

be merely fortuitous ; still, in the difficulty and uncertainty which attend all inquiries into the origin of human institutions, we shall do well to keep our minds open to the possibility that after all among the Semites, and perhaps among other peoples, a causal connexion may be discovered to exist between infanticide and ultimogeniture.

§ 11. *Superstitions about youngest Children*

In conclusion it may be worth while to notice a few miscellaneous superstitions attaching to youngest children which have not found a place in the preceding pages.

Various super- stitions attaching e children in Europe, Asia Africa, and the Pacific. According to old German law, the mandrake, a plant to which magical and oracular virtues were ascribed, passed by inheritance on the death of the father to the youngest son, on condition that he buried a morsel of bread and a piece of money with his father's body in the coffin.[1] Similarly we have seen that among the Koryaks of North-Eastern Asia the sacred fire-board, a magical as well as a useful implement, is inherited by the youngest son or the youngest daughter.[2] Among the Ibibios, a tribe of Southern Nigeria, there are more witches than wizards ; and if a witch has children, she always passes her wicked knowledge to one of her daughters, usually to the youngest born.[3] In the Hervey Islands, South Pacific, the firstborn child, whether male or female, was deemed especially sacred. He or she ate separately, and the very door, through which he or she entered the paternal dwelling, became sacred and might be used by no one else. The eldest son inherited the greater part of his father's landed property, and all the younger brothers were bound to submit to his authority. In general, the chieftainship and the priesthood of the clan were held by the firstborn. Nevertheless, " by a curious perversion of ideas, the god was sometimes said to have taken up his abode in the youngest of the family, who was then invested

[1] Grimm, *Deutsche Sagen*² (Berlin, 1865-1866), No. 84, vol. i. pp. 117 *sq.*; J. Grimm, *Deutsche Rechtsalterthümer*³ (Gottingen, 1881), p. 475. Compare Ch. Elton, *Origins of English History*, pp. 219-221. As to the mandrake,

see below, vol. ii. pp. 372 *sqq.*
[2] Above, p. 476. Compare p. 475 as to the Chukchee.
[3] (Mrs.) D. Amaury Talbot, *Woman's Mysteries of a Primitive People* (London, 1915), p. 162.

by the clan with all the honours due to the firstborn. This was resorted to whenever the feebleness of intellect or lack of energy on the part of the real leader exposed the tribe to destruction."[1] However, in this case the transference of the rights of the eldest to the youngest was clearly a temporary expedient designed, by a sort of legal fiction, to commit the reins of power to stronger hands, and to justify the supersession of an incapable ruler.

Among the Akikuyu of British East Africa the ruling elders are charged with various religious duties, such as the offering of sacrifices and the cleansing of the people from the taint of ceremonial pollution. One of their most important functions is to purify the country from disease. Many measures are adopted for that salutary purpose, but the principal is this. A root or bulb called *kihoithia* is scooped out of the ground, and certain butterflies and insects are put in it, after which it is buried in some muddy place. This must be done by a man who is the last born of his mother, that is, his mother must be past the age of childbearing.[2]

Among the Taiyals, a tribe of mountaineers in the interior of Formosa, when the new grain is cooked for the first time, the youngest boy of the family must eat some of it before the others. When he has done so, the other members of the family follow his example. The food prepared from the new grain may not be given to strangers; further, it may not be consumed all at once, it must furnish the material for two meals. "All these superstitions," we are told, "involve a form of magic by which plentifulness of the crop is secured. A portion of the new crop is kept within the house and it is eaten until the new moon appears; the rest is placed in a store-room, whence it should not be removed before the new moon rises. This is also a form of magic to secure fertility. Like the moon, it must not wane, but wax."[3] If this explanation of the customs in question is correct, the

[1] Rev. William Wyatt Gill, *Life in the Southern Isles* (London, N.D.), pp. 46 *sq.*

[2] Hon. Charles Dundas, "The Organization and Laws of some Bantu tribes in East Africa," *Journal of the Royal Anthropological Institute*, xlv. (1915) pp. 246 *sq.*

[3] Shinji Ishii, "The Life of the Mountain People in Formosa," *Folklore*, xxviii. (1917) p. 123.

reason why the youngest boy eats the new grain before his elders may be a notion, that the crop will last the longer for being first eaten by that member of the family who may naturally be expected to live the longest ; by sympathetic magic he communicates his prospect of longevity to the grain which he takes into his body.

ADDENDA

Pt. i. Ch. iv. The Great Flood

PAGE 168.   With the ancient Greek tradition of a great inundation, consequent on the sudden opening of the Bosphorus and the Dardanelles, we may compare a modern Turkish tradition, which has been recorded at Constantinople.

The Turks say that Iskender-Iulcarni, by whom they mean Alexander the Great, lived before Moses and conquered both the East and the West.   In the course of his conquests he sent to demand tribute from Katifé, Queen of Smyrna, whose ruined castle bears her name (*Katifé-Calessi*) to this day.   But the queen not only refused the demand but threatened, in very insulting language, to drown the king if he persisted in pressing it.   Enraged at her reply, the conqueror resolved to punish the queen for her insolence by drowning her in a great flood.   "I will open the Bosphorus," said he, "and make of it a strait."   For that purpose he employed both Moslem and infidel workmen, from which we gather that, according to popular Turkish tradition, Mohammed must have lived, not only before Alexander the Great, but even before Moses.   Calmly overlooking this slight chronological difficulty, the story proceeds to relate that the infidel workmen received only one-fifth of the pay which rewarded the exertions of the true believers.   So the canal was in process of excavation.   But when it was nearly completed, Iskender, for some unexplained reason, reversed the proportions of the pay, giving the true believers only one-fifth of what he paid to the infidels. Consequently, the Moslems withdrew in disgust, and the heathen were left alone to finish the canal.   The strait of the Bosphorus was about to be opened, when the current of the Black Sea swept away the frail remaining dyke and drowned the infidels who were at work in the great trench.   The inundation spread over Bithynia, the kingdom of which Smyrna was the capital, and several cities of Africa.   Queen Katifé perished in the waters.   The whole world would soon have been engulfed, if ambassadors from every land had not implored Iskender-Iulcarni to save mankind from the threatened catastrophe.   So he commanded to pierce the Strait of Gibraltar in order to let the water of the Mediterranean escape into

567

the ocean.   When that new canal was opened, the drowned cities of
Asia Minor reappeared from the bed of the sea.

Ever since that flood a town of Asia Minor, situated some way
inland from Smyrna, has been known in the Turkish tongue by the
name of Denizli, which signifies "City on the Sea."   But the towns
of Africa remained beneath the waves.   To this day, on the coast
of Africa, you can see the ruins of the cities under water.   The
Black Sea used to cover the greater part of Mount Caucasus.
After the piercing of the Bosphorus the isthmus of the Crimea
appeared.   All along the Asiatic coast of the Black Sea, to a
distance of three hours from the shore, you may find at a considerable height the places where ships used to be moored.[1]

Page 241.   A story of a great flood, like that which the natives
of the New Hebrides tell, is related by the natives of Lifu, one of
the Loyalty Islands, which lie to the south of the New Hebrides.
The tale runs thus :—

Story of a
g   oo l
told in
Lifu, one
of the New
Hebrides.
"An old man named Nol made a canoe inland ; the natives
laughed at him for making it so far from the sea, declaring that
they would not help him to drag it to the coast ; but he told them
that it would not be necessary, for the sea would come to it.
When it was finished the rain fell in torrents and flooded the
island, drowning everybody.   Nol's canoe was lifted by the waters
and borne along by a current ; it struck a high rock which was still
out of the water, and split it in two.   (These two rocks are still
pointed out by the natives : they form the heads of a fine bay on
the north side of the island.)   The water then rushed into the sea
and left Lifu 'high and dry.'

"This tradition may have reference to the time when Lifu,
after the first lift, was a lagoon island like what the island of Uvea
is now.   If so, it shows that this island has been inhabited for a
very long time."[2]

Story of a
great flood
among the
Kaska
Indians of
British
Columbia.
Page 323.   The Kaska Indians, a tribe of the Athapascan stock
in the northern interior of British Columbia, have a tradition of a
great flood which runs as follows :—

"Once there came a great flood which covered the earth.   Most
of the people made rafts, and some escaped in canoes.   Great darkness came on, and high winds which drove the vessels hither and
thither.   The people became separated.   Some were driven far

[1] Henry Carnoy et Jean Nicolaïdes,
Folklore de Constantinople (Paris,
1894), pp. 16-18.
[2] Sidney H. Ray, "The People
and Language of Lifu, Loyalty Islands,"
*Journal of the Royal Anthropological
Institute*, xlvii. (1917) pp. 278 *sq.*,
quoting the Rev. S. Macfarlane, *The
Story of the Lifu Mission* (London,
1873), p. 19.

away. When the flood subsided, people landed wherever they found the nearest land. When the earth became dry, they lived in the places near where they had landed. People were now widely scattered over the world. They did not know where other people lived, and probably thought themselves the only survivors. Long afterwards, when in their wanderings they met people from another place, they spoke different languages, and could not understand one another. This is why there are now many different centres of population, many tribes, and many languages. Before the flood there was but one centre ; for all the people lived together in one country, and spoke one language." [1]

Thus the Kaskan tradition combines the story of a great flood with an explanation of the origin of the diversity of tongues.

Pt. i. Ch. v. THE TOWER OF BABEL

Page 384. A story of an attempt to build a tower that should reach up to the clouds is told also by the natives of Lifu, one of the Loyalty Islands. The tale runs as follows :—

Story of a "tower of babel in Lifu.

"Their forefathers assembled at a place to build, or rather erect, a scaffolding which should reach to the clouds. They had no idea of works in stone, hence their 'tower of Babel' was raised by tying stick to stick with native vines. They laboured on undaunted by the sad consequences of the discovery and stealing of yams underground ; perhaps they anticipated a more agreeable issue to their explorations in the heavens. But, alas, for human expectations ! before the top touched the clouds, the ground-posts became rotten, and the whole affair came down with a crash." [2]

[1] James A. Teit, "Kaska Tales," *Journal of American Folk-lore*, xxx. (1917) pp. 442 *sq.*

[2] Sidney H. Ray, "The People and Language of Lifu, Loyalty Islands,"

Journal of the Royal Anthropological Institute, xlvii. (1917) p. 279, quoting the Rev. S. Macfarlane, *The Story of the Lifu Mission* (London, 1873), pp. 19-20.

END OF VOL. I

Printed by R. & R. CLARK, LIMITED, *Edinburgh.*

PASSAGES OF THE BIBLE

Chosen for their Literary Beauty
and Interest

By Sir J. G. FRAZER

FELLOW OF TRINITY COLLEGE, CAMBRIDGE
AUTHOR OF 'THE GOLDEN BOUGH'
'PSYCHE'S TASK,' ETC.

New and Enlarged Edition. Large Crown 8vo.
Cloth. Price 3s. 6d. net.

SOME PRESS OPINIONS OF THE FIRST EDITION

"Considering its object, the selection of passages by Mr. Frazer is nearly as perfect as could be desired. Hardly a verse or song that rings in any one's memory but will be found here."—*Bookman.*

"Mr. Frazer's selections are, as was to be expected, made with care and taste, and he has prefixed to each of them an appropriate heading." —*Athenæum.*

"He has given us a fascinating book, the perusal of which cannot fail to invest the Bible, even for many of those who know it best, with a fresh interest and significance."— *Westminster Gazette.*

"Mr. Frazer has chosen his passages well. Stowed modestly away at the end of this volume are to be found some excellent notes, the fruit of diligence and learning."—*Realm.*

"Mr. Frazer appends a few pages of notes illustrative of customs and scenes. These, as was to be expected, are excellent, and make us wish he had extended them."—*British Weekly.*

"The notes are simply admirable."—*National Observer.*

"The thanks, not only of all who love the Bible for the truth's sake, but of those also who, as yet, recognise in it only the first classic in the world, the most ancient of all written records, and the purest literature existing in human language, are due to Mr. Frazer for his painstaking and successful volume, the perusal of which cannot fail to elevate the soul, and inspire the loftiest conceptions of the ways and works of the Most High."—*English Churchman.*

PUBLISHED BY
ADAM AND CHARLES BLACK, LTD., SOHO SQUARE, LONDON, W.